KUNIYOSHI

KUNIYOSHI

FROM THE ARTHUR R. MILLER COLLECTION

Timothy Clark

ROYAL ACADEMY OF ARTS

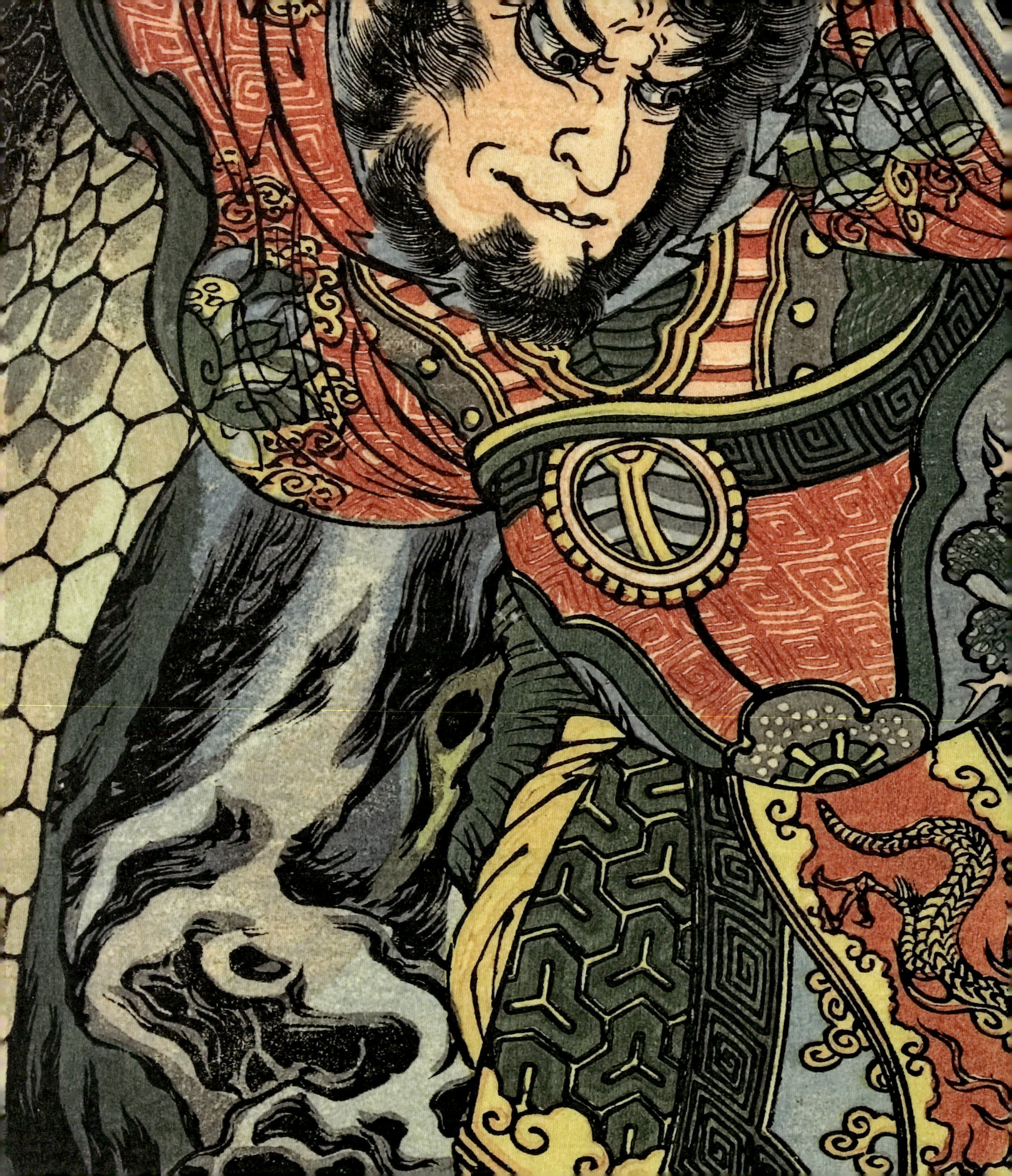

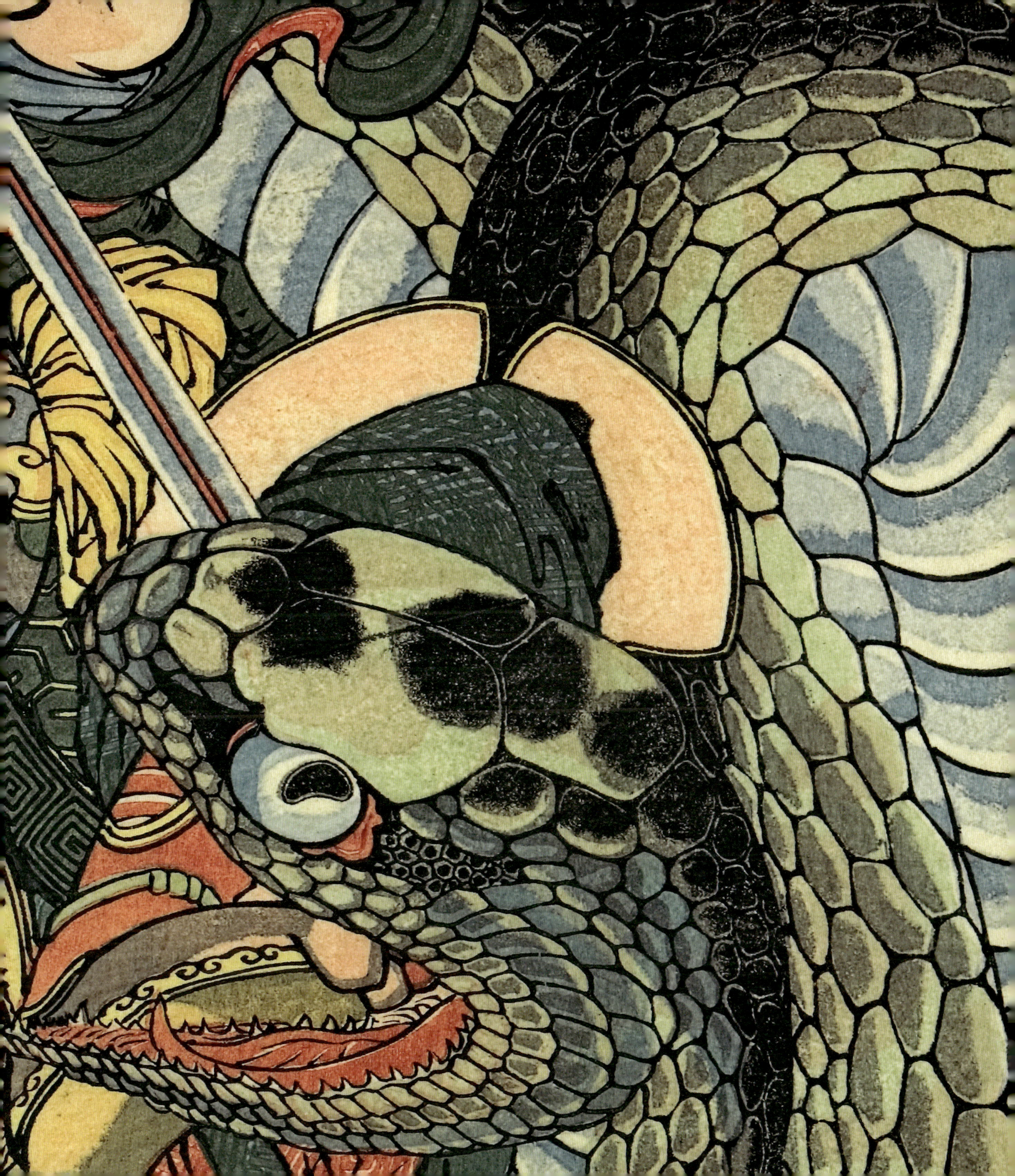

First published on the occasion of the exhibition 'Kuniyoshi: From the Arthur R. Miller Collection'

Royal Academy of Arts, London
21 March – 7 June 2009

Japan Society, New York
12 March – 13 June 2010

Supported by

Canon

Travel partner

Cox & Kings

2009 Season supported by

JTI

This exhibition has been organised by the Royal Academy of Arts in collaboration with Arthur R. Miller and The British Museum.

The Royal Academy of Arts is grateful to Her Majesty's Government for agreeing to indemnify this exhibition under the National Heritage Act 1980, and to Resource, The Council for Museums, Archives and Libraries, for its help in arranging the indemnity.

EXHIBITION CURATORS
Timothy Clark
Israel Goldman
Adrian Locke
assisted by Sarah Lea

EXHIBITION ORGANISATION
Lucy Adams

PHOTOGRAPHIC AND COPYRIGHT CO-ORDINATION
Miranda Bennion

CATALOGUE
ROYAL ACADEMY PUBLICATIONS
Lucy Bennett
David Breuer
Carola Krueger
Sophie Oliver
Peter Sawbridge
Nick Tite

Copy-edited and proofread by
Michael Foster

Designed by
Isambard Thomas

Colour origination by
DawkinsColour

Printed in Italy by
Graphicom

British Library Cataloguing-in-Publication Data
A catalogue record for this book is available from the British Library

ISBN 978-1-905711-40-6 (hardback)

ISBN 978-1-905711-41-3 (paperback)

Distributed outside the United States and Canada by Thames & Hudson Ltd, London

Distributed in the United States and Canada by Harry N. Abrams, Inc., New York

LENDERS TO THE EXHIBITION
American Friends of the British Museum
Andō Osamu
British Museum, London
Fitzwilliam Museum, Cambridge
National Museums Scotland, Edinburgh
Jeffrey Pollard and Ooi-Thye Chong
Takashima Masao
Victoria and Albert Museum, London

ACKNOWLEDGEMENTS
The curators extend their grateful thanks to the following individuals, without whose assistance this exhibition would not have been possible: Jude Ahern, Belle, Katherine Brooks, Ann Brownell Sloane, Rosina Buckland, John Carpenter, Rupert Faulkner, Joanne Harwood, Ishigami Aki, Andrew Lo, Mary Redfern, Cecilia Treves, Hiromi Uchida, Jane Wilkinson, Anna Wu

DETAILS
Endpapers: cat. 123
Title page: cat. 45
Pages 4–5: cat. 29
Pages 8–9: cat. 142
Pages 12–13: cat. 38
Pages 16–17: cat. 148
Page 33: cat. 8
Pages 292–3: cat. 146

PHOTOGRAPHIC ACKNOWLEDGEMENTS
All works of art are reproduced by kind permission of the owners. Unless noted otherwise below, all works are: © Trustees of the British Museum. Photo Art Research Center, Ritsumeikan University, Kyoto.

Boston, © 2009 Museum of Fine Arts: p. 243; Cambridge, Fitzwilliam Museum: cat. 129; Edinburgh, © National Museums Scotland: cats 22, 27; London, © British Library Board: figs 6, 8; London, © Trustees of the British Museum: cats 1, 24, 25, 29, 88, 100, 110, 130, 136, fig. 1; London, © V&A Images/Victoria and Albert Museum: cats 15, 16, 79, 90, 124, figs 13–15; © the Arthur R. Miller Collection. Photo Art Research Center, Ritsumeikan University, Kyoto: figs 2–5, 9–12, 16; Nagoya-shi, © Andō Osamu Collection. Photo Art Research Center, Ritsumeikan University, Kyoto: cats 131, 132; New York, © Jeffrey Pollard and Ooi-Thye Chong Collection. Photo Art Research Center, Ritsumeikan University, Kyoto: cats 108, 109; Tokyo, © Takashima Masao Collection. Photo Art Research Center, Ritsumeikan University, Kyoto: cats 78, 85, 120, 133, fig. 7

EDITORIAL NOTE
Japanese terms and names are transliterated in accordance with the Hepburn system of Romanisation. Some terms used in the publication are explained in the Glossary. Japanese personal names, both pre-modern and modern, appear with the family name (or business name or studio name) preceding the given name, art name, author name etc. Reversal of this order is indicated in the Index by a comma between the names ('Kuniyoshi, Utagawa' etc.).

Unless otherwise indicated, ages are given in accordance with pre-modern Japanese practice, which considered people to be one at birth, their age increasing by one year at every New Year.

English translations of titles of prints and series of prints are given before the transliterated Japanese, which appears in parentheses. Quotation marks around an English title indicate that it has been translated directly from the print. Titles of books and plays are given in Japanese, followed by an English translation in parentheses.

Dimensions are given with the Japanese names for the standard formats in which books and prints were generally issued appearing before dimensions in centimetres, height before width. The Japanese terms are explained in the Glossary.

The Japanese language was generally read from right to left in pre-modern times, and images were also typically 'read' in that direction. Catalogue entries for multi-sheet works are therefore described and numbered from right to left (cat. 41.2, 41.1 etc.).

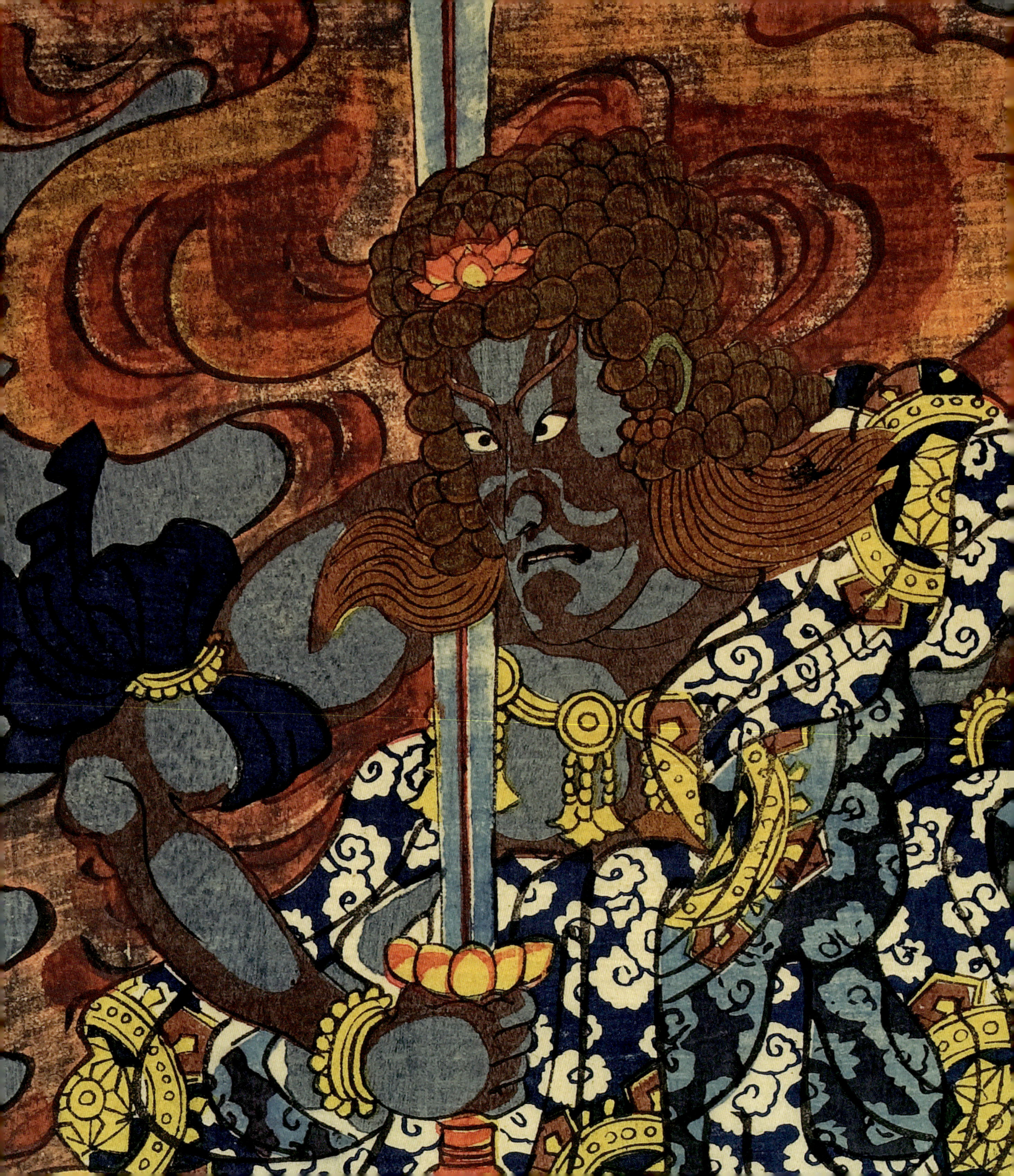

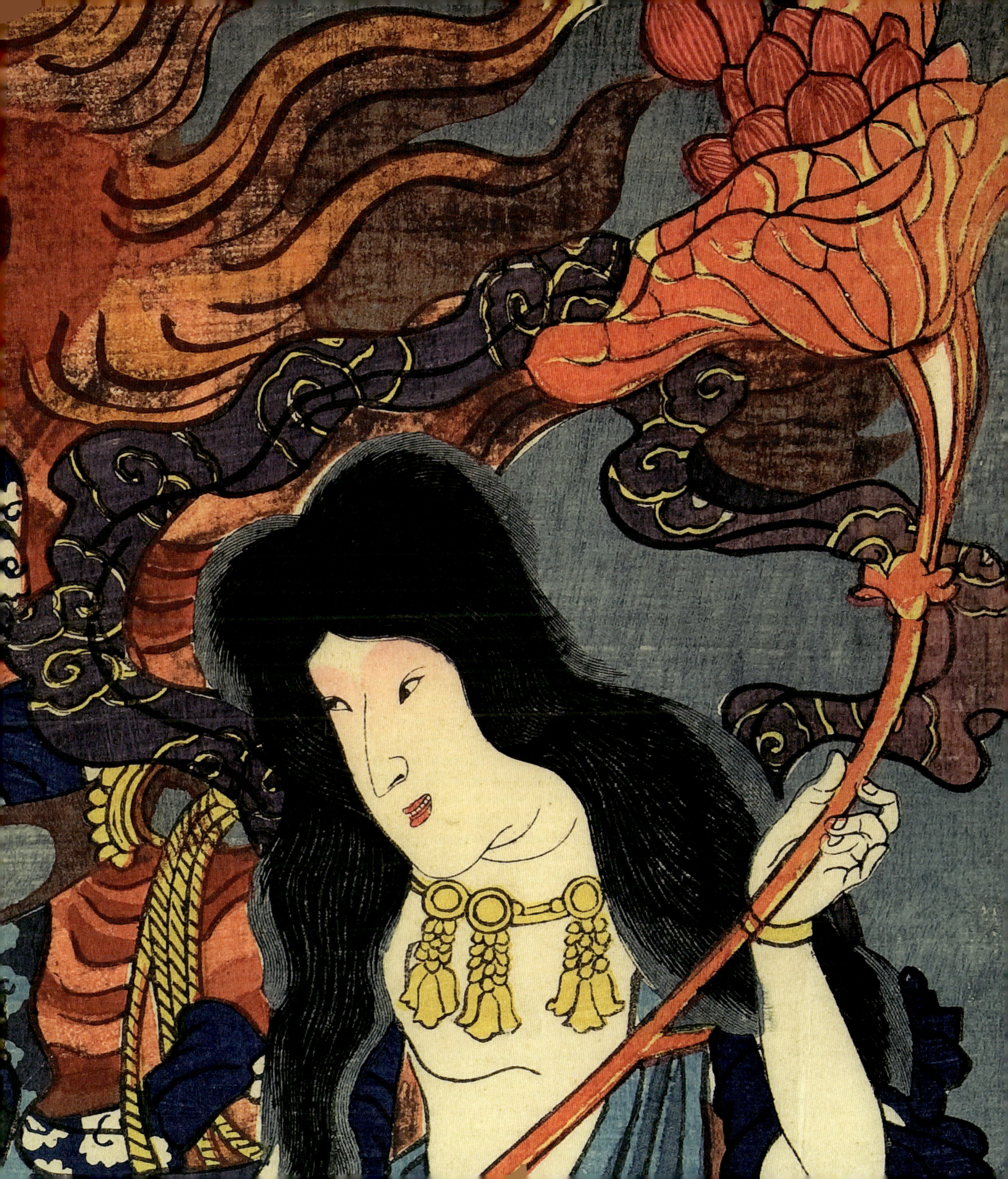

President's Foreword

Since the splendour and magnificence of 'The Great Japan Exhibition: Art of the Edo Period 1600–1868' (1981), the Royal Academy has mounted a series of smaller, more focused exhibitions of Japanese art in its Sackler Wing of Galleries. 'Hokusai: Prints and Drawings' (1991) and 'Hiroshige' (1997) examined the art of woodblock printmaking in the nineteenth century, and 'The Dawn of the Floating World 1650–1765: Early Ukiyo-e Treasures from the Museum of Fine Arts, Boston' (2001) looked back to the origins of the floating world school.

Long recognised in Japan as an artist of equal stature to Hokusai and Hiroshige, Utagawa Kuniyoshi (1797–1861) remains relatively unknown in the West. In redressing the balance, this exhibition presents an overview of Kuniyoshi's artistic production through an examination of his varied subject-matter: from his early depictions of the Chinese heroes of *The Water Margin*, which made his name in the 1820s, to his revolutionary use of the triptych format; and from Western-influenced landscapes to his numerous depictions of beautiful women.

The extraordinarily generous gift being made by Arthur R. Miller, the eminent American lawyer and legal scholar, to the American Friends of the British Museum of his entire collection of nearly two thousand Kuniyoshi prints has afforded us a unique opportunity to elevate the artist's profile. We are delighted to have worked with the British Museum on the project and grateful to the Chairman of the AFBM, Francis Finlay. It is very fitting that the exhibition will be shown at Japan Society, New York, a year from now and we would like to thank its director, Joe Earle, for helping to facilitate this.

The exhibition has been skilfully curated by Timothy Clark, Head of the Japan Section in the Department of Asia at the British Museum, with Israel Goldman, the highly respected collector and dealer in Japanese prints and drawings. Adrian Locke, of the Royal Academy, has also been deeply involved. Mr Clark and Mr Goldman have worked tirelessly to further our understanding of Japanese art and we are honoured to have collaborated with them. Mr Clark's examination of Kuniyoshi's output reveals an artist at the height of his powers, whose subtlety enabled him to circumvent censorship by using historical and other imaginative subject-matter to refer to current events.

This exhibition also pays tribute to the invaluable contribution to Kuniyoshi scholarship made by Basil W. Robinson (1912–2005), Keeper of the Metalwork Department at the Victoria and Albert Museum. As Keeper Emeritus, Mr Robinson was responsible for establishing the museum's Far Eastern Department and, as a collector and scholar of Kuniyoshi, he regularly corresponded with Professor Miller about the artist.

The Royal Academy would like to thank Neil MacGregor, Director of the British Museum, and Jan Stuart, the Keeper of its Department of Asia, for their help in making this exhibition possible. We are also very grateful to His Excellency Ebihara Shin, Ambassador of Japan, for generously agreeing to be patron of the exhibition. We acknowledge the help offered by Okaniwa Ken and Mizutori Mami, respectively the Director and former Director of the Japan Information and Cultural Centre, London, and Akama Ryō, Director of the Art Research Center, Ritsumeikan University, Kyoto. We extend our gratitude to the lenders to the exhibition: the American Friends of the British Museum; the Victoria and Albert Museum, London; the British Museum, London; the Fitzwilliam Museum, Cambridge; the National Museums Scotland, Edinburgh; Jeffrey Pollard and Ooi-Thye Chong; Takashima Masao; and Andō Osamu. In addition we would like to acknowledge the help given by Katsuhara Ryōta in negotiating loans from Japanese collections.

The Royal Academy is extremely grateful to Canon for its generous support of this exhibition. We would also like to thank our Exhibition Travel Partner Cox & Kings, The Japan Foundation and The Great Britain Sasakawa Foundation for additional support. Finally, we thank JTI, our season supporter of exhibitions in the Sackler Wing of Galleries.

Sir Nicholas Grimshaw CBE
President, Royal Academy of Arts

Foreword

Utagawa Kuniyoshi (1797–1861) was an extraordinarily gifted artist of great versatility, capable by turns of evoking pathos at the doomed fate of a samurai hero, humour with the antics of animals impersonating humans, seduction by feisty-spirited beauties from Japan's epic past, and calm contemplation of byways in his native city of Edo (now Tokyo). He created designs for literally thousands of art prints at prices almost all could afford, which were produced by publishers to the most exacting standards for colour woodblock that the world has ever seen. Like Daumier, he lampooned his rulers, but got away with it; like Van Gogh, he collected exotic prints from halfway round the world and was inspired by them to revolutionise his art. While drawing on centuries of Japanese aesthetic achievement, his personality and creative instincts led him to break the mould and lead ukiyo-e, the 'art of the floating world', towards the foreign and the modern.

Professor Arthur R. Miller of New York, the eminent lawyer and legal scholar, has assembled an extraordinary collection of prints that demonstrates the full breadth of Kuniyoshi's genius and encourages assessment with new eyes. Advised and encouraged over several decades by the British Kuniyoshi scholar Basil W. Robinson (1912–2005), Professor Miller set out to reassemble as many complete sets of Kuniyoshi's prints as possible. He searched assiduously in London and New York for prints with fresh, unfaded colours, as close as possible to the artist's original conception.

We are all in Professor Miller's debt for the beauty and interest of this magnificent collection, which he has promised and is in the process of giving to the American Friends of the British Museum. We eagerly anticipate that over time the entire Miller Collection of almost two thousand colour prints by Kuniyoshi will become part of the permanent collection of the British Museum. Expert digital photography of the collection by colleagues at the Art Research Center of Ritsumeikan University in Kyoto will allow us to share these prints online with the public.

Warm thanks are due to Israel Goldman, Japanese print specialist, friend and adviser to Professor Miller. Mr Goldman also has often shared his expertise with the British Museum and has given generously of his deep knowledge to Timothy Clark, who is both the curator of this exhibition and in charge of the British Museum's Japanese collections. We also wish to acknowledge the earlier scholarship on Kuniyoshi by Basil Robinson and Suzuki Jūzō and thank Iwakiri Yuriko, Ellis Tinios and Paul Griffith for their extensive advice.

Since the 'Great Japan' show of 1981–82, the Royal Academy has played a key role in introducing Japanese art to the UK through its special exhibitions. The leading nineteenth-century masters of the Japanese print – Hokusai, Hiroshige and now Kuniyoshi – have had their works elegantly displayed in the RA's Sackler Wing of Galleries. The public benefits greatly by enjoying these exhibitions in addition to being able to study the permanent Japanese collections at the British Museum's Mitsubishi Corporation Galleries and the Victoria and Albert Museum's Toshiba Galleries.

The British Museum is very glad to be collaborating with the Royal Academy on this occasion and we appreciate the cordial and professional assistance received from Charles Saumarez Smith, Adrian Locke and the staff at the RA in exhibiting Professor Miller's historic gift to the nation. Our Japanese Section has been extremely active over the years in co-operating with colleagues from the UK, Japan and around the world to shed new light on the history of that country's splendid cultural achievements. This fascinating exhibition is another manifestation of that strong and ongoing commitment.

Neil MacGregor
Director, The British Museum

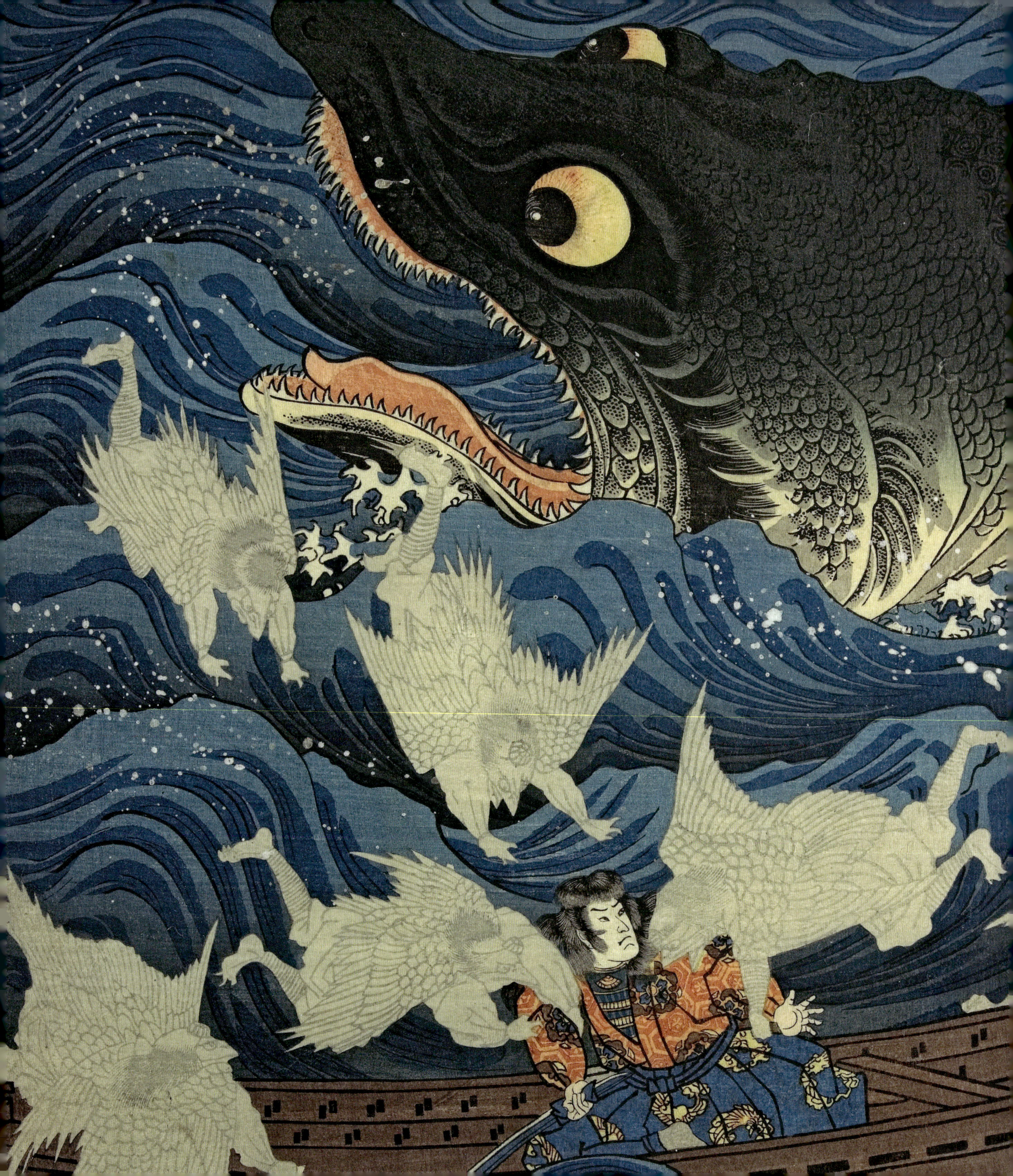

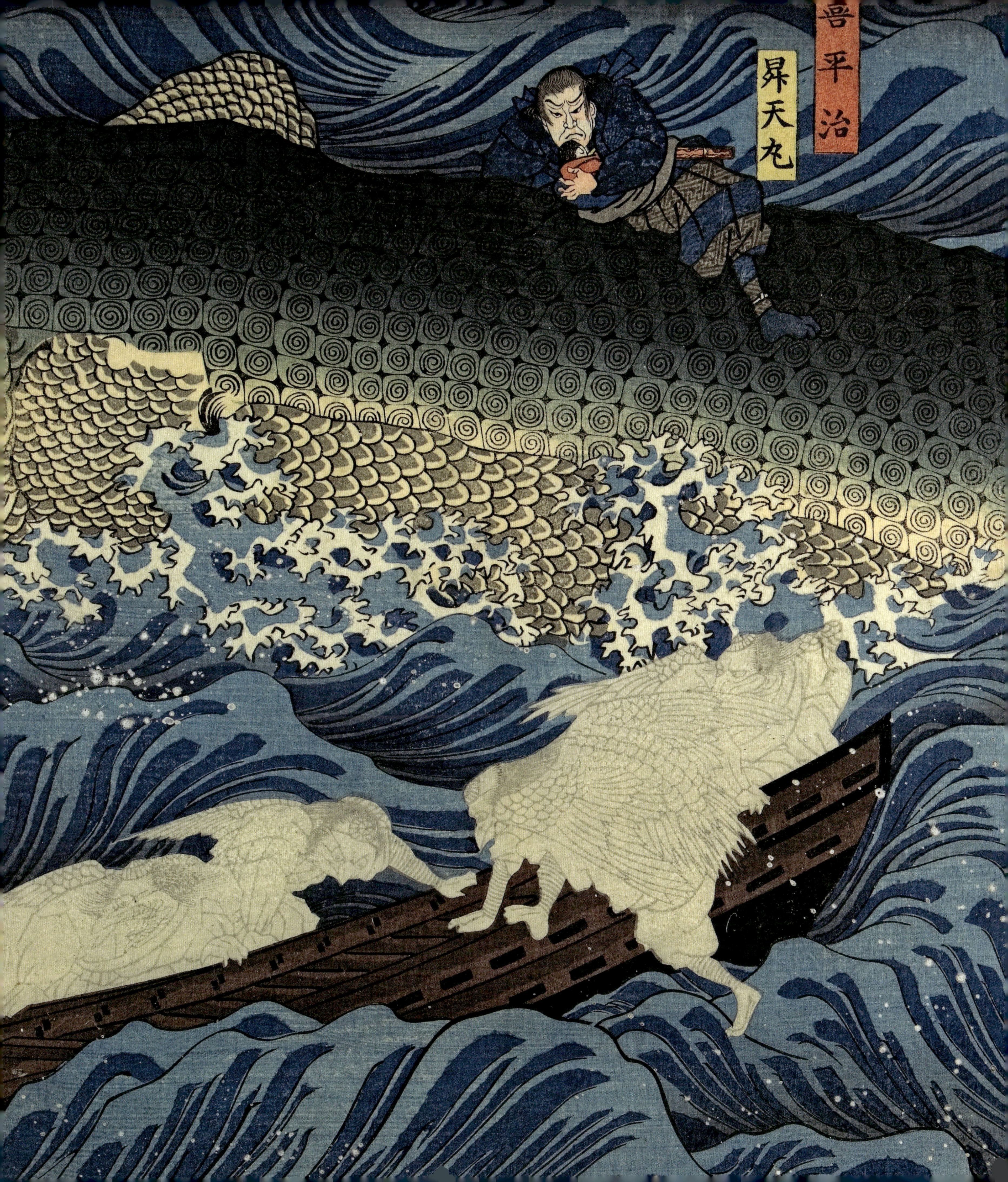
平治
昇天丸

Foreword

My passion for collecting the prints of Utagawa Kuniyoshi is so interrelated with London that leaving them in the care of the British Museum and having them exhibited at the Royal Academy seems most appropriate. My love affair with Kuniyoshi's work began when I wandered into Richard Kruml's former print gallery near Brown's Hotel almost thirty years ago. In those days I periodically came to London to moderate televised Socratic dialogues on a programme called *Hypotheticals*, first on Granada and later on BBC2.

I confessed to Richard that I had no background in the art form but had been attracted to it by a former student (now my colleague at New York University), Linda Silberman, who had acquired prints by Tsukioka Yoshitoshi, one of Kuniyoshi's pupils. Kruml sat me down with more than one hundred prints and said, 'Just select the ones you like.' After protesting my total ignorance, I sheepishly compiled a number of prints and, lo and behold, many of my choices were by Kuniyoshi. This very clever technique resulted in my first purchase – and I never stopped. Despite my television fee, I always left London considerably poorer than when I arrived!

Why Kuniyoshi? The answer must be in my DNA. The warrior and battle prints are dramatic, powerful, heroic. (Sir Harold Evans, former editor of *The Times* and the *Sunday Times*, and a veteran of participating in my inquisitorial TV moderations, claims that my gladiatorial personality attracts me to the samurai.) Yet, Kuniyoshi's landscapes and portrayals of women are serene and often graceful and delicate.

London connections continued. Since I have no background in Japanese culture, art or language, I naturally studied the 1961 and 1982 books on Kuniyoshi by Basil W. Robinson, the renowned Keeper of the Metalwork Department at the Victoria and Albert Museum. These volumes were invaluable in helping me to understand what my eyes found so attractive in the prints and in giving me some appreciation of the collaborative skills of the artist, block-cutter and printer who produced them.

I had the great fortune to be introduced to Mr Robinson, then in retirement, by another Londoner, my good friend Israel Goldman, from whom, along with Kruml, many of the prints in my collection (and this exhibition) were acquired. 'Robbie' and I remained pen-pals until his passing in 2005. His gracious and tolerant mentoring extended beyond his books and resolved many of my questions about acquisitions that were mysterious to me. (Robbie loved to chide me when I failed to identify actors in the Kabuki prints, and their engravers and publishers, but acknowledged his pleasure at solving the mysteries my prints presented.) In 1996 I suggested that his book *Kuniyoshi: The Warrior Prints* be supplemented, and after discussion he agreed to prepare the manuscript and I produced and distributed it.

Thus it is with love for the genius of Kuniyoshi (and the craftsmen who assisted him), and with enormous gratitude to the modest, self-styled ex-'museum man' and two gifted London print dealers who opened the door and have led me along the pathway all these years, that I make the fruits of my gathering available for the public at large to study and enjoy.

Arthur R. Miller
New York City

Sponsor's Preface

Canon Europe is proud to support 'Kuniyoshi', a unique exhibition that celebrates and explores the imagination of one of Japan's greatest and best-known woodblock printmakers.

At Canon we are passionate about the power of the image. Images are at the heart of what we do, and this association with the Royal Academy continues our long tradition of supporting culture and society through the arts. Canon is a Japanese company, and innovation and creativity are the cornerstones of our global business. We are delighted to be involved with this exhibition, which reflects our focus on empowering people to unlock their own creative potential, and will surely fascinate and inspire its audience.

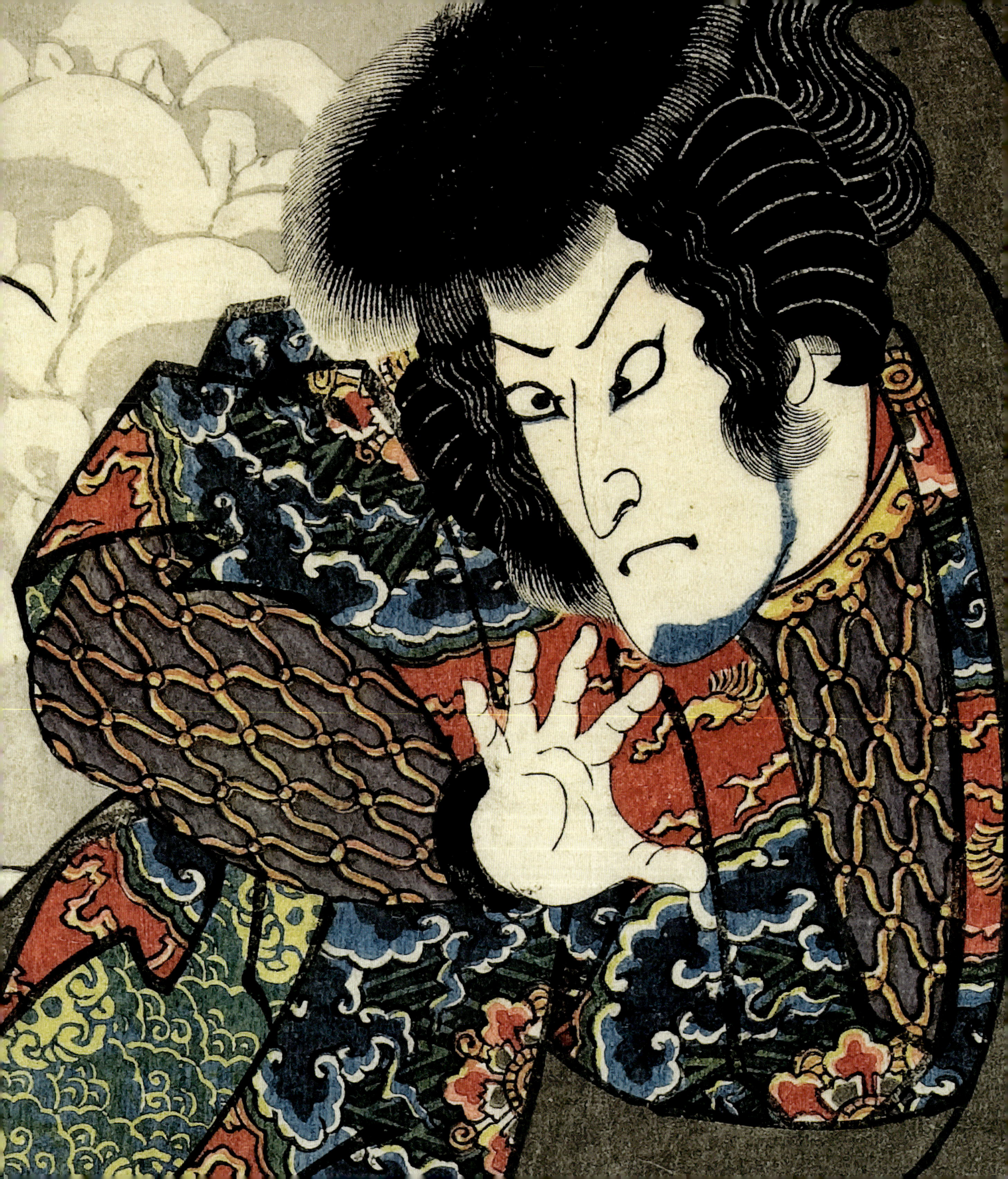

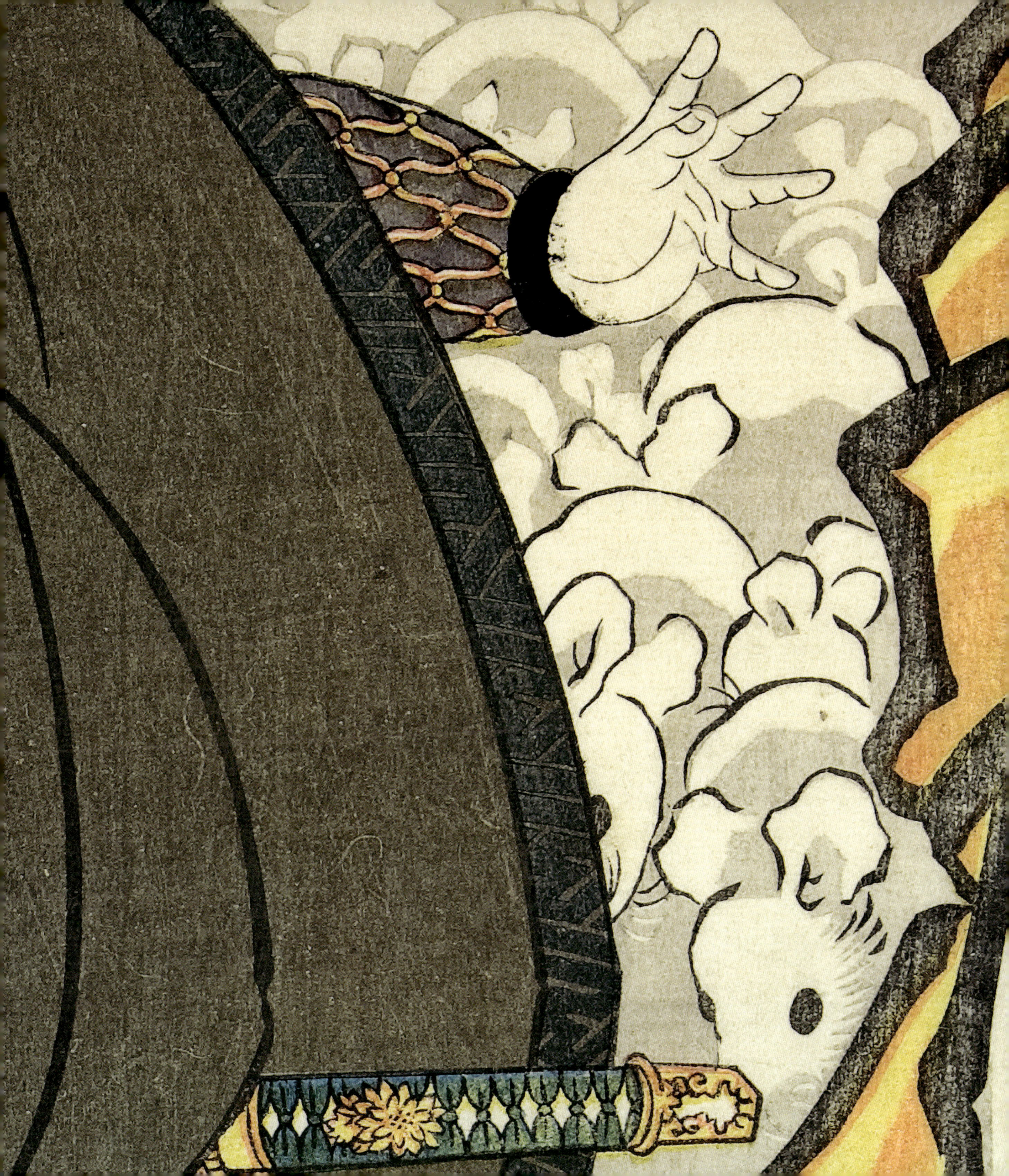

KUNIYOSHI AND CENSORSHIP

Utagawa Kuniyoshi (1797–1861) was one of four leading artists of the popular 'pictures of the floating world', or ukiyo-e, school who were active in Edo (modern Tokyo) in the early to mid-nineteenth century, the final decades of the Edo period (1600–1868). The other three were Katsushika Hokusai (1760–1849), Utagawa Kunisada (1786–1864; known as Toyokuni III after 1844)[1] and Utagawa Hiroshige (1797–1858). All were accomplished painters and prolific book illustrators, in addition to being the designers of many thousands of colour woodblock prints that have transmitted their art and reputations around the globe.

Kuniyoshi is documented as the son of a dyer, Yanagiya Kichiemon of Shirogane-chō in the Nihonbashi district.[2] As a child of seven or eight, he taught himself to draw by copying illustrations in books by Kitao Shigemasa (1739–1820) and Kitao Masayoshi (1764–1824). At the age of eleven a picture by him, 'Shōki the demon-queller holding a sword' (*Shōki tsurugi o saguru zu*), was praised by Utagawa Toyokuni I (1769–1825), who around 1811 accepted him at the age of about fifteen into his studio, by then the largest and most influential of the ukiyo-e school. Relations with Toyokuni I were not always smooth, it seems, and for a time Kuniyoshi may have lodged and studied with Utagawa Kuninao (1793–1854), a more senior pupil. His earliest surviving works are illustrations for a novel in *gōkan* (combined-volume) format that was published in 1814.

For more than a decade, until the late 1820s, Kuniyoshi appears to have struggled to find a distinctive artistic path. Works from this period, mostly book illustrations and Kabuki actor prints, are relatively small in number. Two notable prints of the late 1810s or early 1820s, both favourably received at the time, are the triptychs 'The Ghost of Taira no Tomomori' (*Taira no Tomomori bōrei no zu)* and 'Rōben Waterfall, Ōyama Sekison Temple' (*Ōyama Sekison Rōben no taki no zu*).[3] The latter includes, on the far right, what may be a self-portrait of a heavily tattooed Kuniyoshi bathing boisterously with a crowd of other pilgrims beneath the sacred waterfall.

Kuniyoshi's career was transformed by the success of his first major print series, 'One of the 108 Heroes of the Popular *Water Margin*' (*Tsūzoku Suikoden gōketsu hyakuhachinin no hitori*) of *c.* 1827–30, each design of which features a muscular, sometimes splendidly tattooed Chinese warrior in an energetic pose (cats 3–10). Henceforth, images of Chinese and Japanese warriors in stirring episodes from history were to become the artist's forte.[4] In the 1840s, in particular, he created a succession of glorious warrior and mythological triptych prints in which a single large motif spreads dramatically across all three sheets – a major artistic innovation (for example, cats 20–2, 24, 25, 27, 29).

By the nineteenth century ukiyo-e prints were being issued in vast quantities, in terms both of designs and impressions. They were a key medium of expression and communication in popular culture. Kuniyoshi may have designed as many as ten thousand prints in a career of almost half a century.[5] Kunisada, perhaps the most prolific graphic artist of all time, probably produced in excess of thirty-five thousand.[6] Both were ably assisted by their pupils. An official investigation of 1853 records that Kuniyoshi worked at home, assisted by two artist-daughters and three or four other pupils (see p.30). A memorial stele erected in his honour in 1873 lists sixteen deceased pupils and twenty-five still living (almost all their names begin with 'Yoshi').[7] Kunisada may have had as many as sixty pupils and assistants working in his studio in his later years.[8]

Ukiyo-e prints were purchased primarily by artisans and merchants (together known as 'townspeople'), the lowest-ranking social

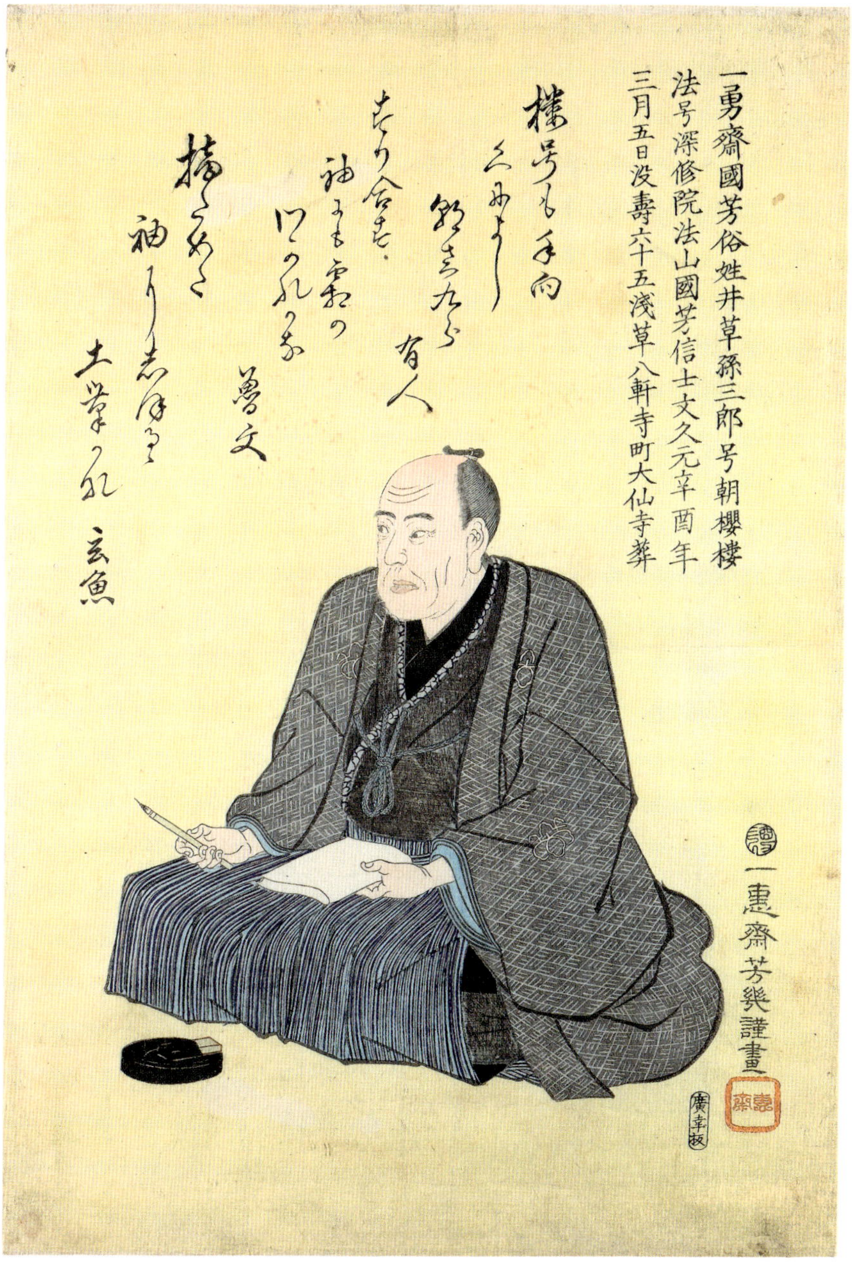

Fig. 1
Utagawa Yoshiiku (1833–1904), Memorial portrait of Kuniyoshi, third month, 1861. Colour woodblock print, published by Hirookaya Kōsuke, 36.4 × 25.4 cm.
The British Museum, London, JA 1912.4-16.0222

groups in the official Confucian hierarchy of samurai–farmer–artisan–merchant, but there is ample evidence that many samurai admired them as well. Edo was probably the largest city in the world, with more than one million inhabitants. It was a vast arena of ritual, display, work and play for samurai and townspeople alike, a highly developed consumer economy with rates of literacy that compared favourably with those of any European city of the period.

Hokusai, Hiroshige, Kunisada and Kuniyoshi each developed specialities of subject-matter and style: the first two are celebrated for their very different treatments of landscape, Kunisada for his prints of actors and beautiful women, and Kuniyoshi for his warrior and comic subjects. Many factors determined such specialisation: the artist's personal inclination; competition between publishers to create and control niche markets; fads and fashions in popular culture, notably Kabuki theatre; influences from popular literature and from other schools of visual art; foreign influences; and technical innovations. Another key, sometimes overriding, factor was government control.

Official censorship of popular printed materials was customary policy during the Tokugawa shogunate.[9] Censorship was particularly stringent during and immediately after the 'Tenpō reforms' of 1841–43. In comparison with his rivals mentioned above, Kuniyoshi is admired particularly for the wide range of his subject-matter and the unique, even eccentric power of his artistic imagination. Examining his achievement in relation to the restrictions imposed by censorship highlights the richness and inventiveness of his art. With him, as with Kitagawa Utamaro (d. 1806), there is a real sense that censorship acted as a catalyst of radical change and growth. Kuniyoshi seems to have possessed the independent, occasionally forthright personality thought typical of an 'Edokko', an artisan or merchant son of Edo. Increased censorship appears to have encouraged in him a spirit of opposition. Resistance was possible only within clearly defined limits, which Kuniyoshi regularly tested but, as a rule, did not breach. His fellow townspeople certainly interpreted some of his most famous prints as critical of the shogunate and its policies. Indeed, this became the key factor in these works' notoriety and commercial success.

In the discussion that follows I focus on Kuniyoshi's art at two key points in his mature career, around 1842–43 and around 1853, and explain some of the mechanics of production that enabled the colour woodblock print to flourish as a genuinely popular art form. I draw extensively on recent studies by Iwakiri Yuriko and others that have done much to expand and clarify our understanding of Kuniyoshi and the world of Edo publishing in which he was such a dynamic force.

New publishing regulations as part of the Tenpō reforms

In the sixth month of 1842 the following instruction was sent from the office of the North City Magistrate (*Kita machibugyō*) to the city official in charge of illustrated books and prints (*ezōshi-kakari nanushi*):

> Producing single-sheet prints of Kabuki actors, prostitutes and geisha – known as 'brocade pictures' [*nishiki-e*] – is detrimental to public morals. It is forbidden to sell either new examples or existing stocks. In the case of illustrated novels in *gōkan* format the following are wasteful and needlessly expensive: intricate designs, likenesses [*nigao*] of actors, themes relating to Kabuki plays, the use of colour printing on covers and wrappers. Existing stocks of this kind must not be sold; actor likenesses and Kabuki themes must cease. Works should be composed in accordance with [the values of] loyalty and fidelity, to promote virtue among children and women… When new examples are printed they must be presented to the senior city official [*machi-doshiyori*] Tate Ichiemon for his approval.[10]

This was a calculated attack by the authorities on publishers and sellers of popular books and colour woodblock prints, who relied for most of their income on scenes from Kabuki plays, images from the pleasure quarters and illustrated novels in *gōkan* format. The decree was but one small element in a wholesale crackdown implemented by the samurai government from the fifth month of 1841 to the ninth month of 1843 and generally called the 'Tenpō reforms' (after the era in which they occurred, the Tenpō era [1830–44]). The main reform policies, spearheaded by senior councillor Mizuno Tadakuni (1794–1851), comprised exhortations to frugality, the suppression of popular culture, the abolition of merchant guilds and the enforcement of lower prices.[11]

Kabuki theatre was a particular target of the reforms. After the Nakamura and Ichimura theatres in Edo burned down in the twelfth month, 1841, the government compelled all three licensed theatres[12] to move from the centre of the city to Saruwaka-machi in Asakusa, a merchant neighbourhood close to the northern outskirts. The Ichimura was the first to reopen there, in the ninth month of 1842. In addition, an example was made of 'superstar' actor Ichikawa Danjūrō VII (1791–1851), who was banished from Edo from the sixth month, 1842, for infringing sumptuary laws. He was obliged to perform elsewhere, mainly in Osaka, until 1849, when he was pardoned and permitted to return to Edo.

The Tokugawa shogunate implemented a general ban both on depicting in words or images contemporary events with political ramifications and on commenting 'inappropriately' on the ruling class and their ancestors in recent centuries. By Kuniyoshi's time a great many news sheets were being generated anonymously in the form of monochrome woodblock prints called 'tile prints' (*kawara-ban*) because they were crudely printed. Censorship had been strengthened and codified in two earlier series of reforms, in the Kyōhō era (1716–36) and the Kansei era (1789–1801), and again following a specific case in 1804 (see p. 26). The main effects, felt each time for only a few years, involved the suppression of explicit erotica, a temporary reduction in luxury printing techniques and a tightening of the general bans mentioned above. The complete ban in 1842 on prints of actors, courtesans and geisha – the celebrities of popular culture – was unusually draconian in comparison with previous crackdowns. Strict enforcement did not begin to be relaxed until about 1846. The longer-term effects of the Tenpō reforms on print culture were profound, as publishers and artists constantly modified their strategies in response to changes in government and society.[13]

The decline of the shogunate

In the 1850s and '60s the 'pax Tokugawa', the stable samurai regime set up in the early seventeenth century, began to crumble. It was challenged from without by the encroachments of foreign powers seeking to establish trade relations and from within by inexorable economic forces of change and by new ideologies that questioned the legitimacy and aptitude of the Tokugawa to continue ruling in the name of the emperor. Rulers and populace alike were alarmed by increasingly regular sightings of foreign ships in Japanese waters, and the shogunate perceived Britain's defeat of China in the First Opium War of 1839–42 as a warning. Negotiations forced on Japan by the USA in 1853–54 led to a treaty of

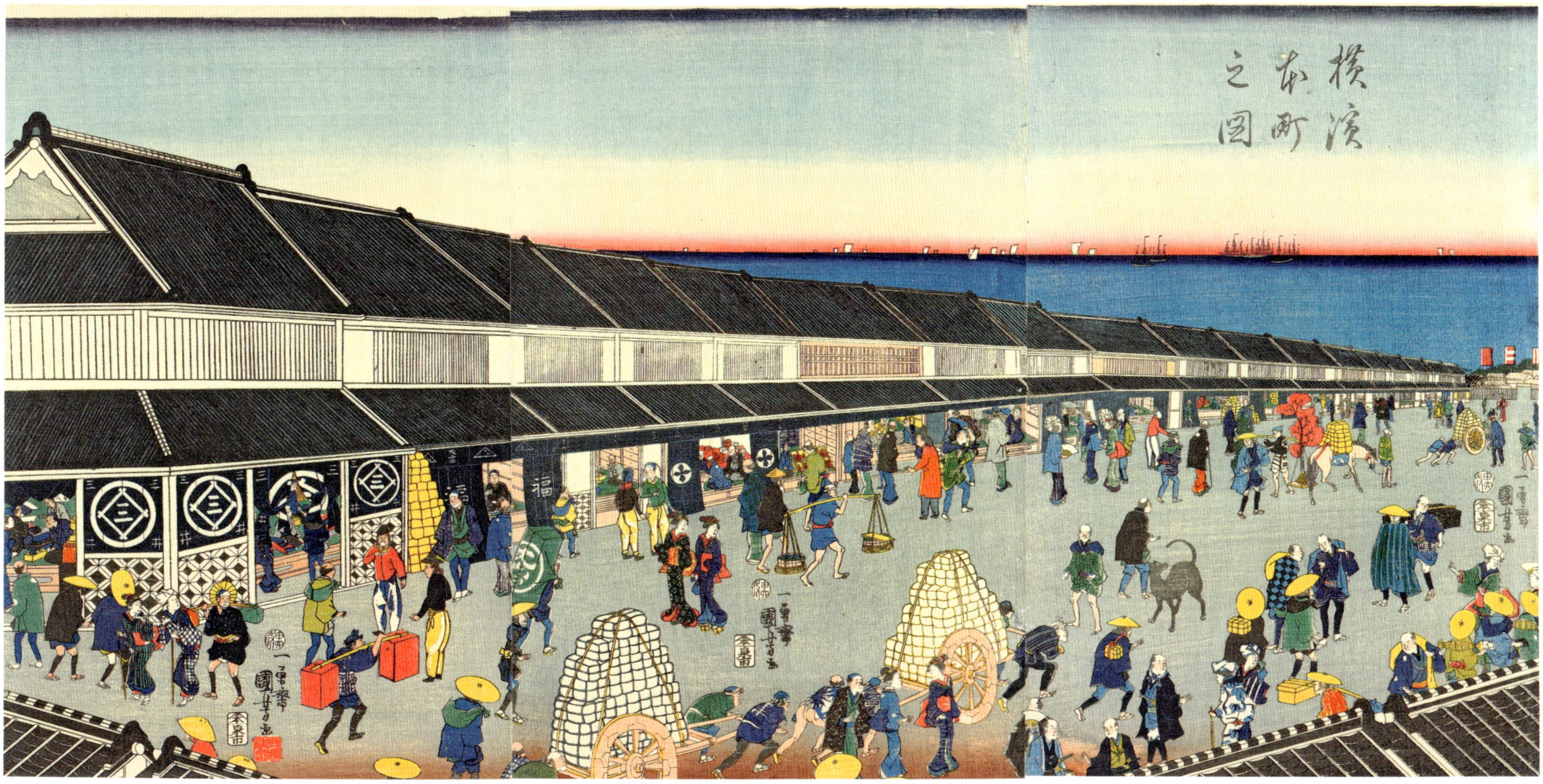

Fig. 2
Kuniyoshi, 'Picture of Honchō in Yokohama' (*Yokohama Honchō no zu*), sixth month, 1860. Colour woodblock triptych, published by Izumiya Ichibei, 36.4 × 24.3 [R], 36.3 × 25.2 [C], 36.3 × 24.3 cm [L].
The Arthur R. Miller Collection 20306

'peace, amity and commerce', which was followed in 1858 by similar treaties with the Netherlands, Russia, Britain and France. In 1859 the first of a small number of ports was opened for trade with foreigners: Kuniyoshi lived just long enough to design, in 1860, a general view of the centre of Yokohama, the newly established 'treaty port' closest to Edo (fig. 2). The 1860s saw a power struggle within the elite between supporters of the shogunate and 'loyalists', who promoted a return to imperial rule. In addition, there were those who favoured continuing to accommodate foreigners so as to modernise Japan with the help of their knowledge, and others who agitated vociferously, and sometimes violently, for their complete expulsion. The turmoil culminated in 1867–68 in a civil war that resulted in the overthrow of the shogunate and the establishment of a new, modernising government in the name of the emperor – events known as the 'Meiji restoration'.

Kuniyoshi did not live to witness all these developments. He had suffered a stroke in the autumn of 1855, at about the time a devastating earthquake hit Edo, and he was plagued by bouts of illness throughout his final years. He died at his home at Genyadana in Nihonbashi district on the fifth day of the third month, 1861, aged sixty-five (sixty-four by Western reckoning). His ashes were interred at the Nichiren sect temple Daisen-ji in Asakusa. A sensitive memorial portrait by his pupil Yoshiiku is probably the most accurate likeness (fig. 1). Kuniyoshi had produced several playful self-portraits in the course of his career (cat. 129 is one) but, modestly, he almost always hid his face from the viewer.

Kuniyoshi's initial responses to the Tenpō reforms

Detective work by Iwakiri Yuriko has done much to clarify how censorship developed after 1842 and how publishers and artists responded to the new challenges.[14] The censorship mechanisms in operation prior to the Tenpō reforms had been implemented in 1791. Inspection was carried out by a rota of minor officials (*gyōji*) who were all members of the guild of publishers of popular fiction and prints (*jihon ezōshi-doiya nakama*). The industry was therefore required to police itself. This system was embodied from 1791 to 1842 in a small, round, printed seal containing the character *kiwame* ('examined') that appeared on most prints (see also the entry for cat. 15).

Trade guilds were abolished in the twelfth month of 1841, and censorship by the publisher's guild seems to have ended in the third month of the following year. The publishing regulations of the sixth month, 1842, quoted above, decreed that new designs be 'presented to the senior city official [*machi-doshiyori*] Tate Ichiemon for his approval'. Iwakiri's researches suggest that in the subsequent months censors applied their personal seal as an indication of approval to rough preparatory drawings (*shita-e*), rather than to the final, block-ready drawing (*hanshita-e*). Hence, the seals were not carved into the printing block and did not appear on the published prints.[15] Not until the eleventh month was a stipulation added requiring the censor to mark the block-ready drawing with his personal seal. Under the new system the censor was a neighbourhood official appointed by the authorities (a *nanushi*), rather than a publisher. His seal was cut into the printing block in the place he had applied it to the drawing and therefore formed part of the finished print. The small, oval personal seal reading 'Fu' near the bottom of each sheet of Kuniyoshi's 'Battle of the Chess Pieces' (*Koma-kurabe banjō taiheiki*; fig. 9), for example, belonged to Fukatsu Ihei, a *nanushi* in the Koami-chō neighbourhood. Iwakiri has demonstrated that, in practice, censors' personal seals probably did not start to appear on prints until the New Year of 1843. Hence, prints published between the fourth and twelfth months of 1842 bore no censorship seals. Thereafter, from the New Year of 1843 to the end of 1846, as the post of censor rotated each month among a group of between five and nine *nanushi*, the seal of a specific individual appeared on all the prints approved in that month.

In addition to producing confirmation that prints were issued without censorship seals for a nine-month period in 1842, Iwakiri has tentatively identified each censor in almost every month of the years 1843 to 1846.[16] This permits prints issued in the period immediately following the Tenpō reforms to be dated much more accurately than before, and this, in turn, has enabled Iwakiri to show how the ebb and flow of censorship directly affected the kinds of print published.

A strikingly large number of prints by Kuniyoshi appeared during the nine months when censorship seals were not in use. Iwakiri lists no fewer than twenty-four series issued after the ban on prints of actors, courtesans and geisha imposed in the sixth month of 1842, grouping them according to subject: children (seven series), beauties (five series), warriors (three series), comic subjects (eight series) and fish (one series). In addition, all but one of the fifty-eight known designs in the series 'One Hundred Poems by One Hundred Poets' (*Hyakunin isshu no uchi*; cats 91–7), along with fourteen sheets from the series 'Twenty-four Paragons of Filial Piety for Children' (*Nijūshi-kō dōji kagami*; fig.3, cats 98–101), lack a censor's seal and are thought to have been issued at this time.

The work Kuniyoshi produced in the shadow of the new publishing regulations is remarkable for its thematic range and inventiveness. He was an ardent cat-lover, and one of the wittiest of his comic series from this time, 'Cats Forming Written Characters' (*Neko no ateji*), shows sleek felines shaping themselves into written phonetic graphs, so as to 'spell out', as it were, the names of certain species of fish. Five designs are known. In 'Bonito' (*Katsuo*) the cat at the top wears a paper bag marked 'sweets' as a hat (fig.4). The others arrange themselves languidly and artfully, two of them clutching the enticing bonito. The title cartouche is formed by a bonito, a fishnet and a garnish of dwarf bamboo leaves. Kuniyoshi's signature is framed by a gourd-shaped *Yoshi* cartouche in the form of a cat collar, complete with bell. Despite the wealth of witty detail, the overall concept is compellingly simple. The long-suffering townspeople of Edo doubtless savoured the artist's stylish nonchalance in the teeth of government repression.

The new publishing regulations exhorted artists 'to promote virtue among children and women'. Kuniyoshi's series 'Crazy Pictures for Children, to Educate Them about True Sayings' (*Jitsugo-kyō kyōga dōgaku*) embodies a topsy-turvy take on some well-worn homilies. In contrast to the sophistication of 'Cats Forming Written Characters', the style is deliberately crude and farcical. In 'Father and mother are like heaven and earth, your lord and your teacher are like the sun and moon' (*Fubo wa tenchi no gotoshi, shikun wa jitsugetsu no gotoshi*; fig.5), for instance, the children appear anything but demure and respectful, laughing at their teachers and crying when their mother falls over (their father seems to have died, and looks down from heaven). A chronicle of significant events of the period, *Bukō nenpyō* (*Edo Chronology*), mentions that 'during [the Tenpō] era, in colour prints it was the "crazy pictures" [*kyōga*] of the floating-world artist Utagawa Kuniyoshi and the landscapes of Ichiryūsai Hiroshige that were popular'.[17] Kuniyoshi's *kyōga* greatly influenced later artists. Kawanabe Kyōsai (1831–1889), for

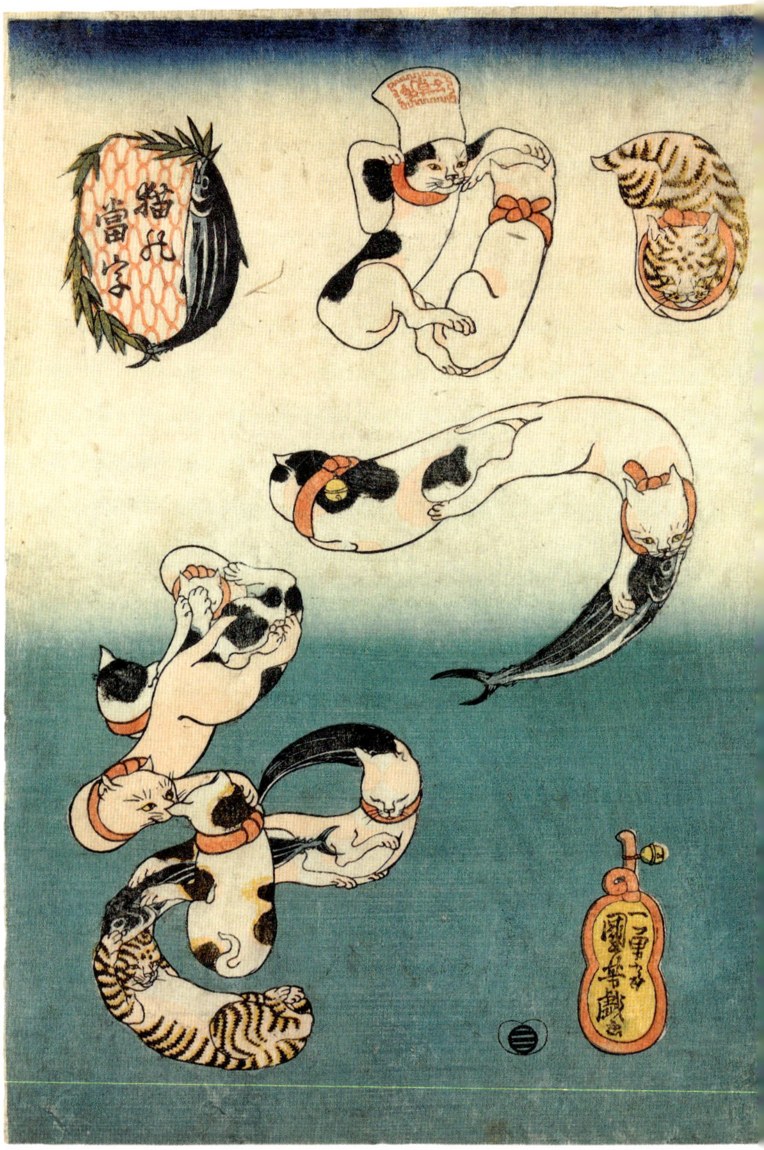

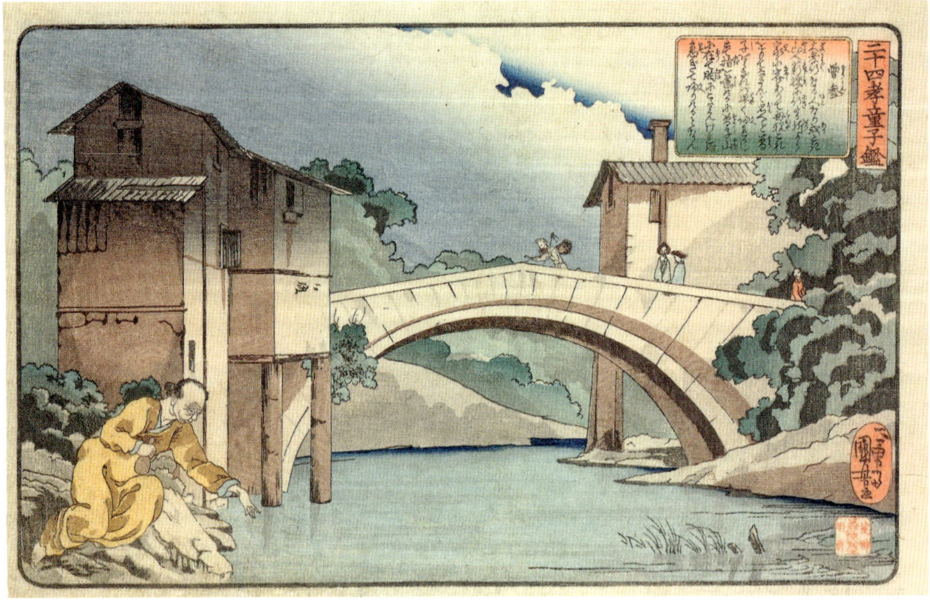

Fig.3 LEFT
Kuniyoshi, 'Sō Shin (Zeng Can)', from the series 'Twenty-four Paragons of Filial Piety for Children' (*Nijūshi-kō dōji kagami*), c. 1843. Colour woodblock print, published by Wakasaya Yoichi, 24.6 × 36.7cm.
The Arthur R. Miller Collection 16903

Fig.4 ABOVE
Kuniyoshi, 'Bonito' (*Katsuo*), from the series 'Cats Forming Written Characters' (*Neko no ateji*), c. 1842. Colour woodblock print, published by Ibaya Senzaburō, 36.2 × 25.3 cm.
The Arthur R. Miller Collection 00901

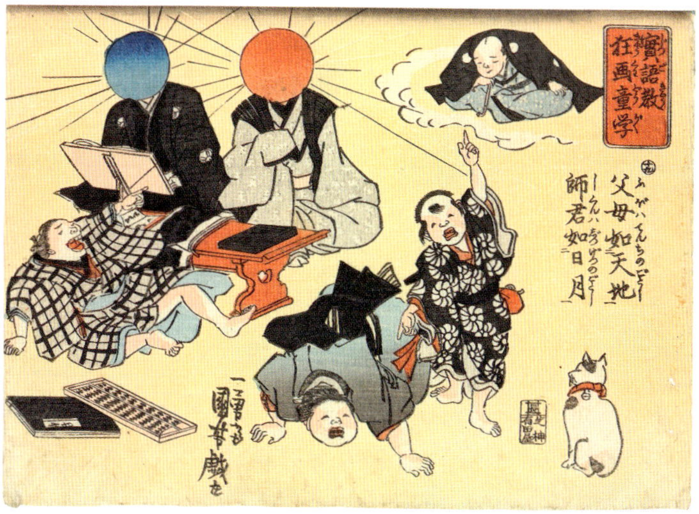

Fig. 5
Kuniyoshi, 'Father and mother are like heaven and earth…' (*Fubo wa tenchi no gotoshi…*), from the series 'Crazy Pictures for Children, to Educate Them about True Sayings' (*Jitsugo-kyō kyōga dōgaku*), 1842–43. Colour woodblock print, published by Aritaya Sei'emon, 18 × 25.3 cm.
The Arthur R. Miller Collection 05004

Fig. 6 RIGHT
Jan (Johannes) Nieuhof (1618–1672), 'Houses of government officials and artists [in Batavia]' (*Stats Meesters en Konstenars Woningen*), from *Gedenkwaerdige Zee- en Lant-Reize door de voornaemste Landschappen van West en Oost Indien*, Amsterdam, 1682, fol.
The British Library, London, 147.h.5

example, who was briefly his pupil around 1837, established a career in the late 1850s by creating pictures of this kind, using an art-name, Kyōsai, that means 'crazy studio'.[18] Kuniyoshi habitually signed works in this genre with the phrase 'Playfully painted by …' (… *giga*). This has led some scholars to refer to his comic works as 'playful pictures' (*giga*), but *kyōga* is the more historically accurate term.[19]

The series 'Twenty-four Paragons of Filial Piety for Children' represents Kuniyoshi's most serious attempt to comply with the moral demands of the new publishing regulations. In the eyes of the authorities no subject could have been better suited to 'promoting virtue' among children than these Chinese stories about young people who went to unusual lengths to honour their parents. Surprisingly, in view of the Chinese origin of the subjects, the artist chose to experiment with a 'European' style. One of the tales concerns Zeng Can, who was gathering firewood in the mountains when he felt a pang of pain in his chest and instinctively realised that his aged mother was struggling alone at home to entertain an unexpected visitor and had bitten her finger (fig. 3). Kuniyoshi sets the scene in an Italianate landscape, with Zeng hurrying home across the bridge in the distance and his mother stooping to fill a flask with water from the river. The low viewpoint, the foreshortening and the cast shadows create a radically 'foreign' ambience. Kuniyoshi doubtless copied the essentials of the composition from a European print, but no specific model has been identified.

Kuniyoshi's European sources

The matter of Kuniyoshi's European sources has long intrigued scholars. The earliest substantial biography of the artist, compiled by Iijima Kyoshin, appeared in 1894 in *Ukiyo-eshi Utagawa retsuden* (*Biographies of Floating-world Artists of the Utagawa School*). It contains a brief anecdote attributed to a certain Kurita, who visited the artist at his home at Genyadana, where he lived from about 1847. The conversation turned to 'Western pictures' (*seiyō ga*). Kuniyoshi reached into a box and took out several hundred Western images he had collected, including 'illustrated newspapers' (*e-iri shinbun*). Kurita wondered where on earth Kuniyoshi could have obtained them, but did not supply the answer.[20]

Kuniyoshi was certainly influenced by earlier Japanese paintings and prints in Europeanised styles, among them copperplate prints by Aōdō Denzen (1748–1822) and the woodblock printed book *Kōmō zatsuwa* (*Dutch Miscellany*) of 1787.[21] Katsumori Noriko has identified a Dutch printed illustration as the source of a composition that belongs among Kuniyoshi's most Western: 'The Night Attack, Act Eleven of *Treasury of Loyal Retainers*' (*Chūshingura jūichi-danme youchi no zu*), issued in the early 1830s (cat. 79). The illustration, by Jan (Johannes) Nieuhof, appears in the book *Gedenkwaerdige Zee- en Lant-Reize door de voornaemste Landschappen van West en Oost Indien*, published in Amsterdam in 1682 (fig. 6).[22] Additional research has shown that Kuniyoshi reworked illustrations from this book for at least three of his print projects over a period of twenty years.[23]

At the end of 1852 Kuniyoshi produced a series of half-length portraits (*shōzō*) of heroes from the Chūshingura story, a vendetta culminating in a nocturnal attack by forty-seven loyal samurai of the Akō fief (see also cats 41–9, 79). Perhaps because these men lived closer to the artist's own times than any of his other warrior subjects, he portrayed them as realistically as possible, modelling them convincingly and employing chiaroscuro and foreshortening. The pinpoints of light on each eyeball enliven the facial expressions. Indeed, the portrait of the men's leader, Ōboshi Yuranosuke, which shows the hilts of his twin swords pointing almost directly at the viewer, is so vivid that a link with early Japanese experiments with photography has been suggested (see the entry for cat. 46). What is certain is that Kuniyoshi returned to Nieuhof's book as a source for this series. Katsuhara Ryōta has shown that three published designs and one unpublished drawing copy parts of illustrations in the volume that depict the

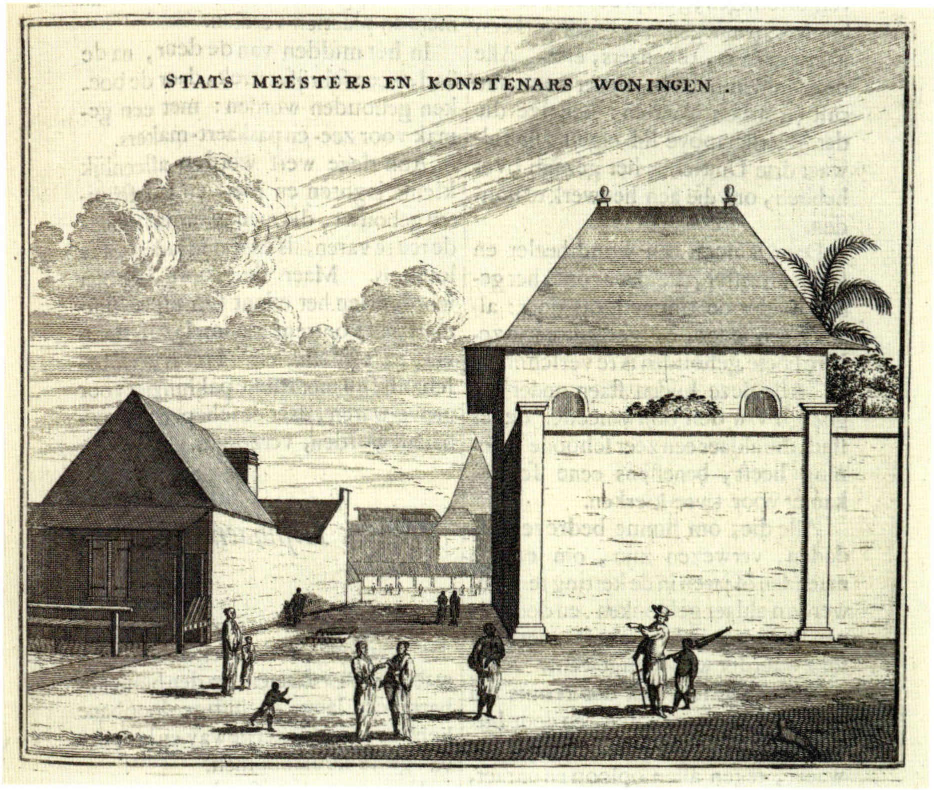

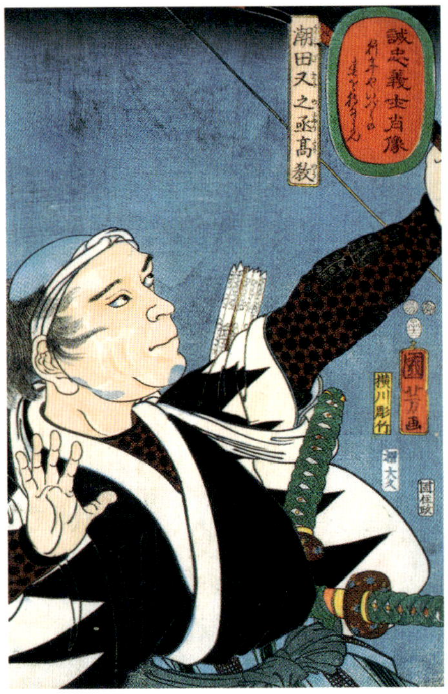

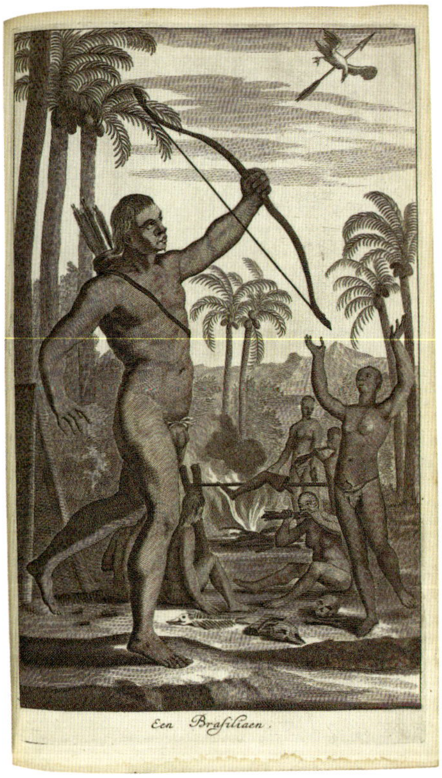

Fig. 7 TOP
Kuniyoshi, 'Ushioda Matanojō Takanori', from the series 'Portraits of Loyal and Righteous Samurai' (*Seichū gishi shōzō*), twelfth month, 1852. Colour woodblock print, published by Sumiyoshiya Masagorō.
Takashima Masao Collection, Japan

Fig. 8 ABOVE
Nieuhof, 'A Brazilian' (*Een Brasiliaen*), from *Gedenkwaerdige Zee- en Lant-Reize*…
The British Library, London, 147.h.5

indigenous peoples of the East and West Indies.[24] In this way Nieuhof's figure of a naked Brazilian hunter metamorphosed into a Japanese samurai archer, the warrior Ushioda Takanori (figs 7, 8). Kuniyoshi had turned to the same illustration some ten years earlier, borrowing the Brazilian woman with her arms stretched upwards for a figure in 'Dong Yong' from the series 'Twenty-four Paragons of Filial Piety for Children' (cat. 99). His corrections to the preparatory drawing show that he deliberately changed the angle of her leg (cat. 100).

Implementation of the new publication regulations

In the eleventh month of 1842, when *nanushi* censors were instructed to apply their seals of approval to block-ready drawings, other, more detailed instructions were being issued from the North City Magistrate's office: the number of colours used in a print must be limited to seven or eight, the price per sheet must not exceed sixteen *mon* (about the same as a double helping of *soba* noodles) and continuous compositions must not extend over more than three sheets. At the same time, explicitly 'erotic goods' (*kōshoku no shina*, i.e. books and prints) were forbidden.[25]

Since the tenth month of 1842 several artists, including Kuniyoshi, had contributed to a spate of prints in which children acted out famous theatrical scenes as a surrogate for the banned Kabuki subjects.[26] Doubtless because the new rules were not being observed strictly enough, six artists – Keisai Eisen (1790–1848), Kuniyoshi, Kunisada, Utagawa Sadahide (1807–1873), Hiroshige and Utagawa Yoshitora (active c. 1836–1887) – were summoned by the *nanushi* Murata Sahei to the magistrate's office in the third month of 1843 and made to sign a declaration that they would not design the following: erotic books, likenesses of Kabuki actors, images of courtesans and female geisha, works on theatrical subjects, pictures in which dancing women and children took on the guise of adults and, finally, biographical illustrations of wise women and virtuous wives, along with images of other faithful women.[27] This last must have come as something of a surprise to Kuniyoshi, because in 1842 he had begun the series 'Biographies of Wise Women and Virtuous Wives' (cats 53–5) to address – at least ostensibly – the demand of the new regulations for works promoting 'loyalty and fidelity'. The declaration makes it clear that officials objected to the fact that women were being drawn 'in contemporary fashions' (*imayō sugata*).

With publishing regulations finalised, there followed until the end of the Edo period a steady stream of official investigations into infringements, with miscreants punished by fine, handcuffing or house arrest. The authorities' view of these is embodied in the case documents surviving in *Shichū torishimari ruishū, Shomotsu nishiki-e no bu* (*Collection of City Prosecutions: Book and Colour Print Section*; henceforth '*City Prosecutions*').[28] An alternative perspective on some of the cases recorded there can be acquired from *Fujiokaya nikki* (*Fujiokaya Diary*), a chronicle of significant public events kept by the bookseller Sudō (Fujiokaya) Yoshizō from 1804 to 1868.[29] Because Fujiokaya worked in the publishing industry, his diary is particularly rich in information about books and prints – what was popular, what had been suppressed – and his accounts can quite often be linked to extant works. He may well have been related to the publishers Fujiokaya Hikotarō and Fujiokaya Keijirō, who issued many important works by Kuniyoshi (including cats 21, 30, 32).[30]

'Riddle pictures'

The ban on pictures of children dancing in imitation of theatrical scenes seems to have been issued in the fifth month of 1843.[31] Publishers must now have been in desperate need of other subjects. Kuniyoshi responded by developing a novel, sophisticated kind of 'crazy picture' that satirised the times in an oblique or diffuse way, making censorship difficult. These images soon came to be referred to in official documents as 'riddle pictures' (*hanji-mono* or *hanji-e*). The most famous example, and one of Kuniyoshi's most celebrated prints, is 'The Earth Spider Conjures Up Demons at the Mansion of Minamoto Raikō' (*Minamoto no Yorimitsu-kō no yakata ni tsuchigumo yōkai o nasu zu*; cats 124, 125), which was published in the eighth month of 1843. *Fujiokaya nikki* and other contemporary sources make it clear that the image was read by the public as a satire on the Tenpō reforms. The ailing warrior Raikō (Yorimitsu) was generally identified with the ineffectual Shogun Tokugawa Ieyoshi (ruled 1837–53), while Urabe no Suetake, the retainer seated in front of him, was associated with the senior councillor Mizuno

Tadakuni (1794–1851), the hated chief architect of the reforms. Viewers would equate each demon taking part in the battle conjured up by the evil Earth Spider with a social group or a profession that was suffering under the reforms. Yet different people invested the picture with different detailed meanings, and this lack of explicitness helped deflect censorship. Kuniyoshi's publisher eventually took fright at the design's scandalous success and withdrew it voluntarily, avoiding punishment for himself and the artist. However, several publishers and artists who produced pirated versions of this notorious image were subjected to handcuffing or fines (see the entry for cats 124 and 125).[32]

The Earth Spider triptych was not Kuniyoshi's first 'riddle picture'. *City Prosecutions* recounts the case of the triptych 'Battle of the Chess Pieces: Prosperity and Great Peace across the Board', published in the seventh month, 1843, in which a battle takes place between two armies of warriors whose 'heads' consist of pieces used in the game *shōgi*, a kind of chess (fig. 9). It was quickly rumoured to have hidden meanings because several of the chess pieces bore strange names written with 'composite characters' (*yose-ji*) and because the arrow fired into a shield recalled the saying 'Everything's crooked and neither arrow nor shield can deflect it' (*Subete monogoto, sujigai nite ya mo tate mo tamaranu*) – in other words, we cannot put up with things as they are. Since the design had been passed by the censor, neither Kuniyoshi nor the publisher Gusokuya was punished. But when a samurai had another set of blocks cut and two booksellers sold a combined total of some nine hundred pirated impressions, officials intervened in the tenth month and ordered them to stop sales.[33]

Shortly after publication of the Earth Spider triptych the political tide began to turn. In the intercalary ninth month of 1843 Mizuno Tadakuni was dismissed from his post as senior councillor. However, the architect of reforms now regarded by many as too harsh was reinstated in the sixth month, 1844, only to be dismissed a second time in the second month of 1845 and forced to retire in the ninth month of that year. By 1846 restrictions on prints were being relaxed and, in the second half of the year, Kabuki prints with actor likenesses started to reappear. Indeed, the city magistrate's office announced in the eleventh month of 1846 that Kabuki prints could now be issued again – the face-saving euphemism 'in the form of dance scenes' (*odori keiyō*) was used – provided they included neither the actor's name nor his acting crest. Iwakiri suggests that these changes reflected not only a shift in the domestic political climate, but also the authorities' anxiety about the arrival in Uraga bay (not far from Edo) in 1845, and again in 1846, of US ships seeking trade relations. Actor prints would now seem to have been regarded as the lesser of two evils in comparison with 'riddle pictures', which might sensationalise the foreign menace and arouse public alarm.[34]

Kuniyoshi's print 'Ichikawa Danjūrō VIII as Ishikawa Goemon', from the series 'Sibling Pictures: Comparison of Thirty Selected Trees and Flowers' (*E-kyōdai mitate sanjū bokuka sen*), published in the ninth month of 1845 (fig. 10), was among the earliest actor likenesses to be produced at this time, more than one year before the ban was officially relaxed. None of the other fifteen portraits identified by Iwakiri in the series can be recognised by the face alone, but the features reflected in the mirror in this design are unmistakably those of Edo's leading actor. He is matched with a gourd plant, and this confirms his identity, because gourd patterns were often used by the Danjūrō line of actors on their clothing and accessories. The authorities tolerated direct

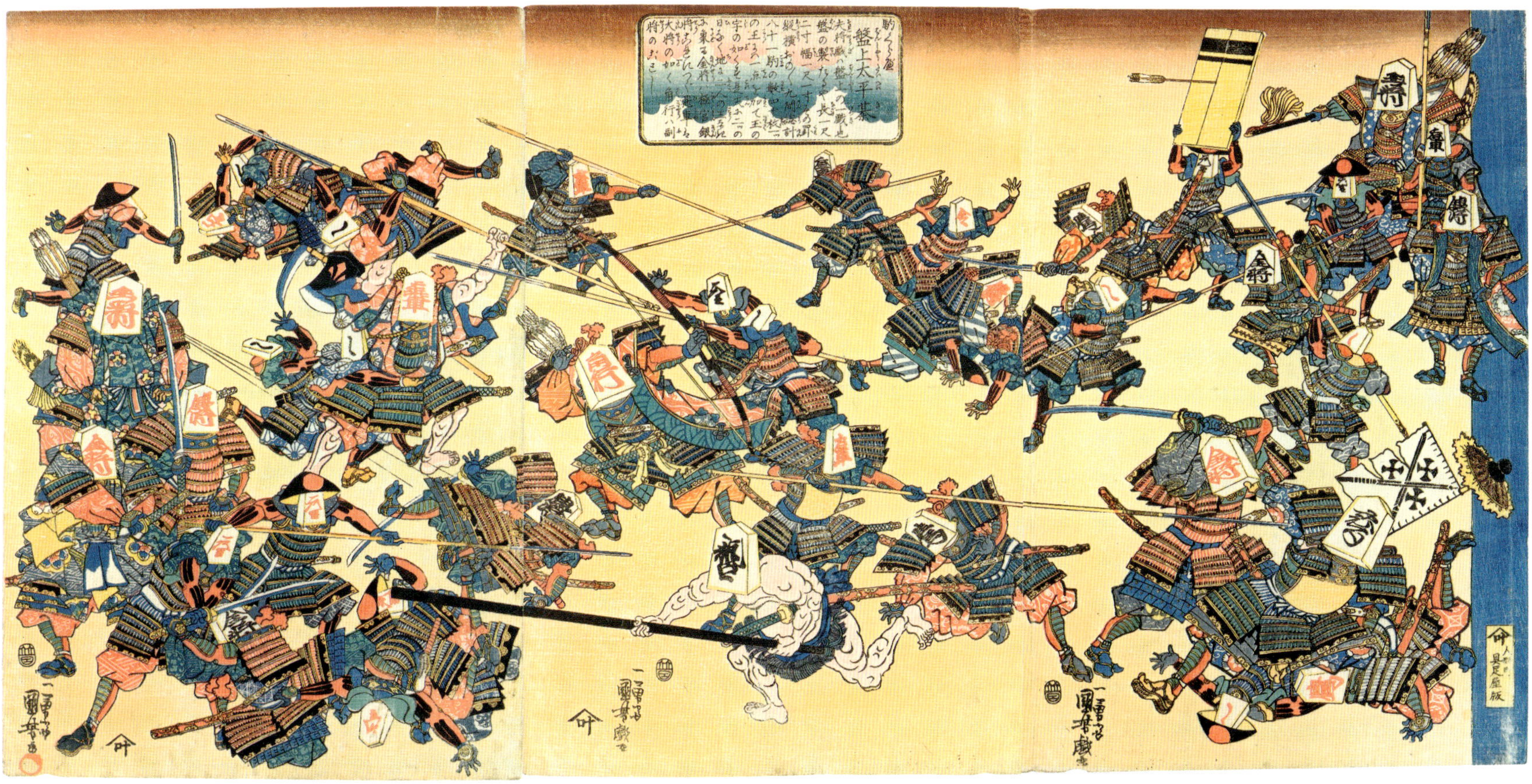

Fig. 9
Kuniyoshi, 'Battle of the Chess Pieces: Prosperity and Great Peace across the Board' (*Koma-kurabe banjō taiheiki*), seventh month, 1843.
Colour woodblock triptych, published by Gusokuya Kahei, 36.8 × 25.4 [R], 37 × 25.4 [C], 36.9 × 25.6 cm [L].
The Arthur R. Miller Collection 18408

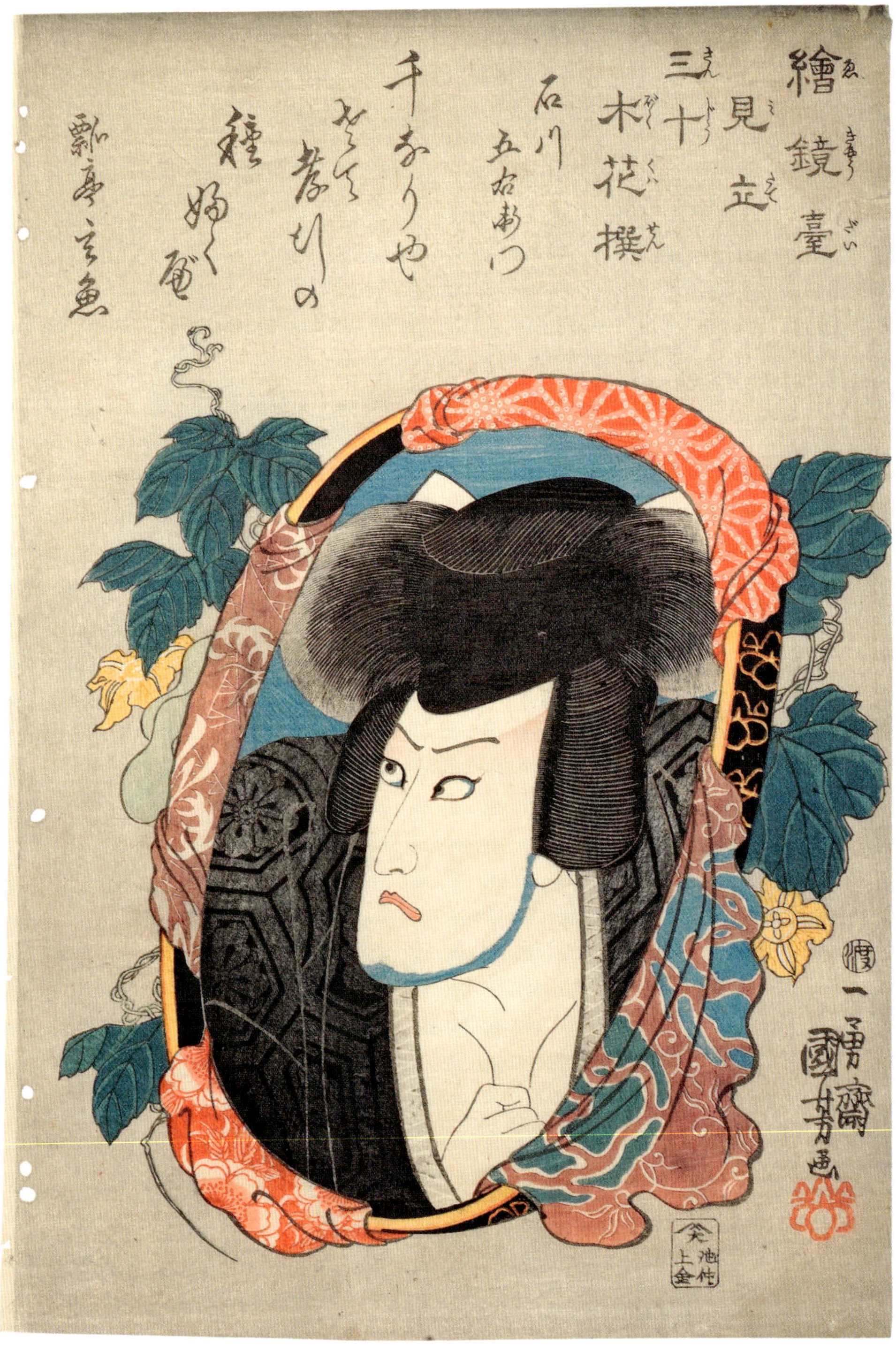

Fig. 10
Kuniyoshi, 'Ichikawa Danjūrō VIII as Ishikawa Goemon', from the series 'Sibling Pictures: Comparison of Thirty Selected Trees and Flowers' (*E-kyōdai mitate sanjū bokuka sen*), ninth month, 1845. Colour woodblock print, published by Jōshūya Kinzō, 36.2 × 24.8 cm.
The Arthur R. Miller Collection 12702

depictions of Danjūrō VIII for a reason: in the fifth month, 1845, they had publicly praised him and given him a cash award for his admirable filial piety towards both his father, Danjūrō VII (who was still living in exile in Osaka), and his mother. Was the government perhaps trying to curry favour with a disgruntled public?

Warrior prints and censorship

Since warrior prints were not a prime target of the Tenpō reforms, Kuniyoshi was in a better position than rival artists to weather the censorship storm. Indeed, a number of his most spectacular triptychs on warrior and mythological subjects were produced in 1845 and 1846, including the famous Skeleton Spectre triptych (cat. 25) and 'Oniwaka-maru about to kill a giant red carp' (*Oniwaka-maru to ō-higoi*; cat. 22). Nevertheless, the authorities considered warrior images to be potentially just as dangerous as prints on other subjects.

In the fifth month of 1804 the artists Utamaro and Toyokuni I (Kuniyoshi's teacher), along with their publishers, were punished for issuing colour prints in Edo that featured and named the warrior leader Toyotomi Hideyoshi (1536–1598), a key figure in the reunification of Japan after more than a century of civil war. The prints were inspired by a best-selling illustrated novel about Hideyoshi and his times, *Ehon Taikōki* (*Picture Book: Tales of the Regent*), which had been published in Osaka in seven volumes from 1797 to 1802 with no objections from the authorities. In 1804, however, both the novel, written by Takeuchi Kakusai (1770–1826) and illustrated by Okada Gyokuzan (1737–1812), and the spin-off prints were banned and withdrawn from sale. At the same time, a regulation was issued to the guild of publishers of popular fiction and prints proscribing images of warriors – including their name and family crest – who had lived from the Tenshō era (1573–92) onwards.[35] The Tokugawa regime was particularly sensitive about references to Toyotomi Hideyoshi and his descendants, whom the Tokugawa had all but eliminated in 1615 while consolidating their power. By dint of his own efforts Hideyoshi had risen from humble origins to become the supreme ruler of Japan and was a figure of immense appeal to a wide public, but for roughly a quarter of a century after the regulation of 1804 almost no images relating to him were produced.

Strong circumstantial evidence exists to suggest that Kuniyoshi admired Hideyoshi. For one thing, from c. 1831 the artist regularly used a gourd-shaped cartouche around his signature, sometimes forming it from the graphs for *yo-shi* (fig. 11). Then, from c. 1844, he adopted a seal following his signature that turned a *yoshi* character into stylised paulownia blossoms (fig. 12). The cartouche almost certainly alluded to Hideyoshi's 'thousand gourd standard' (*sennari hyōtan no umajirushi*), the seal to the imperial paulownia crest that Hideyoshi used as regent (*kanpaku*).[36] Furthermore, it was Kuniyoshi who took the first tentative steps to revive Hideyoshi imagery in the 1830s, and it was he and his pupils who led the full-scale boom in the Ka'ei era (1848–54). It is hard to interpret these phenomena as anything other than an expression of anti-Tokugawa sympathies, although, perhaps not surprisingly, Kuniyoshi never stated this explicitly.

The earliest Hideyoshi-related images by Kuniyoshi occur in the series 'One of Eight Hundred Heroes of *The Water Margin* of Japan' (*Honchō Suikoden gōyū/gōketsu happyakunin no hitori*), published in 1830–36, but they had to be transposed to different historical periods. Thus, the print of c. 1830–32 that ostensibly shows Kashiwade no Hanoshi, a sixth-century envoy to

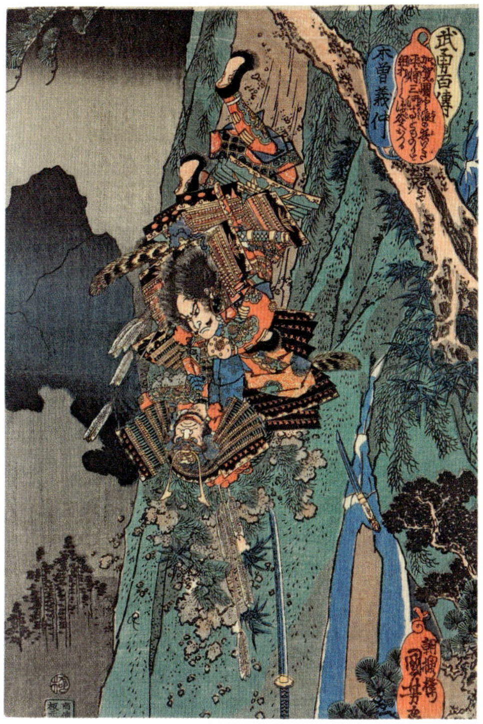

Fig. 11
Kuniyoshi, 'Kiso Yoshinaka [actually Katō Kiyomasa and Yamaji Shōgen]', from the series 'One Hundred Biographies of Military Heroes' (*Buyū hyakuden*), c. 1836. Colour woodblock print, published by Fujiokaya Hikotarō, 36.1 × 24.6 cm.
The Arthur R. Miller Collection 10901

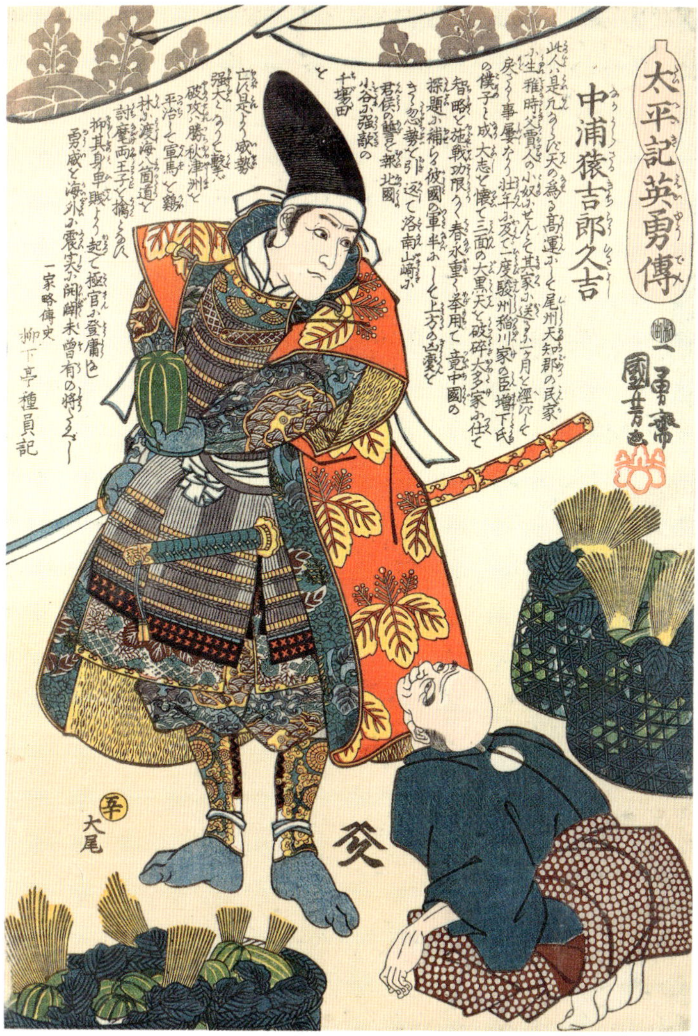

Fig. 12
Kuniyoshi, 'Nakaura Sarukichirō Hisayoshi [actually Toyotomi Hideyoshi]', from the series 'Heroes of the Great Peace' (*Taiheiki eiyūden*), 1848–49. Colour woodblock print, published by Yamamoto Heikichi, 35.8 × 24.8 cm.
The Arthur R. Miller Collection 05619

Korea, was read as a portrait of Hideyoshi's general Katō Kiyomasa (1562–1611), who led the invasions of Korea in the 1590s and took part in a famous tiger hunt there (cat. 12). All five prints known from the series 'One Hundred Biographies of Military Heroes' (*Buyū hyakuden*) of *c.* 1836 allude to well-known scenes from the illustrated biography of Hideyoshi, *Ehon Taikōki*, but again they had to be set in earlier eras. One bears the title 'Kiso Yoshinaka' (1154–1184) and the text states that he is shown fighting the Taira warrior Mikawa-no-kami Tomonori (fig. 11). In fact, this is a familiar *Ehon Taikōki* scene depicting an episode during the battle of Shizugadake (1583), when Kiyomasa and Yamaji Shōgen tumble down into a valley, locked in mortal combat. The Hideyoshi connection is signalled to the viewer by the three gourds around the titles, top right, and the *Yoshi* gourd cartouche around Kuniyoshi's signature, bottom right. To varying degrees Kuniyoshi based the five designs in this series on Gyokuzan's illustrations in *Ehon Taikōki*, adapting the compositions to the vertical format and adding colour.[37]

Less rigorous implementation of the Tenpō reforms from around 1846 brought about an increase in published images on all subjects, including warrior prints. The two most popular themes in performances given at this time by public storytellers (*kōdanshi*) were Chūshingura, the thinly fictionalised version of the famous vendetta by forty-seven loyal retainers of the Akō fief in 1701–03, and tales relating to Hideyoshi. It is no accident, then, that in the second half of the 1840s Kuniyoshi embarked on two series of warrior portraits, accompanied by biographies, that illustrated these very themes: 'Biographies of Loyal and Righteous Samurai' (*Seichū gishi den*) of 1847, with biographies written by Eisen (Ippitsuan Kakō; cats 41–4),[38] and 'Heroes of the Great Peace' (*Taiheiki eiyūden*) of 1848–50 (fig. 12; cats 39, 40), with texts by the storyteller and writer Ryūkatei Tanekazu.[39] A printed note on a design in the former series, which was published by Ebiya Rinnosuke, indicates that the artist began drawing the designs early in the seventh month of 1847 and completed them on the fourteenth day of the twelfth. A passage in *Fujiokaya nikki* records that sales began on the fourteenth day of the seventh month and that new designs continued to be distributed into the third month of 1848. Some eight thousand impressions of each of the fifty-one designs were printed and sold, amounting to a staggering 408,000 sheets and making the series 'the greatest hit and most widely praised of recent years'.[40]

Kuniyoshi followed a similar formula in 'Heroes of the Great Peace', with each portrait of a standing warrior accompanied by a short biography at the top, and this series also seems to have been well received by the public. Advertising copy in a catalogue of available books and prints issued by the publisher Yamamoto Heikichi in 1850 boasts that the series was still being printed and that it was enjoying unusually brisk sales.[41] The series title invokes the world of *Taiheiki* (*Chronicle of the Great Peace*), a major literary work describing events of the mid-fourteenth century, and Kuniyoshi was also obliged to use aliases to disguise the identities of his late sixteenth-century warriors. That did not prevent him from telling in these fifty prints the whole sequence of events from *Ehon Taikōki* with unprecedented boldness, starting with Oda Nobunaga (1534–1582), the warrior who commenced the process of reunification around 1560, and ending with Hideyoshi.

Hideyoshi's common alias of Nakaura Sarukichirō Hisayoshi appears on this last print (fig. 12). The middle nickname alluded to his monkey-like features, but Kuniyoshi portrays him as a dignified figure, superbly attired in armour as he receives a melon from a grateful (and adoring) farmer before the battle of Yamazaki. Hideyoshi cuts the melon to pieces with his sword, demonstrating the inevitable fate of all who seek to betray him.[42] Once again, the series cartouche is gourd-shaped, and Hideyoshi's surcoat and the curtain are emblazoned with his crest of paulownia blossoms. In 1844, when Kuniyoshi's senior in the Utagawa school, Kunisada, brazenly assumed the name of their deceased teacher, Toyokuni,[43] Kuniyoshi quickly abandoned the *toshidama* ring-seal of the school and adopted the red paulownia seal seen beneath his signature here (called the *Yoshikiri* seal, the character *yoshi* appearing in the shape of paulownia flowers). In doing so, he distanced himself from Kunisada, so as not to be thought his pupil, and, simultaneously, declared his sympathy for his historical hero, Hideyoshi. *Fujiokaya nikki* noted that from the spring of 1849 a large number of *Taikōki* (i.e. Hideyoshi) prints were being issued, a vogue that continued to the end of the Edo period.[44]

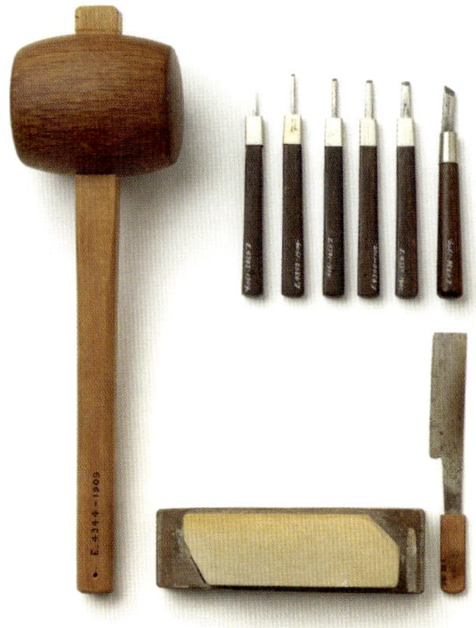

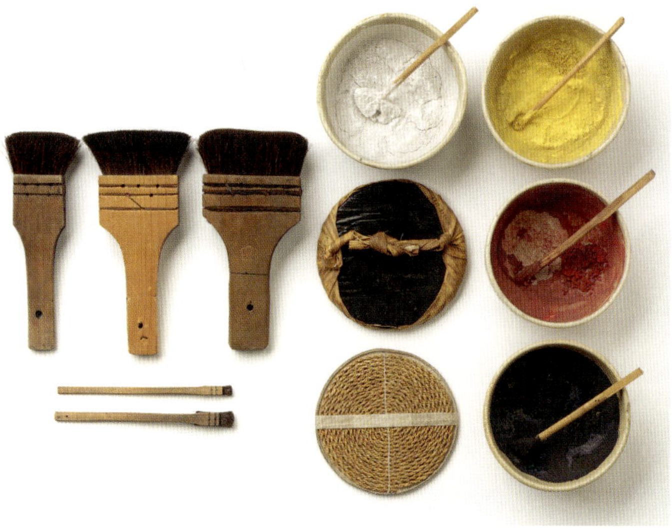

Fig. 13
Selection of woodblock-cutter's tools, c. 1900?
Victoria and Albert Museum, London, E.4344-1909 (mallet), E.4345-1909 (whetstone), E.115-1915 (small saw), E.4333–43-1909 (knives, chisels and gouges)

Fig. 14
Selection of woodblock printer's tools, c. 1900?
Victoria and Albert Museum, London, E.4348-1909 (printer's pad), E.125-1915 (printer's pad case), E.4324, 4326, 4327, 4331, 4332-1909 (printer's brushes)

Artist and publisher, block-cutter and printer

How was Kuniyoshi able to design as many as ten thousand prints in his career? And how did a publisher manage to produce 408,000 impressions of just one series in eight months? Such questions cannot be answered without some knowledge of the process by which colour woodblock prints were made.[45]

Kuniyoshi would be commissioned by a publisher to supply a neat, 'block-ready' brush drawing (*hanshita-e*) on thin paper that could be glued to the printing block for cutting. Two very rare surviving block-ready drawings, for warrior prints that were never published, are included here (cats 15, 16). At the bottom they bear the small impressed trademark (a vertical line with a circle on the right) of the publisher (Yamaguchiya Tōbei) and, next to this, an impression of the small censorship seal reading '*kiwame*' (examined). In quite a few places corrections have been made by pasting on irregular pieces of thin paper and redrawing the areas patched in this way.

Like other artists, Kuniyoshi frequently did several stages of preparatory drawings (*shita-e*) in ink on paper before tracing the block-ready version for the block-cutter. His drawings are often compelling in their dynamism, which is perhaps why many more have been preserved than in the case of other artists.[46] At an unknown date, perhaps around the time of his death, his rough sketches (*sōkō*) were collected in at least sixty albums, each containing about thirty to fifty drawings. Two complete albums have survived in their original form in the Victoria and Albert Museum, London (see also the entry for cat. 109). The warrior drawing on the right in fig. 15 is an initial idea for a portrait of the warrior Saitō Katsuoki in the series 'Heroes of the Great Peace' of 1848–50, discussed above.[47]

On receiving block-ready drawings, the block-cutter pasted them face-down onto smooth blocks of hard mountain cherrywood, cut vertically, along the grain. He then used a variety of chisels, gouges and knives to cut through the back of the drawing, carving away the areas of the design not to be printed and leaving delicate ridges of wood to print the outlines (fig. 13).[48] A series of proof impressions were taken from this 'key-block' (or 'line-block'), into which was cut a right-angled mark in one corner and a long mark near the top of one edge. These 'registrations marks' would be cut in exactly the same place in relation to the design on each of the individual colour blocks. During printing, the corner of the paper was positioned inside the right-angled mark and the edge of the paper aligned with the long mark. This simple but effective registration method had been perfected by the mid-eighteenth century and was known as the *kentō*. The notches forming the two marks are clearly visible on the left of the printing block included here (cat. 131).

On a set of proof impressions taken from the key-block Kuniyoshi would indicate where he wanted each colour to print – generally by painting the areas with red ink – and would write notes on any patterns or printing effects required. He returned these annotated proofs to the block-cutter, who, together with his assistants, used them to carve a set of colour blocks. All the blocks were then transferred to the workshop of the printer and his team, who were quite separate specialist craftsmen. Kuniyoshi and his publisher were doubtless keen to approve a model colour scheme for the earliest impressions, but no eyewitness accounts of this part of the production process seem to have survived.

The printer began by taking impressions from the key-block, before using the *kentō* system to print the colours one after another so that they fitted neatly inside the outlines. The colours consisted of vegetable dyes, mineral pigments and, latterly, chemical pigments (Prussian blue was used extensively after about 1830). They were applied to the block with printer's brushes of various sizes, the bristles made from specially conditioned horsetail hair (fig. 14). Powdered colours were mixed with water and a tiny amount of rice-paste binder, to add lustre. They were placed in small bowls and lined up next to where the printer was working, seated cross-legged with the block laid horizontally at a slight angle in front of him. Thick, handmade mulberry paper (*kōzo*) of high, presentation quality (*hōsho*) was lightly sized with alum and kept slightly damp ready for printing. Paper made in Echizen province (the eastern part of modern Fukui prefecture) was the most favoured. Another key tool was the 'printer's pad' (*baren*), the core of which consisted of a coil of rope made from tightly twisted bamboo-leaf fibres. The pad fitted into a shallow dish made from many layers of glued paper, waterproofed with coatings of persimmon juice and then toughened with an exterior coating of black lacquer. A bamboo leaf was wrapped around the pad and twisted to form a rope grip across the back.

Apprenticeships for block-cutters and printers could last up to ten years. Printers spent much of this time learning to apply the *baren* to the back of the paper with the pressure and sensitivity necessary to obtain a good impression from the block (no printing press or other mechanical device was used). Gradation printing (*bokashi*), as seen especially in landscapes (fig. 3), required the printer to coax a small amount of pigment into a specially dampened area of the block as he was printing and demanded enormous skill.

Kuniyoshi in 1853

The diptych 'Miracle of Masterpieces by Floating-world Matabei' (*Ukiyo Matabei meiga no kidoku*; fig. 16) of 1853 was one of Kuniyoshi's most notorious works, on a par with the Earth Spider triptych of 1843. Like the artist's slightly earlier 'self-portrait' triptych (1848; cat. 129), it ostensibly featured the legendary painter Ukiyo ('Floating-world') Matabei, who was thought to have invented the kind of popular souvenir painting known as 'Ōtsu pictures' (*Ōtsu-e*). Matabei's paintings were so vivid, it was said, that the characters portrayed came to life. In the diptych, as in the print of 1848, Kuniyoshi grafted 'likeness pictures' (*nigao-e*) of Kabuki actors onto all the figures, including Matabei, seated on the right, who appears in the guise of Ichikawa Kodanji IV. As noted above, by the eleventh month of 1846 the authorities were tacitly agreeing to the renewed publication of actor prints, so censorship on these grounds was no longer an issue either in the triptych of 1848 or the diptych of 1853.

City Prosecutions records that the block-ready drawing for the Matabei diptych was approved by the censors on the sixth day of the sixth month, 1853, and that it went on sale in the middle of that month. *Fujiokaya nikki* states that it was available for purchase from the eighteenth day of the seventh month, and that from the first of the eighth month sales exploded.[49] Sixteen hundred impressions were being printed every day to meet the demand. Examination of surviving impressions confirms that the print must have been produced in very large quantities.

Fig. 15
Kuniyoshi, 'Kuniyoshi rough sketches, no. 48' (*Kuniyoshi sōkō, yonjū-hachi*), assembled c. 1860? Scrapbook pasted with sketches, ink on paper, 32.6 × 22.5 cm (covers).
Victoria and Albert Museum, London, D.1194-1210-'89

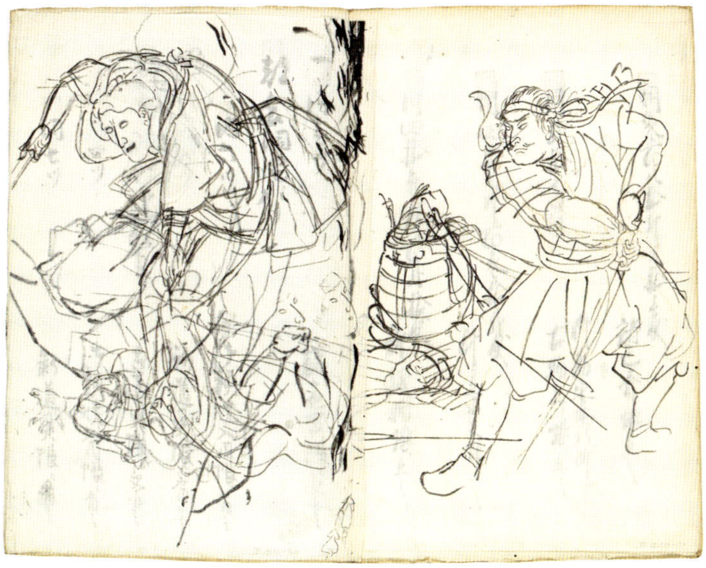

The Miller Collection contains impressions from two quite different sets of blocks. The first (18217; fig. 16), though in good condition, with bright, unfaded colours, exhibits white gaps between the brown of Matabei's robe and its outline – an imprecise fit testifying to block wear. The Museum of Fine Arts, Springfield, Massachusetts, owns an extremely late impression, taken after many more thousands had been printed and the blocks had become considerably more worn.[50] Many of the outlines have disappeared completely and the colour blocks are fitting very badly. The second impression in the Miller Collection (18204) was clearly printed from different blocks, since some small details are not quite as well articulated as in Miller 18217. Recut editions could be produced by sacrificing impressions of the prints, using these, rather than new block-ready drawings, to carve a fresh, almost line-perfect set of blocks – a technique known as 'overlaid carving' (*kabuse-bori*). Printing from several sets at the same time obviously expanded the quantity of impressions at a rapid rate.

The Matabei diptych owed much of its extraordinary success to the timing of its publication. On the third day of the sixth month, 1853, a squadron of four US battleships under the command of Commodore Matthew Perry had steamed into Uraga bay and rumours of a 'foreign invasion' reached the city the following day. In a detailed discussion of the print in relation to these momentous events the historian Minami Kazuo doubted that Kuniyoshi would have had time to design a print in response to the Americans' arrival and present it to the censors by the sixth day of the month, but the matter is surely open to question.[51] Another key factor in the work's popularity was the unexpected death, on the twenty-second day of the sixth month, of the twelfth shogun, Tokugawa Ieyoshi (1793–1853), whose period of rule, starting in 1837, had been dominated by the hated Tenpō reforms. His passing destabilised an already tense situation, and, as they had ten years earlier with the Earth Spider triptych, people began reading into Kuniyoshi's image what they wanted to see. Perhaps Ukiyo Matabei represented Tokugawa Nariaki (1800–1860), lord of Mito? Maybe the Young Falconer with '*kan*' written on his sleeve stood for the soon-to-be-appointed thirteenth shogun, Iesada (1824–1858), a sickly individual nicknamed 'Kan Kubō' (Nervous Kid Shogun)? Could Wisteria Maiden (*Fuji-musume*) be Lady Fujinoe, a powerful figure in the shogun's harem? And did Monkey and Catfish symbolise the Americans? *Fujiokaya nikki* offers detailed explanations of the hidden meaning of each figure, but another contemporary source provides quite different interpretations.[52]

As with the Earth Spider triptych, the authorities were alarmed not only by the question of who was 'really' represented, but also by the generally unsettling effect of the 'false rumours' (*fuhyō*) the image generated. In the eighth month of 1853 they overrode the censor's approval and ordered the publisher to cease selling the prints and to destroy both the blocks and any remaining stocks. The operating censors were all dismissed and replaced. A later document records that Kuniyoshi and his publisher were fined, but *City Prosecutions* mentions no such punishment.[53]

Also in the eighth month of 1853 the North City Magistrate's office ordered Kuniyoshi to be subjected to investigation. A rather detailed report submitted that month by a 'secret investigator' (*onmitsu-mawari*) appears in *City Prosecutions*. The preamble states: 'It came to official notice that the artist Kuniyoshi of Shin-Izumichō made drawings for print designs that gave rise to false rumours. I was asked to investigate his daily behaviour and his reputation. There follows a summary of information about him that resulted from my secret enquiries'.[54] This is one of the most important contemporary sources about the artist, written just two years before the stroke that all but put an end to his career. The report discusses the Matabei diptych, but also gives information on Kuniyoshi's character, family and living conditions.
It mentions his relationship with his patron and long-time friend, the merchant Morota (Enshūya) Sakichi (the *kyōka* poet Umenoya Kakuju, 1801–1865),[55] who owned a feedstuff business. Further, the investigator describes Kuniyoshi's eccentric behaviour at a 'calligraphy and painting party' (*shogakai*) organised by Umenoya.[56] The document merits a full translation, but for present purposes a synopsis must suffice.

The report begins by sketching the background to the case, explaining how the Tenpō regulations prevented Kuniyoshi from continuing to design actor prints. Because of his great talent he received orders for 'weird and unusual pictures' (*kikai no zu*, i.e. satirical prints on topical subjects). Banning such designs merely increased their popularity and their publisher's

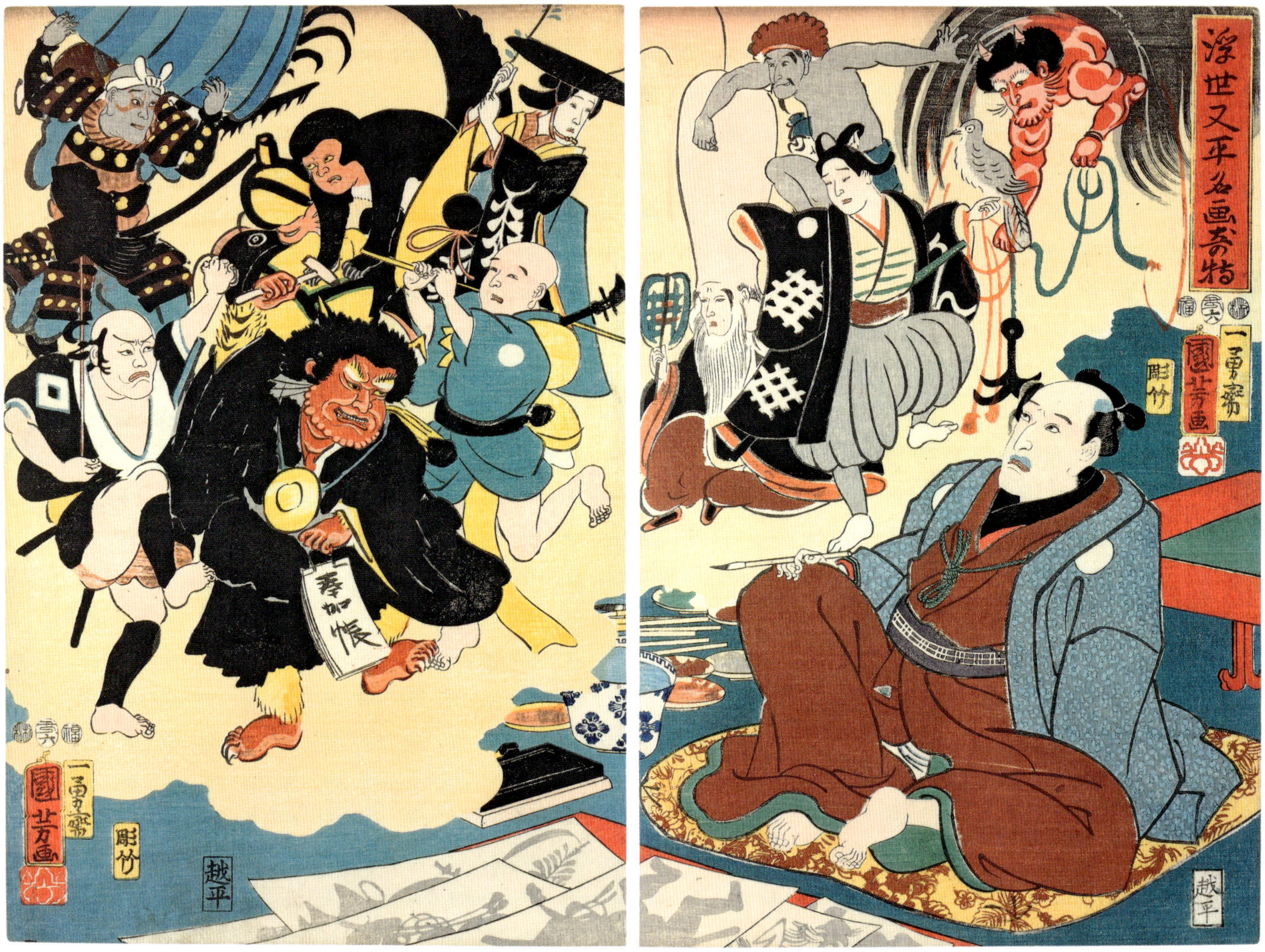

Fig. 16
Kuniyoshi, 'Miracle of Masterpieces by Floating-world Matabei' (*Ukiyo Matabei meiga no kidoku*), sixth month, 1853. Colour woodblock diptych, published by Koshimuraya Heisuke, 35.7 × 24.4 [R], 35.7 × 24.4 cm [L].
The Arthur R. Miller Collection 18217

profits. When prints 'in the form of dance scenes' (i.e. Kabuki prints) were permitted again, he stopped producing weird pictures, but the actor likenesses of 'Toyokuni [III]' (Kunisada) were better than his, so Kuniyoshi constantly devised unusual subjects to earn a living.

As with most ukiyo-e artists, the investigator claims, Kuniyoshi's character was fundamentally that of a craftsman (*shokunin*). His manners were rough (*yahi*) and he was open-hearted (*kattatsu*). Even when a publisher offered him a large sum of money, he would accept an order only if it appealed to him. The ideas for his prints were not his alone: he consulted 'Sashichi' (probably an error for 'Sakichi', the poet Umenoya), a close friend of his who also devised comic skits, festival dances and parades.

His home at Shin-Izumichō Shindō was 2.5 *ken* (about 4.5m) wide and 6 *ken* (about 11m) deep.[57] Eight or nine people lived there. His family did not own many changes of clothes because he gave much of the money he earned to his pupils. On the twenty-fourth day of the sixth month last, 'Sashichi' arranged a calligraphy and painting party at the restaurant of Kawachiya Hanzaburō. (This could have been done for Kuniyoshi's benefit, the proceeds acquired from paying guests going to him.) Kuniyoshi did a magnificent painting of a Chinese *Water Margin* hero on paper covering an area of some thirty tatami mats. To do the shading, he took off his unlined summer kimono (*hitoe-mono*) and, working almost naked, soaked the robe with ink and used it like a giant brush.

The report now turns to the Matabei diptych. It describes how the design was passed by the censor and how the composition is unusually clever, based ostensibly on the plot of the puppet play *Keisei Hangonkō* (*Courtesan of the Hangon Incense*).[58] A list is given of the actors whose likenesses are embedded in the design. The investigator mentions the triptych 'Ōtsu Pictures for the Times: A Rare Thing You've been Waiting For' (*Toki ni ōtsu-e kitai no maremono*; cat. 129) of 'three or four years ago' and observes that the subject did not cause any false rumours. But things were different with the present diptych, which had indeed given rise to such rumours. Otherwise, Kuniyoshi did not appear to be engaging in any unlawful activities.

At the beginning of his report the investigator lists the people living at the house in Shin-Izumichō. In addition to Kuniyoshi (Magosaburō, aged fifty-six), there were his wife, Sei (aged thirty-eight), their daughters Tori (fifteen) and Yoshi (twelve), a mother (Sei's?) named Yasu (seventy-two) and three or four pupils. No cats are mentioned. By this date the artist's daughters were already working alongside their father, contributing, for example, small inset landscapes to 'Auspicious Pictures of Land and Sea' (*Sankai medetai zue*), a series of half-length beauties published in 1852 (cats 71–3).[59]

Notwithstanding scrutiny by the secret investigator, Kuniyoshi seems to have been more fortunate in his skirmishes with the censors than other artists and publishers, apparently escaping serious punishment. This is all the more remarkable in that he often took the lead in circumventing the publication regulations of the Tenpō reforms and played a crucial role in developing 'riddle pictures' and other forms of visual satire. Kuniyosh's avoidance of official censure surely bears eloquent witness to the flexibility and spontaneity of his approach to art, to his willingness not only to adapt to the times, but also to make the times adapt to him.

NOTES

The author wishes gratefully to acknowledge generous assistance in the preparation of this essay and catalogue from Iwakiri Yuriko, whose many publications on Kuniyoshi have transformed our understanding of his art.

1 In 1844 Kunisada assumed the title Toyokuni II, ignoring the achievements of Utagawa Toyoshige (?1802–?1835), who had used the name Toyokuni from c. 1825 to 1834, following the death of their mutual teacher, Utagawa Toyokuni I (1769–1825). Historians therefore refer to Kunisada as Toyokuni III when discussing his post-1844 activities.

2 The most detailed discussion of Kuniyoshi's life and the relevant sources is found in Suzuki 1992, particularly pp. 244–9. A comprehensive account has been given in English by Amy Newland, 'Kuniyoshi's Life and Work', in Amsterdam 1998, pp. 9–34. Ages are given in the present publication in accordance with the traditional Japanese reckoning, which assumes that a baby is one at birth. Ages are therefore generally one year in advance of those given according to the Western system.

3 Suzuki 1992, nos. 12, 13.

4 Basil Robinson's landmark study of 1982, *Kuniyoshi: The Warrior Prints*, provides a comprehensive guide to this aspect of the artist's career. See also the typescript supplement produced by Robinson and Arthur R. Miller in 1996.

5 Personal communication from Iwakiri Yuriko.

6 Personal communication from Ellis Tinios.

7 Suzuki 1992, p. 249.

8 Tinios 1996, p. 45.

9 For ukiyo-e and censorship, see Thompson 1991, the catalogue of a groundbreaking exhibition on the subject. See also GUDHJ, vol. 3, pp. 120–4.

10 Quoted in Minami 1974, p. 18.

11 For a historical summary, see Bolitho 1989.

12 The other licensed Kabuki theatre was the Morita-za, which sometimes used the name Kawarasaki-za.

13 For summaries of the effects on ukiyo-e of the Kyōhō and Kansei reforms, see Clark et al. 2001, pp. 26–8, and Asano and Clark 1995, text vol. pp. 40–5, respectively. Much of the information presented here on the effects of the Tenpō reforms derives from Minami 1973, Minami 1974 and Iwakiri 2002.

14 See Iwakiri 2002.

15 Iwakiri 2007, pp. 89–91.

16 A table suggesting which censor was on duty in most months of the period 1843–46 appears in Iwakiri 2002, pp. 32–3.

17 Quoted in Suzuki 1992, p. 253.

18 Kyōsai used this art-name until 1871, when he switched to one with characters meaning 'enlightened studio'; see Clark 1993, pp. 20–2.

19 A wide selection of Kuniyoshi's *kyōga* is presented and interpreted in Inagaki 1991.

20 Iijima 1894/1941, pp. 280–1.

21 Oka 1992, pp. 155–76.

22 Katsumori 2000, fig. 13. Katsumori identifies further sources of Kuniyoshi's imagery in illustrations to *Aesop's Fables*, printed in a large number of editions in many European languages from the late fifteenth century onwards. Ibid., pp. 25–9.

23 Katsumori 2000; Katsuhara 2006. See also the entries for cats 46–8.

24 Katsuhara 2006.

25 Minami 1974, pp. 19–20.

26 Iwakiri 2002, p. 8.

27 Minami 1974, p. 23.

28 *Shichū torishimari ruishū*.

29 *Fujiokaya nikki*, esp. vols. 2–5, 1988–89.

30 Minami 1973, p. 5.

31 Iwakiri 2002, p. 10.

32 Minami 1973a.

33 Minami 1974, pp. 26–7; Iwakiri 2002, p. 10.

34 Iwakiri 2002, pp. 25–7.

35 Minami 1981; Machida 2003, pp. 193–4.

36 Suzuki 1985, p. 125; Varshavskaya 2005, pp. 22–3.

37 Machida 2003, pp. 182–3, 194.

38 Weinberg 2000.

39 Varshavskaya 2005.

40 *Fujiokaya nikki*, vol. 3, 1998, p. 246.

41 The catalogue appeared in the *gōkan* book *Usumurasaki Uji no akebono*, published in 1850; quoted in Suzuki 1992, p. 270, n. 45.

42 Varshavskaya 2005, p. 158.

43 See note 1.

44 *Fujiokaya nikki*, vol. 3, 1988, p. 457.

45 The most detailed historical description of the woodblock technique in English is Tokuno 1892/1982. The most extensive Japanese source is Ishii 1929/2005.

46 For a monograph on Kuniyoshi's drawings, see Forrer 1988.

47 For the finished print, see Varshavskaya 2005, no. 6, pp. 70–1.

48 The block-cutter's and printer's tools illustrated here were acquired for the Victoria and Albert Museum in 1909 by the Kyoto art dealer Inada Hogitarō, who established premises in London that year. See Faulkner 2001, p. 13.

49 *Shichū torishimaru ruishū*, vol. 21, 1994, pp. 122–36; *Fujiokaya nikki*, vol. 5, 1989, pp. 352–5.

50 Thompson 1991, fig. 38.

51 Minami 1973, pp. 12–13.

52 Minami 1973, p. 12, includes a table of the differing readings of the image given in *Fujiokaya nikki* and on the small labels attached to an impression formerly owned by Mitamura Engyo.

53 The document is *Zoku Taihei nenpyō*, referred to in Minami 1973, p. 13.

54 *Shichū torishimaru ruishū*, vol. 21, 1994, p. 129. The present summary of the investigator's report is based on pp. 129–34.

55 The report consistently, and probably mistakenly, records Umenoya's given name as 'Sashichi', rather than Sakichi. See Iwakiri 1992, part 1, p. 3.

56 For a detailed study of the relationship between Umenoya and Kuniyoshi, see Iwakiri 1992, parts 1 and 2.

57 A small sketch of the house by Hasegawa Keiseki (1842–1932) is reproduced in Amsterdam 1998, fig. 10.

58 As early as 1708 Chikamatsu Monzaemon had included the Ōtsu painter Ukiyo Matabei, or 'Matabei the Stutterer' (Domo Matabei), as a character in his puppet play *Keisei Hangonkō* (*Courtesan of the Hangon Incense*), which was later adapted for Kabuki. By Kuniyoshi's day, various Ōtsu figures had become established characters in Kabuki dance.

59 Suzuki 1992, p. 247, provides more information about Kuniyoshi's family. He remarried after his first wife, Sei, died in 1856. His second wife, name unknown, died during the Keiō era (1865–68). His daughters, Tori and Yoshi, were born in 1839 and 1842 respectively.

CATALOGUE

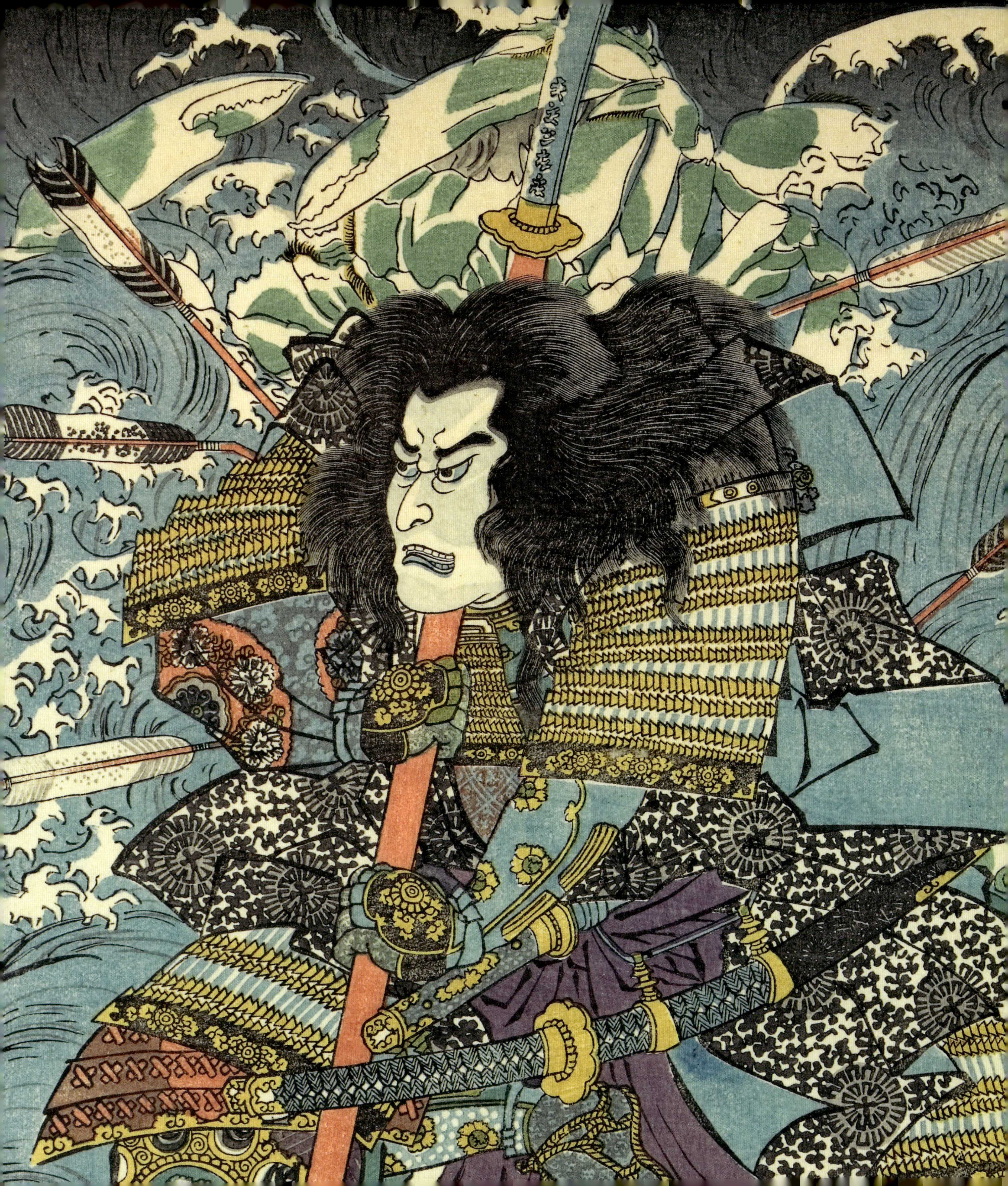

1

WARRIORS

Kuniyoshi belonged to the artisan class: he was not a samurai. How was it, then, that he came to create some of the most heroic and memorable images of Japanese warriors? The subject was clearly congenial to him, and 'warrior pictures' (*musha-e*) were an expanding genre in which he could carve out a leading position within the highly competitive world of popular printmaking. But broader historical currents surely had an impact as well.

During the first half of the nineteenth century, foreign powers made increasingly frequent attempts to end the policy of regulated seclusion that had been pursued by Japan since the late 1630s. In particular, Russian, US and British warships and traders were now often seen in Japanese waters. After the defeat of China by Britain in the First Opium War of 1839–42 Japan feared she might be next. Against this background of anxiety about possible foreign encroachment, images of valiant warriors from the past must have been reassuring to samurai and non-samurai alike. They must also have served as a sustained admonishment to Japan's present rulers to be militarily vigilant and see off any foreign threat. In this context, the themes that Kuniyoshi and his publishers selected for warrior designs become significant.

Kuniyoshi achieved his first great success *c.* 1827–30, with a series popularly known as *Suikoden*, which featured muscular, sometimes heavily tattooed heroes from the Chinese tale *The Water Margin* (cats 3–10). There is evidence that both the artist and his friend and patron Umenoya Kakuju (1801–1865) identified with the Chinese hero Kyūmonryō Shishin, who had nine dragons tattooed on his body; indeed, the idea for the series may have been developed with Umenoya (Iwakiri 1992a, pp. 3–6). The tale's heroes were outlaws who did battle with other brigands and the imperial forces, in accordance with their own moral code.

Scenes of military exploits often overlapped with wider historical narratives, since Japan had been ruled since 1185 by a succession of military regimes. The subjects often contained a strong mythological or supernatural element. Indeed, Kuniyoshi's warrior imagery formed part of a rich continuum of popular media that served a generally literate and well-educated public and included Kabuki theatre, so-called 'playful literature' (*gesaku*), public storytelling (*kōdan*) and street amusements (*misemono*). As his career developed, the artist frequently took inspiration from new genres of popular illustrated fiction, from adventure stories in the *yomihon* ('books for reading') genre by Takizawa Bakin (1767–1848), then from novels in the *gōkan* ('combined-volume') format that superseded these.

Kuniyoshi depicted warriors from all periods, often pitting them in violent combat against giant creatures as well as samurai. He sometimes spread the scenes over a triptych print, unifying the composition in innovative and striking ways with a single large element that crossed all three sheets. A favourite source of subjects was the civil wars of 1180–85 between the Minamoto and Taira clans, in particular the exploits of Minamoto no Yoshitsune (Ushiwakamaru, 1159–1189) and his henchman, the warrior monk Benkei (cats 21–4). Two other themes he returned to many times, especially in his later years, were the reunification wars of the late sixteenth century, centring on the warrior leader Toyotomi Hideyoshi (1536–1598; p. 27, fig. 12; cats 39, 40), and the vendetta of forty-seven loyal samurai from the Akō fief in 1701–03, popularly known as 'Chūshingura' (*Treasury of the Loyal Retainers*; cats 41–9). Both were politically sensitive subjects. Even when the strict censorship introduced by the Tenpō reforms of 1841–43 began to be relaxed around 1846, convention still obliged Kuniyoshi to use aliases when referring to post-1573 heroes and, generally, to set their exploits in more ancient times.

A comprehensive guide to Kuniyoshi's warrior prints is provided by Basil W. Robinson's *Kuniyoshi: The Warrior Prints* (Robinson 1982). See also the typescript supplement produced by Robinson and Arthur R. Miller in 1996.

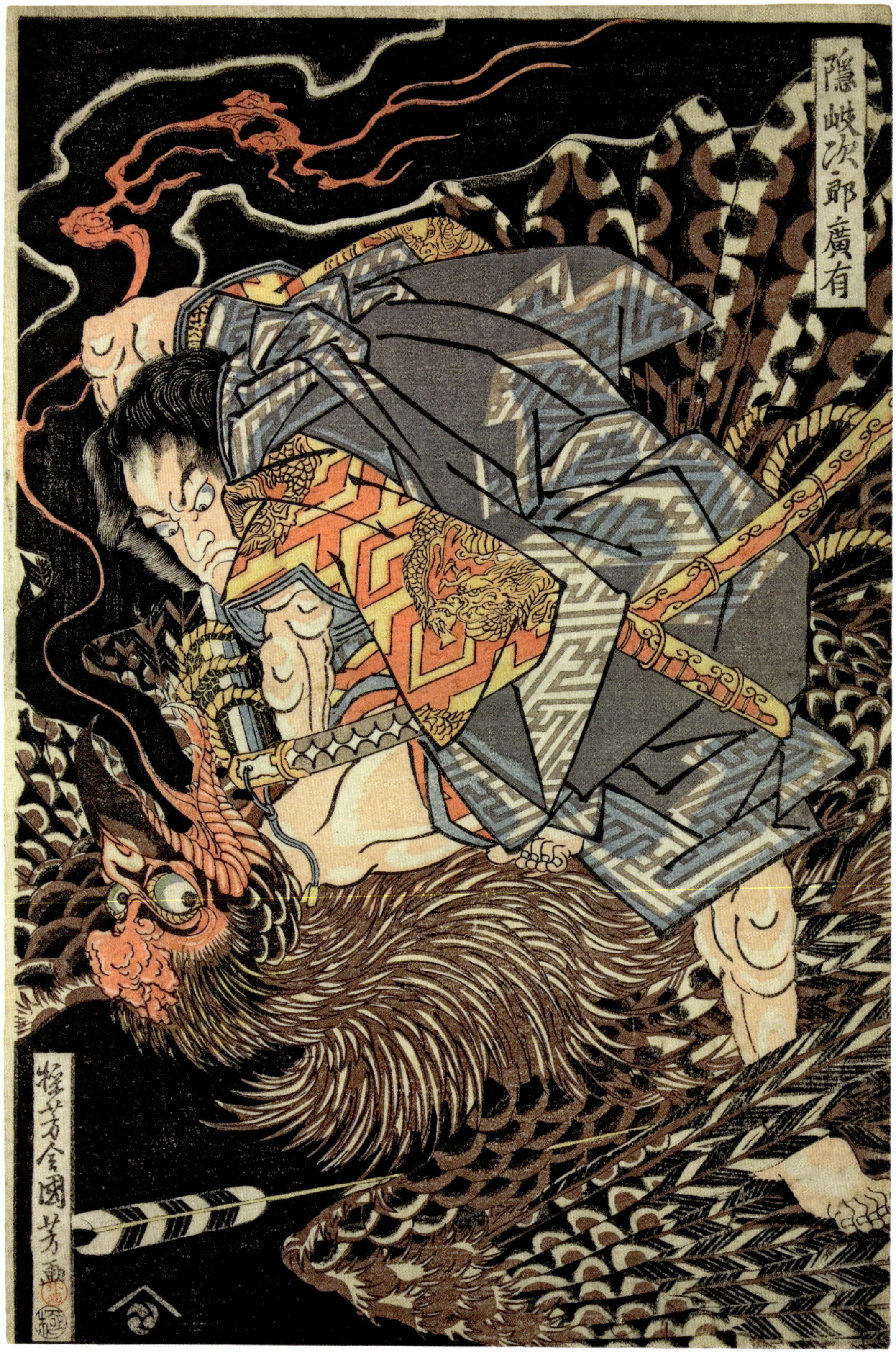

1

Oki no Jirō Hiroari kills a monster bird

late 1810s

Colour woodblock, *ōban*, published by Nishimuraya Yohachi, 37.6 × 25.7 cm

PRINT TITLE
'Oki no Jirō Hiroari'

ARTIST'S SIGNATURE
Saihōsha Kuniyoshi ga

CENSORSHIP SEAL
kiwame

COLLECTOR'S SEAL
Hayashi Tadamasa

American Friends of the British Museum (The Arthur R. Miller Collection) 21201

REFERENCES
Robinson 1961, no. 7 (with the mark of publisher Izumiya Ichibei); Robinson 1982, no. S1a.2; Suzuki 1992, no. 77; Nagoya 1996, no. 8; Amsterdam 1998, no. 6 (this impression); Machida 2003, no. 148; Isao 2008, p. 8

Enveloped in darkness, the warrior Oki no Jirō Hiroari pins a monster bird under one knee and drives the point of his sword into its throat. The bird struggles to grasp the sword with one claw, while flames dart from its mouth. Piercing one wing is the mighty arrow that has brought it down.

The story comes from the famous military chronicle *Taiheiki* (*Chronicle of the Great Peace*, 1340s–1371). In the autumn of 1334 there was pestilence in Kyoto, and each night a monster bird would appear above Shishinden palace and cry out 'How long? How long?' (*itsu made itsu made*). Fire and lightning issued from its beak. Oki no Jirō Hiroari shot it down, as commanded by the emperor. The monster had the head of a human, the body of a snake, a serrated beak-tip and knife-like claws. Its wingspan was some sixteen feet. The subject had already appeared in late eighteenth-century book illustrations by Shunshō, Shigemasa (Machida 2003, p. 136) and Sekien, but this may be the first time it was used for a single-sheet print. Kuniyoshi emphasises the monster's birdlike appearance and draws it thrust on its back, forced into the corner of the design by the violence of the hero's attack.

This is one of the earliest surviving prints that Kuniyoshi signed with the unusual name 'Saihōsha' preceding 'Kuniyoshi'. Five designs are known with this combined signature, including a triptych of Kabuki actors that has been dated to a performance in the eleventh month, 1816 (Isao 2008, p. 9). Four of the five, among them the present print, were published by Nishimuraya Yohachi. Similar subjects of mortal combat between man and beast had appeared in prints by Katsukawa Shun'ei (1762–1819) and his pupil Shuntei (1770–1820), which feature muscular, hirsute warriors with bulging eyes. Kuniyoshi would make such confrontations his forte (see, for example, cats 2, 12, 13). The impression formerly in the Robinson Collection (Robinson 1961, no. 7) seems to be a later printing, made after the blocks had been sold to the firm of Izumiya Ichibei.

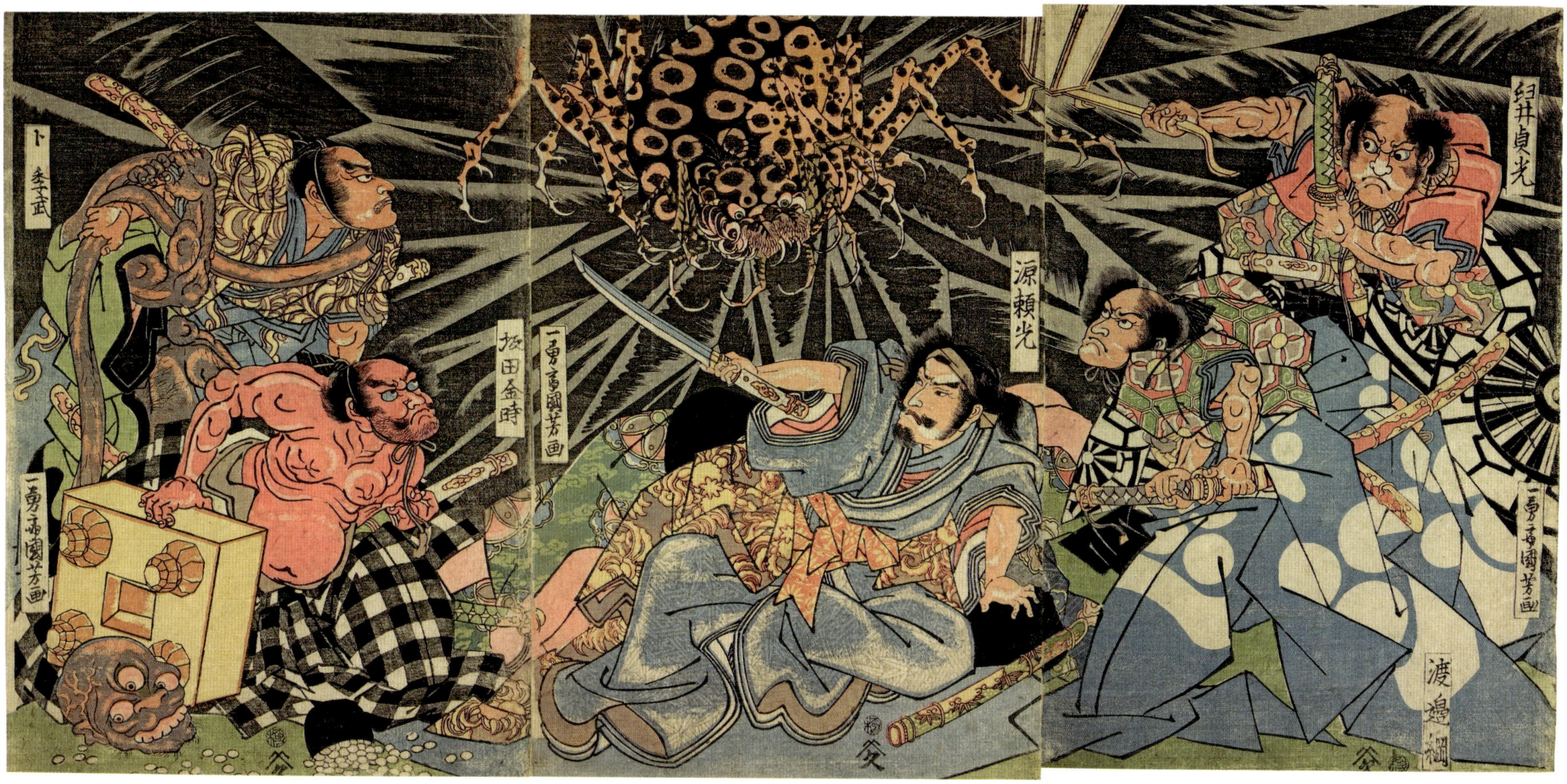

2

Minamoto no Raikō and his retainers battle with the Earth Spider

early 1820s

Colour woodblock, *ōban* triptych, published by Yamamoto Heikichi, 36.7 × 26 [R], 36.7 × 26 [C], 36.6 × 26 cm [L]

ARTIST'S SIGNATURE
Ichiyūsai Kuniyoshi ga

CENSORSHIP SEAL
kiwame

American Friends of the British Museum (The Arthur R. Miller Collection) 20904

REFERENCES
Robinson 1982, no. T4, pl. 34; Mainichi Shinbunsha 1995, no. 1; Amsterdam 1998, no. 2

The warrior hero Minamoto no Yorimitsu (or Raikō, d. 1021; centre) rises from his sickbed and draws his sword to fight off the giant Earth Spider, or Tsuchigumo, which attempts to snare him with a thousand threads of its web. His bodyguards, nicknamed the 'Four Heavenly Kings' (Shitennō), reach for their swords and hurry to defend him. (They are named on the print, from right to left, Usui no Sadamitsu, Watanabe no Tsuna, Sakata no Kintoki and Ura[be] no Suetake.) The story, familiar from several well-known medieval military chronicles and a Nō play, was elaborated in the art, drama and literature of the Edo period. For instance, a Kabuki dance first performed in 1765 added two features: Usui and Sakata were shown playing a game of *go*, and the Earth Spider was able to conjure up a series of demons and monsters to attack the warriors (Machida 2003, p. 149). The present version includes a comic touch, Sakata distractedly crushing with a heavy wooden *go* board the head of a long-necked, three-eyed monster that has wrapped itself around Urabe and, in the process, spilling white *go* stones over the floor.

In the original version of the tale the Four Heavenly Kings follow a blood trail left by the Earth Spider to its cave, where they crush it with a great tree. This is the scene illustrated in an earlier single-sheet print by Shun'ei (1806?; Machida 2003, no. 70) and a triptych by Shuntei (early 1810s; ibid., no. 95). The later version of the story, featuring the sickbed, *go* game and demons, is treated in a triptych of the 1810s by Utagawa Kuninaga (d. 1827). This shows Raikō in the nightclothes and headband of an invalid, as he and the other heroes are assailed from all sides by monsters and demons in a mansion interior depicted with deep perspective recession (The British Museum JA 1907.5-31.0524; HUT vol. 3, 1988, no. 2). Kuniyoshi's triptych intensifies the sensationalism of the stand-off between Raikō and the spider and uses the angular threads of the web to tie in the rest of the composition. This impression is particularly fresh, with bright, unfaded pink on the figures, the spider and the long-necked monster. Other impressions have a darker web in the background (Amsterdam 1998, no. 2). Kuniyoshi returned to the subject in 1843, endowing it with very different, topical meanings (cats 124, 125).

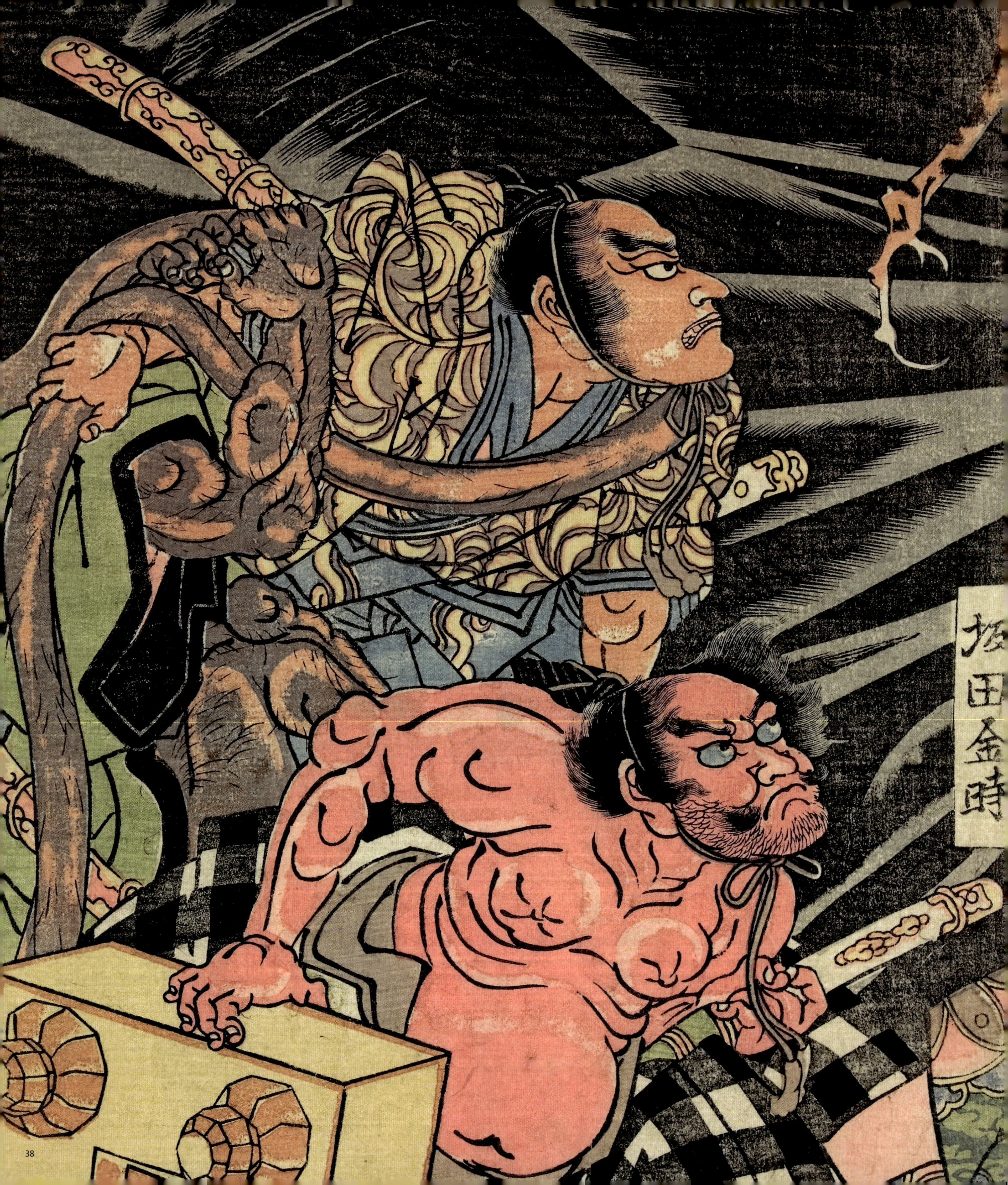
坂田金時

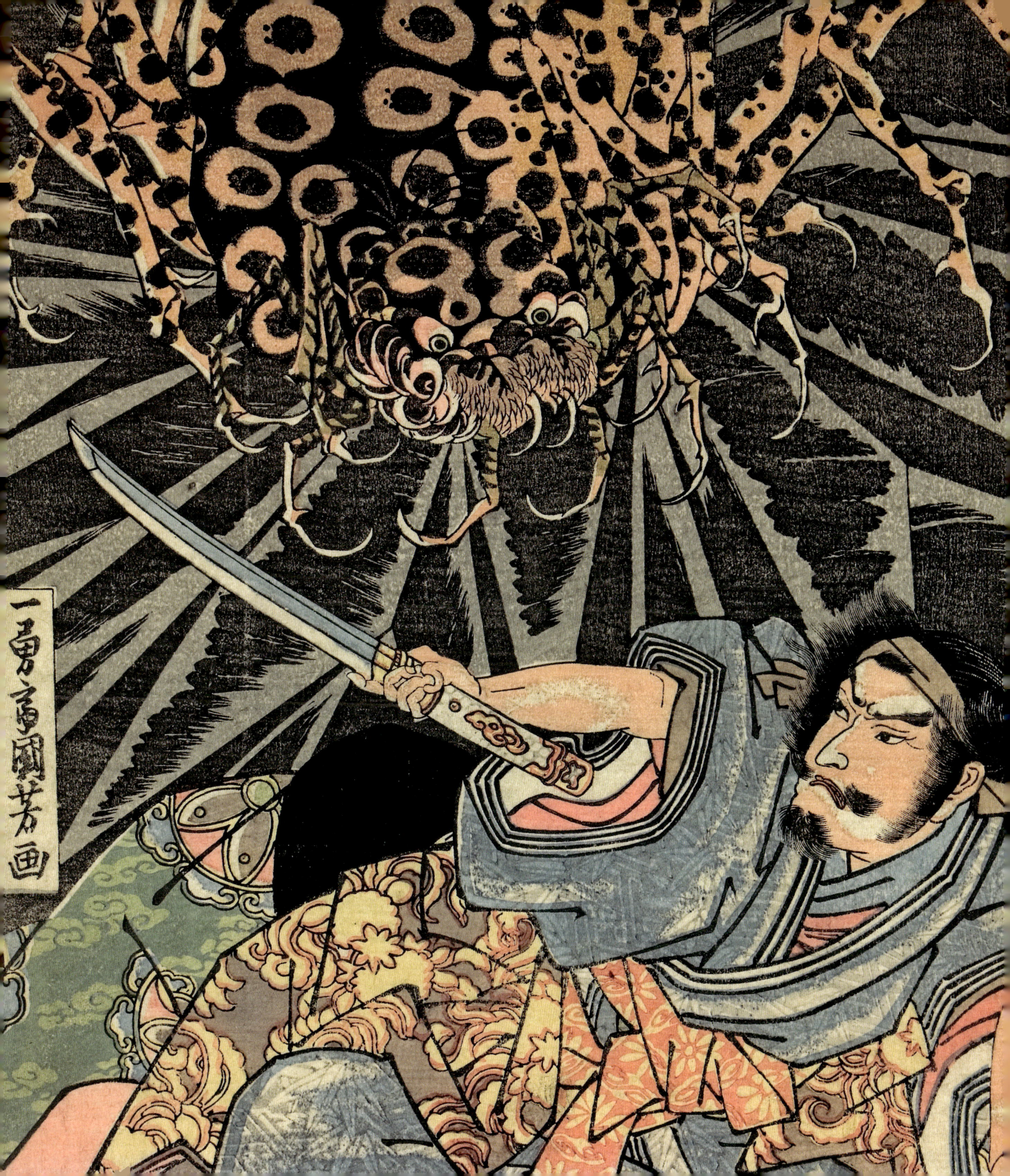
一勇斎國芳画

ONE OF THE 108 HEROES OF THE POPULAR *WATER MARGIN*

(Cats 3–10)

Shuihu zhuan (*The Water Margin*, Jap. *Suikoden*) is among the best-loved adventure stories of China. Its one hundred or more chapters tell the often violent and lurid tale of a band of heroes living in an impregnable hideout at Liangshan marsh – 'a fortress within a valley ringed by mountain peaks within a lake within a marsh' (Plaks 1987, p.312). At first the brigands combat injustice in accordance with their own moral code, but later they come to serve the emperor, battling against other outlaw bands. Their number eventually rises to 108, some joining through idealism, others coerced, all known by a nickname. Each of their thirty-six leaders is associated with a particular 'star of heaven', and each of the seventy-two seconds-in-command with a 'star of earth'. Their supreme leader is Song Jiang (Jap. Sō Kō).

The story, sometimes described as a vernacular novel in episodes, is set at the end of the Northern Song period (960–1125). The events were described in various genres at various times, as an oral tale in the Southern Song period, for example, as a prose work, *Xuanhe yishi* (*Forgotten Events of the Xuanhe Period*), in the thirteenth century, and as a drama in the Yuan period. The full-length novel appeared in the sixteenth century.

The novel first became known in Japanese literary circles in the early eighteenth century, and was soon being translated into Japanese as *Suikoden*, a literal rendering of the Chinese title, *Biographies of the Water Margin [Heroes]*. By 1773 the author Tatebe Ayatari (1718–1773) was transferring the setting to ancient Japan, in his *Honchō suikoden* (*Native Water Margin*). *The Water Margin* reached its widest audience in the early nineteenth century, in an adaptation in the popular genre of *yomihon* ('books for reading') written by Takizawa Bakin (1767–1849) and illustrated by Katsushika Hokusai (1760–1849). *Yomihon* are long, serial novels interspersed with full-spread illustrations rich in an almost gothic atmosphere of fantasy. Bakin and Hokusai's collaboration bore the title *Shinpen Suiko gaden* (*New Illustrated Edition of the Water Margin*) and was issued in ninety-one volumes – nine parts of ten or so volumes each – over two periods, 1805 to 1807 and 1828 to 1838. In 1828 authorship switched to Takai Ranzan, and in *c.* 1838 the illustrations were taken over by Taitō II.

Hokusai's dynamic and imaginative illustrations were printed in tones of grey. Their exotic settings, costumes, armour, weapons and other accessories served as an important model for Kuniyoshi's single-sheet colour prints. Other colour-printed illustrations of the heroes by Hokusai and his pupil Totoya Hokkei (1780–1850) also probably predate Kuniyoshi's prints (Klompmakers 1998, p.28, n.10). Bakin wrote another, female version of the story, *Keisei Suikoden* (*Courtesan Water Margin*), and the success of this publication and other *Suikoden*-related texts from 1825 onwards seems to have encouraged the production of Kuniyoshi's print series, issued by the same publisher as Bakin's book, Kagaya Kichibei (or Kichiemon) of Ryōgoku.

Kuniyoshi is thought to have begun the series 'One of the 108 Heroes of the Popular *Water Margin*' (*Tsūzoku Suikoden gōketsu hyakuhachinin no hitori*) in 1827, with just five designs featuring six heroes, including cat. 3. Seventy-four prints are currently known, and publication is likely to have continued over several years (Suzuki 1985, p.120; Klompmakers 1998, pp.27–8). The prints group into four triptychs (for example, cat.6), five diptychs (one of them vertical) and fifty-two single-sheet designs. Why the series was never completed, despite the enormous continued popularity of the theme, has never been established. Similarly, the status of a group of ten detailed drawings with colour that closely follow the style of the prints, but depict more heroes, is unclear. Each print gives the nickname and name of the hero next to the title cartouche. Elsewhere on the sheet there appears a short biographical note or a brief account of the episode illustrated.

After more than a decade struggling to establish his career, Kuniyoshi finally achieved success with the publication of these *Suikoden* designs. The series revitalised the genre of the warrior print, in the further development of which Kuniyoshi took the lead. The *Suikoden* prints are full of artistic vigour, the figures threatening to burst the confines of the sheet. Some of the designs contain striking Western-style features in addition to the many exotic Chinese-style elements. Another notable aspect is the prominence given to tattoos on the heroes' bodies. (Fifteen men have tattoos, as opposed to six in the original Chinese novel.) Street toughs and firemen in Edo apparently copied the style of the tattoos in the prints, and this style has formed the mainstream of full-body tattooing in Japan ever since (Klompmakers 1998, pp.35–7).

In 1998 Klompmakers reproduced all the surviving designs in colour, commented on them in detail and included a series of introductory essays. The present entry relies for much of its information on her publication, which places the prints in an order based on the chronological appearance of the heroes in the novel. The principal Japanese source is an exhibition catalogue of the former Riccar Art Museum, with a commentary by Suzuki Jūzō later summarised by Suzuki (Riccar 1979; Suzuki 1992, pp.192–3). Suzuki elsewhere presents evidence supporting a date of 1827 for the inception of the series (Suzuki 1985, pp.120–1). Robinson lists the prints in alphabetical order of the main hero depicted and names publications and collections containing various impressions (Robinson 1982, pp.102–4).

3

The Chinese military strategist Wu Yong

1827–30

Colour woodblock, *ōban*, published by Kagaya Kichibei (or Kichiemon), 38.9 × 26.7 cm

SERIES TITLE
'One of the 108 Heroes of the Popular Water Margin' (*Tsūzoku Suikoden gōketsu hyakuhachinin no hitori*)

PRINT TITLE
'Chitasei Go Yō [Wu Yong]'

ARTIST'S SIGNATURE
Ichiyūsai Kuniyoshi ga

CENSORSHIP SEAL
kiwame

American Friends of the British Museum (The Arthur R. Miller Collection) 10011

REFERENCES
Riccar 1979, no. 2; Springfield 1980, no. 7; Robinson 1982, no. S2.11; Brussels 1989, no. 864; MSU 1991, no. 59; Suzuki 1992, no. 81; Klompmakers 1998, no. 9; Machida 2003, no. 154

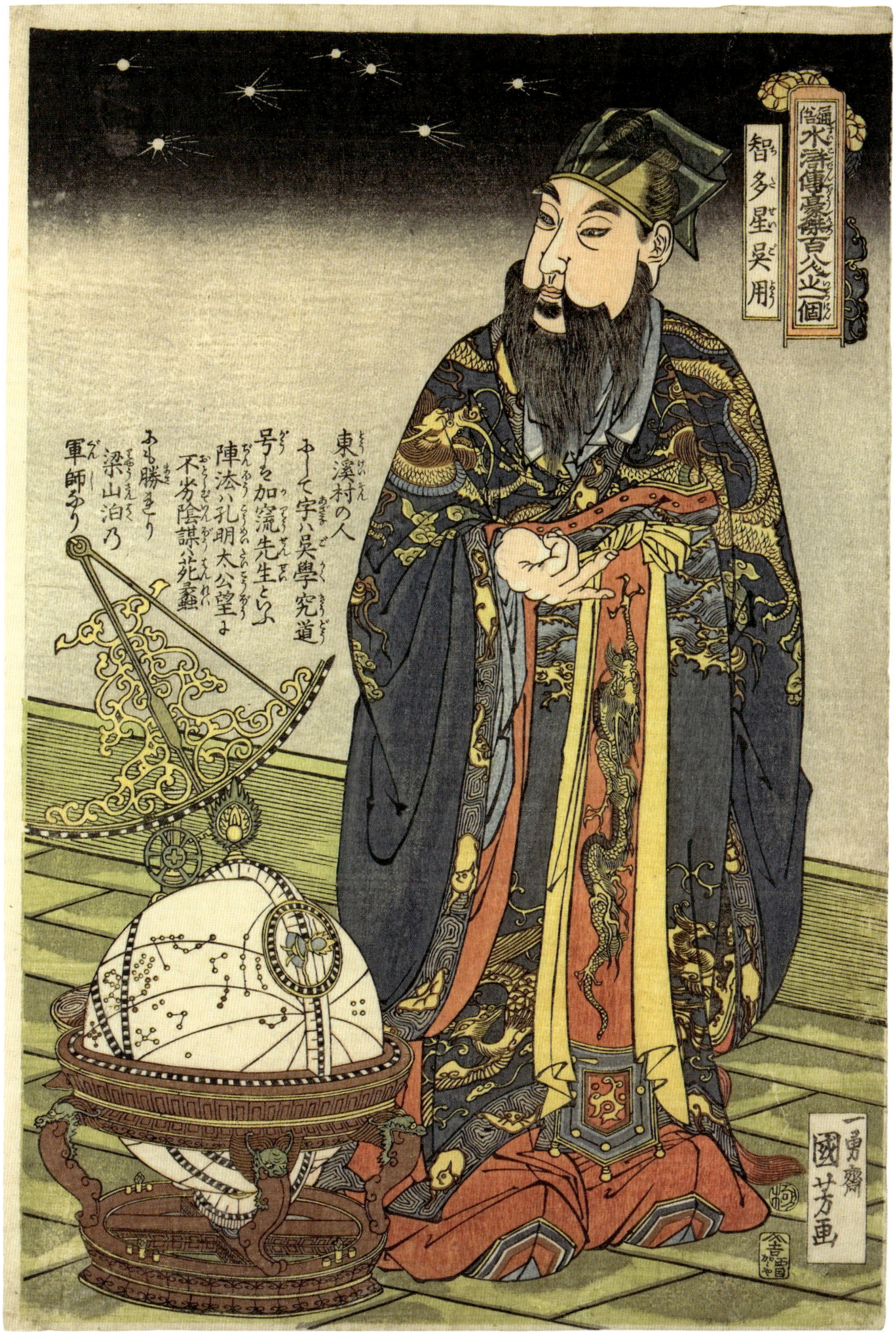

The inscriptions on the print describe Wu Yong as the 'military strategist' of the Liangshan marsh gang and give his nickname as 'The great intelligence (Clever star)'. He is one of a group of seven heroes who, early in the tale, plot successfully to steal treasures belonging to the evil governor of Beijing. (Beijing is here another name for Daming prefecture in the Northern Song period.) Wu Yong's tactics lead to victories over two imperial armies sent to recover the treasures. The print shows him counting with one hand, apparently making an astronomical calculation (stars are visible in the sky) with the assistance of a quadrant and a celestial globe, which appear next to him. Kuniyoshi's image agrees broadly with the description of Wu Yong in the novel as having finely shaped eyebrows, a white face and a long beard. The brocade robes, richly decorated with dragons, and the diaphanous hat befit a scholar, and the pose is notably dignified and static compared with the others in the series. This is one of five designs named in the 1868 manuscript *Shin zōho ukiyo-e ruikō* (*New Supplement to 'Thoughts on Ukiyo-e'*) as the first in the series and issued 'at the end of the Bunsei era [1818–30]' (Yura 1979, p. 222).

4

The Chinese warriors Mu Chun [L] and Xue Yong [R] fighting

1827–30

Colour woodblock, *ōban*, published by Kagaya Kichibei (or Kichiemon), 38.7 × 26.3 cm

SERIES TITLE
'One of the 108 Heroes of the Popular *Water Margin*' (*Tsūzoku Suikoden gōketsu hyakuhachinin no hitori*)

PRINT TITLE
'Shōsharan Boku Shun [Mu Chun] [R] and Byōtaichū Setsu Ei [Xue Yong] [L]'

ARTIST'S SIGNATURE
Ichiyūsai Kuniyoshi ga

CENSORSHIP SEAL
kiwame

American Friends of the British Museum (The Arthur R. Miller Collection) 10008

REFERENCES
Riccar 1979, no. 60; Robinson 1982, no. S2.8; Klompmakers 1998, no. 20; King and Iwakiri 2007, no. 146

Xue Yong (clothed, right) is a travelling medicine seller. He takes the side of Song Jiang, leader of the brigands, in an argument with a village headman called Mu Chun (tattooed, left). Grabbing Mu's hair, Xue gives him a heavy beating. The headman had taken exception to Song Jiang's breaking of village rules by giving Xue Yong money to buy food. Xue's medicines, staff and money are scattered on the ground and Mu's robe has been pulled off to reveal a spectacular tattoo of a dragon rising from the sea and disgorging a walled mansion. Not mentioned in the novel, the tattoo seems to have been invented by Kuniyoshi. Xue is eventually reconciled with Mu Chun and his brother Mu Hong (see cat. 6L), and later all three join the Liangshan brigands. Xue Yong is nicknamed 'Sick tiger', Mu 'The lesser one whom no obstacle can stay'. Some of the *Water Margin* brigands are playfully labelled in this way as 'sick/deficient' or 'lesser/junior' versions of earlier heroes (Plaks 1987, pp. 320–1).

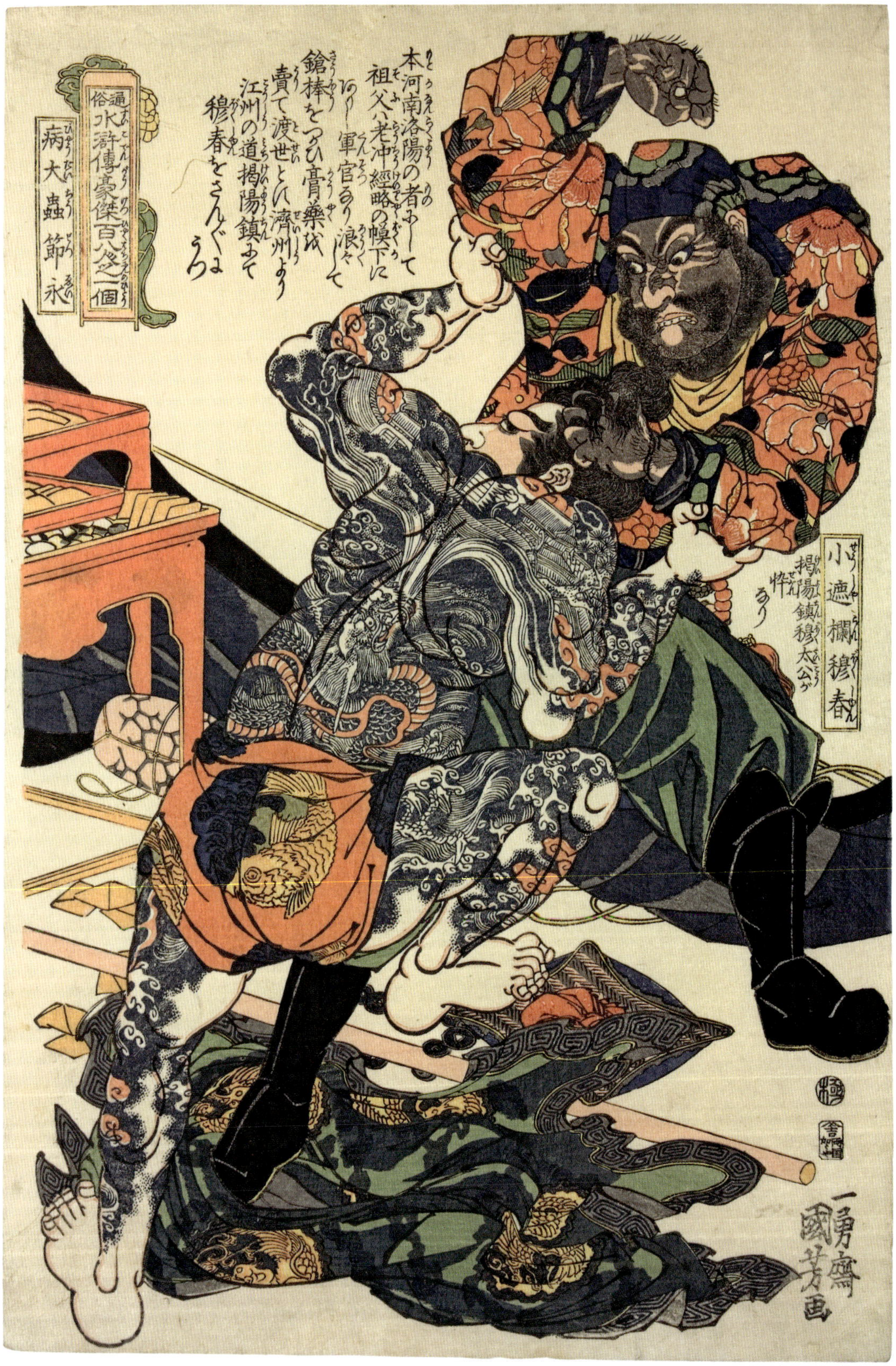

5

The Chinese female warrior Hu Sanniang fights using two swords

1827–30

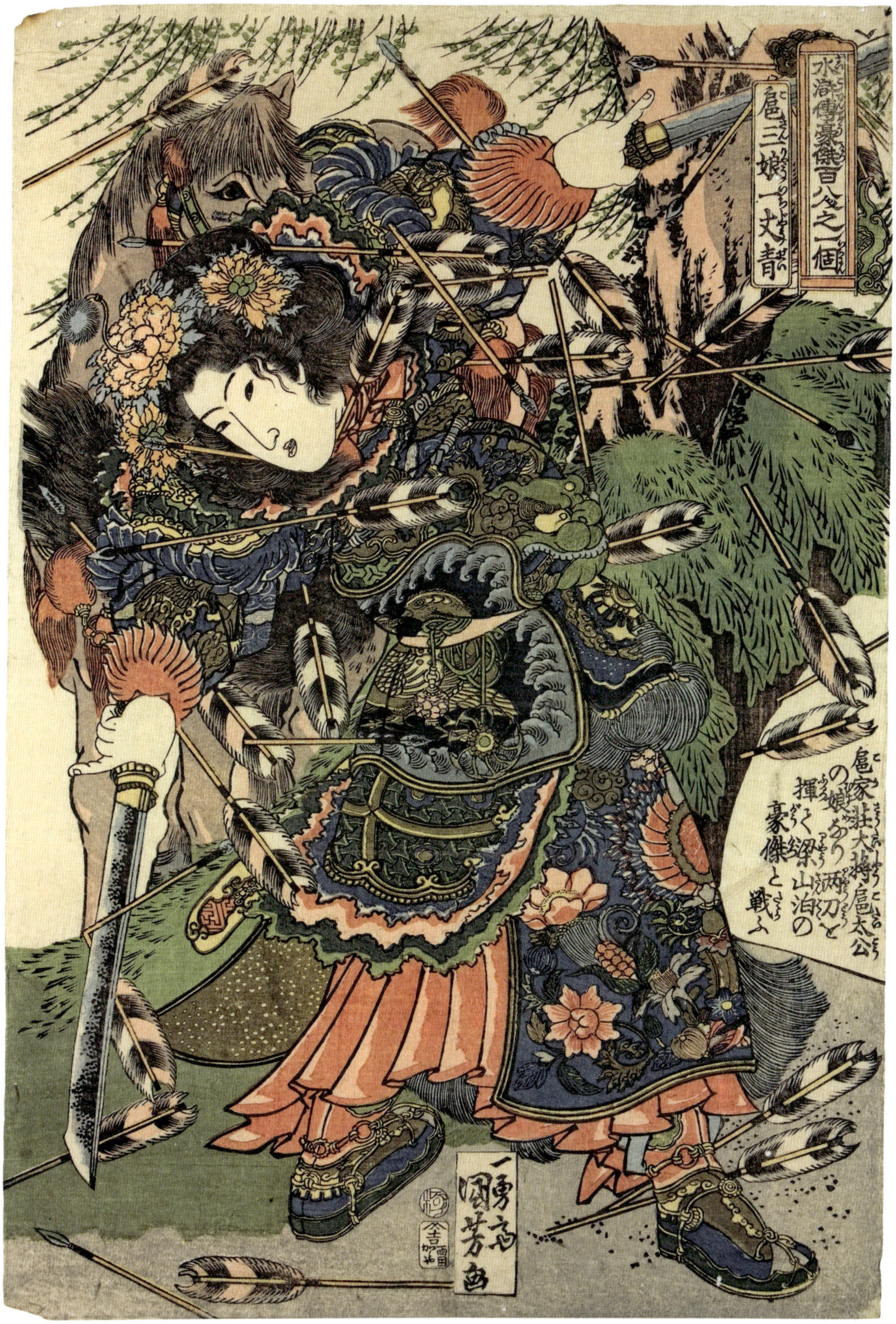

Colour woodblock, *ōban*, published by Kagaya Kichibei (or Kichiemon), 38.7 × 26.7 cm

SERIES TITLE
'One of the 108 Heroes of the Popular *Water Margin*' (*Tsūzoku Suikoden gōketsu hyakuhachinin no hitori*)

PRINT TITLE
'Ko Sanryō Ichijōsei' [Hu Sanniang]'

ARTIST'S SIGNATURE
Ichiyūsai Kuniyoshi ga

CENSORSHIP SEAL
kiwame

American Friends of the British Museum (The Arthur R. Miller Collection) 10034

REFERENCES
Riccar 1979, no. 50; Springfield 1980, no. 12; Robinson 1982, no. S2.37; Klompmakers 1998, no. 25

Hu Sanniang is one of three female warriors depicted by Kuniyoshi in this *Suikoden* series. She is formidable in battle, simultaneously wielding two swords that glitter like the sun and moon. Here she uses them to cut through a hail of arrows, twisting her body to face in the opposite direction to her feet. Her horse is tethered behind a grassy bank. The text describes her fighting the Liangshan brigands, so the episode depicted must take place just before her capture by the hero Lin Chong. Song Jiang, leader of the band, eventually fulfils an earlier promise by making her the wife of the diminutive Wang Ying. In this way Hu Sanniang became a member of the band of 108 heroes. The meaning of her nickname, 'Ten foot green', apparently derived from the name of an earlier male bandit, is obscure (Plaks 1987, p. 321).

6

Fight between the Chinese warriors Liu Tang [R], Lu Junyi [C], Li Ying [L] and Mu Hong [L]

1827–30

Colour woodblock, *ōban* triptych, published by Kagaya Kichibei (or Kichiemon), 38.6 × 26.3 [R], 38.7 × 26.3 [C], 37.1 × 26.5 cm [L]

SERIES TITLE
'One of the 108 Heroes of the Popular *Water Margin*' (*Tsūzoku Suikoden gōketsu hyakuhachinin no hitori*)

PRINT TITLES
'Sekihatsuki Ryū Tō [Liu Tang]' [R], 'Gyokukirin Ro Shungi [Lu Junyi]' [C], 'Hakutenchō Ri Ō [Li Ying] [L] and Bossharan Boku Kō [Mu Hong] [L]'

ARTIST'S SIGNATURE
Ichiyūsai Kuniyoshi ga

CENSORSHIP SEAL
kiwame

American Friends of the British Museum (The Arthur R. Miller Collection) 10052 (r), 10016 (c), 10002 (l)

REFERENCES
Riccar 1978, no.45; Riccar 1979, nos 1, 7, 16; Robinson 1982, nos S2.2, S2.17, S2.5; HUT, vol.3, 1988, no.43; Klompmakers 1998, no.39a-c

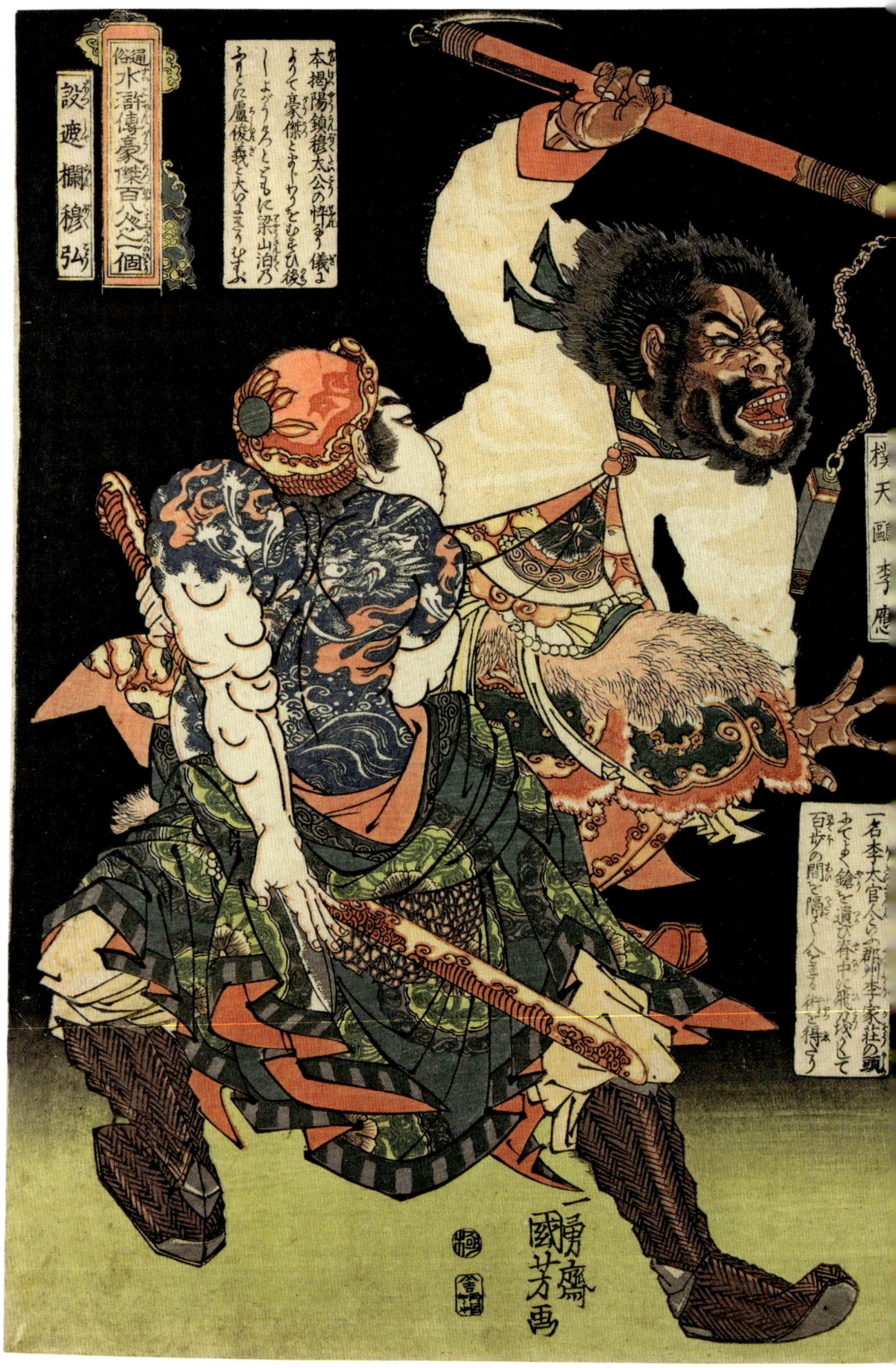

This grand three-sheet print shows Lu Junyi (centre), a wealthy man and skilled warrior from Beijing, fighting with three heroes from the Liangshan band. He has been tricked by Wu Yong (see cat.3) into leaving his family: his baggage appears in carts on the right sheet. His nickname is 'Jade qilin' (a *qilin* is an auspicious mythological creature). On the right sheet is Liu Tang, nicknamed 'Red-hair devil', who joined the brigands as one of seven warriors involved in the theft of treasures belonging to the Beijing governor. On the left sheet are Li Ying ('Eagle who smites the heavens'), wielding a chain mace above his head, and Mu Hong ('He whom no obstacle can stay'), his heavily tattooed back turned towards the viewer as he draws his sword. Mu Hong is the brother of Mu Chun (see cat.4). After many more vicissitudes, Lu Junyi finally becomes a leader of the Liangshan band, second in status only to Song Jiang.

Kuniyoshi distributes the violent poses across the composition with striking bravura, with Li Ying's grimace and flying hair constituting one of the most ferocious images in the whole series. Li's robe has been given a furred texture by elaborate blind printing, while the background must have been printed several times to achieve such a rich black.

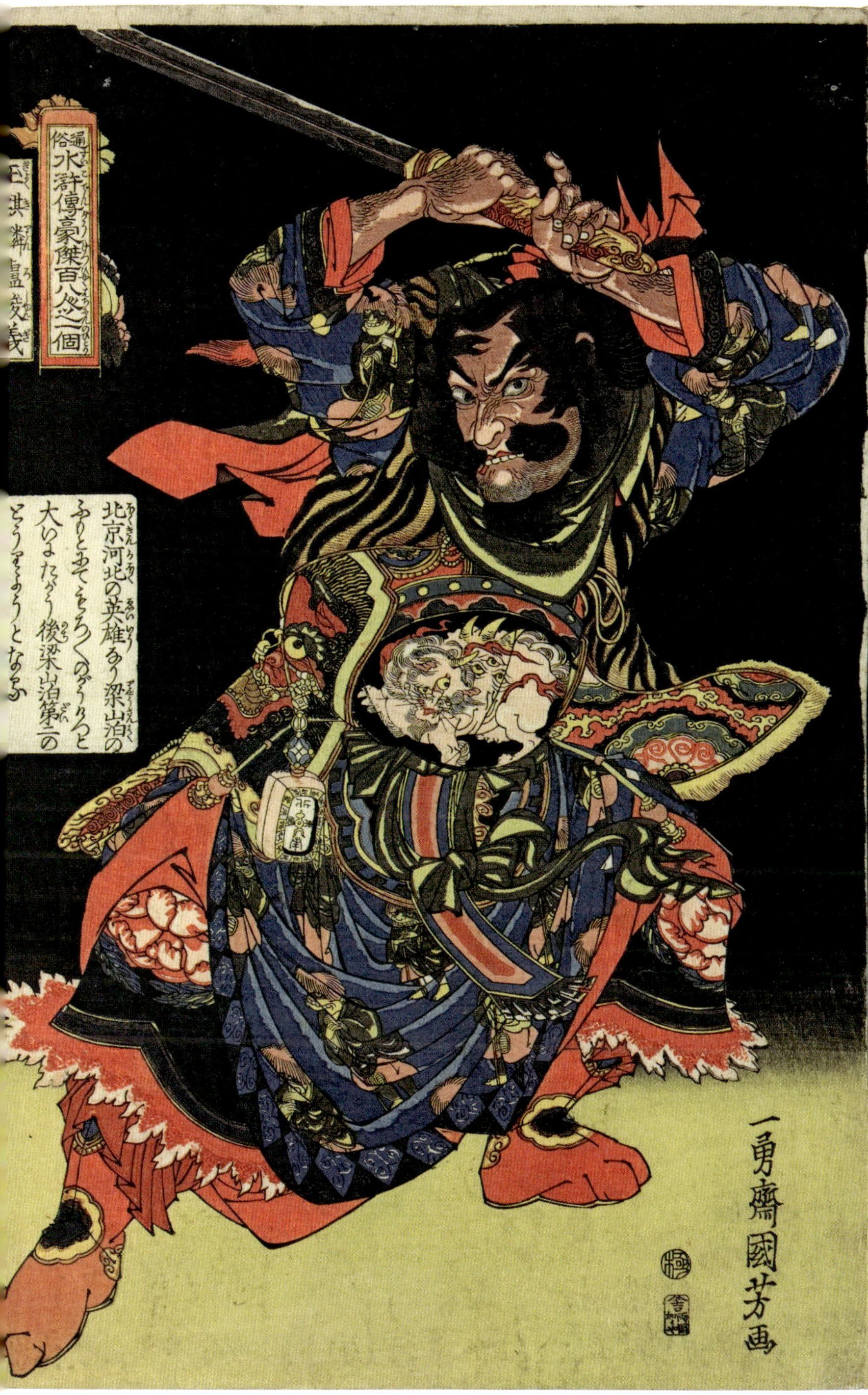
通俗水滸傳豪傑百八人之一個
玉麒麟盧俊義
北京河北の英雄なり梁山泊の
一勇齋國芳画

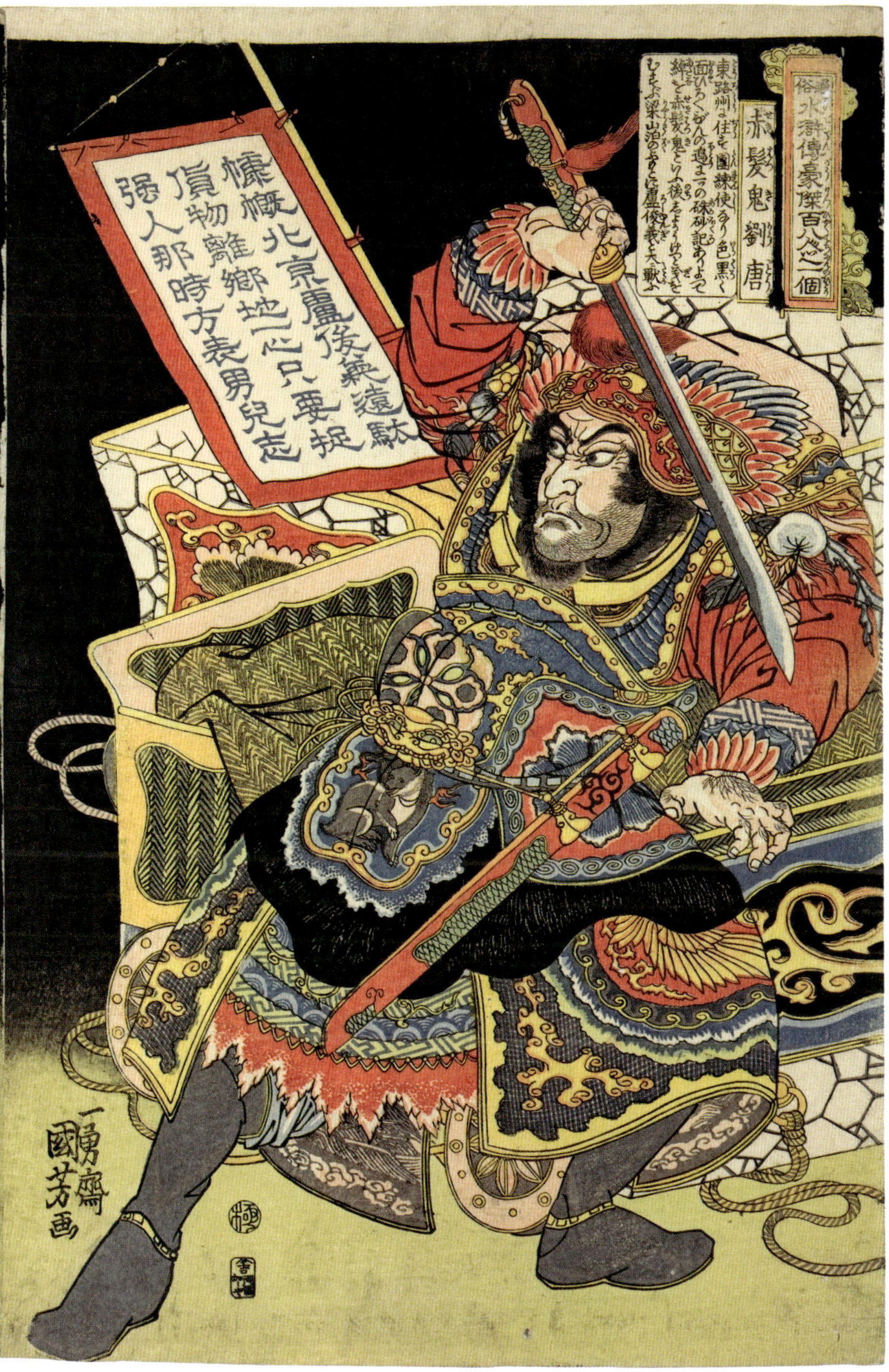
通俗水滸傳豪傑百八人之一個
赤髮鬼劉唐
慷慨北京盧俊義遠駄
貨物離鄉地一心只要捉
强人那時方表男兒志
一勇齋國芳画

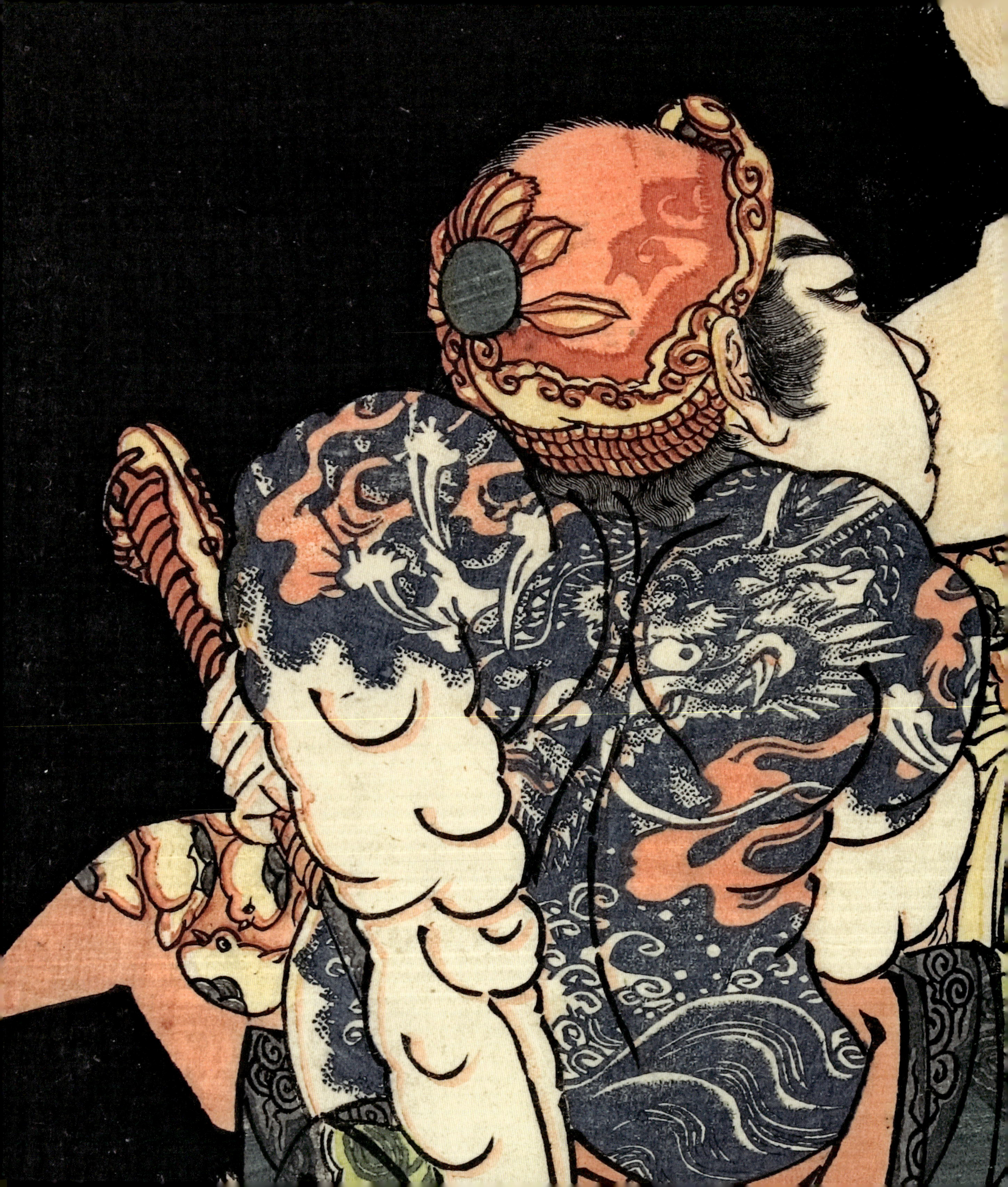

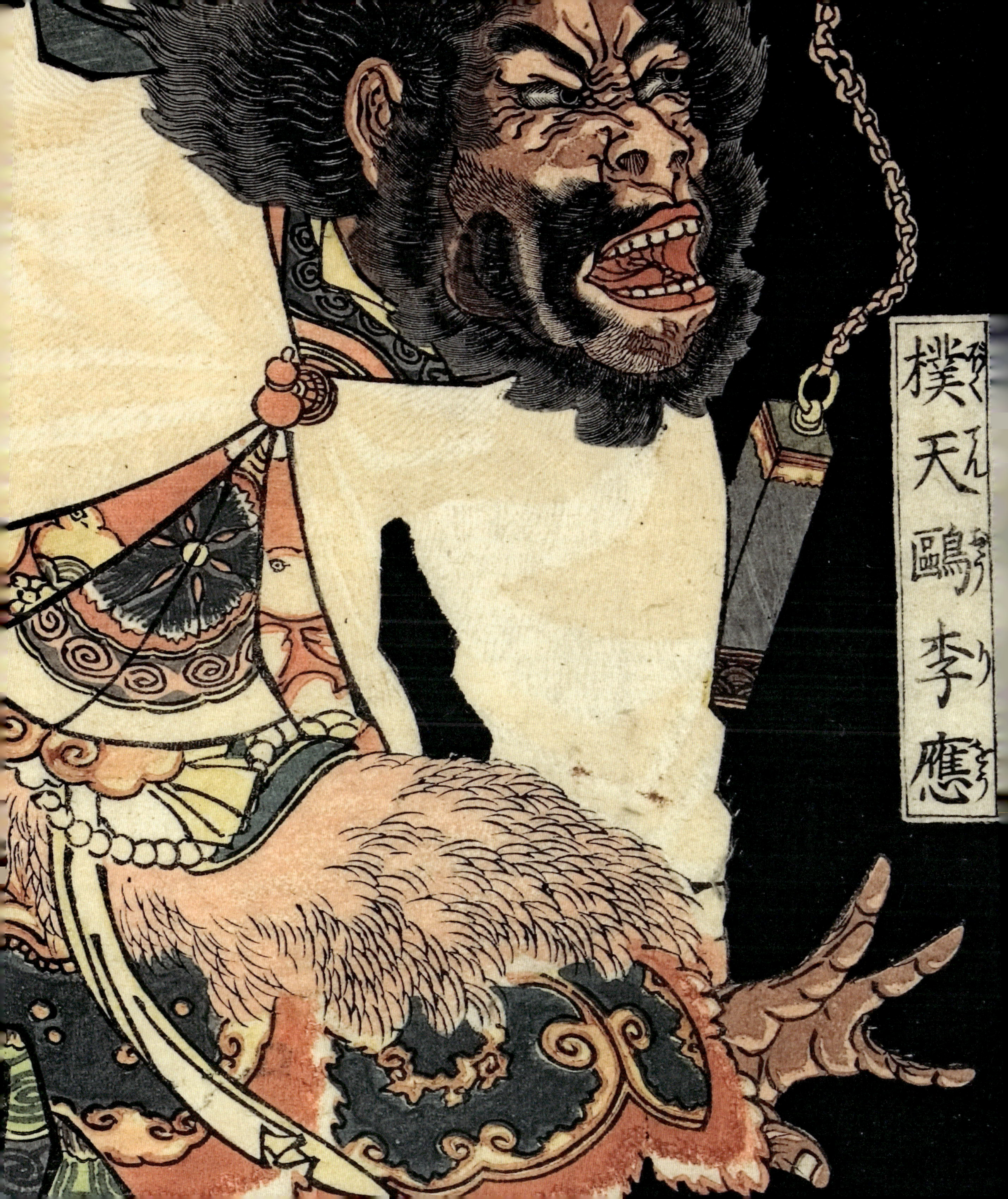
樸天鵰李應

7

The Chinese warrior Zhang Shun smashes a water gate

1827–30

Colour woodblock, *ōban*, published by Kagaya Kichibei (or Kichiemon), 37.2 × 25.1 cm

SERIES TITLE
'One of the 108 Heroes of the Popular *Water Margin*' (*Tsūzoku Suikoden gōketsu hyakuhachinin no hitori*)

PRINT TITLE
'Rōrihakuchō Chō Jun [Zhang Shun]'

ARTIST'S SIGNATURE
Ichiyūsai Kuniyoshi ga

CENSORSHIP SEAL
kiwame

American Friends of the British Museum (The Arthur R. Miller Collection) 10043

REFERENCES
Riccar 1979, no. 27; Springfield 1980, no. 13, pl. 1; Robinson 1982, no. S2.49; MSU 1991, no. 60; Suzuki 1992, no. 82; Itabashi 1994, Kuniyoshi no. 30; Nagoya 1996, no. 21; Klompmakers 1998, no. 56; Ōta 1999, no. 17; Machida 2003, no. 155; Isao 2008, p. 18

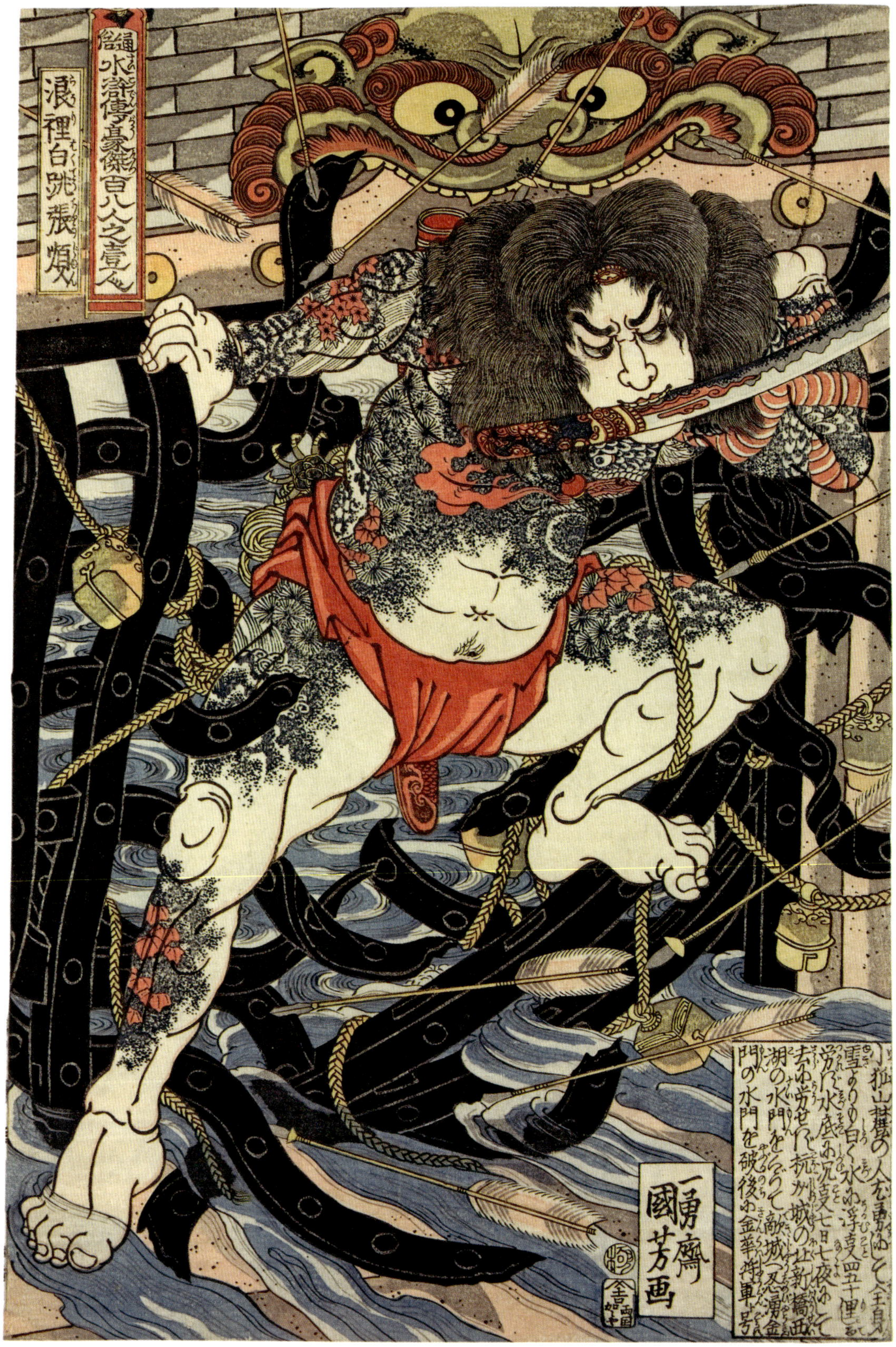

The muscular, spectacularly tattooed hero Zhang Shun has smashed his way through the Yongjin water gate. He is attacking Hangzhou city, where enemies of the Liangshan band have taken refuge. Sword clenched between his teeth, Zhang seems oblivious to the arrows that rain down on him from the city guards, who have been alerted by the roped alarm bells tied around the water gate. He will later die from his injuries. The staring eyes of the stylised lion's head above the gate serve to accentuate the fiercely determined expression on Zhang's face, and each limb of the hero pushes in a different direction so as to suggest tremendous strength.

Zhang Shun and his brother Zhang Heng began their outlaw career by extorting money from travellers who boarded their ferryboat. Zhang Shun later became the owner of a fish market. The inscription states that his skin is as white as snow and that he can float in water effortlessly for a distance of forty to fifty *li* (about 100 to 120 miles). This may explain his nickname, 'White leaper in the waves'. His all-over body tattoo, which features a large snake, pines, vines and a waterfall, is not mentioned in the original Chinese novel.

The colours in this and other early impressions tend to be light. They subsequently became darker, with the wall above the water gate switching to blue (for example, in the impression in the British Museum, 1906.12-20.01301). This darkening – and coarsening – of the colours increased still further in the reprint edition of *c.* 1845 published by Ibaya Senzaburō and described and illustrated by Klompmakers (1998, p. 172).

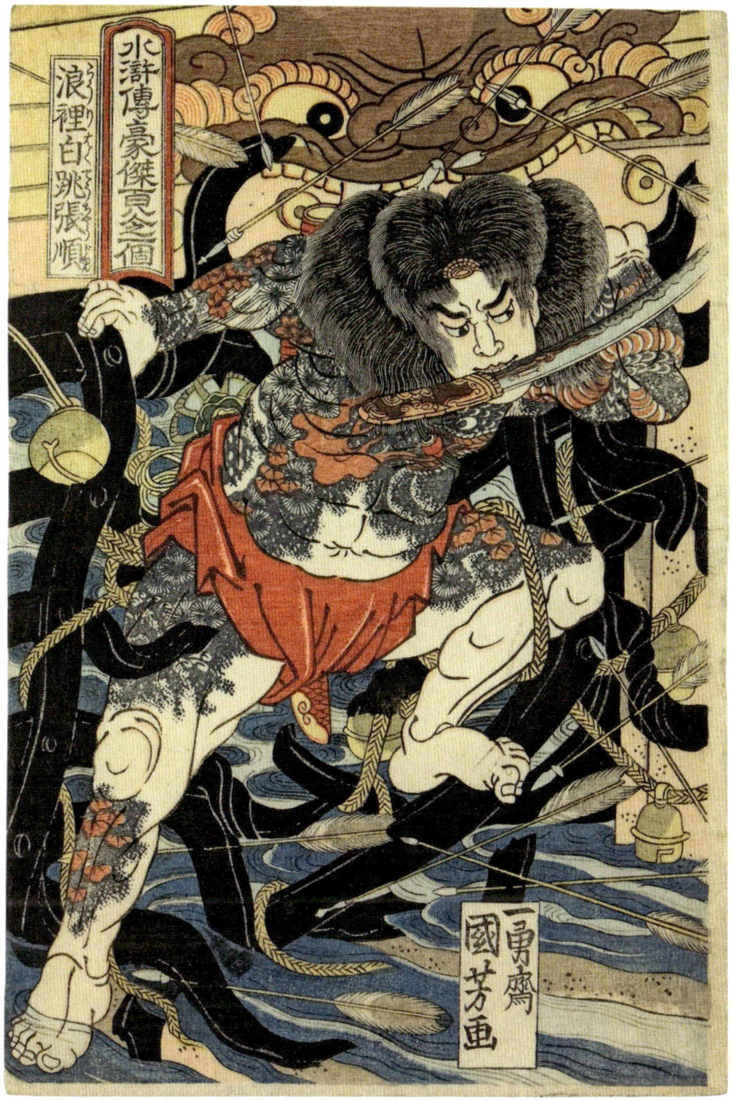

8

The Chinese warrior Zhang Shun smashes a water gate

1827–30?

Colour woodblock, *yotsugiri-ban*, no publisher's seal, 18.9 × 13 cm

SERIES TITLE
'One of the 108 Heroes of *The Water Margin*' (*Suikoden gōketsu hyakuhachinin no hitori*)

PRINT TITLE
'Rōrihakuchō Chō Jun [Zhang Shun]'

ARTIST'S SIGNATURE
Ichiyūsai Kuniyoshi ga

COLLECTOR'S SEAL
Theodor Scheiwe (*verso*)

American Friends of the British Museum (The Arthur R. Miller Collection) 10305

REFERENCES
Klompmakers 1998, p. 185

This version of the subject depicted in cat. 7 is one quarter as large (*yotsugiri-ban*) and provides concrete evidence of the enormous popularity of Kuniyoshi's *Suikoden* prints, particularly the most striking designs. The similar colouring suggests a date close to that of the larger print, but the lack of either a publisher's mark or a censorship seal (where one would expect the *kiwame* ['examined'] seal) may indicate a pirated edition. Certainly, the relationship between the various motifs is a little awkward in comparison with the full-size version, although this impression is printed on fine, thick paper.

The present print comes from an apparently unrecorded series. It bears some resemblance to a small-format *Suikoden* series with figures of about the same size, but also featuring wide decorative borders. Suzuki states that this series was published by Yamazaki Kinbei and gives the total size of the sheets as 24.5 × 17 cm – that is, *koban* format (Riccar 1979, suppl. no. 24). Robinson lists twelve designs, describing them, perhaps mistakenly, as in the *chūban* format (Robinson 1982, series S2a). Nineteen designs are mentioned in the Amsterdam catalogue of 1998 (p. 185). The Miller Collection contains four designs from the series with decorative borders (10301–04). Many of the prints in that series bear the Mura censorship seal, implying that they were issued in the early 1840s. Perhaps a *yotsugiri-ban* series of *c.* 1830 was reprinted at that time, with the format of the originals increased to *koban* through the addition of printed decorative borders.

9

The Chinese warrior Ruan Xiaowu fights underwater

1827–30

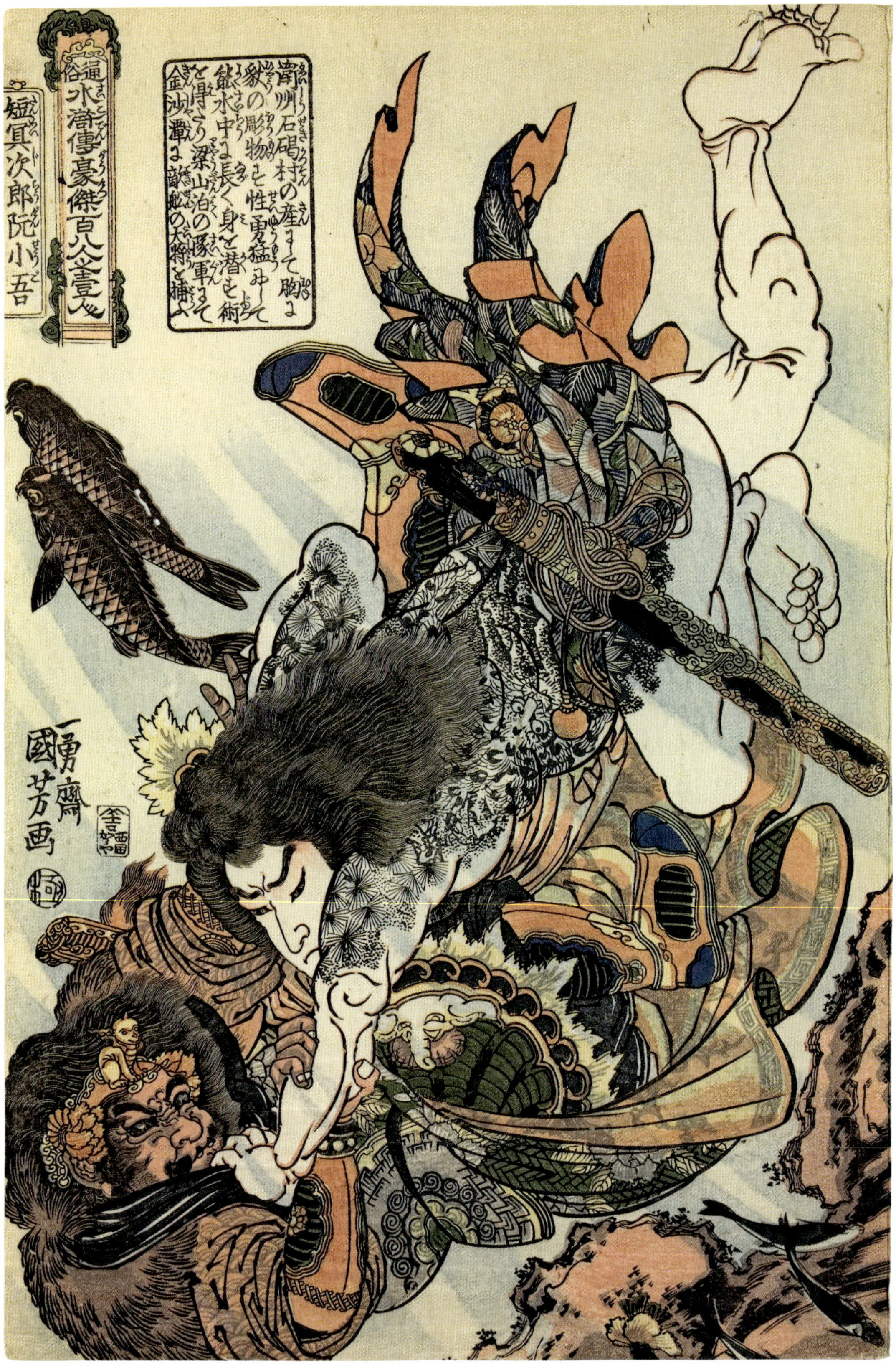

Colour woodblock, *ōban*, published by Kagaya Kichibei (or Kichiemon), 36.7 × 24.8 cm

SERIES TITLE
'One of the 108 Heroes of the Popular *Water Margin*' (*Tsūzoku Suikoden gōketsu hyakuhachinin no hitori*)

PRINT TITLE
'Tanmeijirō Gen Shōgo [Ruan Xiaowu]'

ARTIST'S SIGNATURE
Ichiyūsai Kuniyoshi ga

CENSORSHIP SEAL
kiwame

American Friends of the British Museum (The Arthur R. Miller Collection) 10062

REFERENCES
Riccar 1978, no. 48; Riccar 1979, no. 26; Springfield 1980, no. 10; Robinson 1982, no. S2.69; Suzuki 1992, no. 85; Itabashi 1994, Kuniyoshi no. 32; Mainichi Shinbunsha 1995, no. 2; Klompmakers 1998, no. 52; Smithsonian 2002, no. 71; Shōtō 2003, no. 150; Isao 2008, p. 14

In one of the most dynamic designs of the *Suikoden* series the tattooed hero Ruan Xiaowu grapples underwater with an adversary – probably the commander of an enemy fleet (Klompmakers 1998, p. 162). Fish scatter in alarm. Ruan, nicknamed 'Short-lived second master', is one of three brothers who, early in the *Water Margin* tale, take part in the successful plot by seven brigands to steal treasures from the governor of Beijing. The Ruan brothers were subsequently among the first 108 heroes to settle at Liangshan marsh. Xiaowu, the middle brother, is particularly good at swimming underwater for long periods, perhaps because he was originally a fisherman and salt smuggler (see also cat. 50.3). The inscription mentions a leopard tattooed on his chest, a feature clearly visible in Kuniyoshi's design.

Some impressions of this print have heavier blue waves extending higher in the composition and sometimes printed over a pale blue background filling the entire sheet. The colours in this fine early impression appear somewhat faded in comparison with an example in the Museum of Fine Arts, Boston (64.800), which has deeper reds and yellows.

10

The Chinese warrior Ding Desun kills a giant snake

1827–30

Colour woodblock, *ōban*, published by Kagaya Kichibei (or Kichiemon), 37.9 × 26.5 cm

SERIES TITLE
'One of the 108 Heroes of the Popular *Water Margin*' (*Tsūzoku Suikoden gōketsu hyakuhachinin no hitori*)

PRINT TITLE
'Chūsenko Tei Tokuson [Ding Desun]'

ARTIST'S SIGNATURE
Ichiyūsai Kuniyoshi ga

CENSORSHIP SEAL
kiwame

REFERENCES
Robinson 1961, no. 10; Riccar 1978, no. 46; Riccar 1979, no. 59; Robinson 1982, no. S2.13; Klompmakers 1998, no. 60; King and Iwakiri 2007, no. 147

American Friends of the British Museum (The Arthur R. Miller Collection) 10013

The hero Ding Desun grips his sword with both hands and thrusts it into the gaping mouth of a giant snake that is attacking him. The reptile's body completely encircles the figure so as to create an electrifying stand-off between the gazes of man and monster, linked by the sword. Ding will later suffer a painful death from the snake's poisonous bite. The inscription states that the episode took place on a mountain road in Qinzhou and mentions that the warrior, nicknamed 'Arrow-wounded tiger', is skilled at throwing forked darts while riding on horseback. Ding was an ally of Zhang Qing, and the pair were subdued by the Liangshan brigands only with great difficulty and eventually persuaded to join them. The colours of this impression are especially well preserved.

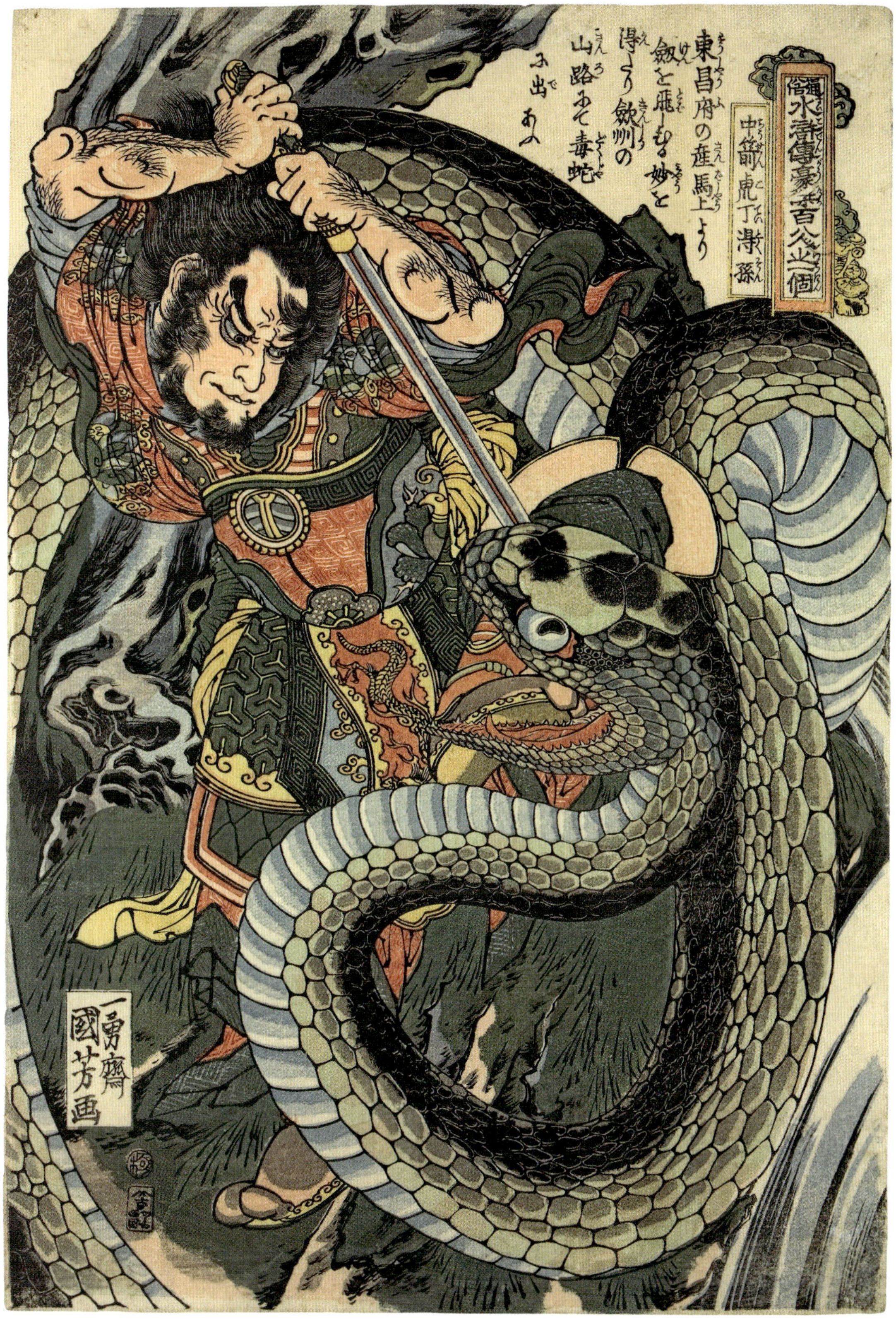

108 HEROES OF THE POPULAR *WATER MARGIN*

(Cat. 11)

Evidence for the continuing popularity of the *Water Margin* (*Suikoden*) theme in the late 1840s is provided by this series of medium-sized (*chūban*) portraits of the 108 heroes of the Liangshan marsh. By this time Kuniyoshi's style has matured considerably from the explosive vigour of his first great series, produced from 1827 to 1830 for the publisher Kagaya Kichibei (or Kichiemon) (cats 3–10). Unlike the earlier prints, the present series, published by Yamamoto Heikichi, has fully printed backgrounds and rich, deep colours. The figures are also smaller in scale and more poised and naturalistic. Robinson lists twenty-four designs, all of them represented in the Miller Collection (10201–25). The Riccar exhibition catalogue of 1979 illustrates twenty-three in black and white; the twenty-fourth depicts Ruan Xiaowu (Jap. Tanmeijirō Gen Shōgo).

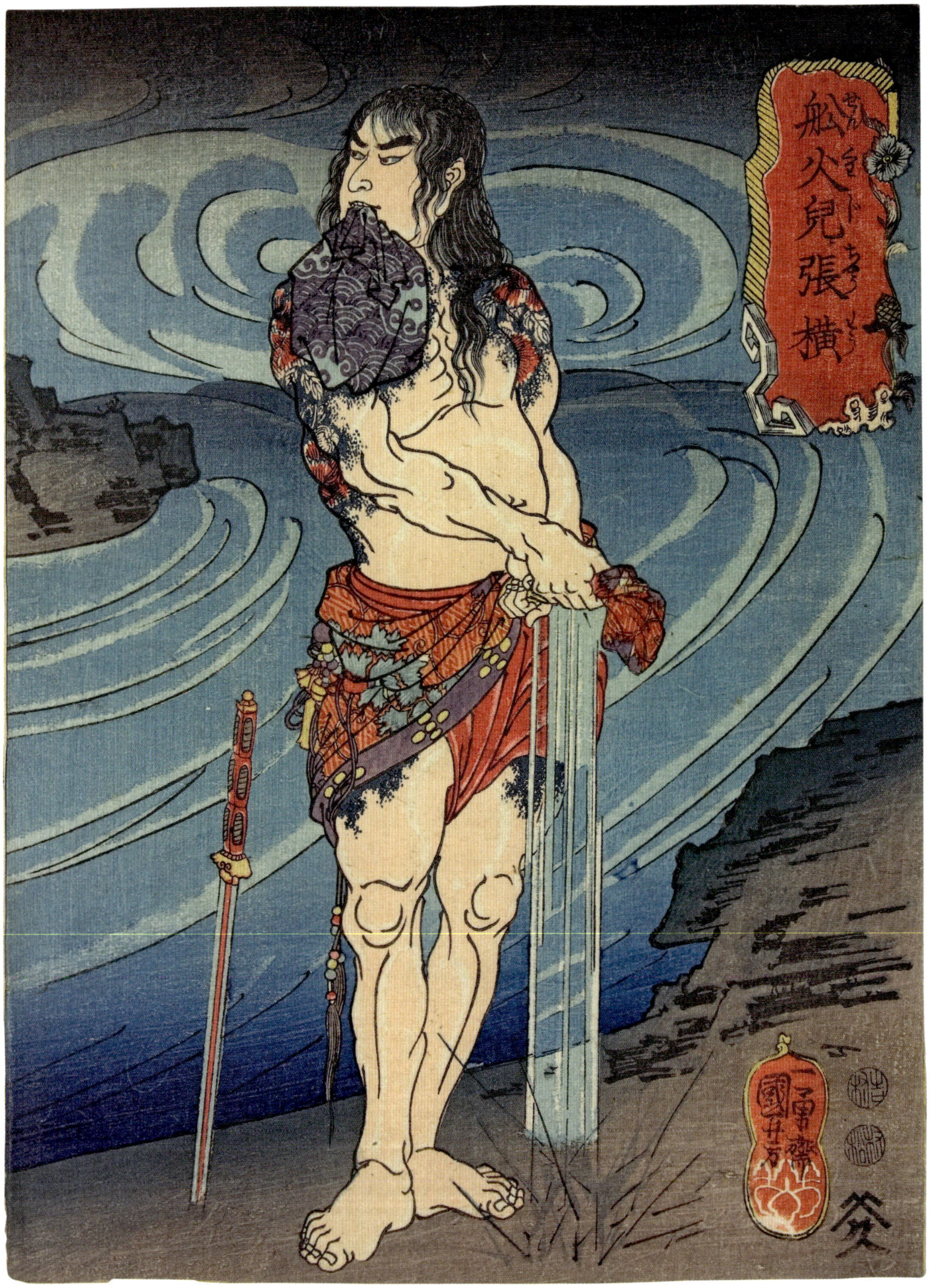

11

The Chinese warrior Zhang Heng

1847–48

Colour woodblock, *chūban*, published by Yamamoto Heikichi, 24.5 × 18.2 cm

SERIES TITLE
'108 Heroes of the Popular *Water Margin*' (*Tsūzoku Suikoden gōketsu hyakuhachinin*) [not on this print]

PRINT TITLE
'Senkaji Chō Ō [Zhang Heng]'

ARTIST'S SIGNATURE
Ichiyūsai Kuniyoshi ga (in gourd-shaped *Yoshi* cartouche)

ARTIST'S SEAL
Yoshikiri

CENSORS' SEALS
Muramatsu and Yoshimura

American Friends of the British Museum (The Arthur R. Miller Collection) 10221

REFERENCES
Riccar 1979, suppl. no. 9; Robinson 1982, no. S47.20; Amsterdam 1998, no. 71

Zhang Heng, a ferryman, is the brother of Zhang Shun (see cats 7, 8). This print shows the moment of his revenge for his brother's death, which, as depicted in cat. 7, had occurred at Yongjin water gate by order of the enemy general Fang Tianding [Jap. Hō Tentei]. The spirit of the dead Shun has entered Heng's body, enabling him to emerge suddenly from the water and attack their unsuspecting enemy. Magnificently tattooed like his brother, Heng wrings out his loincloth, while holding in his teeth a bundle wrapped in cloth. The bundle contains the severed head of General Fang. The cartouche, top right, gives the hero's name, but for unknown reasons this design, like several of the others, does not include the series title.

ONE OF EIGHT HUNDRED HEROES OF *THE WATER MARGIN* OF JAPAN

(Cats 12–14)

Following the success of the 1827–30 series 'One of the 108 Heroes of the Popular *Water Margin*' (cats 3–10), the publisher Kagaya must have looked for further ways of capitalising on the popularity of the *Water Margin* theme. Tatebe Ayatari (1718–1773) had already transferred the setting of the stories to ancient Japan in his 1773 novel *Honchō Suikoden* (*Native Water Margin*). The present series features Japanese heroes from all historical periods, depicted in the medium of the colour woodblock print. The range is wide: some designs show heroes of recent popular fiction (cat. 14), others contain hidden references to subjects forbidden by censorship regulations (cat. 12). The style and the method of presentation continue seamlessly those of the earlier series, which had depicted Chinese brigands.

The series title indicates that the aim was to catalogue eight hundred Japanese heroes rather than 108 Chinese, and this doubtless reflects national pride (in other contexts '800' has the generic meaning of 'a lot'). In the event, far fewer designs were produced. Robinson lists twenty-seven, which he divides into three groups (Robinson 1982, series S4). More recently, Iwakiri Yuriko has written a detailed article on the series, reproducing all thirty known designs and discussing their possible sources (Iwakiri 2001). She, too, divides them into three groups, in accordance with the dates of publication she ascribes to them: A (1830–32), B (1833–35) and C (*c.* 1836). Group A she subdivides into three further groups, each with the title in a different calligraphic style. She also notes that the word for 'heroes' in the title was changed from *gōyū* to *gōketsu* after twelve designs had been published. Block-ready preparatory drawings survive for several more designs showing Japanese heroes in a similar style (see cats 15, 16). These were prepared in 1833–35 for a rival publisher, Yamaguchiya Tōbei, and they do not include a series title.

12

The Japanese warrior Kashiwade no Hanoshi kills a tiger in Korea

1830–32

Colour woodblock, *ōban*, published by Kagaya Kichibei (or Kichiemon), 37 × 25.6 cm

SERIES TITLE
'One of Eight Hundred Heroes of *The Water Margin* of Japan' (*Honchō Suikoden gōyū happyakunin no hitori*)

PRINT TITLE
'Kashiwade no Hanoshi'

ARTIST'S SIGNATURE
Ichiyūsai Kuniyoshi ga (in gourd-shaped cartouche)

CENSORSHIP SEAL
kiwame

American Friends of the British Museum (The Arthur R. Miller Collection) 02806

REFERENCES
Robinson 1982, no. S4a.8; Iwakiri 2001, no. 16; Machida 2003, no. 72

The short text on the print states that Kashiwade was an envoy sent to the Korean kingdom of Baekje during the reign of Emperor Kinmei (ruled 539–571). When a wild tiger eats a child in Kashiwade's party, the warrior tracks it into snow-covered mountains and kills it. Kuniyoshi repeats the familiar and effective composition of a hero forcing his foe down into the bottom left corner of a design. Despite the text, viewers in the 1830s would have immediately read the image as a portrait of the warrior general Katō Kiyomasa (1562–1611) and the scene as a famous tiger hunt that took place during the Japanese invasions of Korea in the 1590s. The print follows convention by depicting Kiyomasa, who led the invasions by order of the ruler Toyotomi Hideyoshi, with an unusual high court cap as part of his helmet, fronted by horns. In addition, his military crests – a 'snake-eye' ring and 'trailing wisteria' – are clearly alluded to in the pattern on his robe. Censorship regulations banned explicit references to warriors who lived later than the Tenshō era (1573–92) because the ruling Tokugawa family had all but obliterated Hideyoshi's descendants and were highly sensitive about mentions of him, let alone expressions of sympathy. Nevertheless, depictions of Hideyoshi-related subjects, even if clandestine, remained very popular (see also pp. 26–7).

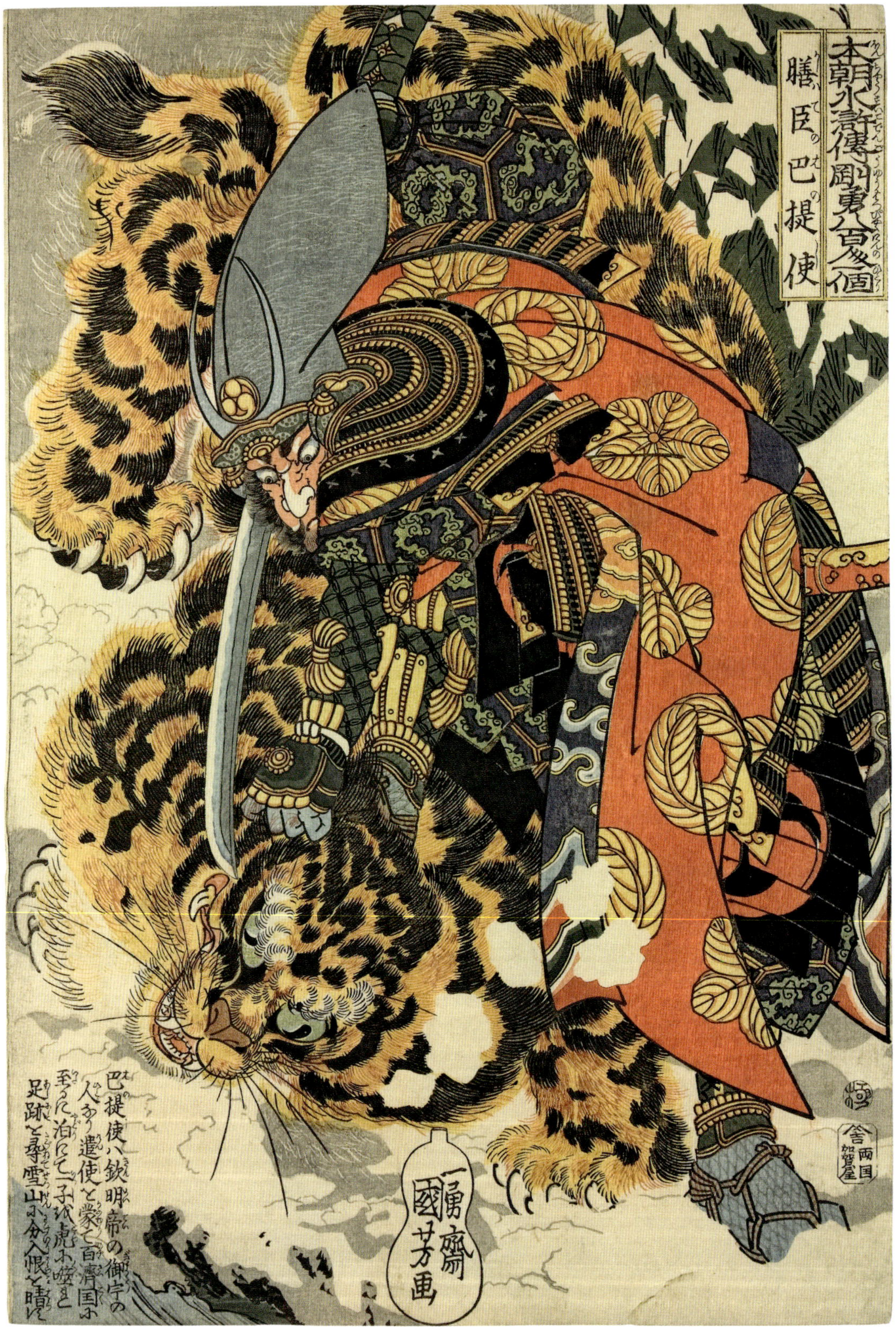

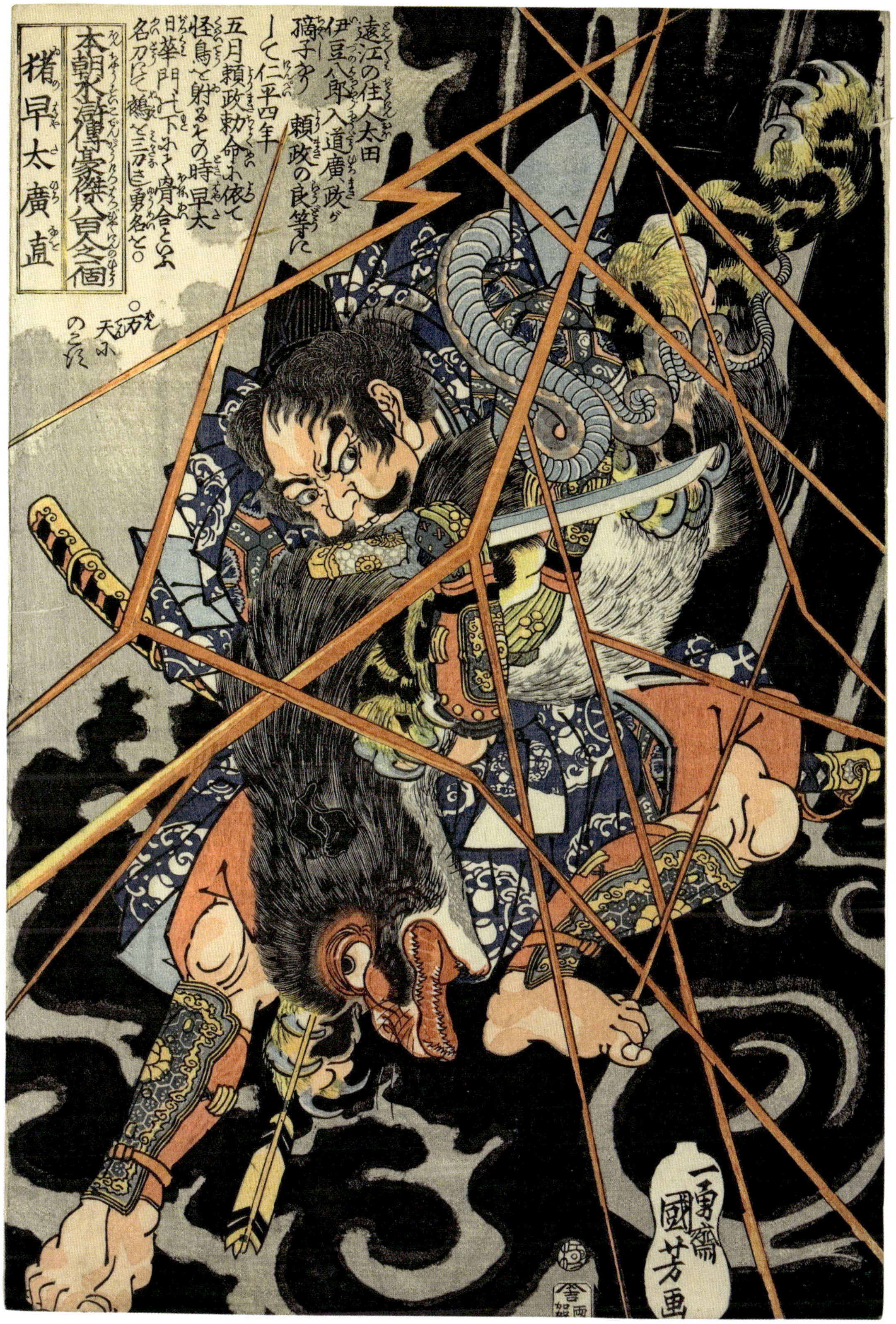

13

The Japanese warrior I no Hayata Hironao kills the *nue* monster

1830–32

Colour woodblock, *ōban*, published by Kagaya Kichibei (or Kichiemon), 37 × 25.7 cm

SERIES TITLE
'One of Eight Hundred Heroes of *The Water Margin* of Japan' (*Honchō Suikoden gōketsu happyakunin no hitori*)

PRINT TITLE
'I no Hayata Hironao'

ARTIST'S SIGNATURE
Ichiyūsai Kuniyoshi ga (in gourd-shaped cartouche)

CENSORSHIP SEAL
kiwame

American Friends of the British Museum (The Arthur R. Miller Collection) 02805

REFERENCES
Robinson 1982, no. S4a.6; Suzuki 1992, no. 89; Mainichi Shinbunsha 1995, no. 10; Amsterdam 1998, no. 13; Iwakiri 2001, no. 1; Shōtō 2003, no. 51

Sometime in the Ninpyō era (1151–54) the emperor's sleep was disturbed night after night by a forbidding black cloud hovering over his palace. I no Hayata helped his lord, the warrior hero Minamoto no Yorimasa (1104–1180), to remove this threat. Yorimasa shot arrows into the cloud and out tumbled an extraordinary monster called the *nue*. As described in several medieval military chronicles, it had the head of a monkey, the body of a racoon dog (*tanuki*), the legs of a tiger and the tail of a snake. I no Hayata immediately set upon the monster and killed it with his sword.

In this extremely animated design the stricken *nue* hurtles to the ground amid swirling black clouds and jagged lightning. I no Hayata grasps the monster in both arms and is about to stab it with his short sword. Teeth bared in fierce concentration, he seems almost to bite the beast. The warrior's leg is planted resolutely in one corner of the design, while the tiger-like leg of the *nue* stretches into the other, the bizarre body of the monster forming a powerful diagonal.

The subjugation of the *nue* was a common theme in shrine votive paintings (*ema*) as well as in warrior prints (Machida 2003, p. 148). In the early 1820s Kuniyoshi had designed a triptych print of the incident that shares some features with the present version (ibid., no. 186).

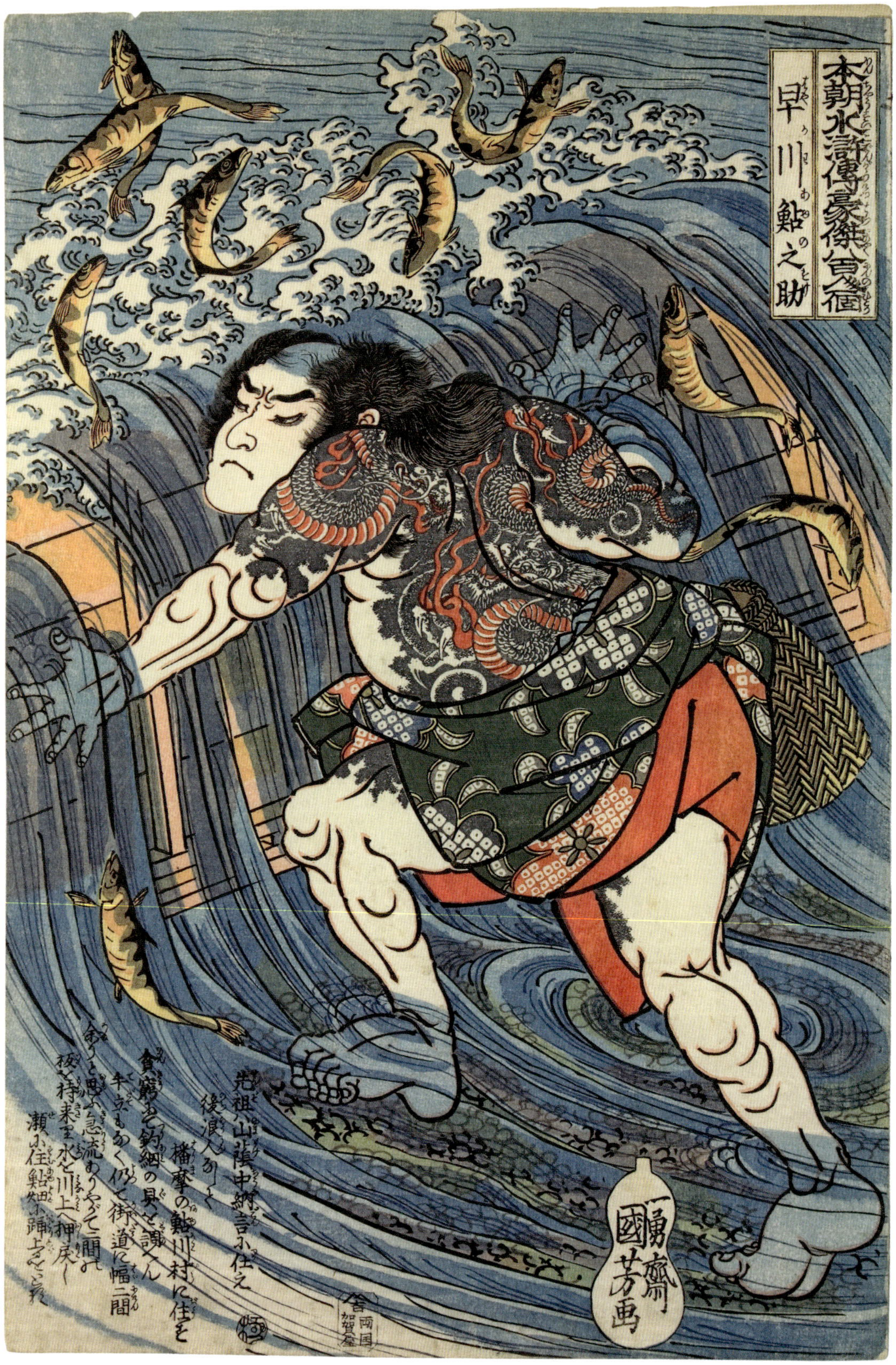

14

The Japanese warrior Hayakawa Ayunosuke makes a fish-trap

1830–32

Colour woodblock, *ōban*, published by Kagaya Kichibei (or Kichiemon), 37.8 × 25.8 cm

SERIES TITLE
'One of Eight Hundred Heroes of *The Water Margin* of Japan' (*Honchō Suikoden gōketsu happyakunin no hitori*)

PRINT TITLE
'Hayakawa Ayunosuke'

ARTIST'S SIGNATURE
Ichiyūsai Kuniyoshi ga (in gourd-shaped cartouche)

CENSORSHIP SEAL
kiwame

American Friends of the British Museum (The Arthur R. Miller Collection) 02802.

REFERENCES
Robinson 1982, no. S4a.2;
Mainichi Shinbunsha 1995, no. 9;
Iwakiri 2001, cover illus.;
Machida 2003, no. 162

The text states that Hayakawa is a masterless samurai who lives in Ayukawa ('Trout river') village in Harima province. So poor that he cannot afford to buy fishing tackle or a net, he picks up a plank more than six metres long and pushes it against the heavy current. This forces the fish out of the water and into the riverside fields. Grimacing from the effort and displaying a magnificent body tattoo of coiling dragons amid rain clouds, Hayakawa strides inexorably upstream, while trapped fish dance in the shallows above his improvised weir. Particularly effective are the areas where the clear blue water flows rapidly over the 'weir', Hayakawa's limbs and the pebbles on the riverbed.

The subject was of quite recent vintage: Hayakawa was a character from a popular illustrated novel, *Ehon Sarashina sōshi* (*Picture Book: Sarashina Tale*), published in 1810 with text by Ritsujōtei Kiran and pictures by Ishida Gyokuzan. Kuniyoshi and his publishers were clearly keen to expand the repertoire of Japanese heroes to cater for the growing audience for warrior prints (Machida 2003, p. 126).

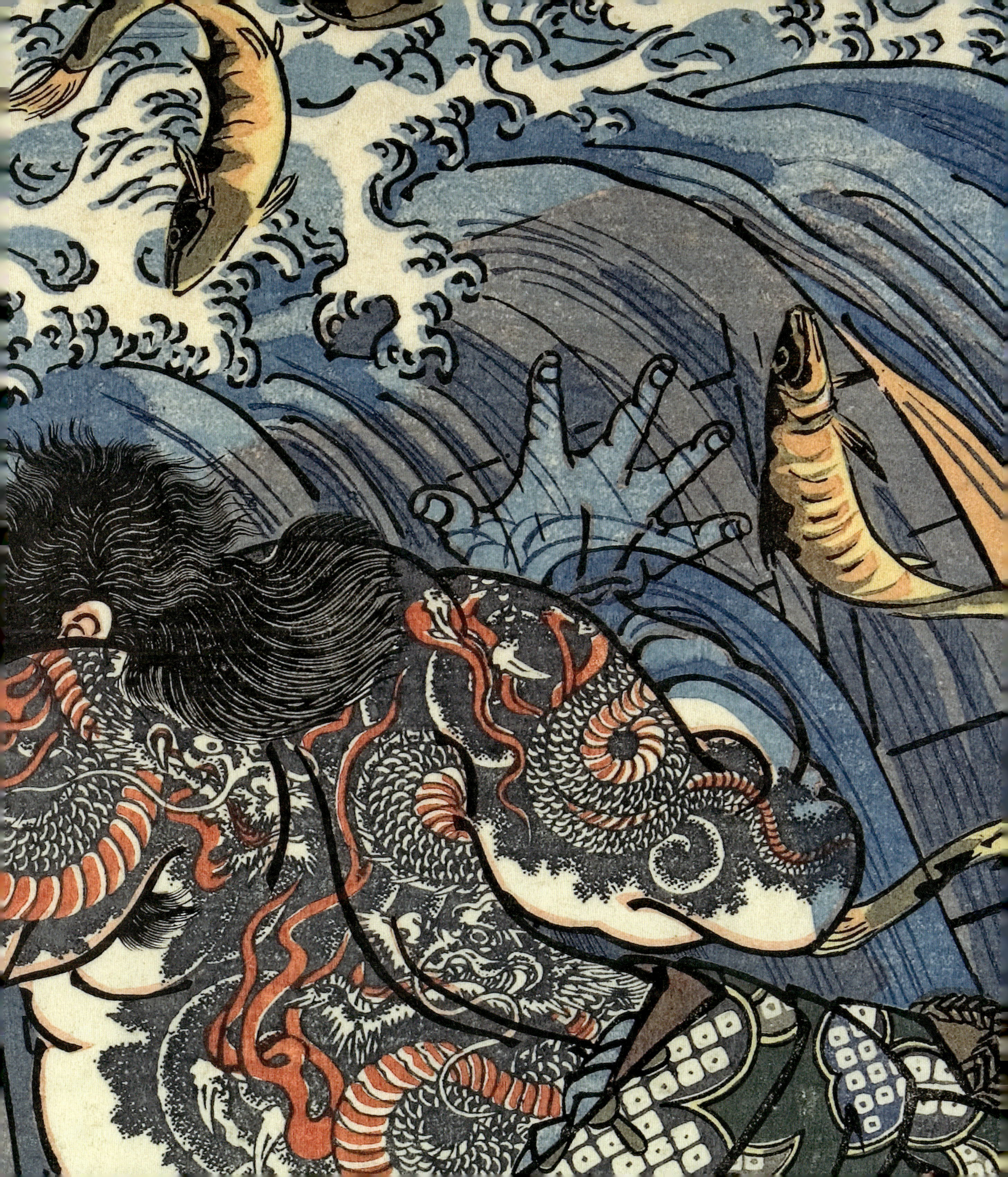

15

Block-ready drawing for an unpublished print 'Sanjō Kokaji Munechika'

1833–35

Ink and slight colour on paper, 39.3 × 26.4 cm

ARTIST'S SIGNATURE
Ichiyūsai Kuniyoshi ga
(in irregular cartouche)

CENSORSHIP SEAL
kiwame (actual seal impression)

PUBLISHER'S SEAL
Yamaguchiya Tōbei
(actual seal impression)

Victoria and Albert Museum, London, E.2250-1909

REFERENCES
Robinson 1961, no. 85; Forrer 1988, no. 41; HUT, vol. 5, 1989, no. 202

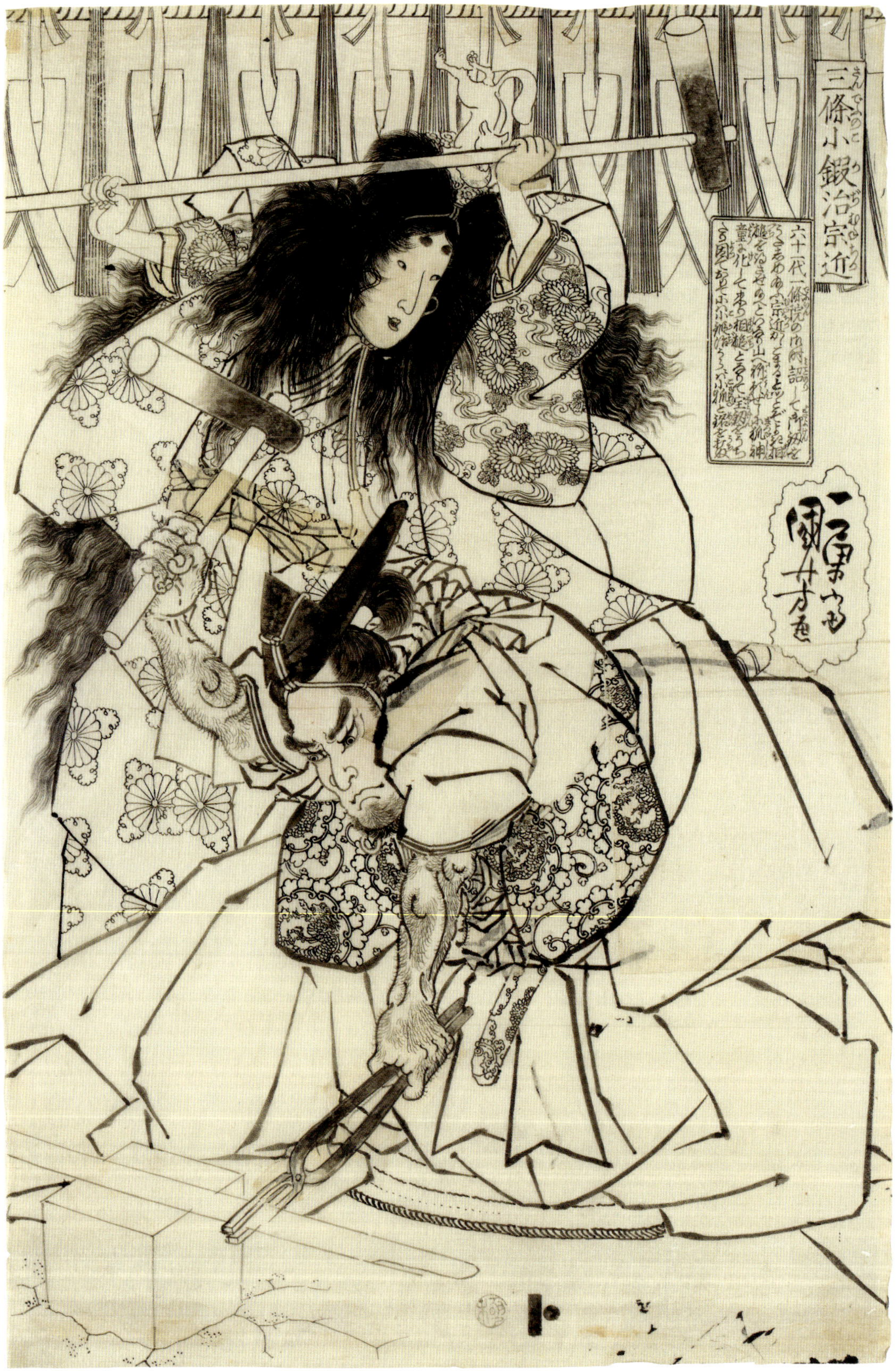

The renowned sword-smith Munechika (active in the late Heian period, 984–1185) beats the red-hot blade he is forging in his workshop at Sanjō in Kyoto. His actions are echoed by a boy with flowing hair. The boy's cap bears the emblem of a running fox, indicating that he is the Fox God of Mt Inari, who has taken this form in order to assist the smith. Suspended ritual paper streamers signify that the forging is a sacred activity performed in a purified place. Munechika had prayed at Mt Inari to improve his hammering technique, and the sword he is fashioning will be named 'Little Fox' (*Ko-gitsune*) in honour of the deity. The inscription on the print states that these events took place during the reign of Emperor Ichijō (986–1011).

This drawing, along with cat. 16, is among the few 'block-ready pictures' (*hanshita-e*) to have survived. Made by Kuniyoshi in his studio for colour woodblock prints that were never published, they are line-perfect images ready to be glued face down on the cherrywood printing block for the professional block-cutter to start carving the key- or line-block, with which the outlines of the design will be printed. Since the cutter carves through the back of the drawing, it is routinely destroyed during preparation of the block. Even the tiniest details are depicted in the drawing, which includes all the texts and the minute glosses that run down the side of the written characters to aid comprehension. Impressions from two small but important seals appear at the bottom of the drawing in the centre. That on the right consists of a thick vertical line with a circle beside it and is the trademark of the publisher Yamaguchiya Tōbei. The fainter, circular seal on the left contains the stylised character *kiwame* ('examined') and shows that the design has been passed by the official censor. From 1791 to 1842 censorship duties were performed in monthly rotation by a different member of the wholesale publishers' guild. Publishers were thus required by the authorities to police the designs of their peers.

The National Museum of Ethnology, Leiden, possesses a rough, first-stage preparatory drawing of this subject that shows every indication of being from the hand of Kuniyoshi himself (Forrer 1988, no. 40). Many differences exist between that drawing and the block-ready version, so it is not certain if the two are directly related.

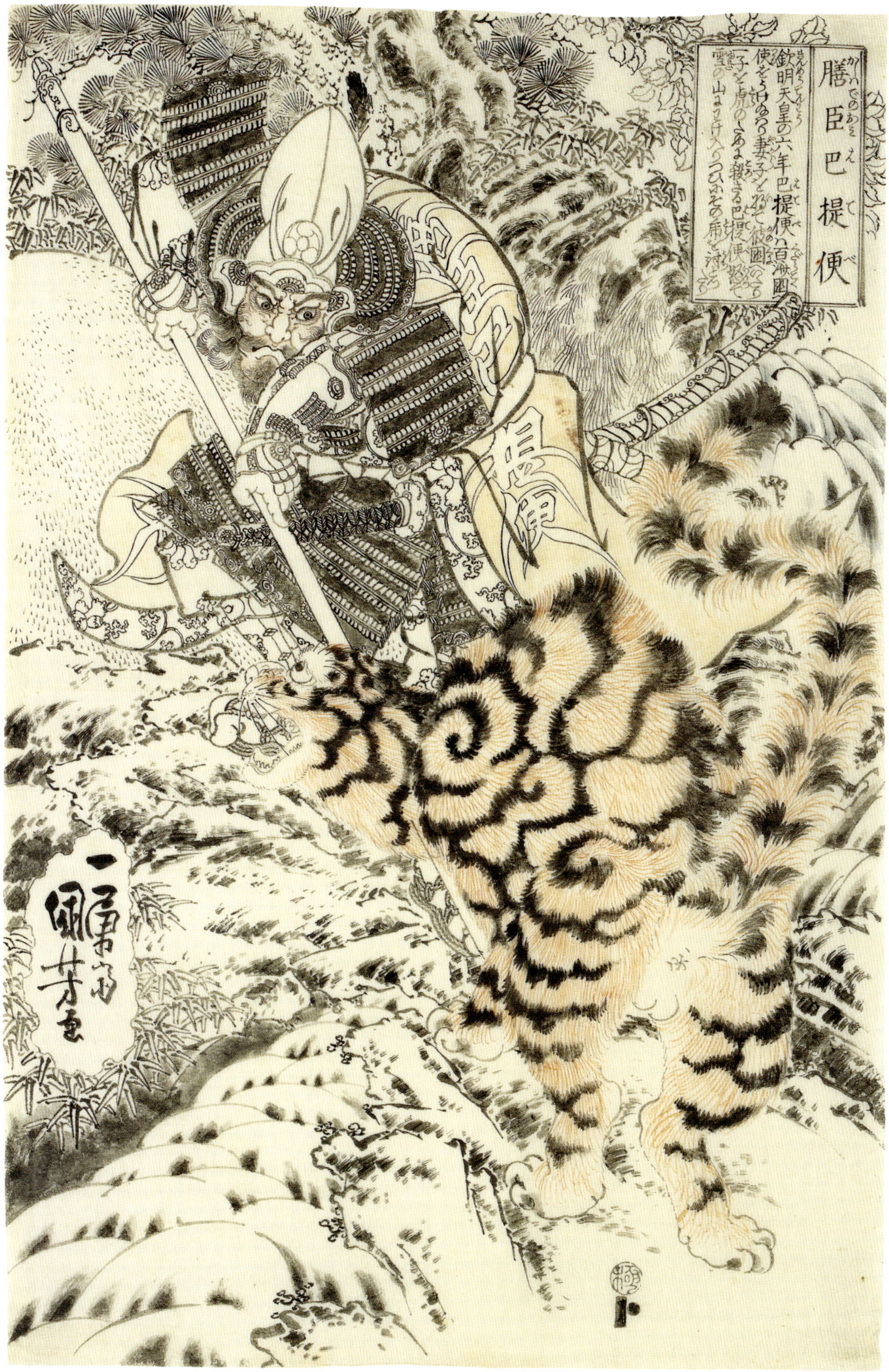

16

Block-ready drawing for an unpublished print 'Kashiwade no Omi Hatebe'

1833–35

Ink and slight colour on paper,
39.6 × 26.5 cm

ARTIST'S SIGNATURE
Ichiyūsai Kuniyoshi ga
(in irregular cartouche)

CENSORSHIP SEAL
kiwame (actual seal impression)

PUBLISHER'S SEAL
Yamaguchiya Tōbei
(actual seal impression)

Victoria and Albert Museum, London,
E.2251-1909

REFERENCES
Robinson 1961, no.84; HUT, vol.5, 1989, no.201; V&A 1991, no.89

This is a slightly later version of the subject described under cat. 12. Ostensibly it shows the warrior Kashiwade killing a tiger in Baekje, Korea, during the reign of Emperor Kinmei (ruled 539–571), as recounted in the ancient history *Nihon shoki* (*Chronicle of Japan*, 720). However, it was intended to be read as an image of the warrior general Katō Kiyomasa (1562–1611) leading a tiger-hunt in Korea during the Japanese invasions of the 1590s – a subject that could not be treated directly as it contravened censorship laws (see p.26). In contrast to cat. 12, in which the warrior and tiger are drawn so close to the picture plane that they seem about to burst upon the viewer, the tiger's body and the waterfall in the present drawing lead the eye deep into pictorial space, where, guided by the diagonal of his spear, it eventually meets the warrior. Such a composition embodies a new development in Kuniyoshi's style, a new maturity in his art.

All the rich detail of the rocks, plants and water, not to mention the warrior's armour and tiger's fur, has been carefully drawn for the block-cutter. Like cat. 15, the sheet bears the publisher's and censor's seals, impressed just below the tiger's hind legs. Although these two drawings seem never to have appeared in print form, the same publisher issued three prints that show Japanese warriors in a similar style (Robinson 1982, series S1C, nos 8–10), among them 'Wada no Heida Tanenaga kills a giant python' (Miller Collection 21209).

17

Ariō-maru kills a giant octopus

1833–35

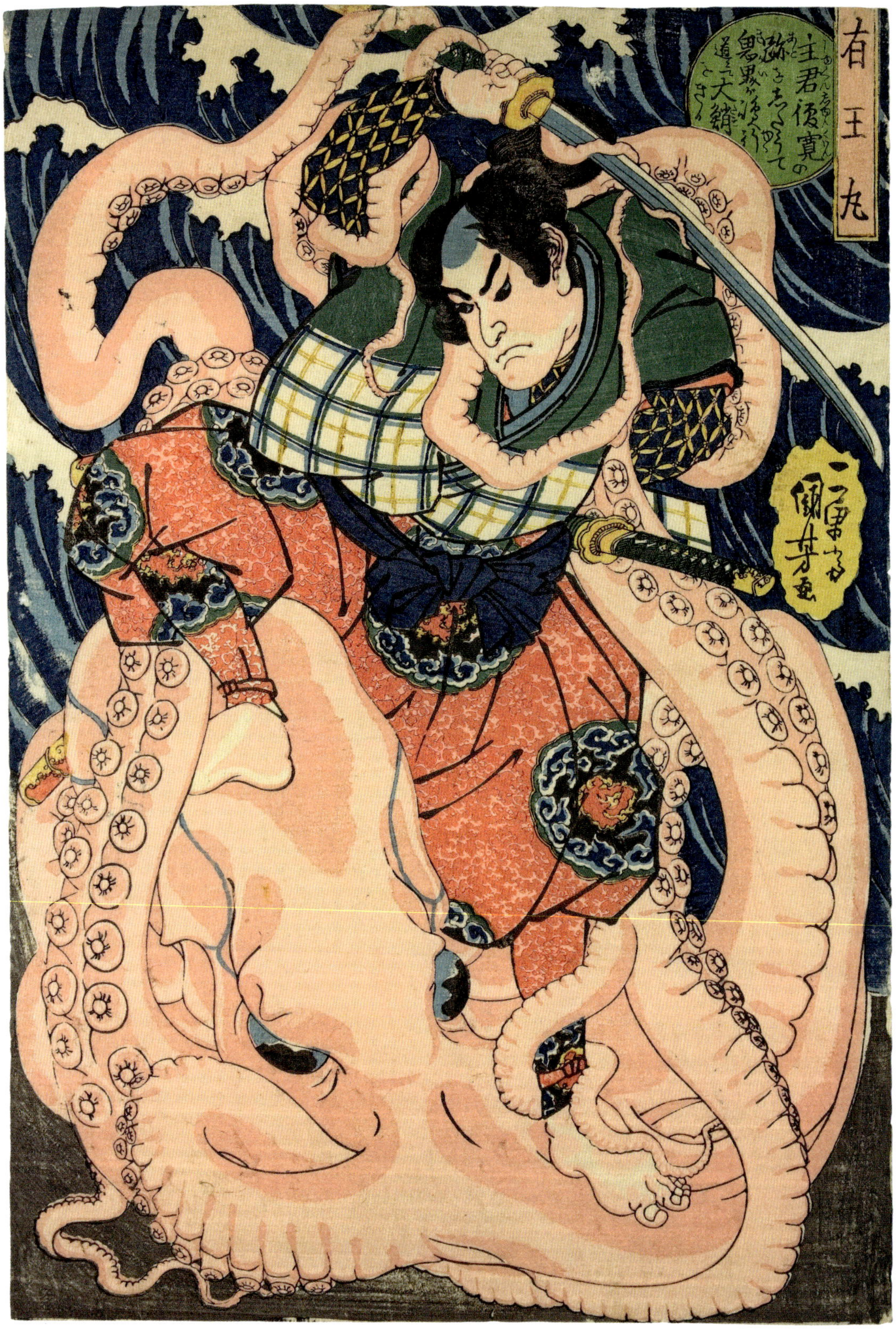

Colour woodblock, *ōban*, no publisher's mark [originally published by Kawaguchiya Chōzō], 37.8 × 26.4 cm

PRINT TITLE
'Ariō-maru'

ARTIST'S SIGNATURE
Ichiyūsai Kuniyoshi ga (in irregular cartouche)

CENSORSHIP SEAL
kiwame

American Friends of the British Museum (The Arthur R. Miller Collection) 21211

REFERENCES
Robinson 1982, no. S1c.13; HUT, vol. 3, 1988, BW no. 45 (key-block impression); Yamaguchi 1991, Kuniyoshi no. 23; Nagoya 1996, no. 28

In Japanese medieval military chronicles Ariō was originally a child servant of Priest Shunkan (d. 1179) who gave particularly loyal service during Shunkan's banishment and death on Kikai island. The adult hero shown in the present print seems to have been developed by Kuniyoshi from a character in Bakin's 1808 novel *Shunkan sōzu shima monogatari* (*Tale of Priest Shunkan on the Island*), which contained illustrations by Toyohiro (Nagoya 1996, p. 231). The inscription, top right, tells how Ariō killed a giant octopus during his journey to Kikai island to join his master. This brief literary episode served as the seed for an intense pictorial struggle between man and beast, with Ariō's neck, limbs and sword-hilt ensnared by the octopus's coiling tentacles.

Earlier printings of the design have a red, not green, circular cartouche for the inscription and show red lead pigment, not strong pink, on Ariō's leggings (Nagoya 1996, no. 28). The seashore (?) at the bottom of the design is printed black rather than grey, and into it is carved in white reserve the name and trademark of the publisher Kawaguchiya Shōzō. This was removed before the present impression was taken, suggesting that the blocks had been sold to another publisher. The British Museum owns an impression taken from the key-block (JA 1906.12-20.01317) – one of seven Kuniyoshi key-block impressions formerly in the collection of Arthur Morrison (Binyon 1916, Kuniyoshi nos 109–15, pp. 535–6). The long registration mark (*hikitsuke*) can be seen at the top, to the right of the series title. A certain degree of wear and some breaks in lines indicate that this impression was not taken before the original colour blocks were carved. In other words, it cannot be considered a true 'proof' impression (*kyōgō-zuri*) for the first printing.

Robinson lists this warrior print with others lacking a series title that were issued by various publishers in the mid-1830s (Robinson 1982, series S1c). The other design in this group published by Kawaguchiya Shōzō, 'Han-no-ue Danjō kills a giant salamander', is in the Miller collection (21210), and a key-block impression of it is among the ex-Morrison group at the British Museum (JA 1906.12-20.01316).

18

Sakata Kaidō-maru wrestles with a giant carp

c. 1837

Colour woodblock, *ōban*,
published by Kagaya Kichibei
(or Kichiemon),
37.8 × 26 cm

PRINT TITLE
'Sakata Kaidō-maru'

ARTIST'S SIGNATURE
Ichiyūsai Kuniyoshi ga
(in irregular cartouche)

CENSORSHIP SEAL
kiwame

American Friends of the British Museum
(The Arthur R. Miller Collection) 21215

REFERENCES
Riccar 1978, no. 55; Springfield 1980, no. 22; Robinson 1982, no. S1d.1; Amsterdam 1984, no. 217a&b; Suzuki 1992, no. 220; Nagoya 1996, no. 33; Amsterdam 1998, no. 19; Madison 2007, no. 101; King and Iwakiri 2007, no. 148; Isao 2008, p. 47

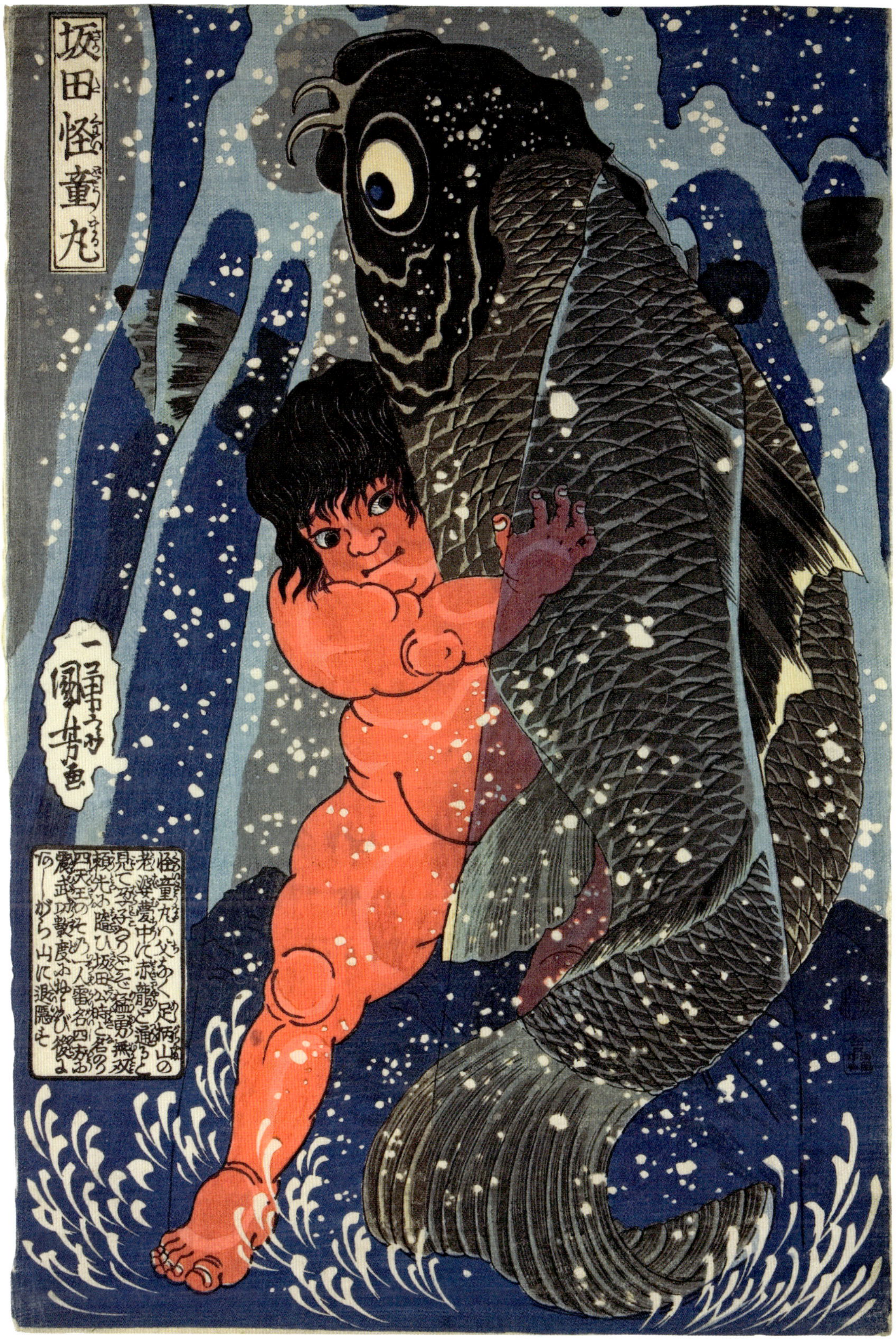

Naked, red-bodied strong-boy Kaidō-maru wrestles under a waterfall with a giant carp. He is also known as Kintarō and, as an adult warrior hero, as Sakata no Kintoki (see cat. 2). White bubbles of foam dance through the design and a strikingly beautiful film of pale blue water passes over the carp's back. The inscription reads: 'Kaidō-maru had no father and it is said he was born of the old woman of Mt Ashigara after she saw him pass by in a dream with a red dragon. His bravery was without match and he became a follower of [Minamoto no] Yorimitsu, taking the name Sakata no Kintoki. One of the so-called Four Heavenly Kings, his thunderous name resounded in all directions. After many exploits of military valour, he retired back to Mt Ashigara'. A slightly earlier, *surimono* version of the subject, by Hokkei, dates from the 1820s and appears to be the first example of a newly invented episode involving Kaidō-maru (Chiba 1997, no. 283). A carp leaping up a waterfall after many attempts was a symbol of manly perseverance, and carp streamers were flown for the Boys' Festival in the fifth month of each year.

The Rijksmuseum in Amsterdam possesses a key-block proof of the design that once belonged to the architect Frank Lloyd Wright. In it the bubbles are printed as black dots, so as to ensure that when colour blocks were cut from similar proofs the bubbles would be carved in exactly the correct shapes and positions (Amsterdam 1984, no. 217b). At least four different printings of the finished design are known. The earliest has yellow printed on the signature and inscription cartouches; the next, as here, omits this yellow; the third introduces a small white rectangle at bottom right to make the publisher's mark and *kiwame* censorship seal more clearly visible; the fourth is a reprint from the 1840s by Ibaya Senzaburō.

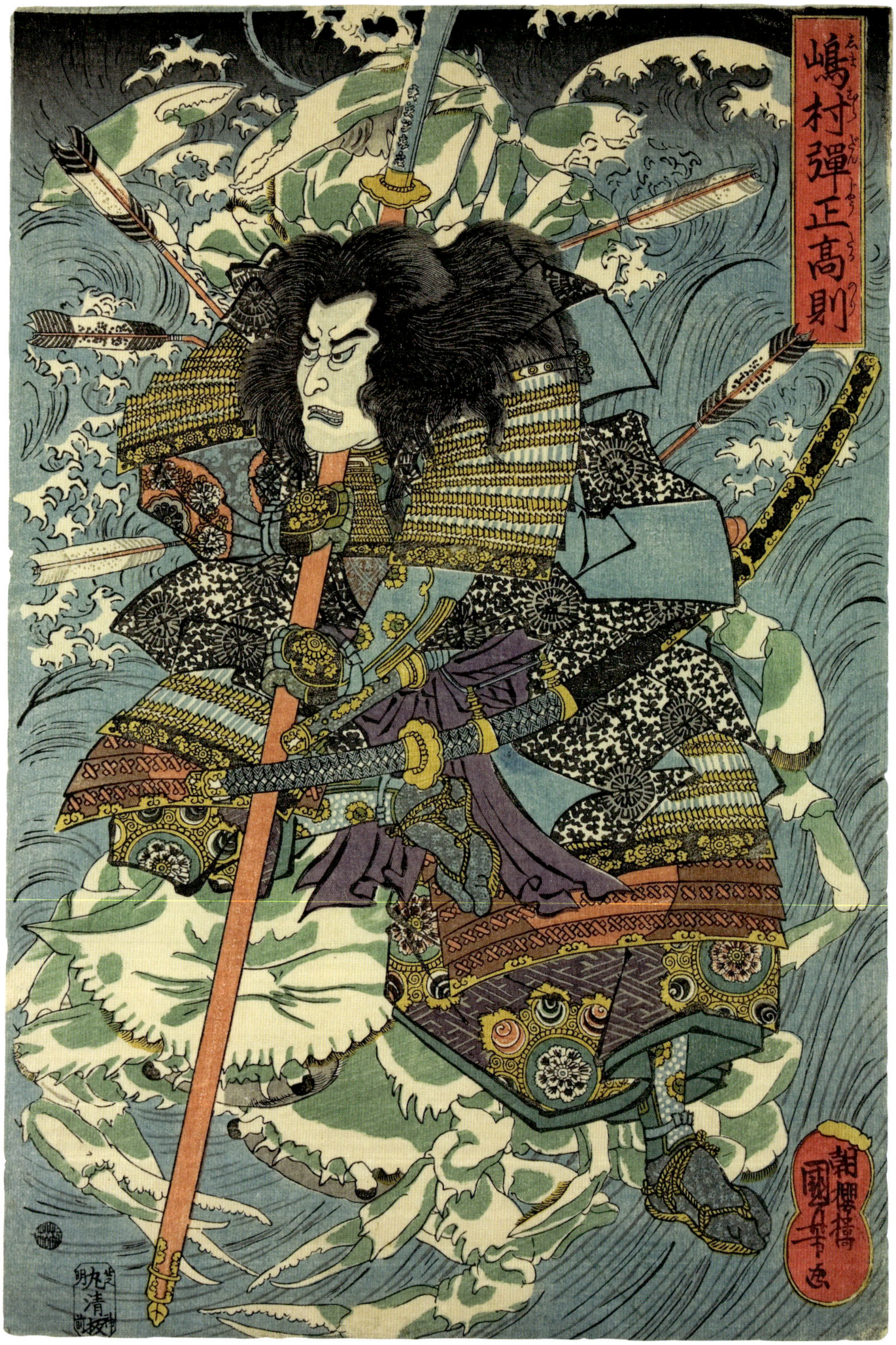

19

Ghost of the drowned warrior Shimamura Danjō Takanori, and crabs

1843–44

Colour woodblock, *ōban*, published by Maruya Seijirō, 37.6 × 25.8 cm

PRINT TITLE
'Shimamura Danjō Takanori'

ARTIST'S SIGNATURE
Chōōrō Kuniyoshi ga (in gourd-shaped *toshidama* cartouche)

CENSORS'S SEAL
Muramatsu

American Friends of the British Museum (The Arthur R. Miller Collection) 21225

REFERENCES
Joly 1908, p. 316, pl. facing p. 352; Robinson 1982, no. S1f.12; Amsterdam 1998, no. 39; King and Iwakiri 2007, no. 150

Shimamura Danjō Takanori was a retainer of warlord Hosokawa Takakuni. In 1531 he took part in a battle against the forces of Miyoshi Nagamoto (Kaiun) in the vicinity of Amagasaki. Fighting to save his lord, he was drowned in the nearby Nozato river, Settsu province. According to legend, the shells of the crabs in this area bear markings that resemble Shimamura's features. (For a similar story, involving the 'Heike crabs', see cat. 30.)

In this print the drowned warrior has the pale blue features of a ghost. Shot through with arrows, he leans resolutely on the shaft of a halberd while half sitting on the backs of two giant crabs. Another crab appears from among the waves behind him. Robinson classified this as one of the last single-sheet warrior prints by Kuniyoshi that does not belong to a series and believed that the design was drawn several years before publication of the print (Robinson 1982, p. 102).

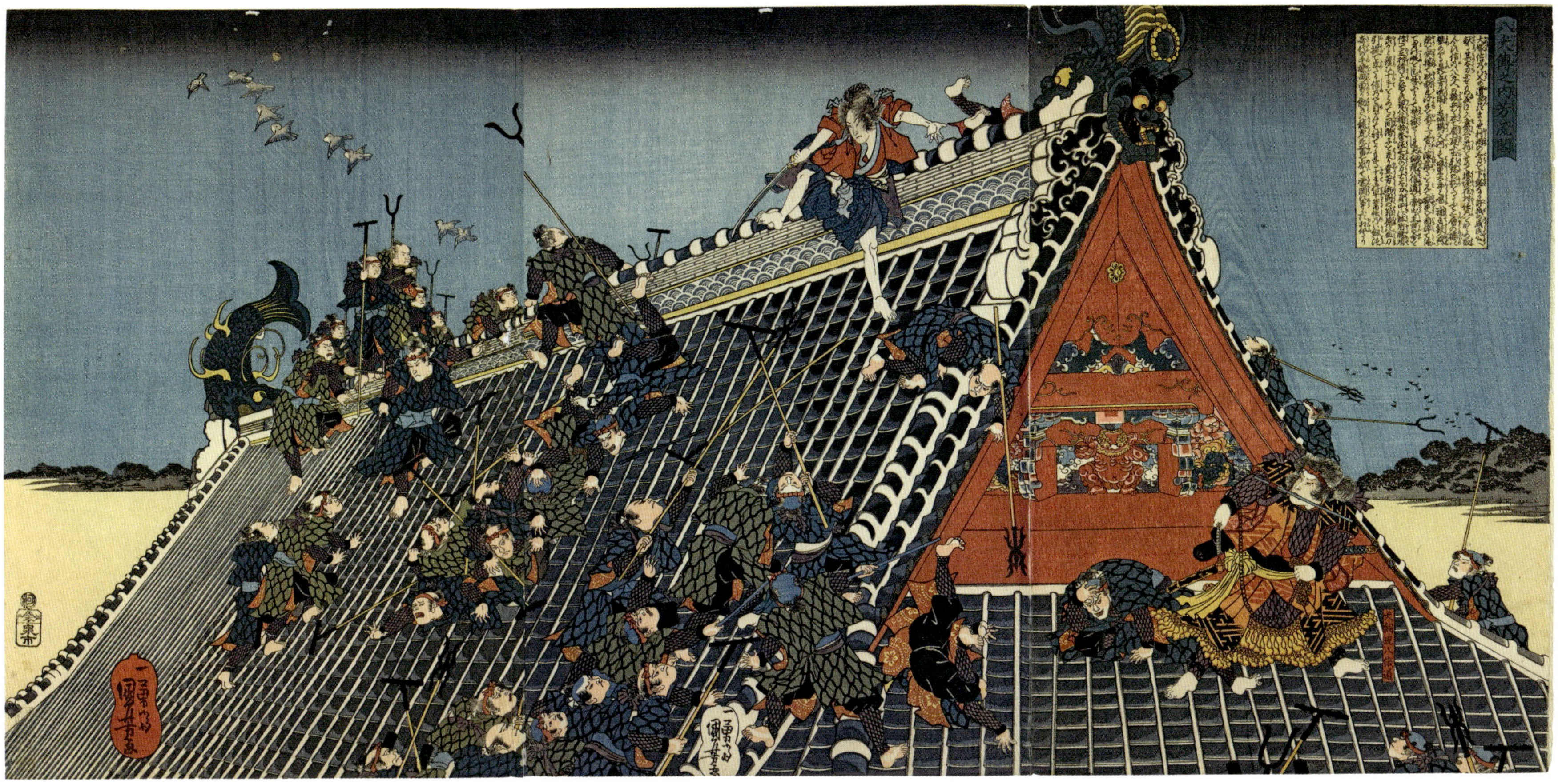

20

Fight on the roof of Hōryū tower

1840

Colour woodblock, *ōban* triptych, published by Izumiya Ichibei, 36.9 × 25.7 [R], 36.7 × 25.9 [C], 36.9 × 25.7 cm [L]

PRINT TITLE

'Hōryū Tower from *Tale of the Eight Dogs*' (*Hakkenden no uchi Hōryūkaku*)

ARTIST'S SIGNATURE

Ichiyūsai Kuniyoshi ga (in gourd-shaped cartouche)

CENSORSHIP SEAL

kiwame

American Friends of the British Museum (The Arthur R. Miller Collection) 18312

REFERENCES

Springfield 1968, no. 123; Riccar 1978, no. 90; Springfield 1980, no. 87; Robinson 1982, no. T41, pl. 43; HUT, vol. 3, 1988, BW no. 31; Yamaguchi 1991, Kuniyoshi no. 3; Suzuki 1992, no. 99; Nagoya 1996, no. 40

Over a large tiled roof a fierce combat rages between Inuzuka Shino, who balances near the ridge on the centre sheet, sword in hand, and Inukai Kenpachi, who stands on the lower roof on the right sheet, metal truncheon gripped in his mouth. The other figures, clambering up or tumbling down the roof, are constables under the command of Kenpachi, who has been ordered by Lord Nariuji to capture Shino, a man falsely accused of spying. The setting is the huge roof of Hōryū tower, a three-storey fortification on the banks of the Tone river.

This is one of the best-loved scenes in the novel *Nansō Satomi hakkenden* (*Tale of the Eight Dogs of the Satomi of Nansō*). This rambling adventure story, written by Bakin and illustrated by Yanagawa Shigenobu and others, was published serially from 1814 to 1842, eventually extending to 106 volumes in nine parts. It tells how in the fifteenth century eight warrior brothers, all the magical offspring of a dog called Yatsubusa and a princess called Fusehime, fought to restore the fortunes of the Satomi clan of Kazusa province. The main theme underpinning this extraordinarily popular work was the reward of virtue and feudal loyalty and the punishment of vice, with each brother representing a traditional Confucian virtue. Later versions of the *Eight Dogs* frequently abridged the tale. Kuniyoshi was the first to make it the subject of ukiyo-e prints, in his series *One of Eight Hundred Heroes of The Water Margin of Japan* of 1830–36 (see cats 12–14). The story was adapted as a Kabuki play for the first time in 1836, and the swarm of constables on the roof in the print does indeed recall the massed fights often seen in Kabuki performances.

One of Kuniyoshi's most striking artistic innovations in the 1840s and early 1850s was to unify the triptych print format by means of a large motif spanning all three sheets. The present example is one of the earliest. A surviving letter written by Bakin on the sixth day of the sixth month, 1840, to his friend Ozu Keisō (1804–58) of Ise Matsuzaka comments in some detail on the publication of this print. Mentioning that the triptych was selling well, Bakin went on to say that, according to his information, it was unlikely to be printed in great numbers, because it required many colour blocks. Since the publisher, Izumiya, was located quite far away, in the Shiba district, Bakin had purchased a copy at a bookshop in Denma-chō. The retail price was high: 38 *mon* per sheet or 118 *mon* for the complete triptych (Suzuki 1992, p. 195).

This impression comes from the earliest printing, in which the Tone river in the background is pale yellow and the wood-grain pattern in the sky on the right sheet is notably strong. In later printings the river changed to blue fading upwards into white (for instance, Suzuki 1992, no. 99), before becoming plain, undifferentiated blue.

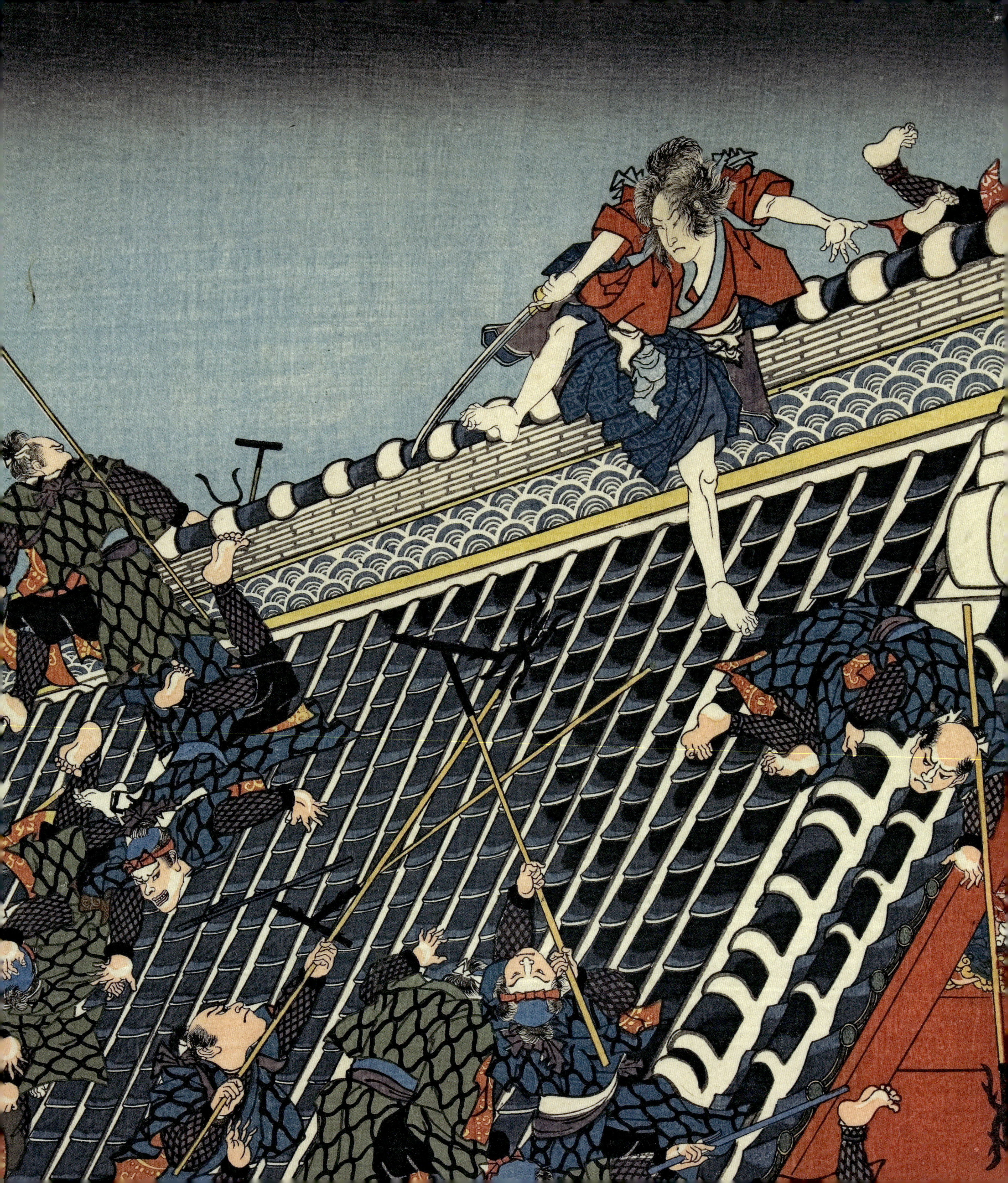

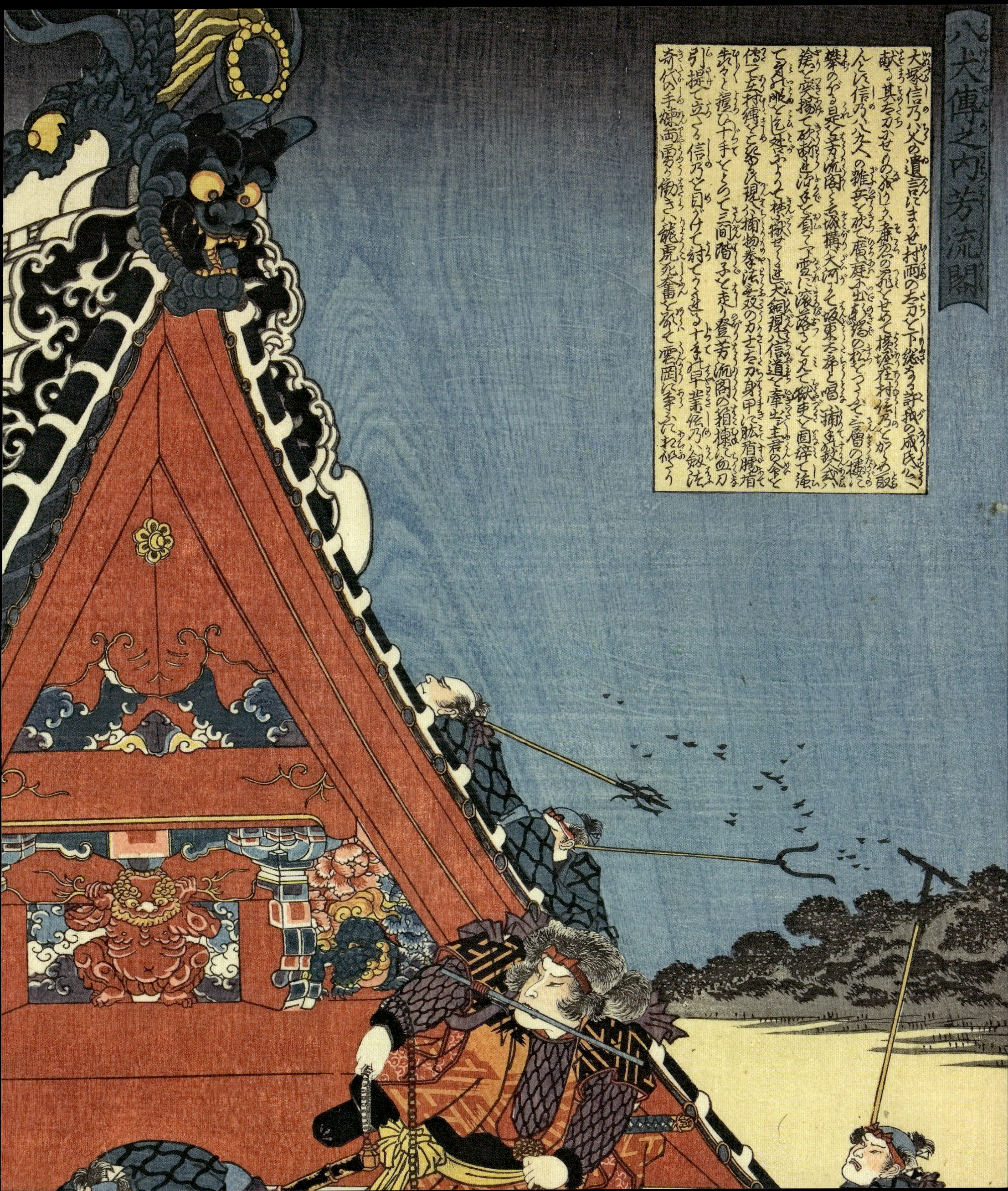
八犬傳之内芳流閣

21

Benkei and Ushiwaka-maru fight on Gojō bridge

c. 1839

Colour woodblock, *ōban* triptych, published by Fujiokaya Hikotarō, 36.9 × 25.8 [R], 37.2 × 25.7 [C], 37.1 × 25.9 cm [L]

PRINT TITLE
'*Biography of Yoshitsune*: Gojō Bridge' (*Yoshitsune ichidaiki Gojō-no-hashi no zu*)

ARTIST'S SIGNATURE
Ichiyūsai Kuniyoshi ga (in irregular cartouche, right sheet)

CENSORSHIP SEAL
kiwame

American Friends of the British Museum (The Arthur R. Miller Collection) 20604

REFERENCES
Robinson 1961, no. 45; Robinson 1963, no. 4; Springfield 1968, no. 52; Riccar 1978, no. 91; Springfield 1980, no. 93; Robinson 1982, no. T47, pl. 40; Suzuki 1992, no. 129; Baur 1994, no. G386; Amsterdam 1998, no. 20

The warrior monk Benkei was of giant stature. Picking fights with travellers who crossed Gojō bridge in Kyoto, he swore to collect from them one thousand weapons. After he had amassed 999, he faced the teenage Ushiwaka-maru as his next opponent. Nimble of foot and trained in swordplay by the *tengu* of Mt Kurama, Ushiwaka succeeded in defeating Benkei, who promptly became his devoted follower. Ushikawa went on to become the warrior hero Minamoto no Yoshitsune (1159–89). This is one of the earliest and finest of the many triptych prints that Kuniyoshi devoted to the exploits of Yoshitsune and Benkei.

As early as 1552 a painter of the Kano school had presented a votive panel of this subject to Itsukushima shrine (Machida 2003, p. 140) and nearly all ukiyo-e print artists who produced warrior prints tried their hand at it. What sets Kuniyoshi's version apart is the dramatic way in which Gojō bridge spans all three sheets of the triptych. The great bridge turns into the picture and leads the eye past Benkei and along the cloak he is spearing towards Ushiwaka, who seems almost to be dancing on the red railing. The third character, on the right sheet, is named as Onmaya no Kisanda Sadakiyo and was apparently introduced into the story by Kuniyoshi, perhaps to balance the composition. Through the pillars of the bridge can be seen temporary teahouses on the Kamo river and the hills of Higashiyama, marking the eastern extent of Kyoto. Geese fly close to a full moon and bats flit about the bridge.

The earliest printings of the design have a diagonal band of deep blue with wiped edges, which passes across a lighter blue river (see, for example, Robinson 1982, pl. 40). In those printings all the mountains have a gradated band of black across their summits, and gradated black is also used on the top half of the bridge pillars. The present impression must therefore come from a somewhat later printing.

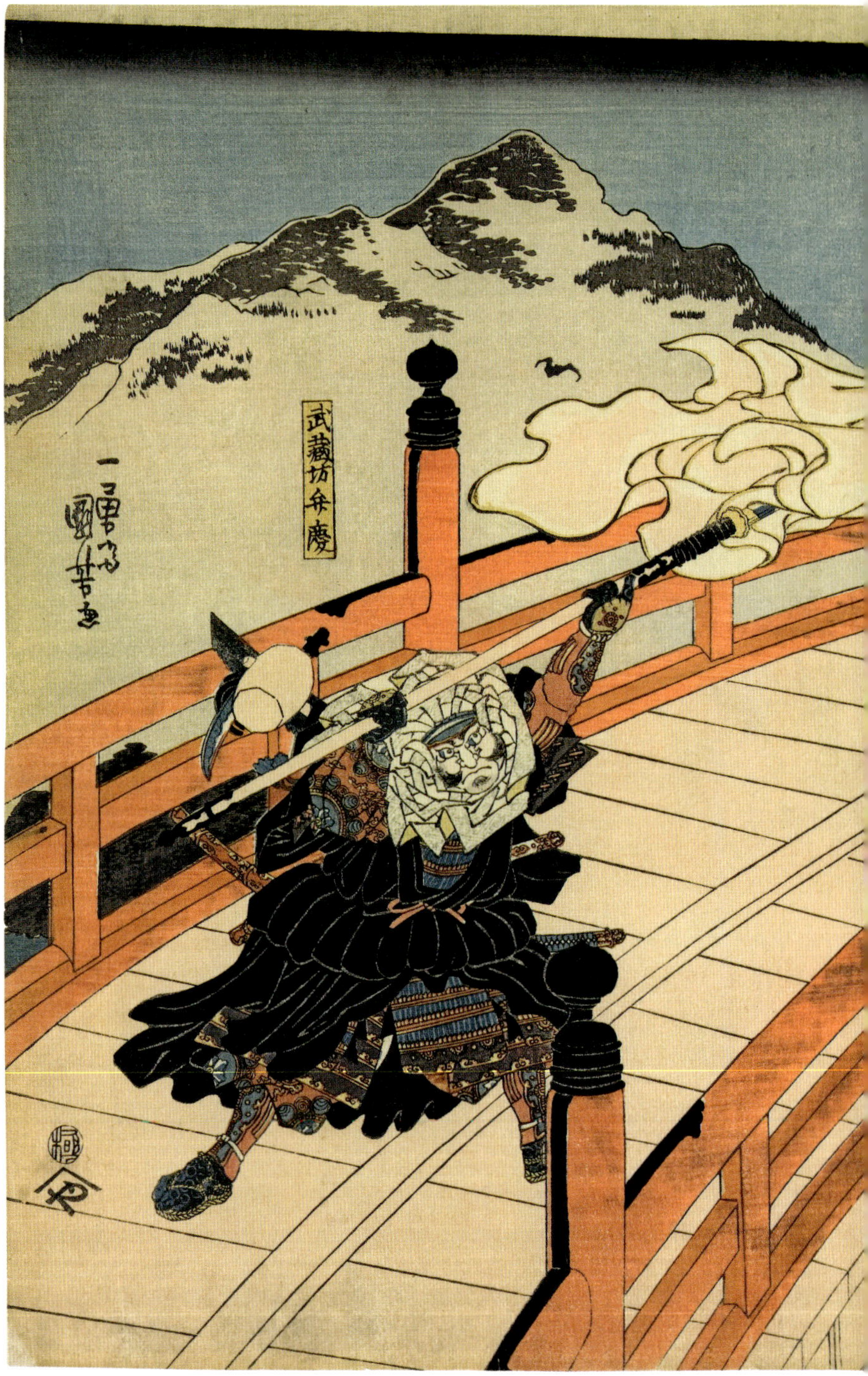

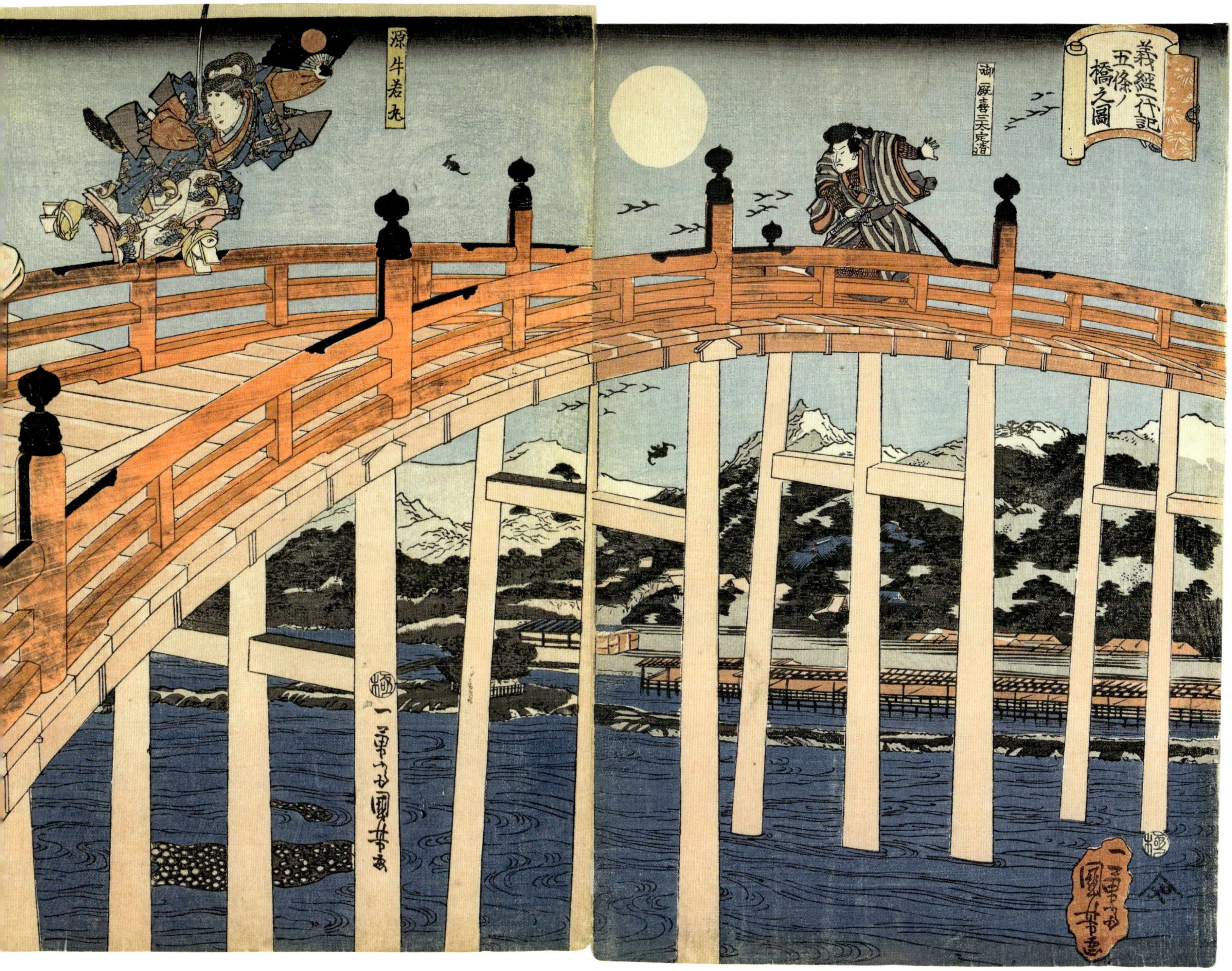
義經一代記
五條ノ橋之圖
御厩喜三太定清
源牛若丸
一勇斎國芳画
一勇斎國芳画

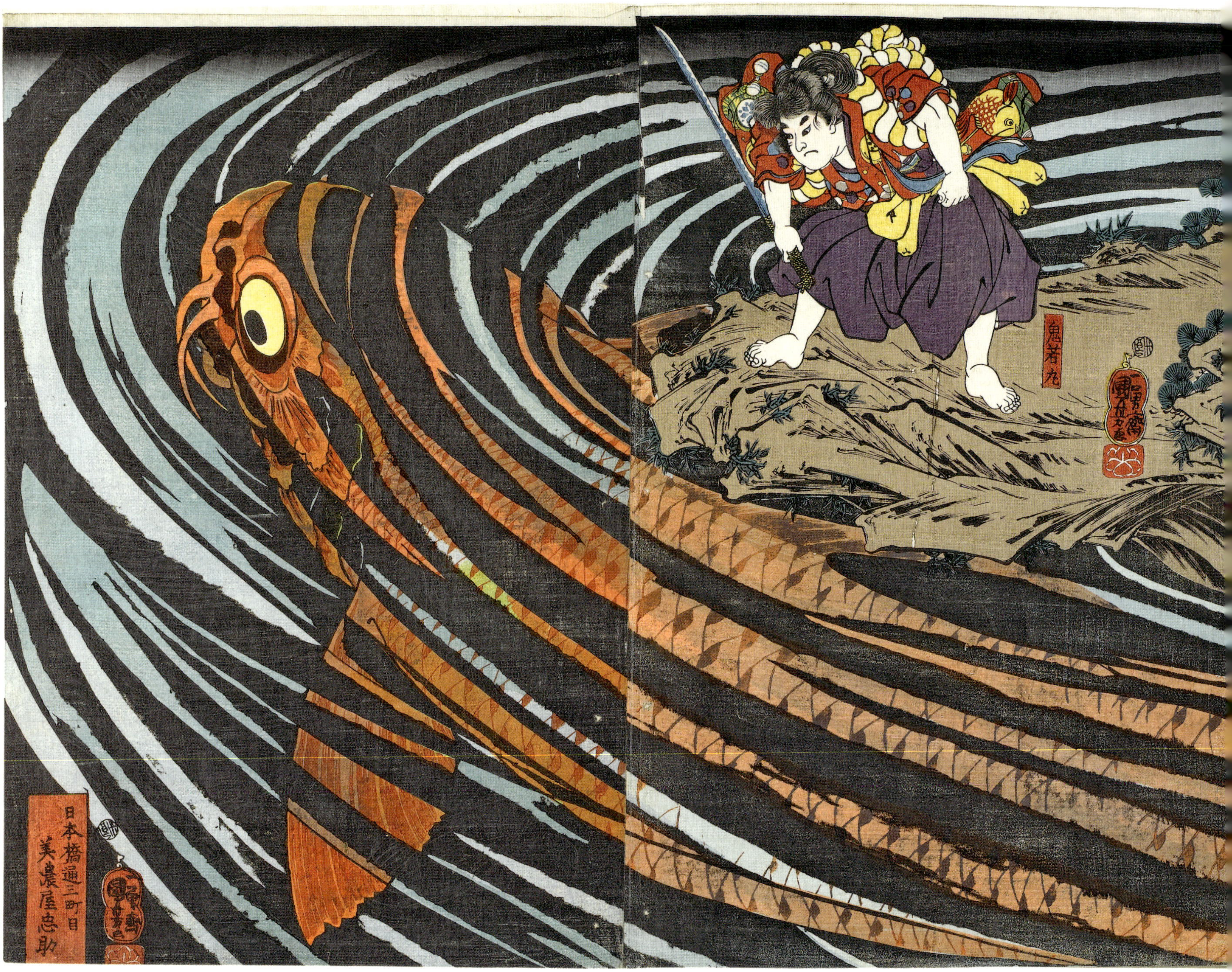
鬼若丸
日本橋通三町目
美濃屋忠助

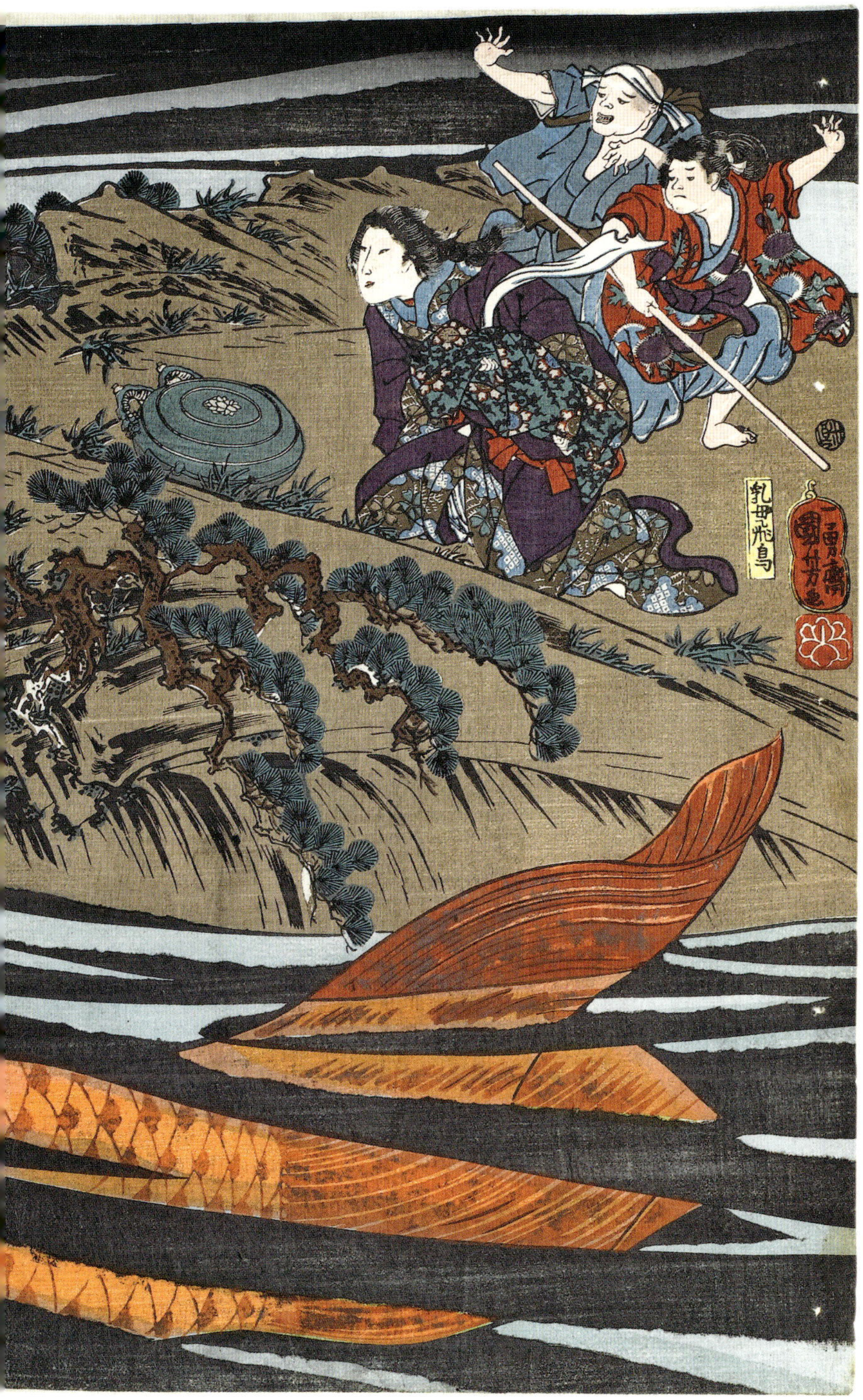

22

Oniwaka-maru about to kill a giant red carp

1845–46

Colour woodblock, *ōban* triptych, published by Minoya Chūsuke, 36.5 x 73.8 cm

ARTIST'S SIGNATURE
Ichiyūsai Kuniyoshi ga (in gourd-shaped *Yoshi* cartouche)

ARTIST'S SEAL
Yoshikiri

CENSORS'S SEAL
Mera

Courtesy of the Trustees of National Museums Scotland, A.1887.745.68.1.2–4

REFERENCES
Riccar 1978, no.98; Springfield 1980, no.122; Robinson 1982, no.T171, pl.54; HUT, vol.5, 1989, no.48; Keyes 1989, no.57; Suzuki 1992, no.72; Itabashi 1994, Kuniyoshi no.21; Mainichi Shinbunsha 1995, no.53; Nagoya 1996, nos 52–3; Amsterdam 1998, no.68; Machida 2003, no.192

Oniwaka-maru was the childhood name of Benkei (see cat.21) while he was an acolyte at Hieizan monastery, Kyoto. In this print he stares down intently into eddying water, waiting for the right moment to dive in and attack a monstrous carp gliding just below the surface. To the right are two alarmed child companions and Oniwaka's wet-nurse, Asuka, who kneels beside a large bronze gong. Oniwaka has presumably just struck the gong to attract the carp, then tied the gong rope around his shoulders to pull back the sleeves of his robe, the child's pattern of which charmingly includes a toy fish. Suzuki notes the telling detail of the rope wrapped around the hilt of Oniwaka's sword to stop it slipping from his immature grip (Suzuki 1992, p.191). No old text describing this episode has been discovered among the legends concerning Benkei's childhood. The inscription on a slightly later version of the scene by Kuniyoshi, a single-sheet print from the series 'Sixteen Stories of Musashi-bō [Benkei]' (*Jūroku Musashi-bō*, c.1848–50), tells how Oniwaka (Benkei) killed a monster carp that was haunting a pond at Hieizan (Machida 2003, p.137; Robinson 1982, no.S68.3).

As with the bridge triptych (cat.21), a single large motif – the sinister carp – serves to unify the three sheets and electrify the composition. The pattern of ragged eddies achieved in the water, partly by abrading the block used for the black ripples (a technique known as *ita-bokashi*), is a tour de force. The National Museum of Ethnology, Leiden, possesses a preparatory drawing by Kuniyoshi for an apparently unpublished triptych in which Oniwaka clings onto the back of the giant carp and stabs it (Forrer 1988, no.57).

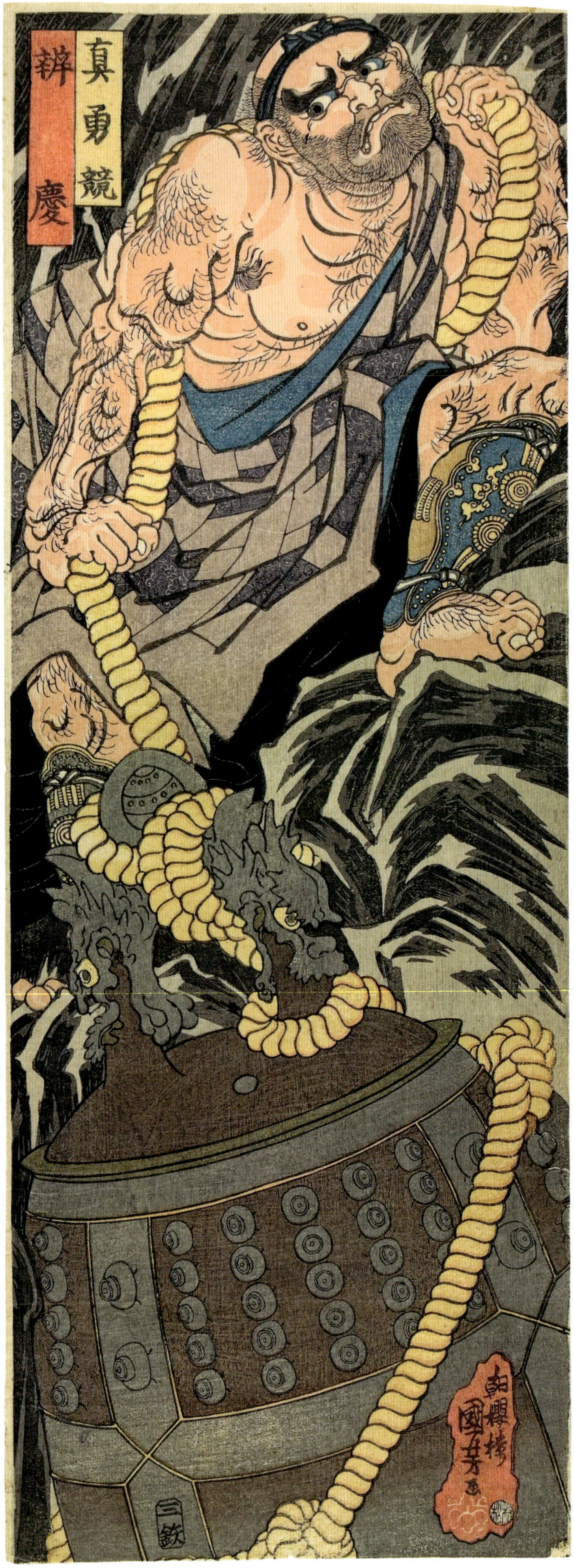

23

Benkei drags the bell of Mii temple up Mt Hiei

1845–46

Colour woodblock, tall *ōban*, published by Mikawaya Tetsugorō, 49.2 × 18.5 cm

SERIES TITLE
'Comparisons of True Courage' (*Shin'yū kurabe*)

PRINT TITLE
'Benkei'

ARTIST'S SIGNATURE
Chōōrō Kuniyoshi ga (in irregular cartouche)

ARTIST'S SEAL
Yoshikiri

CENSORS'S SEAL
Muramatsu

American Friends of the British Museum (The Arthur R. Miller Collection) 02001

REFERENCES
Riccar 1978, no.83; Springfield 1980, no. 146; Robinson 1982, no. S49.1; Suzuki 1992, no. 139; Mainichi Shinbunsha 1995, no. 44; Amsterdam 1998, no. 56

In a Herculean demonstration of strength the warrior monk Benkei drags the huge bronze bell of Mii temple up the slopes of Mt Hiei, Kyoto. It is said that he pulled the bell so forcefully that its protruding metal ornaments wore flat. Benkei's muscular body is set against an almost sheer cliff, and the extraordinary strength required for the exploit is etched in the grimace on his face. He wears both a Buddhist monk's stole (*kesa*), across one shoulder, and military shin guards – a combination symbolising Benkei's dual status as monk and warrior. A thick, knotted rope snakes up the picture, serving as a unifying element within the composition.

The print comes from a group of ten in the unusual tall *ōban* (*naga-ōban*) format, all published by Mikawaya Tetsugorō. Four bear the series title 'Comparisons of True Courage' (*Shin'yū kurabe*), six the title 'Tales of Successive Heroes' (*Retsumō den*). Within each of these groups half the designs were originally published c. 1845–46 with the single Mura censorship seal, the other half with *aratame* censorship seals giving the dates of the ninth and tenth months of 1856. The style of the signature is uniform on all ten prints, suggesting that they were designed together in the mid-1840s. For unknown reasons publication of half the prints must have been delayed until 1856. This is made particularly clear by the image of Kintarō and a black bear from the *Retsumō den* group, which has both a Mura censorship seal and a date seal for the tenth month, 1856 (Nagoya 1996, no. 61). Robinson lists all the designs, many of which are illustrated by Suzuki in the Nagoya City Museum exhibition catalogue (Robinson 1982, series S48 and S49; Suzuki 1992, nos 138–43; and Nagoya 1996, nos 58–63).

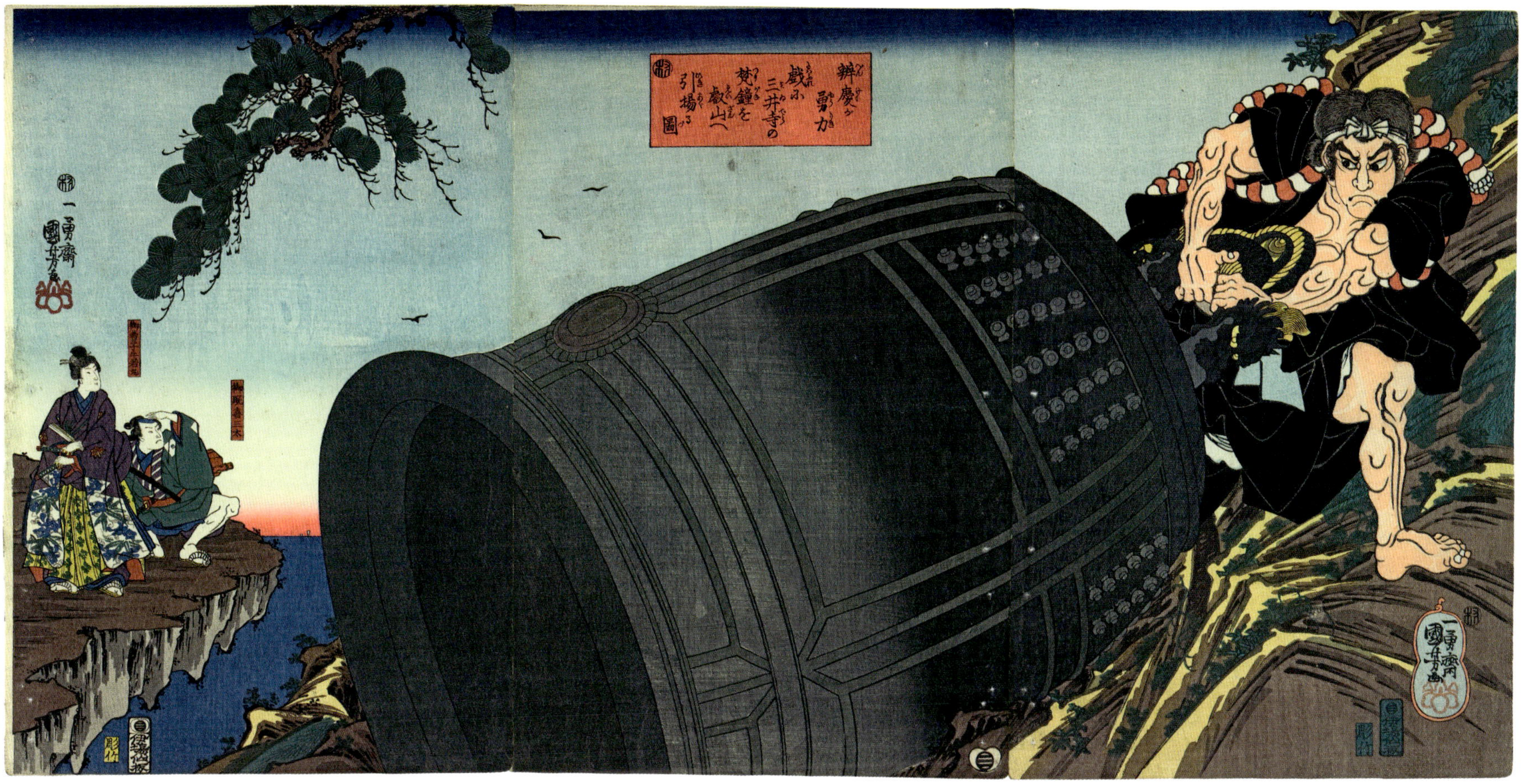

24

Benkei drags the bell of Mii temple up Mt Hiei

1845–46

Colour woodblock, *ōban* triptych, published by Ibaya Senzaburō, 37.2 × 25.3 [R], 37.1 × 25.2 [C], 37.2 × 25.3 cm [L]

PRINT TITLE
'Benkei's Heroic Strength: Playfully Dragging the Bell of Mii Temple up Mt Hiei (*Benkei ga yūriki tawamure ni Miidera no tsurigane o Eizan e hikiaguru zu*)

ARTIST'S SIGNATURE
Ichiyūsai Kuniyoshi ga (in gourd-shaped *Yoshi* cartouche, right sheet)

ARTIST'S SEAL
Yoshikiri

CENSORS'S SEAL
Mura

BLOCK-CARVER
Hori-Take

The British Museum, JA 1915.8-23.0921(1-3)

REFERENCES
Riccar 1978, no. 101; Springfield 1980, no. 145; Robinson 1982, no. T150; Yamaguchi 1991, Kuniyoshi no. 6; Suzuki 1992, no. 73; Nagoya 1996, nos 55–6

This triptych version of the episode in which Benkei drags the huge bronze bell of Mii temple up the slopes of Mt Hiei, Kyoto, dates from around the same time as the tall *ōban* (cat. 23). Benkei's exploit is watched from a distance by 'Onzōshi' (The Young Master) Ushiwaka-maru, the future Yoshitsune, and his crouching retainer Onmaya no Kisanda. These additional figures were apparently Kuniyoshi's invention. Down below, the waters of Lake Biwa spread off into the distance. The exact textual origins of the story have not been determined: it seems to be an Edo-period conflation of an older tale in *Taiheiki* (*Chronicle of the Great Peace*), in which monks steal the bell from the temple and hurl it to the bottom of a valley, with an episode in which Benkei hangs a temple bell from a pine tree and signals military strategies at the battle of Ichinotani (Nagoya 1996, pp. 235–6). Suzuki points out that Kuniyoshi must have been influenced by Hokusai's book illustration of the same subject in his *Wakan ehon sakigake* (*Picture Book of Military Valour in China and Japan*) of 1836 and by a warrior print, also by Hokusai, in which a black robed priest ties a red and white rope around a giant bell (Suzuki 1992, p. 191; the print is illustrated in Nagoya 1991, no. 74).

This is one of the earliest triptychs by Kuniyoshi to feature a single large motif spanning all three sheets. Doubtless because of the overwhelming presence of the bell some commentators have found the image lacking in movement. On the other hand, the careful curving of the gradation in the boundary between light and dark grey on the bell grants it an appropriate and memorable solidity.

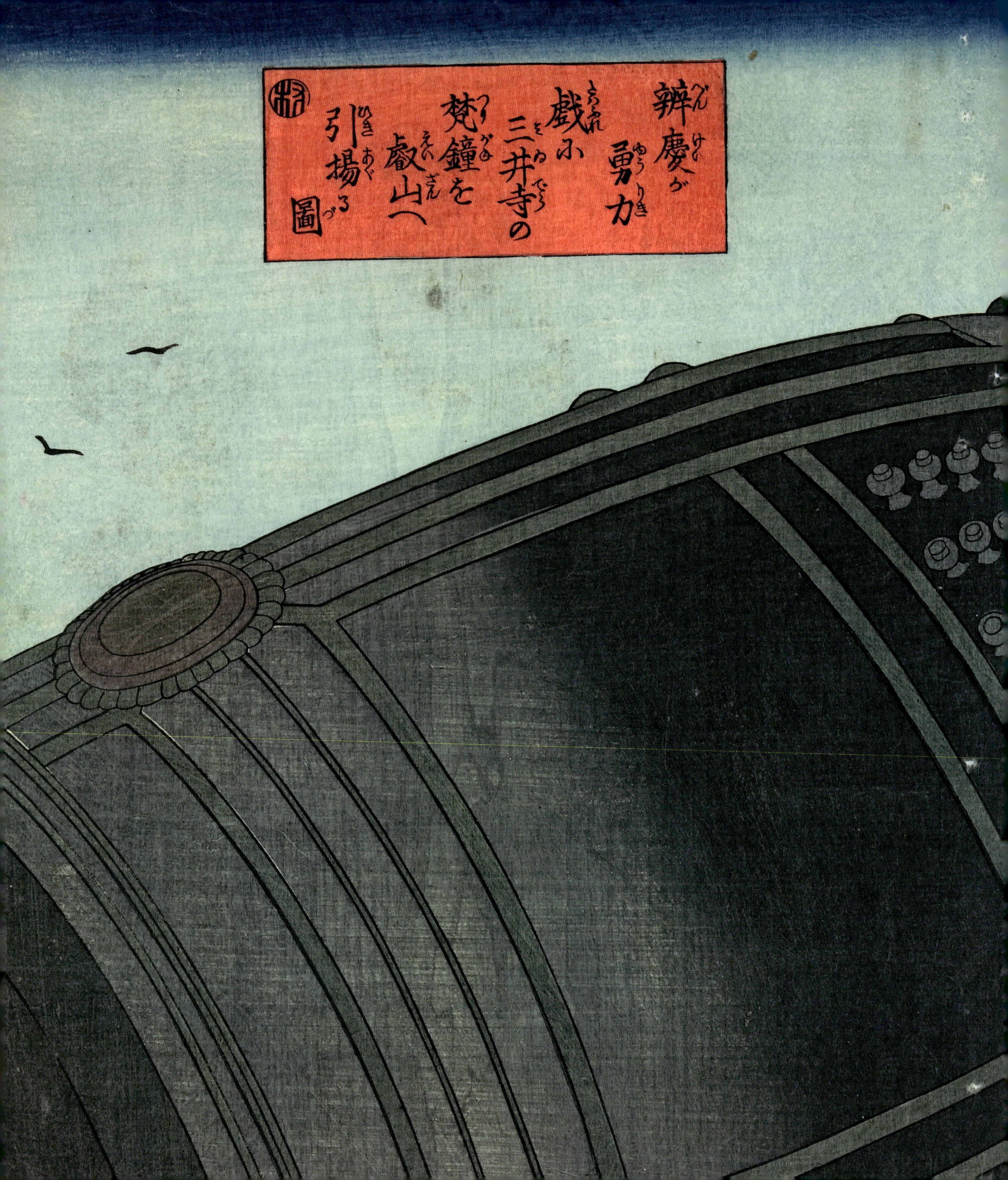
辨慶が勇力
戯に三井寺の梵鐘を叡山へ引揚る圖

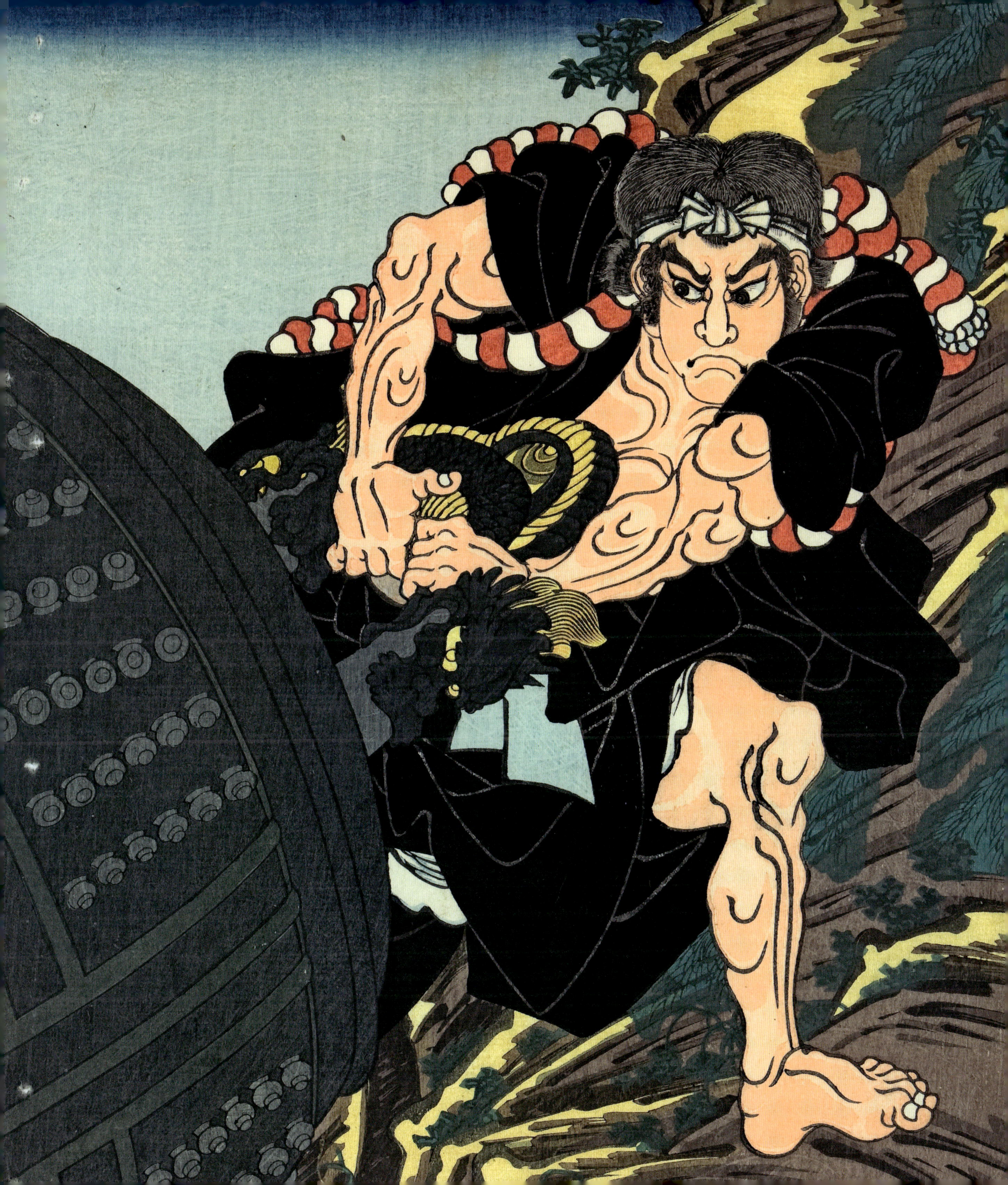

25

Mitsukuni defies the skeleton spectre conjured up by Princess Takiyasha

1845–46

Colour woodblock, *ōban* triptych, publisher unidentified, 37.2 × 25.1 [R], 37 × 25.3 [C], 37.2 × 25.3 cm [L]

ARTIST'S SIGNATURE
Ichiyūsai Kuniyoshi ga (in gourd-shaped *Yoshi* cartouche)

ARTIST'S SEAL
Yoshikiri (right sheet only)

CENSORS'S SEAL
Watari

The British Museum, JA 1915.8-23.0915, 0916

REFERENCES
Robinson 1961, no. 43; *Ukiyo-e taikei* 1974, nos 36–8; Riccar 1978, no. 100; Robinson 1982, no. T138, pl. 52; HUT, vol. 3, 1988, no. 48; HUT, vol. 5, 1989, BW, no. 31; Suzuki 1992, no. 70; Baur 1994, no. G394; Mainichi Shinbunsha 1995, no. 57; Nagoya 1996, nos 50–1; Amsterdam 1998, no. 53; Machida 2003, no. 191; King and Iwakiri 2007, no. 151; Isao 2008, pp. 32–3

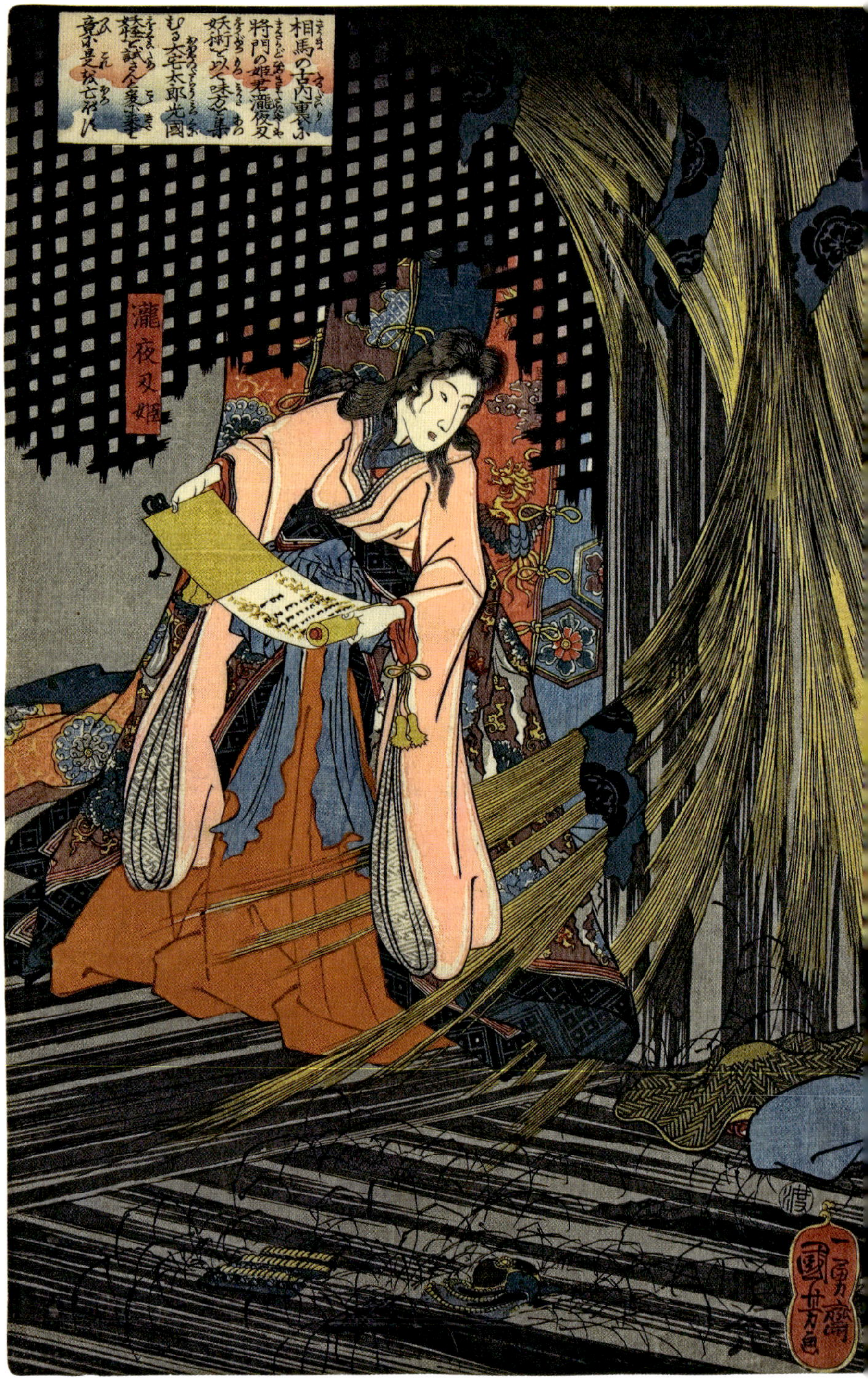

With a chillingly lifelike attitude a giant skeleton looms out of the blackness to menace the warrior Mitsukuni below, pulling back tattered reed blinds with its bony fingers. This fearsome apparition has been conjured up by the sorceress Princess Takiyasha, who spies on the scene from the left as she reads from a scroll of spells. The setting is the ruined palace of Sōma at Sashima in Shimōsa province, where the doomed pretender Taira no Masakado (d. 940) had in former times established a palace in rivalry to the legitimate imperial court in Kyoto. Beautiful Takiyasha is his surviving daughter, and the warrior hero Ōya no Tarō Mitsukuni has been sent by his lord Minamoto no Yorinobu to destroy her evil power.

The immediate source for the story was a *yomihon* of 1806, *Utō Yasukata chūgi den* (*Tales of Faithful Utō Yasukata*). That illustrated novel features several hundred skeletons, which divide into two armies and fight a battle. Kuniyoshi's penchant for compositions that linked the three sheets of a triptych by means of a single large motif surely led him to focus on just one skeleton. Suzuki suggests Hokusai's print of *c.* 1831–32 showing the skeleton of Koheiji pulling down a mosquito net with bony fingers as one important model (Suzuki 1992, p. 190; the print is illustrated in TNM 2005, no. 389). He also mentions documented public performances at Asakusa in the third month, 1847, in which one Yanagawa Itchōsai (Bungo no Daijō) manipulated models with supernatural subjects, perhaps featuring a full-scale model of a skeleton. Suzuki has often raised the intriguing question of the possible influence on Kuniyoshi's work of sensational popular displays (*misemono*), although in the present case the performances slightly post-date the print. Illustrations in imported European medical or art treatises would constitute a much more specific visual source, and one that would explain the anatomical accuracy of Kuniyoshi's skeleton. Dutch drawing manuals, such as Samuel van Hoogstraten's *Inleyding tot de Hooge Schoole der Schilderkonst* of 1678, sometimes include illustrations of skeletons in animated poses, but no precise model of this kind has been discovered.

This impression has bright, largely unfaded colours. In what seem to be the earliest printings a darker black pigment of granular character appears on the skeleton's ribs in the centre of the chest, in the eye sockets and on the temple. In later printings the band of wiped black disappears from across the top of the composition and the eye sockets are a deeper blue.

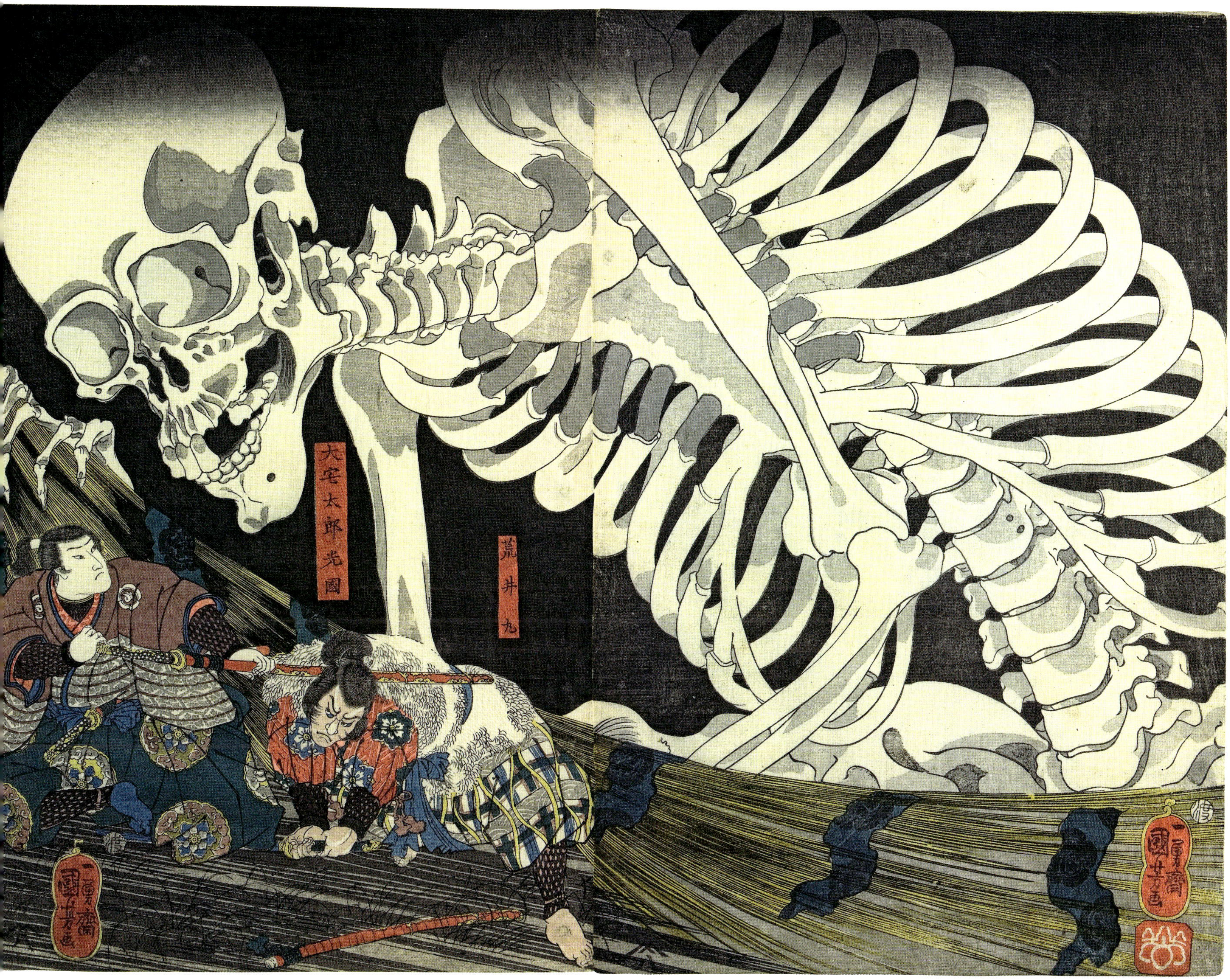
大宅太郎光國
荒井丸
一勇齋國芳画
一勇齋國芳画

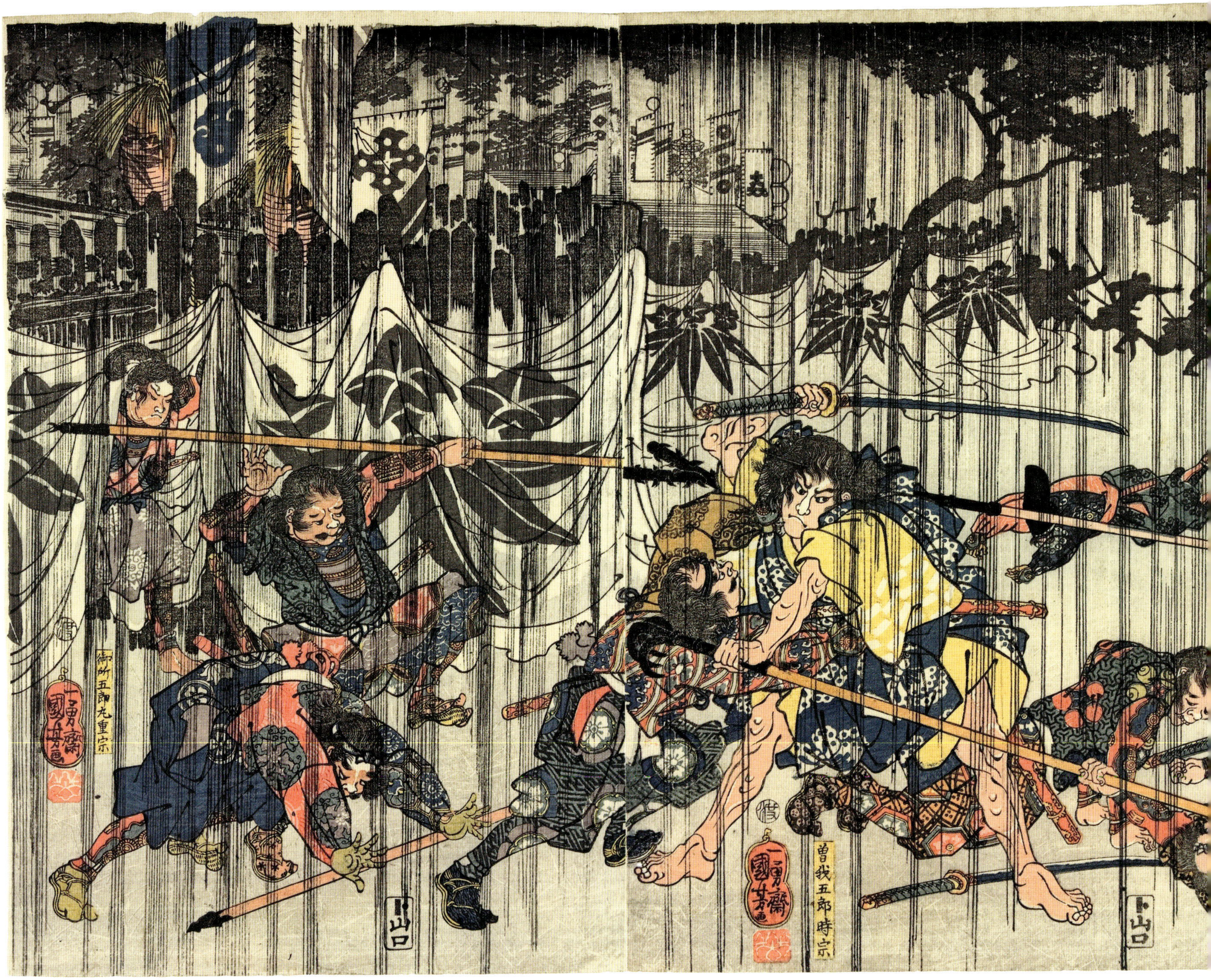
御所五郎丸重宗
一勇斎國芳画
曽我五郎時宗
一勇斎國芳画

26

The Soga brothers achieve their revenge at the base of Mt Fuji

1845–46

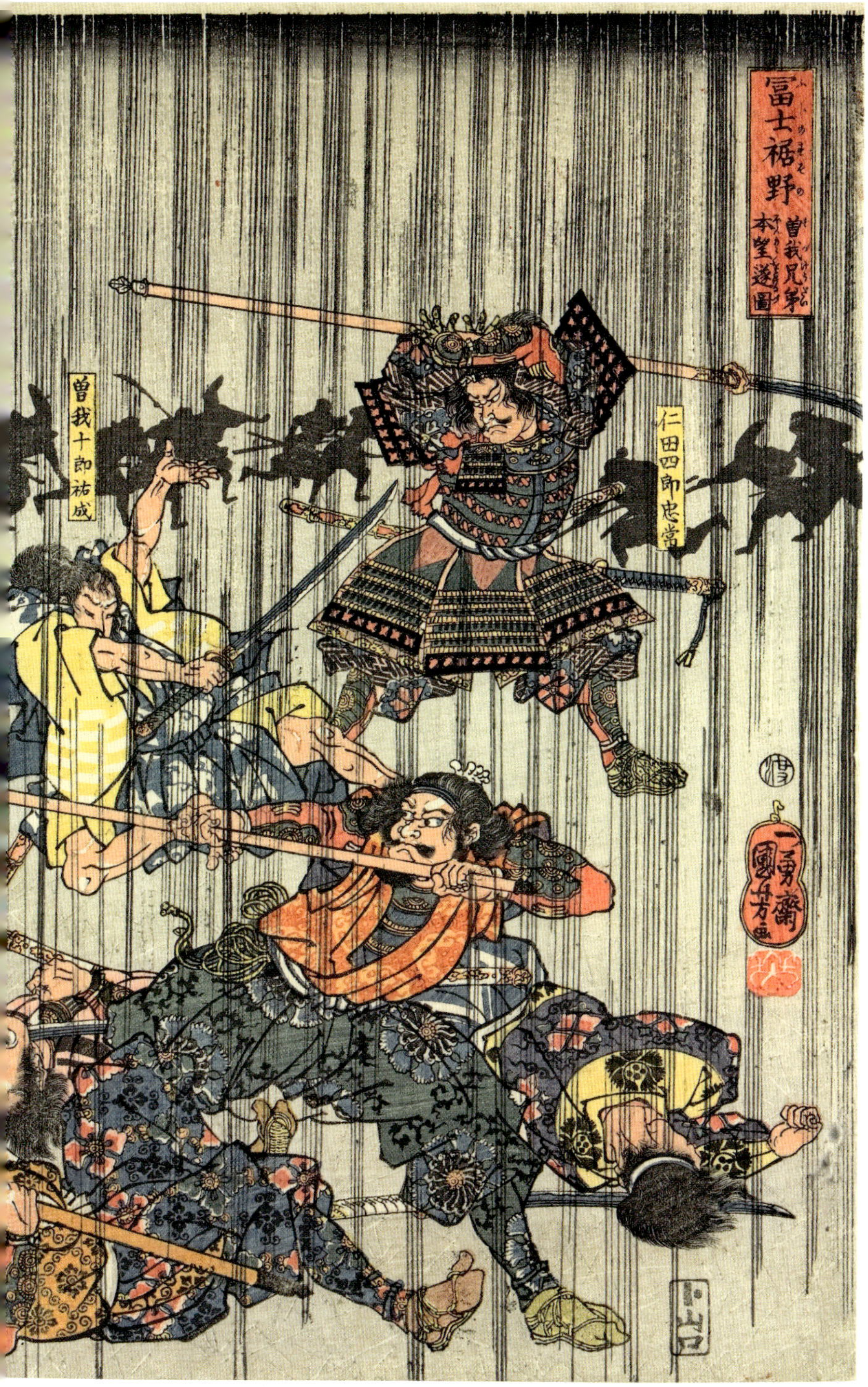

Colour woodblock, *ōban* triptych, published by Yamaguchiya Tōbei, 37.2 × 25.7 [R], 37.4 × 25.5 [C], 37.5 × 24.8 cm [L]

PRINT TITLE
'The Soga Brothers Achieve their Revenge on the Plain at the Base of Mt Fuji' (*Fuji no susono Soga kyōdai honmō o togeru zu*)

ARTIST'S SIGNATURE
Ichiyūsai Kuniyoshi ga (in gourd-shaped *Yoshi* cartouche)

ARTIST'S SEAL
Yoshikiri

CENSOR'S SEAL
Watari

American Friends of the British Museum (The Arthur R. Miller Collection) 19001

REFERENCES
Robinson 1961, no.44;
Robinson 1982, no.T159;
HUT, vol. 3, 1988, BW, no.33

The revenge of the Soga brothers Jūrō and Gorō on their father's murderer, Kudō Suketune, was one of the most celebrated of all warrior vendettas. Kudō had treacherously killed their father, the famous wrestler Kawazu no Saburō, when they were young boys, and the pair were then raised by Soga no Tarō. Planned for eighteen years, their revenge finally came about in 1193, while Kudō was accompanying Shogun Minamoto no Yoritomo on a great hunting expedition on the moor at the base of Mt Fuji. Bursting into Kudō's tent during a violent storm, they were able to surprise and kill him. The scene in the print shows Jūrō and Gorō attempting to fight off Yoritomo's warriors after the alarm has been raised. They wear matching yellow and blue robes, patterned with plovers and butterflies respectively. Jūrō, on the right sheet, will presently be killed by his opponent Nitta no Shirō Tadatsune, while Gorō, in the centre, will be captured by Yoritomo's young bodyguard, Gosho no Gorōmaru Shigemune, who is emerging from the curtained enclosure on the left. The rendering of pouring rain, which, diplomatically, obscures neither the protagonists' faces nor the artist's signatures, represents a tour de force by the block-cutters.

The classic version of this famous story was recorded in *Soga monogatari* (*Tales of the Soga Brothers*) in the mid-fourteenth century. Reworked in various dramatic and literary forms, the story of Jūrō and Gorō and their revenge on Kudō eventually became one of the most common types of Kabuki play during the Edo period, when it was much embroidered with love interest. Kuniyoshi particularly favoured the revenge scene: Robinson lists six different triptychs on the subject (Robinson 1982, p.25).

27

Miyamoto Musashi kills a great whale

1847–48

Colour woodblock, *ōban* triptych, published by Kawaguchiya Shōzō, 36.5 x 75.3 cm

ARTIST'S SIGNATURE
Ichiyūsai Kuniyoshi ga (in gourd-shaped *Yoshi* cartouche)

ARTIST'S SEAL
Yoshikiri

CENSORS' SEALS
Mera and Murata

Courtesy of the Trustees of National Museums Scotland, A.1887.745.68.4.43–45

REFERENCES
Riccar 1978, no. 108; Springfield 1980, no. 183; Robinson 1982, no. T208; Suzuki 1992, no. 4; Mainichi Shinbunsha 1995, no. 56; Nagoya 1996, nos 66–7; Amsterdam 1998, no. 69 (this impression); Machida 2003, no. 193; King and Iwakiri 2007, no. 153; Isao 2008, pp. 68–9

Musashi rides a great whale, poised to make a two-handed stab with his sword into the creature's back. Kuniyoshi skilfully fills the three sheets of the print so that the nose is in one corner and the tail bends round to fit into another. The liveliness of the surging sea is amplified by the fanciful white dots on the whale's massive body. The ragged edges of the areas of black and grey, achieved by abrading the printing block (*ita-bokashi*), well suggest the rough folds of the creature's thick skin. The present impression lacks a band of wiped black across the middle of the whale on the centre and right sheets, perhaps indicating a slightly later printing.

The inscription states that Musashi accomplished his feat off Hizen province (which comprised parts of modern Saga and Nagasaki prefectures) in the far west of Japan. The whale is a *semi-kujira*, designated in English as the North Pacific Right Whale, which can grow to as much as eighteen metres in length and weigh one hundred tons: Kuniyoshi has thus in no way exaggerated its size. This is but one of many heroic exploits attributed to Musashi in Edo-period literature and public storytelling, carried out as he travelled around the country perfecting the art of swordsmanship. The historical Miyamoto Musashi (1584?–1645) founded the 'Two Sword' (*Nitō*) school and was a highly original ink-painter who used the art-name Niten.

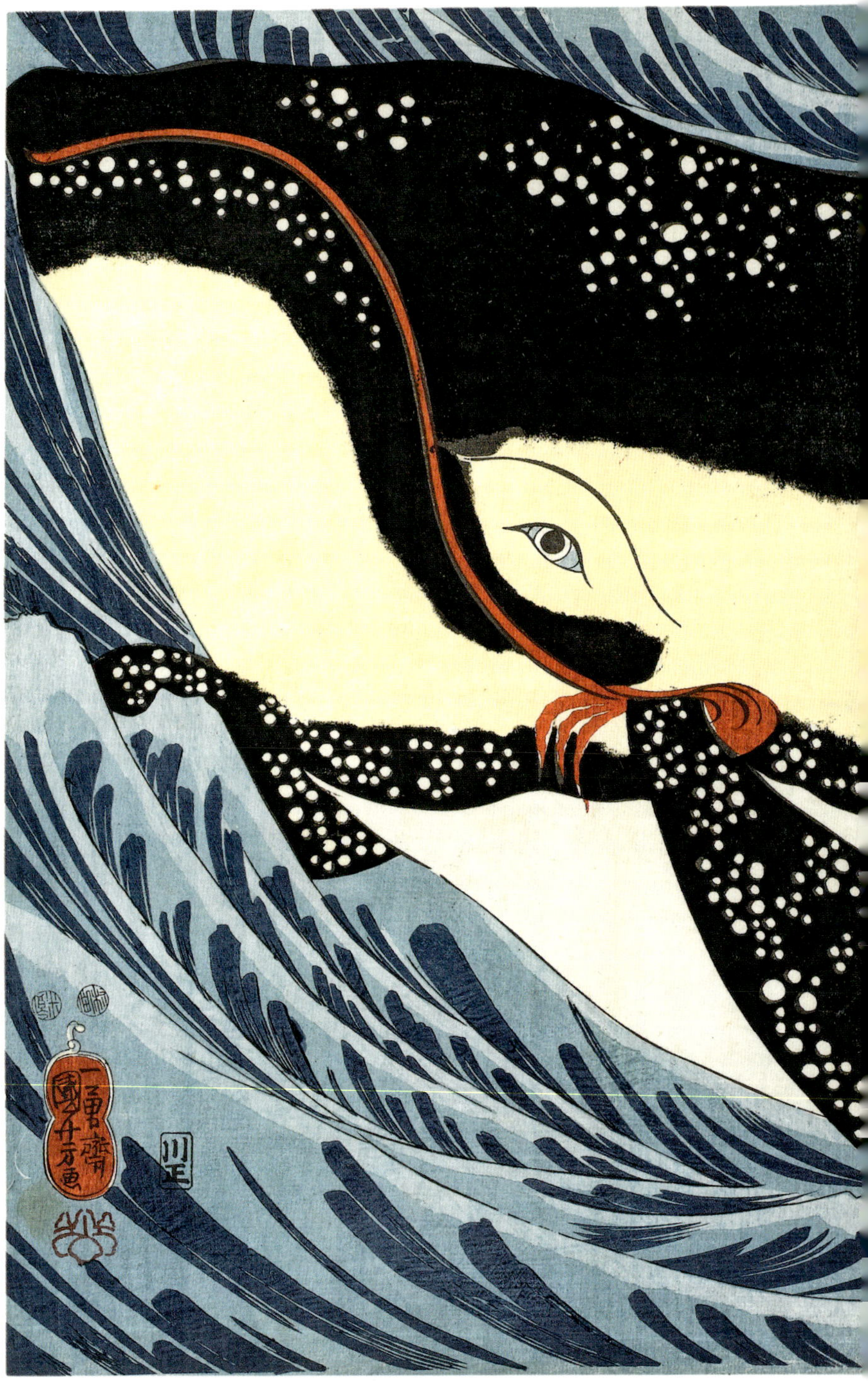

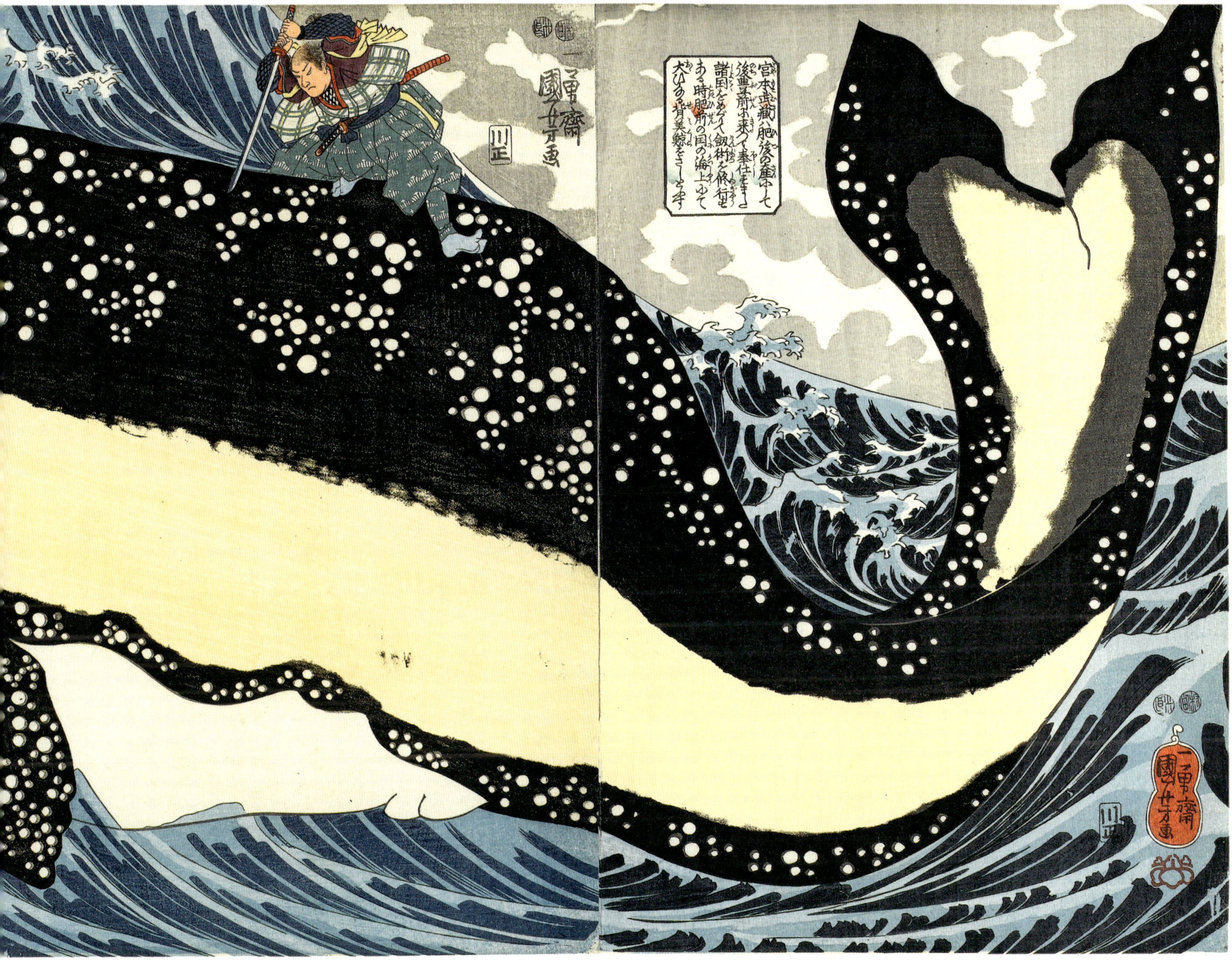
宮本武蔵ハ肥後の産にて
後豊前に来つて奉仕ます
諸国をめぐりて剣術を修行せ
ある時肥前の国の海上にて
大ひなる背美鯨を
一勇齋國芳画

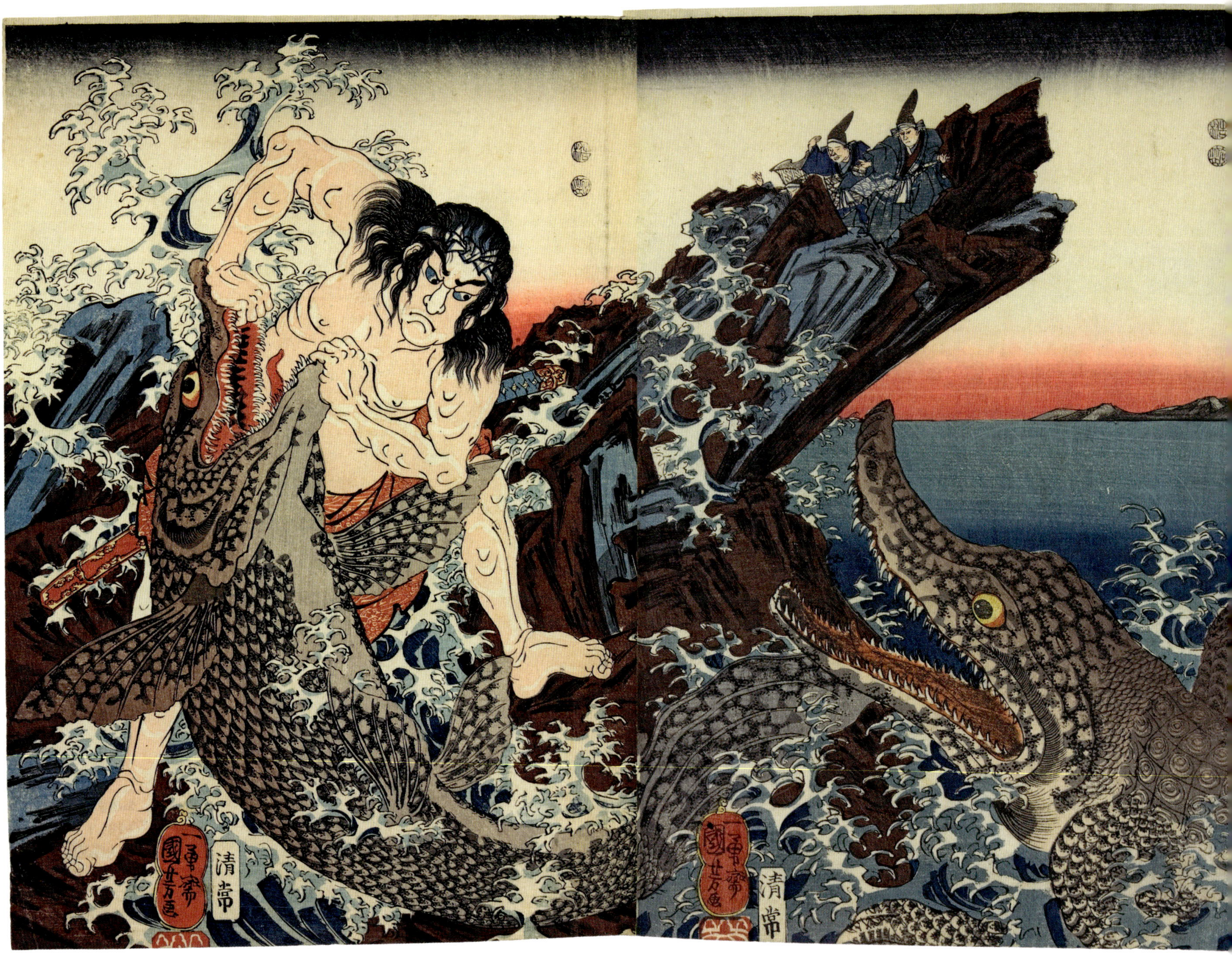
一勇斎國芳画
清常
一勇斎國芳画
清常

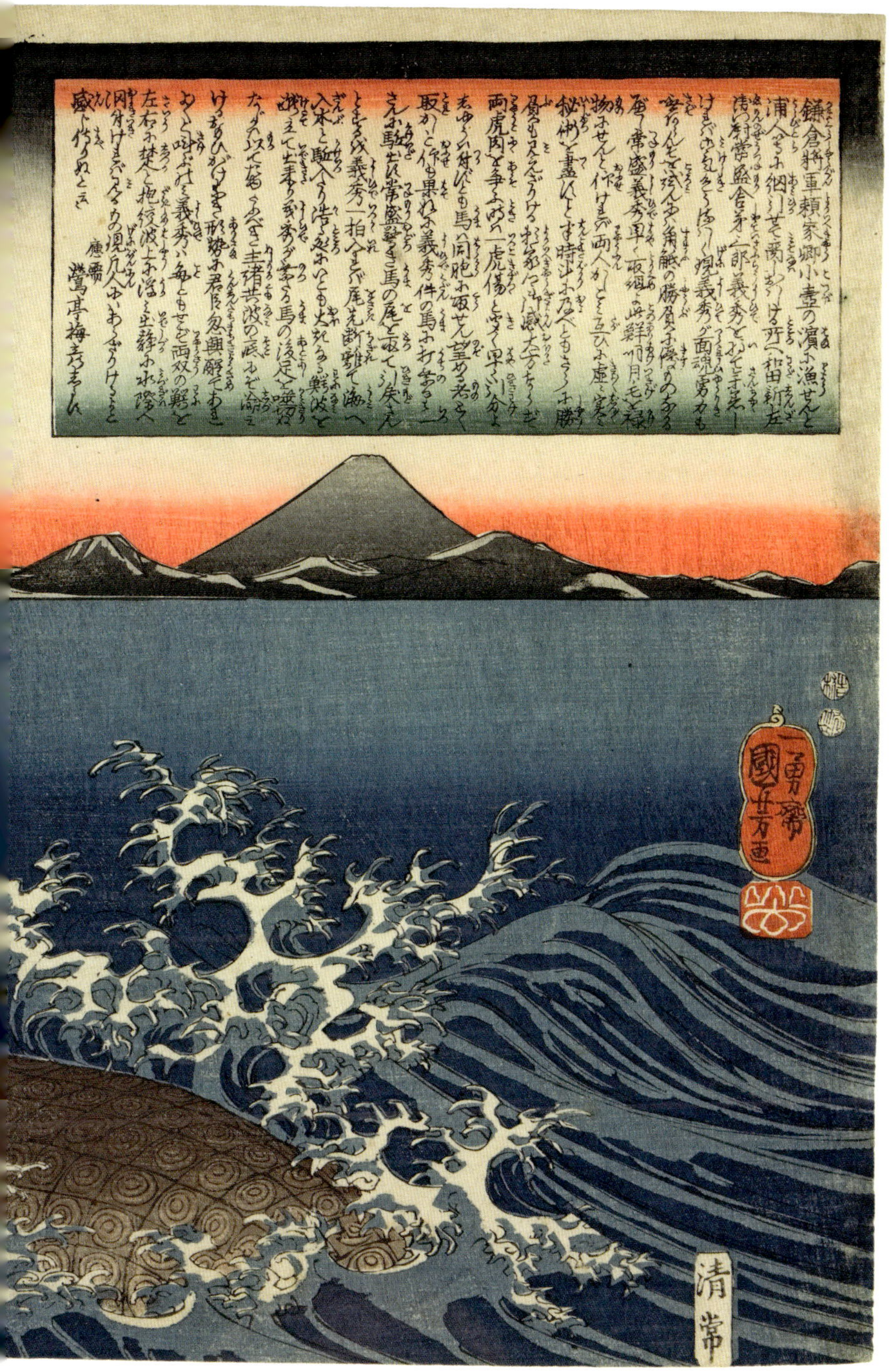

28

Asaina Saburō Yoshihide wrestles with two crocodiles at Kotsubo beach, Kamakura

1849

Colour woodblock, *ōban* triptych, published by Shimizuya Tsunejirō, 36.3 × 25.6 [R], 35.4 × 25.4 [C], 35.7 × 25.2 cm [L]

ARTIST'S SIGNATURE
Ichiyūsai Kuniyoshi ga
(in gourd-shaped
Yoshi cartouche)

ARTIST'S SEAL
Yoshikiri

CENSORS' SEALS
Kinugasa and Yoshimura

American Friends of the British Museum
(The Arthur R. Miller Collection) 19303

REFERENCES
Robinson 1982, no. T218, pl. 56;
Machida 2003, no. 196;
King and Iwakiri 2007, no. 157

Muscular Asaina prizes open the jaws of a crocodile, his legs braced on the rocky coastline while waves splinter spectacularly all around him. Watching from a distant rocky promontory are Shogun Minamoto no Yoriie and several retainers. Mt Fuji can be seen far away, across Sagami bay.

The episode brought to life here is said to have taken place in the year 1200 (Machida 2003, p. 135). When Yoriie visited Kotusbo beach, Kamakura, he commanded the strongman Asaina Saburō to engage in a trial of strength with Wada Shinzaemon-no-jō Tsunemori. The version of the story on the print was written by Ōtei Umehiko, whom the who's who *Gei'en ichiran* of 1850 lists as a poet living in Iida-machi, Edo. His account relates that, at one point in the combat, Asaina rode his horse into the waves, whereupon a crocodile seized one of its back legs. Much to the consternation of the assembled retainers, Asaina immediately jumped into the sea and disappeared beneath the waves. Suddenly, he reappeared, grasping a crocodile under each arm and dragging them to the shore in an unprecedented display of strength.

It might be objected that crocodiles (*wani*) do not live in the sea and have legs, not flippers, but that does nothing to diminish Kuniyoshi's achievement in creating a stirring and memorable scene of combat between strongman and beast. His treatment of the waves surely echoes Hokusai's famous 'Great Wave' print of c. 1830–33.

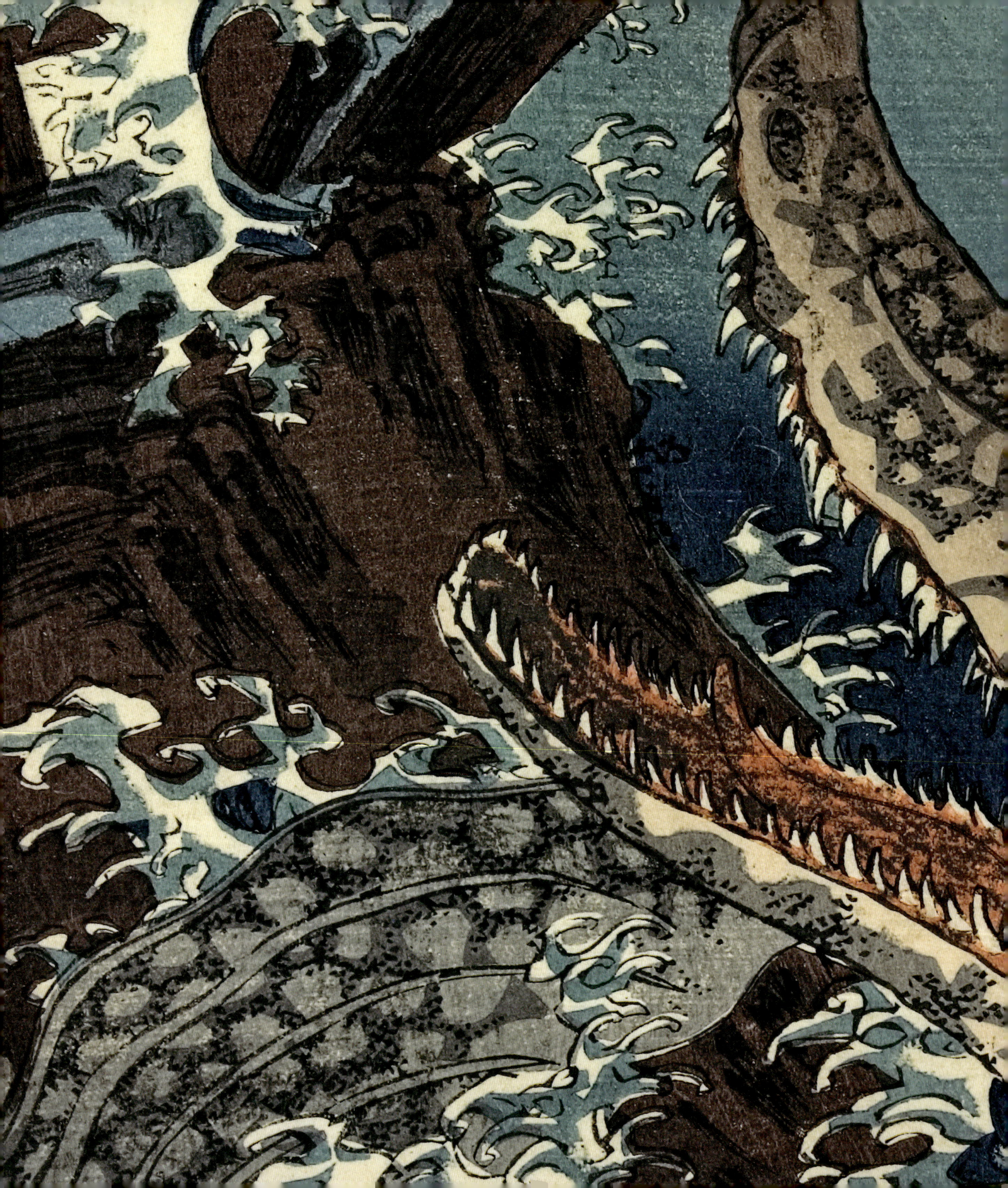

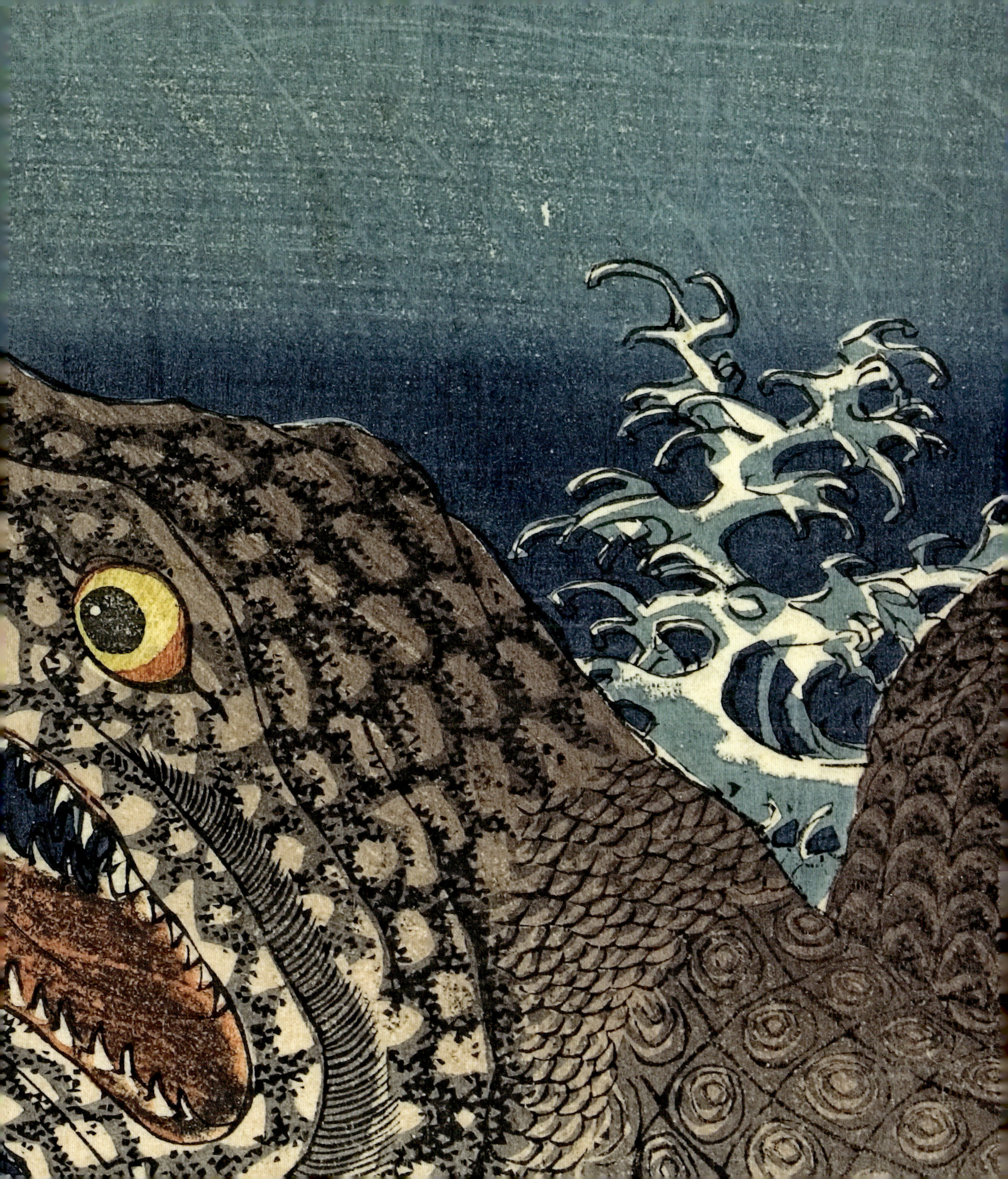

29

Tametomo rescued from suicide by *tengu*

1851

Colour woodblock, *ōban* triptych, published by Sumiyoshiya Masagorō, 36.5 × 25.2 [R], 36.5 × 25.2 [C], 36.5 × 25 cm [L]

PRINT TITLE
'Retired Emperor Sutoku sends his followers to rescue Tametomo' (*Sanuki-no-in kenzoku o shite Tametomo o sukuu zu*)

ARTIST'S SIGNATURE
Ichiyūsai Kuniyoshi ga (in gourd-shaped *Yoshi* cartouche)

ARTIST'S SEAL
Yoshikiri

CENSORS' SEALS
Mera and Watanabe

The British Museum, JA 1906.12-20.01339

REFERENCES
Robinson 1961, no. 58; Riccar 1978, no. 103; Springfield 1980, no. 173; Robinson 1982, no. T263, fig. 16; HUT, vol. 3, 1988, BW, no. 29; HUT, vol. 5, 1989, no. 47; V&A 1991, no. 90; Yamaguchi 1991, Kuniyoshi no. 29; Suzuki 1992, no. 69; Itabashi 1994, Kuniyoshi no. 23; Mainichi Shinbunsha 1995, no. 55; Nagoya 1996, nos 68–9; Amsterdam 1998, no. 89; Shōtō 2003, no. 135; Isao 2008, pp. 66–7

This magnificent design combines three separate episodes from the shipwreck suffered by the hero Tametomo on a voyage from Kyushu to Kyoto. On the right sheet Princess Shiranui, Tametomo's wife, has thrown herself into the sea as a sacrifice to placate the storm, but to no avail. The action then shifts to the left sheet, where the desperate Tametomo is saved from committing ritual suicide by mythical creatures called *tengu*, half bird and half man, who have been sent to rescue him by the spirit of Emperor Sutoku. Finally, in the centre sheet Tametomo's retainer Kiheiji cradles his master's infant son Sutemaru in his arms as the two are saved from drowning by a giant 'crocodile-shark' (*wani-zame*). The crocodile-shark had first tried to kill the pair, but was then pacified by the spirits of a dead husband and wife, loyal retainers of Tametomo, flying into its mouth. This sequence of events is presented simultaneously in a highly dramatic design, full of movement, in which giant sea creature, boat and roiling sea are all instantly legible to the informed viewer. To add visual excitement, dots of white pigment have been flicked onto the surface of the print in the areas of the sea. The pigment must be white lead, as it has started to tarnish black in some places.

The fantastical events depicted in the triptych were derived from the serial novel *Chinsetsu yumihari-zuki* (*Strange Tales of the Bow Moon*), written by Bakin and illustrated by Hokusai. The relevant section of this exceptionally popular work appeared in 1808. The historical Minamoto no Tametomo (1139–70) was a warrior highly skilled at archery who held sway first in Kyushu, then on the island of Izu Ōshima. He had been banished to the island after the Hōgen rebellion of 1156 (a civil war fought between the factions of Retired Emperor Sutoku and Emperor Go-Shirakawa) and eventually committed ritual suicide there.

The form of the giant crocodile-shark, with its distinctive patterned scales, seems to have been adapted by Kuniyoshi from an illustration of a caiman (a beast resembling an alligator) in *Kōmō zatsuwa* (*Dutch Miscellany*) of 1787, edited by Morishima Chūryō.

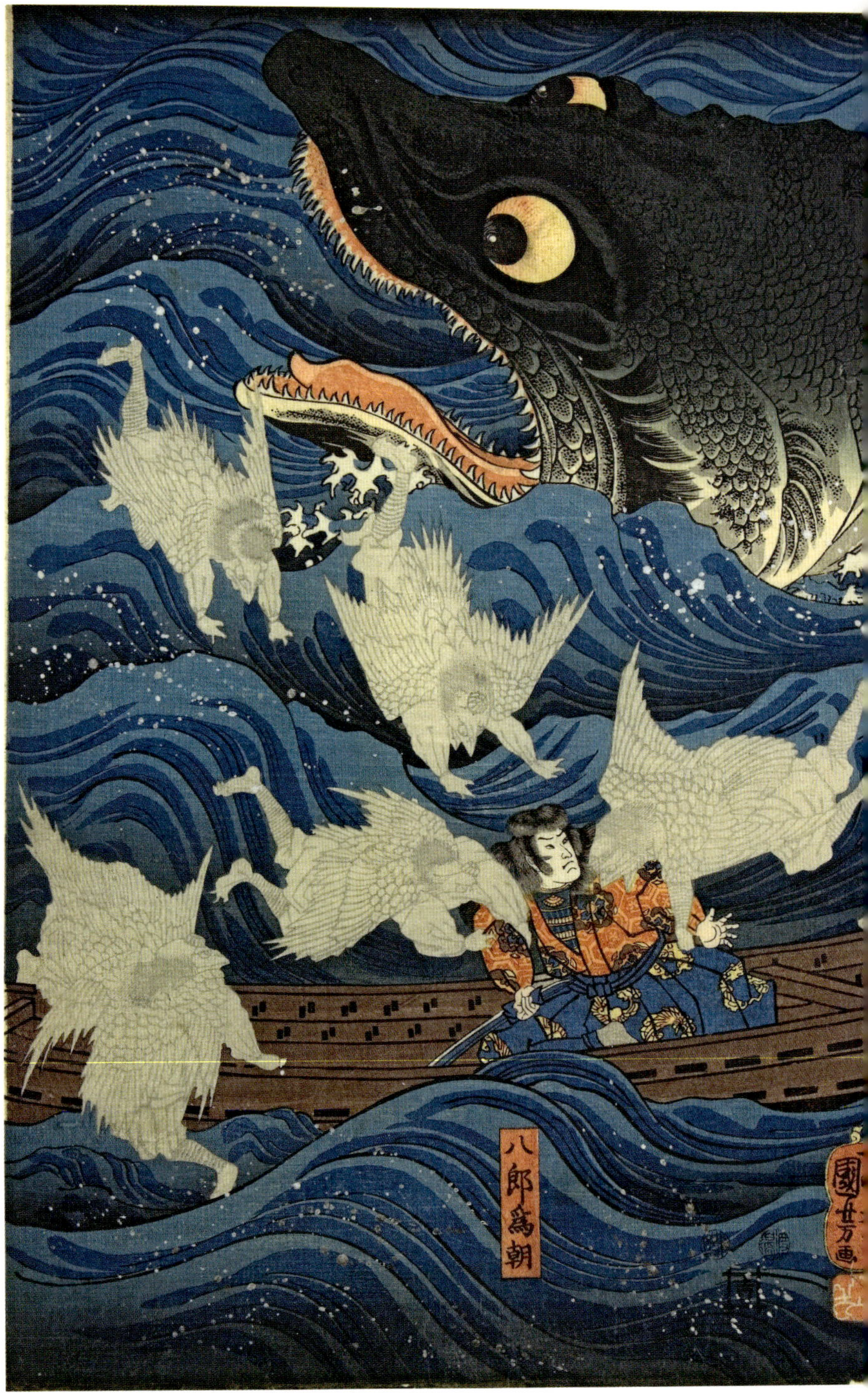

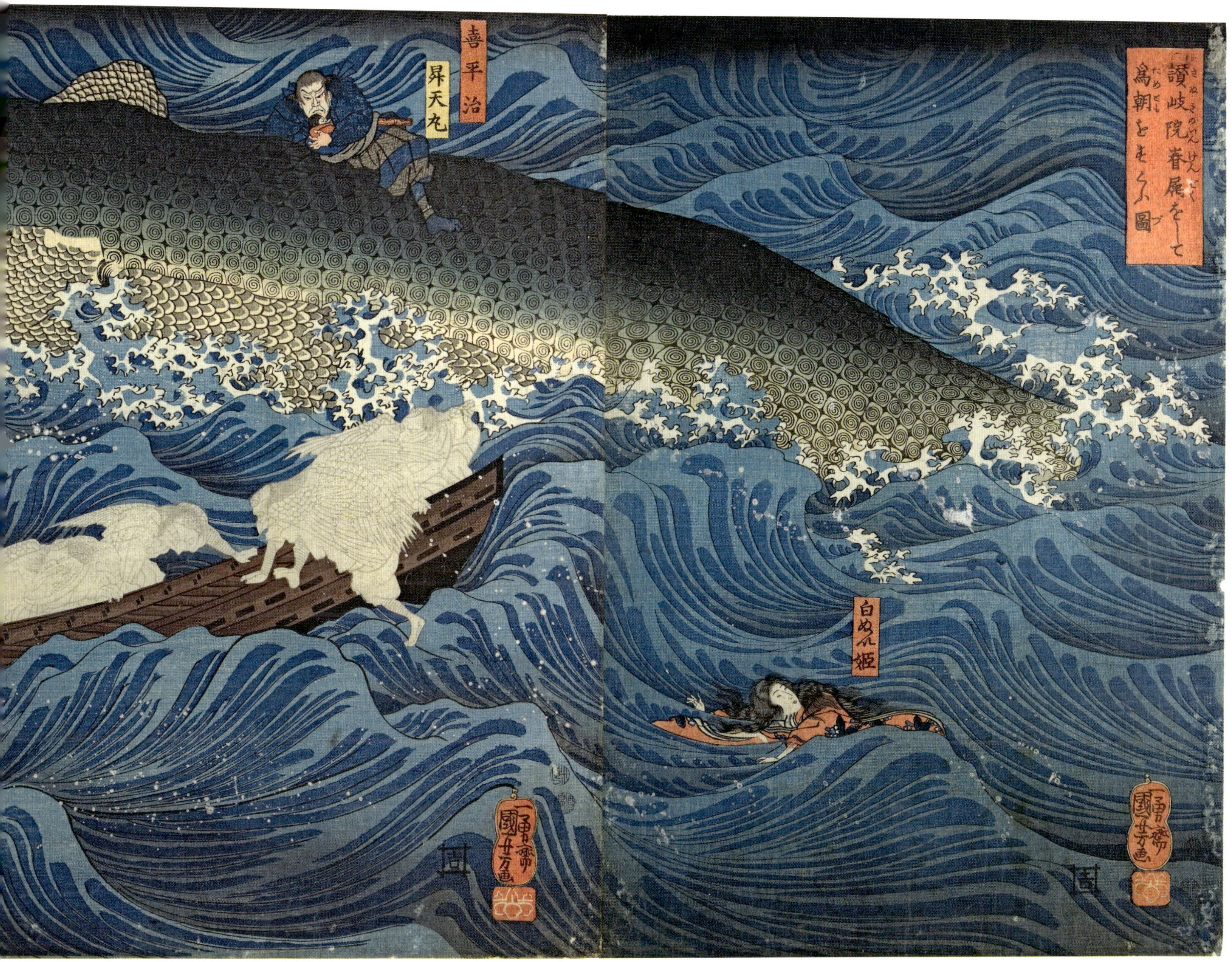
讃岐院眷属をして為朝をすくふ圖
喜平治
昇天丸
白ぬれ姫

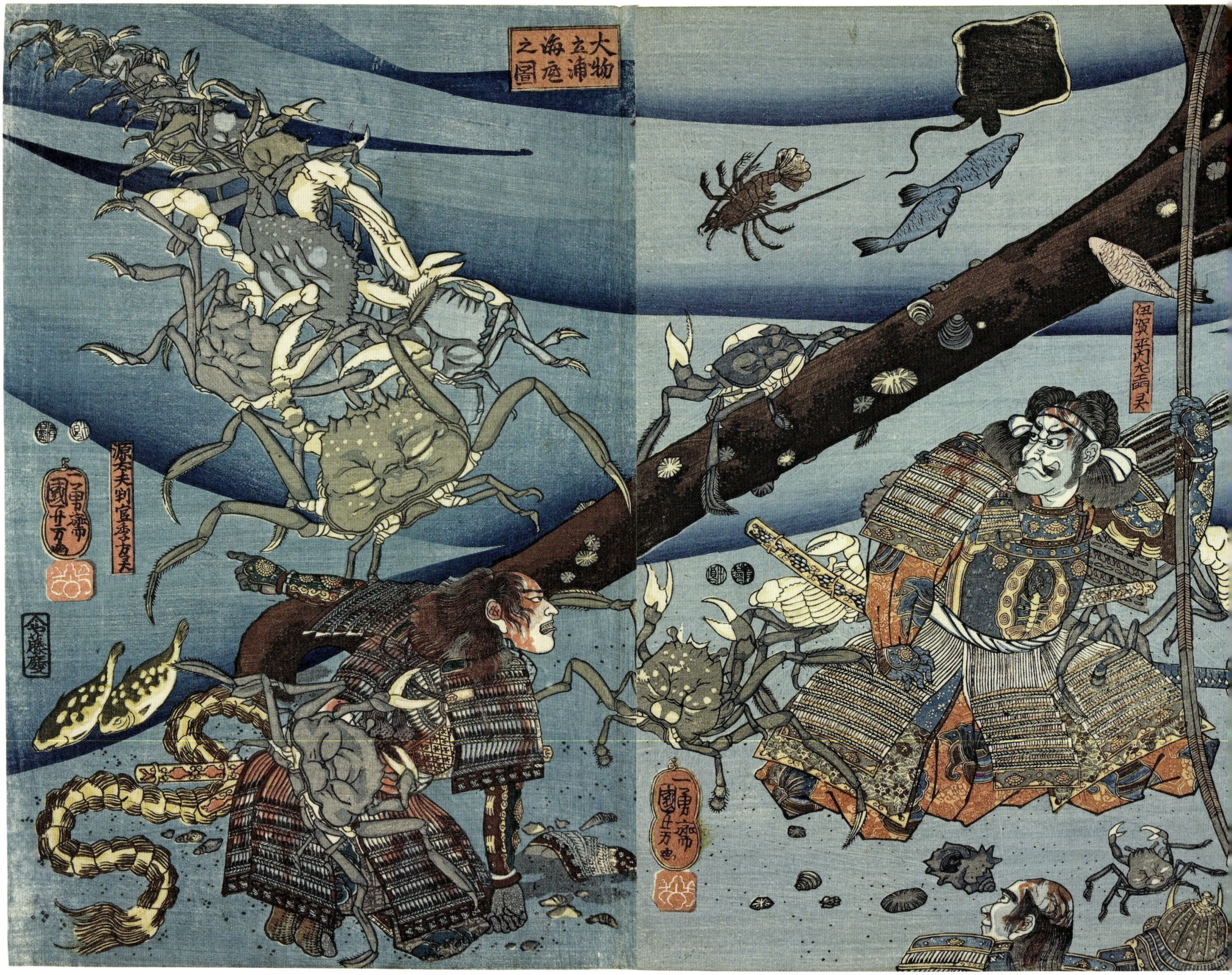
大物之浦海底之圖

30

Ghosts of the Taira warriors on the seabed at Daimotsu bay

1851

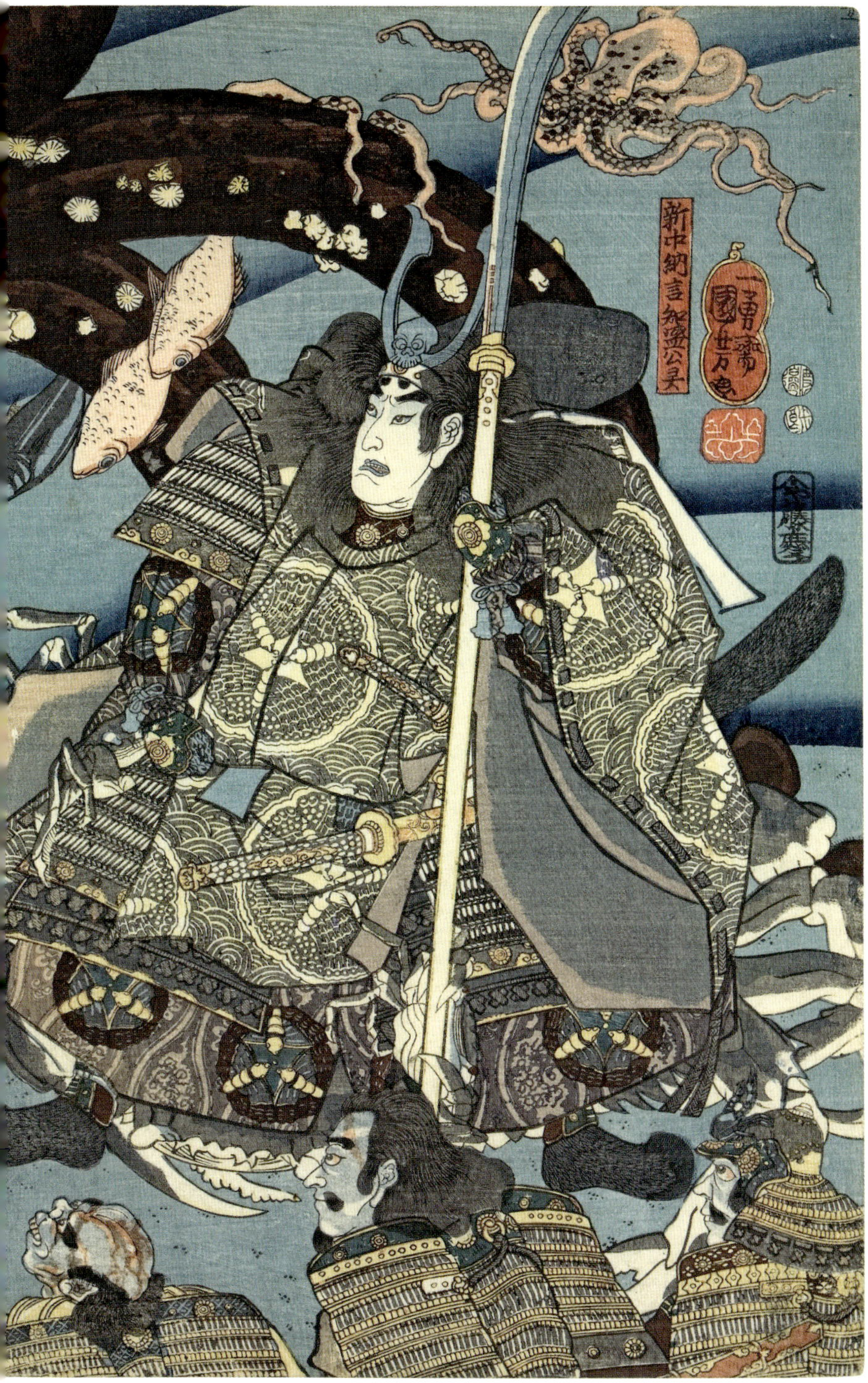

Colour woodblock, *ōban* triptych, published by Fujiokaya Keijirō, 36.4 × 25.3 [R], 36.3 × 24.3 [C], 36.3 × 24.6 cm [L]

PRINT TITLE
'The Sea Bed at Daimotsu Bay' (*Daimotsu-no-ura kaitei no zu*)

ARTIST'S SIGNATURE
Ichiyūsai Kuniyoshi ga (in gourd-shaped *Yoshi* cartouche)

ARTIST'S SEAL
Yoshikiri

CENSORS' SEALS
Mera and Watanabe

American Friends of the British Museum (The Arthur R. Miller Collection) 20104

REFERENCES
Hillier 1976, no. 841; Riccar 1978, no. 107; Springfield 1980, no. 1984; Robinson 1982, no. T266, fig. 22; Suzuki 1992, no. 74; Nagoya 1996, no. 72; Amsterdam 1998, no. 88; Shōtō 2003, no. 86

This is one of Kuniyoshi's most pleasingly macabre conceptions, in which ghosts of drowned warriors of the Taira clan sit on the seabed of Daimotsu bay, Settsu province (part of modern Hyōgo prefecture), as they plot revenge on Yoshitsune. Their blue faces indicate their ghost status and most are still bloodied around the head from wounds sustained some months earlier in 1185 during their catastrophic defeat at the naval battle of Dannoura in Nagato province. On the right is the Taira commander Tomomori. When defeat became apparent at Dannoura, he tied himself to a giant anchor and cast himself into the sea. On the centre and left sheets are his generals Iga no Heinaizaemon and Gendaifu no Hōgan Suekata, the latter pointing to the column of 'Heike crabs' they have summoned, each with the features of a drowned Taira warrior visible in the markings on its back ('Heike' is an alternative name for the Taira clan). The sinister-looking animals will be sent to attack Yoshitsune's ship (see cat. 31). Close inspection reveals an ever greater number of them: Tomomori seems to be seated on a giant one and another crawls up Suekata's back. Shells are encrusted on the anchor and a veritable aquarium of fish and sea creatures glides across the background. The wiped bands of Prussian blue waves were omitted from later printings (for example, the ex-Vever Collection impression illustrated in Hillier 1976, no. 841).

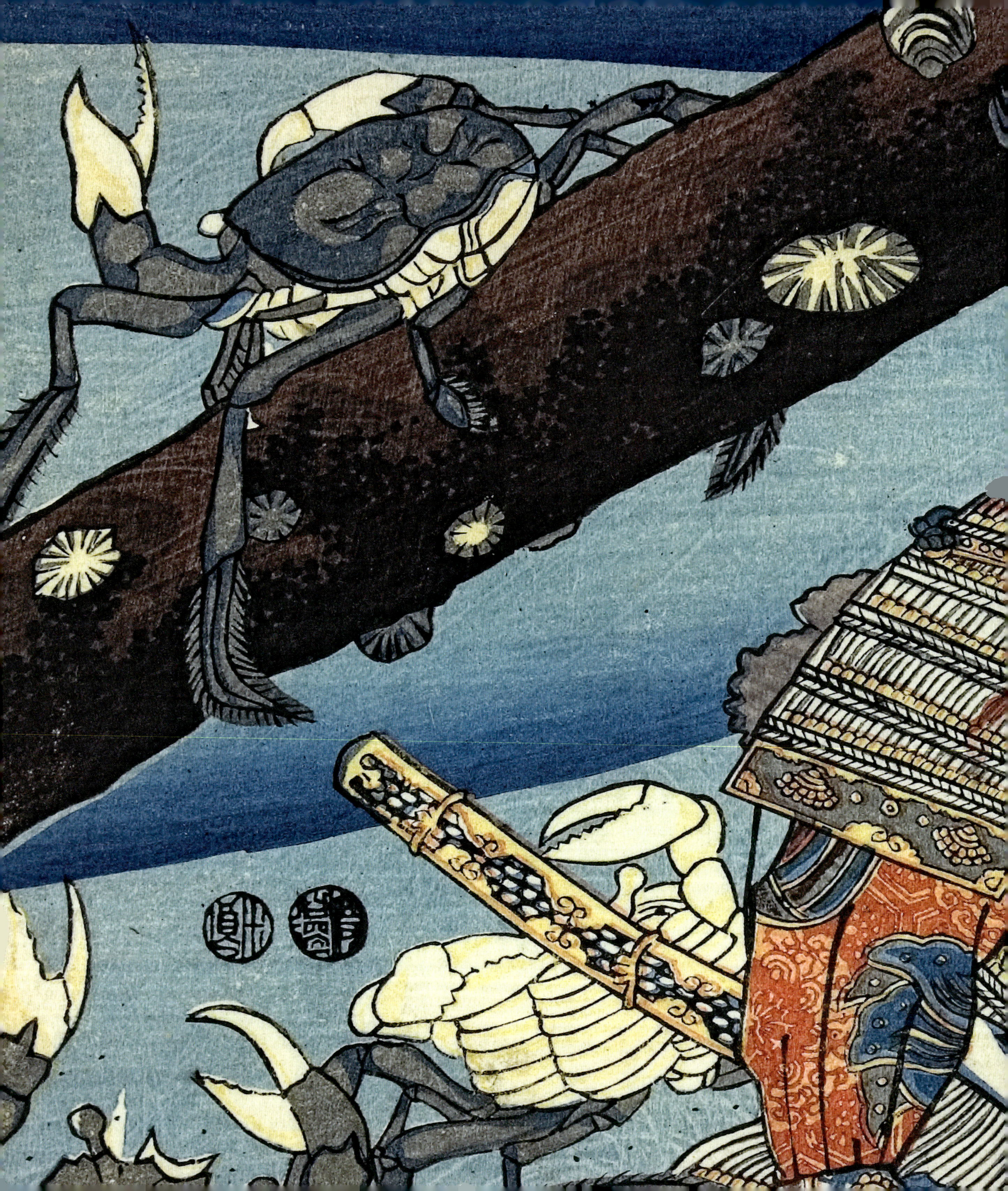

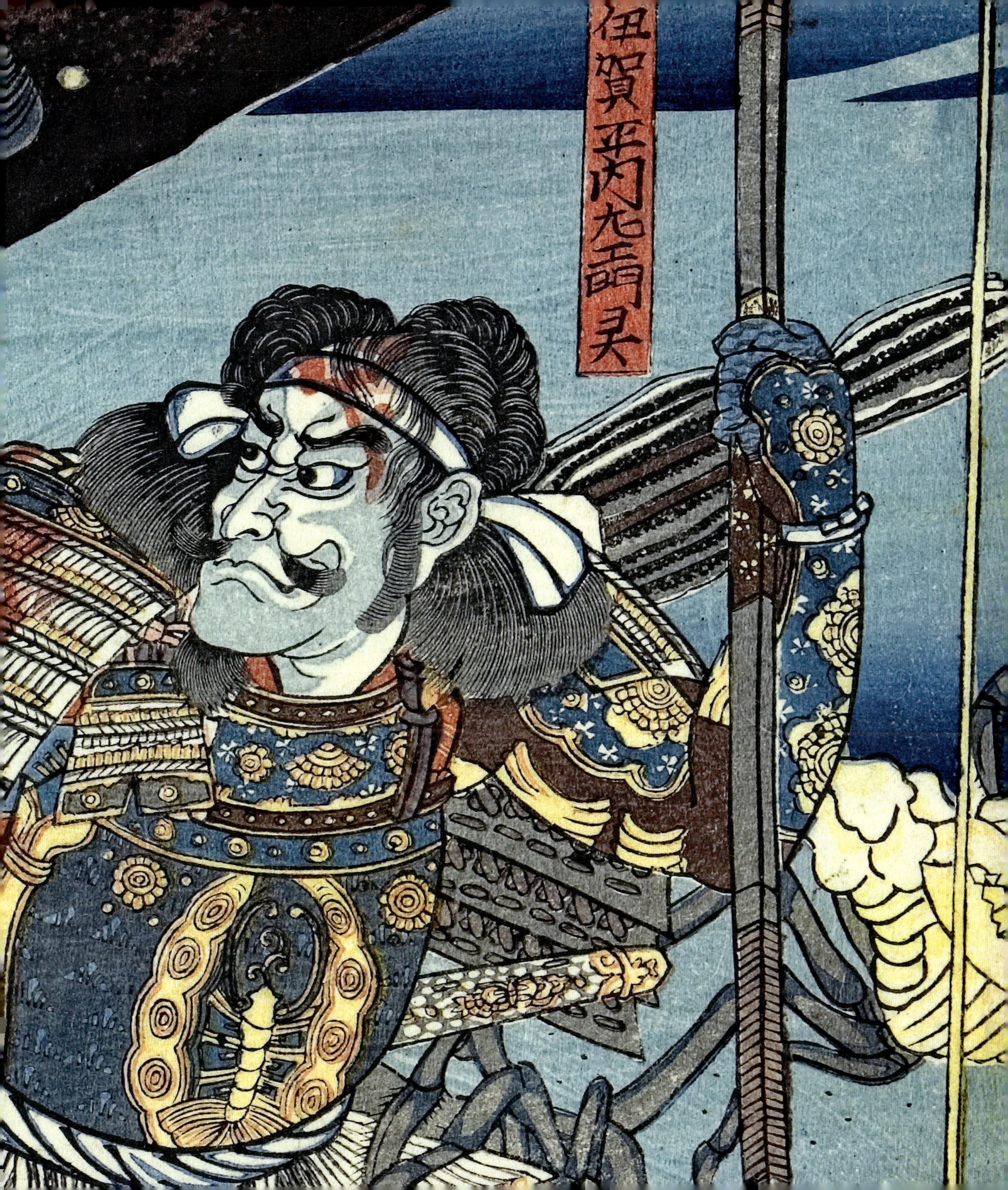
伊賀平内左衛門尉

31

Yoshitsune's ship is attacked by ghosts of the Taira warriors at Daimotsu bay

c. 1851

Colour woodblock, *ōban* triptych, published by Enshūya Hikobei, 35.8 × 24.8 [R], 35.8 × 24.8 [C], 35.9 × 24.8 cm [L]

ARTIST'S SIGNATURE
Ichiyūsai Kuniyoshi ga (in gourd-shaped *Yoshi* cartouche)

ARTIST'S SEAL
Yoshikiri

CENSORS' SEALS
Fuku and Muramatsu

American Friends of the British Museum (The Arthur R. Miller Collection) 20609

REFERENCES
Springfield 1968, no. 98; Riccar 1978, no. 104; Springfield 1980, no. 185; Robinson 1982, no. T242; Keyes 1984, pl. 156; HUT, vol. 3, 1988, BW, no. 30; Suzuki 1992, no. 71; Itabashi 1994, Kuniyoshi no. 24; Mainichi Shinbunsha 1995, no. 54; Nagoya 1996, nos 70–1; Amsterdam 1998, no. 86; Machida 2003, no. 194

The ship carrying Yoshitsune and his band of loyal warriors pitches into a mountainous wave; the sail is already half down and the rigging in tatters. Many of the retainers fall about in alarm, and only Yoshitsune, seated in the centre, and Benkei, standing at the stern, remain alert to the danger about to engulf them. The ghosts of their former enemies, the drowned Taira warriors, gather menacingly at the rear of all three sheets, rendered sinisterly in silhouette: they have conjured up the stormy sea and are preparing to attack the ship (see also cat. 30). The seafarers are saved by warrior monk Benkei's quick thinking: he rubs a string of Buddhist prayer beads between his palms and intones an exorcism, which causes the storm and phantoms to disappear. Minamoto no Yoshitsune had defeated the Taira at the naval battle of Dannoura in 1185. Now he is fleeing the jealous wrath of his brother Yoritomo. After surviving a surprise night attack by Yoritomo's forces at Horikawa palace, Kyoto, Yoshitsune and his band boarded the ship at Daimotsu bay in Settsu province to escape to distant Kyushu.

Kuniyoshi designed four triptychs on this subject, each for a different publisher (they are listed in Robinson 1982, p. 24). In formal terms this is the most mature: the ship, great wave and their collision are all powerfully three-dimensional, with broadly wiped Prussian blue and mica lines in the waves. In contrast the forms of the ghosts appear wraithlike, made all the more uncanny by sombre colours and subtle wiping. This is an early printing: most of the ghosts' eyes were filled in progressively in later versions, and finally their horns were cut off (see, for instance, the impression in the Bigelow Collection, Museum of Fine Arts, Boston, 11.30566a-c). The reason for these changes is unknown.

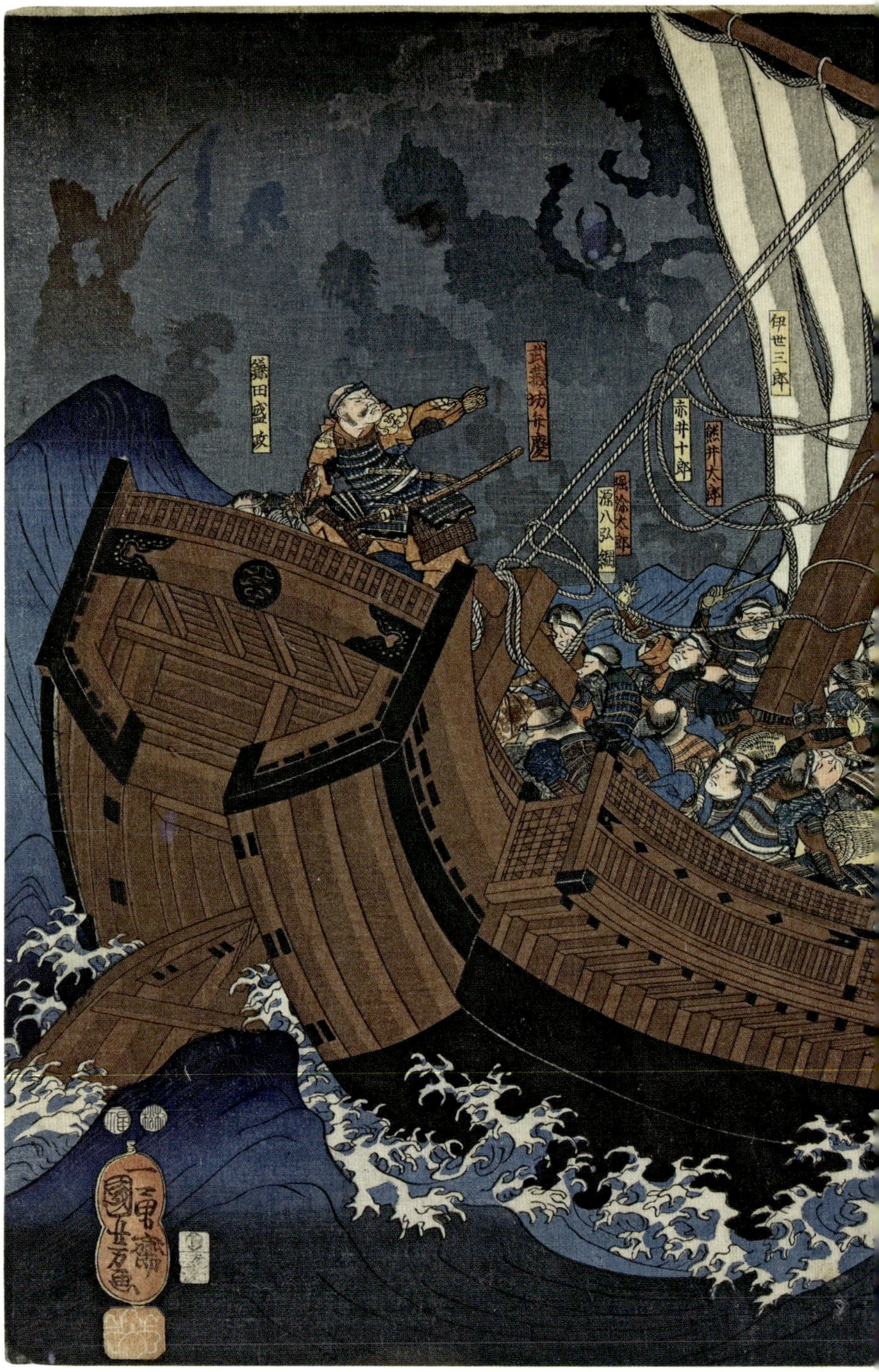

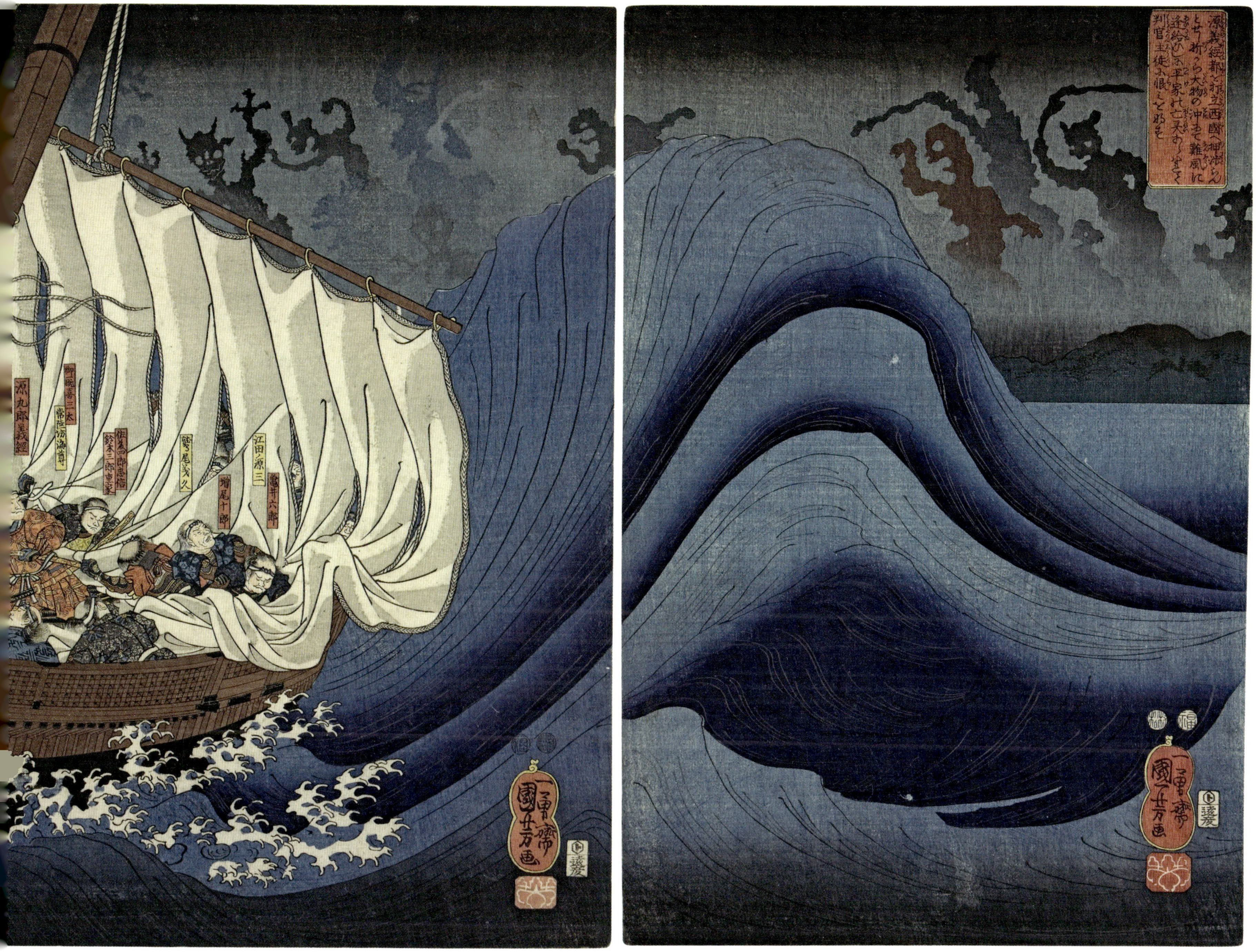
源九郎義經
御厩喜三太
常陸坊海尊
佐藤四郎忠信
鈴木三郎重家
鷲尾義久
江田ノ源三
増尾十郎
亀井六郎
一勇斎國芳画
一勇斎國芳画

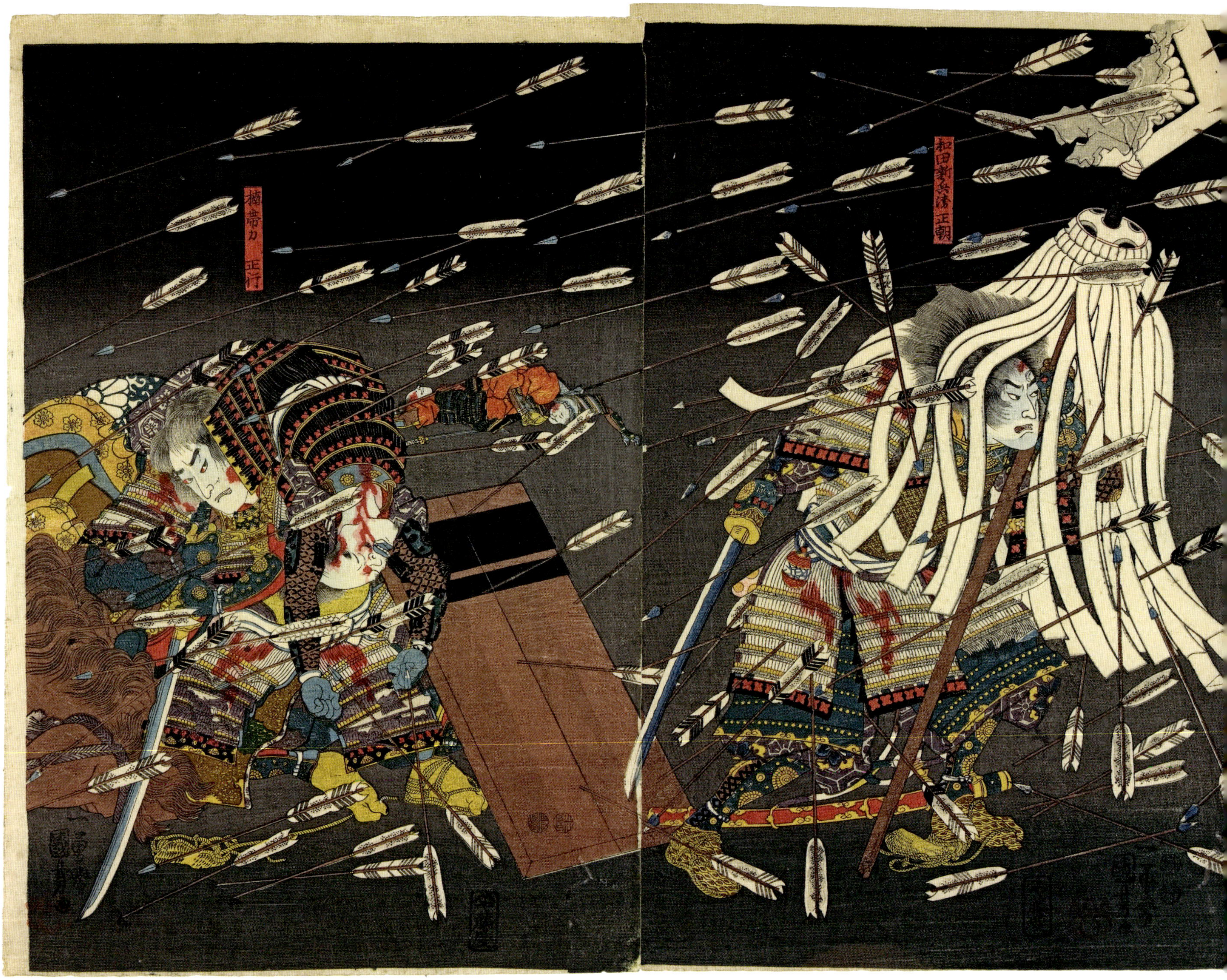

楠帯刀 正行
和田新兵衛 正朝

32

Last stand of the Kusunoki heroes at Shijō-Nawate

1851

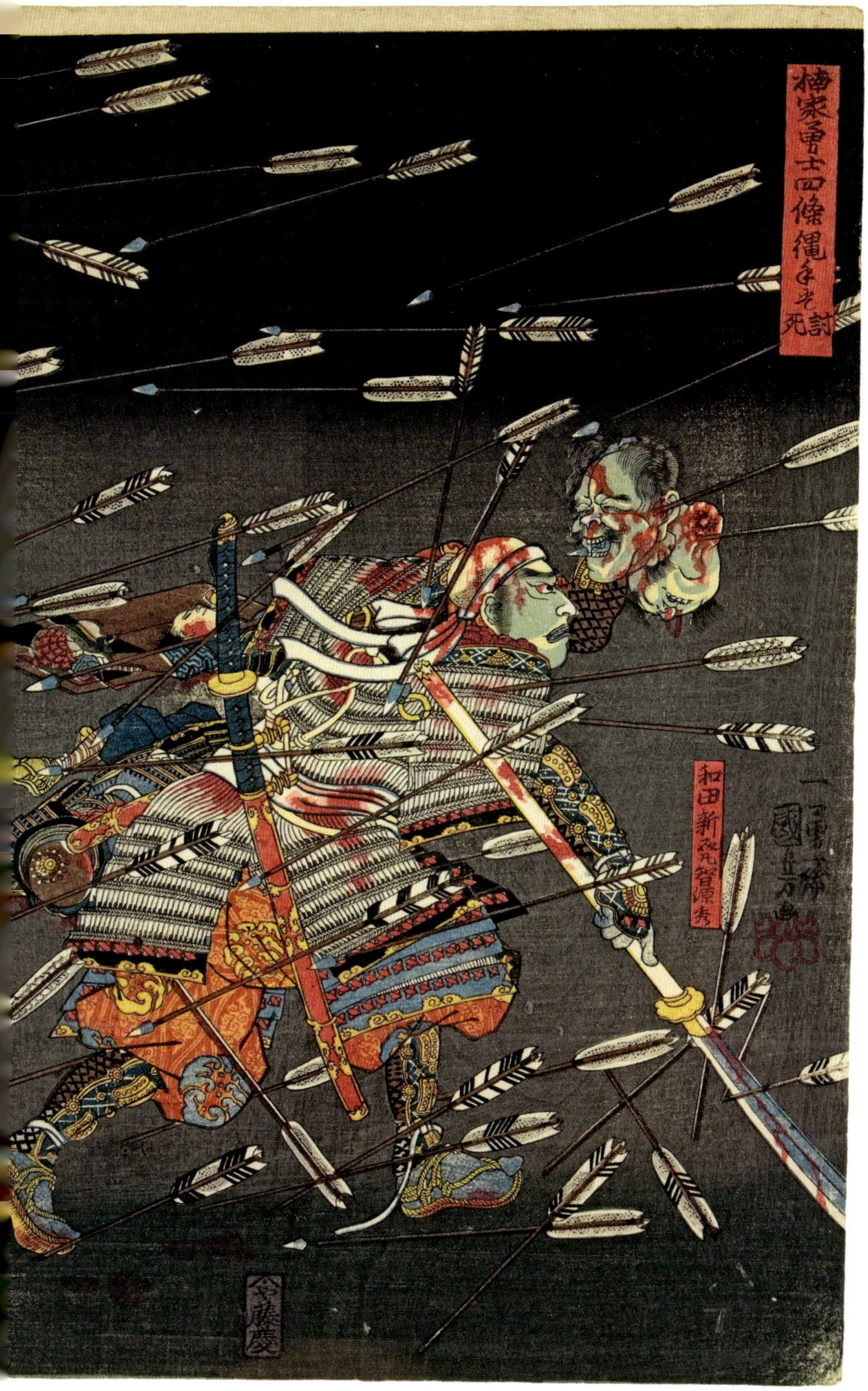

Colour woodblock, *ōban* triptych, published by Fujiokaya Keijirō, 38 × 26.2 [R], 38.2 × 25.7 [C], 38 × 25.8 cm [L]

PRINT TITLE
'Last Stand of the Kusunoki Heroes at Shijō-Nawate' (*Nanke yūshi Shijō-Nawate nite uchijini*)

ARTIST'S SIGNATURE
Ichiyūsai Kuniyoshi ga

ARTIST'S SEAL
Yoshikiri

CENSORS' SEALS
Mera and Watanabe

American Friends of the British Museum (The Arthur R. Miller Collection) 18402

REFERENCES
Robinson 1961, no. 59; Riccar 1978, no. 106; Springfield 1980, no. 179; Robinson 1982, no. T271, pl. 59; HUT, vol. 5, 1989, no. 40; V&A 1991, no. 92

The doomed warriors of the Kusunoki clan advance with grim resolution in the teeth of a thick hail of arrows. Wada Shinbochi Kenshū (here 'Genshū') leads, brandishing two enemy heads as trophies. Next comes his younger brother, Wada Shinbei Masatomo, leaning against a tattered battle standard. Bringing up the rear is Kusunoki Masatsura, their leader, who rests for a moment against a fallen horse, shielding himself with the body of a dead warrior. Traditional accounts of the battle state that Masatsura and his younger brother, Masatoki, killed one another when they realised that all was lost; the body may therefore be Masatoki's. All the Kusunoki warriors are heavily wounded and dripping with blood, their pallid blue faces indicating that they are soon to depart this world. In this still vivid and unfaded impression of the print warriors and arrows stand out dramatically against the dark and sensitively gradated background. Two more fallen samurai can be glimpsed in the middle distance.

According to the military chronicle *Taiheiki* (*Chronicle of the Great Peace*), the battle took place on the fifth day of the first month, 1348, at Shijō-Nawate in Kawachi province. The army of the Southern Court, comprising some three thousand men commanded by Masatsura, was vastly outnumbered by the six thousand Northern Court troops of Ashikaga Takauji, who obliterated them under their leader Kō no Moronao.

In 1857 two related triptychs by Kuniyoshi were published by a firm with the trademark 'Aito' (Miller 18403). These have sometimes been regarded as a continuous six-sheet composition, but, as Iwakiri Yuriko points out, the two triptychs bear date seals four months apart. She further notes that the slightly earlier one, dated fourth month, 1857, is in a style similar to that of the triptych reproduced here. It would seem, then, that in 1857 'Aito' took over publication of a triptych design created by Kuniyoshi c. 1851 and asked the artist to supply another to match (HUT, vol. 5, 1989, p. 224).

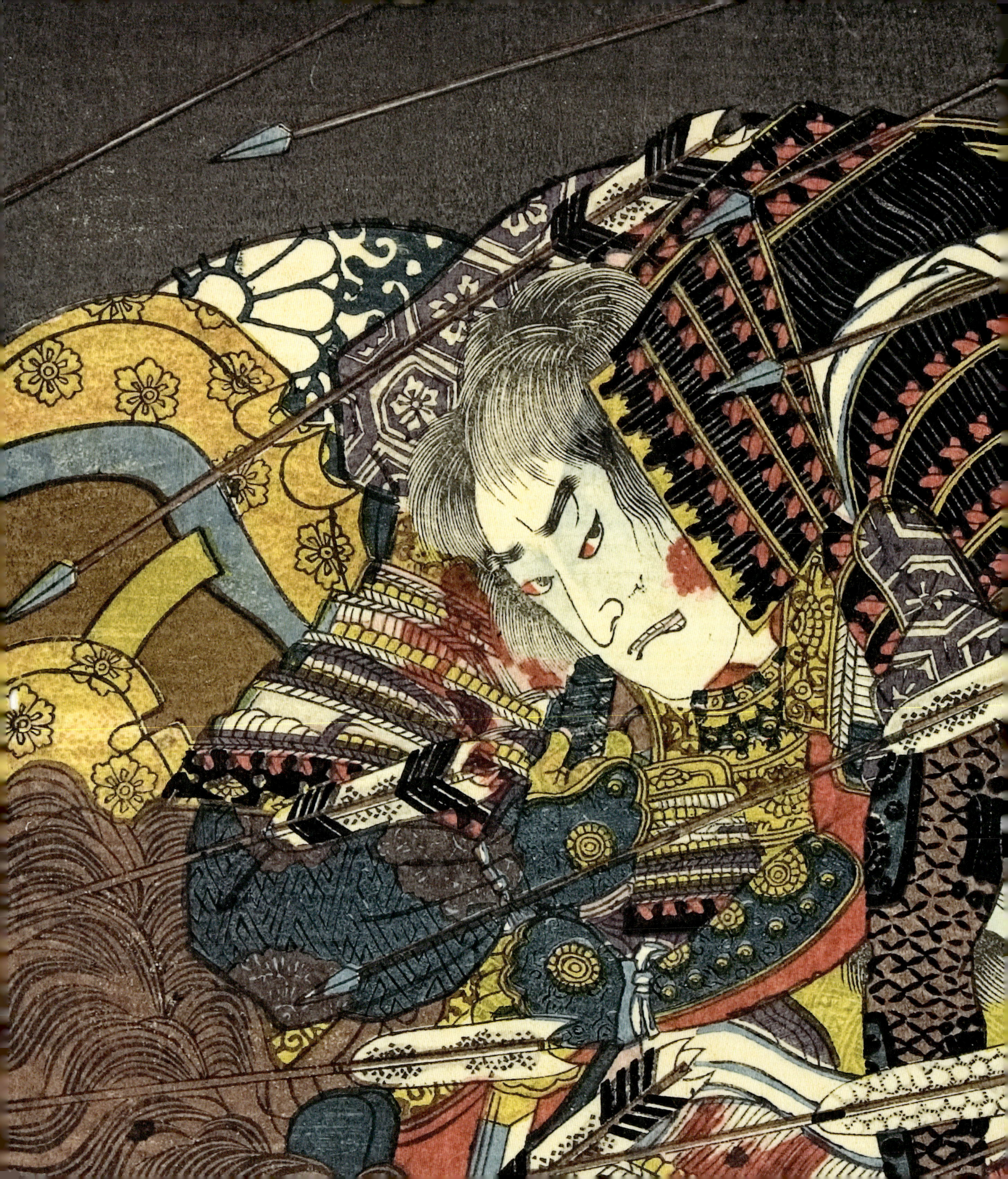

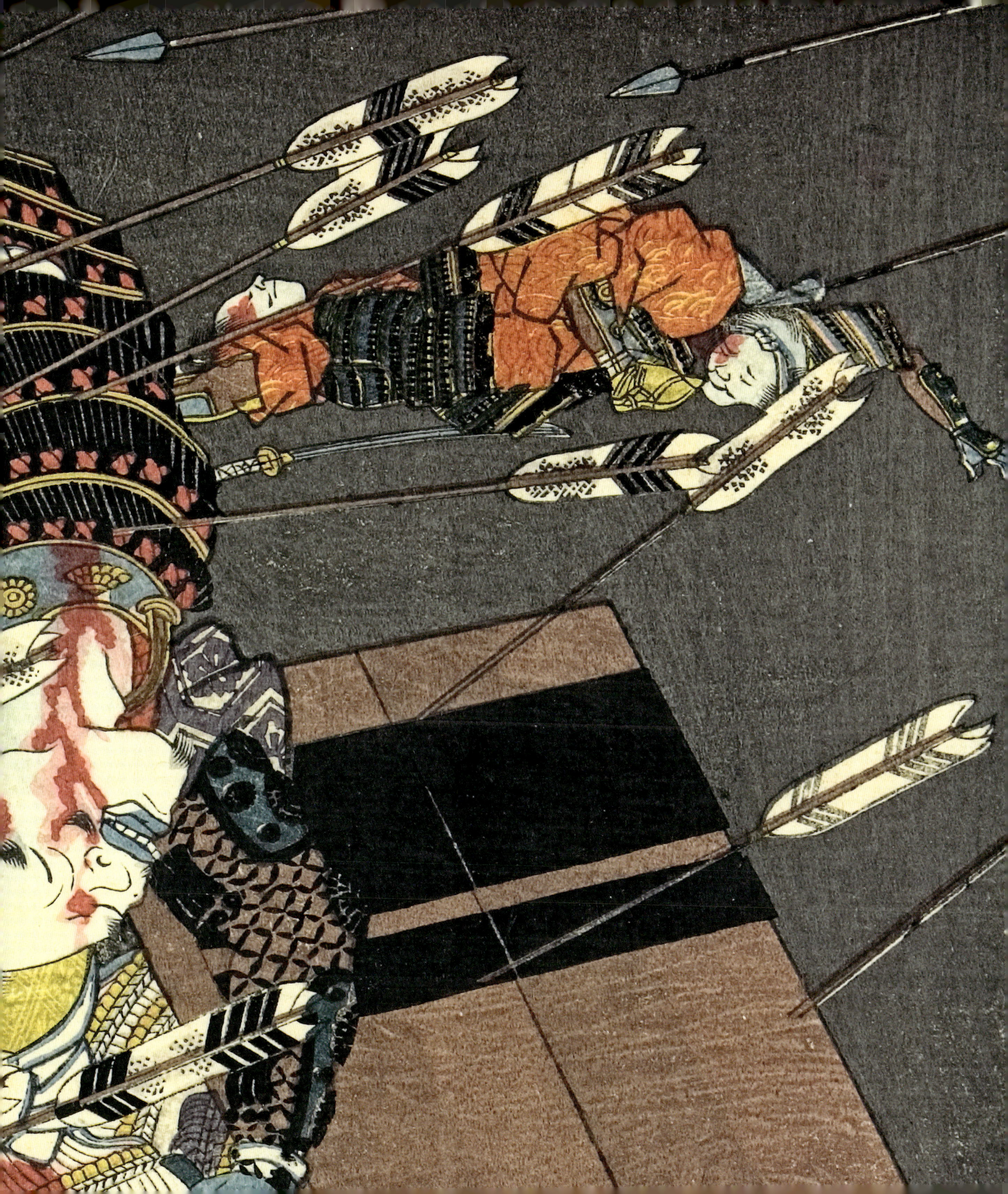

33

Monk Mongaku does penance in Nachi waterfall

1851–52

Colour woodblock, vertical *ōban* triptych, published by Sumiyoshiya Masagorō, 37.3 × 26 [T], 37.5 × 26 [C], 37.6 × 25.6 cm [B]

ARTIST'S SIGNATURE
Ichiyūsai Kuniyoshi ga (in gourd-shaped *Yoshi* cartouche)

ARTIST'S SEAL
Yoshikiri

CENSORS' SEALS
Kinugasa and Murata

American Friends of the British Museum (The Arthur R. Miller Collection) 19212

REFERENCES
Robinson 1961, no. 60a; Riccar 1978, no. 122; Springfield 1980, no. 166; Robinson 1982, no. T253, pl. 64; Nihon Ukiyo-e Kyōkai 1990, no. 1–76; Suzuki 1992, no. 1; Baur 1994, no. G395; Mainichi Shinbunsha 1995, no. 61; Nagoya 1996, no. 76; Amsterdam 1998, no. 87; Machida 2003, no. 201; Isao 2008, p. 72

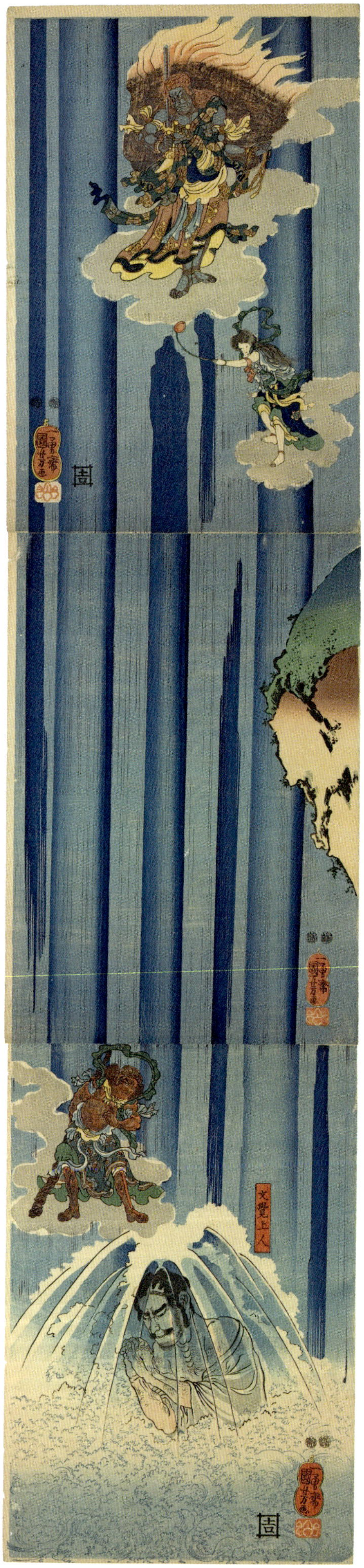

Half immersed in water, the monk Mongaku stands at the base of Nachi waterfall and clasps his hands in a ritual gesture. He is performing this extremely austere religious act to atone for murder. It is mid-winter, and the mid-thirteenth-century chronicle *Heike monogatari* (*The Tales of the Heike*) tells how after seven days at the waterfall Mongaku lost consciousness until revived by the intervention of the deity Fudō Myōō (the Buddhist 'Immovable King of Light'; top sheet) and Fudō's child attendants Kongara (top) and Seitaka (bottom). Miraculously, the water then felt warm to Mongaku and he was able to endure the full twenty-one-day physical trial. With its sheer drop of 133 metres, the awesome Nachi waterfall (in modern Wakayama prefecture) was a key sacred site in medieval Shintō-Buddhist practice, and remains much venerated today.

Mongaku (1139–1203) had committed the murder in his earlier, secular life. As the young warrior Endō Musha Moritō, he had obsessively pestered Kesa Gozen, wife of Watanabe Wataru. She resorted to a desperate strategy to put an end to his unwanted attentions. After persuading Moritō to kill Watanabe, she impersonated her sleeping husband and was murdered in his place, thus preserving her honour intact. This was the dreadful crime that caused Moritō to quit the world of the warrior and become a monk (see Robinson 1982, p. 26, for a more extensive account of the tale).

Kuniyoshi was the first artist to use the extremely unusual vertical-triptych format for warrior subjects: in the present work and in another of similar date, 'Fight at Mt Yoshino' (Suzuki 1992, no. 2). In the Mongaku image the attenuated format strikingly suggests the long drop of the waterfall, with the centre sheet daringly containing nothing but cascading water and an outcrop of rock.

This impression comes from the second printing, in which intricately curling lines of blue foam have been added at the bottom. In the first printing this effect had been achieved by embossing, which was perhaps felt to be visually too subtle (Suzuki 1992, no. 1).

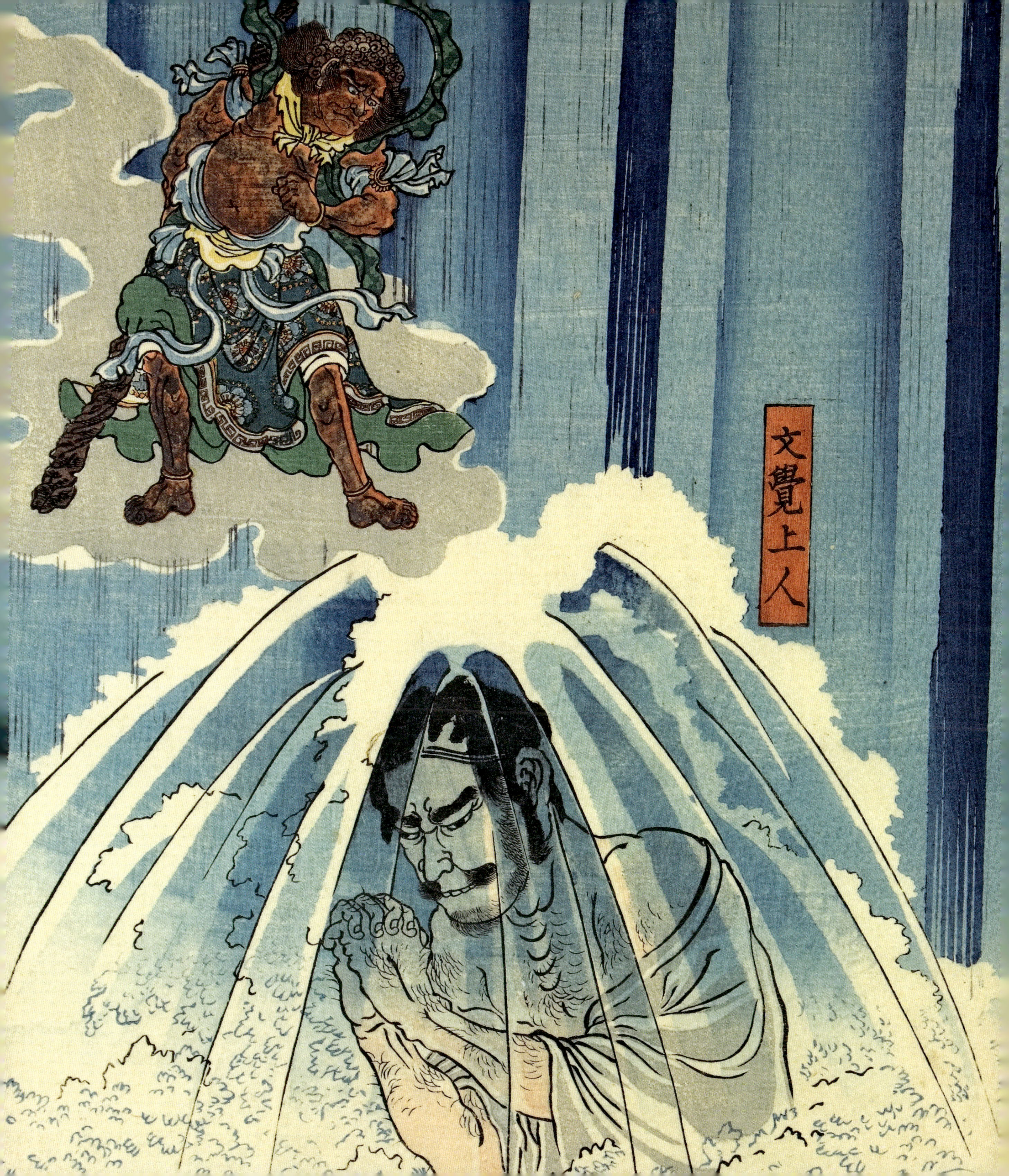
文覺上人

ONE HUNDRED HEROIC GENERALS IN BATTLE AT KAWANAKAJIMA, SHINANO PROVINCE

(Cats 34–6)

Kawanakajima (literally, 'island between the rivers') is the name given to a series of five battles fought in the period 1553–64 for control of northern Shinano province (modern Nagano prefecture) between the forces of warlords Takeda Shingen of Kai and Uesugi Kenshin of Echigo. The fourth and largest battle, ultimately indecisive, took place on a triangular island in the shallows at the confluence of the Sai and Chikuma rivers. The name of the island, Kawanakajima, was later applied to all five battles waged in the area. They occurred during the 'period of warring provinces' (*sengoku jidai*), when the weakness of the Ashikaga shogunate's central government in Kyoto led to escalating conflicts among regional warlords.

Robinson lists twelve designs, seven relating to the Takeda clan, five to the Uesugi, including a presumed, but as yet undiscovered portrait of Uesugi Kenshin (Robinson 1982, series S34). Four publishers seem to have collaborated on the project. All the designs feature the bold half-length portrait of a warrior, close to the viewer and in a dynamic pose. Their style is characterised by fine cutting of bushy hair, whiskers and eyebrows, by thick, calligraphic drapery lines and by bulbous eyes with white pupils. Across the top of each print silhouetted armies do battle near a distant river.

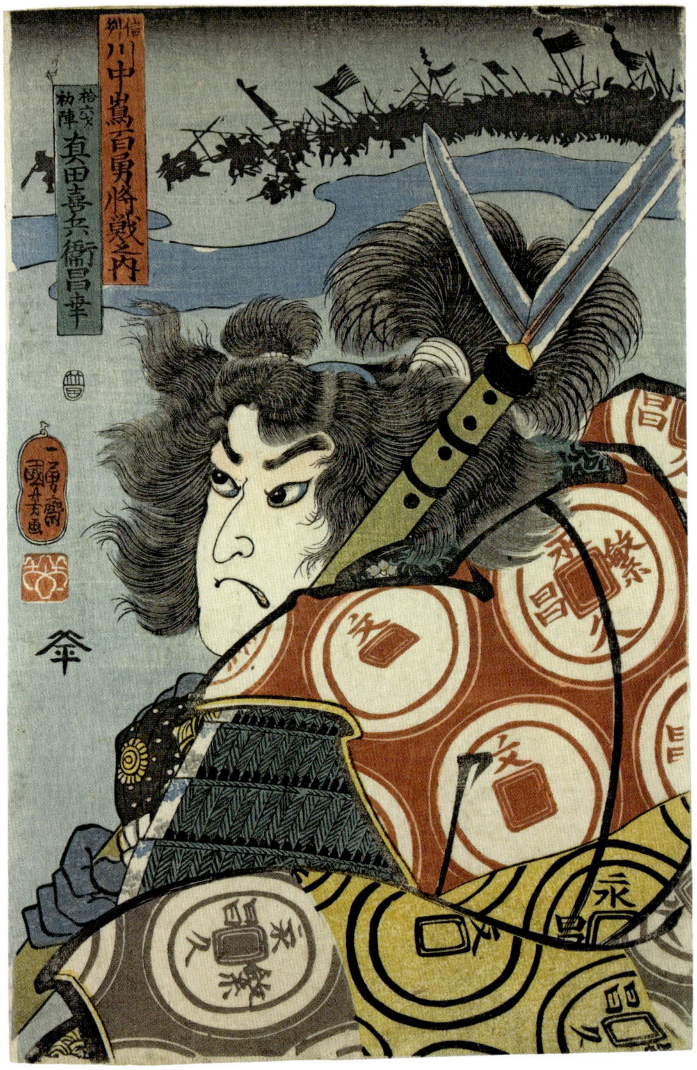

34

Sixteen year-old warrior Sanada Masayuki

1845–46

Colour woodblock, *ōban*, published by Yamashiroya Heisuke, 37.9 × 25.4 cm

SERIES TITLE
'One Hundred Heroic Generals in Battle at Kawanakajima, Shinano Province' (*Shinshū Kawanakajima hyaku yūshō sen no uchi*)

PRINT TITLE
'Sanada Kihei Masayuki, sixteen years, first time in battle' (*Jūroku-sai uijin Sanada Kihei Masayuki*)

ARTIST'S SIGNATURE
Ichiyūsai Kuniyoshi ga (in gourd-shaped *Yoshi* cartouche)

ARTIST'S SEAL
Yoshikiri

CENSOR'S SEAL
Fu

American Friends of the British Museum (The Arthur R. Miller Collection) 10506

REFERENCES
Robinson 1982, no. S34.7; Ōta 1999, no. 44; Shōtō 2003, no. 126

Sanada Masayuki (1547–1611) fought on the Takeda side. Above the warrior's name is an annotation stating that he is sixteen (fifteen by Western reckoning) and participating in his first battle. According to *Kōyō gunkan* (*Military Exemplars of Kai Province*), a book of military strategy, this was at the fourth battle at Kawanakajima, which took place in 1561. Sanada's forelock has not yet been shaved off to mark his coming of age. Despite his inexperience, he is said to have inflicted many casualties on the Uesugi forces (Shōtō 2003, p. 98).

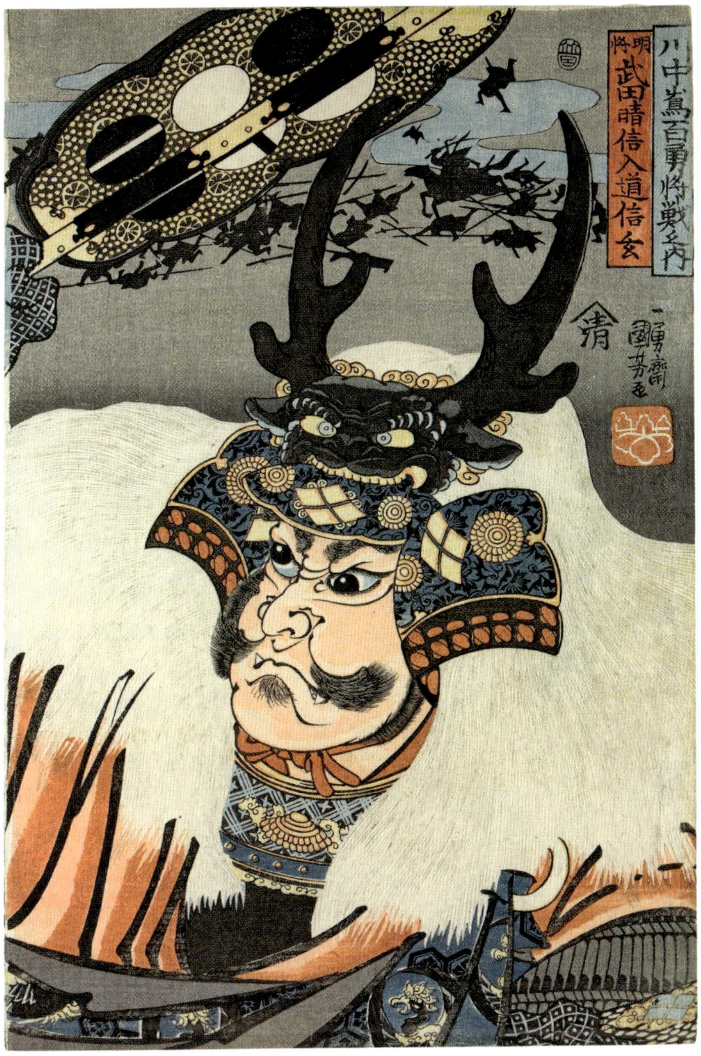

35

Famous general Takeda Shingen

1845–46

Colour woodblock, *ōban*, published by Shimizuya Naojirō, 36.9 × 25 cm

SERIES TITLE
'One Hundred Heroic Generals in Battle at Kawanakajima' (*Kawanakajima hyaku yūshō sen no uchi*)

PRINT TITLE
'Famous general, Takeda Harunobu Nyūdō Shingen' (*Meishō Takeda Harunobu Nyūdō Shingen*)

ARTIST'S SIGNATURE
Ichiyūsai Kuniyoshi ga

ARTIST'S SEAL
Yoshikiri

CENSOR'S SEAL
Fu

American Friends of the British Museum (The Arthur R. Miller Collection) 10501

REFERENCES
Robinson 1982, no. S34.1; Amsterdam 1998, no. 37

The warlord Takeda Shingen (1521–1573), leader of the Takeda army in the Kawanakajima conflict, is shown wearing his customary helmet topped with a grimacing monster, deer antlers and a flowing white main of hair – the hair here embossed deeply into the paper. He brandishes a war-fan (*gunbai*) above his head. This probably alludes to the famous moment in the fourth battle when Uesugi Kenshin launched a surprise attack on Shingen's headquarters, suddenly riding his horse Tsukige straight towards his enemy and cutting at Shingen with his mighty sword – a blow that Shingen successfully parried with the metal war-fan.

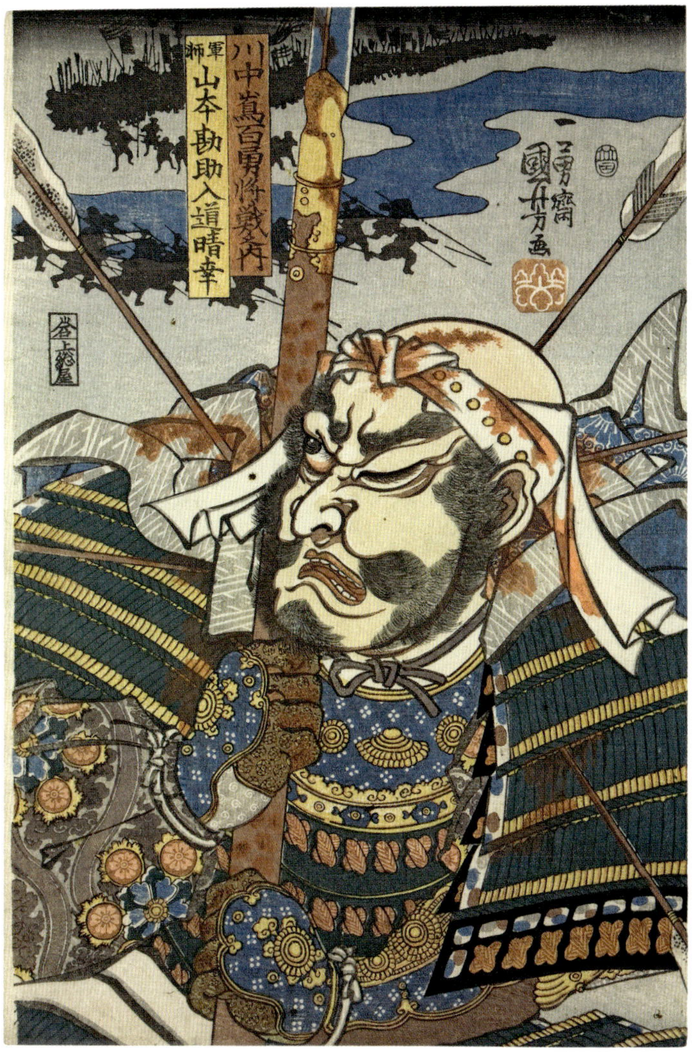

36

Military strategist Yamamoto Kansuke

1845–46

Colour woodblock, *ōban*, published by Kazusaya Iwazō, 36.7 × 25 cm

SERIES TITLE
'One Hundred Heroic Generals in Battle at Kawanakajima' (*Kawanakajima hyaku yūshō sen no uchi*)

PRINT TITLE
'Military strategist, Yamamoto Kansuke Nyūdō Haruyuki' (*Gunshi Yamamoto Kansuke Nyūdō Haruyuki*)

ARTIST'S SIGNATURE
Ichiyūsai Kuniyoshi ga

ARTIST'S SEAL
Yoshikiri

CENSOR'S SEAL
Fu

American Friends of the British Museum (The Arthur R. Miller Collection) 10504

REFERENCES
Robinson 1982, no. S34.4

General Yamamoto Kansuke (?1493–1561), who is shown after losing the use of one eye, was one of Takeda Shingen's five leading retainers and a military strategist. His plan for the fourth battle of Kawanakajima, in 1561, failed. To redeem his honour Kansuke attacked the enemy directly with a band of men and fought ferociously, before finally being overcome and killed. The print shows his desperate last moments. (See also cat. 37.)

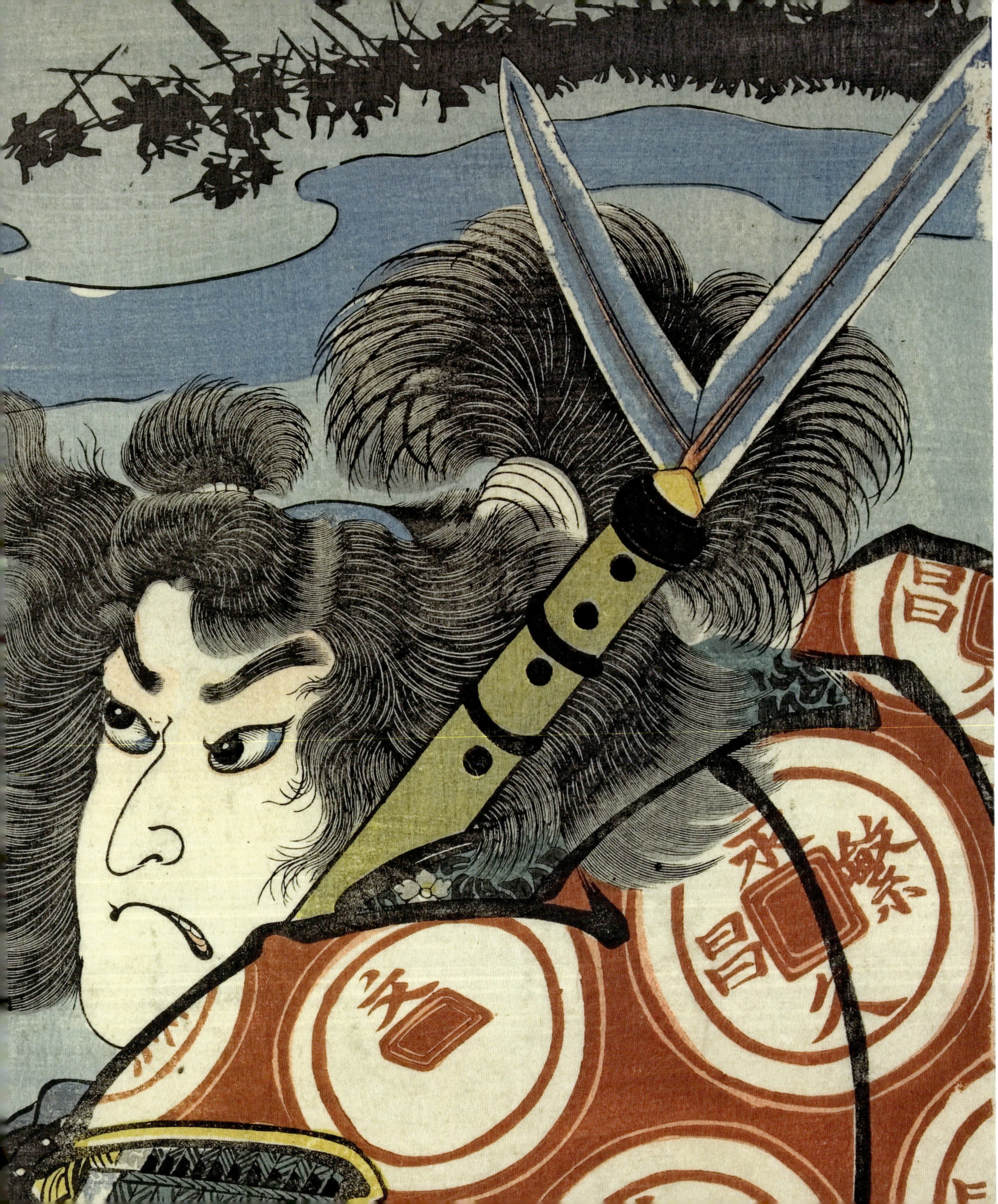

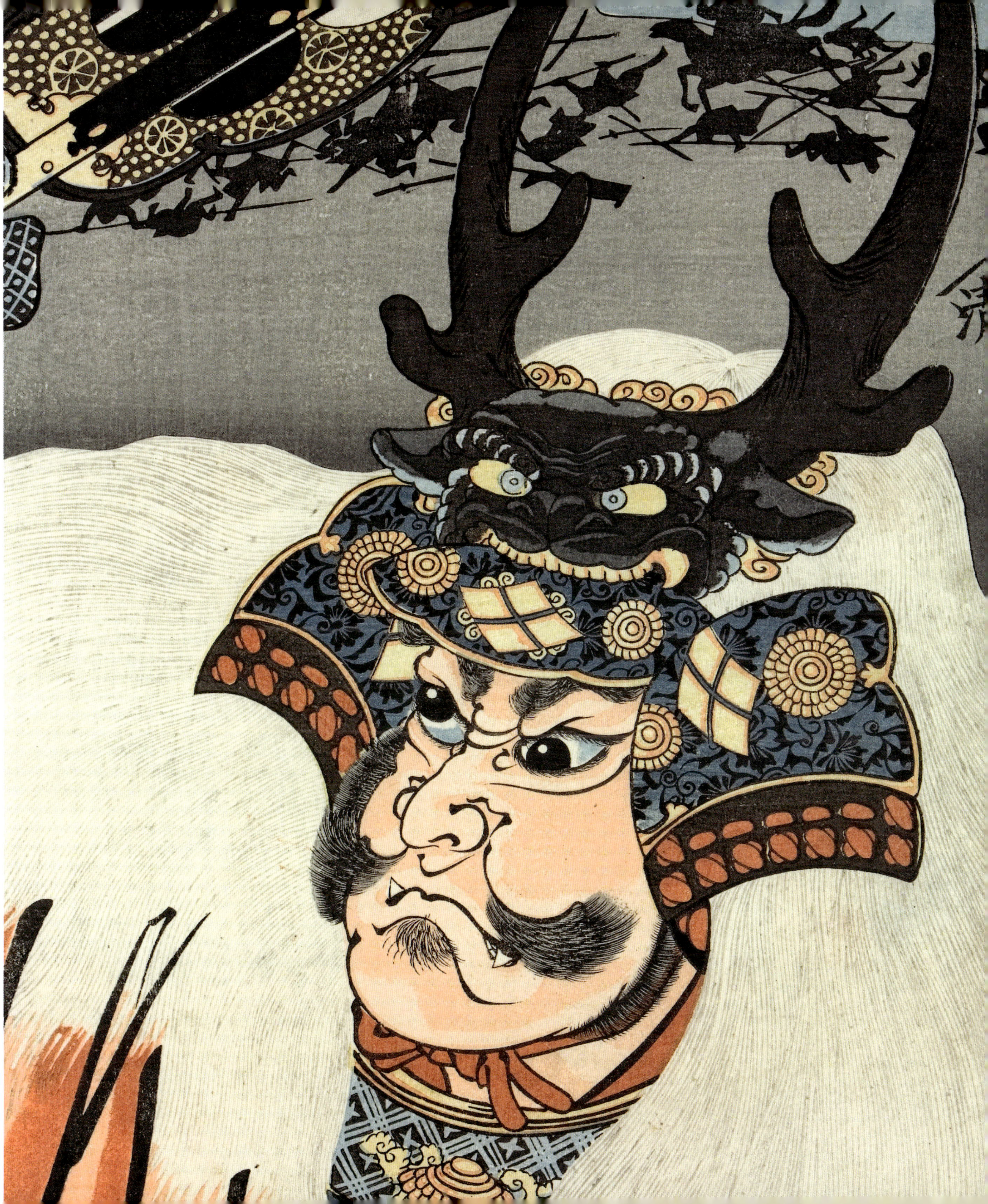

BIOGRAPHIES OF HEROIC GENERALS OF KAI AND ECHIGO PROVINCES

(Cats 37, 38)

The series relates to the same historical events as cats 34–6: the five Kawanakajima battles fought in the period 1553–64 between Takeda Shingen and Uesugi Kenshin. Each print features a full-length figure of a general, with a short biographical sketch above that generally includes a description of the climactic moment depicted. As with many other prints by Kuniyoshi in this form, some texts in the series are by Ryūkatei Tanekazu and others by Ippitsuan. Ryūkatei Tanekazu (1807–1858) was a pupil of the leading popular writer Ryūtei Tanehiko and well known for his public recitations of military tales (texts by him also appear on cats 39, 40). Ippitsuan was a pen name used by the ukiyo-e artist Keisai Eisen (1791–1848), texts by whom are included in cats 42–5. Kuniyoshi first employed the format of a single figure with text above in the series 'Biographies of One Hundred Famous Heroes' (*Meikō hyakuyū den*) of *c.* 1843–44 (Robinson 1982, series S31) and continued to use it for the rest of the 1840s.

The subtitle of the series suggests that the plan was to produce prints of forty-eight generals, twenty-four each from the Takeda and Uesugi sides. Robinson (1982, series 63) identifies ten Takeda generals and eight Uesugi. He suggests that impressions bearing the number in the series could belong to slightly later printings, the numbers presumably added as the prints were issued. Two more Uesugi generals have since been identified: Yamayoshi Genba-no-jō Chikafusa (Miller 15011) and Honjō Echizen-no-kami (Robinson and Miller 1996, p. 5; Iwakiri, personal communication).

37

The warrior Yamamoto Kansuke leaning on a spear

c. 1848

Colour woodblock, *ōban*, published by Sumiyoshiya Masagorō, 36.4 × 25.9 cm

SERIES TITLE
'Biographies of Heroic Generals of Kai and Echigo Provinces, Twenty-four Generals of the Takeda Clan' (*Kōetsu yūshō den, Takeda-ke nijūshi-shō*)

PRINT TITLE
'No. 3, Yamamoto Kansuke Nyūdō Dōkisai Haruyuki'

ARTIST'S SIGNATURE
Ichiyūsai Kuniyoshi ga

ARTIST'S SEAL
Yoshikiri

CENSORS' SEALS
Muramatsu and Yoshimura

American Friends of the British Museum (The Arthur R. Miller Collection) 15003

REFERENCES
Robinson 1982, no. S63.3

General Yamamoto Kansuke, who had lost the use of one eye, acted as a military strategist for the Takeda clan. This print shows his last stand at the 1561 battle of Kawanakajima. One foot braced on a severed enemy head, he leans defiantly on his spear, even though his head is badly wounded and several arrows have pierced his armour. The text describes how the Takeda forces were seriously threatened by the Uesugi tactic of *kuruma-gakari*, whereby troops attacked relentlessly in never-ending rotations. Taking responsibility for his failed battle plan, Yamamoto led seventy-five warriors against the large Uesugi army of Nagao Yoshikage. Although badly wounded, Yamamoto attacked seven times before falling in battle. (See also cat. 36.)

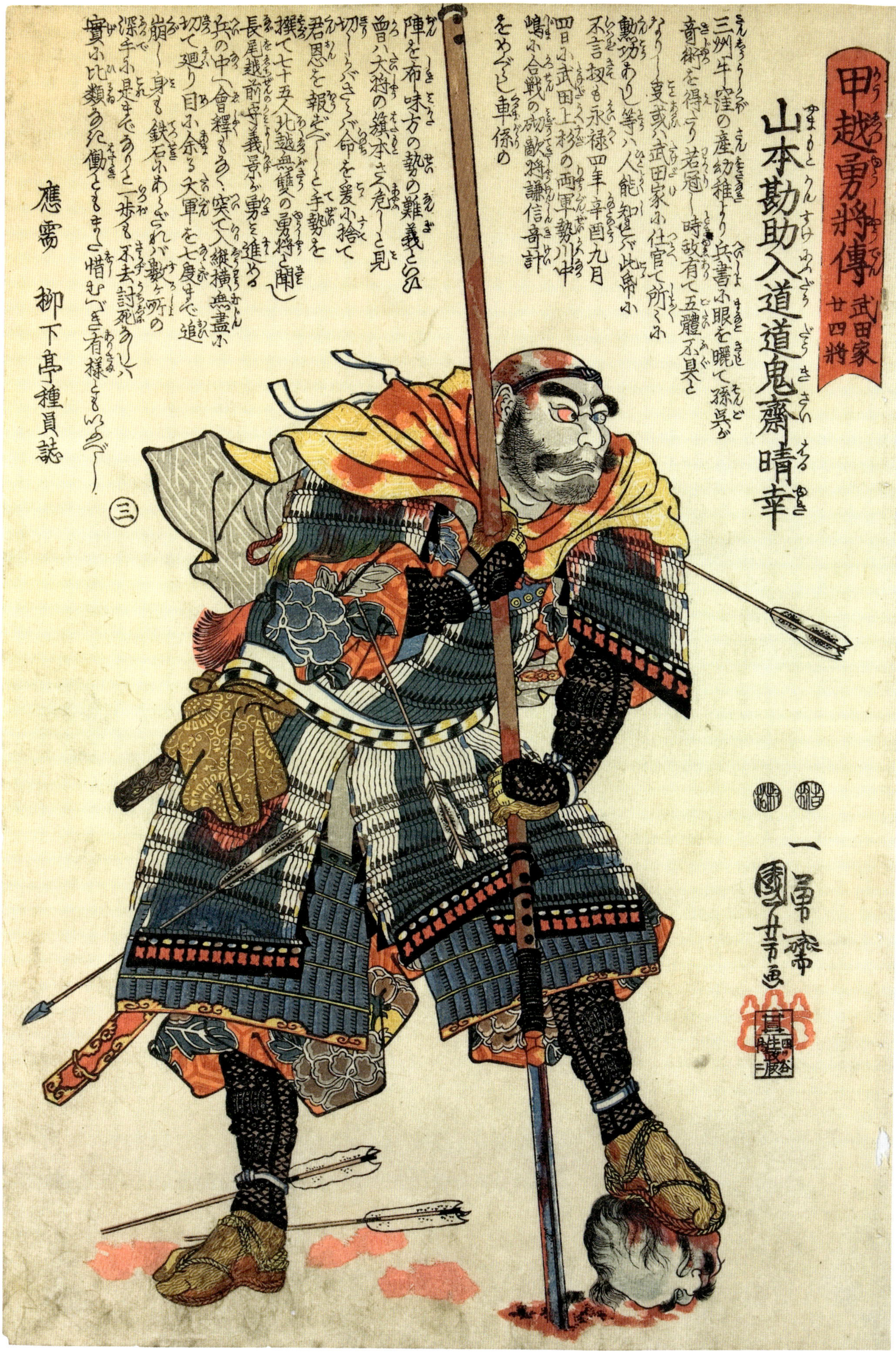
甲越勇將傳
武田家廿四將
山本勘助入道道鬼齋晴幸
應需 柳下亭種員誌
一勇齋國芳画

38

The warrior Morozumi Masakiyo kills himself in battle

c. 1848

Colour woodblock, *ōban*, published by Sumiyoshiya Masagorō, 36.6 × 25.7 cm

SERIES TITLE
'Biographies of Heroic Generals of Kai and Echigo Provinces, Twenty-four Generals of the Takeda Clan' (*Kōetsu yūshō den, Takeda-ke nijūshi-shō*)

PRINT TITLE
'No. 23, Morozumi Bungo-no-kami Masakiyo, One of Three Heroic Deaths in Battle' (*San uchijini no uchi, Morozumi Bungo-no-kami Masakiyo*)

ARTIST'S SIGNATURE
Ichiyūsai Kuniyoshi ga

ARTIST'S SEAL
Yoshikiri

CENSORS' SEALS
Mera and Murata

American Friends of the British Museum (The Arthur R. Miller Collection) 15009

REFERENCES
Springfield 1968, no. 109; Riccar 1978, no. 63; Springfield 1980, no. 162; Robinson 1982, no. S63.9, pl. 20; Keyes 1989, no. 226; Amsterdam 1998, no. 80; King and Iwakiri 2007, no. 158

Morozumi Bungo-no-kami Masakiyo (d. 1561), a general of the Takeda clan, is generally known to modern historians as Morozumi Toramitsu. The text describes how his forces were blown to pieces by landmines planted by the enemy in a dry riverbed. Morozumi suffered terrible burns and could barely walk. As sparks continued to rain down, he ripped off his armour from both arms, stabbed the point of his sword into his mouth and threw himself into the explosion: 'never before had such a death been known in battle'. Kuniyoshi focuses on Morozumi's ferocious expression immediately before he meets his end, as a mine explodes in front of him. Flashes from the explosion splinter across his body in a vortex of complex pictorial effects. A fine spray of red-brown pigment has been blown onto the epicentre of the blast, probably using a split bamboo tube as an atomiser.

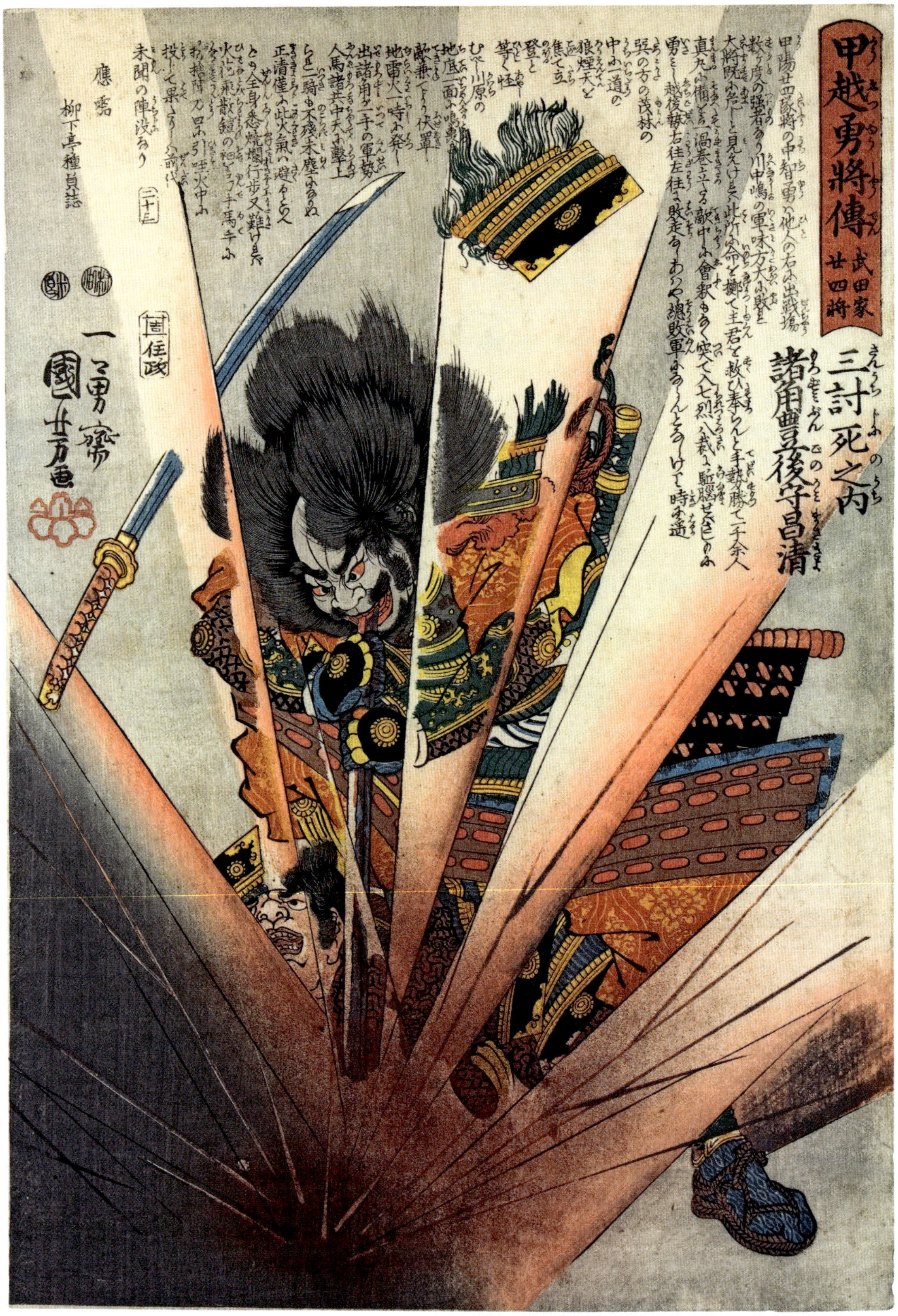

HEROES OF THE GREAT PEACE

(Cats 39, 40)

People in Kuniyoshi's day took enormous interest in the epic events leading to the establishment in 1603 of the Tokugawa shogunate – that is, the regime under which they still lived. Beginning in 1560, the military successes of the warlords Oda Nobunaga (1534–1582), Toyotomi Hideyoshi (1536–1598) and Tokugawa Ieyasu (1542–1616) led progressively to the reunification of the country, following more than a century of ruinous civil war. It was the character and biography of Hideyoshi, in particular, who rose from low-ranking samurai to all-powerful ruler, that held tremendous fascination for the popular imagination. But in 1615 the Tokugawa attacked Hideyoshi's son Hideyori (1593–1615) and wiped out most of the Toyotomi clan. In future centuries the Tokugawa were extremely sensitive about direct public references to these events of the early seventeenth century. In 1804, for example, Utamaro, Toyokuni and other artists and writers were punished for producing prints relating to *Ehon taikōki* (*Picture Book: Tales of the Regent*,1797–1802), an illustrated biography of Hideyoshi that had been a runaway best-seller before being banned that year by the authorities. At the same time, they renewed a ban on references in popular art and literature to warriors who lived later than 1573.

Taiheiki (*Chronicle of the Great Peace*, 1340s–71) was a major literary work that recounted the attempt by Emperor Go-Daigo (1288–1339) to restore imperial rule. It appears in the title of Kuniyoshi's print series as a thinly veiled reference to *Taikōki*, the biography of Hideyoshi, which still could not be mentioned explicitly. Similarly, the identities of the warriors depicted were disguised by giving them different names that sounded a little like the originals. Employing subterfuge of this kind, the series treats in detail all the major military figures and events of the reunification wars of the late sixteenth century, from the early victories of Nobunaga in 1560 to the death of Hideyoshi in 1598. It begins, symbolically, with a portrait of Ōta Kazusa-no-suke Taira no Harunaga kō (the historical Oda Nobunaga) and ends with one of Nakaura Sarukichirō Hisayoshi (an alias for Toyotomi Hideyoshi; p.27, fig.12). Kuniyoshi generally selects a pivotal moment in the career of the warrior depicted, which is then explained as part of the 'brief family chronicle' (*ikke ryaku denshi*) written by Ryūkatei Tanekazu and printed above the figure (for Tanekazu, see cats 37, 38). Although Kuniyoshi had begun making covert allusions to the life of Hideyoshi in his prints as early as the mid-1830s – in the series *Yōbu hakkei* (*c.*1836) and *Buyū hyaku den* (*c.*1836; p.26, fig.10) – the present set was by far the most ambitious and blatant. Evidence exists to suggest that Kuniyoshi sympathised or otherwise identified with Hideyoshi (see pp.26–7).

Elena Varshavskaya has produced an exemplary monograph on this series, reproducing all fifty known designs in generally fine impressions, giving a detailed commentary on each print and publishing a full translation of the biography that appears on them (Varshavskaya 2005). Her introductory essay discusses in depth the historical events portrayed and the wide-ranging cultural ramifications of their adaptation in Kuniyoshi's images and Tanekazu's texts. She also illustrates five preparatory drawings in the National Museum of Ethnology, Leiden, that relate to the series (ibid., pp.49–51). Many of the prints are numbered and Varshavskaya follows this order in her book. Robinson (1982, series S62) lists the prints alphabetically according to the warrior's name and provides information on the location of impressions in collections and publications.

39

The warrior Sasai Masanao on the trunk of a pine tree

1848–50

Colour woodblock, *ōban*, published by Yamamoto Heikichi, 36.8 × 25.9 cm

SERIES TITLE
'Heroes of the Great Peace' (*Taiheiki eiyūden*)

PRINT TITLE
'Sasai Ukon Masanao'

ARTIST'S SIGNATURE
Ichiyūsai Kuniyoshi ga

ARTIST'S SEAL
Yoshikiri

CENSORS' SEALS
Mera and Murata

American Friends of the British Museum (The Arthur R. Miller Collection) 05628

REFERENCES
Robinson 1963, no. 22; Robinson 1982, no. S62.37; Varshavskaya 2005, no. 11

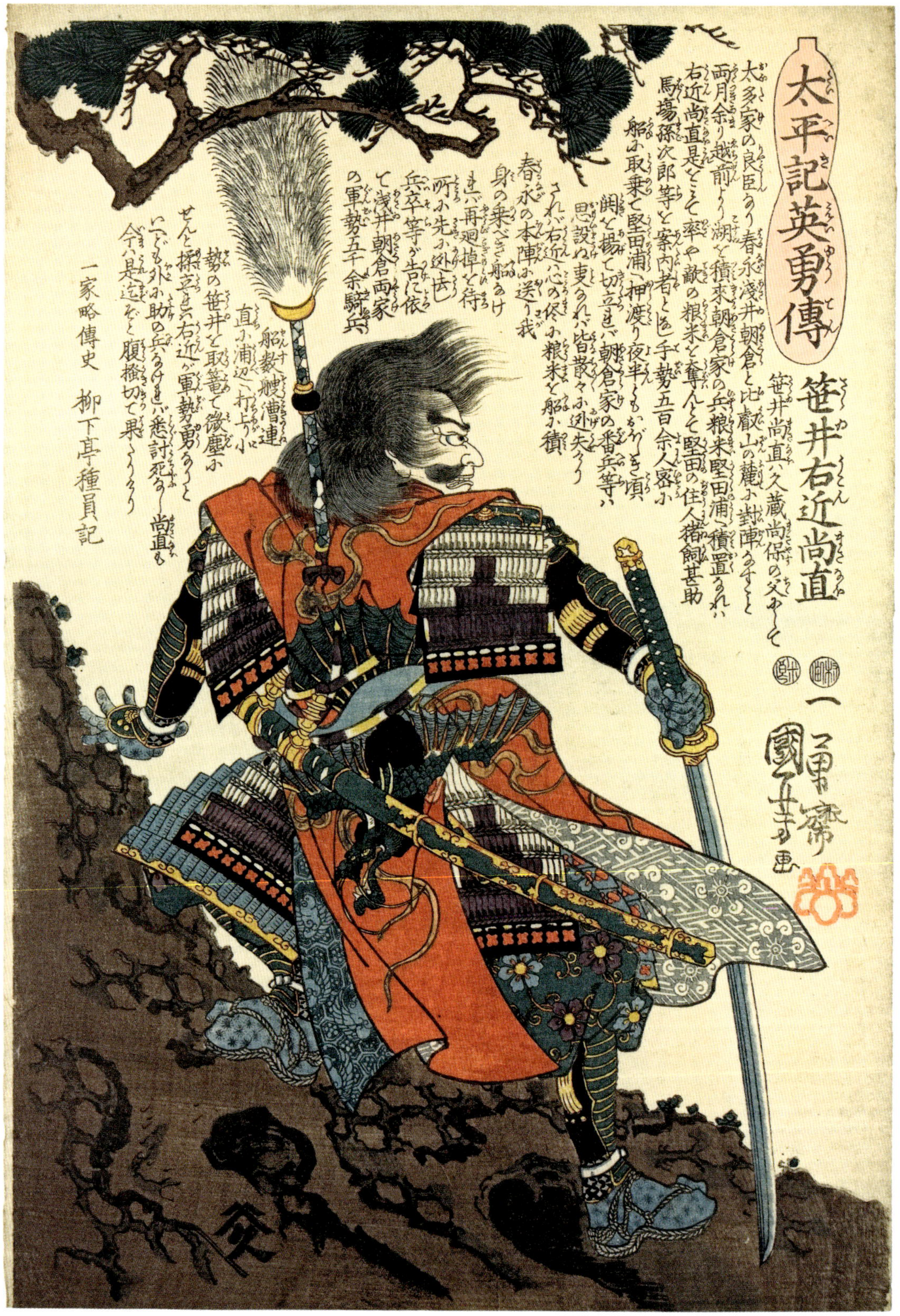

The warrior Sasai Masanao (representing the historical figure Sakai Ukon Masanao, d. 1570) has climbed onto the inclined trunk of the ancient pine tree at Karasaki, on the shores of Lake Biwa. He grimaces defiantly at the forces of the Asai and Asakura families, who will shortly overwhelm his troops and massacre them. The brilliant surcoat (*jinbaori*) he wears over his armour bears a bold design of a winged dragon.

The text explains that Sasai (Sakai), a retainer of the Ōta family (Oda Nobunaga), staged a daring night raid on the Asakura clan's grain supplies at Katata bay on Lake Biwa. While waiting for the return of the ship transporting the stolen grain to Harunaga's (Nobunaga's) camp, he was attacked by the regrouped Asai and Asakura troops. With a cry of 'Now, this is my last!' (*Ima wa kore made zo!*) Sasai drives his sword into his stomach and kills himself.

40

The warrior Sasai Masayasu caught in gunfire

1848–50

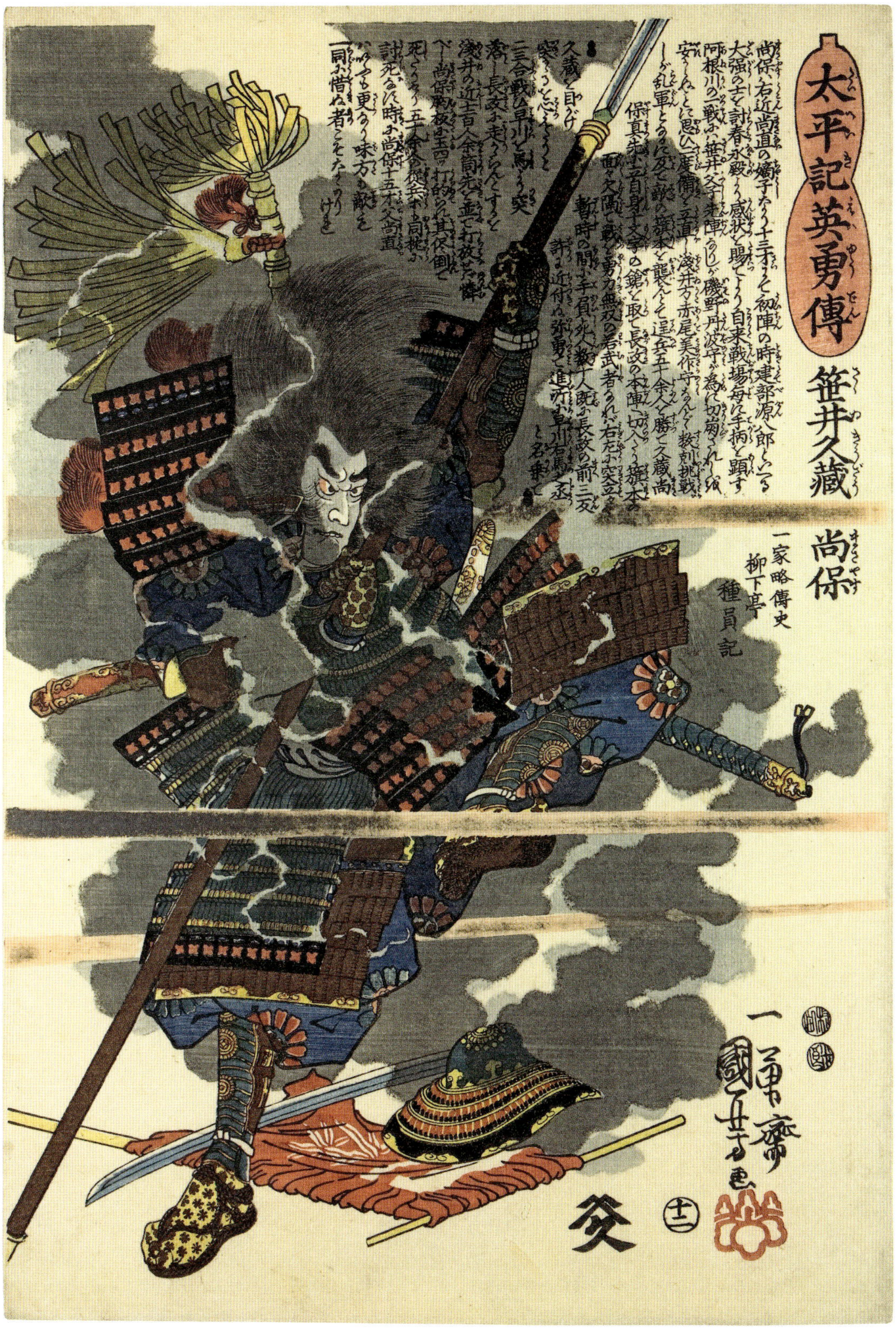

Colour woodblock, *ōban*, published by Yamamoto Heikichi, 37.3 × 25.9 cm

SERIES TITLE
'Heroes of the Great Peace' (*Taiheiki eiyūden*)

PRINT TITLE
'No. 12, Sasai Kyūzō Masayasu'

ARTIST'S SIGNATURE
Ichiyūsai Kuniyoshi ga

ARTIST'S SEAL
Yoshikiri

CENSORS' SEALS
Mera and Murata

American Friends of the British Museum (The Arthur R. Miller Collection) 05627

REFERENCES
Robinson 1961, no.62; Riccar 1978, no.60; Springfied 1980, no. 181; Robinson 1982, no.S62.36; Amsterdam 1998, no.73; Varshavskaya 2005, no.12

Sasai Masayasu (representing the historical figure Sakai Kyūzō Narishige, ?1555–1570) is caught in a barrage of gunfire as he tries to reach and attack the enemy leader, Asai Nagamasa, in the latter's headquarters. The text describes how four bullets pierce his breastplate and kill him. Some fifty of his followers die in the same barrage. Friend and foe alike lament his death, as the young warrior was only fifteen years old. Masayasu, like his father, Sasai Masanao (Sakai Masanao), depicted in cat.39, is a loyal retainer of Ōta Harunaga (Oda Nobunaga).

This is one of the most memorable designs in the series, with Masayasu's face uncannily illuminated amid clouds of gun smoke. His pose, with one leg raised, suggests determination to rush forward, even as he is knocked backwards by the hail of shot. The smoke has deliberately been printed with ragged edges and partly obscures the detail of his armour. Masayasu's spear cuts a strong, resolute diagonal through the horizontal traces of the bullets surrounding him.

LOYAL AND RIGHTEOUS SAMURAI: ORIGINS (Cat. 41)
BIOGRAPHIES OF LOYAL AND RIGHTEOUS SAMURAI (Cats 42–4)
BIOGRAPHIES OF LOYAL AND RIGHTEOUS HEARTS (Cat. 45)

These three series all relate to the Akō vendetta of 1701–03, which is popularly referred to as 'Chūshingura' ('Treasury of the Loyal Retainers'). That name comes from the title of the best-loved puppet/Kabuki play based on the historical events, the eleven-act *Kanadehon chūshingura* (*Calligraphy Primer of the Treasury of Loyal Retainers*), written in 1748 by Takeda Izumo and two other playwrights. Unusually for the Edo period, this vendetta prompted widespread debate throughout Japan, owing to the collision it encapsulated between old-fashioned values of samurai family honour and the more modern, legalistic thinking of the Tokugawa shogunate. Embellished versions of the incident began appearing in popular literature, theatre and art almost immediately, burgeoning into a cultural phenomenon that grew and embraced new genres in the eighteenth, nineteenth and even twentieth centuries (a comprehensive account of the 'cultural capacity' of Chūshingura is given in Smith 2003). Names and settings had to be changed to evade official intervention, but the Chūshingura story was too notorious for the authorities to suppress or censor its dissemination effectively. For many, Chūshingura became – and remained – a paradigm of samurai behaviour and this created a huge market for popular imagery relating to the tale. Kuniyoshi was not the first ukiyo-e artist to produce Chūshingura prints, but, as in his treatment of many other warrior themes, he was the most prolific and the most systematic. Together, for example, these three series, feature all the main protagonists. For once, Kuniyoshi was depicting scenes of military prowess relatively close to his own time, rather than re-imagining them from the distant past.

On the fourteenth day of the third month, 1701, the young lord of Akō, Asano Naganori, drew his sword in a corridor of Edo castle and attempted to kill Kira Yoshinaka, a shogunal protocol official. Asano's motivation is unclear and Kira was only slightly wounded, but the shogunal authorities responded severely because the incident had occurred within the precincts of the shogun's castle. Asano was ordered to commit ritual suicide that same day, his domain was confiscated and his retainers were disbanded, becoming 'wave men' (*rōnin*), or masterless samurai. Not only did Kira escape punishment; much to the disgust of the Akō retainers and large sections of samurai opinion, he was also praised for the 'restraint' he had shown in not responding with his own sword. For almost two years the former retainers of Asano went their separate ways, bided their time and hatched their secret plans. Then, one snowy night in the twelfth month of 1702, forty-seven of them, led by the senior retainer, Ōishi Kuranosuke, launched a surprise attack on Kira's mansion at Honjo in Edo. They killed Kira, cut off his head, marched across the city to the temple of Sengaku-ji to present the head to the grave of their dead lord and then surrendered to the authorities. After weeks of debate within the government, these 'righteous samurai' (*gishi*) were condemned to death, but permitted the honour of committing ritual suicide. They were buried in graves surrounding Asano's at Sengaku-ji which still exist.

Within just a few years of the Akō vendetta the leading playwright, Chikamatsu Monzaemon, wrote the puppet play *Goban taiheiki* (*Go-board Chronicle of the Great Peace*, 1710), which circumvented censorship by transposing the events back to the fourteenth century. The oldest surviving print on the subject, depicting a disguised Kabuki version of the final attack on Kira, has been dated to the New Year, 1711: 'The Shida Revenge Night Attack' (*Shida kaikei no youchi*) by a Torii school artist (Art Research Center, Ritsumeikan University, Kyoto, UP1303). Most later versions of the story in literature and drama took up the device of setting the events in the distant past. That is true of the puppet/Kabuki play *Kanadehon chūshingura*, which in turn coloured some later treatments of the story by introducing several female characters and subplots to provide love interest.

Other major categories of Chūshingura-related texts are also important for understanding the background to Kuniyoshi's prints. First, many contemporary manuscript accounts, or 'true records' (*jitsuroku*), were widely copied and circulated on the assumption – often quite false – that they recounted the historical facts accurately (information conveyed in manuscript form was less likely to be censored). Second, from the mid-eighteenth century onwards there was a boom in oral tales (*kōdan*) describing the 'individual stories' (*meimeiden*) of the righteous samurai and the 'outside stories' (*gaiden*) of characters associated with them. Finally, an important illustrated novel (*yomihon*) entitled *Ehon chūshingura* (*Picture-book Chūshingura*), published in Osaka in 1800 and written and illustrated by Hayami Shungyōsai (d. 1823), introduced a new strand into the Chūshingura narrative.

The texts on Kuniyoshi's prints draw on several of these traditions. For example, they tell the 'individual stories' of the Chūshingura characters in the manner of *kōdan* recitations (with disguised names different from those used in the Kabuki plays) and they are written by two authors of popular illustrated fiction, Ippitsuan Kakō (better known as the ukiyo-e artist Keisai Eisen, 1791–1848) and Shōtei Kinsui (1797–1862).

'Biographies of Loyal and Righteous Samurai' (*Seichū gishi den*; cats 42–4), published by Ebiya Rinnosuke, is the most frequently encountered of the three series included here. The book *Chūshin meimei gaden* (*Illustrated Biographies of Each of the Loyal Retainers*), with text by Eisen and illustrations by Kuniyoshi, was published in 1848, so the series must have been either a parallel venture or a spin-off. It seems to be the only one completed, with a total of fifty-one prints. It was tremendously successful, with some eight thousand impressions of each design sold (see also p.27). Weinberg reproduces all fifty-one sheets in colour, accompanied by full translations by Alfred H. Marks of the biographical texts (Weinberg 2000). The prints, almost all numbered in small circles next to the publisher's mark, show each of the forty-seven loyal retainers, one per sheet. They wear the striking black and white 'dog-tooth'-patterned robes customarily used on stage for the scene of the final attack and many are depicted in dynamic combative poses. The four additional characters are Kō no Moronao (the historical Kira Yoshinaka), Enya Hangan (Lord Asano Naganori), Teraoka Hei'emon Nobuyuki, a loyal follower who was permitted to join the band at the last moment, and Jinzaburō, a servant who supplied refreshments to the samurai during the attack. For unknown reasons two quite different versions were produced of the Ōboshi Rikiya Yoshikane design (Weinberg 2000, nos 1.2, 1.2a). The series title on some impressions of the prints depicting Kira and Enya includes the phrase 'The cause of…' (*…no okori*), explaining that the actions of these two men set the saga in motion. The protagonists are all identified by disguised versions of their historical names different from those used in the stage plays – a common ploy for circumventing censorship regulations that forbade the treatment of contemporary events or the naming of warriors who lived after 1573. The strikingly lifelike poses of the figures vividly evoke the events and would seem to be Kuniyoshi's invention: they are certainly not derived from theatrical convention.

Print no.50, the portrait of Yoshita Chūzaemon Kanesuke, includes a printed note next to Kuniyoshi's signature stating that the artist began to draw the series early in the seventh month and completed it on the fourteenth day of the twelfth month. A publisher's inscription on the same print confirms that these dates relate to the rat year (1847) and expresses the hope that the forthcoming *gaiden* issue will also find favour. This probably refers to the next series described here.

'Biographies of Loyal and Righteous Hearts' (*Seichū gishin den*; cat.45), also published by Ebiya Rinnosuke, continues where the previous series left off. It tells the stories of peripheral Chūshingura characters: the family members and servants of the loyal retainers. Weinberg reproduces seventeen of the eighteen known designs in colour, along with translations by Marks of their biographical texts (Weinberg 2000). The prints are numbered. No.16, a portrait of Yatō Chōsuke Noritsugu missing from Weinberg's catalogue, is included in the Miller Collection (15413).

'Loyal and Righteous Samurai: Origins' (*Seichū gishi hottan*; cat.41) is by far the rarest of the three series. The six designs bearing this title in the Miller Collection (15252–57) are the largest known group. Though they have generally been considered in conjunction with the two series already described, they were issued by a different, much less important publisher: Kameya Iwakichi of Asakusa. The word 'origins' (*hottan*) in the title draws attention to their function: they explain the prehistory of the tale, before Enya's assault of Kira in Edo castle. Three of the six prints in the Miller Collection have the numbers one to three printed in red, but they appear to constitute a single-sheet print of Konami, daughter of Kakogawa (*Kakogawa no musume Konami*, 15256), and a diptych depicting Momonoi Wakasanosuke Naotsune (right; 15253) and Kakogawa Honzō Yukikuni (left; 15254). Two of the remaining designs in the Miller Collection perhaps constituted a diptych and they are presented as such here. The final print shows Lady Kaoyo, wife of Lord Enya (*Enya no okugata Kaoyo-gozen*; 15257). Given that Kameya Iwakichi was a minor publisher compared with Ebiya Rinnosuke, these 'origin' prints may have been a further spin-off from the series featuring the forty-seven loyal retainers.

41.1

Lord Kō no Moronao [R]

1847–48

Colour woodblock, *ōban*, published by Kameya Iwakichi, 36.1 × 24.9 cm

SERIES TITLE
'Loyal and Righteous Samurai: Origins' (*Seichū gishi hottan*)

PRINT TITLE
'Kō no Musashi-no-kami Moronao'

ARTIST'S SIGNATURE
Ichiyūsai Kuniyoshi ga

ARTIST'S SEAL
Yoshikiri

CENSORS' SEALS
Muramatsu and Yoshimura

American Friends of the British Museum (The Arthur R. Miller Collection) 15255

REFERENCES
Robinson 1961, no. 64; Robinson 1982, no. S55.1

41.2

Lord Enya Hangan [L]

1847–48

Colour woodblock, *ōban*, published by Kameya Iwakichi, 36.2 × 25.2 cm

SERIES TITLE
'Loyal and Righteous Samurai: Origins' (*Seichū gishi hottan*)

PRINT TITLE
'Enya Hangan Takasada'

ARTIST'S SIGNATURE
Ichiyūsai Kuniyoshi ga

ARTIST'S SEAL
Yoshikiri

CENSORS' SEALS
Muramatsu and Yoshimura

American Friends of the British Museum (The Arthur R. Miller Collection) 15252

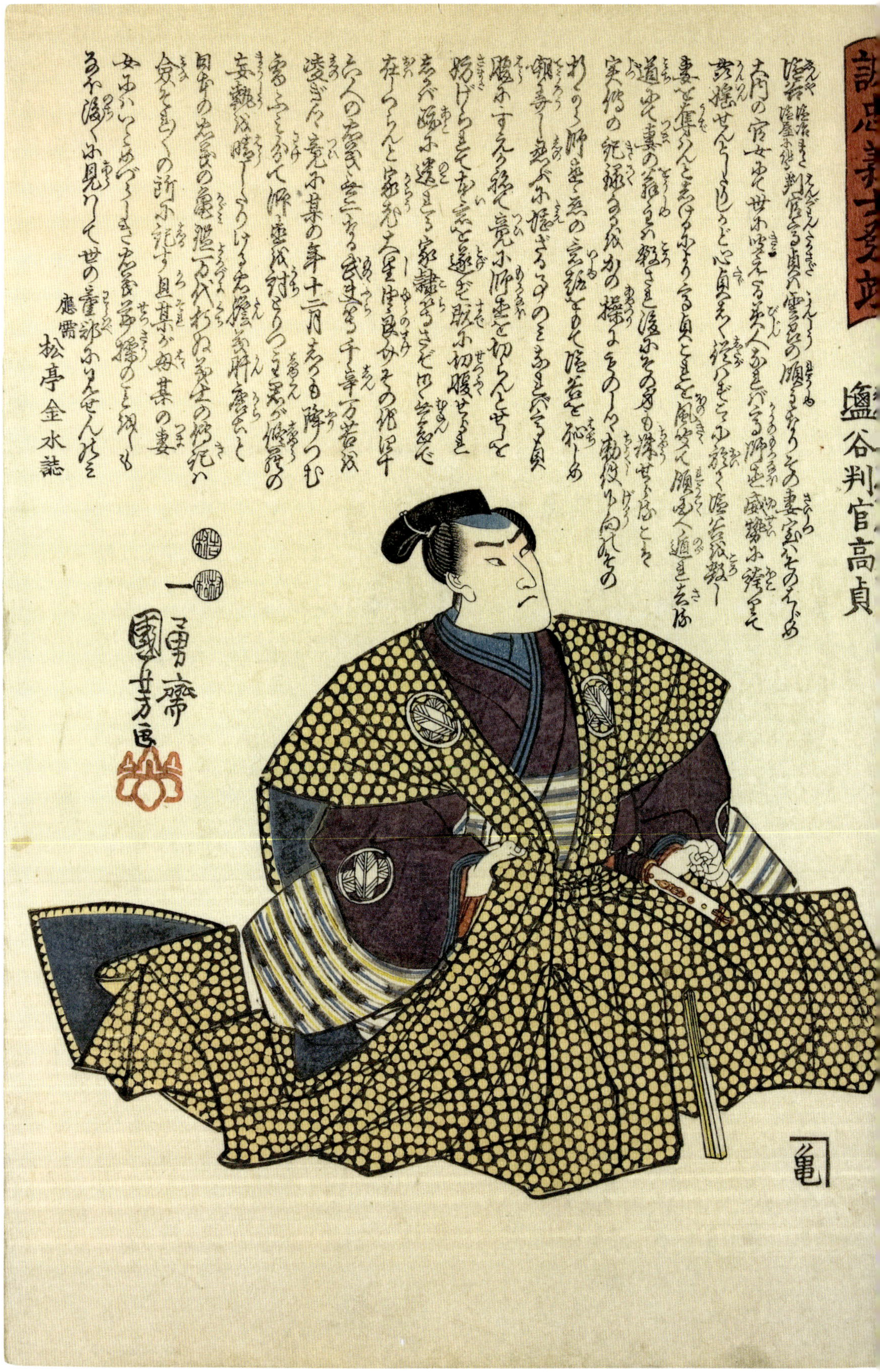

41.2

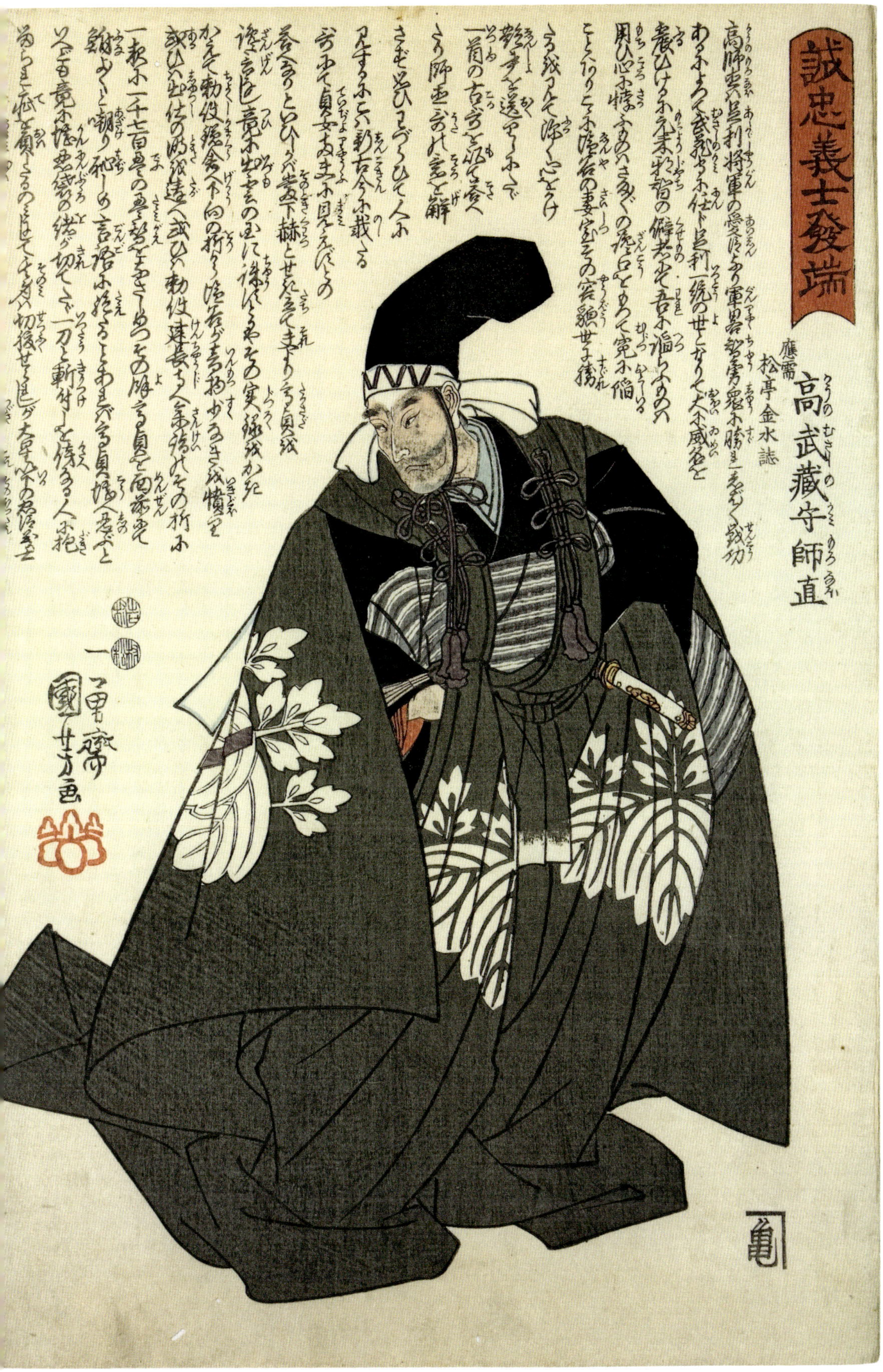

41.1

The two prints may have been intended to form a diptych. In that arrangement they suggest an angry confrontation between Lord Kō no Moronao (the historical Kira Yoshinaka), who stands on the right in formal robes, ready to meet an imperial envoy, and the younger Lord Enya Hangan (the historical Asano Naganori), seated on the left, who glares up at his enemy.

The troubled relations between these men sparked off the Akō vendetta, the events that became known in the artistic realm as the Chūshingura tale. The text on both prints tells the same basic story, switching the emphasis to the character portrayed in each case. The writer, Shōtei Kinsui, distinguishes between those parts of the story based on 'true records' (*jitsuroku*) and those resulting from the efforts of popular authors to rewrite it 'in all kinds of plays' (*zatsugeki*). According to Kinsui, the 'true' part can be summarised as follows. Lady Kaoyo is extremely beautiful. Lord Moronao is smitten, even though Kaoyo is married to Lord Enya. Moronao sends her suggestive letters, but she rebuffs his approaches with a single, barbed classical poem. Angered, Moronao plots to kill Enya and steal his wife. Enya decides to hide Kaoyo in his Izumo domain, but the shogun believes the slanders spread by Moronao and sends retainers to kill her.
The more 'fictional' parts of the story include episodes in which Moronao insults and bullies Enya during the visit of an imperial envoy to Kamakura in the fourteenth century (to which the story has been transposed, as decreed by convention). In one of these he orders Enya to organise the replacement of seventeen hundred tatami mats at the temple Kenchō-ji in the course of a single night. Enya, goaded beyond endurance, eventually strikes Moronao with his sword. Restrained by those around him, he cannot kill his tormentor and is ultimately forced to commit ritual suicide. Returning to the familiar Akō/Chūshingura story, Kinsui next relates how Enya's senior retainer, Ōboshi Yuranosuke, assembles a band of forty-six other loyal followers. On a snowy night in the twelfth month 'of a certain year' they kill Moronao and avenge their lord. 'These righteous samurai will serve as models of faithful loyalty for ten thousand generations, in both China and Japan.' This version of the story differs notably from the familiar puppet/Kabuki play *Kanadehon chūshingura*, which in Act Three shows the two main characters confronting one another in the pine-tree room of Edo castle.

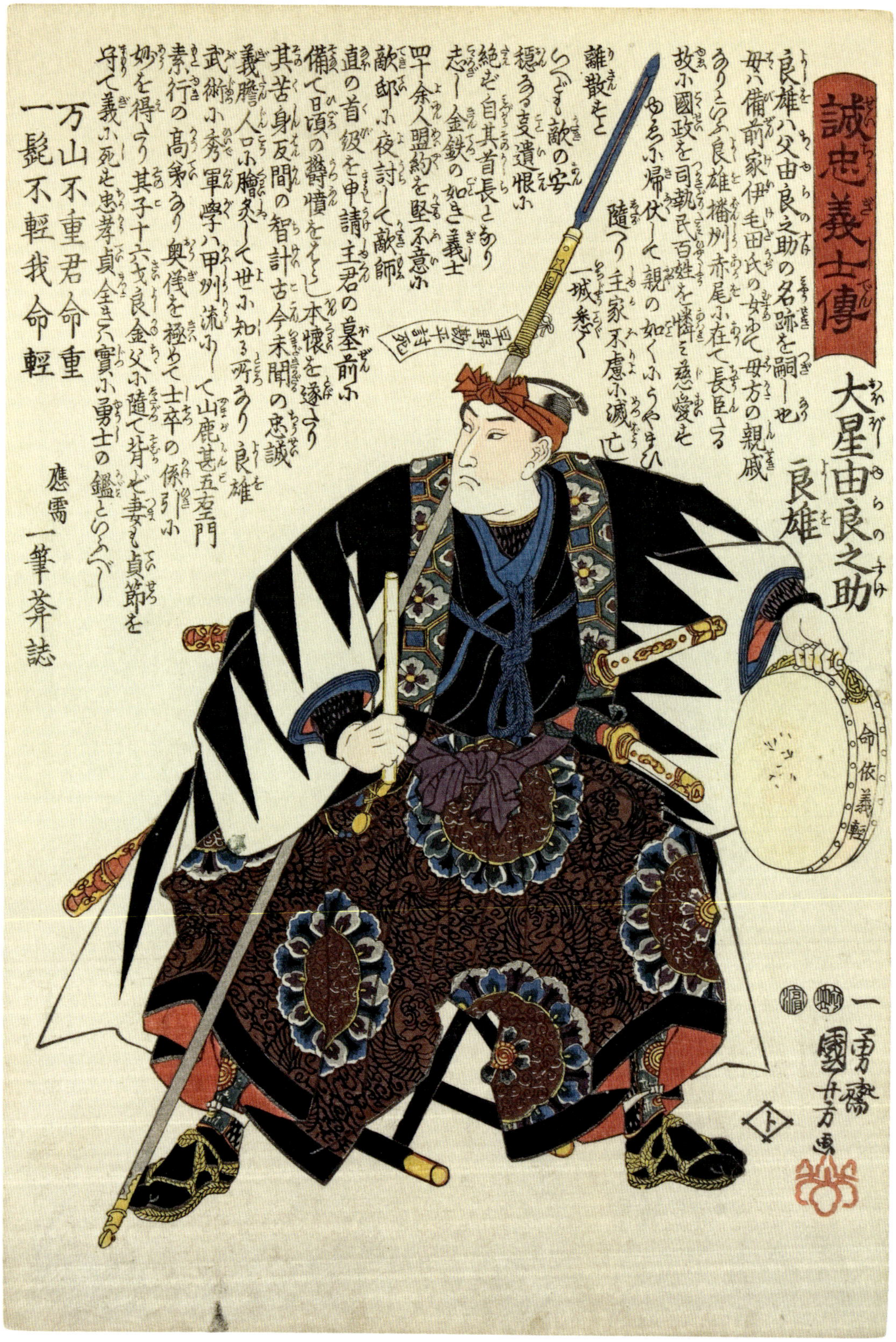

42

Ōboshi Yuranosuke, leader of the loyal retainers

1847

Colour woodblock, *ōban*, published by Ebiya Rinnosuke, 36.2 × 25 cm

SERIES TITLE
'Biographies of Loyal and Righteous Samurai' (*Seichū gishi den*)

PRINT TITLE
'Ōboshi Yuranosuke Yoshio'

ARTIST'S SIGNATURE
Ichiyūsai Kuniyoshi ga

ARTIST'S SEAL
Yoshikiri

CENSORS' SEALS
Hama and Kinugasa

American Friends of the British Museum (The Arthur R. Miller Collection) 15201

REFERENCES
Springfield 1980, no. 143; Robinson 1982, S54.1; Weinberg 2000, no. 1.1

Ōboshi Yuranosuke Yoshio (the historical Ōishi Kuranosuke Yoshitaka, aged forty-five at his death) is the senior retainer of deceased Lord Enya and the leader of the plot to avenge him. Seated on a campaign stool, he is holding a war drum, ready to signal the band of loyal retainers to carry out their night attack. He wears the distinctive black and white 'dog-tooth'-patterned jacket and rich brocade trousers customary in this scene. The inscription tells of Yuranosuke's family background and how he came to serve the 'Akao' (Akō) clan. It outlines the events of the vendetta and describes Yuranosuke's prowess in various military arts. Praise is accorded to his sixteen-year-old son, Yoshikane, and his wife (see cat. 45), both of whom sacrificed themselves for the cause. Finally, two stirring lines of poetry are quoted: 'One's lord's life is heavier than ten thousand mountains / One's own life is lighter than a hair' (trans. Alfred H. Marks, in Weinberg 2000).

A label attached to Yuranosuke's spear reads 'Hayano Kanpei, dead in battle'. In the Chūshingura play Kanpei commits ritual suicide in the mistaken belief that he has unintentionally killed his future father-in-law (whereas, in fact, he has killed his father-in-law's murderer). To honour his memory, dead Kanpei's name is nonetheless included among those of the forty-seven loyal retainers.

43

Loyal retainer Sugenoya Masatoshi

1847

Colour woodblock, *ōban*, published by Ebiya Rinnosuke, 37.1 × 25.3 cm

SERIES TITLE
'Biographies of Loyal and Righteous Samurai' (*Seichū gishi den*)

PRINT TITLE
'No. 33, Sugenoya Sannojō Masatoshi'

ARTIST'S SIGNATURE
Ichiyūsai Kuniyoshi ga

ARTIST'S SEAL
Yoshikiri

CENSORS' SEALS
Muramatsu and Yoshimura

American Friends of the British Museum (The Arthur R. Miller Collection) 15233

REFERENCES
Robinson 1982, S54.33; Weinberg 2000, no. I.33

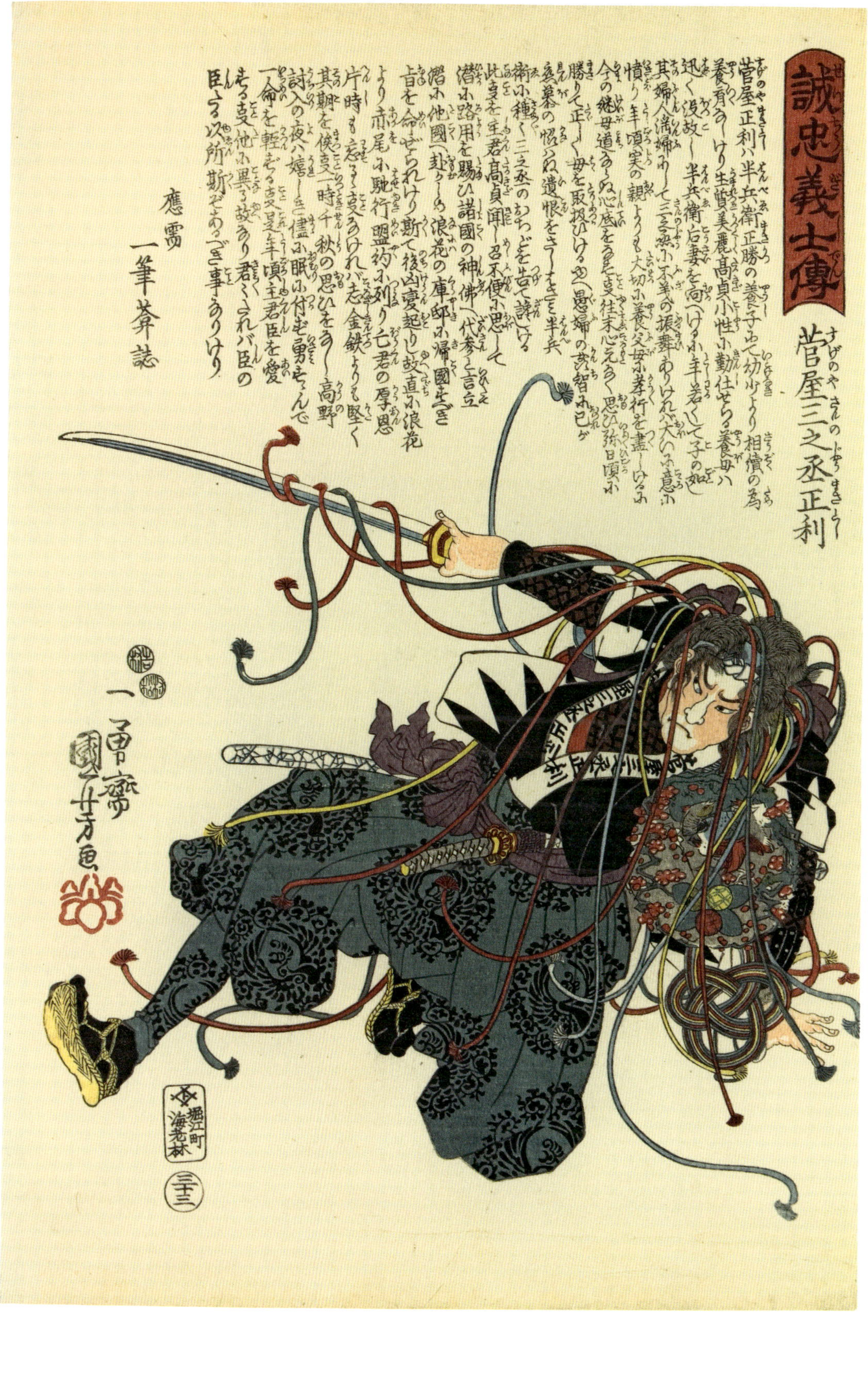

Sugenoya Sannojō Masatoshi (the historical Sugaya Hannojō Masatoshi, aged forty-four at his death) is shown entangled in the tassels of a 'scented ball' (*kusudama*), a decoration hung in rooms to provide fragrance. The tassels part to show his resolute expression as he braces himself on the ground with one hand and one knee, while continuing to point his sword at an unseen enemy. The text tells how he behaved correctly as a youth when his stepmother made improper advances. It also stresses his 'incomparable love' for his lord and relates how, 'when the night of the attack came, he couldn't sleep for joy' (trans. Alfred H. Marks, in Weinberg 2000).

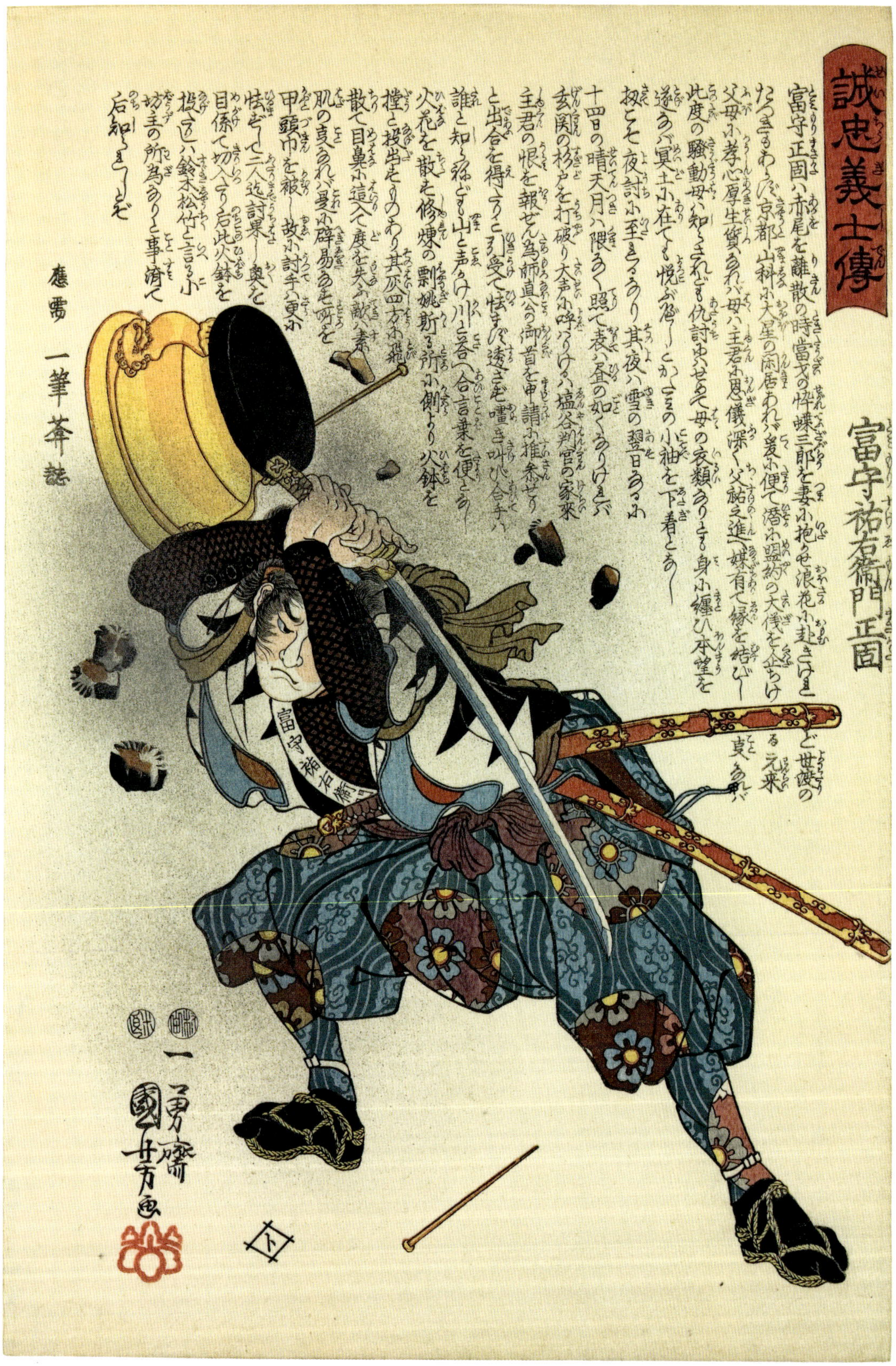

44

Loyal retainer Tomimori Masakata

1847

Colour woodblock, *ōban*, published by Ebiya Rinnosuke, 37.4 × 25.6 cm

SERIES TITLE
'Biographies of Loyal and Righteous Samurai' (*Seichū gishi den*)

PRINT TITLE
'Tomimori Suke'emon Masakata'

ARTIST'S SIGNATURE
Ichiyūsai Kuniyoshi ga

ARTIST'S SEAL
Yoshikiri

CENSORS' SEALS
Mera and Murata

American Friends of the British Museum (The Arthur R. Miller Collection) 15227

REFERENCES
Robinson 1982, S54.27; Amsterdam 1998, no.67; Weinberg 2000, no.I.27; Machida 2003, no.202

Tomimori Suke'emon Masakata (the historical Tominomori Suke'emon Masayori, aged thirty-four at his death) ducks to avoid a metal brazier hurled at him. Coals, ash and a pair of metal fire tongs fly in all directions. As the text says, 'he got [ash] in his nose and mouth' (trans. Alfred H. Marks, in Weinberg 2000). It also mentions how Tomimori wore a piece of his mother's clothing close to his skin during the attack, so 'he would go happily to the land of the dead'.

45

Ishijo, wife of Ōboshi [Yuranosuke] Yoshio

1848

Colour woodblock, *ōban*,
published by Ebiya Rinnosuke,
37.6 × 25.6 cm

SERIES TITLE
'Biographies of Loyal
and Righteous Hearts'
(*Seichū gishin den*)

PRINT TITLE
'No. 1, Ishijo, wife of Ōboshi
Yoshio [Yuranosuke]'
(*Ōboshi Yoshio no naishitsu Ishijo*)

ARTIST'S SIGNATURE
Ichiyūsai Kuniyoshi ga

ARTIST'S SEAL
Yoshikiri

CENSORS' SEALS
Hama and Kinugasa

American Friends of the British Museum
(The Arthur R. Miller Collection) 15401

REFERENCES
Robinson 1982, S56.1;
Weinberg 2000, no. II.1

This is the first print in the series 'Biographies of Loyal and Righteous Hearts' (*Seichū gishin den*), which features the wives, daughters, sons and servants of the loyal retainers. Ishijo is the uncomplaining wife of their leader, Ōboshi Yuranosuke. Samurai women were expected to practise the martial arts, and Ishijo is shown here knocking over a smoking set with a lunge of her halberd. The inscription describes how she faithfully cared for the children, kept the house spotless and safeguarded the family documents while Ōboshi was away planning the vendetta. On hearing of the successful killing of Moronao, she entrusted the children to relatives and followed her husband by committing suicide. The text concludes: 'She was a model samurai wife, a heroic and virtuous woman for all ages' (trans. Alfred H. Marks, in Weinberg 2000).

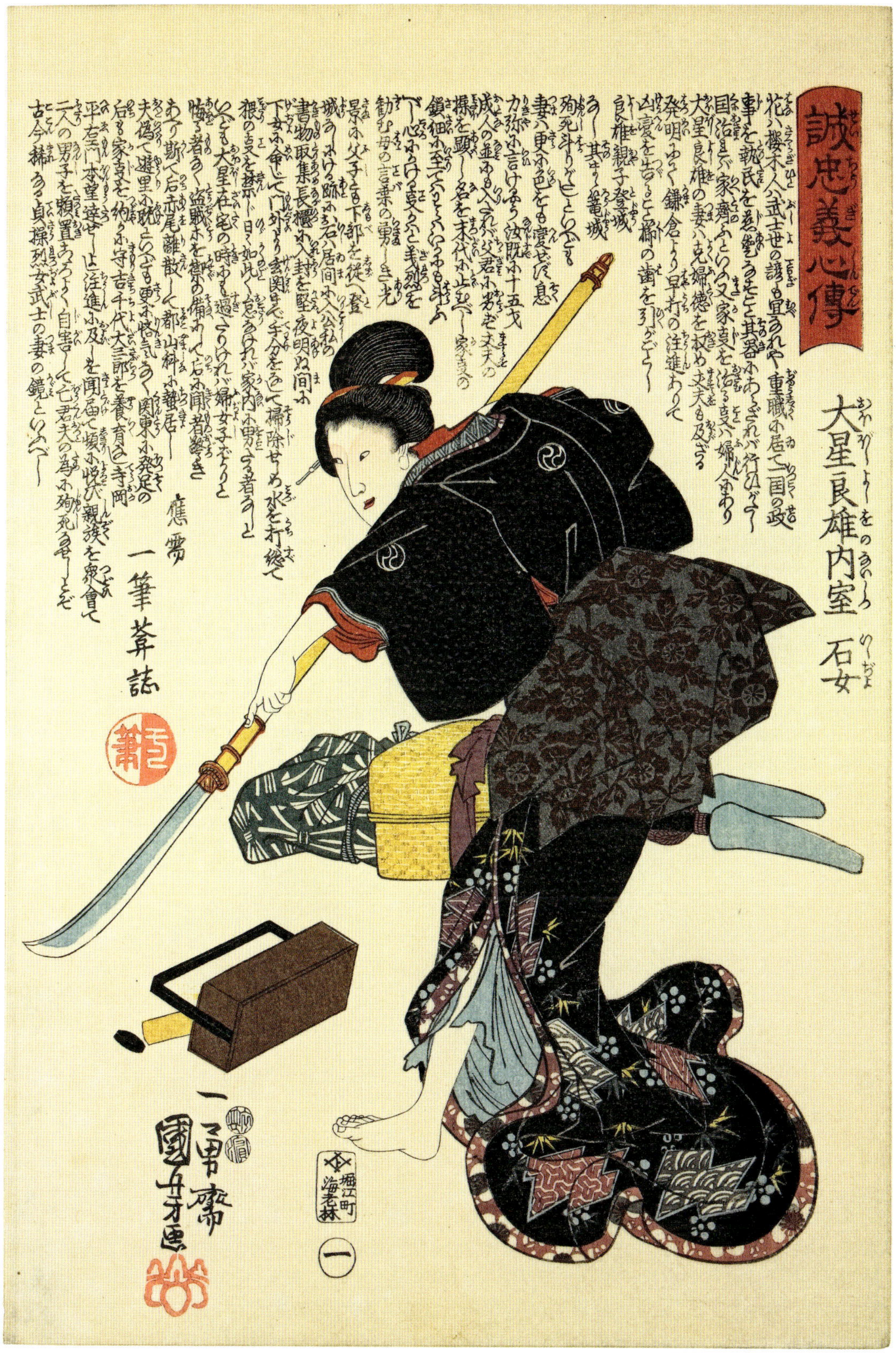

PORTRAITS OF LOYAL AND RIGHTEOUS SAMURAI

(Cats 46–8)

The series features half-length portraits of members of the band of forty-seven loyal retainers, depicted during their revenge attack on the mansion of Kō no Moronao (the historical Kira Yoshinaka) at Honjo in Edo on a snowy night. A haiku poem appears on each print between the series title and the name of the warrior. (For the Akō vendetta/Chūshingura drama, see also the entries for cats 41–5.)

Kuniyoshi's work quite frequently testifies to a strong interest in Western art. That interest is particularly marked in this series: the 'portraits' (*shōzō*) include modelling and chiaroscuro in the facial features, strong foreshortening of some elements and generally plausible poses (albeit within a narrow depth of field). Kuniyoshi's contacts with the photographer Ugai Gyokusen, mentioned in *Utagawa retsuden*, may be significant in this context (see Iwakiri's comments in Nagoya 1996, p.240). Ugai's photography studio in Edo did not open until 1861, yet pioneering experiments with daguerreotypes had begun in Japan as early as 1848 (Houston 2003, p.312).

Individual models have recently been discovered for three of the published designs from the series and one unpublished preliminary drawing of the warrior Yazama Kihei (National Museum of Ethnology, Leiden). Kuniyoshi apparently copied details of various heads and poses from images of the native inhabitants of the West and East Indies included in a printed book imported from the Netherlands: Jan Nieuhof's *Gedenkwaerdige Zee- en Lant-Reize door de voornaemste Landschappen van West en Oost Indien*, published in Amsterdam in 1682 (Katsuhara 2006; see also pp.23–4). He replaced the bows and arrows, spears, blowpipes and scanty clothing of the native peoples with samurai swords and the loyal retainers' distinctive black and white costume.

A further preliminary drawing, depicting the warrior Fuwa Kazuemon, is known (private collection, Germany; illustrated in Amsterdam 1998, no.270). A block-ready drawing (*hanshita-e*) showing the warrior Onodera Kōemon Hidemasa and bearing censorship and date seals has also survived (private collection, Japan; Nagoya 1996, no.308). The fact that this design was abandoned just before publication has led scholars to suggest that Kuniyoshi's experiments with a pronounced Western style may not have found favour with the print-buying public (Suzuki 1992, p.204). The warriors' names on the prints are close to their historical names, reflecting a relaxation in the early 1850s of the ban on explicit mention of their identity (Smith 2003, pp.23–4). Suzuki details changes made to the names of two warriors between early and later printings so as to make them more historically accurate. Impressions with these altered names bear the 'Suri Ō-Hisa' mark of the printer Ōumiya Hisagorō, but Suzuki warns against assuming that all impressions with that mark come from later printings. All twelve published designs are reproduced in colour in Edo-Tokyo 1999, no.16, pp.170–1.

46

Ōboshi Yuranosuke, leader of the loyal retainers

1852

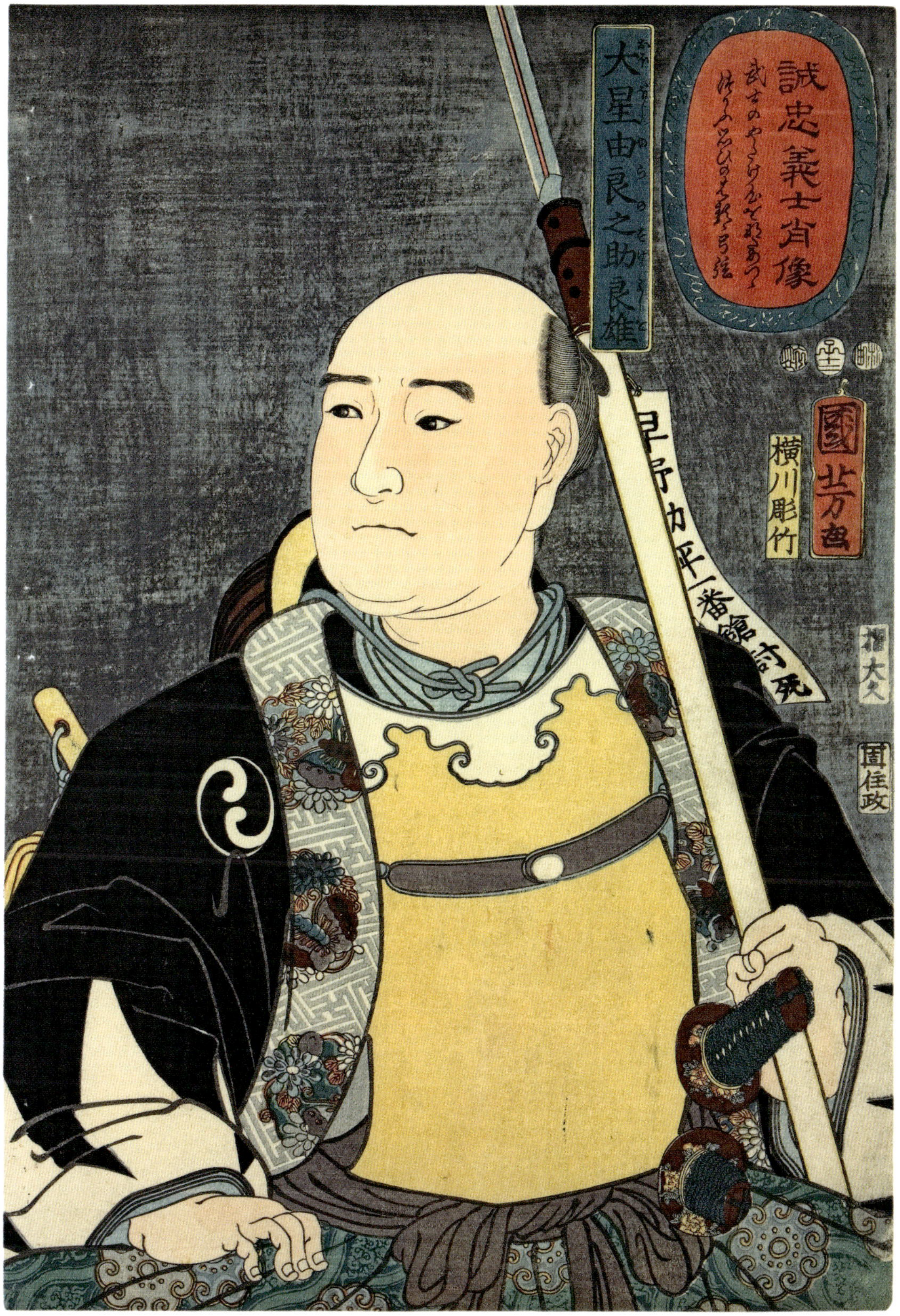

Colour woodblock, *ōban*, published by Sumiyoshiya Masagorō, 35.8 × 24.9 cm

SERIES TITLE
'Portraits of Loyal and Righteous Samurai' (*Seichū gishi shōzō*)

PRINT TITLE
'Ōboshi Yuranosuke Yoshio'

ARTIST'S SIGNATURE
Kuniyoshi ga (in rectangular *Yoshi* cartouche)

BLOCK-CUTTER
Yokokawa Hori-Take

PRINTER
Ōumiya Hisagorō

CENSORS' SEALS
Kinugasa and Murata

DATE SEAL
12th month, 1852

American Friends of the British Museum (The Arthur R. Miller Collection) 11601

REFERENCES
Robinson 1961, no. 69; Springfield 1968, no. 128; Riccar 1978, no. 66; Springfield 1980, no. 187, pl. 8; Robinson 1982, no. S78.1; Yamaguchi 1991, Kuniyoshi no. 57; MSU 1991, no. 70; Suzuki 1992, no. 162; Nagoya 1996, no. 81; Machida 2003, no. 204; Isao 2008, p. 78

As befits the leader of the band of loyal retainers, Ōboshi Yuranosuke is portrayed as a man with noble features. Calm determination can be detected in his steady gaze and the slightly clenched line of his mouth. He appears to be seated on a campaign chair, spear leaning against his shoulder and helmet slung around the back of his head (cf. cat. 42). White lead pigment mixed with blue in the background has tarnished to create a pleasing texture. There are a number of distinctly Western stylistic elements: the slight, sensitive shading of the face around the eyes, which serves to highlight the bridge of Yuranosuke's nose; the white spot of light reflected in the pupils of his eyes (common to the whole series); and the severe foreshortening of the hilts of his twin swords. No other print in the series suggests the influence of photographs more strongly.

47

Loyal retainer Nakamura Masatatsu

1852

Colour woodblock, *ōban*, published by Sumiyoshiya Masagorō, 37.6 × 25.9 cm

SERIES TITLE
'Portraits of Loyal and Righteous Samurai' (*Seichū gishi shōzō*)

PRINT TITLE
'Nakamura Kansuke Masatatsu'

ARTIST'S SIGNATURE
Kuniyoshi ga
(in rectangular *Yoshi* cartouche)

BLOCK-CUTTER
Yokokawa Hori-Take

PRINTER
Ōumiya Hisagorō

CENSORS' SEALS
Kinugasa and Murata

DATE SEAL
12th month, 1852

American Friends of the British Museum (The Arthur R. Miller Collection) 11605

REFERENCES
Robinson 1982, no. S78.6; Suzuki 1992, no. 164; Itabashi 1994, Kuniyoshi no. 42; Mainichi Shinbunsha 1995, no. 64; Nagoya 1996, no. 82; Amsterdam 1998, no. 98; Ōta 1999, no. 78; Smithsonian 2002, no. 93; Isao 2008, p. 78

Nakamura Kansuke Masatatsu (the retainer's historical name, sometimes read as Masatoki) shields his face with one hand and the hilt of his sword in order to fend off a hand-brazier (*te-aburi*) that has been flung at him. White pigment has been blown onto the surface of the print to represent the cloud of ash from the brazier. Masatatsu bites his lower lip and squints to prevent the ash getting in his eyes. With its vivid sense of a powerful body turning in space, the print has rightly been lauded as one of the most dynamic in the series. A telling detail is the pierced paulownia design in the wall of the brazier: it represents the family crest of Kō no Moronao, soon to be put to death.

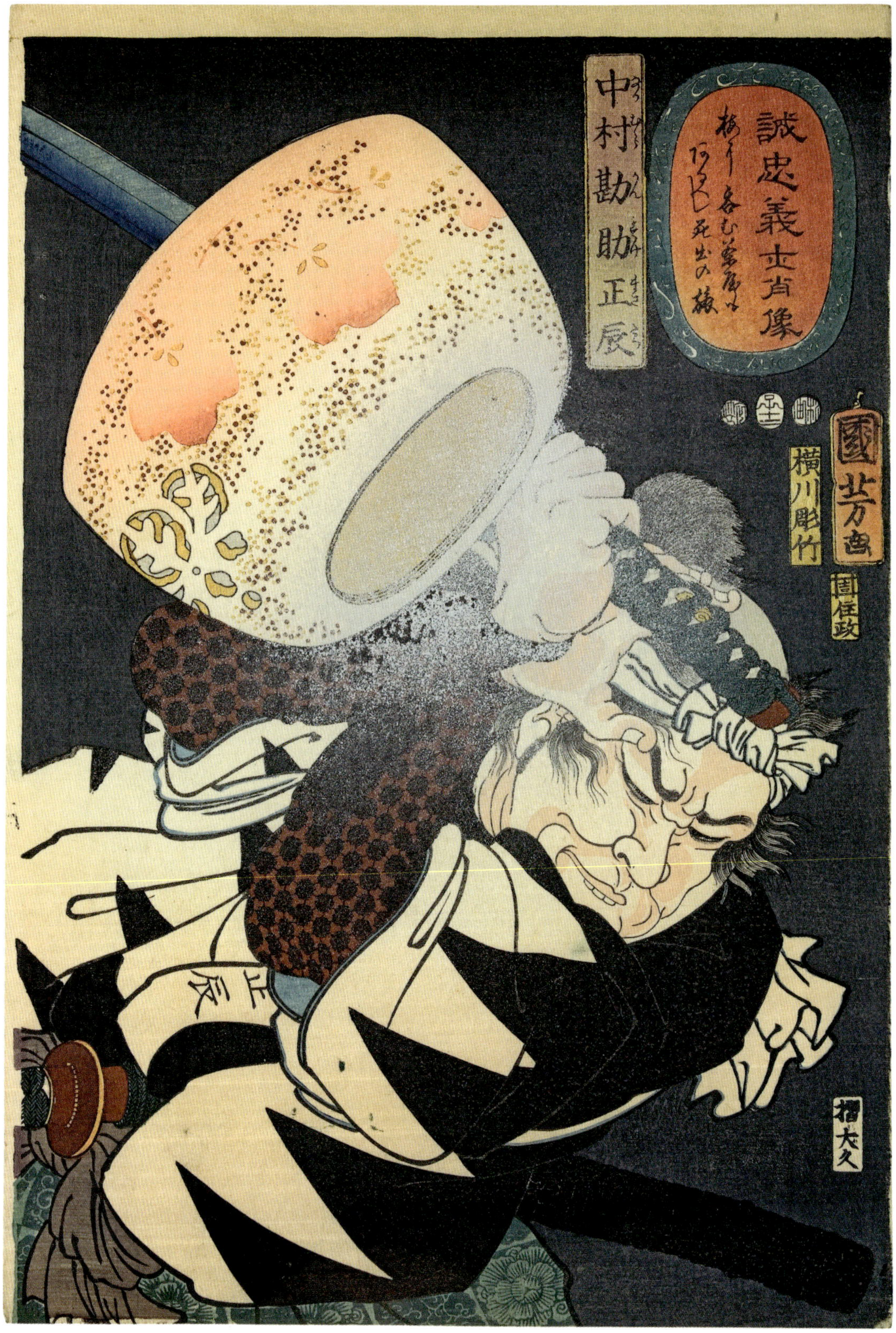

48

Loyal retainer Yatō Norikane

1852

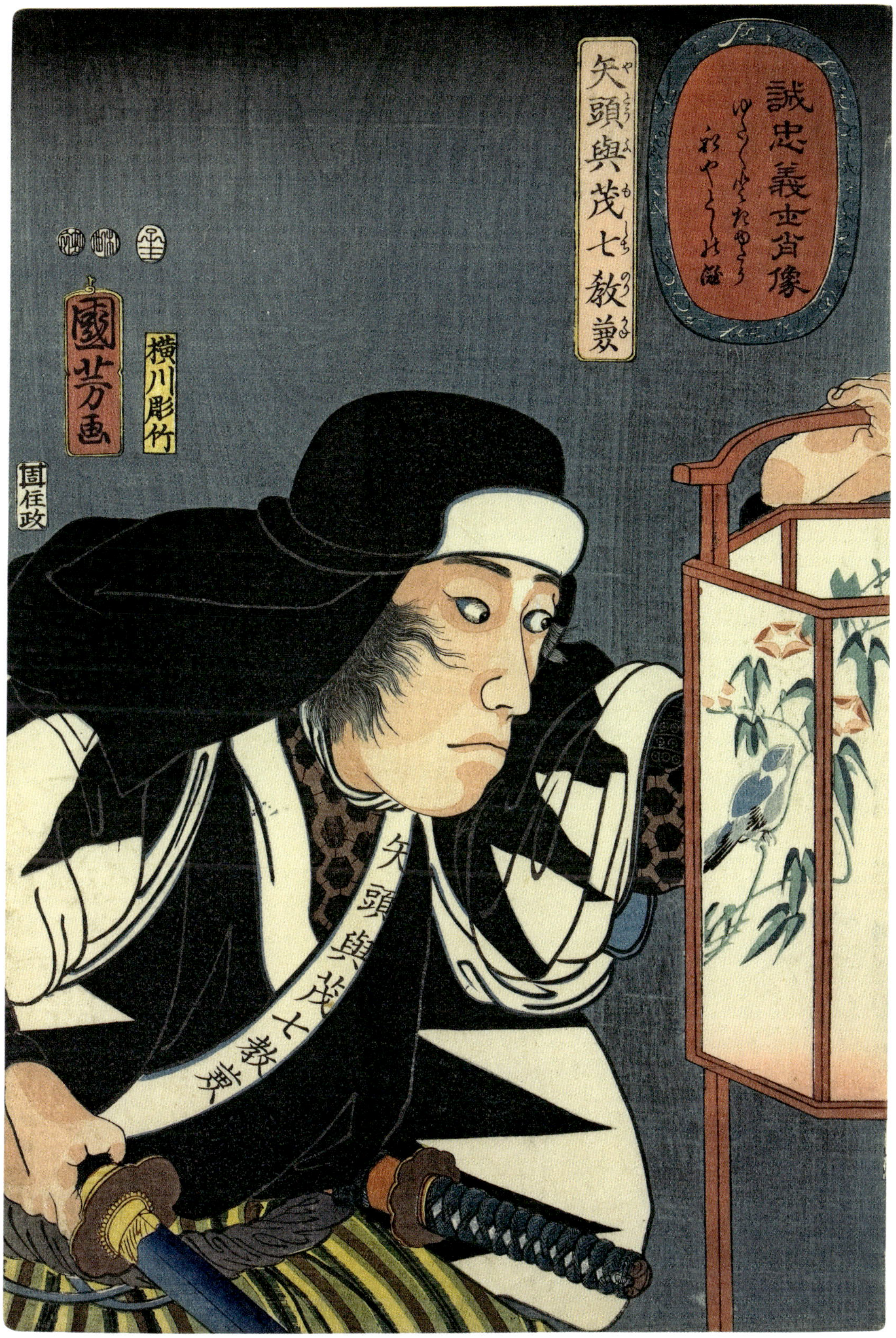

Colour woodblock, *ōban*, published by Sumiyoshiya Masagorō, 36.3 × 24.7 cm

SERIES TITLE
'Portraits of Loyal and Righteous Samurai' (*Seichū gishi shōzō*)

PRINT TITLE
'Yatō Yomoshichi Norikane'

ARTIST'S SIGNATURE
Kuniyoshi ga
(in rectangular *Yoshi* cartouche)

BLOCK-CUTTER
Yokokawa Hori-Take

CENSORS' SEALS
Kinugasa and Murata

DATE SEAL
12th month, 1852

American Friends of the British Museum (The Arthur R. Miller Collection) 11602

REFERENCES
Riccar 1978, no. 67; Springfield 1980, no. 188; Robinson 1982, no. S78.2; Nagoya 1996, no. 83

Yatō Yomoshichi Norikane (historical name Yatō Uemonshichi Norikane), who was only eighteen at the time of the attack, stares apprehensively as he holds up a standing lantern painted with a design of a bird among morning glory. Yet his firm grip on the scabbard of his sword shows resolution.

49

The loyal retainers attack Moronao's mansion at night

1851–52

Colour woodblock, *ōban* triptych, published by Tsujiokaya Bunsuke, 37.6 × 25.4 [R], 37.5 × 25.5 [C], 37.7 × 25.3 cm [L]

PRINT TITLE
'Treasury of the Loyal Retainers: Picture of the Night Attack' (*Chūshingura youchi no zu*)

ARTIST'S SIGNATURE
Ichiyūsai Kuniyoshi ga

CENSORS' SEALS
Kinugasa and Murata

American Friends of the British Museum (The Arthur R. Miller Collection) 18805

REFERENCES
Robinson 1982, no. T260

The attack by the band of forty-seven loyal retainers on the mansion of Kira Yoshinaka at Honjo in Edo began at about 3 am on the fifteenth day of the twelfth month, 1702, a snowy night. By 6 am it was all over. With Kira's severed head stuck on a pike, the retainers marched across the city to the temple of Sengaku-ji at Takanawa to present it to the grave of their dead lord, Asano Naganori.

This triptych shows the culmination of the vendetta, largely in the manner of theatrical versions of the tale and citing the theatrical names of the characters. The events depicted in the print take place in Act Eleven of the puppet/Kabuki play *Kanadehon chūshingura*. The loyal retainers are all dressed in robes with the familiar black and white 'dog-tooth' design. On the right sheet Kō no Moronao (the historical Kira Yoshinaka) has finally been discovered hiding in a wooden shed, dressed in his night clothes and not defending himself with arms or armour. He has refused the offer of a dagger to commit an honourable suicide, so Ōboshi Yuranosuke, Ōboshi's son Rikiya and other members of the band are about to kill him and cut off his head. In the background, fighting still rages throughout the rooms and corridors of Moronao's mansion, the sliding doors conveniently removed so as to provide a good view.

For an earlier, perspective view showing the initial stages of the attack, see cat. 79.

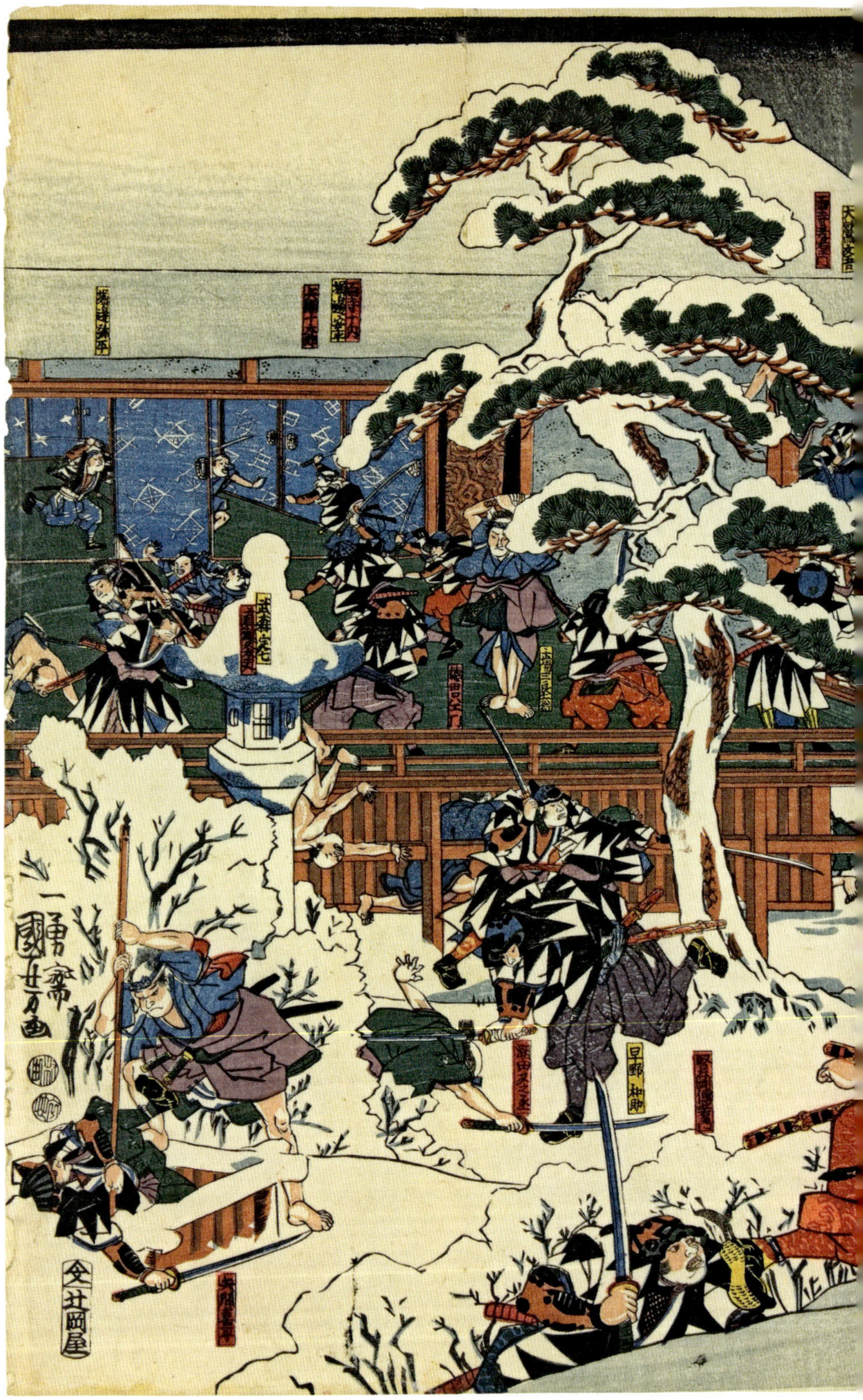

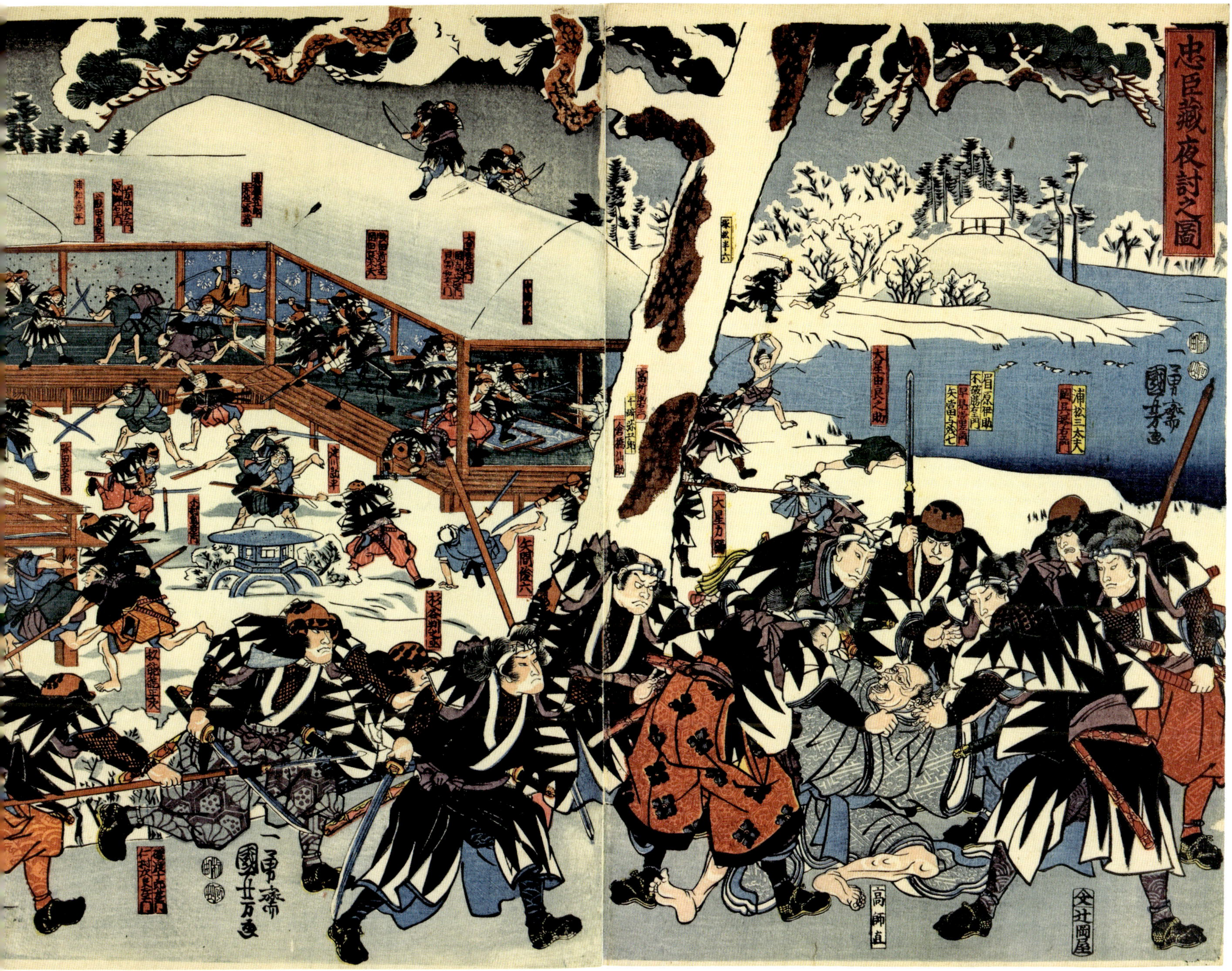
忠臣蔵夜討之圖
大星由良之助
浦松三太夫
大星力弥
高師直
一勇斎國芳画
一勇斎國芳画

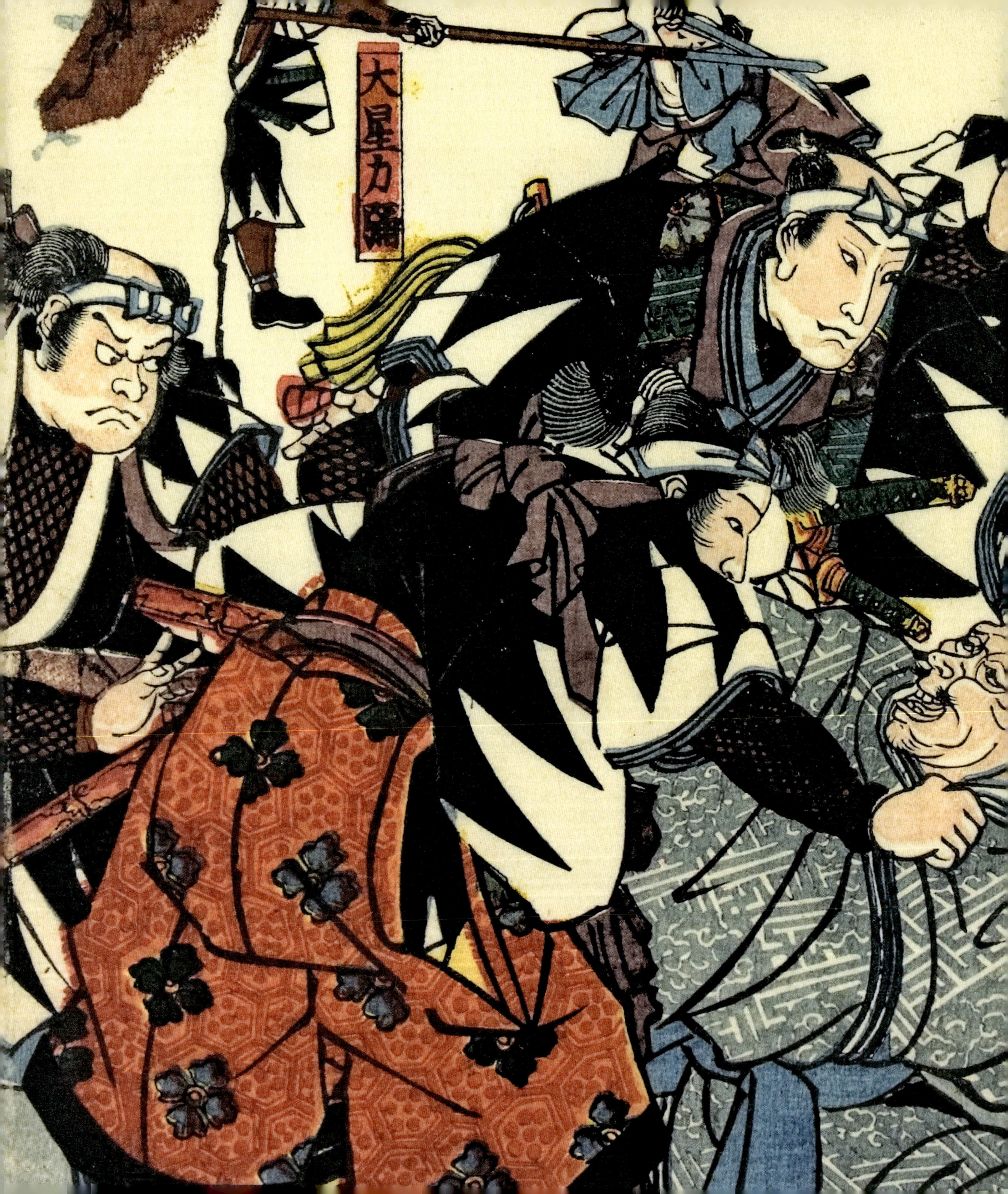
大星力彌

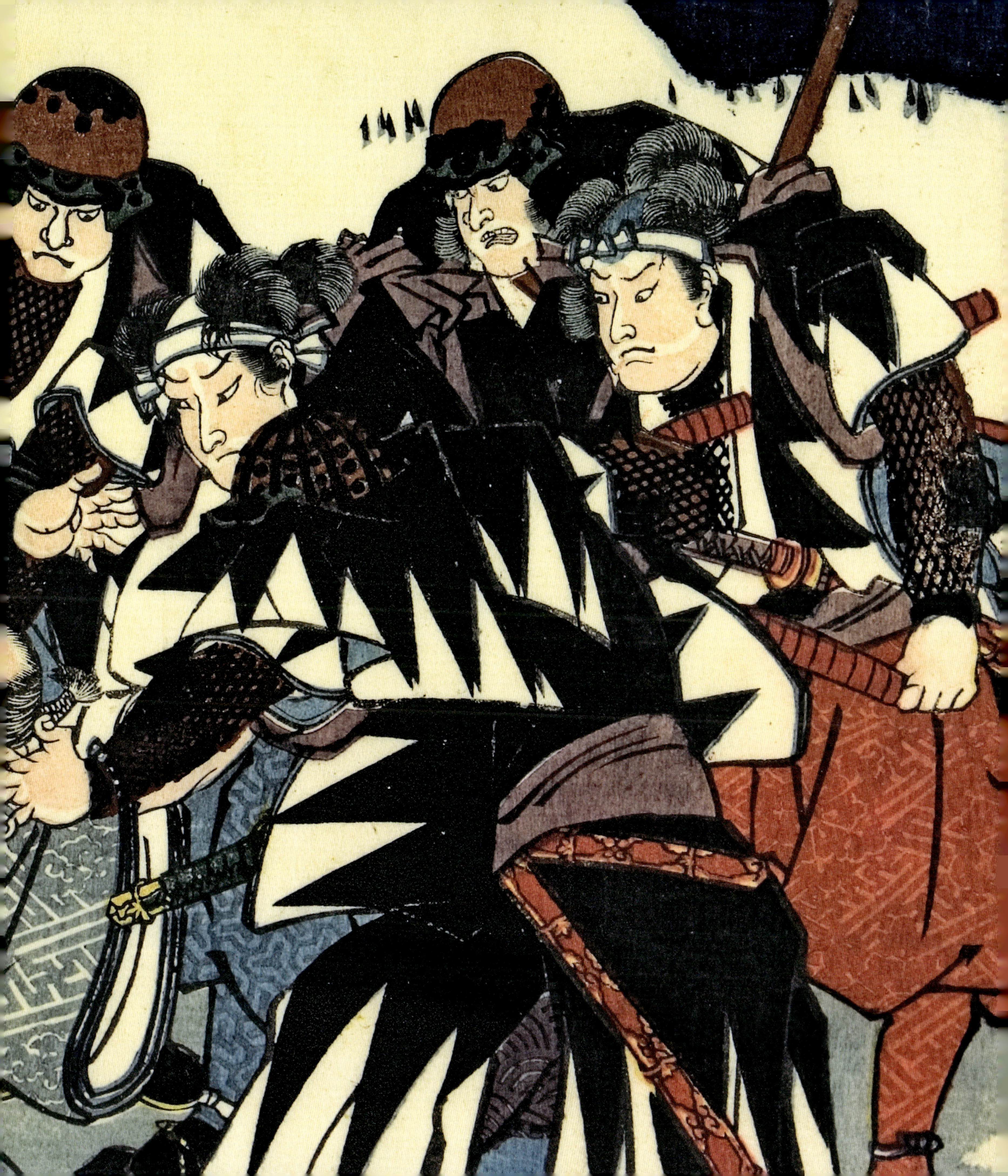

2

BEAUTIFUL WOMEN

The essential dynamic of 'pictures of beautiful women' (*bijin-ga*) was to present a beautiful woman dressed in fine robes in a seductive pose for the delectation of the viewer. The genre had been at the heart of the ukiyo-e ('pictures of the floating world') school since it first developed at the end of the seventeenth century. By Kuniyoshi's times the floating world's economy of desire was sustained by women belonging to a number of professional categories: high-ranked courtesans of Yoshiwara (the single officially authorised pleasure quarter), prostitutes in unlicensed quarters, geisha (entertainers), bathhouse women and shop girls. Different categories of woman were patronised by different townsmen, according to their degree of wealth, and even by some samurai. Images of nudity were rare outside the (prolific) genre of explicitly erotic 'spring pictures' (*shunga*), which gloried in the beauty and vigour of coupling bodies, male and female.

Kuniyoshi's images of beautiful women were unadventurous during the early years of his career, in the 1820s and '30s: the genre was basically considered the preserve of his senior rivals, Kunisada and Eisen. A half-length portrait of a geisha, one of a group of floating-world female types, is representative of this period (cat. 52).

Things changed when new publishing regulations were introduced in the sixth month of 1842 as part of the moralistic Tenpō reforms. The regulations dealt a major blow to the *bijin-ga* genre by banning images of courtesans and geisha, two of its staples. However, the order to 'compose [works] in accordance with [the values of] loyalty and fidelity, to promote virtue among children and women' galvanised Kuniyoshi and his publishers into producing many innovative series featuring famous women from history and ordinary women at work.

'Biographies of Wise Women and Virtuous Wives' (*Kenjo reppu den*; cats 53–5) promoted the exemplary behaviour of heroines such as Hatsuhana, who prayed for a hundred days under a freezing waterfall to cure her husband's illness (cat. 53). This did not prevent Kuniyoshi and other artists being summoned to the city magistrate's office in the third month of 1843: the authorities objected to the fact that women in this and similar series were shown 'in contemporary fashions' (*imayō sugata*; see also p. 24).

The prints in 'Pride of Edo: Comparison of Famous Products' (*Edo jiman meibutsu-kurabe*) are named after neighbourhoods of Edo and the products that could be purchased there, but the focus is clearly on the charming women associated with those products (cat. 59). In designing the images, Kuniyoshi copied several figures from works by Kitagawa Utamaro (d. 1806), who in the 1790s and early 1800s had perfected the art of presenting ordinary working women in an alluring way.

Single standing figures of beautiful women are the most common subject in hanging scroll paintings by artists of the ukiyo-e school. Such pictures were sometimes individually commissioned. Of the sixty-two paintings by Kuniyoshi currently recorded, half show beautiful women (cat. 78).

ELEGANT WOMEN'S *WATER MARGIN*: FROM ONE HUNDRED AND EIGHT FIGURES

(Cats 50, 51)

Kuniyoshi enjoyed enormous success from about 1827 with the series of single-sheet prints of Chinese heroes 'One of the 108 Heroes of the Popular *Water Margin*' (cats 3–10). Soon he was commissioned by two groups of poets of 'crazy verse' (*kyōka*) to design the present series of de luxe prints, or *surimono*, on a related theme, with the poems printed at the top. The basic idea was to show the customs of beautiful women of Kuniyoshi's day, each one with some clever allusion to a hero of the *Water Margin* story. Asano Shūgō has so far identified twenty designs, making this the largest *surimono* series undertaken by the artist (Nagoya 1996, pp. 17–19, 279). Asano divides them into three groups, which he dates tentatively: 1) eight prints of *c.* 1829 bearing two hand-impressed seals, the title seal 'From a Set of One Hundred and Eight' (*Hyaku hachiban no uchi*) under the emblem of the Hisakataya poetry group, which is thought to be a stylised version of the character *amalame* ('heaven'), and the seal of the printer Shinzō; 2) seven more designs for the Hisakataya group, dating from *c.* 1830 and including next to a woodblock-printed title seal the name of the Chinese hero alluded to, some with the Shinzō seal, some without; 3) a five-sheet design for the Taiko poetry club, each sheet showing the drum emblem of the club and the additional title 'Five-sheet Print of Collecting Brine' (*Shiokumi goban-tsuzuki*), both woodblock-printed in red.

Courtesan with a pipe (cat. 51) comes from group 1 and relates to the Chinese hero Shi Jin (Jap. Shi Shin; Chiba 1997, p. 192). The next three *surimono*, which depict women gathering brine to make salt (cat. 50), belong to group 3 and form the three left-hand designs of the five-sheet print (illus. below). The two remaining sheets (not exhibited) show women linked to the heroes Li Jun (Jap. Ri Shun; right of centre; Cracow National Museum, Poland) and Ruan Xiaoqi (Jap. Gen Shōshichi; far right; Gerhard Pulverer Collection, Germany; Nihon Ukiyo-e Kyōkai 1990, no. 2–19). Two sets of all five sheets have been published, one formerly in the collection of Sidney C. Ward (Ward 1976, no. 96), the other illustrated in GUDHJ (vol. 9, 1981, nos 11–15). Asano observes that the five Taiko club *surimono* are known both with and without the Shinzō printer's seal. In general he thinks that specimens with the hand-impressed printer's seal may derive from slightly earlier printings. He also notes that three of the five designs – Ri Shun, Ruan Xiao'er (cat. 50.1) and Ruan Xiaowu (cat. 50.3) – exist in alternative printings with different poems (a not uncommon practice with *surimono*). Keyes records a 'Group A' copy of the sheet on the far left (cat. 50.3) that was made by Tsumura Isakichi in Akashi, near Kobe, in the 1890s (Keyes 1985, p. 518, no. 122).

Surimono were the product of close collaboration among the poets, who commissioned the prints and provided the poems; the printer, who sometimes supervised general production in addition to printing the sheets; and the artist, who contributed the design. The poems contain witty allusions to the chosen theme and celebrate the joys of spring, often by engaging in wordplay. Similarly, the artist may make subtle visual references to the theme in his design. Decoding such hidden verbal and visual clues was one of the pleasures of the New Year holiday for members of small poetry groups (*ren*) and large poetry clubs (*gawa*), who exchanged these special prints among themselves.

The fundamental link between the five-sheet design of women collecting brine and the *Water Margin* tale was that the Chinese heroes alluded to in the prints, who were among the earliest to join the Liangshan band, all had connections to salt, the sea and water (Klompmakers 1998, nos 13a, 14, 35, 58, 59): the three Ruan brothers were salt smugglers before they became fishermen, Li Jun was a good swimmer who could stay underwater for a long time and Zhang Heng was a ferryman. People of the time intimately familiar with the novel will surely have picked up on many other subtle pictorial references, contained in poses, accoutrements, patterns on the women's robes and so forth (see the entries for cats 9, 11).

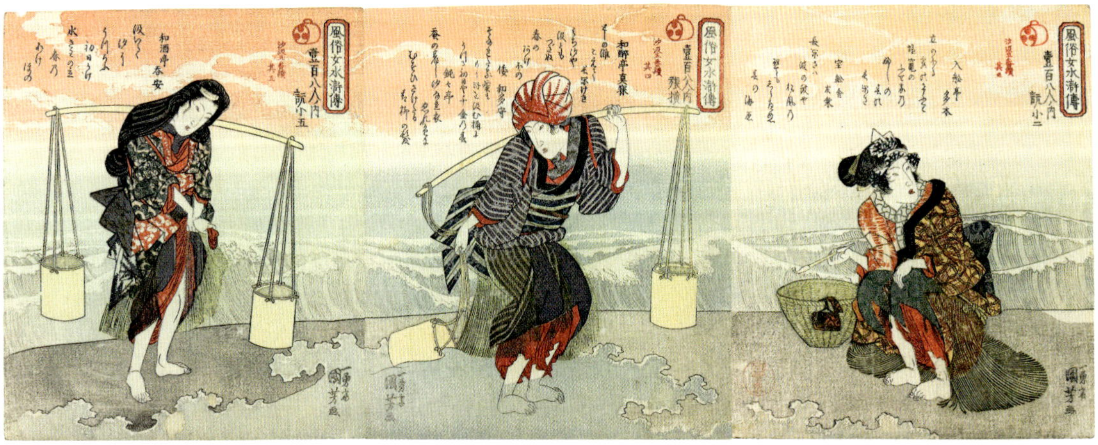

50.1

Crouching woman holding a pipe

1828–30

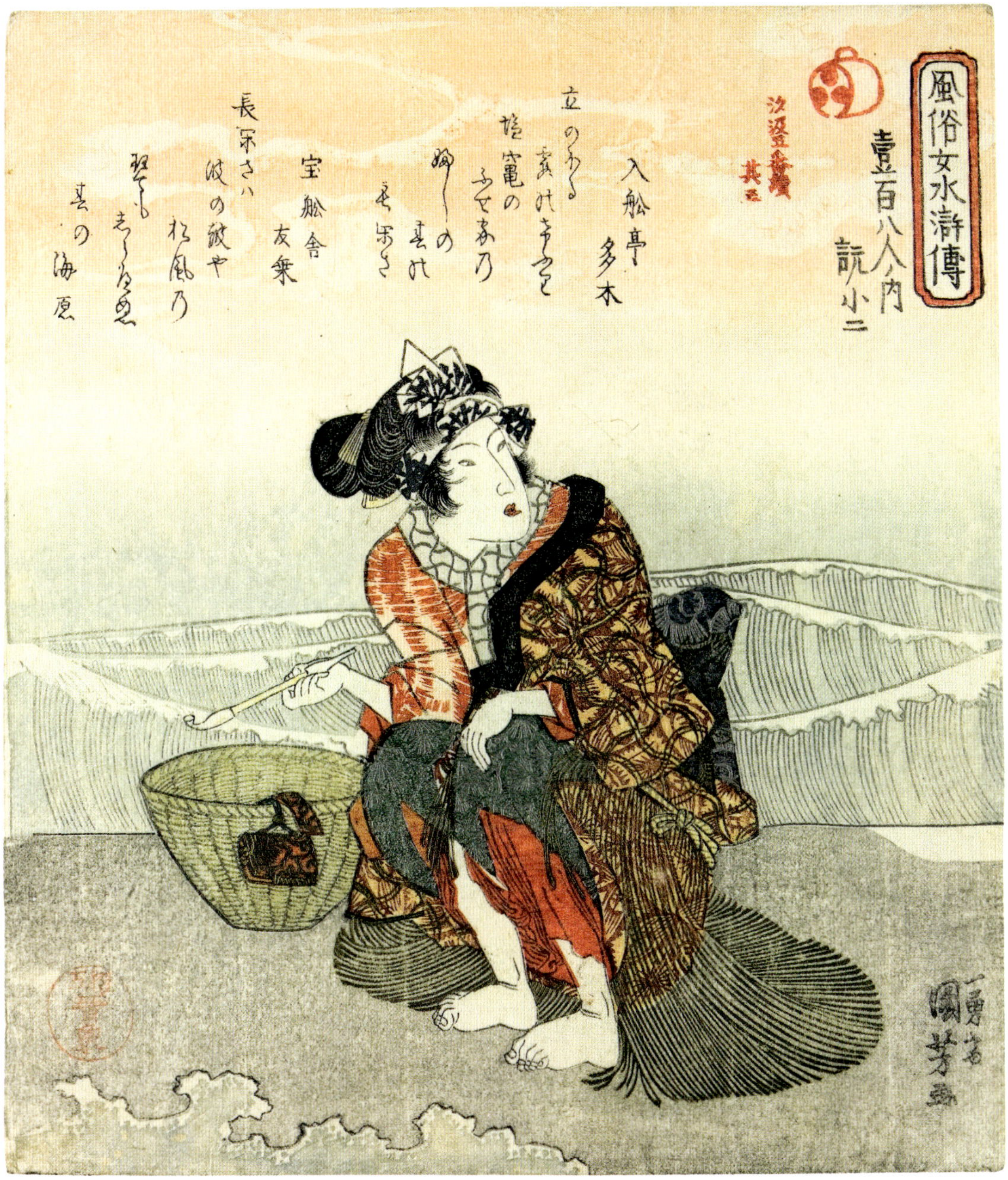

Colour woodblock with embossing and metallic pigment, *shikishi-ban surimono*, 21.2 × 18.6 cm

SERIES TITLE
'Elegant Women's *Water Margin*: From One Hundred and Eight Figures' (*Fūzoku onna Suikoden, ipyakku-hachinin no uchi*)

PRINT TITLE
'Gen Shōji [Ruan Xiao'er]'

ADDITIONAL PRINT TITLE
'Five-sheet print of Collecting Brine, No. 3' (*Shiokumi goban-tsuzuki, sono san*)

ARTIST'S SIGNATURE
Ichiyūsai Kuniyoshi ga

PRINTER
Shinzō

American Friends of the British Museum (The Arthur R. Miller Collection) 21801

REFERENCES
Ward 1976, no. 96; Hillier 1976, no. 845; Nagoya 1996, p. 279, no. 18; Amsterdam 1998, p. 250

This is the centre sheet of the five-part composition, as suggested by the woman's contrapposto pose as she looks back over one shoulder. The title identifies her with the Chinese hero Ruan Xiao'er, the eldest of three warrior brothers who had started out as salt smugglers. Her clothes, though richly patterned, are workmanlike: she wears a cotton headband, an outer robe (from which she has slipped one arm for ease of movement) and the straw skirt common to all the women, here printed with brass powder to suggest gold. On the skirts of her robe a metallic pigment, probably containing tin, has been used to imitate silver. The same pigment appears in the embossed waves, where it reflects the light evocatively. A soft pink sky represents the glow of dawn on New Year's day. The woman is smoking a pipe; a pipe case and tobacco pouch made of brocade or leather hang over the rim of a woven bamboo basket.

The first poem on the far-right sheet makes reference to Akashi, a famous beach not far from the modern city of Kobe which, together with nearby Suma, featured frequently in classical tales. In one such story the sisters Matsukaze and Murasame, who made salt there, were poignantly abandoned by their courtier lover Ariwara no Yukihira. The costumes and general elegance of the female figures in the prints, and the mention of *matsukaze* (pine breeze) in one of the poems, deliberately echo that medieval narrative. The authors of the two poems style themselves Nyūsentei Ōki and Hōsensha Tomonori. Their verses describe the relaxed calm of a beautiful spring morning, smoke rising from a salt kiln like mist, waves lapping on a sea that stretches far into a distance, and a breeze passing through the pines like the sound of a transverse harp (*koto*).

This is the only one of the three sheets that bears the hand-impressed seal of the printer Shinzō and it may thus be a slightly earlier printing than the other two.

50.3

Woman wringing out the hem of her robe

1828–30

Colour woodblock with embossing and metallic pigments, *shikishi-ban surimono*, 21.2 × 18.5 cm

SERIES TITLE
'Elegant Women's *Water Margin*: From One Hundred and Eight Figures' (*Fūzoku onna Suikoden, ipyakku-hachinin no uchi*)

PRINT TITLE
'Gen Shōgo [Ruan Xiaowu]'

ADDITIONAL PRINT TITLE
'Five-sheet Print of Collecting Brine, No. 5' (*Shiokumi goban-tsuzuki, sono go*)

ARTIST'S SIGNATURE
Ichiyūsai Kuniyoshi ga

American Friends of the British Museum (The Arthur R. Miller Collection) 21803

REFERENCES
Ward 1976, no. 96; Kruml 1989, no. 132; Baur 1994, no. G425; Nagoya 1996, p. 279, no. 20; Amsterdam 1998, p. 250

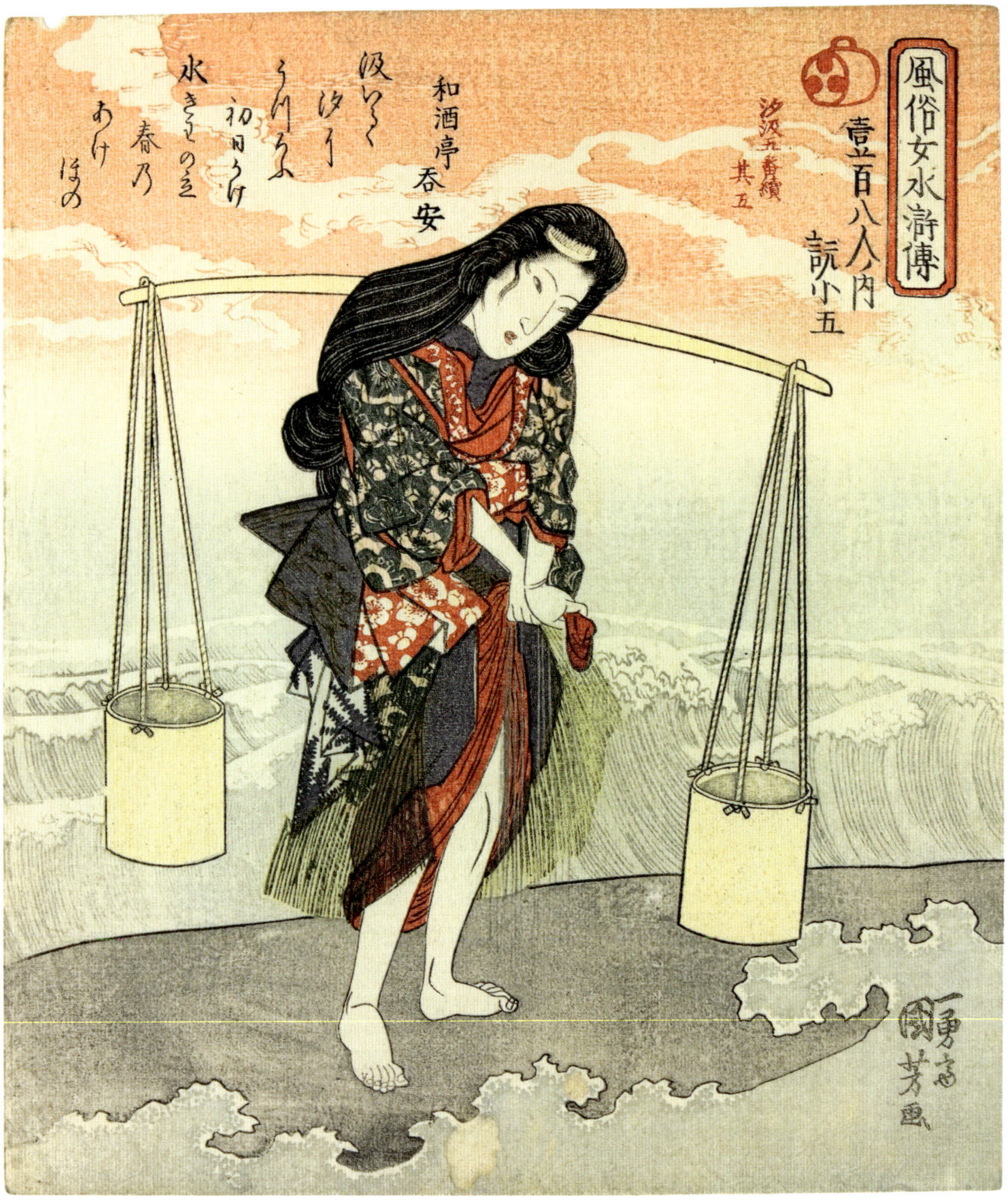

This design appears at the far left of the five-part composition. Perhaps showered with sea spray, the woman wrings out the skirt of her red undergarment. Her hair hangs loose and voluptuous. She is likened in the title to the hero Ruan Xiaowu, whom Kuniyoshi elsewhere depicted fighting underwater (cat. 9). The poem is by Washutei Nomiyasu ('Likes to Drink at the Saké Inn'). It describes the transient light of the New Year's first morning, reflected in the brine that the woman is collecting while the dawn rises over the water's edge.

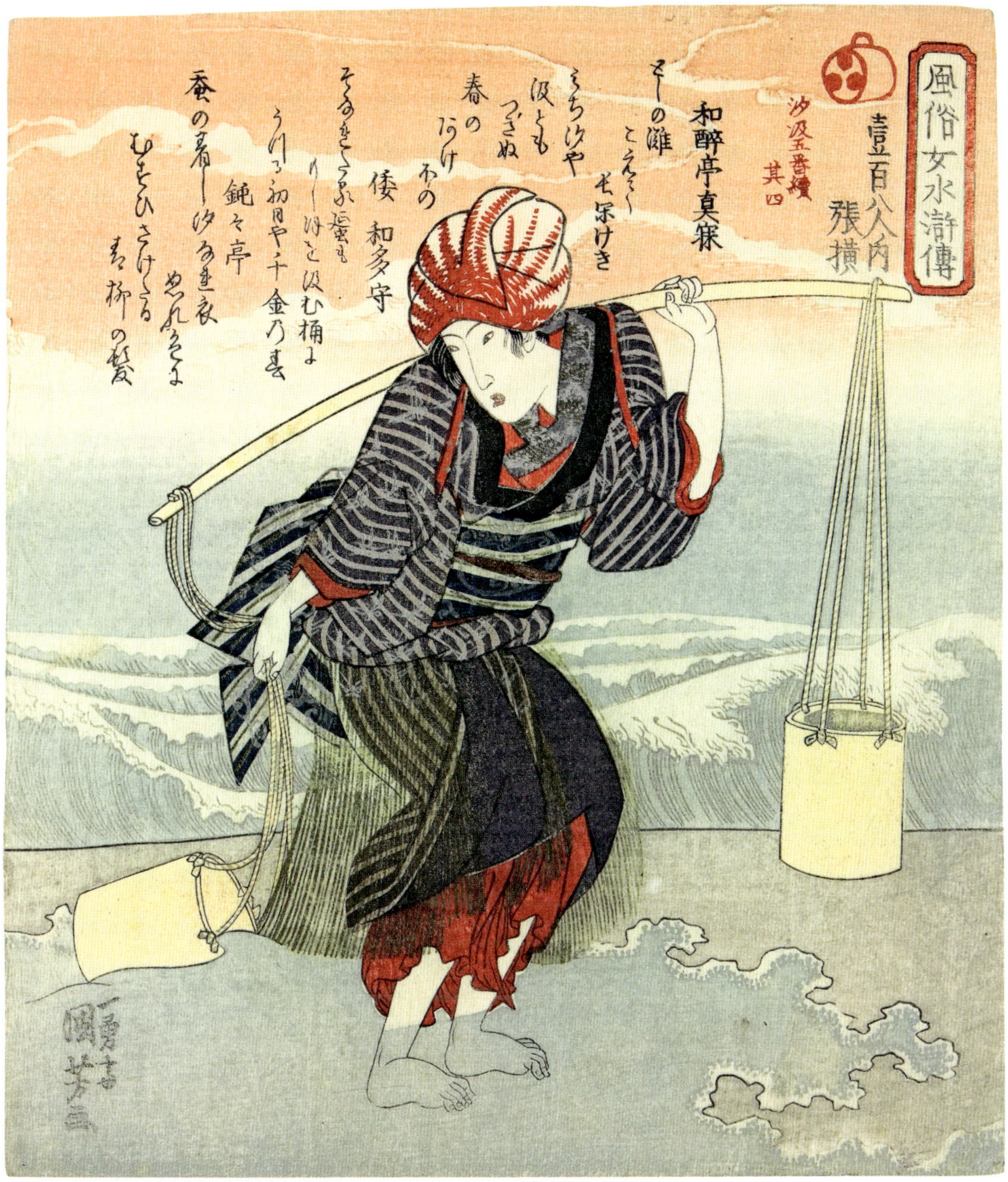

50.2

Woman gathering brine for salt

1828–30

Colour woodblock with embossing and metallic pigments, *shikishi-ban surimono*, 21.1 × 18.7 cm

SERIES TITLE
'Elegant Women's *Water Margin*: From One Hundred and Eight Figures' (*Fūzoku onna Suikoden, ipyakku-hachinin no uchi*).

PRINT TITLE
'Chōō [Zhang Heng]'

ADDITIONAL PRINT TITLE
'Five-sheet print of Collecting Brine, No.4' (*Shiokumi goban-tsuzuki, sono yon*)

ARTIST'S SIGNATURE
Ichiyūsai Kuniyoshi ga

American Friends of the British Museum (The Arthur R. Miller Collection) 21802

REFERENCES
Nihon Ukiyo-e Kyōkai 1974, no. 218; Ward 1976, no. 96; Nagoya 1996, p. 279, no. 19; Amsterdam 1998, p. 250

This sheet occupies the centre-left position in the five-part design. Wearing a head-cloth, the woman scoops brine into one of the buckets balanced on her yoke. Her feet are seen through the transparent pale blue water of the tide pool in which she is standing. The pink and light blue in the sky have survived in pristine condition, even stronger than in cat. 50.1, and metallic pigments are used extensively, as in cat. 50.3.

The woman is identified in the title with the warrior Zhang Heng, a ferryman and strong swimmer (see also cat. 11). The three verses (right to left) are by Wasuitei Masane, Yamato Watamori and Dondontei respectively. They describe how at dawn in springtime the tide is so high and the atmosphere so calm that the brine cannot be fully scooped. Spring is priceless, like the reflection of the first rising sun of the New Year in the water in the bucket. The salt-gatherers' long, untied tresses are wet and alluring, resembling the new, pale green branches of a willow. Matsuri ga Wataru ('Parade Passes By') was the leader of the Taiko ('Drum') club of *kyōka* poets, whose verses appear on all five sheets. He also used the name Dondontei, in imitation of the sound of a drum.

51
Courtesan with a pipe
1828–30

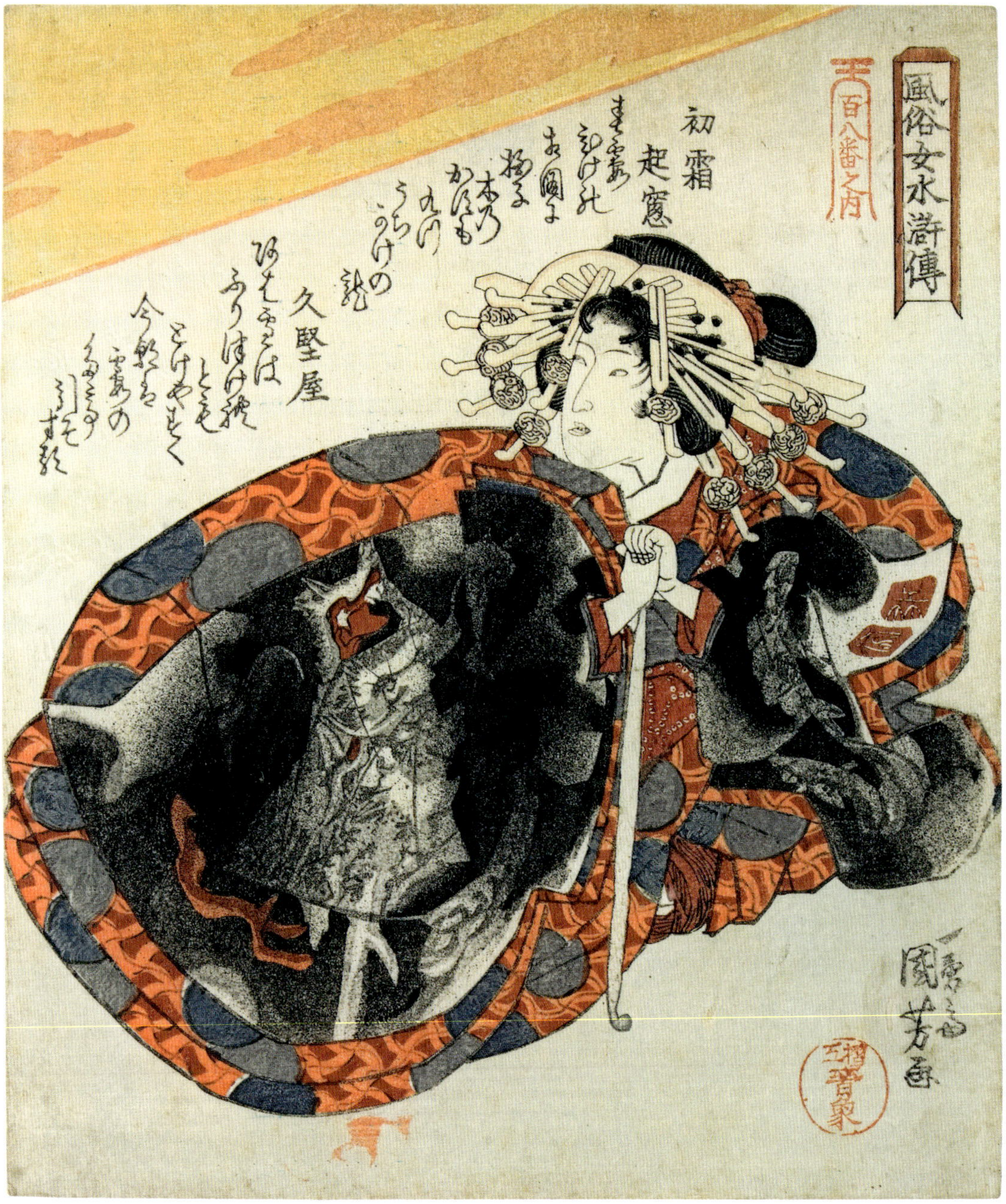

Colour woodblock with embossing and metallic pigments, *shikishi-ban surimono*, 21.2 × 18.3 cm

SERIES TITLE
'Elegant Women's *Water Margin*: One Hundred and Eight Sheets' (*Fūzoku onna Suikoden, hyakuhachi-ban no uchi*)

ARTIST'S SIGNATURE
Ichiyūsai Kuniyoshi ga

PRINTER
Shinzō

American Friends of the British Museum (The Arthur R. Miller Collection) 21701

REFERENCES
Illing 1978, no. 17 (right); Nagoya 1996, p. 279, no. 8; Amsterdam 1998, p. 251

The woman is identified as a high-ranking courtesan by an elaborate arrangement of heavy carved hairpins and combs. She rests her hands on the mouthpiece of a long pipe. Her surcoat (*uchikake*) is decorated with a striking design featuring a large dragon coiling its body amid thunderclouds, its open mouth pointing upwards. This motif alludes to a leading Chinese hero in the *Water Margin* tale, Shin Jin (Jap. Shi Shin), nicknamed 'Nine Dragon Pattern' (Jap. Kyūmonryō) after his magnificent body tattoo. Kuniyoshi had already portrayed Shin in three single prints in the series 'One of the 108 Heroes of the Popular *Water Margin*', each time showing him wielding his favourite weapon, a long pole – represented here by the courtesan's pipe.

The poems are by Hatsushimo Okimado and Hisakataya (Hisakataya Misora, leader of the poetry group). Okimado's verse contains wordplay on the nine dragons of the robe and the ninth hour, signalled by beats of wooden clappers marking the official closing of Yoshiwara pleasure quarter around midnight.

In the lower right corner, next to Kuniyoshi's printed signature, is a circular, hand-impressed red seal that reads 'Printer Shinzō' (*Surikō Shinzō*). *Surimono* bearing this seal in the present series are presumed to be the earliest printings. Keiindō Shinzō is thought to have been a specialist printer and publisher of *surimono*. He also designed them occasionally (one is reproduced in Chiba 1997, no. 179).

52

Geisha

early 1830s

Colour woodblock, *ōban*, published by Kawaguchiya Chōzō, 38.5 × 26.2 cm

ARTIST'S SIGNATURE
Ichiyūsai Kuniyoshi ga

CENSORSHIP SEAL
kiwame

American Friends of the British Museum (The Arthur R. Miller Collection) 21502

REFERENCES
Ukiyo-e taisei 1931, no. 452; Suzuki 1992, no. 230; Mainichi Shinbunsha 1995, no. 97; Nagoya 1996, no. 134

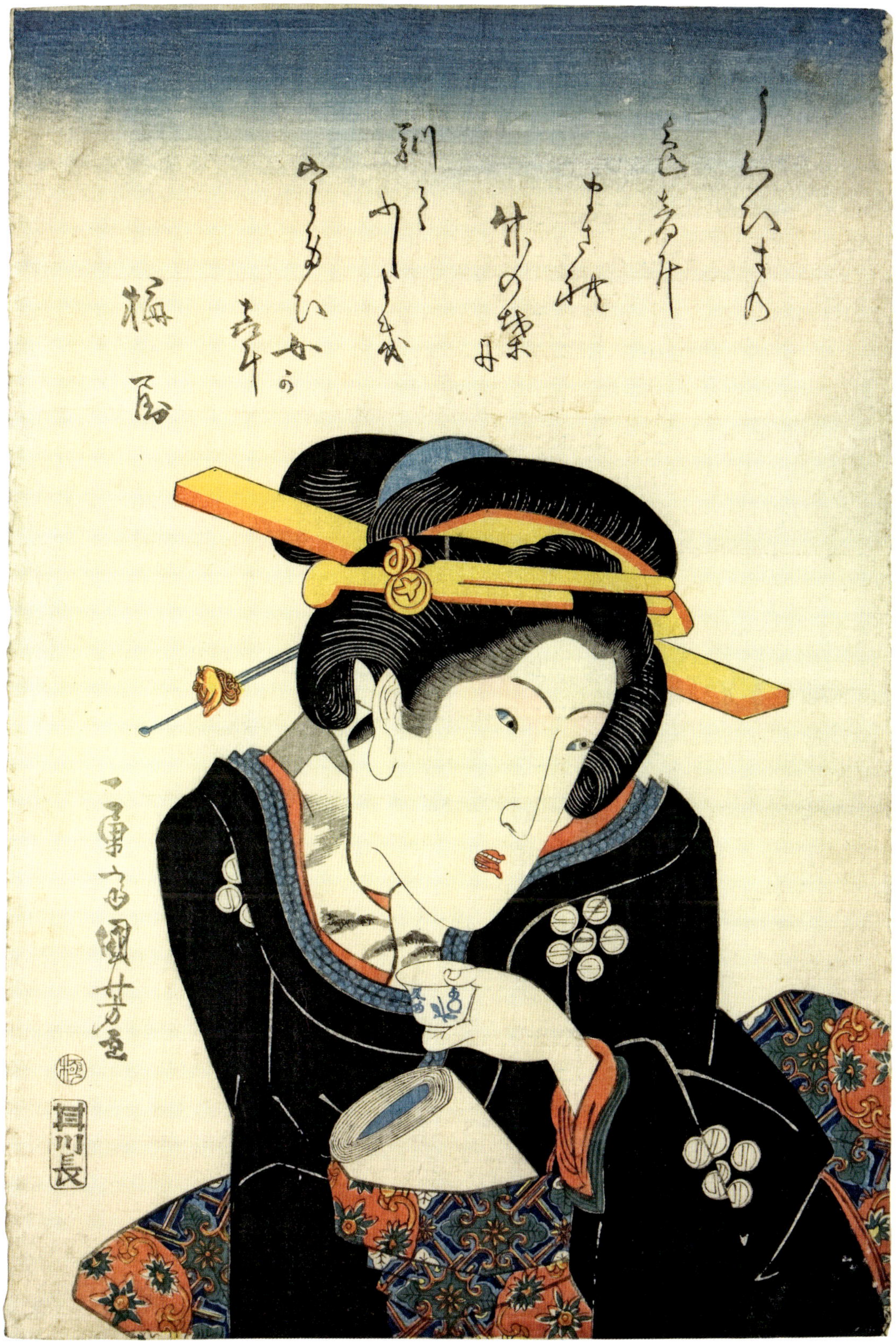

As was the custom with geisha – professional entertainers who played and sang music, and danced, at parties – the woman wears a relatively sombre robe, here black. She has chosen her accessories with a considerable sense of chic, revealed in such small details as the (painted?) design of Mt Fuji and Miho-no-Matsubara on her collar. She has tucked a roll of tissue into her brilliant brocade sash and is holding a small, blue and white porcelain saké cup, perhaps chatting while about to take a drink at the invitation of a guest.

Printed above the figure is a witty *kyōka* poem signed 'Umenoya', full of wordplay praising the skills of the geisha: 'More lovely than / the call of the warbler, / well used to saké, / *shamisen* and song / – voice of the singing girl' (*Uguisu no / irone ni masare / take no ha ni / narete fushiyoki / utaime ga koe*). The poet is Umenoya Kakuju (Kakushi, Morota Sakichi, 1801–65), a lifelong friend and patron of Kuniyoshi (Nagoya 1996, p. 13).

This is one of Kuniyoshi's earliest prints of beautiful women, a genre in which he was competing with several better-established artists, notably Kunisada and Eisen. It comes from a group of four half-length portraits of women of the floating world, all in a similar style and with poems above the figures. The others show a Yoshiwara courtesan with a showy arrangement of heavy hairpins (Nagoya 1996, no. 133), a 'kept woman' (*kakoi*) returning from a public bath (*Ukiyo-e taisei* 1931, no. 452) and a waitress (*karuko*, personal communication from Iwakiri Yuriko).

Two printings of this design are known. One has a band of gradated blue across the top, as here, and may be earlier; the other features a pattern of dripped blue that crosses, and partly obscures, the poem (Nagoya 1996, no. 134).

BIOGRAPHIES OF WISE WOMEN AND VIRTUOUS WIVES

(Cats 53–5)

New regulations concerning colour prints were issued by the shogunate in the sixth month, 1842, as part of the Tenpō reforms. They included an exhortation for works to be 'composed in accordance with [the values of] loyalty and fidelity, in order to promote virtue among children and women' (see also p.20). The same stipulations banned prints of courtesans and geisha, which encouraged artists to explore other kinds of women as the subject of appealing images. Portraits of famous female exemplars from the past suddenly proliferated. The present series is a prime example. Others should also be viewed in this context (see cats 56–8, 62).

Each design presents a famous woman from history with a rectangular cartouche containing a short biography. Thirty-one designs are known (Robinson 1982, series S.20). Only eleven bear censorship seals, eight the single seal of Yoshimura, three the single seal of Muramatsu. This suggests that the series was published around the time of the reforms, perhaps shortly after the regulations had been issued and a new system of censorship by named city officials (*nanushi*) was being introduced (see also p.24)

53
Hatsuhana prays under a waterfall
c. 1842

Colour woodblock, *ōban*, published by Ibaya Senzaburō, 36.4 × 24.8 cm

PRINT TITLE
'Hatsuhana'

SERIES TITLE
'Biographies of Wise Women and Virtuous Wives' (*Kenjo reppu den*)

ARTIST'S SIGNATURE
Ichiyūsai Kuniyoshi ga (in double gourd-shaped cartouche)

American Friends of the British Museum (The Arthur R. Miller Collection) 15606

REFERENCES
Robinson 1963, no.8; Riccar 1978, no.135; Springfield 1980, no.111; Robinson 1982, no.S20.7; Amsterdam 1998, no.32

Hatsuhana was the beautiful wife of the warrior Iinuma Katsugorō. She spent one hundred days under a waterfall praying to the deity Hakone Gongen to cure her husband's disabling illness. Hatsuhana was subsequently killed by Katsugorō's enemy, the evil Takiguchi Kōzuke, but the deity appeared to her husband and healed him. Katsugorō went on to take revenge on Kōzuke, who had also killed his brother. The text on the print relates the essentials of the story, which seems to have been adapted from the plot of the puppet/Kabuki play *Hakone reigen izari no adauchi* (*Hakone Deity: A Cripple's Revenge*), first performed in 1801. This play, in turn, was supposedly based loosely on the vengeance wreaked in 1590 by the warrior Iinuma Hatsugorō on one Katō Kōsuke, who had killed his elder brother (Iizuka 1926, pp.287–8). The text on Kuniyoshi's print praises Hatsuhana's 'fidelity' (*teisetsu*) – the very expression used in the censorship regulations quoted here on page 20.

Praying intently, Hatsuhana appears oblivious to the thundering torrent that beats down upon her, the waters parting to reveal her calm, beautiful features. The splintering cascade harmoniously echoes the shape of her long, loose tresses, and the complex visual effects of the figure as seen through the water have been realised with remarkable skill by the block-cutters and printers.

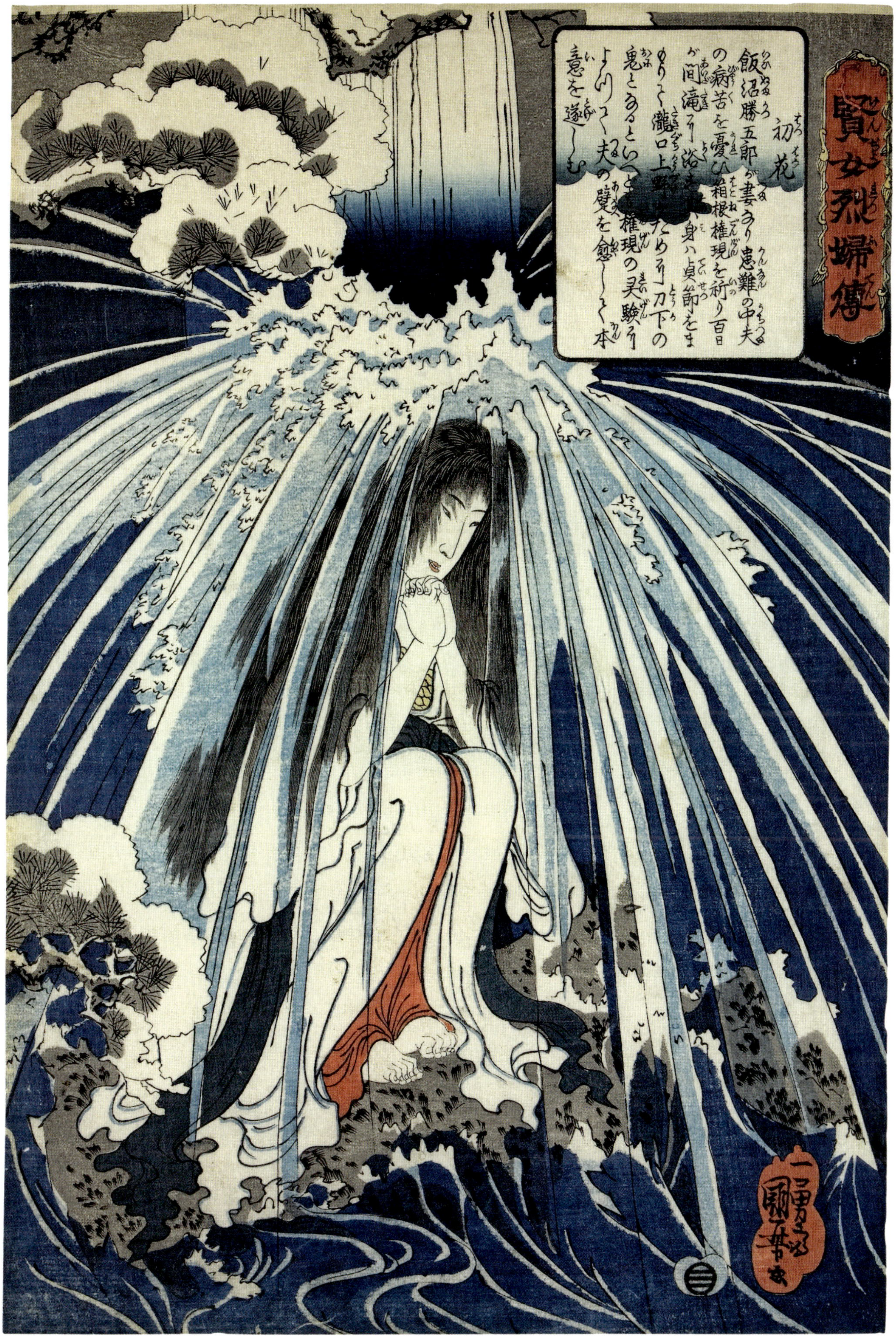
賢女烈婦傳
初花
飯沼勝五郎が妻なり患難の中夫
の病苦を憂ひ箱根権現を祈り百日
が間滝に浴し身ハ貞節をま
もりて瀧口上野ために刀下の
鬼となると権現の霊験に
よりて夫の讐を愈して本
意を遂しむ
一勇斎國芳画

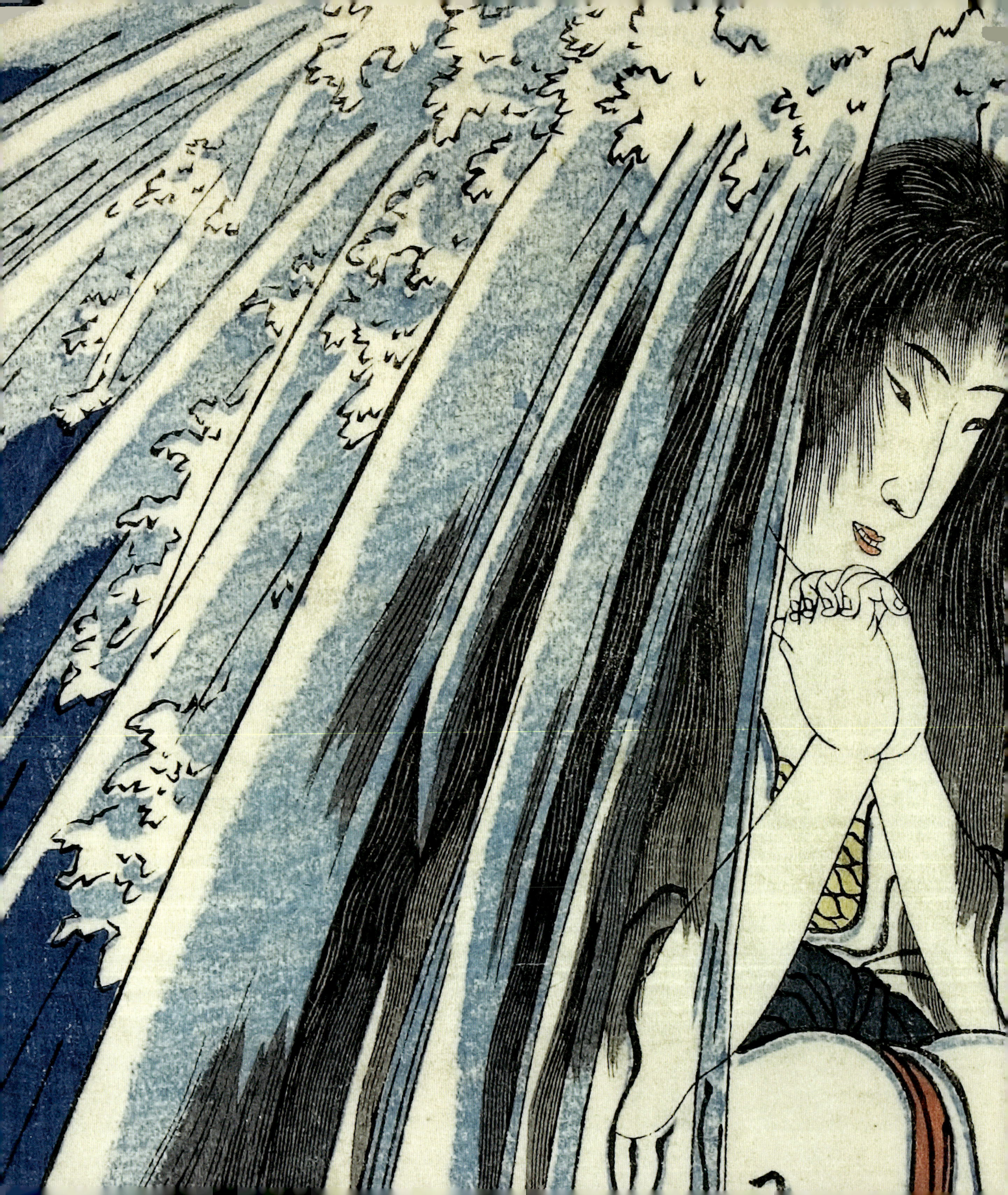

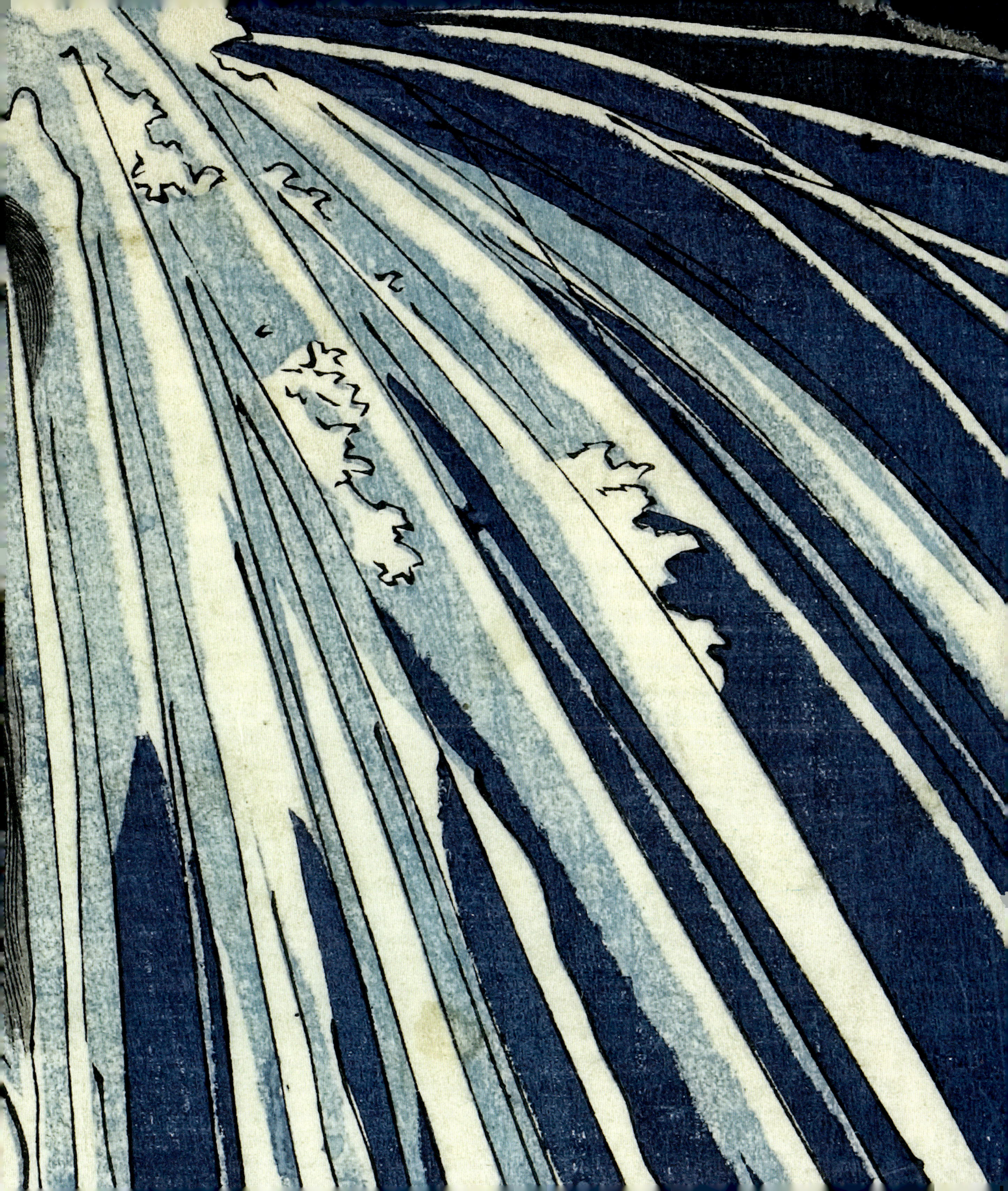

54

Ōiko moves a large rock

c. 1842

Colour woodblock, *ōban*, published by Ibaya Senzaburō, 37.7 × 25.2 cm

SERIES TITLE
'Biographies of Wise Women and Virtuous Wives' (*Kenjo reppu den*)

PRINT TITLE
'Ōiko'

ARTIST'S SIGNATURE
Chōōrō Kuniyoshi ga

American Friends of the British Museum (The Arthur R. Miller Collection) 15615

REFERENCES
Robinson 1982, no. S20.17; Mainichi Shinbunsha 1995, no. 107

Dressed alluringly in a printed cotton robe and red undergarment, Ōiko is secretly moving a great rock 'some six or seven feet square' at night. She is blocking the irrigation of fields belonging to her fellow villagers at Takashima in Ōmi province. The text explains that, out of spite, they had directed the water away from Ōiko's fields and this was her revenge. Next morning they were amazed, and not even the combined strength of several villagers could shift the rock. Only when they apologised profusely to Ōiko did she remove it, easily: 'Her strength was impossible to measure and "Ōiko's water-stopping rock" [*Ōiko no mizuguchi-ishi*] can still be seen there today.'

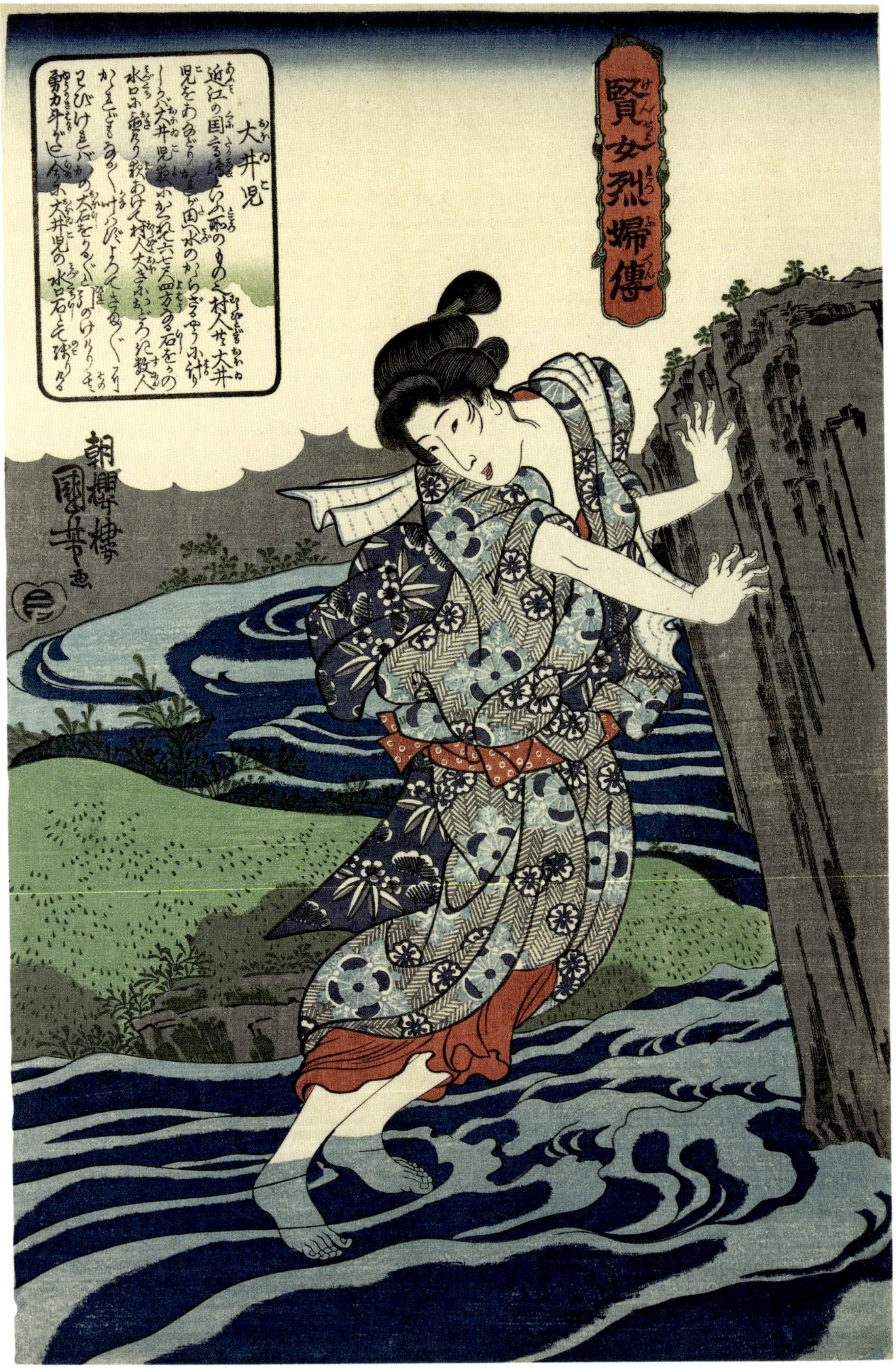

55

Princess Anju collects brine for salt

c. 1842

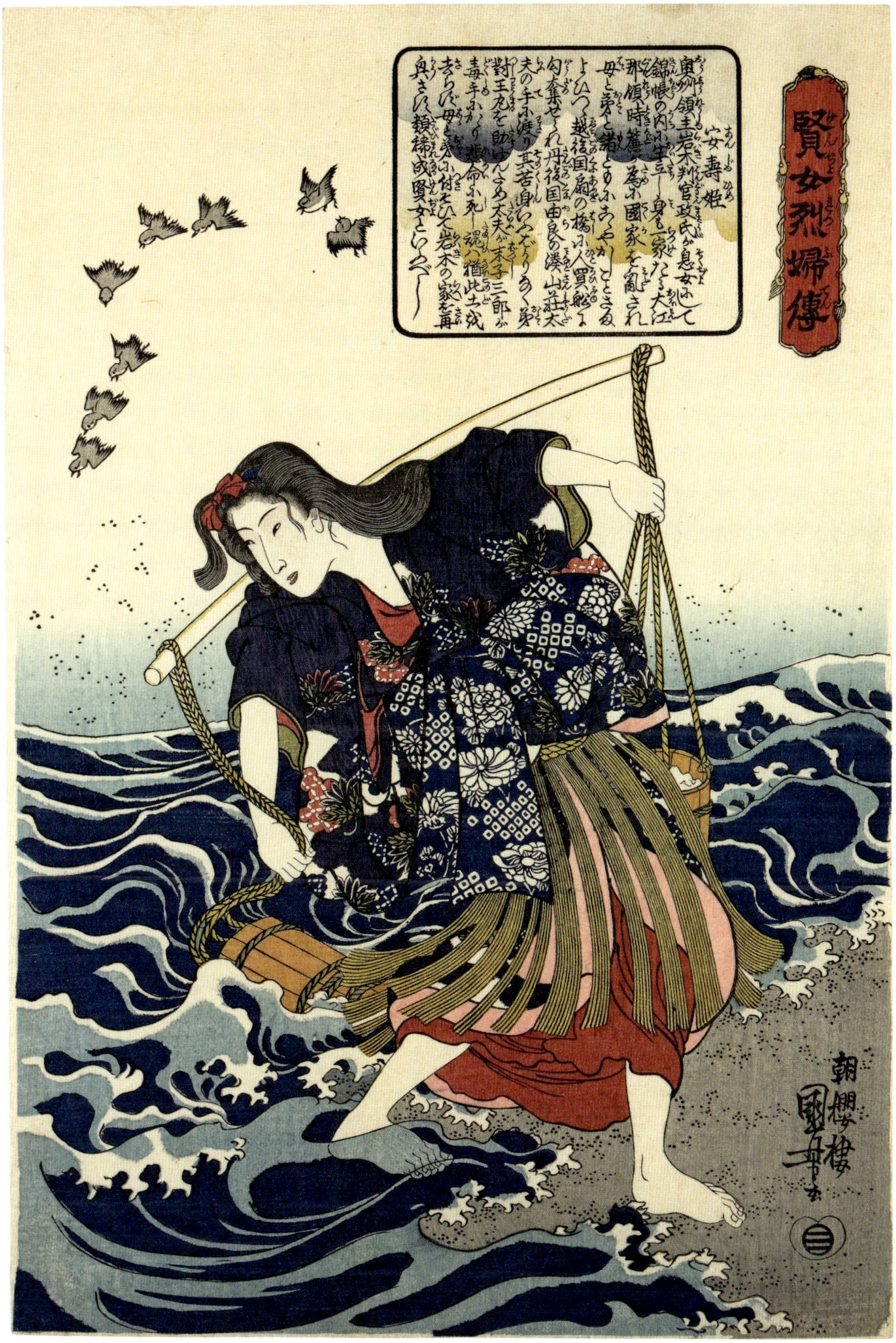

Colour woodblock, *ōban*, published by Ibaya Senzaburō, 37.4 × 25.8 cm

SERIES TITLE
'Biographies of Wise Women and Virtuous Wives' (*Kenjo reppu den*)

PRINT TITLE
'Princess Anju' (*Anju-hime*)

ARTIST'S SIGNATURE
Chōōrō Kuniyoshi ga

American Friends of the British Museum (The Arthur R. Miller Collection) 15601

REFERENCES
Robinson 1982, no. S20.1

The viewer is invited to empathise with the lot of beautiful Princess Anju, a high-born young woman ('brought up within the brocade curtain', as the text on the print puts it) who has been sold into slavery. She is shown struggling to scoop seawater into her yoked pail. The richly patterned robe and the contrast between the brilliant red undergarment and Anju's pure white legs give the image an erotic tinge. The straw skirt was typical work-wear for women who collected salt.

The story was a medieval one, much embellished in Edo-period fiction and drama, and is summarised in the text on the print. Princess Anju is the daughter of Iwaki Hangan Masauji, lord of the northern Mutsu province. With her mother and younger brother, Zushiō-maru ('Tsushiō-maru' on this print), she sets out in search of her father, who has been banished as the result of a false accusation. In Echigo province they are kidnapped and sold into slavery, entering the service of the evil rich man Sanshō-dayū, who lives at the port of Yura in Tango province. Zushiō-maru escapes and Anju is then tortured to death. Her restless spirit stays close to her mother and brother as they restore the fortunes of the Iwaki family. 'She was a wise woman of rare calibre', the text concludes.

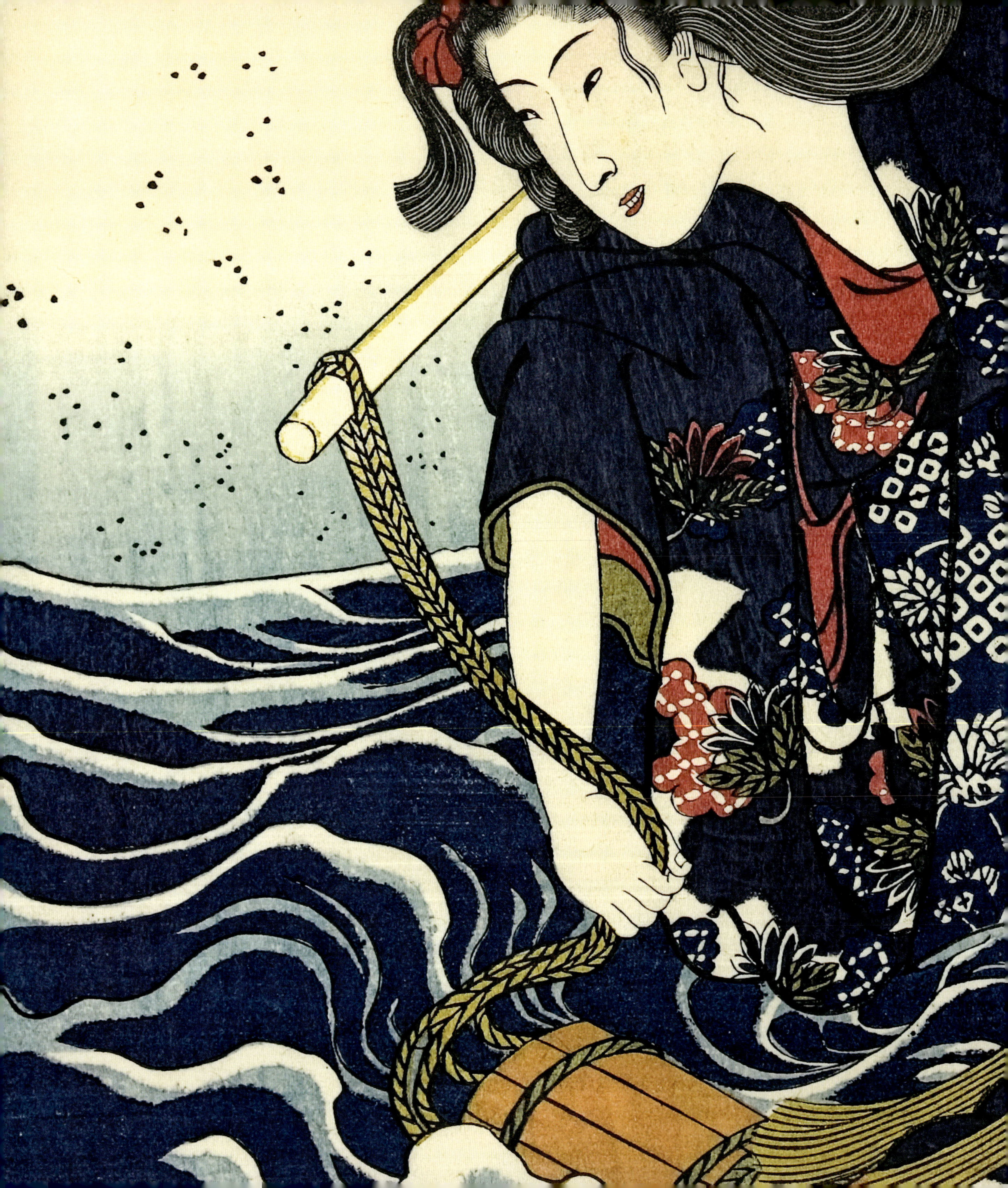

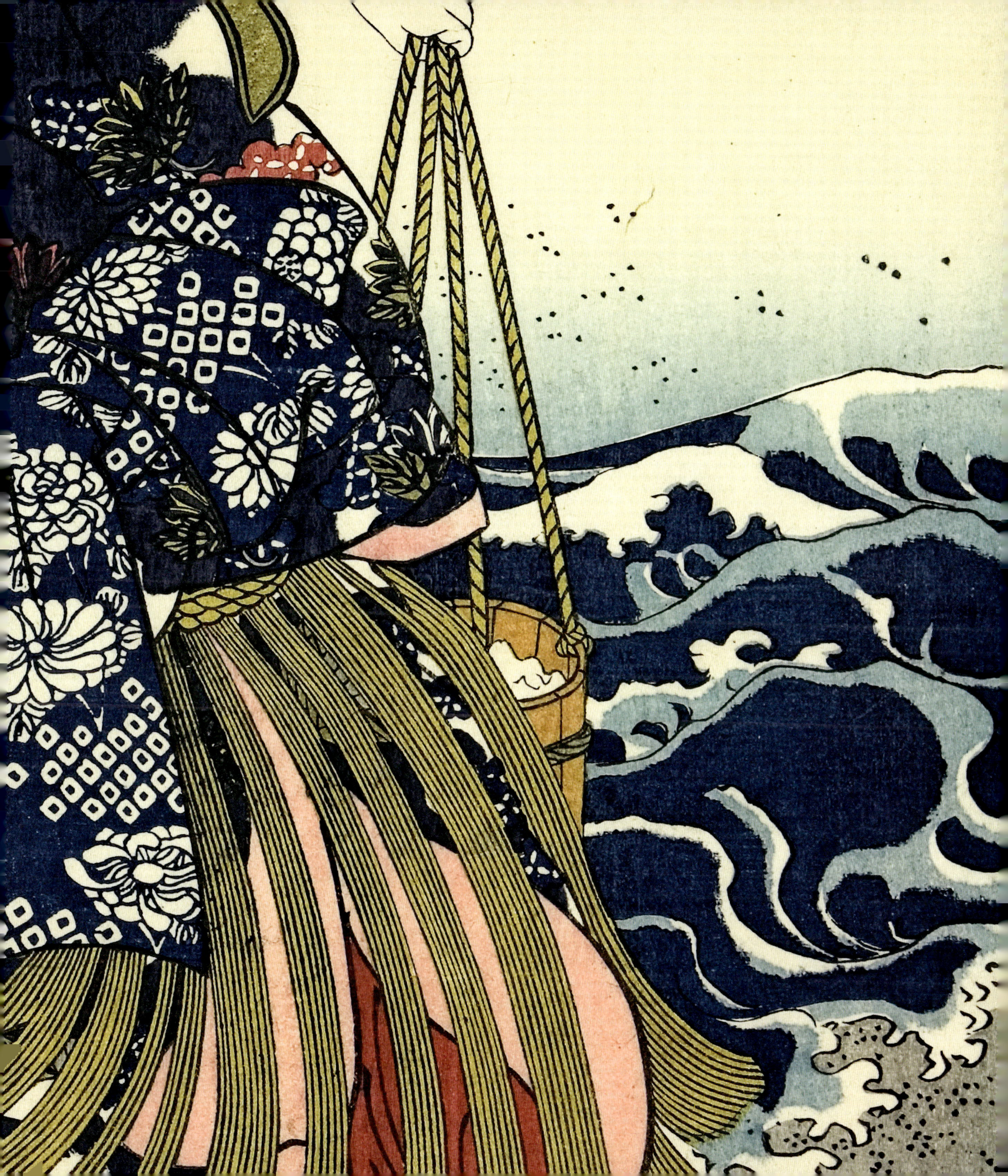

THIRTY-SIX IMMORTALS OF POETRY: MIRRORS OF ETHICS FOR GIRLS

(Cats 56–8)

The title gives the ostensible *raison d'être* of the series: to present girls with models of feminine behaviour as reflected in classical verses by the 'thirty-six immortals of poetry' (exemplary poets originally selected by the courtier and poet Fujiwara no Kintō [966–1041]). In this way Kuniyoshi and his publishers sought to observe the letter, if not the spirit, of the new regulations governing prints described above (pp. 20, 24). Lest there should be any doubt about this, each print not only displays the celebrated classical verses, in elegant calligraphy, but also contains a square cartouche with a moralising text.

The real purpose of the prints was to show attractive young women of different classes and backgrounds in a variety of situations. The reforms seem to have prompted Kuniyoshi to explore a wider range of female types – notably, working women – but he continued to depict them as alluring. This often produces a mismatch between text and image, casting doubt on the sincerity of some of the pious sentiments expressed.

It is not known whether all thirty-six designs were published.

56

Woman struggling against an autumn breeze

1843

Colour woodblock, *ōban*, published by Wakasaya Yoichi, 36.7 × 25.4 cm

SERIES TITLE
'Thirty-six Immortals of Poetry: Mirrors of Ethics for Girls' (*Sanjū-rokkasen dōjo kyōkun kagami*)

PRINT TITLE
'Sarumaru-dayū'

POEM
Ochikochi no / tazuki mo shiranu / yamanaka ni / obotsukanaku mo / yobukodori kana

ARTIST'S SIGNATURE
Ichiyūsai Kuniyoshi ga

ARTIST'S SEAL
toshidama

CENSOR'S SEAL
Take

American Friends of the British Museum (The Arthur R. Miller Collection) 09806

REFERENCES
Springfield 1968, no. 104; Riccar 1978, no. 136; Springfield 1980, no. 106

The young woman grasps her wide-brimmed travelling hat with both hands as she bends forward in a sudden gust of autumn wind. Falling leaves dance around her and a travelling cane lies discarded at her feet. The long, hanging sleeves (*furisode*) of her plain outer robe billow, offering glimpses of a bright plum and bamboo pattern on the red and white garment beneath. The subtle effect of white 'ripples' on the outer robe was achieved by exploiting the natural grain pattern of a printing block carved specially from zelkova wood, a technique known as *keyaki-zuri* (zelkova printing).

Next to nothing is known about the poet Sarumaru-dayū and some scholars doubt his existence. The first lines of the verse here attributed to him chime with the image: 'Lost in the mountains / Not a hint on any side / Whither I should turn, / How uncertain sounds the call / Of the calling bird to me' (trans. Edwin A. Cranston, in Fischer 2000, p. 162). Commenting that it is the way of the world to encompass both the high-born and the lowly, the wise man and the fool, the rich and the poor, the moralising text states that this is like having a full set of furnishings in a home and quotes the saying 'We need companions on a journey and fellow-feeling in life'.

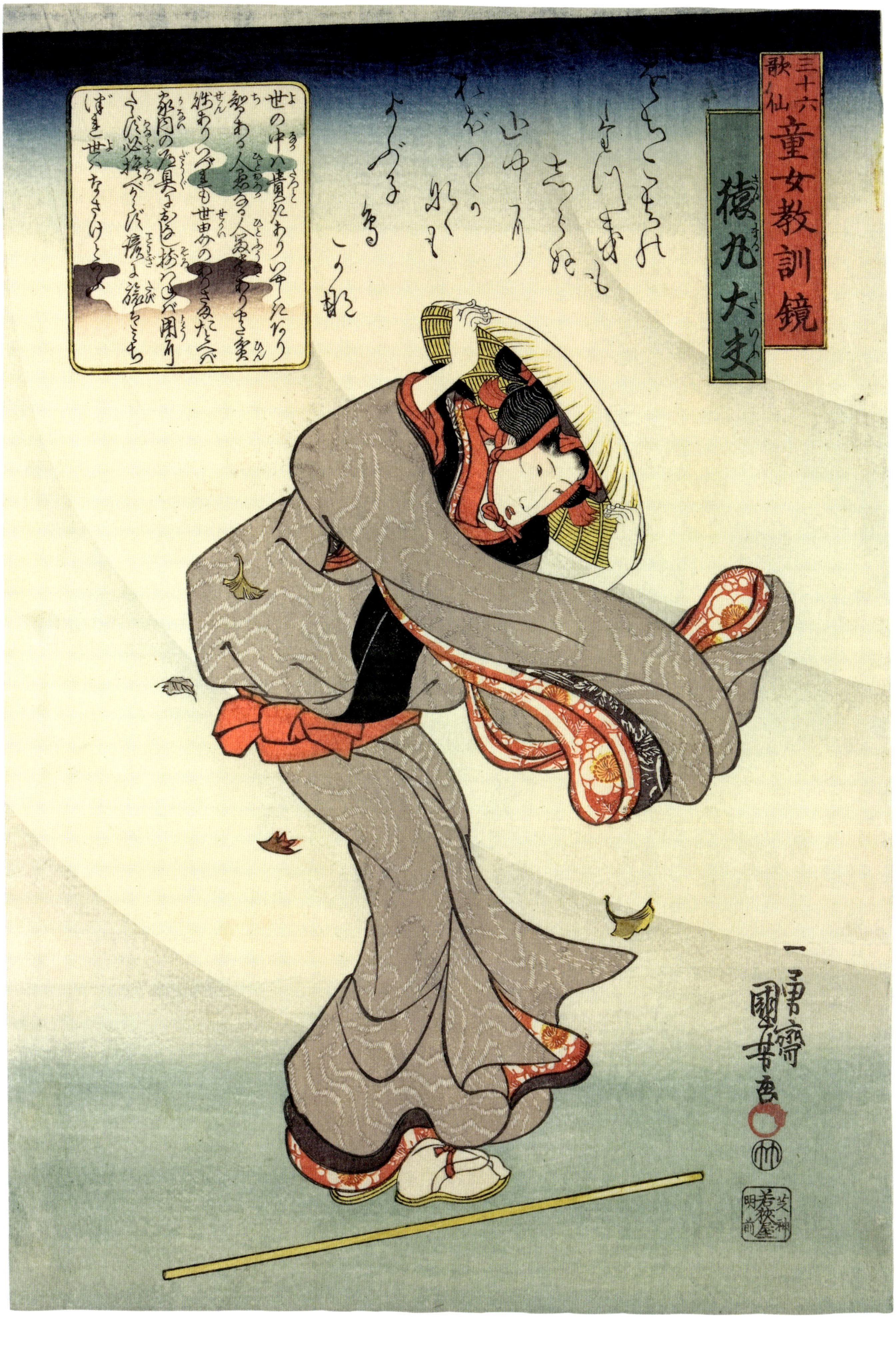
三十六歌仙 童女教訓鏡
猿丸大夫
一勇齋國芳画
芝神明前 若狭屋

57

Woman playing with a cat

1843

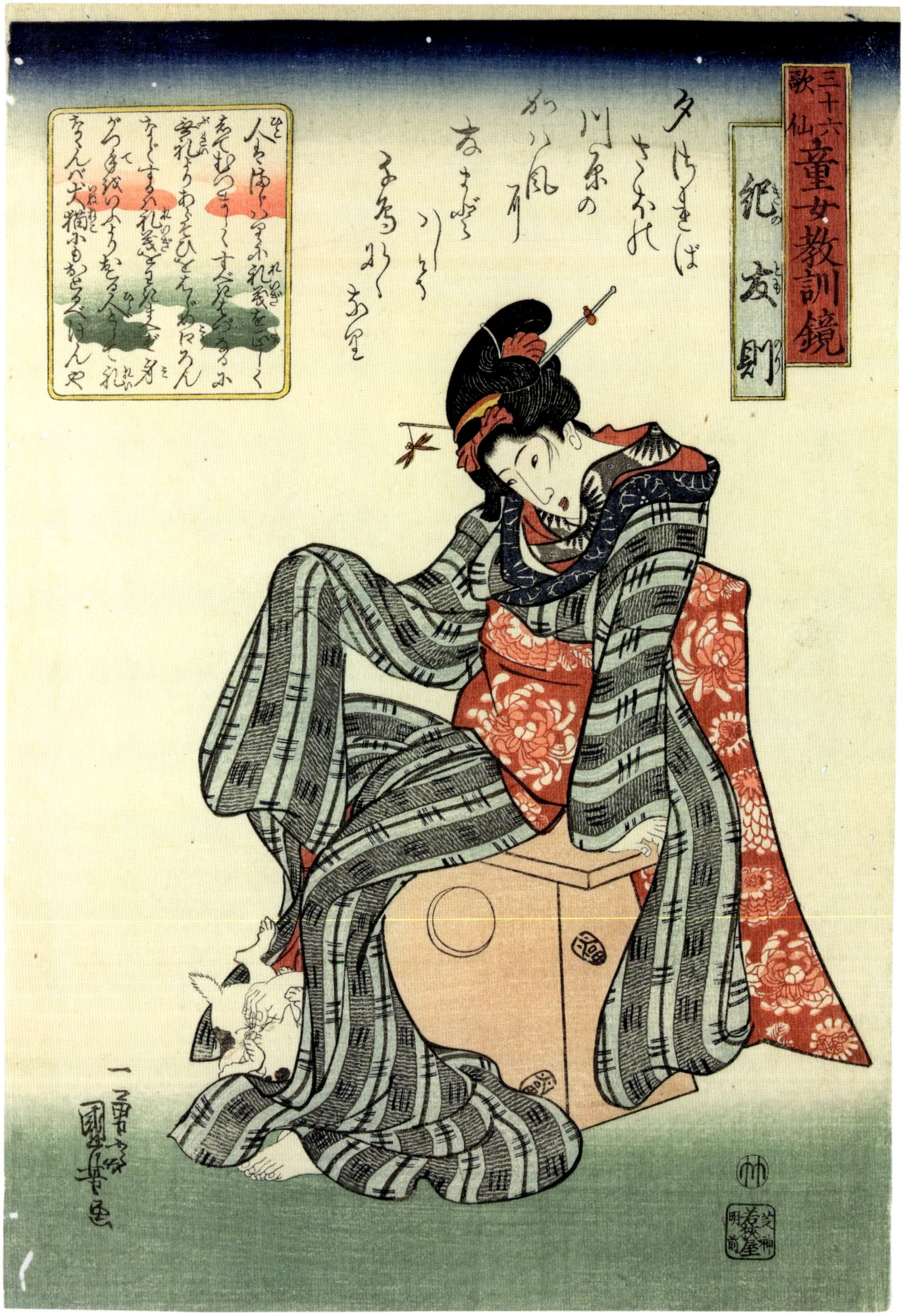

Colour woodblock, *ōban*, published by Wakasaya Yoichi, 36.4 × 25.8 cm

SERIES TITLE
'Thirty-six Immortals of Poetry: Mirrors of Ethics for Girls' (*Sanjū-rokkasen dōjo kyōkun kagami*)

PRINT TITLE
'Ki no Tomonori'

POEM
Yū sareba / Sao no kawase no / kawagiri ni / tomo madowaseru / chidori naku nari

ARTIST'S SIGNATURE
Ichiyūsai Kuniyoshi ga

CENSOR'S SEAL
Take

American Friends of the British Museum (The Arthur R. Miller Collection) 09808

A young woman dangles the long sleeve of her robe to amuse the cat playing at her feet. The connection with the classical verse by Ki no Tomonori (died shortly after 905?) seems tenuous, except that the poem describes companionship between a person and an animal (in this case a bird): 'Has he lost a friend – / The plover raising his cry / In the river mist / As evening shadows fall / On the Sao River bank?' (trans. Helen Craig McCullough, in McCullough 1985, p. 359). The moralising text stresses the importance of proper manners and etiquette in social interaction: rude behaviour causes altercations; arguments erupt when people are unfamiliar with correct manners; and are we not worse than cats and dogs when we behave in a selfish manner, without observing proper etiquette? This tone of mock admonishment doubtless raised a smile among purchasers of the print.

58

Woman weaving

1843

Colour woodblock, *ōban*, published by Wakasaya Yoichi, 36.6 × 25.8 cm

SERIES TITLE
'Thirty-six Immortals of Poetry: Mirrors of Ethics for Girls' (*Sanjū-rokkasen dōjo kyōkun kagami*)

PRINT TITLE
'Chūnagon Asatada'

POEM
Au koto no / taete shi naku wa / nakanaka ni / hito o mo mi o mo / uramizaramashi

ARTIST'S SIGNATURE
Ichiyūsai Kuniyoshi ga

CENSOR'S SEAL
Taka

American Friends of the British Museum (The Arthur R. Miller Collection) 09801

With a gourd-patterned head-cloth protecting her hair from dust, and with her sleeves tied back with braids, the woman focuses intently on her weaving. The woven cloth gathers in a roll held in place by a belt that passes behind the woman's waist, while she operates the loom mechanism by means of a cord attached to her big toe. The classical verse, a disappointed lover's complaint, is by Chūnagon ('Middle Counsellor') Asatada (910–966): 'If there were no such thing / As ever having met her, then / Contrary to all expectations, / Neither her coldness nor my pain / Would I have to resent!' (trans. Joshua S. Mostow, in Mostow 1996, p.272). There is no obvious connection with the picture. Perhaps viewers were to imagine themselves smitten by the weaver's charms? The moralising text warns how obsessive greed can lead people to lose all sense of moderation, as they place all their ingenuity at the service of duping others.

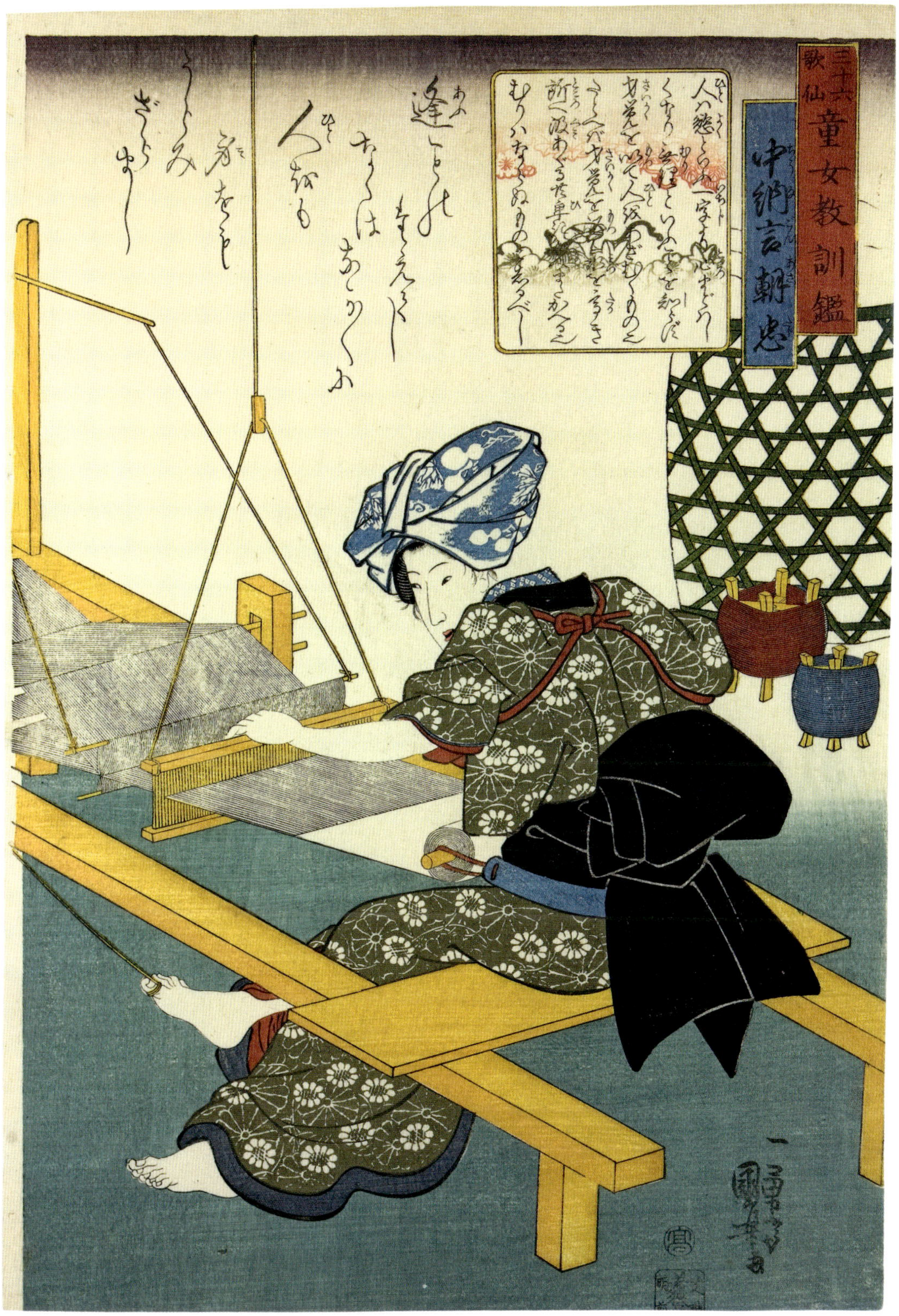

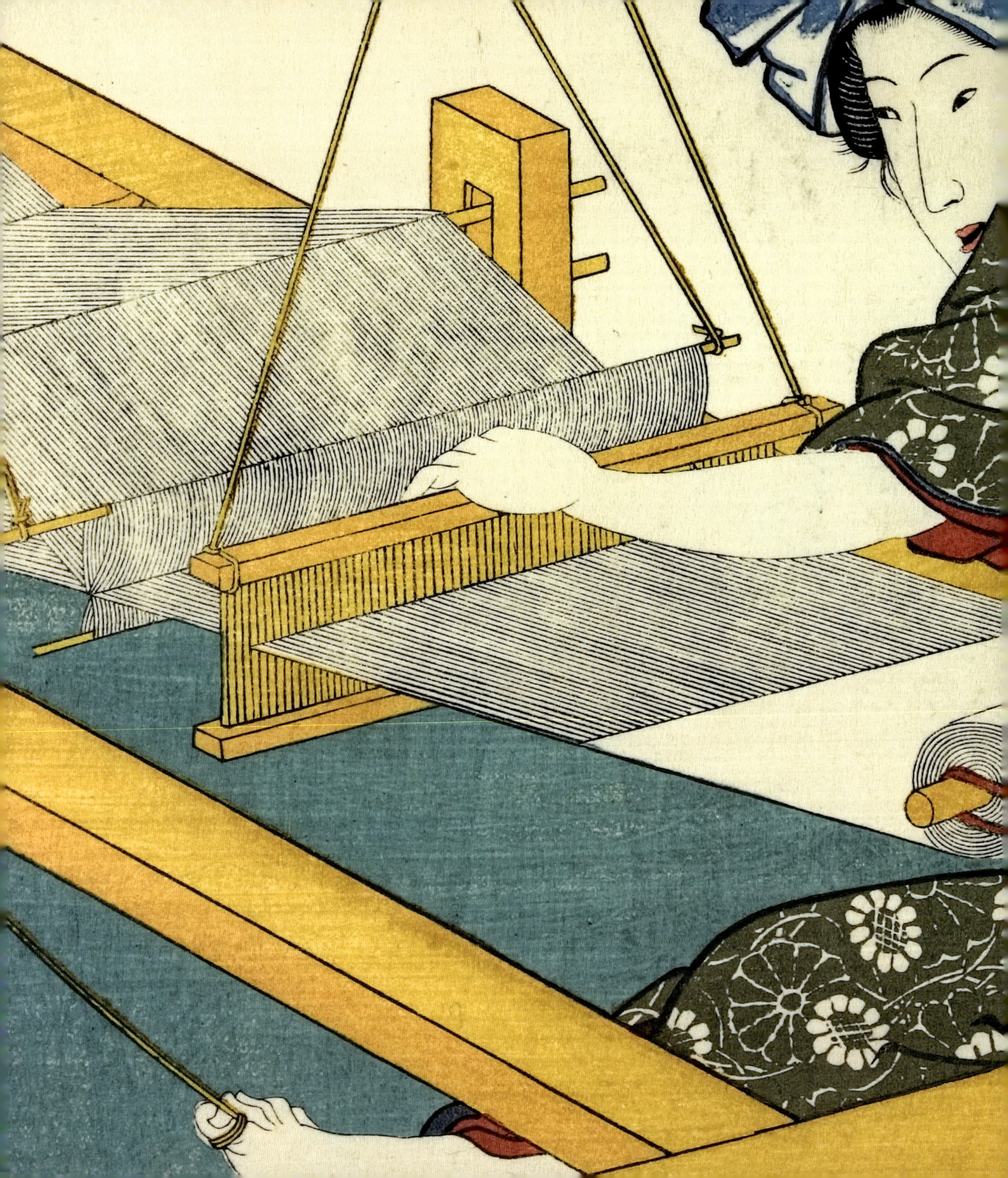

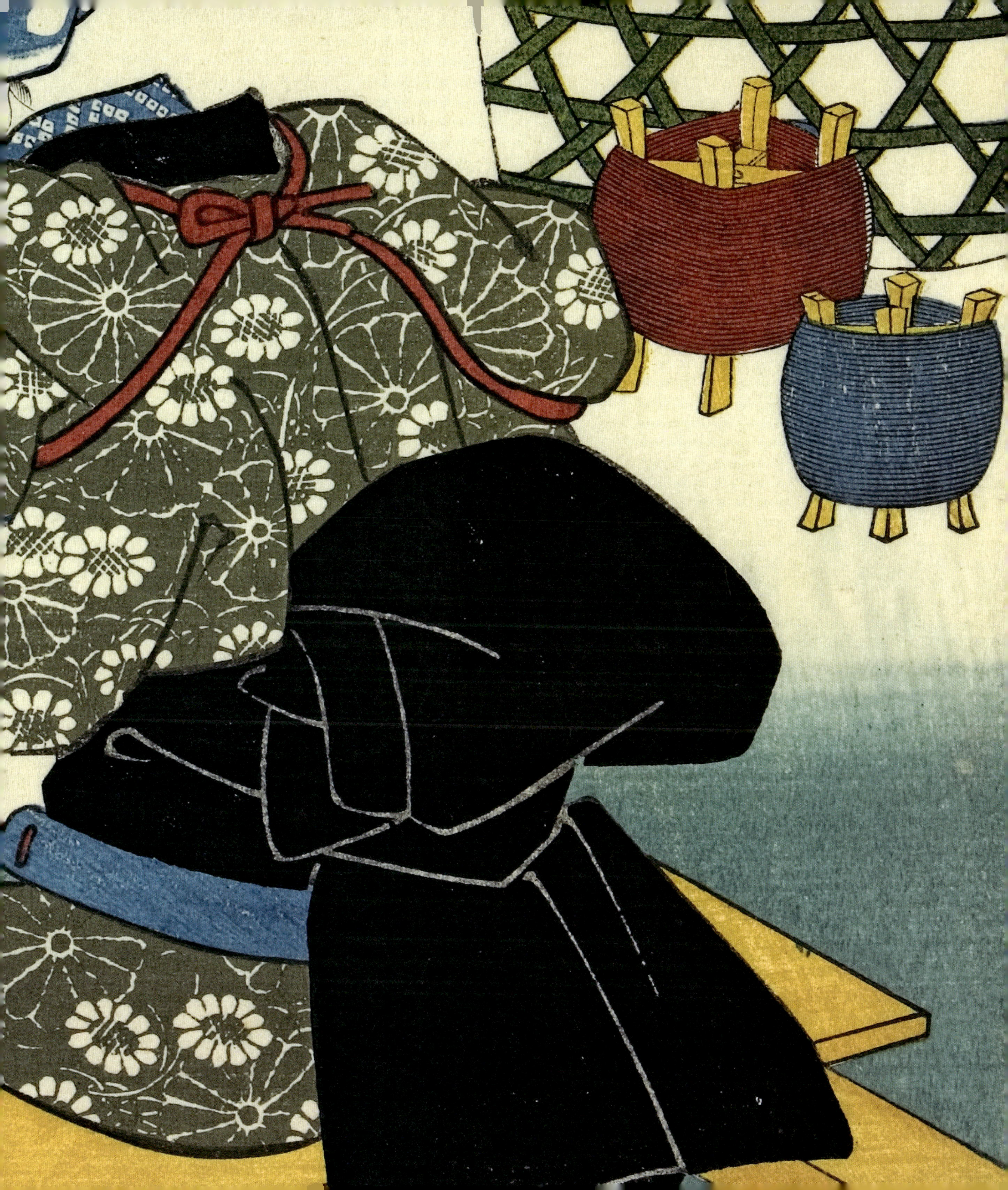

59

Woman blowing the coals of a stove

c. 1844

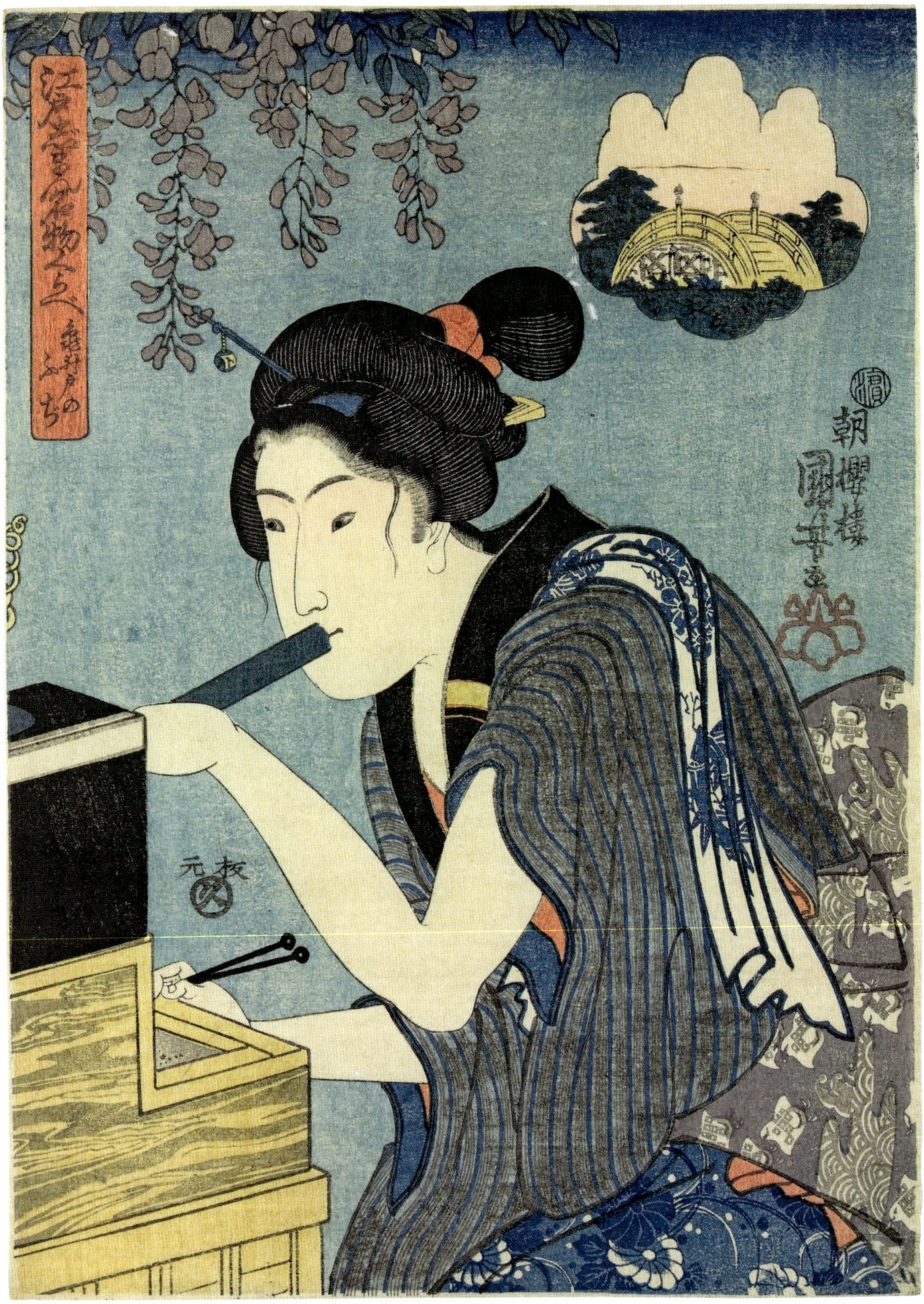

Colour woodblock, *chūban*, published by Ibaya Kyūbei, 25.5 × 18.6 cm

SERIES TITLE
'Pride of Edo: Comparison of Famous Products' (*Edo jiman meibutsu-kurabe*)

PRINT TITLE
'Wisteria at Kameido' (*Kameido no fuji*)

ARTIST'S SIGNATURE
Chōōrō Kuniyoshi ga

ARTIST'S SEAL
Yoshikiri

CENSOR'S SEAL
Hama

American Friends of the British Museum (The Arthur R. Miller Collection) 01501

REFERENCES
Riccar 1978, no. 139; Suzuki 1992, no. 244; Nagoya 1996, no. 140

The young woman blows through a bamboo tube to keep the coals of her stove alight. She tends to her cooking with metal tongs, a cotton towel hung in workmanlike fashion over one shoulder. Wisteria flowers dangle above her, and these, together with the inset picture of a 'drum bridge' (*taiko-bashi*), indicate the location: the Tenjin shrine at Kameido in the district of Honjo, on the east bank of the Sumida river. The deity venerated there is the courtier poet Sugawara no Michizane (deified as Tenjin). Shrines dedicated to him are scattered throughout Japan, all of them copying elements of the original at Dazaifu in Kyushu, especially its semicircular drum bridge. The Kameido Tenjin shrine, now part of Tokyo, is still a popular place in early summer to enjoy refreshments beneath trellises of wisteria blooming beside a pond. The woman in the print is probably serving at a tea stall.

The charming pose is copied from a diptych print by Utamaro, *Kitchen scene* (*c.* 1794–95; illustrated in Asano and Clark 1995, no. 206). As Asano Shūgō has pointed out (in Nagoya 1996, p. 250), Kuniyoshi took over the poses of all four women in the Utamaro design, three in the series to which this print belongs, one in the series 'Auspicious Pictures of Land and Sea' (*Sankai medetai zue*; cats 71–3). Kuniyoshi's young woman is clearly puffing out her cheeks, an engagingly realistic touch.

The print comes from the series 'Pride of Edo: Comparison of Famous Products' (*Edo jiman meibutsu-kurabe*). All its seven known designs (listed in Nagoya 1996, p. 250) have a small inset landscape of a famous tourist spot in Edo (present-day Tokyo) depicted inside a cartouche shaped like stylised paulownia blossoms. The cartouche resembles the artist's *Yoshikiri* seal, which frequently appears, as here, beneath his signature. Viewers of the prints are invited to delight in the famous features of each neighbourhood (wisteria, for instance), but interest naturally focuses primarily on the beautiful women to be encountered there.

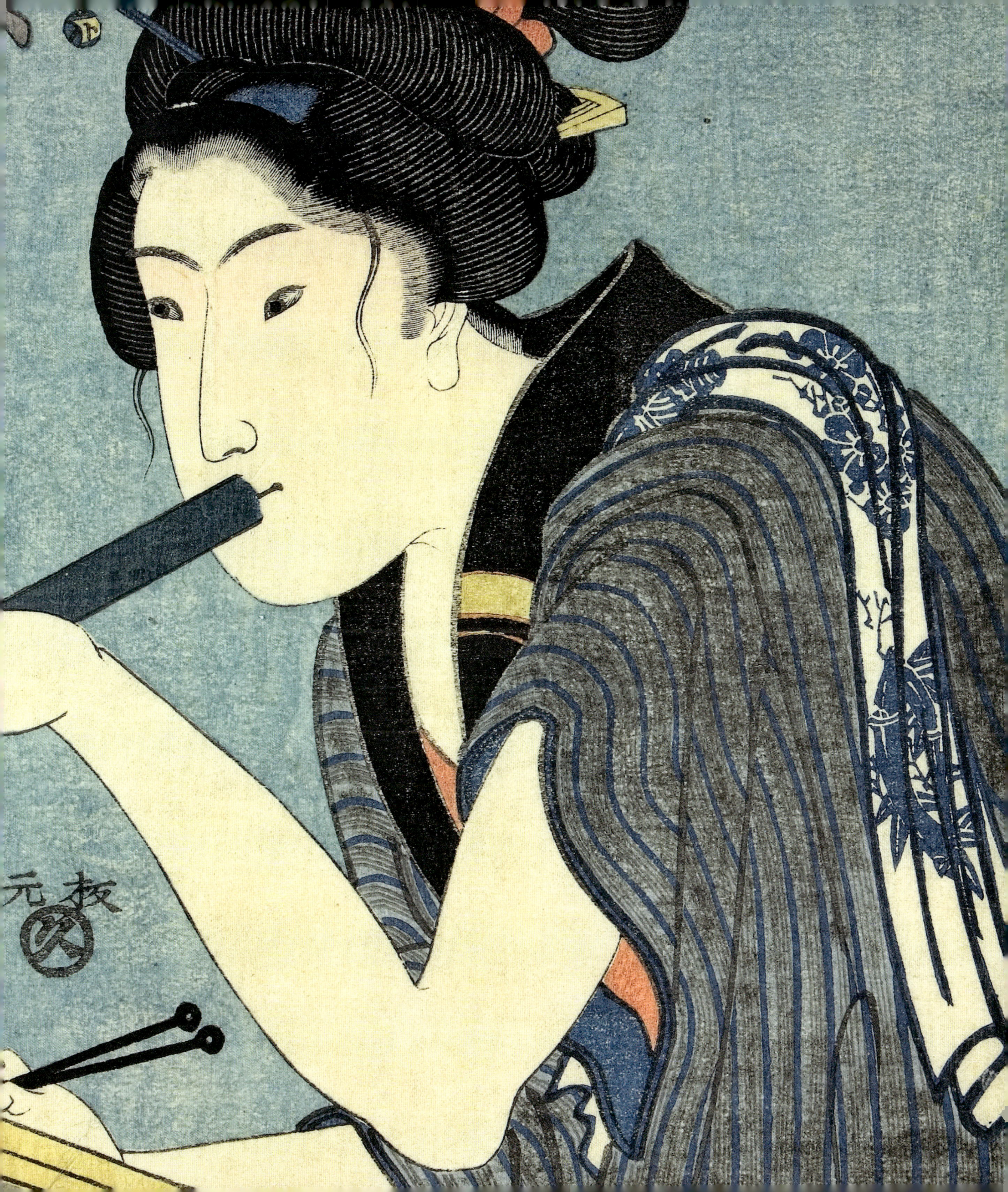
板元

WOMEN LIKENED TO BENKEI, WEARING CHECKS

(Cats 60, 61)

'Benkei check' (*Benkei-jima*) is the name given to bold chequered patterns woven into cotton fabric used for summer robes. Each of the women in the ten known designs from the series wears a garment of this type. In addition, every print contains a playfully hidden 'parody' (*mitate*) of a famous event from the life of the warrior monk Benkei, who sometimes wore clothing with this kind of bold pattern. The witty *kyōka* poem printed above each half-length portrait gives clues to identifying the event. The designs do not bear individual printed titles. Suzuki lists the attributed titles and conjectures that the series may have been sponsored by cloth manufacturers or by the *kyōka* poets (Suzuki 1992, p.214).

The print relating to the 'subscription list' (*kanjinchō*) episode in Benkei's life shows a woman reading a printed calendar for the coming year (parodying the occasion on which Benkei read out a mock list of 'temple subscribers' to dupe guards at a checkpoint and make his escape with his master, Yoshitsune, and their band, disguised as monks). The cover of the calendar bears the date 'Tenpō 15' (i.e. 1844), which provides a clue to the timing of Kuniyoshi's print series (Suzuki 1992, no.249).

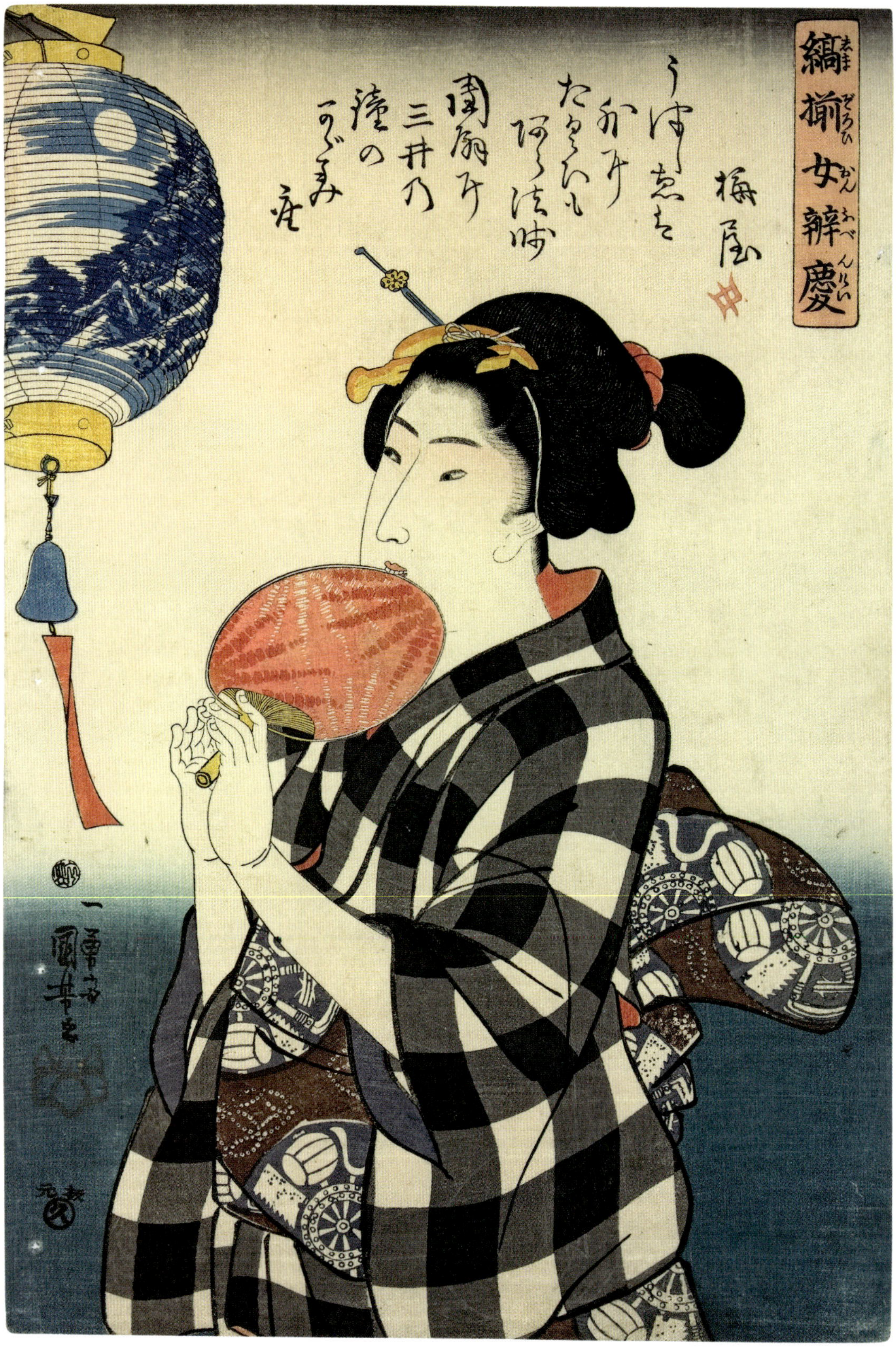

60

Woman admiring a paper lantern

c. 1844

Colour woodblock, *ōban*, published by Ibaya Kyūbei, 36 × 24.9 cm

ARTIST'S SEAL
Yoshikiri

CENSOR'S SEAL
Kinugasa

SERIES TITLE
'Women Likened to Benkei, Wearing Checks' (*Shima-zoroi onna Benkei*)

ARTIST'S SIGNATURE
Ichiyūsai Kuniyoshi ga

American Friends of the British Museum (The Arthur R. Miller Collection) 18002

REFERENCES
Itabashi 1994, Kuniyoshi no. 63; Amsterdam 1998, no. 133

The woman toys with a round fan (*uchiwa*) as she admires the landscape painted on a paper lantern. Her robe is patterned with 'Benkei checks' and her sash bears a bold design that combines the 'seven weapons' typically used by the warrior monk Benkei (mallet, saw, sickle and so forth) with the Buddhist 'wheel of the law' motif often seen on his costume. The small wind-chime bell that hangs from the bottom of the lantern alludes to the episode in the monk's life in which he dragged the giant temple bell of Mii-dera up the side of Mt Hiei (see cats 23, 24). That surely indicates that the landscape painted on the lantern represents Mt Hiei. The *kyōka* poem is by Kuniyoshi's patron Umenoya Kakuju.

61

Woman writing a label for a potted chrysanthemum

c. 1844

Colour woodblock, *ōban*, published by Ibaya Kyūbei, 37.4 × 24.9 cm

ARTIST'S SEAL:
Yoshikiri

BLOCK CARVER
Hori-Renkichi

SERIES TITLE
'Women Likened to Benkei, Wearing Checks' (*Shima-zoroi onna Benkei*)

CENSOR'S SEAL
Hama

ARTIST'S SIGNATURE
Chōōrō Kuniyoshi ga

American Friends of the British Museum (The Arthur R. Miller Collection) 18004

In the 'Naniwa plum tree' episode from Benkei's life he is ordered by Yoshitsune to write a notice board (*seisatsu*) ensuring that no damage is done to an ancient plum tree at Amagasaki near Naniwa (Osaka) said to have been mentioned in a poem by Emperor Nintoku (Machida 2003, p. 146). The young woman in the print, dressed in a cotton robe with bold 'Benkei checks', is about to write a label to insert into the earth of her potted chrysanthemum. The *kyōka* poem was written by Ryūkatei Tanekazu.

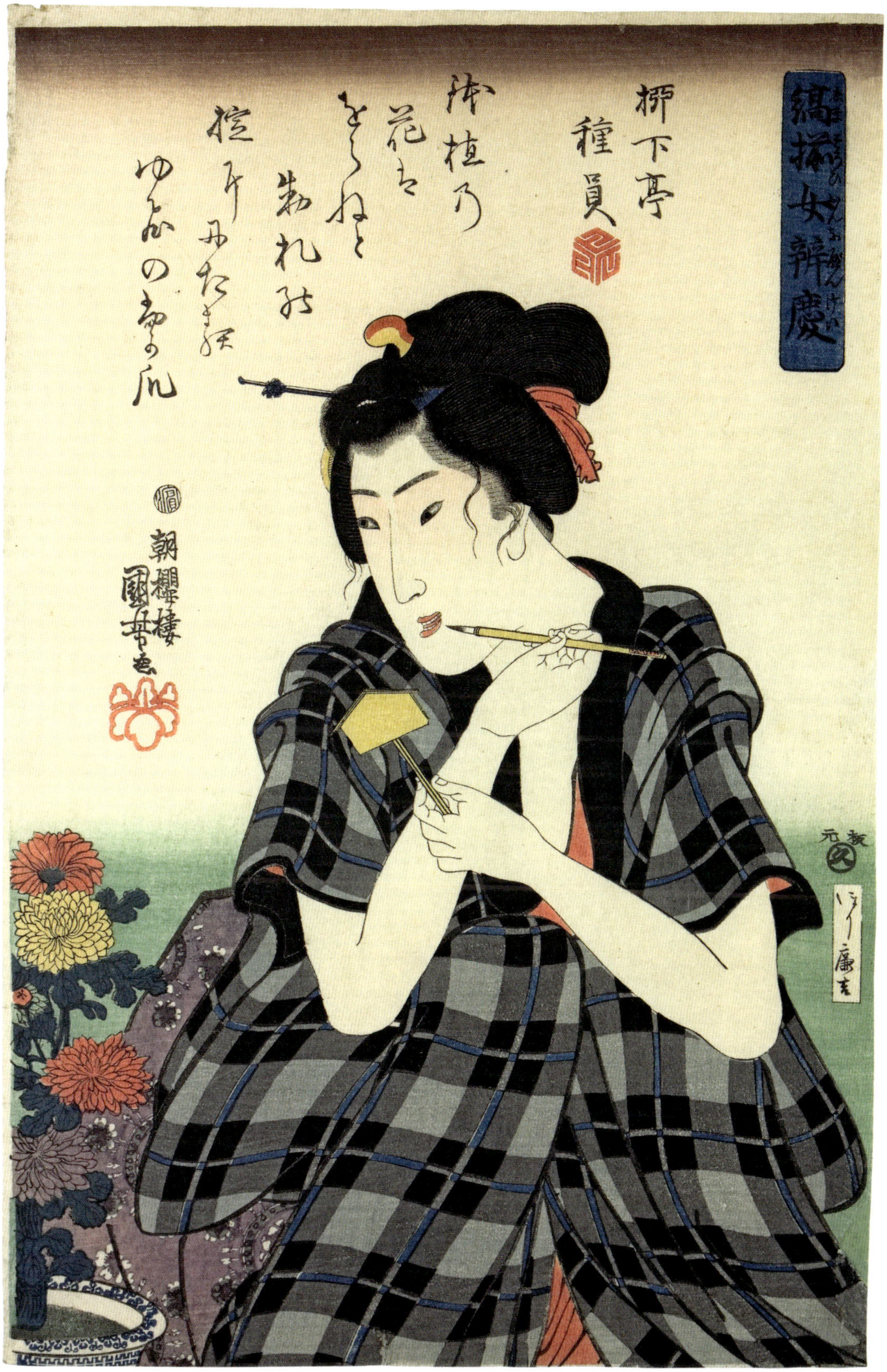

62

The woman Kane stops a runaway horse

1845–46

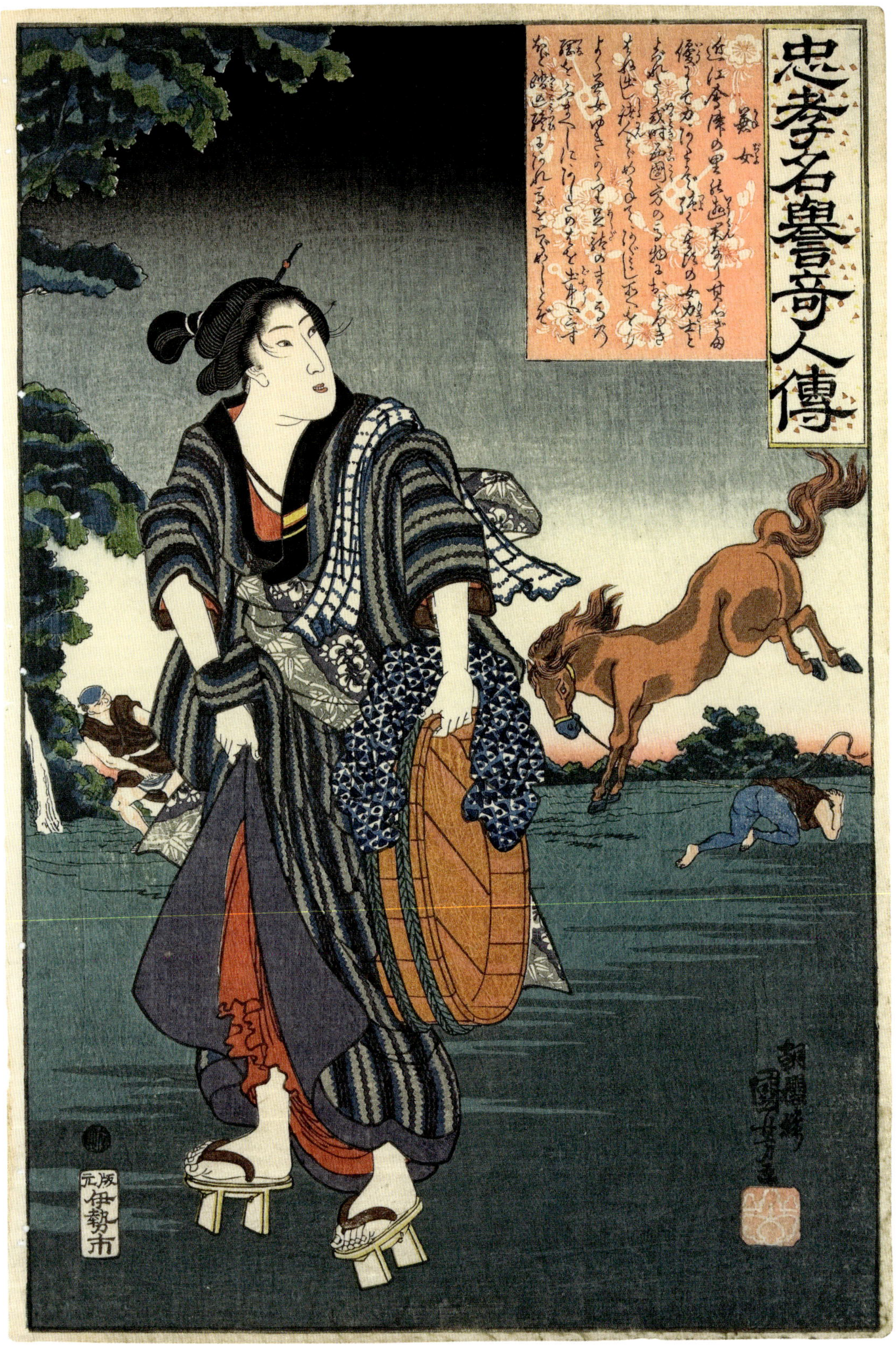

Colour woodblock, *ōban*,
published by Iseya Ichibei,
36.4 × 25 cm

SERIES TITLE
'Biographies of Exceptional Persons of Loyalty and Honour' (*Chūkō meiyo kijin den*)

PRINT TITLE
'Kanejo'

ARTIST'S SIGNATURE
Chōōrō Kuniyoshi ga

ARTIST'S SEAL
Yoshikiri

CENSOR'S SEAL
Kinugasa

American Friends of the British Museum (The Arthur R. Miller Collection) 15505

REFERENCES
Riccar 1978, no. 207; Robinson 1982, no. S35.5; Yamaguchi 1991, Kuniyoshi no. 63; Suzuki 1992, no. 242; Mainichi Shinbunsha 1995, no. 109; Nagoya 1996, no. 146

The printed text explains that Kane was a country prostitute of fine character and unusual strength – just like a woman wrestler – who lived in the village of Kaizu in Ōmi province. She stopped the runaway horse shown in the print simply by stepping on its reins with one of her clogs: the clog sank three inches into the ground. The story originally appeared in *Kokon chōmon-jū* (*Collection of Noteworthy Tales, Past and Present*, compiled in 1254). Kuniyoshi has chosen the moment when Kane notices the bucking horse and decides to act. The animal and the terrified men near it appear far in the distance and, drawn in the European manner, were probably copied from an imported book illustration. Kane, on the other hand, is depicted in conventional ukiyo-e style.

The print is one of eighteen known from the series 'Biographies of Exceptional Persons of Loyalty and Honour' (*Chūkō meiyo kijin den*), issued jointly by Enshūya Matabei and Iseya Ichibei and featuring famous men and women from Japanese history (Nagoya 1996, p. 251). The rather stilted title testifies to the continuing influence of the moral exhortations contained in the print regulations that formed part of the Tenpō reforms (see p. 20).

A recently discovered group of ninety-five printing blocks comprises mainly items for Kuniyoshi designs issued by the publisher Iseya Ichibei. The blocks include nine for the 'Biographies of Exceptional Persons of Loyalty and Honour', among them some of the colour blocks, but not the key-block, for the present design (National Museum of Japanese History, Sakura; personal communication from Ōkubo Jun'ichi).

63

Woman mending a fishing net

1845–46

Colour woodblock, *ōban*, published by Ebiya Rinnosuke, 36.9 × 25.5 cm

PRINT TITLE
'Yui'

SERIES TITLE
'Fifty-three Pairings along the Tōkaidō Road' (*Tōkaidō gojūsan-tsui*)

ARTIST'S SIGNATURE
Ichiyūsai Kuniyoshi ga (in gourd-shaped *Yoshi* cartouche)

CENSOR'S SEAL
Mura

American Friends of the British Museum (The Arthur R. Miller Collection) 04317

REFERENCES
Robinson 1982, no. S44.17; Amsterdam 1998, no. 46; Ōta 1999, no. 92

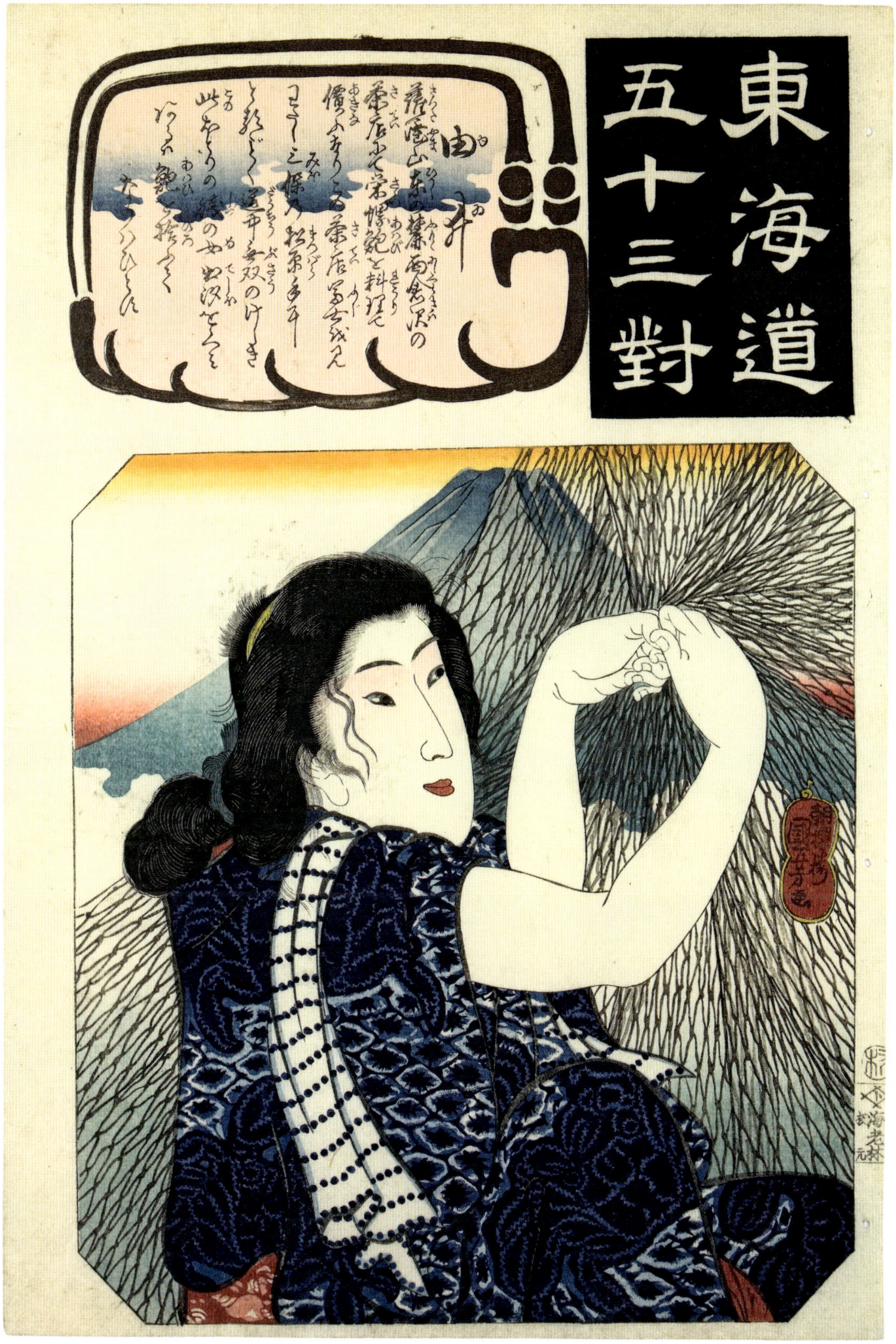

The woman is mending a fishing net through which Mt Fuji can be seen. Her robe is decorated with a tie-dyed indigo design of large crabs; the red sash bears a pattern of seashells. The text in the stylised lobster-shaped cartouche above the image describes a teahouse in the village of Nishi-Kurasawa at the foot of the eastern slopes of Mt Satta. Here, the local culinary delicacy, a kind of shellfish called 'turban abalone' (*sazai-awabi*), could be enjoyed along with an unparalleled view of Fuji and Miho-no-Matsubara. The shellfish were collected at low tide by poor local women.

The print comes from the series 'Fifty-three Pairings along the Tōkaidō Road' (*Tōkaidō gojūsan-tsui*), the 'pairings' perhaps indicating a connection between the name of each post-station on the road and either a legendary event that happened there or another subject associated with the place depicted in the main picture. The Tōkaidō was the principal highway along the Pacific coast, linking the shogun's capital, Edo (modern Tokyo), and the ancient imperial capital, Kyoto. The series has one design for each of the fifty-three stations, an additional print each for Mitsuke, Ishiyakushi and Ōtsu (for unknown reasons) and compositions featuring Nihonbashi and Kyoto that mark the beginning and the end of the road. Robinson lists all fifty-eight prints (Robinson 1982, series S44). The present design is that for Yui, the sixteenth station from Edo. Three leading ukiyo-e artists collaborated on the series, Kuniyoshi producing thirty-one designs, Hiroshige nineteen and Kunisada eight. Some half a dozen publishers cooperated on issuing the prints.

FABRIC-PICTURE BATTLEDORES

(Cats 64, 65)

An *oshi-e* ('pressed picture') consists of carefully cut shapes of different fabrics that have been mounted on paper and assembled into a picture. Sometimes the individual shapes are padded from behind to create a three-dimensional effect. A *hagoita* is a decorated battledore for hitting shuttlecocks in games played during the New Year holidays. By the early nineteenth century battledores with pressed-picture decoration were being made as New Year decorations without any intention of their being used as racquets, which in any case would have been unpractical when the picture was padded. The tradition survives to this day.

The present series of prints presents half-length portraits of famous figures from history. Eight designs are known, half of them depicting women, the other half men or boys (Nagoya 1996, p.243). The series title is written right to left across the top. The 'battledore' functions exclusively as a novel framing device. Kunisada had used it in the early 1820s for images of Kabuki actors. The tall, narrow format, known as *chū-tanzaku*, is achieved by cutting a standard *ōban* sheet vertically in half.

64

Haiku poet Shūshiki

1845–46

Colour woodblock, *chū-tanzaku*, pubished by Ibaya Senzaburō, 37.4 × 12.7 cm

PRINT TITLE
'Shūshiki'

SERIES TITLE
'Fabric-picture Battledores' (*Oshi-e hagoita*)

ARTIST'S SIGNATURE
Chōōrō Kuniyoshi ga

ARTIST'S SEAL
Yoshikiri

BLOCK-CUTTER
Matsushima Fusajirō

CENSOR'S SEAL
Watari

American Friends of the British Museum (The Arthur R. Miller Collection) 22101

REFERENCES
Suzuki 1992, no. 278; Mainichi Shinbunsha 1995, no. 116; Robinson and Miller 1996, no. S35a.4

The haiko poet Shūshiki-jo (d. 1725) of Edo was a pupil of Takarai Kikaku, who, in turn, had been a pupil of the great Matsuo Bashō (1644–1694). At the age of thirteen (twelve by Western reckoning) she composed the following celebrated verse about raucous flower-viewers at Ueno: 'Cherry by the well / Watch out! / Drunk on saké' (*I no hata no / sakura abunashi / sake no yoi*). In Kuniyoshi's print she holds a roll of paper while looking attentively over one shoulder, no doubt poised to compose a verse.

65

Strongwoman O-Kane

1845–46

Colour woodblock, *chū-tanzaku*, pubished by Ibaya Senzaburō, 37.1 × 12.5 cm

PRINT TITLE
'Okane from Ōmi' (*Ōmi no Okane*)

SERIES TITLE
'Fabric-picture Battledores' (*Oshi-e hagoita*)

ARTIST'S SIGNATURE
Chōōrō Kuniyoshi ga

ARTIST'S SEAL
Yoshikiri

CENSOR'S SEAL
Watari

American Friends of the British Museum (The Arthur R. Miller Collection) 22102

REFERENCES
Suzuki 1992, no. 277; Mainichi Shinbunsha 1995, no. 113; Nagoya 1996, no. 106; Robinson and Miller 1996, no. S35a.3; Ōta 1999, no. 91

The story of O-Kane and the bolting horse is discussed in the entry for cat. 62. In that picture, too, O-Kane is shown holding a shallow wooden washing tub under her arm. Red braids (*tasuki*) are tied around her shoulders to keep her sleeves up while she works. Appropriately, the complex blue and white dyed pattern on her cotton robe incorporates a metal horse's bit at the shoulder. The wisps of hair hanging down at her temples indicate that she has arranged her hair casually, for work. O-Kane is portrayed as confident, even assertive – qualities generally admired in the working townswomen of Edo. The arrangement of the features, with long aquiline nose, high-set eyes and lips parted slightly to reveal pearly white teeth, is a hallmark of Kuniyoshi's style, clearly distinguishing his work from that of his major rivals, Kunisada and Eisen.

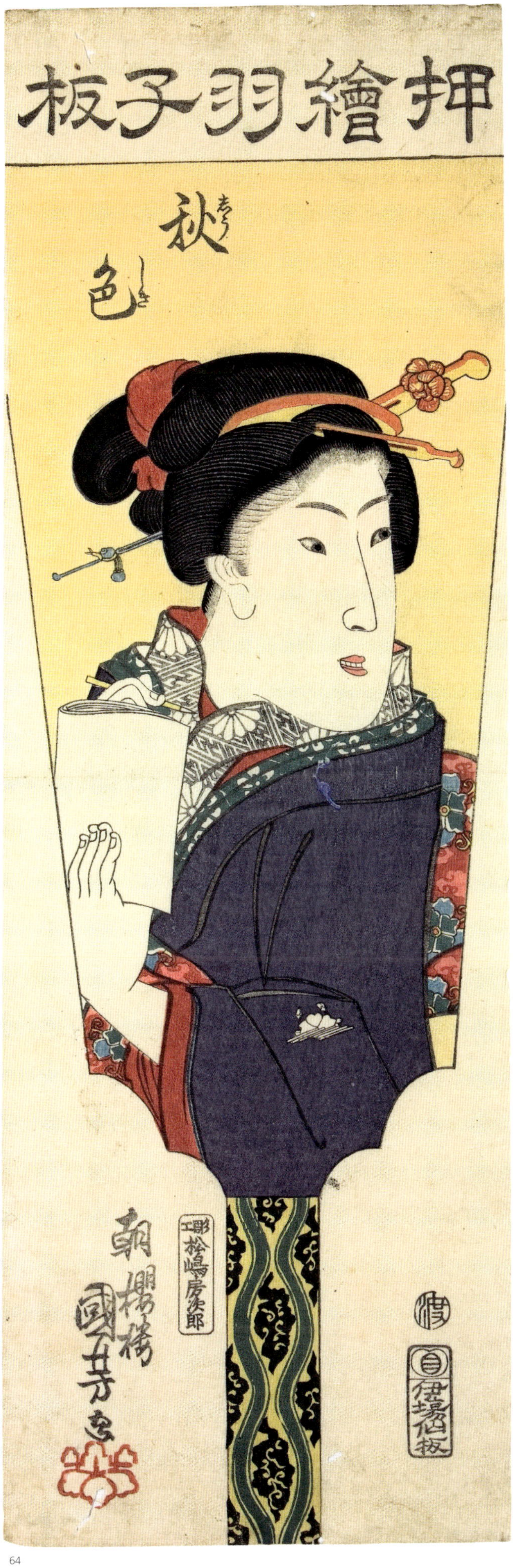

64

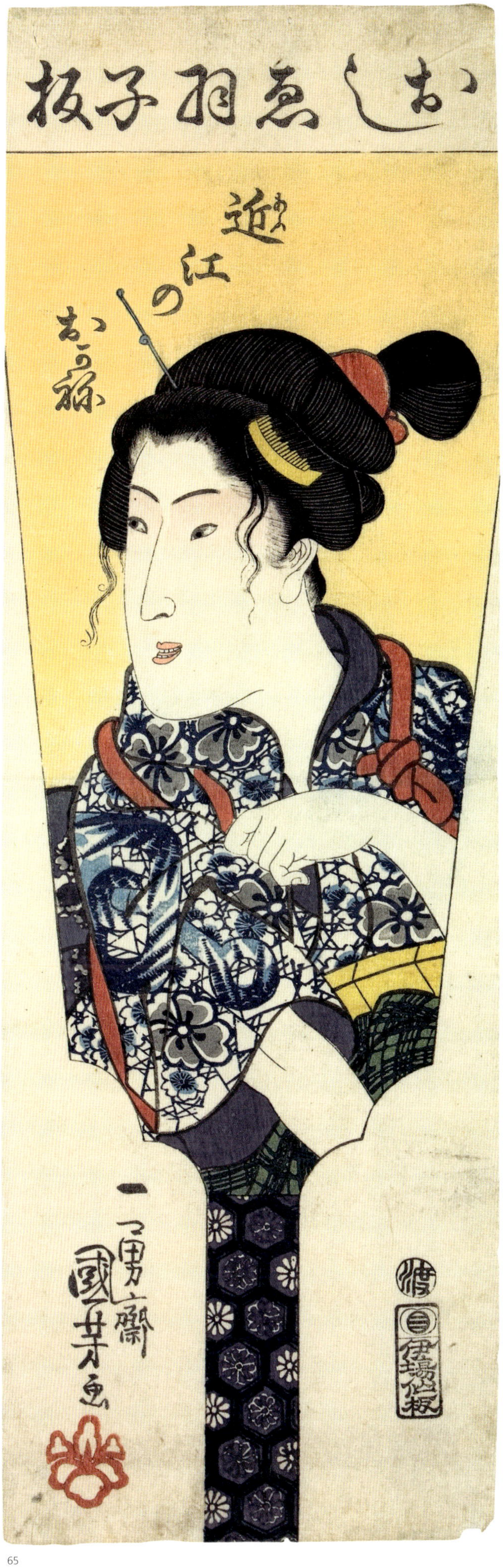

65

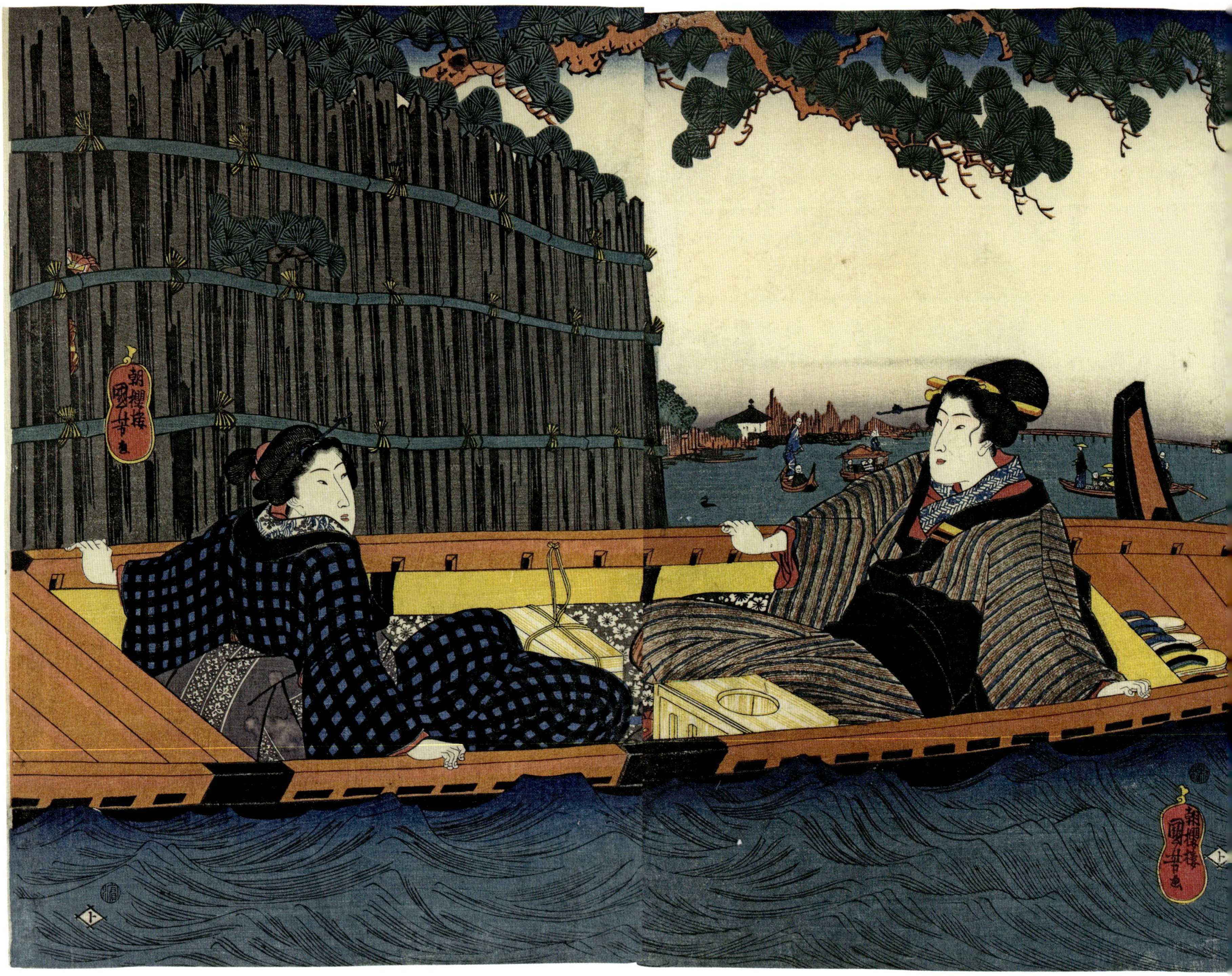

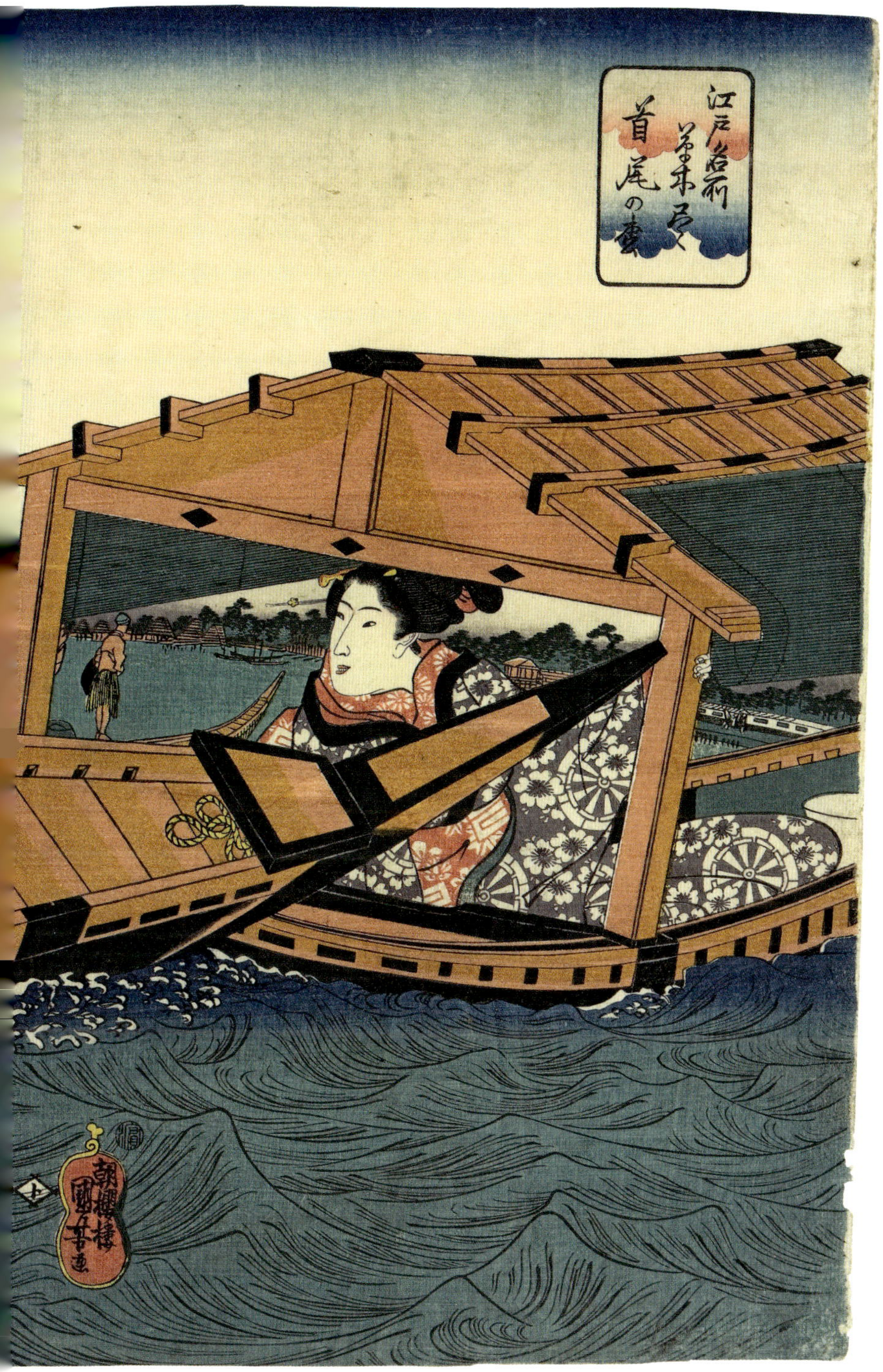

66

Three women in pleasure boats

1843–44

Colour woodblock, *ōban* triptych, published by Ebiya Rinnosuke, 36.9 × 25.4 [R], 36.5 × 25.3 [C], 36.9 × 25.5 cm [L]

SERIES TITLE
'Plants and Trees at all the Famous Places in Edo' (*Edo meisho sōmoku-zukushi*)

PRINT TITLE
'Successful-deal Pine Tree' (*Shubi no matsu*)

ARTIST'S SIGNATURE
Chōōrō Kuniyoshi ga (in gourd-shaped *Yoshi* cartouche)

CENSORS' SEALS
Hama (right, left) and Muramatsu (centre)

American Friends of the British Museum (The Arthur R. Miller Collection) 18617

REFERENCES
Springfield 1980, no.23; Yamaguchi 1991, Kuniyoshi no.60; Suzuki 1992, no.258; Baur 1994, no.G391

Two boats have collided on the choppy waters of the Sumida river in the centre of Edo. The two women in the narrow boat hang on for dear life, while the woman in the roofed pleasure boat looks on in amusement. The narrow vessel is a type of fast river-taxi called a 'boar's tusk boat' (*choki-bune*) after its distinctive shape; the ferryman is to be imagined standing just out of the picture, on the left, manipulating a single oar at the stern. A panoramic view of the river unfolds behind the boats, looking north (upstream) towards Ōkawa bridge on the horizon. The small white square building on the left (west) bank is Komagatadō, a Buddhist temple. Kuniyoshi has paid considerable attention to the detailed depiction of various kinds of boat: a fishing boat, a passenger ferry crossing the river, and more pleasure boats and river-taxis coming downstream towards the viewer.

Above the women's heads stretch the protective branches of 'Successful-deal Pine Tree' (*Shubi no matsu*), a landmark looked out for by travellers up and down the river at its location in front of a row of government warehouses at Kuramae. The tree's name was said to derive from playboy passengers' tales of their exploits in Yoshiwara pleasure quarter, related on their way back to the centre of town the morning after (Hamada 1973, pp.223–4).

This and a further triptych (cat.67) are the only known designs from the series 'Plants and Trees at all the Famous Places in Edo' (*Edo meisho sōmoku-zukushi*).

67

Three women in a hilltop teahouse

1843–44

Colour woodblock, *ōban* triptych, published by Ebiya Rinnosuke, 37.4 × 25.5 [R], 37.2 × 25.3 [C], 36.9 × 25.1 cm [R]

SERIES TITLE
'Plants and Trees at all the Famous Places in Edo' (*Edo meisho sōmoku-zukushi*)

PRINT TITLE
'Autumn Maples at Eight-view Hill in Shinagawa' (*Shinagawa Yakei-zaka no momiji*)

ARTIST'S SIGNATURE
Ichiyūsai Kuniyoshi ga (right sheet), Chōōrō Kuniyoshi ga (centre, left sheets)

CENSOR'S SEAL
Hama

American Friends of the British Museum (The Arthur R. Miller Collection) 18618

The setting is a hill overlooking Edo bay, above Shinagawa post-station on the southern outskirts of Edo. The 'Eight-view Hill' (Yakei-zaka) mentioned in the title survives as a modern place name, close to Ōmori station in Ōta ward, Tokyo. The women on the left and centre sheets, rather breathless after their climb up the hill, are resting at a teahouse, where they are served by a waitress. Their bundles of ripe persimmons and rice cakes in the shape of flower stems (*mochi-bana*) suggest they have been on a pilgrimage to the Meguro Fudō temple. As the title indicates, this was a spot from which to admire the brilliant autumn foliage of maples, seen on the hillside on the right sheet.

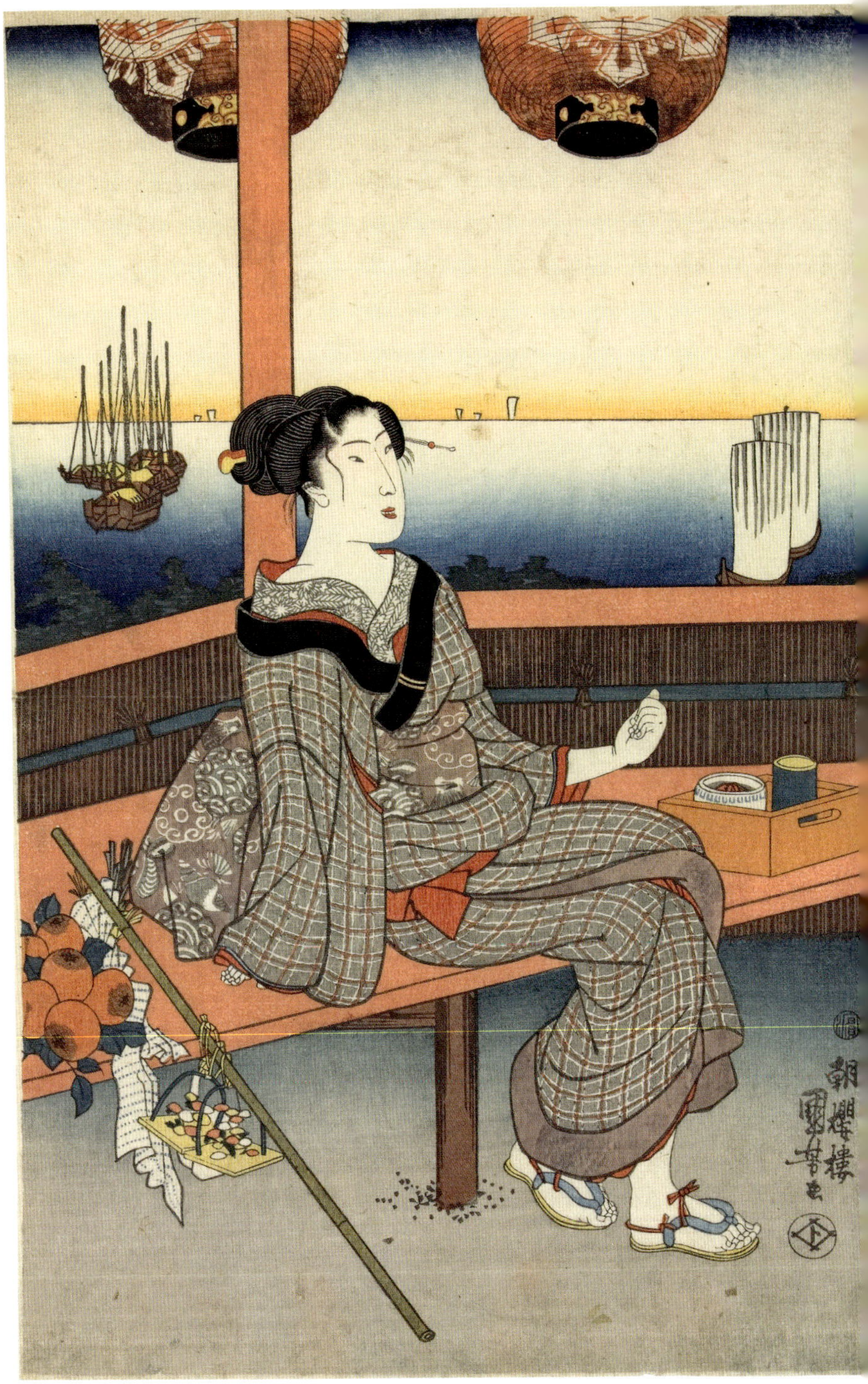

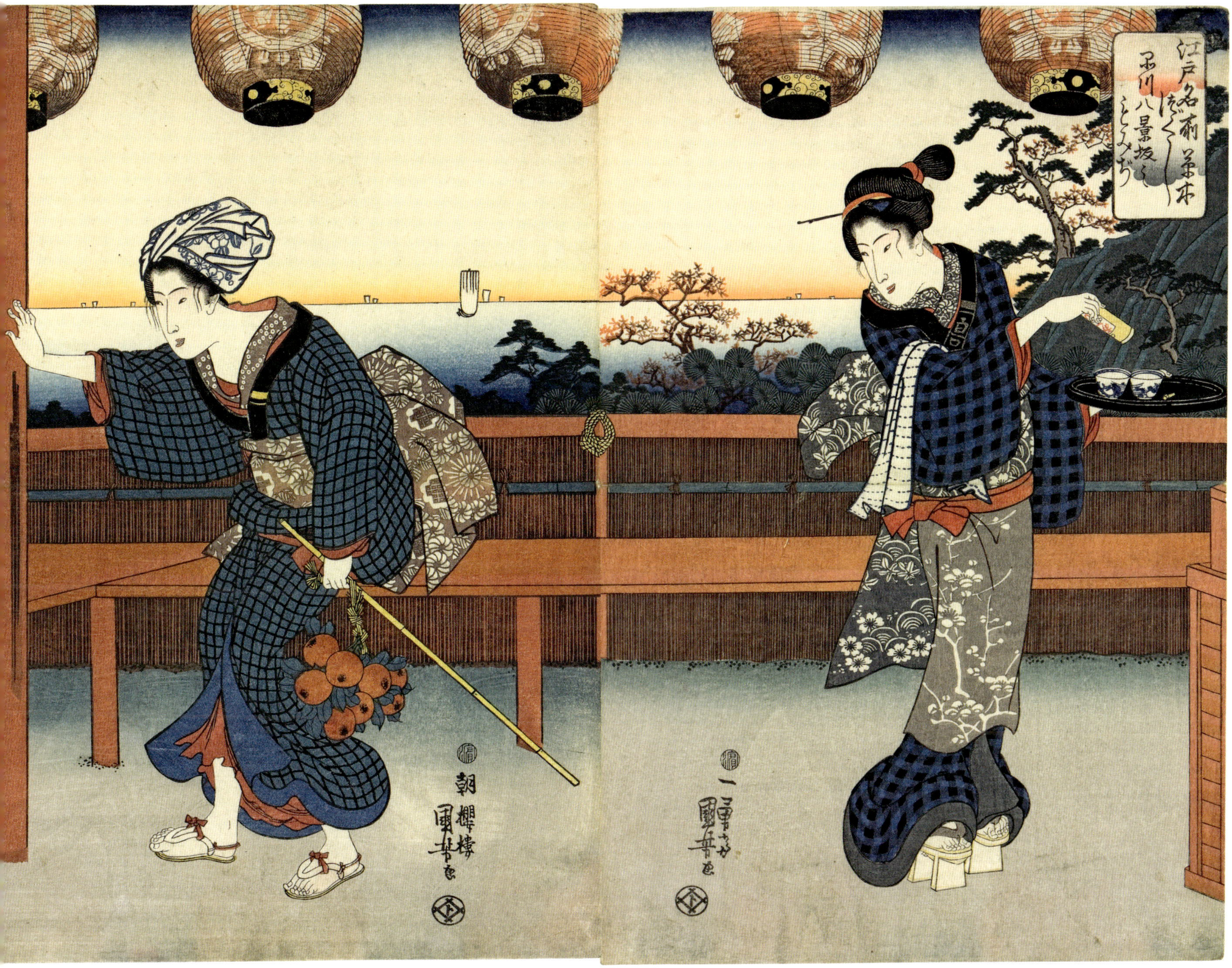
江戸名所茶屋尽し
朝櫻樓國芳画
一勇斎國芳画

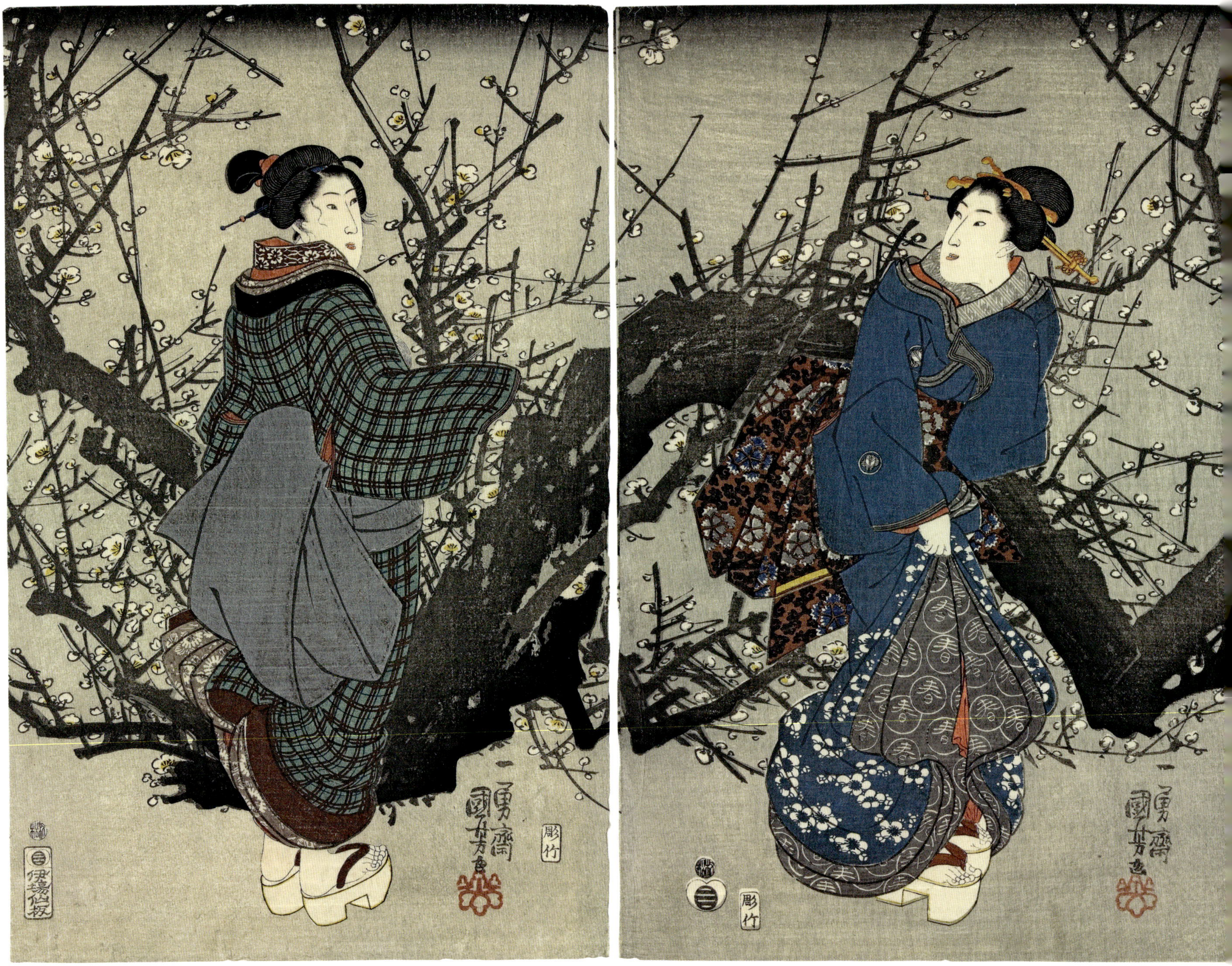
一勇齋國芳画
彫竹
伊場仙板
一勇齋國芳画
彫竹

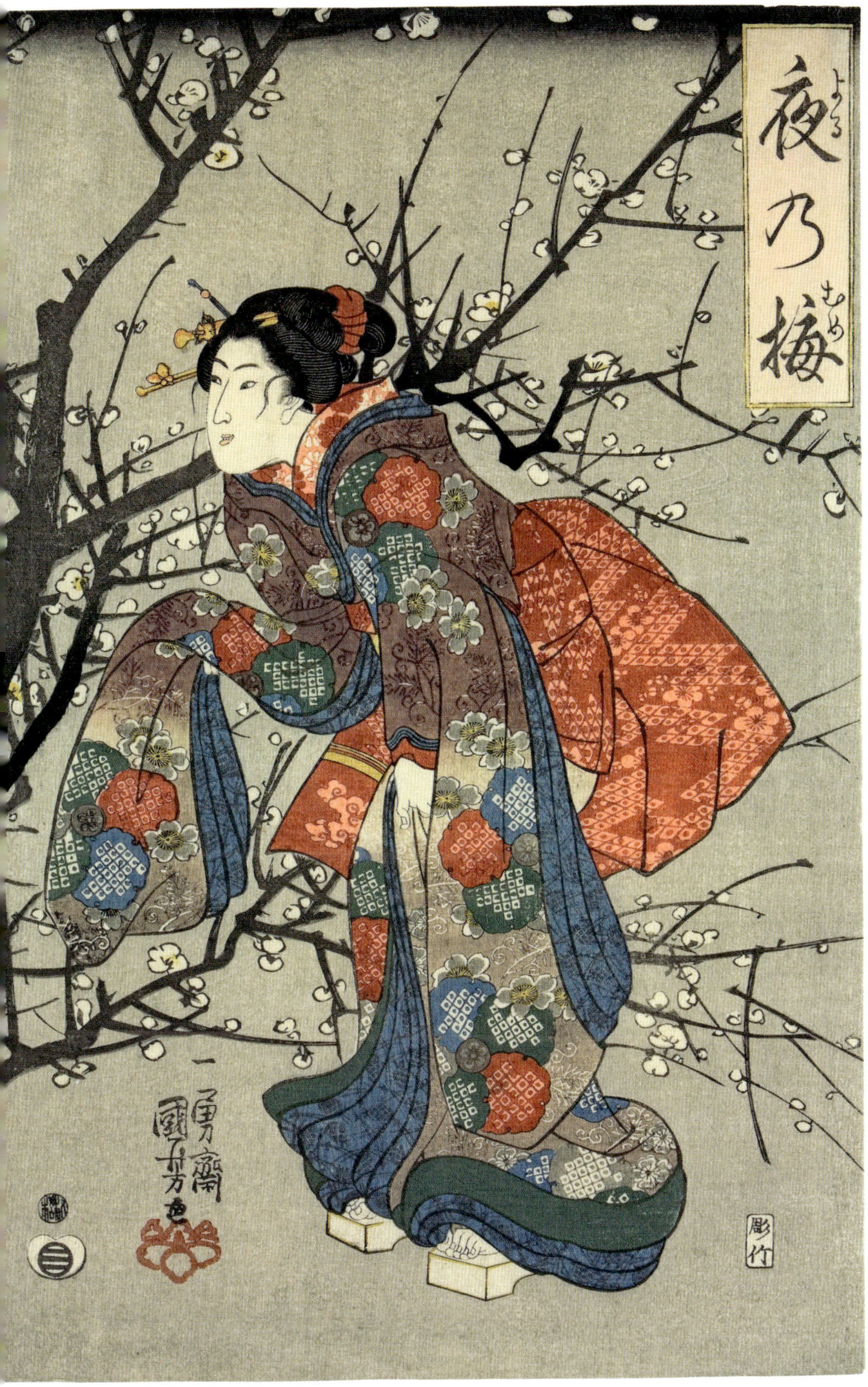

68

Three women by an old plum tree at night

1845–46

Colour woodblock, *ōban* triptych, published by Ibaya Senzaburō, 36.1 × 24.4 [R], 36 × 24.9 [C], 36.1 × 23.5 cm [L]

PRINT TITLE
'Plum Tree at Night' (*Yoru no ume*)

ARTIST'S SIGNATURE
Ichiyūsai Kuniyoshi ga

ARTIST'S SEAL
Yoshikiri

BLOCK CARVER
Hori-Take

CENSOR'S SEAL
Muramatsu

American Friends of the British Museum (The Arthur R. Miller Collection) 18609

REFERENCES
Springfield 1968, no. 36; Riccar 1978, no. 155; HUT, suppl. vol., 1990, no. 67

Three women stand at night next to the spreading trunk and branches of an ancient plum tree that is just coming into bloom. The poses suggest excited admiration. The young woman on the right, for instance, bends forward from the waist and lifts one long, hanging sleeve of her *furisode* to gesticulate with the hand inside. Complex tie-dyeing and past-resist dyeing will have been used to create the design on this robe, which incorporates plum blossoms. The purple skirts of the more mature woman in the centre bears a pattern consisting of the character for 'spring' rendered in white reserve.

The 'Crawling Dragon Plum' (Garyūbai) seen here was a famous attraction of Umeyashiki, a garden located close to the Tenjin shrine at Kameido in Honjo district (see also cat. 59). The trunk of this ancient tree had tilted over onto the ground, where it continued to push down roots, the twisting, constantly proliferating shape prompting its poetic name. Plum was one of the earliest blossoms to appear each spring, and delicate flowers emerging from rugged old trees formed a powerful symbol of renewal. The fragrance of the thousands of blossoms on the Crawling Dragon Plum was almost overpowering and Umeyashiki was always thronged with visitors of all classes at this time of year (Hamada 1973, p. 58).

Kuniyoshi and other ukiyo-e artists produced several versions of the subject, typically featuring one beautiful woman on each sheet of a triptych with the trunk and branches executed across the back with bravura ink-strokes (the Miller Collection contains versions published by Kawaguchiya Uhei [18608] and Yorozuya Kichibei [18610]). Painting plum trees gave Chinese, Korean and Japanese artists – particularly the 'scholar-painters' (*bunjin*) – a chance to show off their brush skills. Sometimes they deliberately split brush hairs so as to suggest gnarled trunks and spiky branches, a technique skilfully imitated here by Kuniyoshi and his block-cutter.

Another printing of the design is known. Formerly in the collection of Theodor Scheiwe, it bears the alternative title 'Plum spring' (*Ume no haru*; illustrated in Christie's 1989a, lot 109).

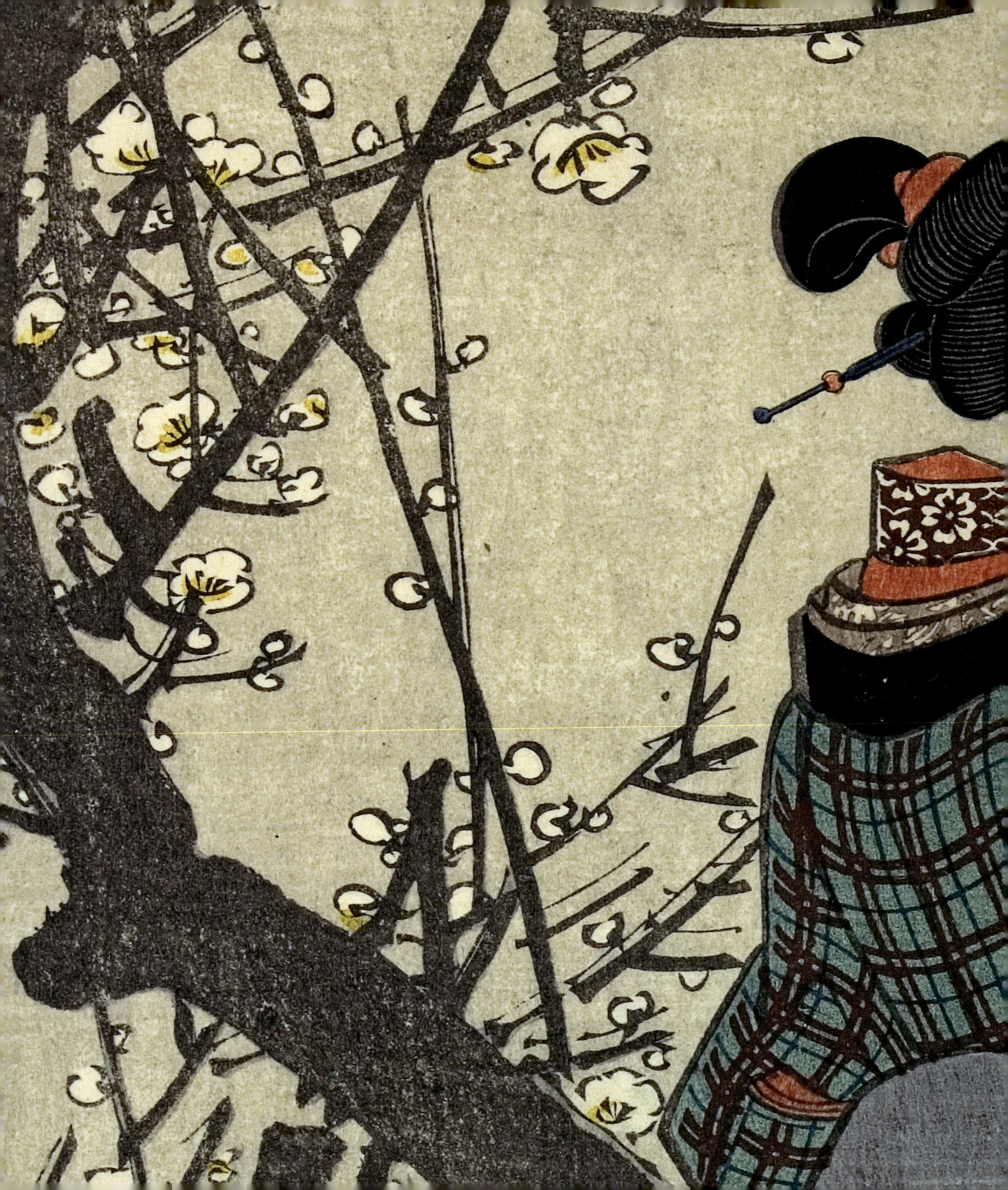

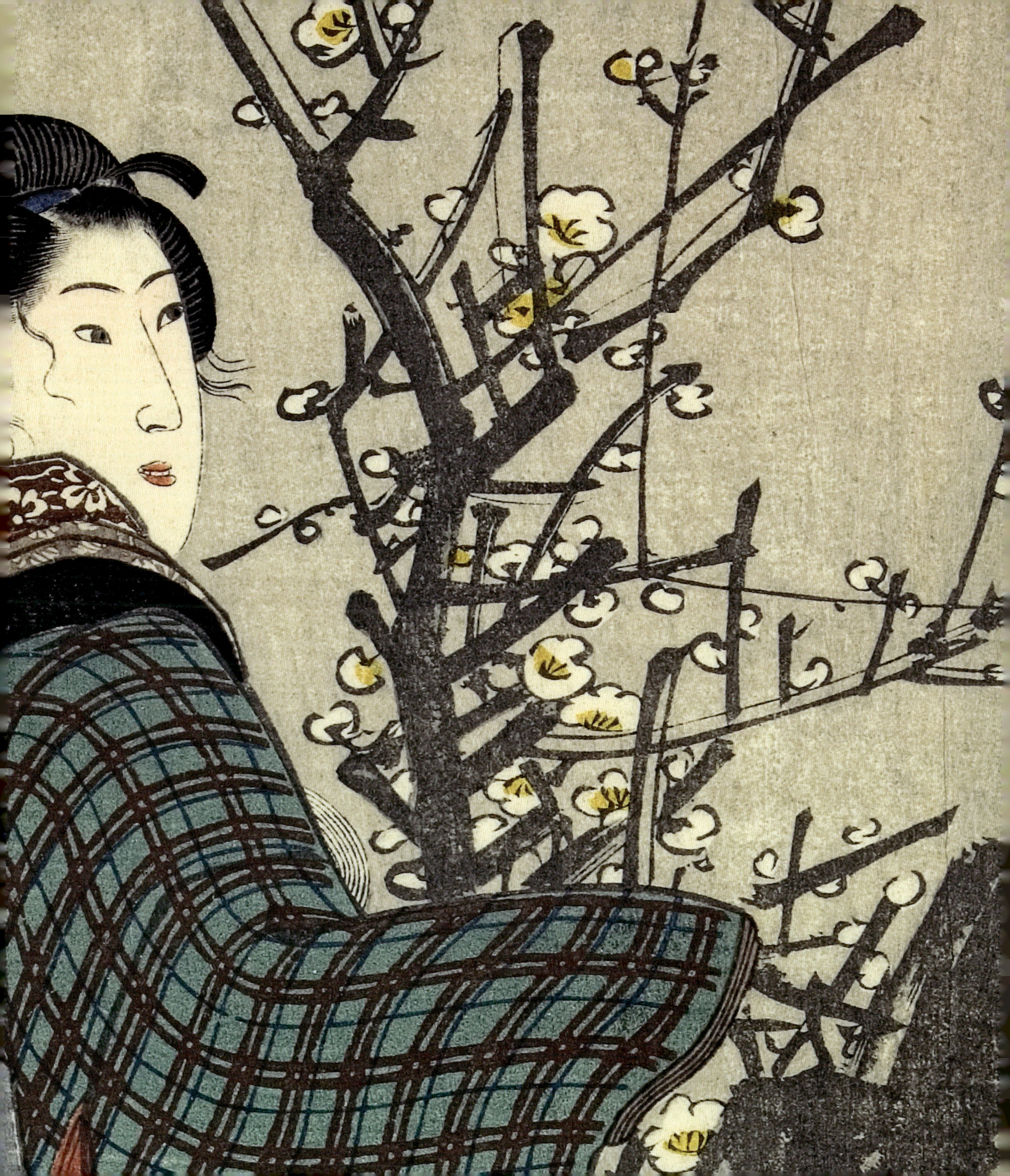

69

Three women collecting brine for salt

1847–48

Colour woodblock, *ōban* triptych, published by Sanoya Kihei, 36.9 × 25 [R], 36.9 × 24.9 [C], 37.2 × 25.3 cm [L]

PRINT TITLE
'Plover Jewel River in Mutsu Province' (*Mutsu no kuni Chidori no Tamagawa*)

ARTIST'S SIGNATURE
Ichiyūsai Kuniyoshi ga

ARTIST'S SEAL
Yoshikiri

CENSORS' SEALS
Mera and Murata

American Friends of the British Museum (The Arthur R. Miller Collection) 18613

REFERENCES
HUT, vol. 5, 1989, BW no. 34; Baur 1994, no. G396

Three women are collecting brine in yoked buckets to make salt. Two more women can be seen farther off, one with pails, the other raking salt flats. A flock of plovers rises from the waters and flies off into the distance in a long, winding formation. As with other versions of the subject by Kuniyoshi, the aim was to present working women in alluring poses expressive of exertion and exhibiting a slight dishabille (see also cats 50, 55, 97). A figure very similar to the woman wringing out her wet red undergarment occurs in a *surimono* print of almost twenty years earlier (cat. 50.3).

The theme of women collecting salt has been combined in this triptych with the ancient subject of 'Six Jewel Rivers' (*Mu-tamagawa*). The six rivers, at various locations throughout Japan, are celebrated in classical poems for their beauty. By Kuniyoshi's day they had also become the subject of popular songs and dances. 'Plover Jewel river' (Chidori no Tamagawa), also known as the Noda Jewel river, links the towns of Shiogama ('Salt Kiln', a name reflecting the river's historical connections with salt-making) and Tagajō in modern Miyagi prefecture, where it flows into the Pacific.

The catalogue of the Baur Collection, Geneva, illustrates all six triptychs in what is in effect a series, though it does not have a title (Baur 1994, nos G396–401). Each displays the name of the province and that of the Jewel river within a snowflake-shaped cartouche.

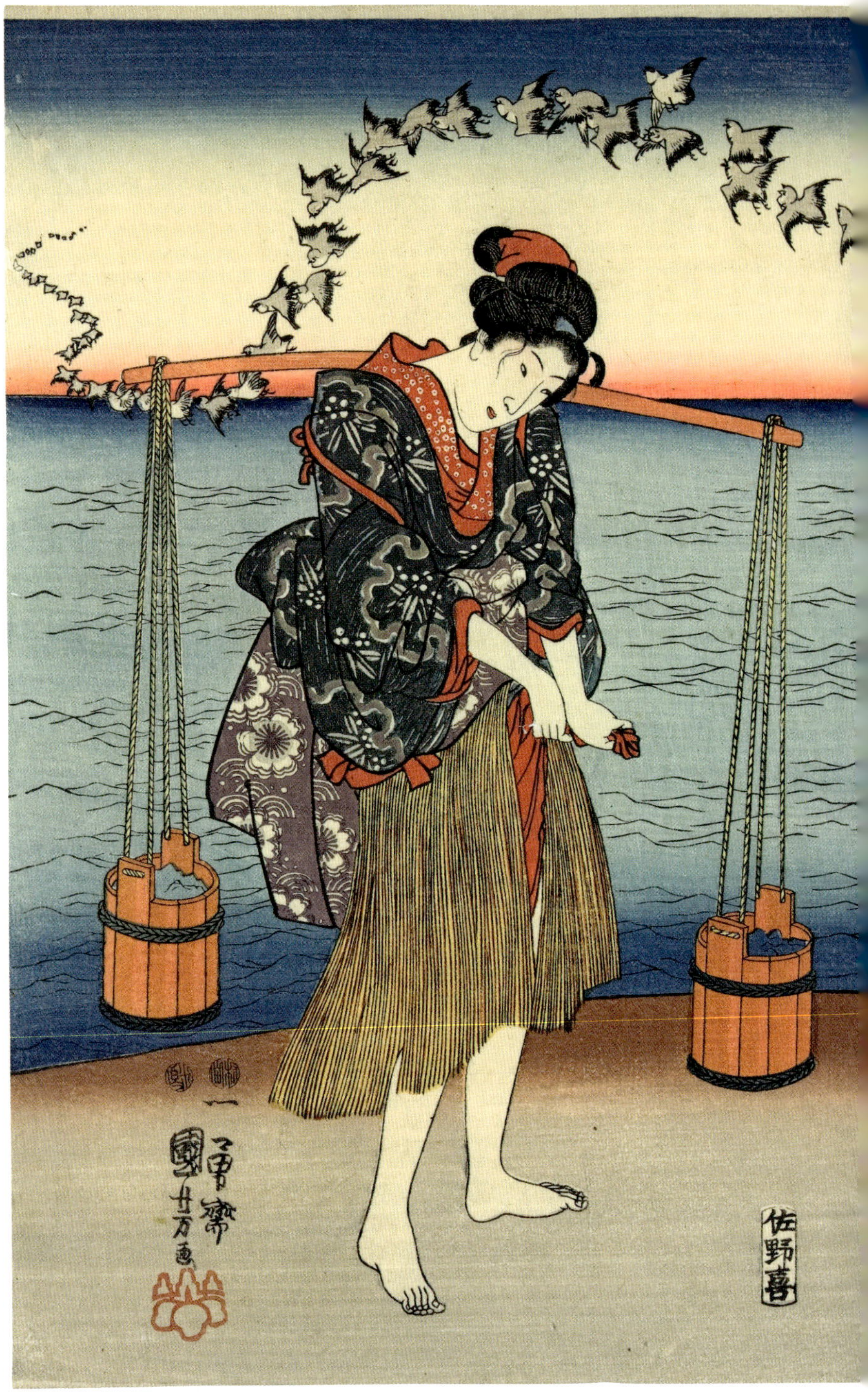

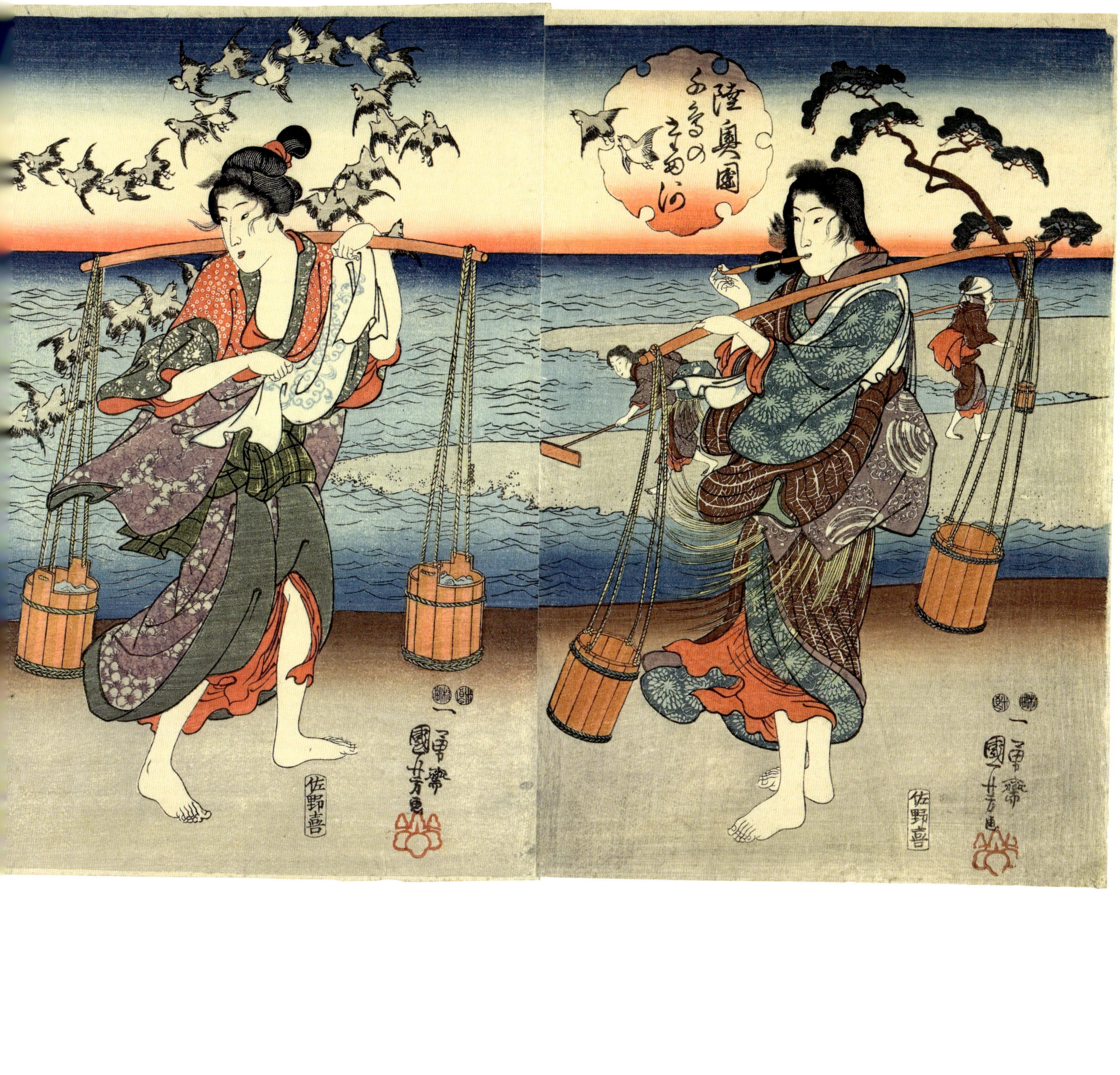
陸奥國
千鳥の玉川
一勇齋國芳画
佐野喜
一勇齋國芳画
佐野喜

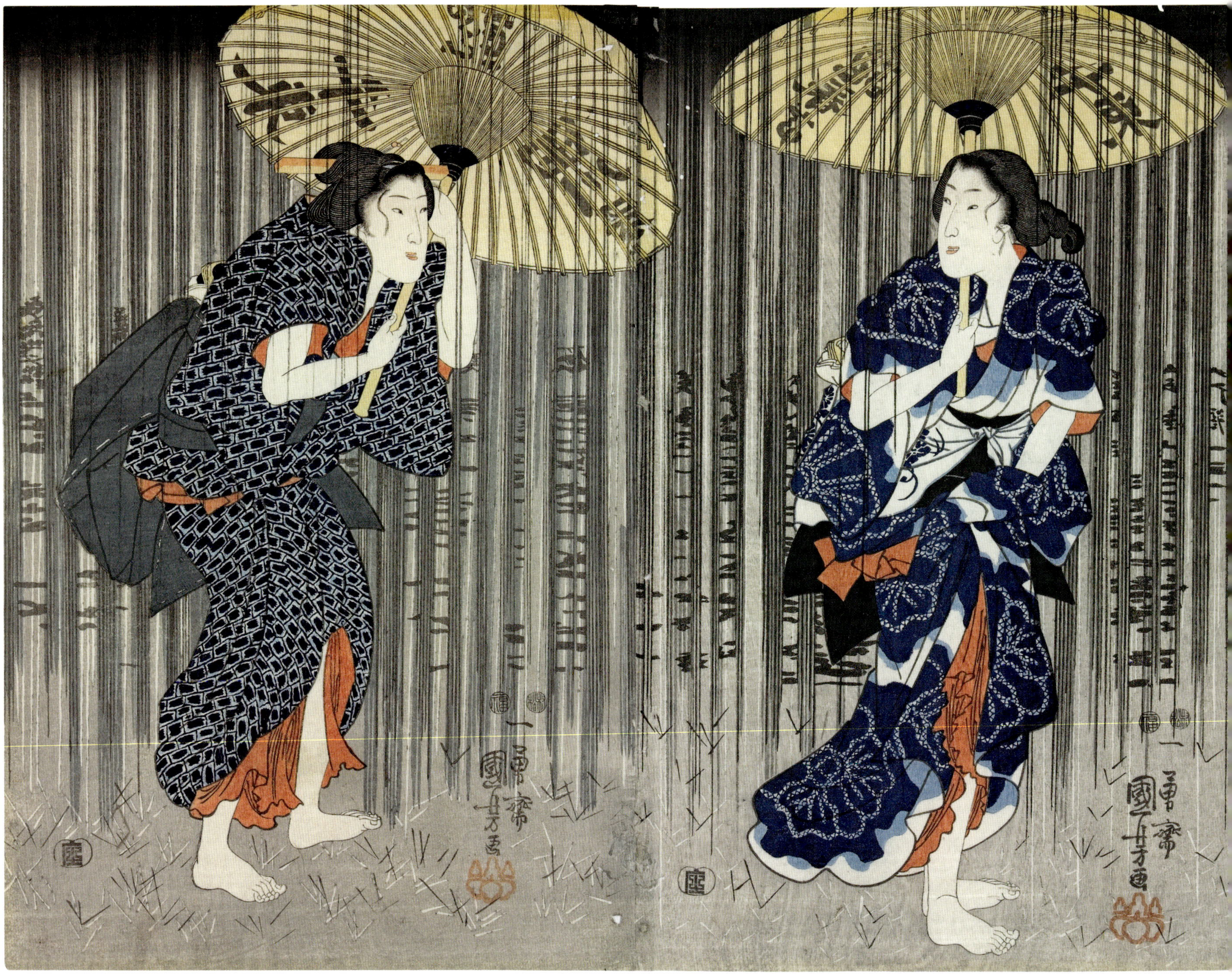
一勇斎國芳画
一勇斎國芳画

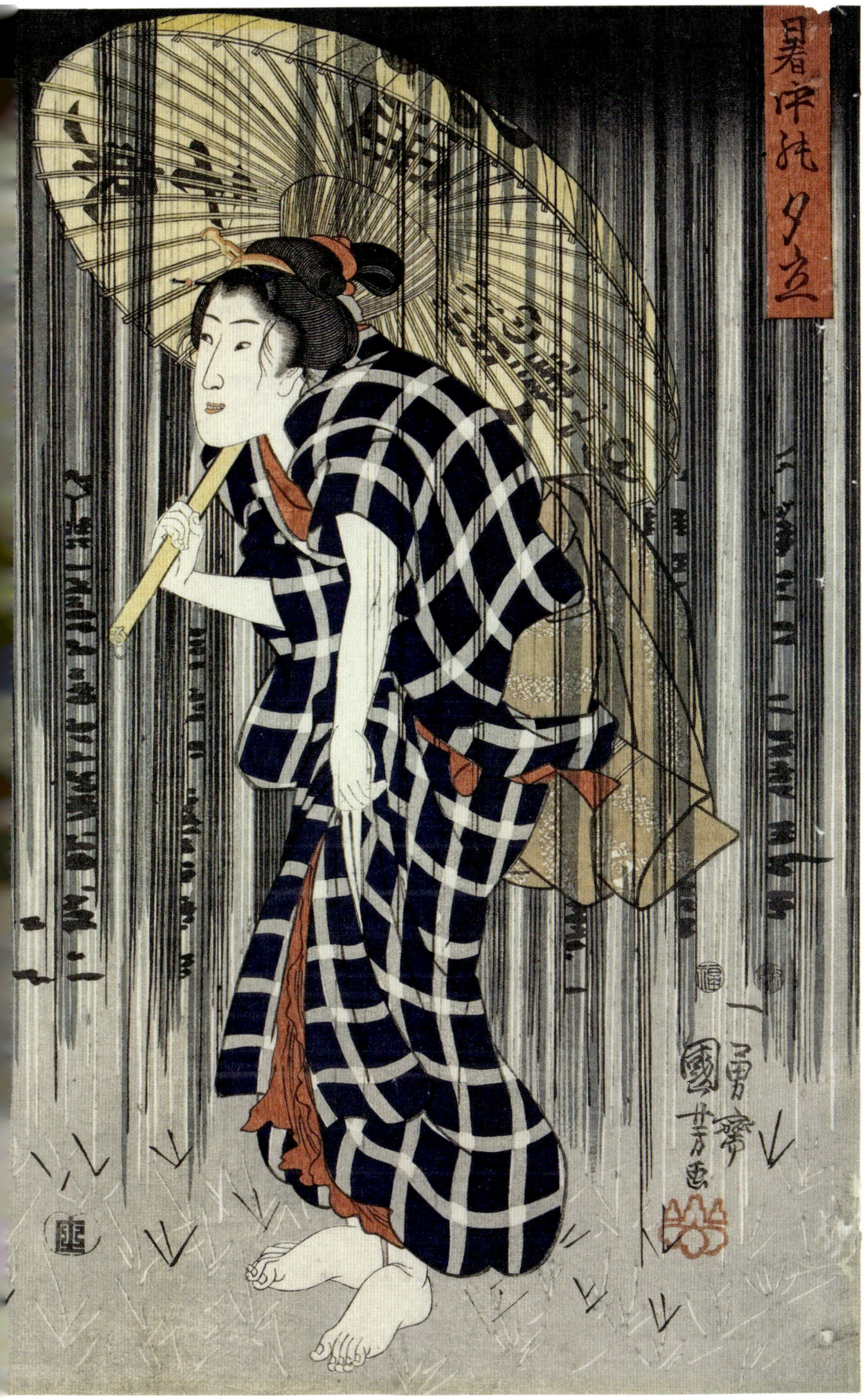

70

Three women with umbrellas in a summer shower

1849–51

Colour woodblock, *ōban* triptych, published by Hayashiya Shōgorō, 36.1 × 24.2 [R], 36.1 × 24.3 [C], 36.2 × 24.4 cm [L]

PRINT TITLE
'Sudden Shower in the Summer Heat' (*Shōchū no yūdachi*)

ARTIST'S SIGNATURE
Ichiyūsai Kuniyoshi ga

ARTIST'S SEAL
Yoshikiri

CENSORS' SEALS
Fuku and Muramatsu

American Friends of the British Museum (The Arthur R. Miller Collection) 18615

REFERENCES
Riccar 1978, no. 157; Springfield 1980, no. 148; Yamaguchi 1991, Kuniyoshi no. 71; Suzuki 1992, no. 261; Baur 1994, no. G406; Itabashi 1994, Kuniyoshi no. 70; Mainichi Shinbunsha 1995, no. 117; Nagoya 1996, no. 165; Amsterdam 1998, no. 149; Ōta 1999, no. 105; Madison 2007, no. 121; Isao 2008, p. 81

The skies have opened and rain pelts straight down around three women. They prefer to go barefoot in this sudden downpour in the steamy heat of mid-summer, rather than ruin their sandals, which are tucked into the back of their sashes. The woman in the centre has even tied a hand towel around her sash to protect it. They all seem to be enjoying the drama of the weather. The umbrellas bear the name Chūshuntei Tagawaya, a famous restaurant in the neighbourhood in front of Daion-ji temple, just to the north-west of Yoshiwara pleasure quarter, that may have sponsored the print. The rice fields glimpsed in the gloom between the shafts of rain are thus probably those near Ryūsen-ji village in the Shitaya district of Edo (Asano Shūgō, in Nagoya 1996, p. 254).

The principal aesthetic satisfaction of the design derives from the complex way in which the rain is depicted. Represented by black, grey and white lines, it appears transparent in the few areas where it passes over the figures. It also splashes up from the ground in places, with some of the splashes rendered in white reserve. The viewer's eyes are also drawn to the bold blue patterns of the cotton summer robes, which suggestively follow the contours of the bodies beneath and bring to mind the fact that Kuniyoshi's father was an indigo dyer by trade.

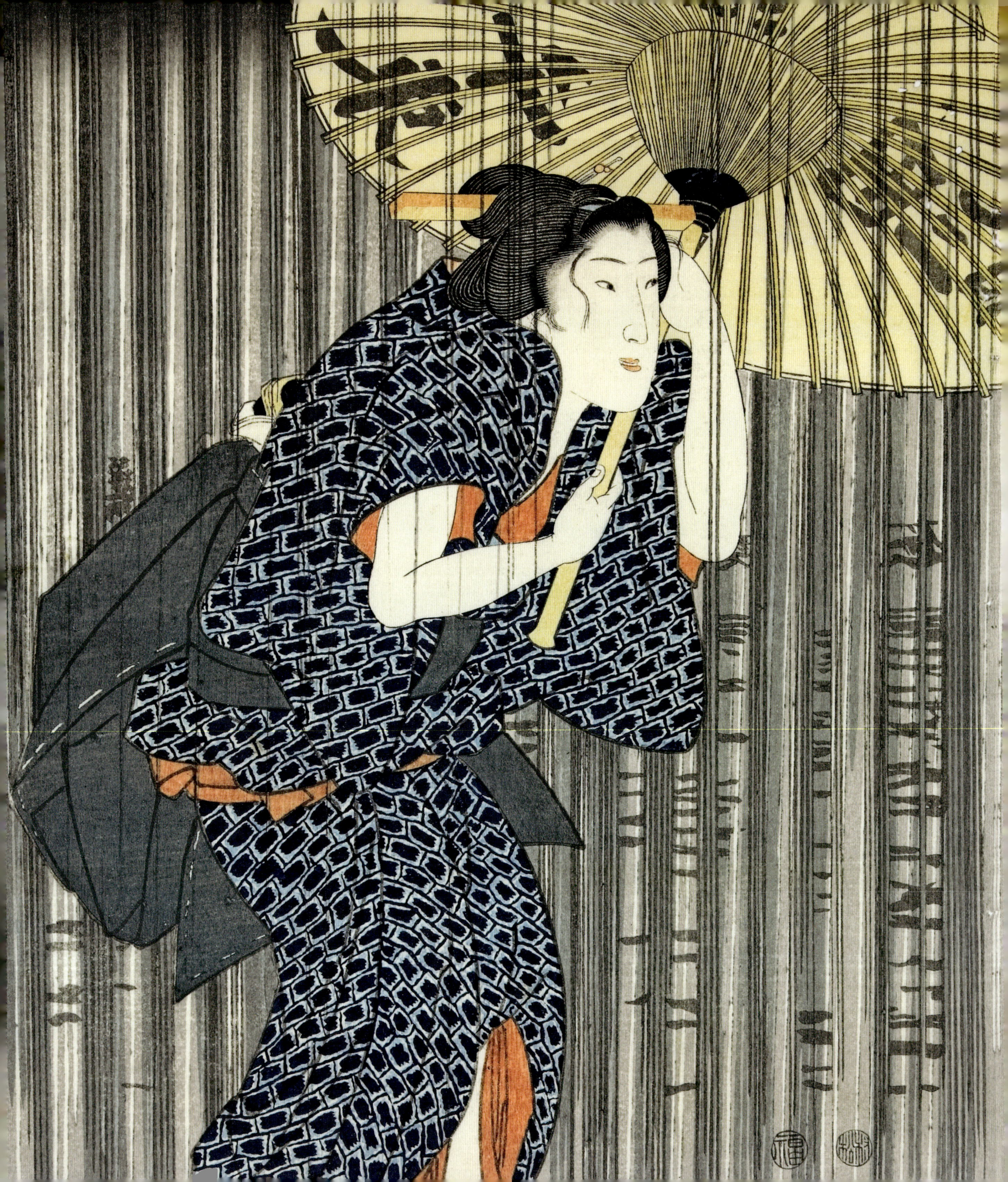

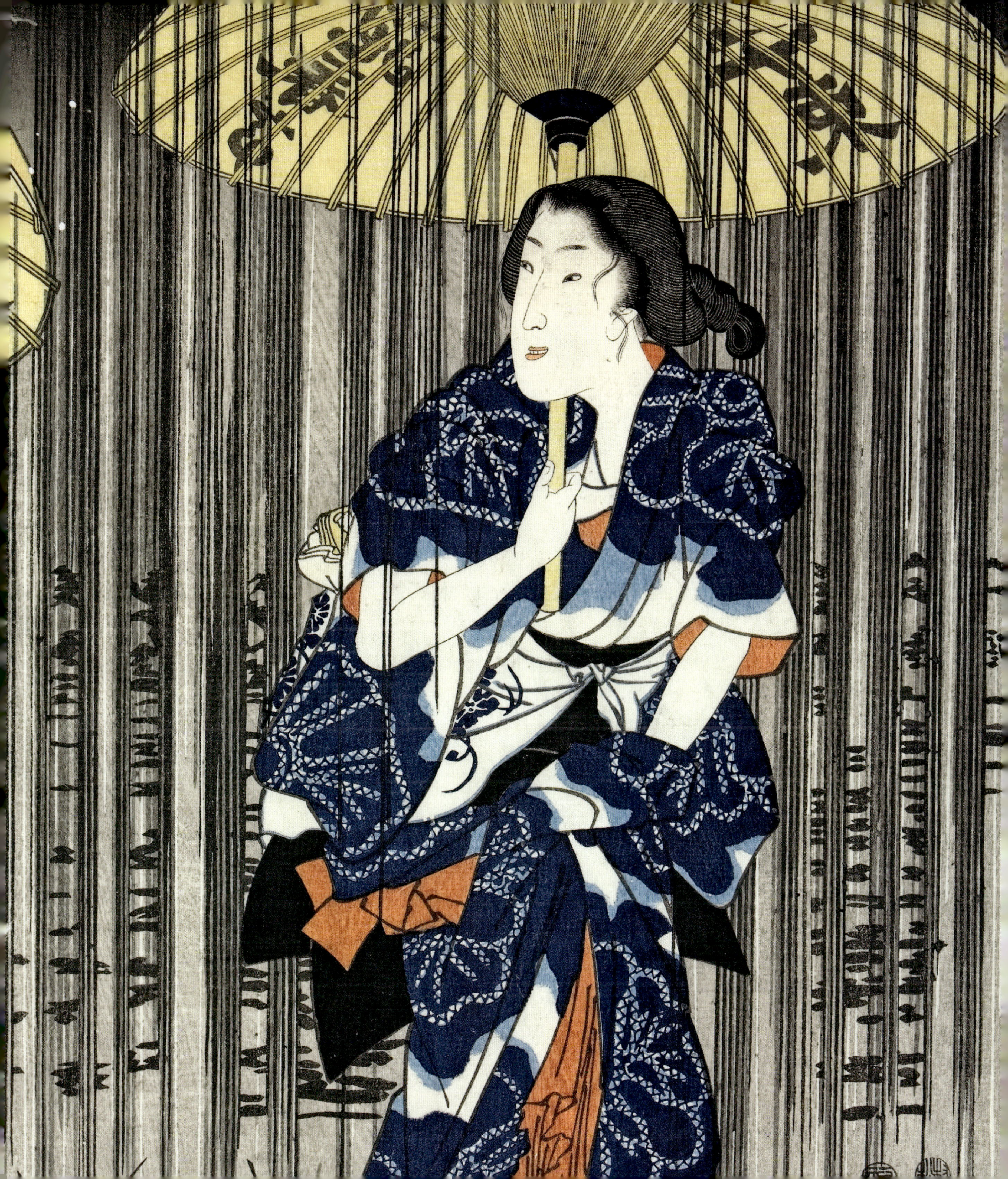

AUSPICIOUS PICTURES OF LAND AND SEA

(Cats 71–3)

The series features half-length portraits of women of different classes and occupations, paired with inset pictures of well-known regional products. The rationale behind the pairings is unclear. The word *medetai* in the title not only means 'auspicious', but in this context also refers to products 'we should be grateful for'. The *-tai* suffix is playfully repeated as the last sound in the subtitle of each print, written on the left within the red (sometimes horizontally banded) title cartouche with decorative floral borders. When *-tai* occurs at the end of a verb it signifies a wish to do something, and there is a sense in some compositions that the woman depicted is impatient or excited. The inset pictures, designed by Kuniyoshi's two daughters and other pupils, have their own titles, which generally combine the name of a province – occasionally also a place – with that of a land or marine product for which it is noted. Many of these are food products.

Each of the designs is numbered. The highest recorded number is seventy, but, since eight items have yet to be accounted for, the total number of currently known designs is sixty-two. (The number of provinces was traditionally given as sixty-eight.) With one exception, each of the inset pictures is individually signed. Sarah Thompson has totalled those responsible for them as follows: forty designs by Kuniyoshi's elder daughter, Tori (1839–?70), four by his younger daughter, Yoshi (1842–?85), nine by Daiji, one by Toriyoshi, six by Yoshiiku (1833–94), one unsigned (presumed to be by Kuniyoshi) and one with an illegible signature. In 1852, when the prints appeared, Tori and Yoshi were aged thirteen and ten respectively (personal communication from Sarah Thompson). The series was issued jointly by five publishers: Sanoya Kihei, Tsutaya Kichizō, Yamaguchiya Tōbei, Jōshūya Kinzō and Mitaya Kihachi. The Miller Collection contains fifty-four of the designs (02101 to 02156, two numbers unused).

71

Woman playing with a cat

1852

Colour woodblock, *ōban*, published by Tsutaya Kichizō, 36.9 × 25.2 cm

SERIES TITLE
'Auspicious Pictures of Land and Sea' (*Sankai medetai zue*)

PRINT TITLE
'No. 7, Ouch! That hurts!' (*Oo, itai*)

INSET LANDSCAPE TITLE
'Giant Octopus at Nameri River, Etchū Province' (*Etchū Namerikawa no ōtako*)

ARTIST'S SIGNATURE
Ichiyūsai Kuniyoshi ga (in gourd-shaped *Yoshi* cartouche)

ARTIST'S SEAL
Yoshikiri

ARTIST'S SIGNATURE ON INSET LANDSCAPE
Yoshitori ga

CENSORS' SEALS
Murata and Kinugasa

DATE SEAL
8th month, 1852

American Friends of the British Museum (The Arthur R. Miller Collection) 02105

REFERENCES
Amsterdam 1998, no. 154; Madison 2007, no. 152

The print, titled 'Ouch! That hurts!', shows a pet cat clawing excitedly at a young woman's robe and nipping her on the chin. The inset picture depicts a large octopus being hunted in the Nameri river in Etchū province (modern Toyama prefecture), which flows into the sea at Toyama bay.

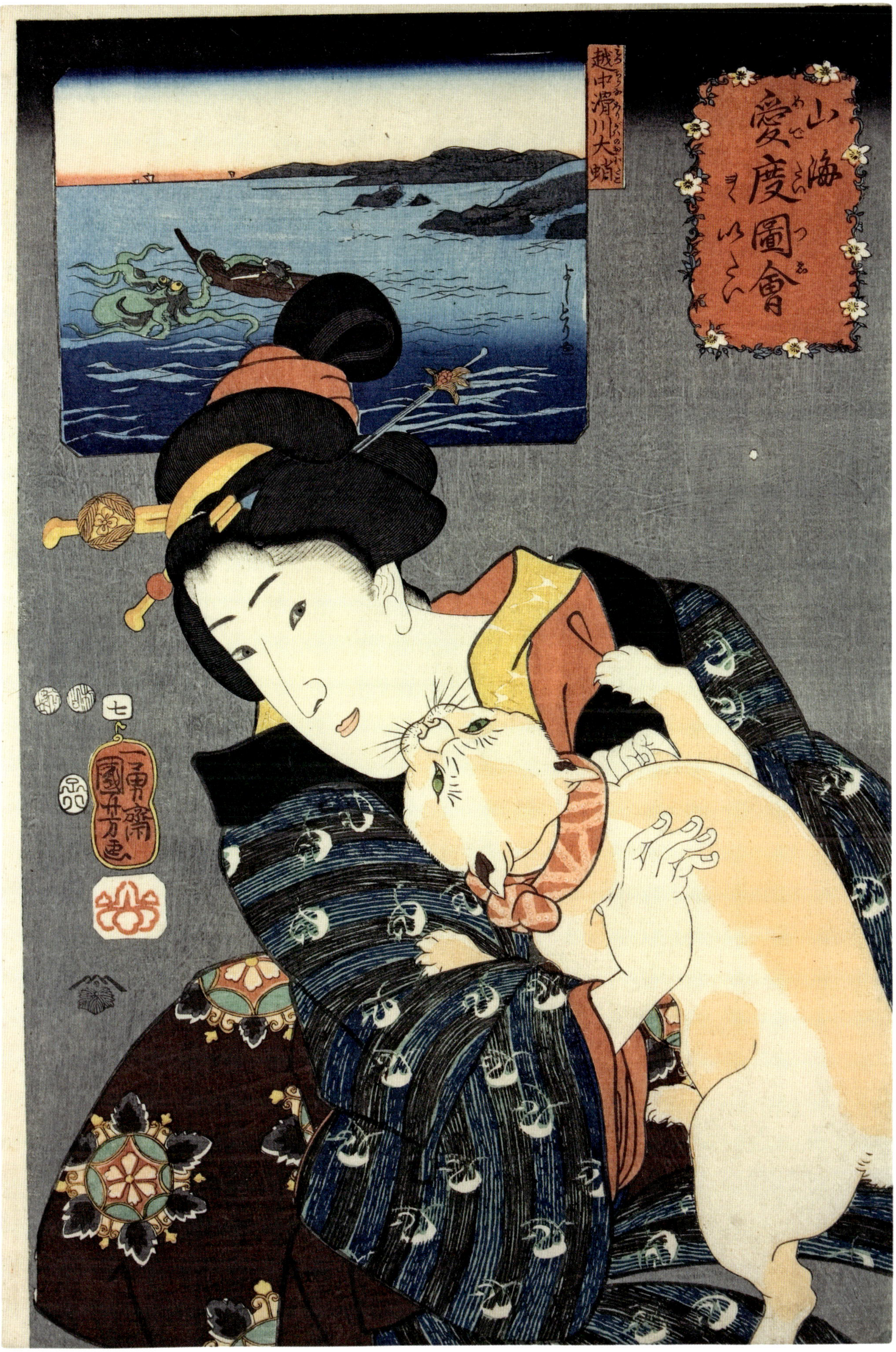
山海愛度圖會
越中滑川大蛸
七
一勇齋國芳画

72

Woman looking at a Kabuki theatre booklet

1852

Colour woodblock, *ōban*, published by Sanoya Kihei, 37.4 × 25.7 cm

SERIES TITLE
'Auspicious Pictures of Land and Sea' (*Sankai medetai zue*)

PRINT TITLE
'No. 2, Can't wait to see it' (*Hayaku mitai*)

INSET LANDSCAPE TITLE
'Whale at Hirado' (*Hirado no kujira*)

ARTIST'S SIGNATURE
Ichiyūsai Kuniyoshi ga (in gourd-shaped *Yoshi* cartouche)

ARTIST'S SEAL
Yoshikiri

ARTIST'S SIGNATURE ON INSET LANDSCAPE
Yoshitori ga

CENSORS' SEALS
Mera and Watanabe

DATE SEAL
7th month, 1852

American Friends of the British Museum (The Arthur R. Miller Collection) 02102

REFERENCES
Riccar 1978, no. 152

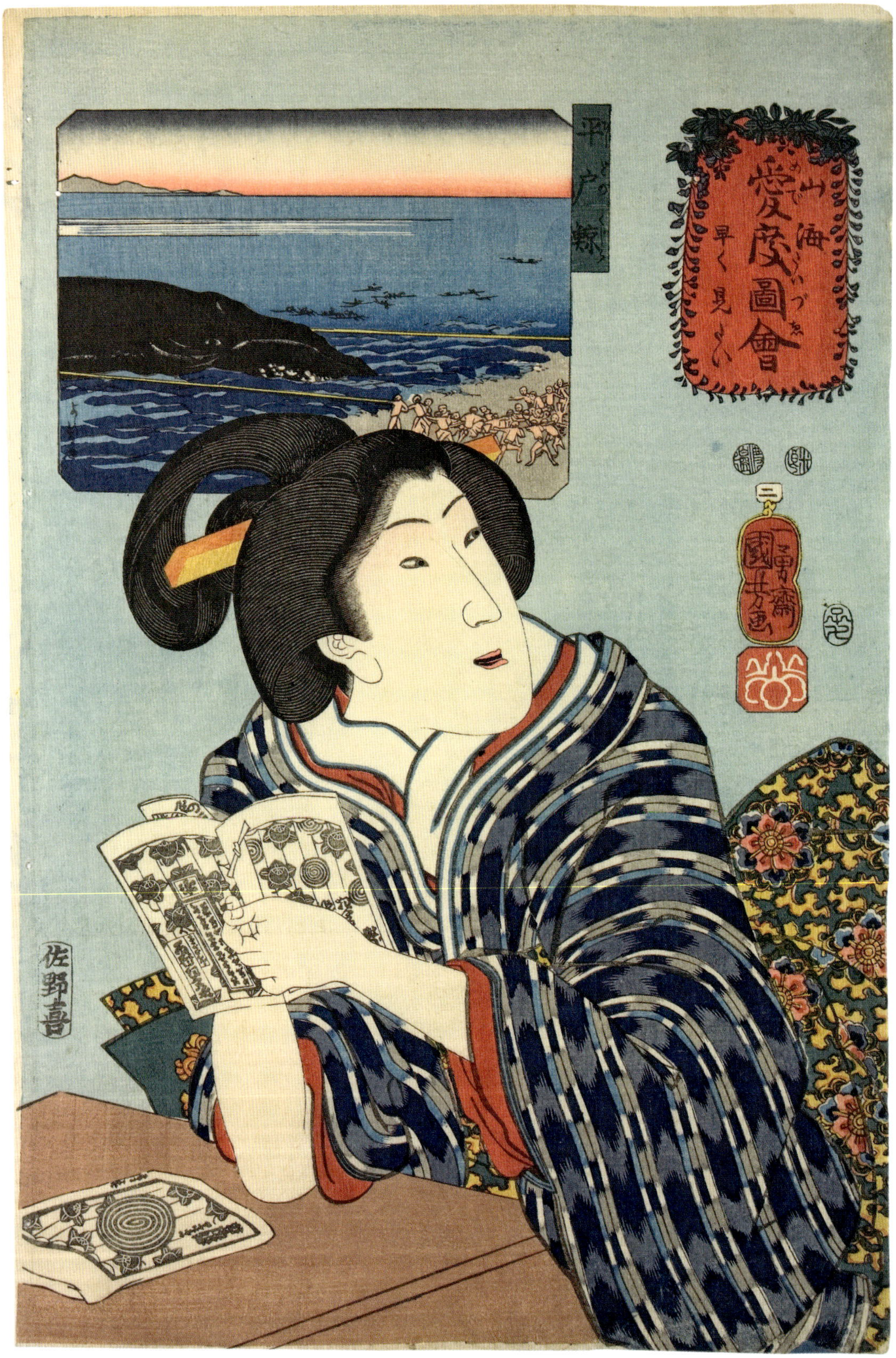

The print title is 'Can't wait to see it', and the woman is looking at an illustrated booklet (*ehon banzuke*) for a Kabuki play. These simply produced programmes were generally designed anonymously. The woman's blackened teeth indicate that she is married. The book's printed wrapper lies on the table and, like the book itself, bears the mandarin orange emblem of the Ichimura theatre. The inset picture shows a hunted whale being dragged onto the beach at Hirado in the north-western part of Kyushu.

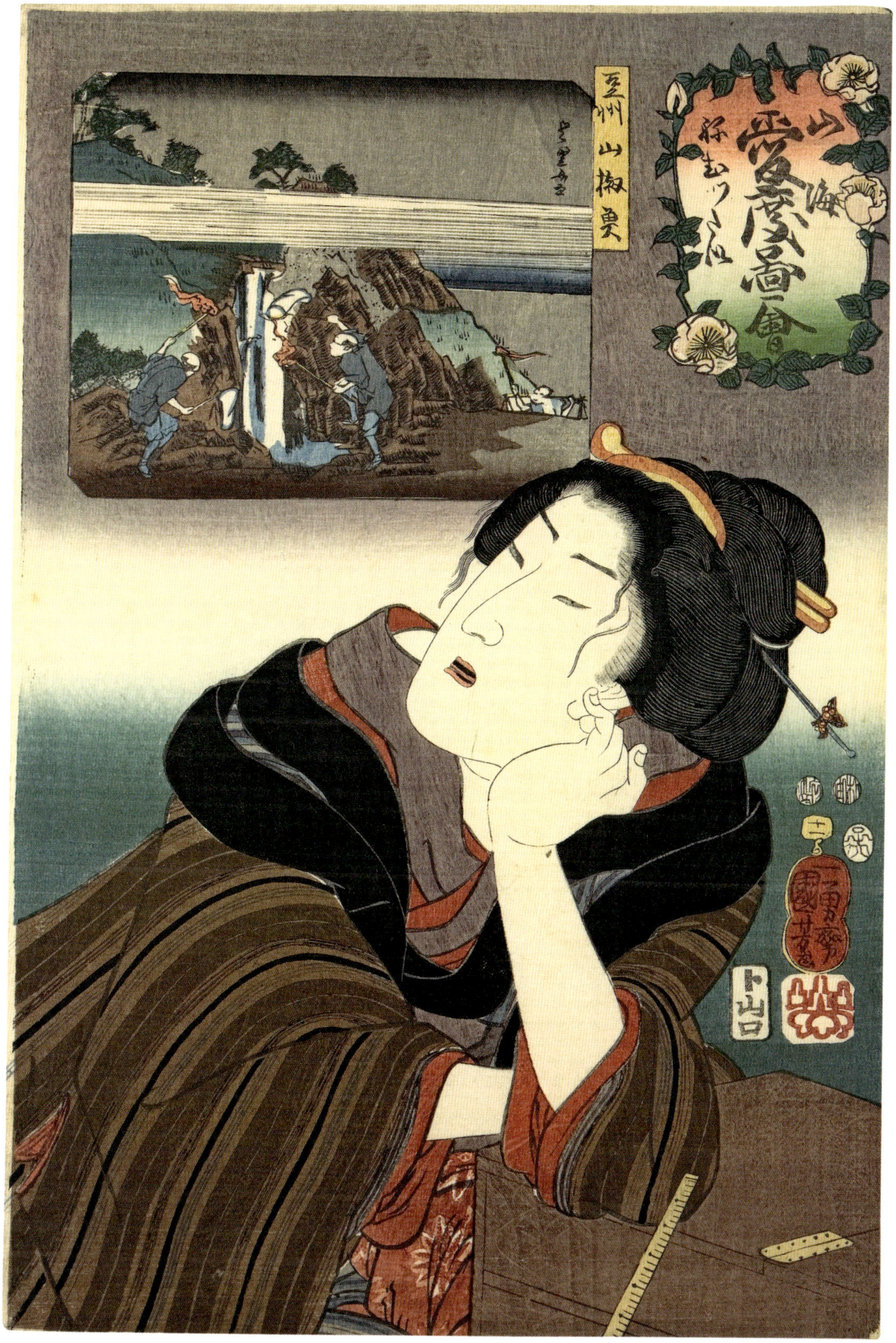

73

Woman dozing by her needlework box

1852

Colour woodblock, *ōban*, published by Yamaguchiya Tōbei, 36.3 × 24.7 cm

SERIES TITLE
'Auspicious Pictures of Land and Sea' (*Sankai medetai zue*)

PRINT TITLE
'No. 11, Sleepy' (*Nemuttai*)

INSET LANDSCAPE TITLE
'Salamanders, Izu Province' (*Zushū sanshō-uo*)

ARTIST'S SIGNATURE
Ichiyūsai Kuniyoshi ga (in gourd-shaped *Yoshi* cartouche)

ARTIST'S SEAL
Yoshikiri

ARTIST'S SIGNATURE ON INSET LANDSCAPE
Torijo ga

CENSORS' SEALS
Murata and Kinugasa

DATE SEAL
8th (?) month, 1852

American Friends of the British Museum (The Arthur R. Miller Collection) 02109

The print title, 'Sleepy' (or 'Wants to sleep'), refers to a married woman wearing a striped winter jacket who is shown resting her chin on one hand as she leans on her sewing box. A wooden ruler has slid off the lid of the box. Kuniyoshi has convincingly captured the woman's sleepy expression, with half-closed, angled eyes and half-open, slackened mouth. Eyelashes, hairline and stray wisps of hair are all very finely cut and printed. The inset picture depicts hunters with torches and scoop nets fishing for salamanders (*sanshō-uo*) at night in a mountain pool below a waterfall in Izu province (the eastern part of modern Shizuoka prefecture).

FAN PRINTS

(Cats 74–7)

A practical necessity in the stifling summer heat, fans could also be attractive personal accessories when they carried a painted or printed picture for the bearer to admire and to show off to others. Since the late eighteenth century half-length portraits of celebrated Kabuki actors or beautiful women had been popular subjects for such images. The two main formats were the round (rigid) fan on a stick (*uchiwa*), used chiefly in summer, and the folding fan with bamboo ribs (*ōgi*), in use throughout the year.

In the nineteenth century nearly all printed fans were in the *uchiwa* format and designed by ukiyo-e artists. With Edo's population amounting to more than one million, the market for these elegant accessories was huge. Yet their ephemeral nature makes it difficult to estimate the total number of designs produced. Fans would generally be discarded when they became soiled or damaged, so relatively few used examples have survived. However, numerous sheets that were never cut and mounted on bamboo supports exist, often in excellent condition. These were presumably purchased and prized for their images, with no intention of having them made into fans. Some may have come from sample books. The *uchiwa* format, in particular, with its characteristic oval shape missing a section at the bottom, presented artists with an unusual challenge. Kuniyoshi, Kunisada and Hiroshige all excelled in creating striking designs for this format. Kuniyoshi, especially, responded with many close-up images of beautiful women, which allowed him to develop further his style of open and appealing facial expressions. Iwakiri Yuriko has discovered more than 360 fan designs of beauties by the artist (personal communication).

The publishing reforms of the Kyōhō era (1716–36) prompted the formation of a merchants' guild for fan-print publishers, the *uchiwa toiya*, which functioned independently of the *jihon toiya*, the guild responsible for standard sheet prints, illustrated books and popular fiction. From about 1811 to 1842 fan prints sometimes bear distinctive date seals not found on ordinary standard sheet prints (they are listed in GUDHJ, vol. 3, 1982, pp. 127–9). When the guild system was temporarily suspended from 1842 to 1851, during the Tenpō reforms, former *uchiwa-toiya* and *jihon toiya* publishers ventured into each other's areas of activity. Only one publication in English has been devoted entirely to fan prints (to an important group by Hiroshige in the Victoria and Albert Museum, London; Faulkner 2001).

74

Woman wearing a headscarf

1849

Colour woodblock, uncut *uchiwa* fan print, published by Ibaya Senzaburō, 22.8 × 29.2 cm

PRINT TITLE
'Parody of Konkai' (*Mitate Konkai*)

ARTIST'S SIGNATURE
Ichiyūsai Kuniyoshi ga (in gourd-shaped *Yoshi* cartouche)

ARTIST'S SEAL
Yoshikiri

CENSORS' SEALS
Kinugasa and Yoshimura

American Friends of the British Museum (The Arthur R. Miller Collection) 22004

The woman grasps a wooden post and leans forward intently, biting the end of her cotton headscarf, which bears a design of a crow and an egret. She wears a thick padded robe (*dotera*). The background is filled with the wheels and shafts of a 'flower cart' (*hana-guruma*), with trailing clematis and circular emblems. The title alerts the viewer to hidden allusions. This print is a *mitate*, a type of image that establishes playful, often tenuous connections between two apparently unrelated subjects.

The sound of the word *Konkai*, which formed the title of a medieval comic play (*kyōgen*), was said to mimic the barking cry of a fox. The play later developed into a Kabuki dance called *Tsuri-gitsune* (*Fox-catching*). Close scrutiny of the border of the title cartouche in the top right corner of the print reveals a snaking rope attached to a circular trap loaded in the centre with bait, probably a dead rat. This is the fox trap featured at the end of the *Konkai/Tsuri-gitsune* story, when a fox spirit disguised as an aged monk admonishes the hunter Hakuzōsu to stop killing its relatives. On its way home the fox–monk cannot entirely suppress its animal nature and is drawn irresistibly to the bait in the last trap set by the hunter. The crow and egret headscarf of Kuniyoshi's woman, and her attitude as she clutches the post, mimic the costume and pose of the fox–monk in the *kyōgen* play. The circular emblems are those commonly found on the leggings (*hakama*) worn by *kyōgen* actors.

Iwakiri Yuriko has identified a total of five fan prints in this series, in which beauties imitate famous scenes from Nō and *kyōgen* plays (personal communication).

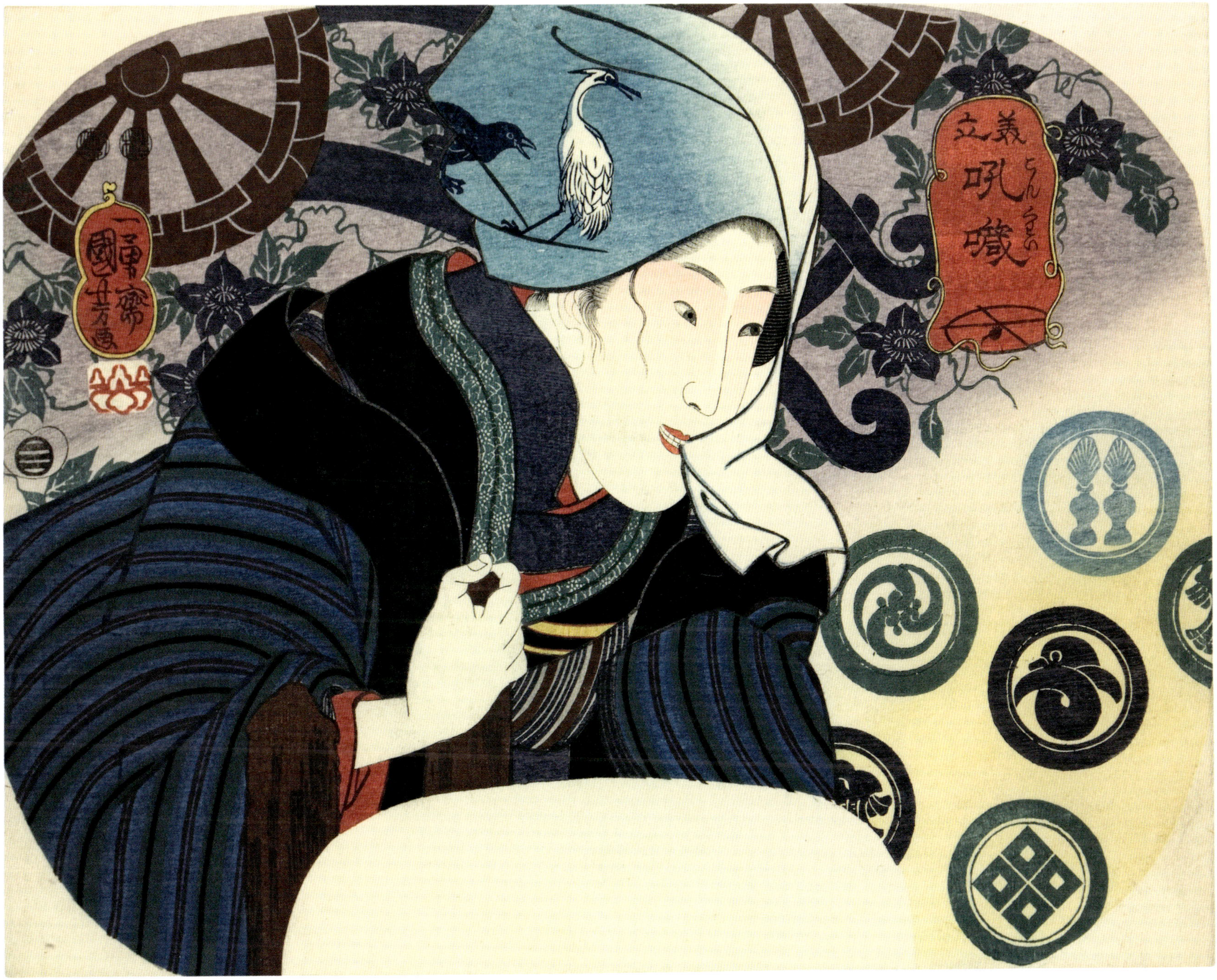
一勇斎國芳画

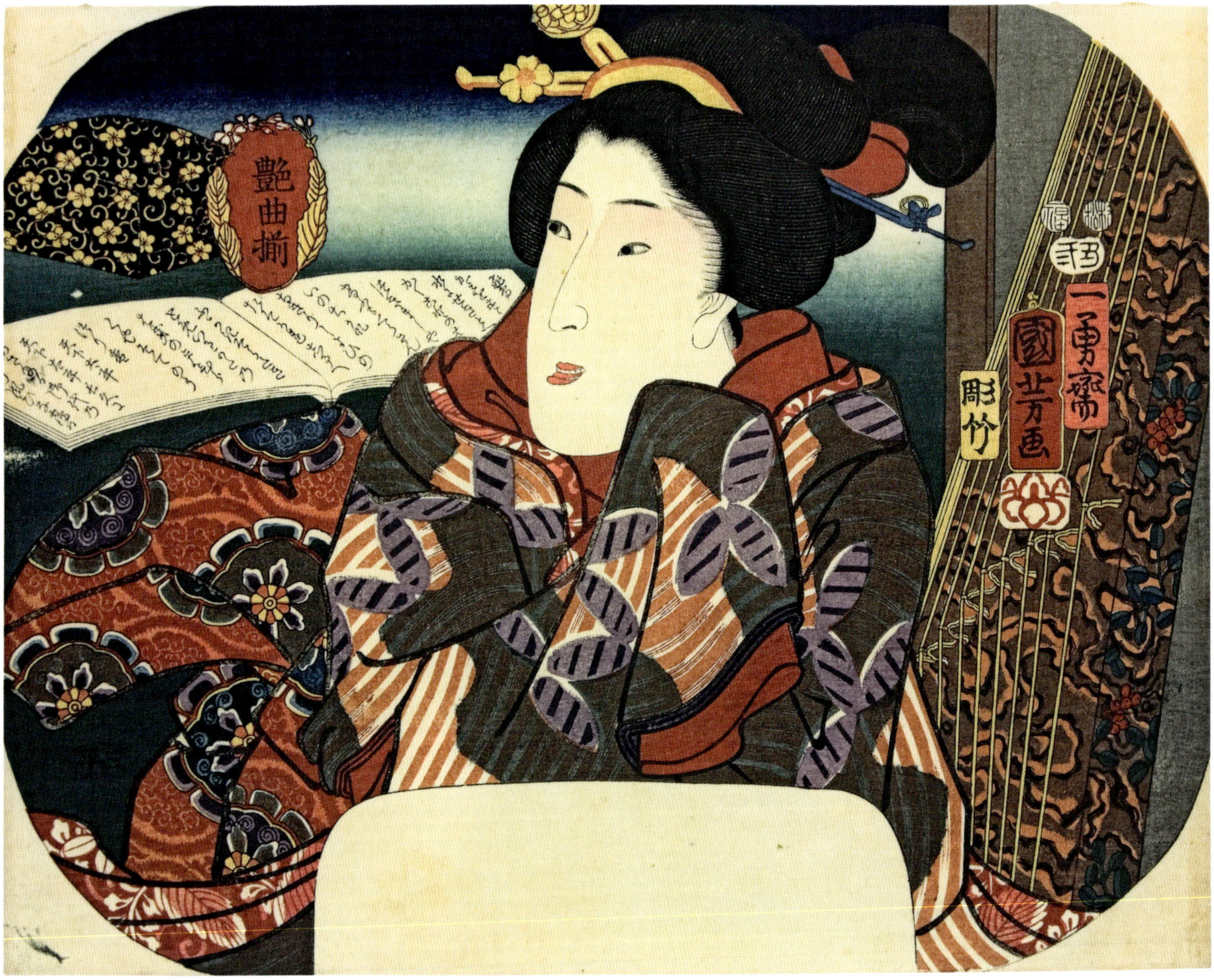

75

Young woman with a *koto*

1853

Colour woodblock, uncut *uchiwa* fan print, published by Sanpei, 22.8 × 29.3 cm

PRINT TITLE
'Set of Voluptuous Melodies' (*Enkyoku-zoroi*)

ARTIST'S SIGNATURE
Ichiyūsai Kuniyoshi ga (in rectangular *Yoshi* cartouche)

ARTIST'S SEAL
Yoshikiri

BLOCK-CUTTER
Hori-Take

CENSORS' SEALS
Fuku and Muramatsu

DATE SEAL
2nd month, 1853

American Friends of the British Museum (The Arthur R. Miller Collection) 22006

The seated young woman is shown with her musical instrument, a transverse harp (*koto*), which leans upright against the wall beside her. She coyly raises one covered hand to her face. Behind her appear an open book with the words of a song and a lacquered box for the instrument's accessories. One of the legible song titles reads *Tenga taihei* (*Peace in the Realm*), a popular work of the *koto* repertoire composed by Yatsuhashi Kengyō (1614–1685).

The print title, 'Set of Voluptuous Melodies', suggests the allure both of music and of the young woman. Iwakiri Yuriko has identified a total of five designs in what appears to be an untitled series (personal communication).

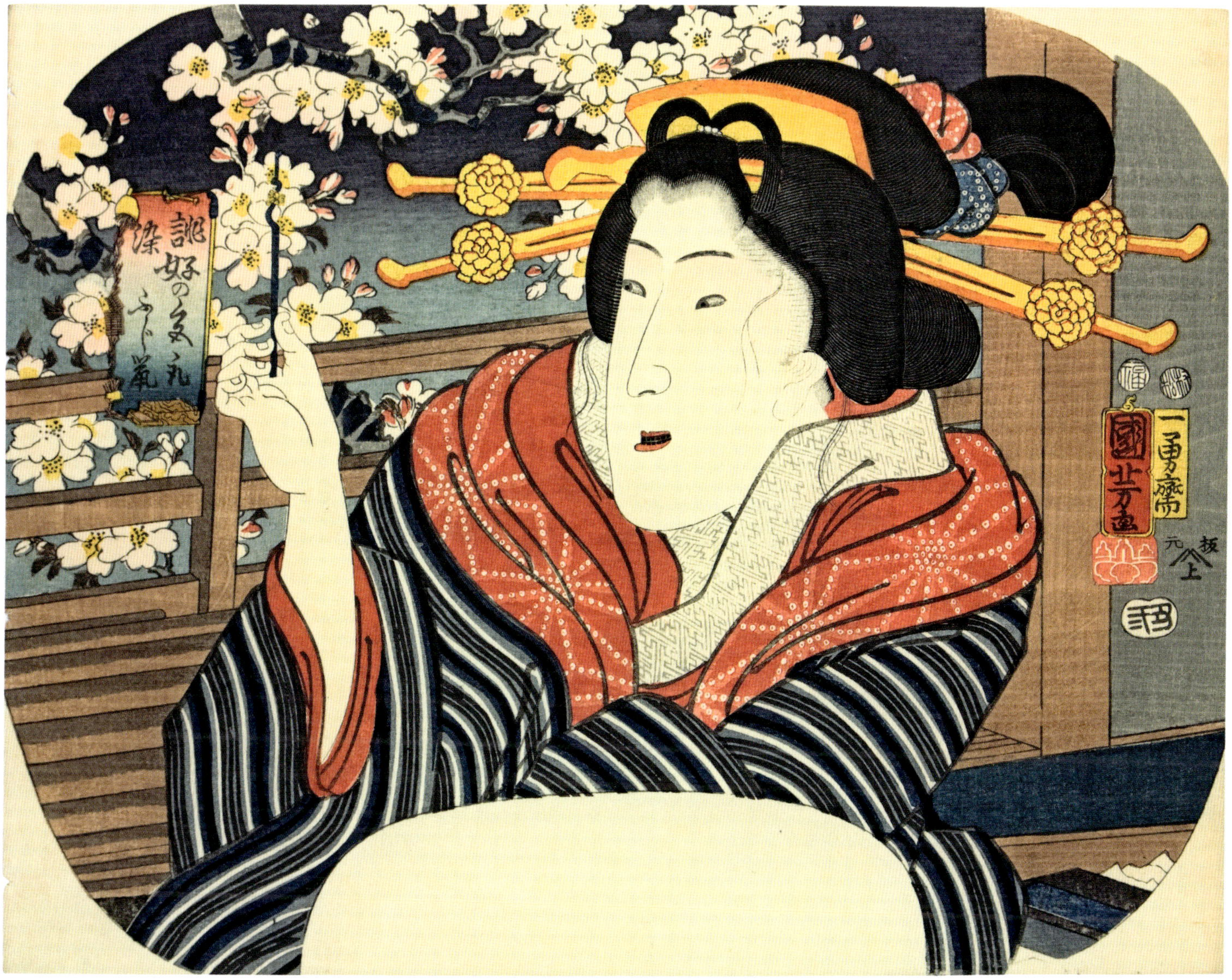

76

Woman viewing cherry blossom at night

1853

Colour woodblock, uncut *uchiwa* fan print, published by Iseya Sōemon, 22.8 × 29.6 cm

SERIES TITLE
'Dyed to order in your favourite colours' (*Atsurae-zome konomi no irodori*)

PRINT TITLE
'Wisteria grey' (*Fuji-nezumi*)

ARTIST'S SIGNATURE
Ichiyūsai Kuniyoshi ga (in rectangular *Yoshi* cartouche)

ARTIST'S SEAL
Yoshikiri

CENSORS' SEALS
Fuku and Muramatsu

DATE SEAL
2nd month, 1853

American Friends of the British Museum (The Arthur R. Miller Collection) 22005

The arrangement of heavy hairpins suggests that this is a courtesan. Wearing a striped robe over red undergarments, she is gazing at night from an upstairs room into the blossoming branches of a cherry tree. She holds a taper in her raised hand. On the floor behind her lie an open fabric pouch and some crumpled tissues.

Fuji-nezumi ('wisteria grey') is a purple-grey colour, perhaps found here among the stripes on the courtesan's robe. The series title ostensibly refers to nothing but fabric dyed in a chosen colour, but the implication is that a woman's favours can be purchased to order as well. That meaning is underscored by the use of the word *iro*, which has strong connotations of both 'colour' and 'sex'.

Iwakiri Yuriko has identified a total of five designs in the series, each print bearing the name of a different colour (personal communication).

77

Courtesan and girl, 1848–51

Colour woodblock, fan-shaped *surimono*, 15.9 × 49.5 cm

ARTIST'S SIGNATURE
Ichiyūsai Kuniyoshi ga

ARTIST'S SEAL
Yoshikiri

American Friends of the British Museum (The Arthur R. Miller Collection) 22003

REFERENCES
Pittsburgh 1976, no. 295; Suzuki 1992, no. 460

A child attendant kneels as she passes to the courtesan a long-stemmed pipe for smoking. The courtesan is dressed in her most elaborate finery – a surcoat bearing a hydrangea design and worn over other densely patterned robes, with a rich brocade sash cascading to the ground in front. She is amusing herself by making strings of artificial flowers, probably for one of the festivals regularly held in Yoshiwara pleasure quarter.

Nearly all fans designed by ukiyo-e artists in the nineteenth century were in the *uchiwa* format, and this is Kuniyoshi's only known design for an *ōgi* fan. Its survival is all the more remarkable in that radiating fold-marks clearly show it to have been used.

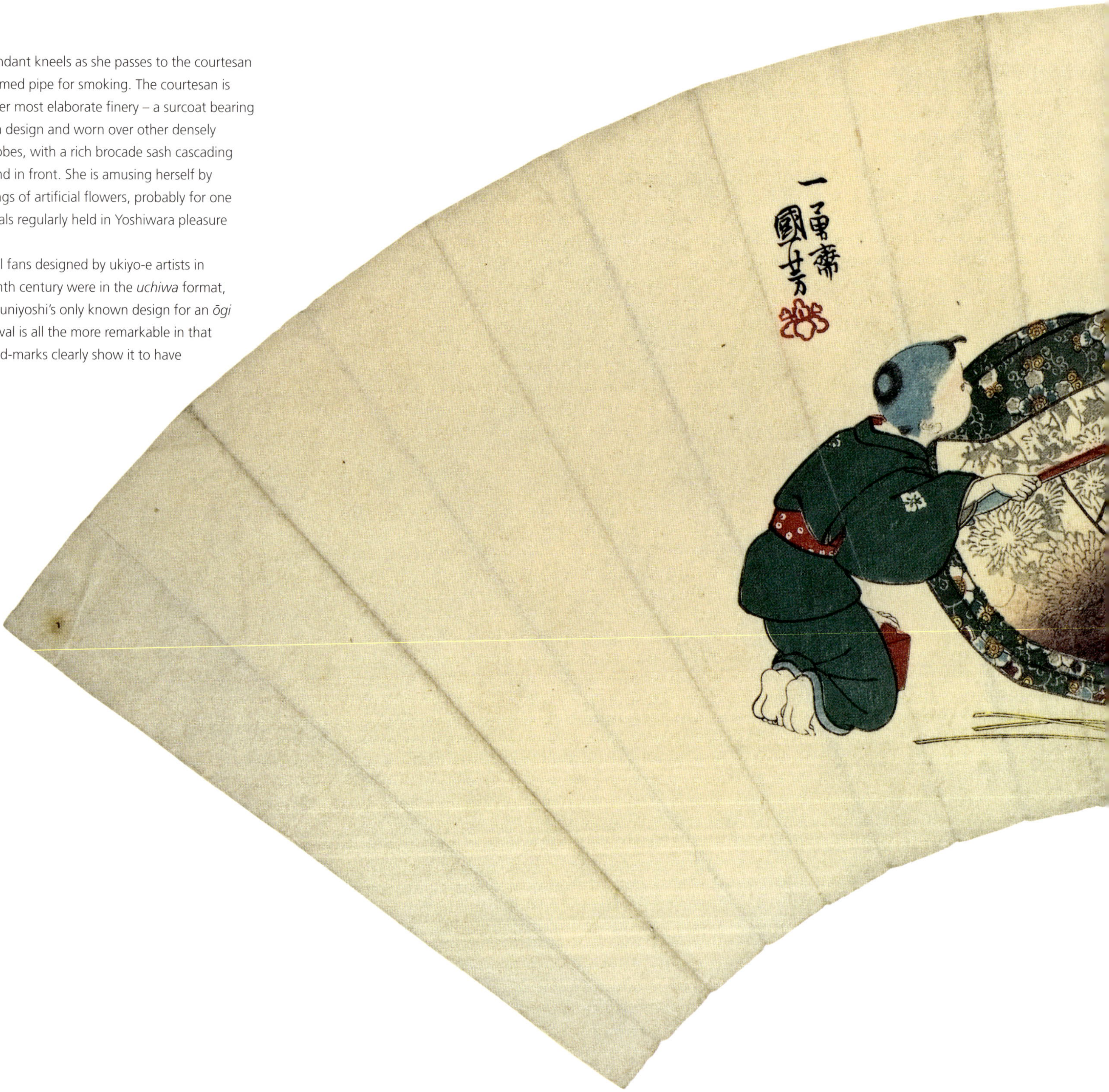

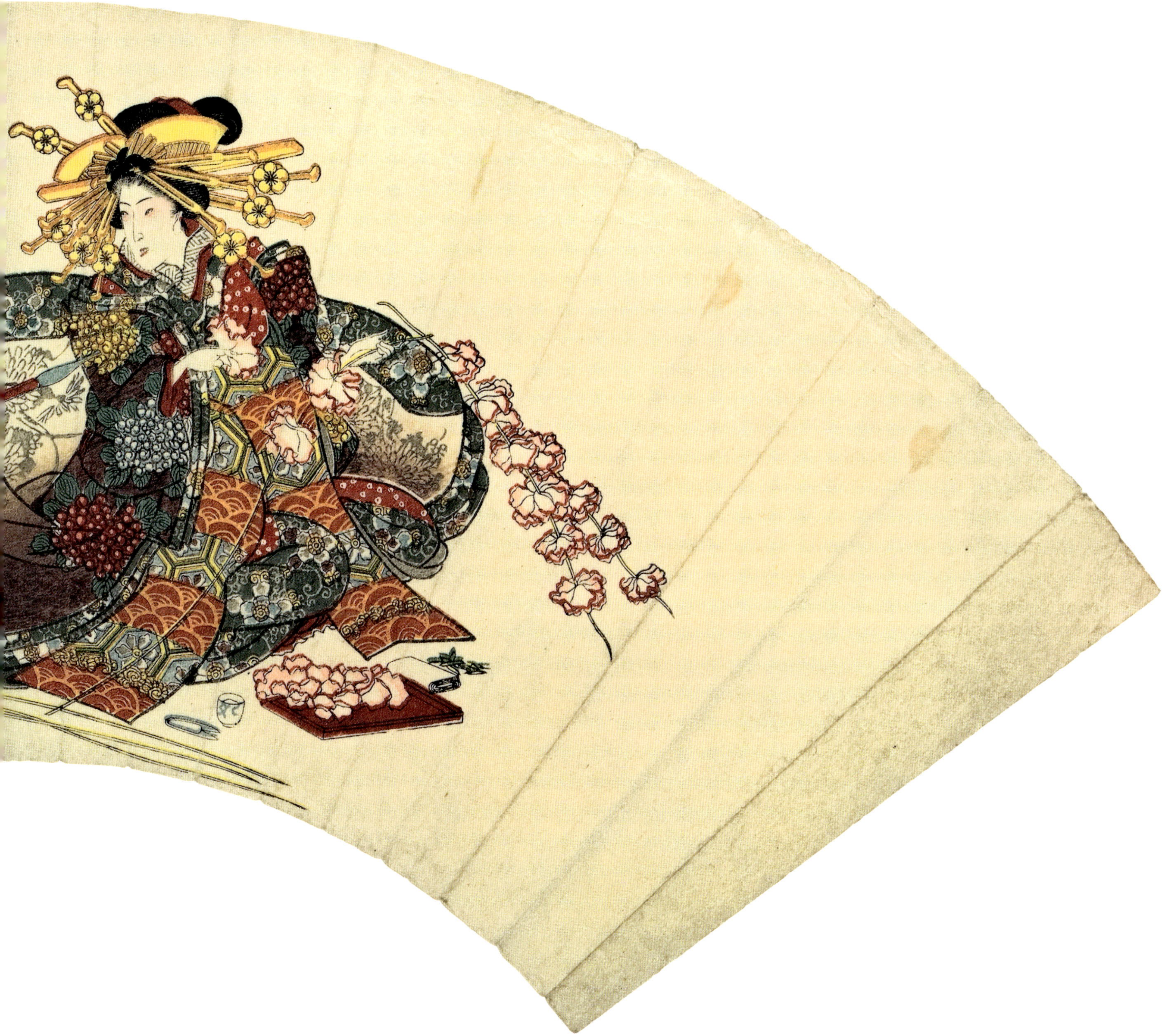

78

Courtesan wearing a robe with Ōtsu pictures

1848–54

Hanging scroll, ink and colour on silk, 87.8 × 29.6 cm

ARTIST'S SIGNATURE
Ichiyūsai Kuniyoshi ga

ARTIST'S SEAL
Kuniyoshi

PROVENANCE
Hirano Seikichi Collection (1983); Azabu Museum of Arts and Crafts, Tokyo (1995)

Takashima Masao Collection, Japan

REFERENCES
Shibui 1983, 'Bunka-Bunsei to Bakumatsu', no.42; NUT 1995, no. 80

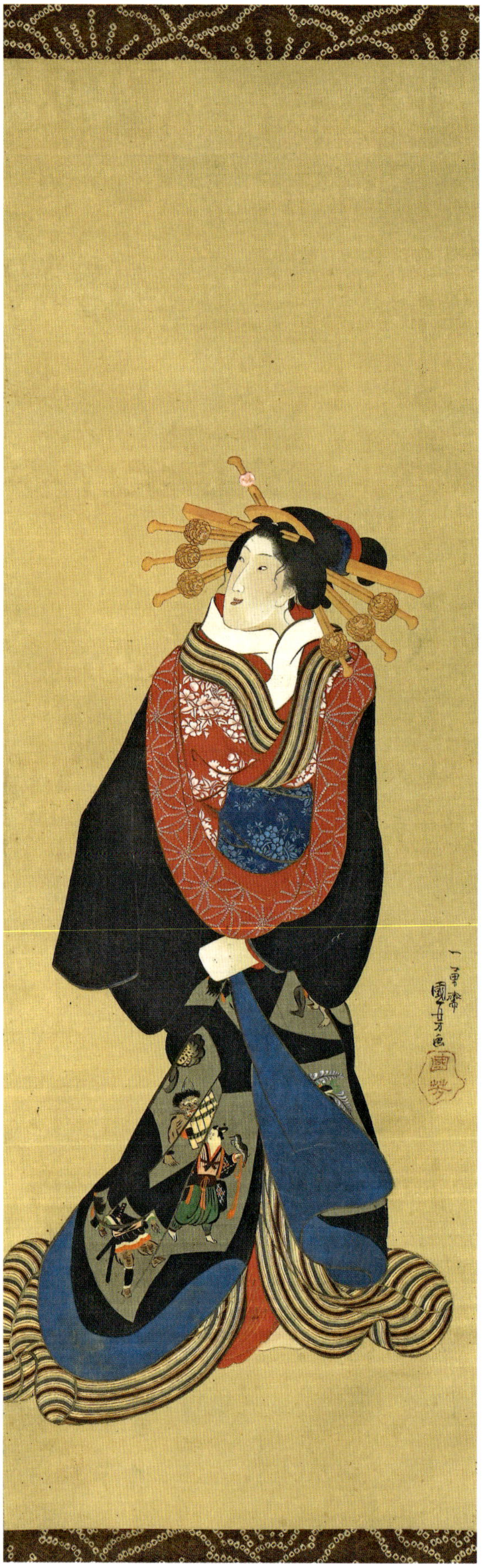

The courtesan glances back cheerfully, perhaps in response to a salutation, as she draws her surcoat (*uchikake*) around her. Her face, with its prominent nose, small eyes and mouth, and open, appealing expression, is drawn in accordance with the conventions of the Utagawa school, as refined by Kuniyoshi's sensibility. Focussing on the figure, with little indication of setting, the artist was especially skilled at suggesting suddenly arrested movement in his paintings of beautiful women.

The courtesan walks barefoot, probably in the chamber of her Yoshiwara apartments, and holds a roll of tissue. Her robes are brilliant scarlet, with a deep blue sash; both colours contrast strikingly with the rich black of the surcoat. A particular feature is the design of Ōtsu folk paintings around the skirts of the surcoat. 'Ōtsu pictures' (*Ōtsu-e*) were popular souvenirs sold to travellers in the environs of the village of that name in Ōmi province (modern Shiga prefecture). They had a stock range of characters brushed in a simple and lively style that seems to have appealed to Kuniyoshi, since he included them in several works roughly contemporaneous with this painting. One of these is a triptych self-portrait that shows the artist executing Ōtsu paintings that come to life (1848; cat. 129). Another, a diptych, depicts the painter Ukiyo ('Floating-world') Matabei, who was thought to have invented the genre, in a similar situation (1853; p. 30, fig. 16). Comparison with these other works permits the four Ōtsu figures revealed tantalizingly in fragments in the present hanging scroll to be identified as, from left to right, Samurai Footman (*yakko*), Thunder Devil (*kaminari*), Young Falconer (*taka-jō wakashu*) and Wisteria Maiden (*fuji musume*).

The most comprehensive listing of Kuniyoshi's autograph paintings contains sixty-two items, half of which are hanging scrolls of beautiful women (Clark, in Amsterdam 1998, pp. 254–61). Many more will undoubtedly be added as a result of further research into this relatively neglected aspect of his oeuvre.

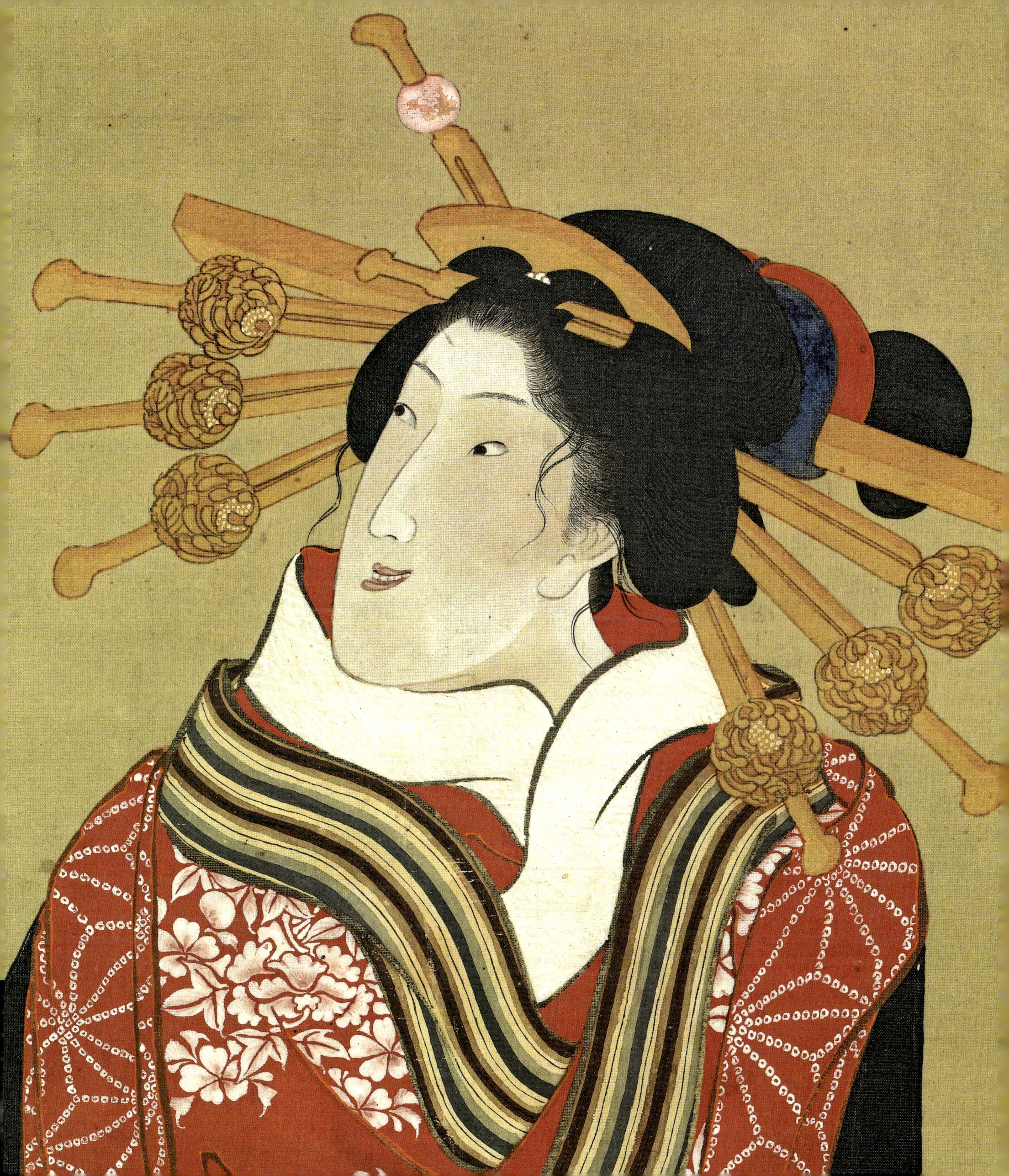

3

LANDSCAPES

Kuniyoshi was not a prolific landscape artist, especially in comparison with his contemporaries Katsushika Hokusai (1760–1849) and Utagawa Hiroshige (1797–1858), who made the genre their forte. However, some of the views of Edo he produced in the early 1830s belong among the greatest of all Japanese landscape prints, their European elements and their eccentric subjects and viewpoints granting them a unique, piquant flavour.

Cityscape prints of Edo had been common since their introduction in the late 1760s by Utagawa Toyoharu (1735–1814), founder of the Utagawa school of artists, to which Kuniyoshi was affiliated. The 1780s had seen the beginnings of a rapid increase in the publication of illustrated gazetteers that described cities and regions throughout Japan. This reflected the growth of travel in all sections of society. Prints showing views outside Edo became popular with Hokusai's series 'Thirty-six Views of Mt Fuji' (*Fugaku sanjū-rokkei*, *c.* 1830–33). This was soon followed by lyrical views of Edo and of places on the Tōkaidō road by Hiroshige, notably his 'Fifty-three Stations of the Tōkaidō' (*Tōkaidō gojūsan-tsugi*) of 1833–34. Kuniyoshi's cityscape prints of Edo seem to have been issued in parallel with Hiroshige's, as publishers vied to exploit this lucrative new genre.

Kuniyoshi's two series of Edo views from the early 1830s include memorable designs with low horizons, ragged clouds, pronounced foreground motifs, unusual subjects or viewpoints and occasional shadows (cats 81–5). This reflects European influence, and the artist may even have been aware of paintings produced in the late eighteenth century by the so-called 'Dutch' school of the Akita fief (*Akita ranga*), which had pioneered the Europeanised style in Japan. He certainly borrowed from popular copperplate prints of landscapes in this style by Aōdō Denzen (1748–1822).

New light has recently been shed on Kuniyoshi's European sources by the discovery that he based the atmospheric night scene 'The Night Attack, Act Eleven of *Treasury of Loyal Retainers*' (cat. 79) on a Dutch book illustration – a view of Batavia (modern Jakarta) by Jan Nieuhof (1618–1672; p. 23, fig. 6). Kuniyoshi adapted other illustrations from the same volume for some of his landscapes in 'foreign' styles, notably the series 'Twenty-four Paragons of Filial Piety for Children' (*Nijūshi-kō dōji kagami*) of 1843 (p. 22, fig. 3; cats 98–101). Kuniyoshi generally adopted this Europeanised style for any images of foreigners, be they Chinese (as in the series just cited), South Asians or Europeans (cat. 102).

Kuniyoshi made a distinctive contribution to the landscape genre in what might be termed his 'poetic landscapes'. A fine example is the series 'One Hundred Poems by One Hundred Poets' (*Hyakunin isshu no uchi*), in which he interprets an anthology of classical poems compiled in the 1230s (cats 91–7). Kuniyoshi brings the poets and their ancient verses vividly to life by setting them in lyrical landscapes. The literary ethos of these prints accorded with the serious, moralising atmosphere of the times: the series was issued in the second half of 1842, in the wake of stringent new publication regulations, introduced in the sixth month of that year, that banned actor, courtesan and geisha prints and encouraged more edifying subjects.

79

The loyal retainers attack Kira Yoshinaka's mansion at night

early 1830s

Colour woodblock, *ōban*,
no publisher's seal,
24.3 × 35.6 cm

PRINT TITLE
'The Night Attack, Act Eleven of *Treasury of Loyal Retainers*' (*Chūshingura jūichi-danme youchi no zu*)

ARTIST'S SIGNATURE
Ichiyūsai Kuniyoshi ga
(in rectangular cartouche)

Victoria and Albert Museum, London,
E.2590-1962

REFERENCES
Springfield 1968, no. 25; *Ukiyo-e taikei* 1974, no. 32; French 1977, no. 52; Riccar 1978, no. 86; Springfield 1980, no. 28; Amsterdam 1984, no. 216; Keyes 1984, pl. 37; Brussels 1989, no. 877; HUT, vol. 5, 1989, BW no. 41 (this impression); HUT, vol. 7, 1990, no. 178; V&A 1991, no. 94 (this impression); TNM 1991, no. 185; Suzuki 1992, no. 63; Itabashi 1994, Kuniyoshi no. 40; Nihon Ukiyo-e Kyōkai 1995, no. 160; Nagoya 1996, no. 193; Amsterdam 1998, no. 211 (this impression)

The scene shows the culmination of the vendetta of 1701–02 that came to be known as 'Chūshingura': the attack on Kira Yoshinaka's mansion by the band of forty-seven loyal retainers on a snowy night (see cat. 49). Some of the loyal samurai pacify the watchdogs with food while others scale the walls of the mansion with a rope ladder. They are directed by their leader, Ōishi Kuranosuke, who stands gesticulating to the right of the ladder. Notwithstanding the full moon, one retainer shines a torch-like lantern up the wall. They all wear the distinctive black and white jackets of theatrical convention, and each miniature figure is drawn in a convincing pose.

Although the title mentions act eleven of the Kabuki version of the story, Kuniyoshi goes to great lengths to present the attack as if it is actually taking place, rather than being performed on stage. He does so in the most 'European' style he can muster: the structures on the street are rendered in dramatically receding perspective, while buildings, figures, dogs and even the rope ladder cast shadows of an appropriate tonality in the moonlight. The print has long been recognised as one of the artist's most experimental.

Katsumori Noriko has identified a Dutch book illustration as the direct source of Kuniyoshi's composition (p. 23, fig. 6; Katsumori 2000). Additional research by Katsuhara Ryōta has shown that Kuniyoshi regularly turned to illustrations in this book in connection with a wide range of prints (Katsuhara 2006). Although he borrowed the composition of the street scene almost line for line, it was an inspired imaginative act to convert a static, black and white engraving into a dramatic, coloured night scene.

The general stylistic similarity between the title and signature cartouches in the present design and those in a series of Edo landscapes with titles taking the form *Tōto… no zu* (cat. 85) suggests that this print was issued around the same time in the early 1830s, quite probably by the same publisher, Yamaguchiya Tōbei. The earliest known printings are almost entirely in grisaille, with a wiped band of pale blue on the horizon (sometimes also half-way up the sky). These impressions do not have pink light emanating from the lantern on the right, but they do show extensive abraded edges (*ita-bokashi*) along the bottom of the clouds (Keyes 1984, pl. 37; TNM 1991, no. 185). One would normally expect printings to have existed with a red seal below the artist's signature, a publisher's seal and the *kiwame* censorship mark, but these features are missing from even the earliest surviving impressions.

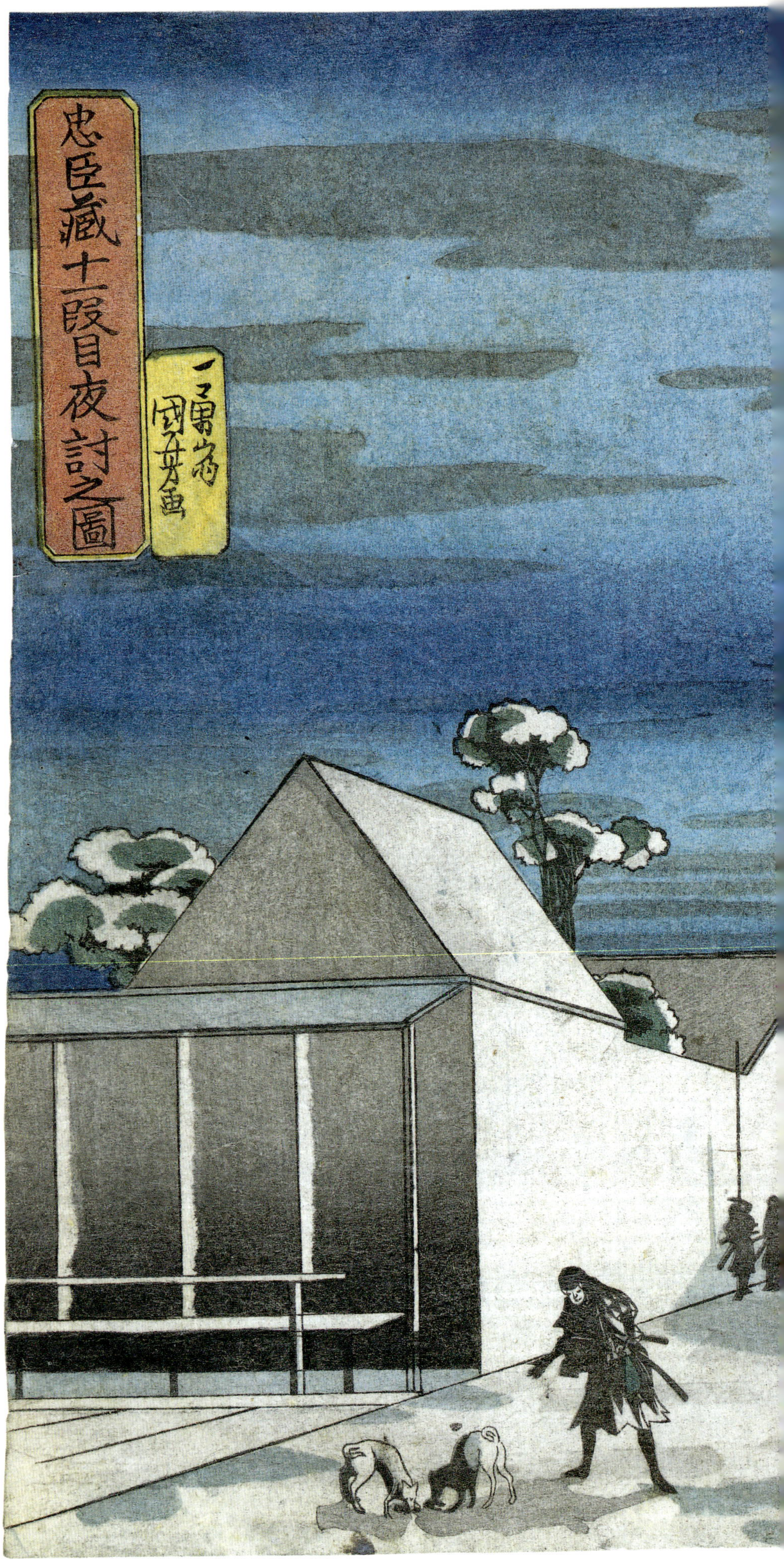

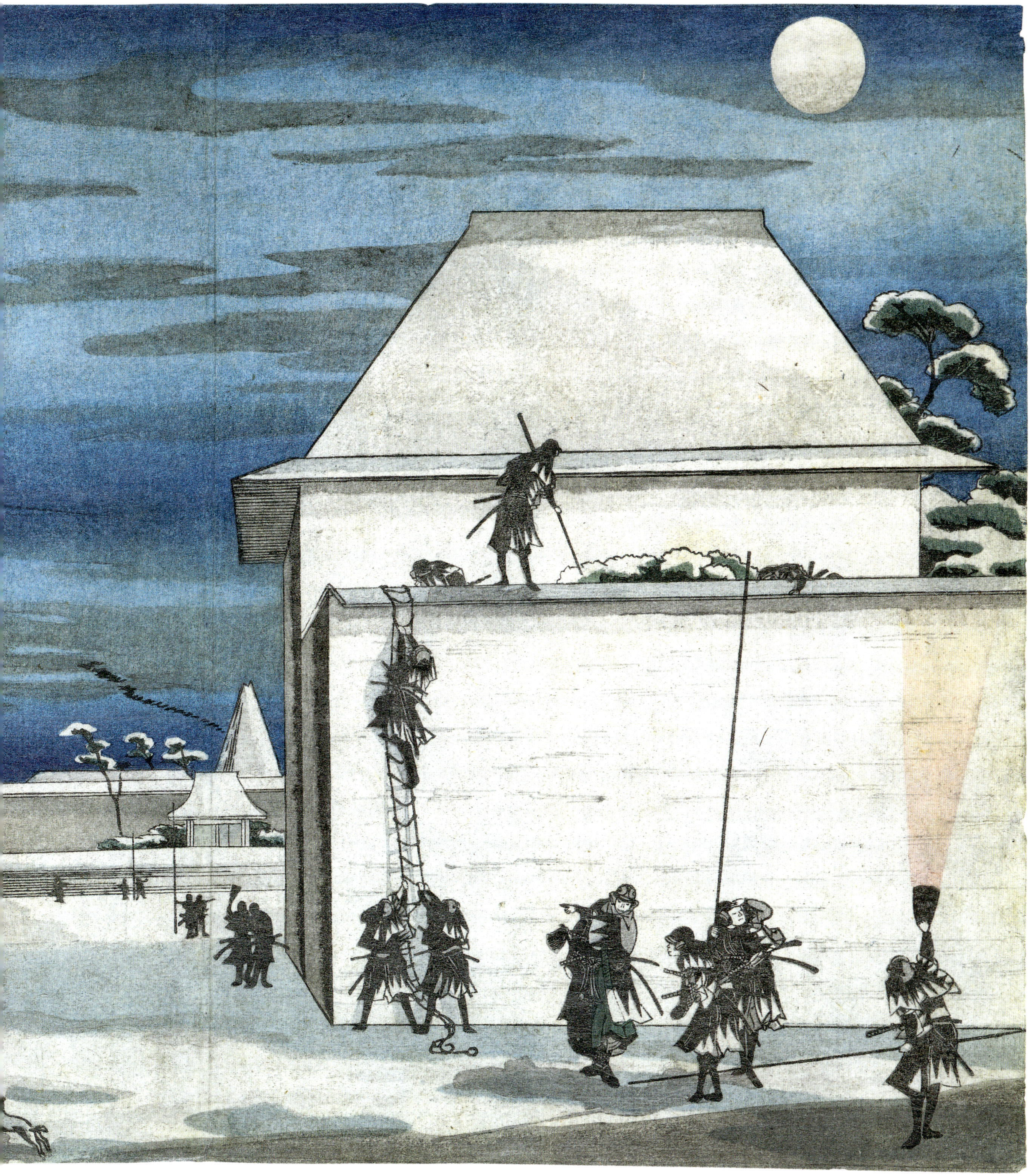

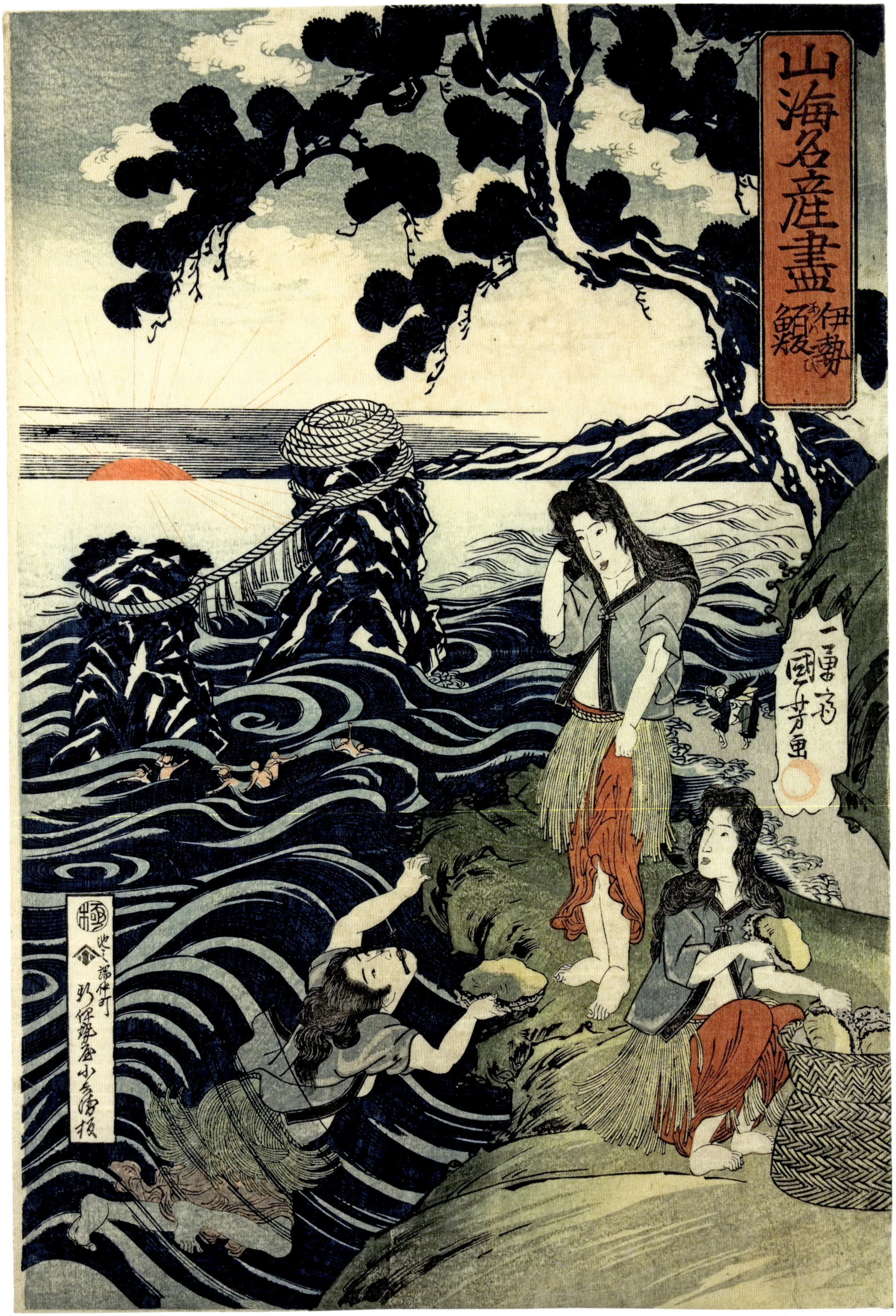
山海名産盡
伊勢 鰒
一勇斎 國芳画

80

Women diving for abalone at Ise

1830–31

Colour woodblock, *ōban*, published by Shin-Iseya Kohei, 38.3 × 26.8 cm

SERIES TITLE
'All the Famous Products of Land and Sea' (*Sankai meisan-zukushi*)

PRINT TITLE
'Ise, Abalone' (*Ise, awabi*)

ARTIST'S SIGNATURE
Ichiyūsai Kuniyoshi ga (in irregular cartouche)

ARTIST'S SEAL
toshidama

CENSORSHIP SEAL
kiwame

American Friends of the British Museum (The Arthur R. Miller Collection) 03403

REFERENCES
Springfield 1980, no. 6; Yamaguchi 1991, Kuniyoshi no. 44; Suzuki 1992, no. 54; Mainichi Shinbunsha 1995, no. 185; Nagoya 1996, no. 169

Three women are diving for abalone (*awabi*) in the sea close to the celebrated 'wedded rocks' (*me-oto iwa*) – 'male' and 'female' rocks joined by a sacred rope – at Futami bay in Ise province. This was a vantage point from which to worship the rising sun, particularly on New Year's morning, and it was generally thronged with pilgrims. In Kuniyoshi's image the women modestly wear short jackets, but in real life the fact that the shell-divers (*ama*) worked with their breasts uncovered formed an important part of their mystique. The shellfish was dried and made into wafer-thin sheets, which were then cut into decorative strips (*noshi*) for attachment to formal gifts.

The title of the series, 'All the Famous Products of Land and Sea' (*Sankai meisan-zukushi*), suggests that the prints aimed to promote local products, yet the ten known designs focus more on the customs surrounding their production. Many are foodstuffs. The style is tentative, with the figures rather awkward and not always smoothly integrated into the image as a whole. Indeed, some figures are known to have been adapted from illustrations by the Osaka artist Shitomi Kangetsu in the 1799 gazetteer *Nihon sankai meisan zue* (*Illustrated Guide to Famous Products of Land and Sea in Japan*). The series nevertheless possesses considerable significance as an indication of the direction in which Kuniyoshi's landscapes were soon to develop. For example, the prints already evince an interest in rendering spatial depth and in three-dimensional modelling. The extensive use of the chemical pigment Prussian (Berlin) blue in part reflects the novelty of its sudden availability, but also signals a willingness to embrace influences from outside Japan (the pigment was manufactured in China and imported; see Smith 2005). Suzuki Jūzō reproduces all ten designs in the series (Suzuki 1992, nos 51–60).

FAMOUS PLACES IN EDO

(Cats 81–4)

This series of ten cityscapes of Edo, all but two of which feature or are located near water, was published by the same firm that issued Kuniyoshi's famous *Suikoden* warrior portraits (cats 3–10). The title refers to 'famous places' (*meisho*), but most of the sites or vantage points are unusual, even eccentric. Each view is contained within a decorative frame of green bamboo. Such frames often signal landscapes in a 'foreign' idiom, and the series is generally regarded as containing many of Kuniyoshi's finest landscapes in a European, or European-influenced, style. Features of this style include a low viewpoint and low horizon line, occasional shadows cast by the sun or moon, reflections on water, three-dimensional modelling of trees and rocks, irregular cloud formations and the emphatic foregrounding of individual motifs. Many of these elements also appear in the series represented here by cat. 85, which is thought to have been issued at about the same time. The present series is dated to the early 1830s on the basis of the form of Kuniyoshi's signature and the assumed chronological proximity to Hiroshige's first horizontal *ōban* series of Edo views, *Tōto meisho*, published by Kawaguchiya Shōzō and reckoned to have been issued *c.* 1831. For illustrations of the complete series, see MSU 1991, nos 1–10.

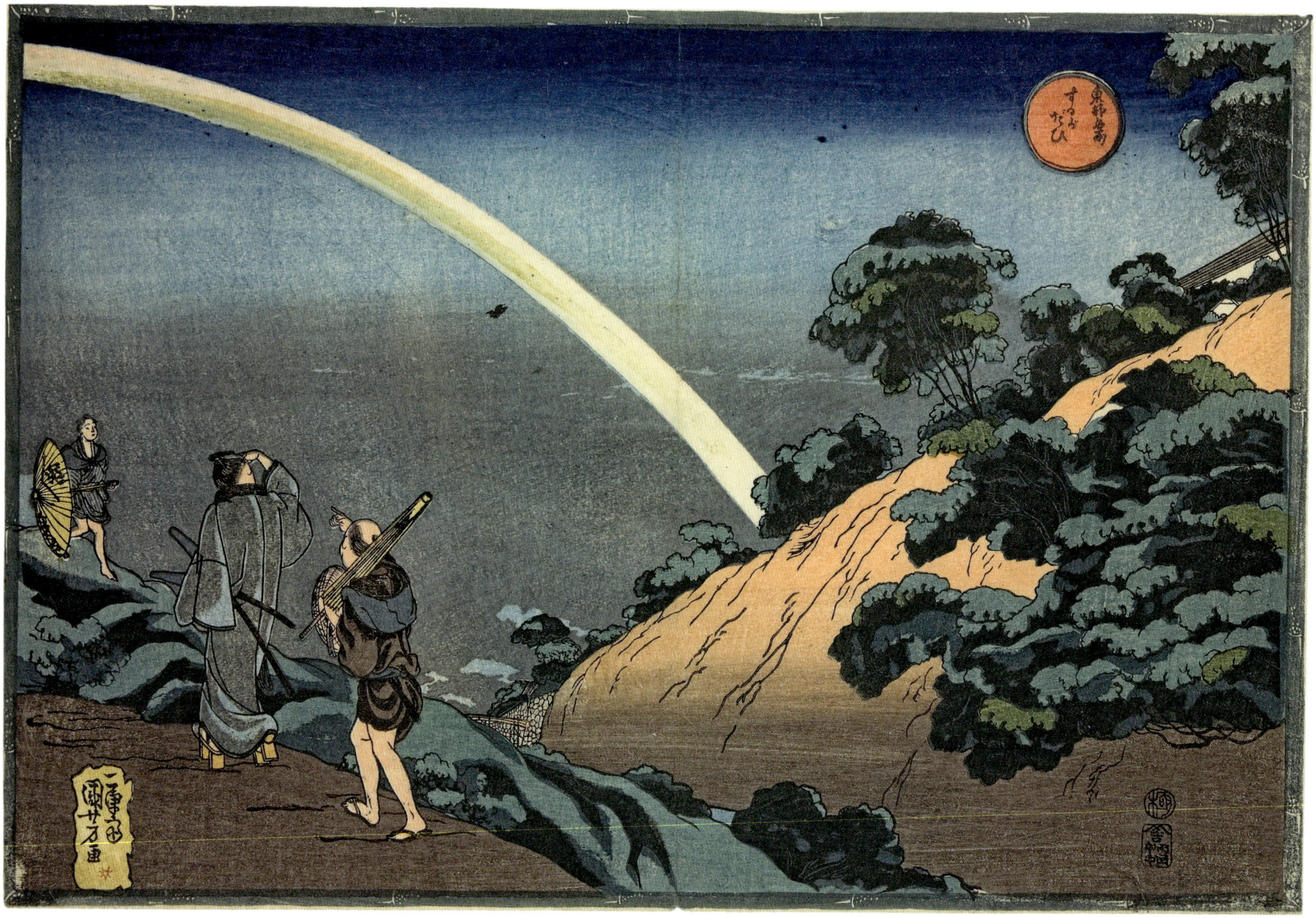

81

Rainbow at Surugadai

early 1830s

Colour woodblock, *ōban*, published by Kagaya Kichibei (or Kichiemon), 24.5 × 36.3 cm

PRINT TITLE
'Surugadai'

SERIES TITLE
'Famous Places in Edo' (*Tōto meisho*)

ARTIST'S SIGNATURE
Ichiyūsai Kuniyoshi ga (in irregular cartouche)

CENSORSHIP SEAL
kiwame

COLLECTOR'S SEAL
Henri Vever

American Friends of the British Museum (The Arthur R. Miller Collection) 03603

REFERENCES
Riccar 1978, no. 13; MSU 1991, no. 3; Suzuki 1992, no. 15; Nihon Ukiyo-e Kyōkai 1995, no. 156; Nagoya 1996, no. 176; Sotheby's 1997, lot. 162 (this impression); Ōta 1999, no. 111

A rainbow is forming after a sudden evening shower and sunlight catches the wooded bank of the Kanda river flowing in the valley below. Three figures are looking at the rainbow, their attention perhaps also caught by a sudden cry from the small silhouetted bird (a cuckoo?). A samurai wearing a long raincoat climbs the slope ahead of his servant, while a boy hurries down in the opposite direction, twirling his open umbrella to shake off the rain. The white outer walls of Yushima Seidō, a Confucian worship hall, can just be seen at the top of the bank on the right: Surugadai was a high-lying district populated mainly by samurai retainers of the shogunate and known for its fine views of Mt Fuji. The bridge-like structure in the far distance has been identified as the Kanda aqueduct (Kanda Jōsui; Nagoya 1996, p. 256). A horizontal flaw in the block used to print the grey in the centre of the sky is apparent in several impressions. An impression formerly in the Grabhorn Collection shows a different light green in the foliage and grassy slope (Nihon Ukiyo-e Kyōkai 1995, no. 156).

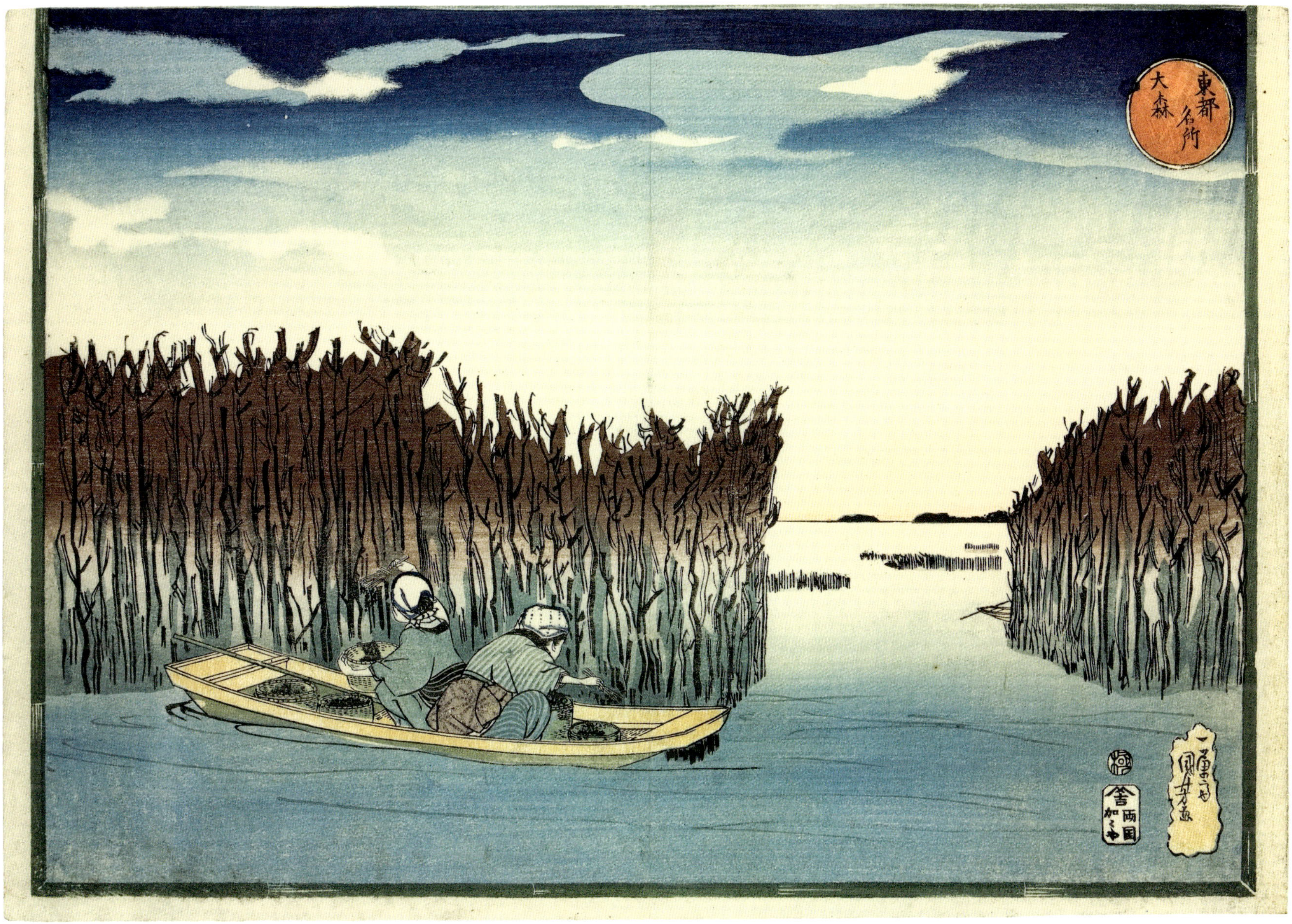

82

Gathering seaweed at Ōmori

early 1830s

Colour woodblock, *ōban*, published by Kagaya Kichibei (or Kichiemon), 25.4 × 36.7 cm

PRINT TITLE
'Ōmori'

SERIES TITLE
'Famous Places in Edo' (*Tōto meisho*)

ARTIST'S SIGNATURE
Ichiyūsai Kuniyoshi ga (in irregular cartouche)

CENSORSHIP SEAL
kiwame

American Friends of the British Museum (The Arthur R. Miller Collection) 03601

REFERENCES
Robinson 1961, no. 18; Springfield 1968, no. 31; Hillier 1976, no. 830; Riccar 1978, no. 7; Springfield 1980, no. 44; HUT, vol. 5, 1989, no. 61; HUT, vol. 7, 1990, BW no. 133; MSU 1991, no. 2; Suzuki 1992, no. 19; Itabashi 1994, Kuniyoshi no. 3; Nihon Ukiyo-e Kyōkai 1995, no. 157; Nagoya 1996, no. 172; Amsterdam 1998, no. 205

The vantage point is low, almost at water level, as the viewer watches two women in a boat gathering fresh seaweed. This activity typically took place on cold winter mornings. Special beds for cultivating seaweed were located in Edo bay, off Ōmori in the southern outskirts of the city, where it grew on the dense clumps of branches seen in the print. Once harvested, it was processed into wafer-thin dried sheets, a well-known product sold in the Asakusa district. The workaday subject of the print has no place in conventional picturesque depictions of 'famous places' (*meisho*) and their related activities.

A pleasing vista opens up between the cultivation beds as the sun rises beyond the horizon. Along with the deep perspective, the irregular cloud formations are hallmarks of the 'European style', their ragged edges achieved by abrading the edge of the printing blocks, a technique called *ita-bokashi*. These abraded edges perhaps imitate the fine parallel lines used at the interface of clouds and sky in European engravings.

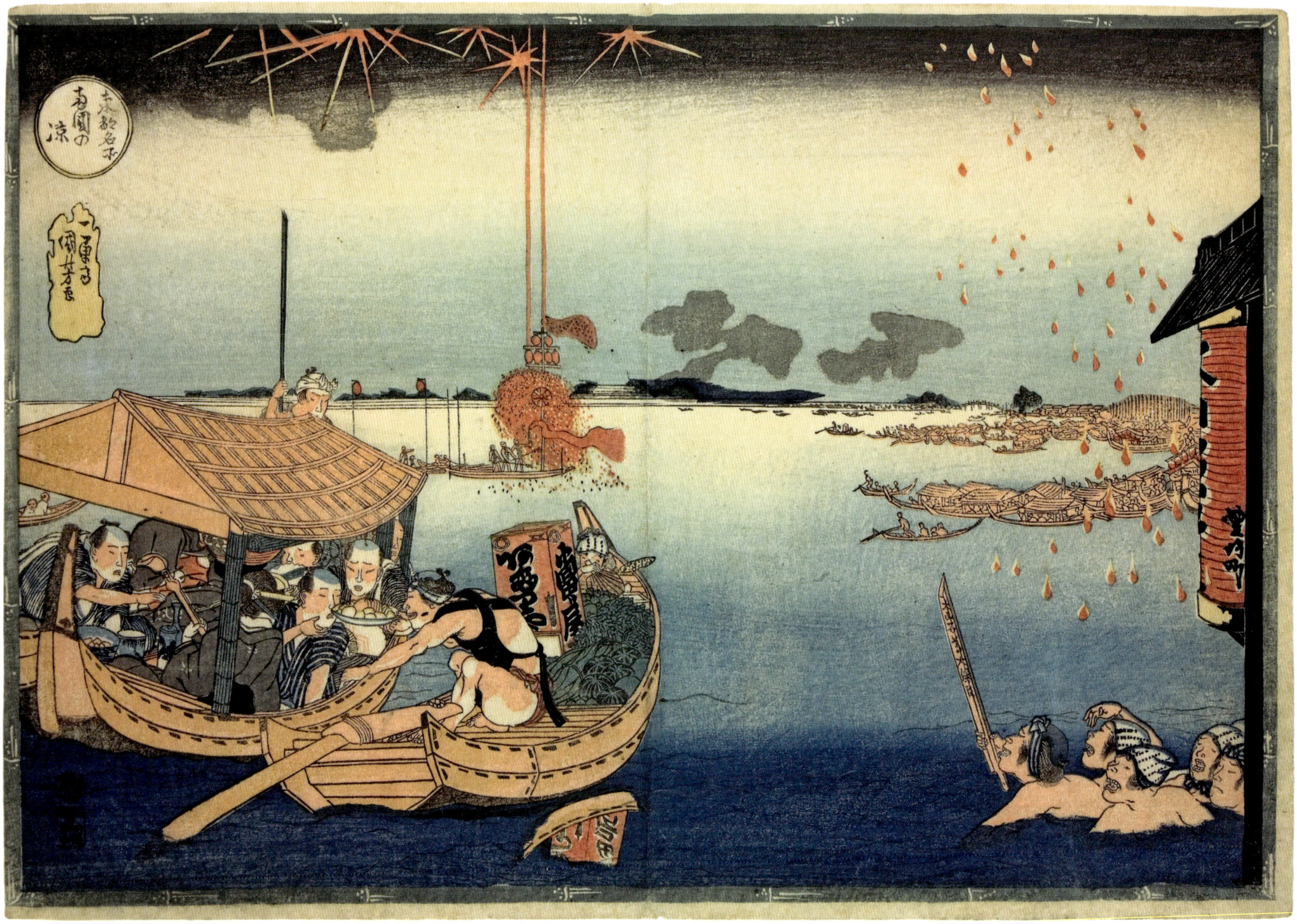

83

Pleasure boats and fireworks at Ryōgoku

early 1830s

Colour woodblock, *ōban*,
published by Kagaya Kichibei
(or Kichiemon),
25.6 × 37.3 cm

PRINT TITLE
'Evening Cool at Ryōgoku'
(*Ryōgoku no suzumi*)

SERIES TITLE
'Famous Places in Edo'
(*Tōto meisho*)

ARTIST'S SIGNATURE
Ichiyūsai Kuniyoshi ga
(in irregular cartouche)

CENSORSHIP SEAL:
kiwame

American Friends of the British Museum
(The Arthur R. Miller Collection) 03605

REFERENCES
Riccar 1978, no. 14; Springfield 1980, no. 45; MSU 1991, no. 9 (this impression); Suzuki 1992, no. 21 (this impression); Itabashi 1994, Kuniyoshi no. 5; Mainichi Shinbunsha 1995, no. 72; Nagoya 1996, no. 180

Ryōgoku ('Two Province') bridge across the Sumida river in central Edo was built in 1661 to link what were then the provinces of Musashi and Shimōsa. It became the most popular place to moor pleasure boats in the summer months, to catch cooling evening breezes from the river and to enjoy the firework displays regularly presented by one of two rival companies, Tamaya and Kagiya. The print shows a vendor supplying a covered boat full of revellers with a dish of fruit and vegetables, some perhaps grilled by his companion. *Shamisen* music played by a geisha animates the party. The foreshortened lines of the boat's roof take the gaze back to a boat in the middle distance, where fireworks are being launched. Spectators are watching from a large flotilla of pleasure boats and barges lined up in the distance. Sparks from the fireworks rain down on a group of workmen, who are purifying themselves by bathing in the river. One of them holds a ritual wooden sword, signalling that they are about to make a pilgrimage to Mt Ōyama, a two-day journey west of Edo (see also cat. 89). Pilgrims were permitted to climb to the very top of the sacred mountain only in the summer. Their ritual ablution always took place at a spot called Koriba, near the eastern end of Ryōgoku bridge. The great bridge is thus presumably to be imagined arching above the scene shown in the print; and that suggests, in turn, that the viewer is looking north, upstream towards Azuma bridge in the far distance. Kuniyoshi's inventive composition encourages the gaze to circle continuously among all the lively activities. A particularly notable detail is the reflection of part of the vendor's lantern and the side of his boat in the foreground water. Although the presence of lanterns and fireworks show this to be an evening or night scene, it is principally the convention of the gradated black band across the top of the print that indicates the darkness.

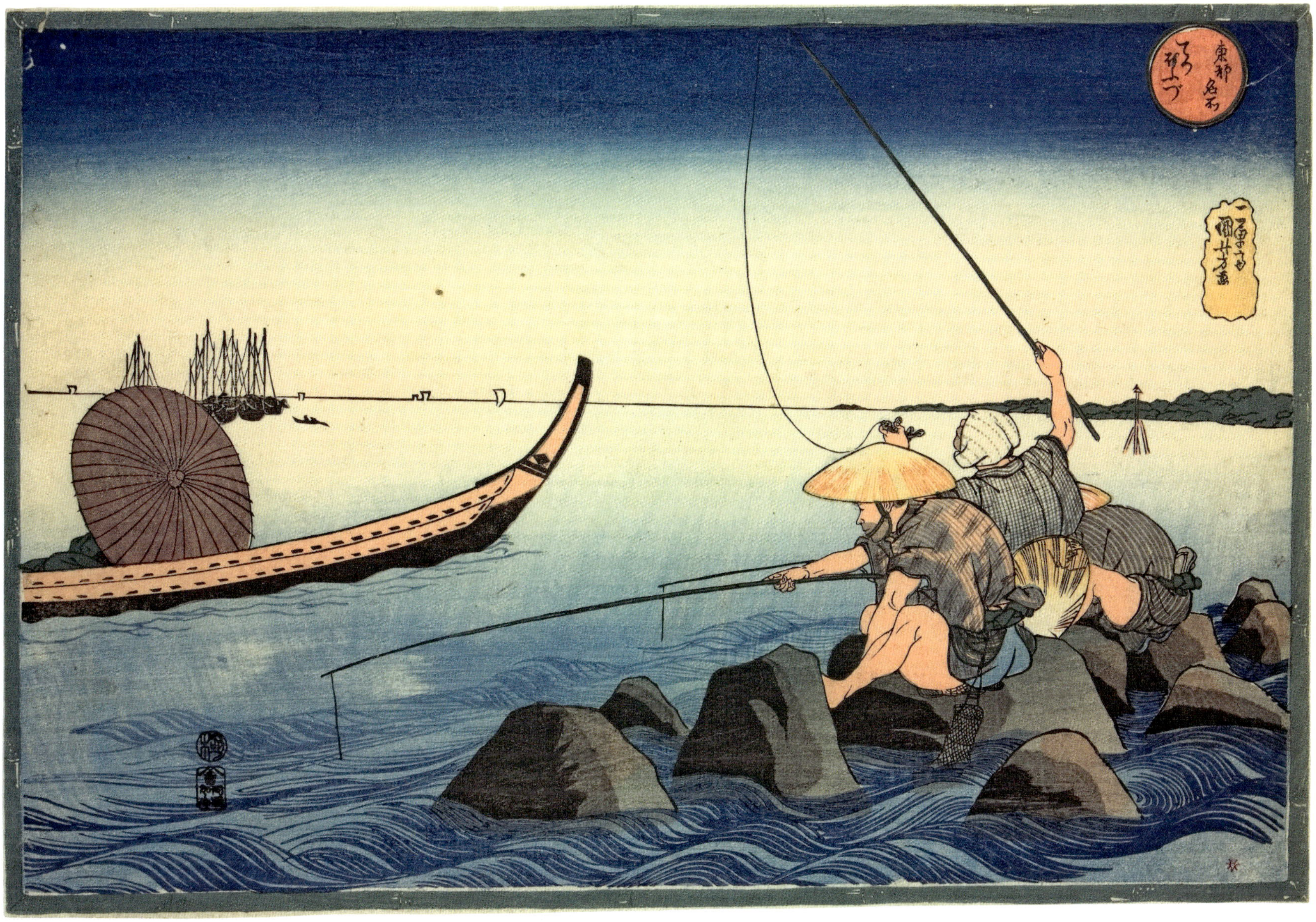

84

Fishermen at Teppōzu

early 1830s

Colour woodblock, *ōban*, published by Kagaya Kichibei (or Kichiemon), 24.6 × 36.4 cm

PRINT TITLE
'Teppōzu'

SERIES TITLE
'Famous Places in Edo' (*Tōto meisho*)

ARTIST'S SIGNATURE
Ichiyūsai Kuniyoshi ga (in irregular cartouche)

CENSORSHIP SEAL
kiwame

COLLECTOR'S SEAL
Henri Vever

American Friends of the British Museum (The Arthur R. Miller Collection) 03604

REFERENCES
Springfield 1968, no. 34; Pittsburgh 1976, no. 297; Hillier 1976, no. 829; Riccar 1978, no. 15; MSU 1991, no. 8; Suzuki 1992, no. 18; Itabashi 1994, Kuniyoshi no. 4; Nagoya 1996, no. 178; Sotheby's 1997, lot. 159 (this impression)

Three workmen enjoy the simple pleasure of fishing on the rocks at Teppōzu. This was an area of reclaimed shoreline, looking out over Edo bay towards Tsukuda island in the distance. The brightly coloured figures, the volumetric shading of their clothes and the complex shadows and coloured shading among the rocks suggest strong sunlight on a summer's day. A narrow 'boar's tooth boat' (*chokibune*) moves into view from the left, the single passenger probably a woman sheltered by her large parasol. With its bold foregrounding of the main motifs and eloquent interplay between the lines of the rods and the boat, this is one of the most satisfying designs in the series. All but invisible on the far left of the horizon is the embossed silhouette of Mt Fuji. This is more pronounced in other impressions. That in the Tanba Collection (Kanagawa Prefectural Museum of Art), for example, shows the sky pale pink along the horizon and has Fuji left in reserve so as to appear white (Suzuki 1992, no. 18). In addition, the wider band of deep Prussian blue in the sky is wiped with a distinct curve at the bottom, which blends into the orange. Finally, the woman's parasol is blue, not purple.

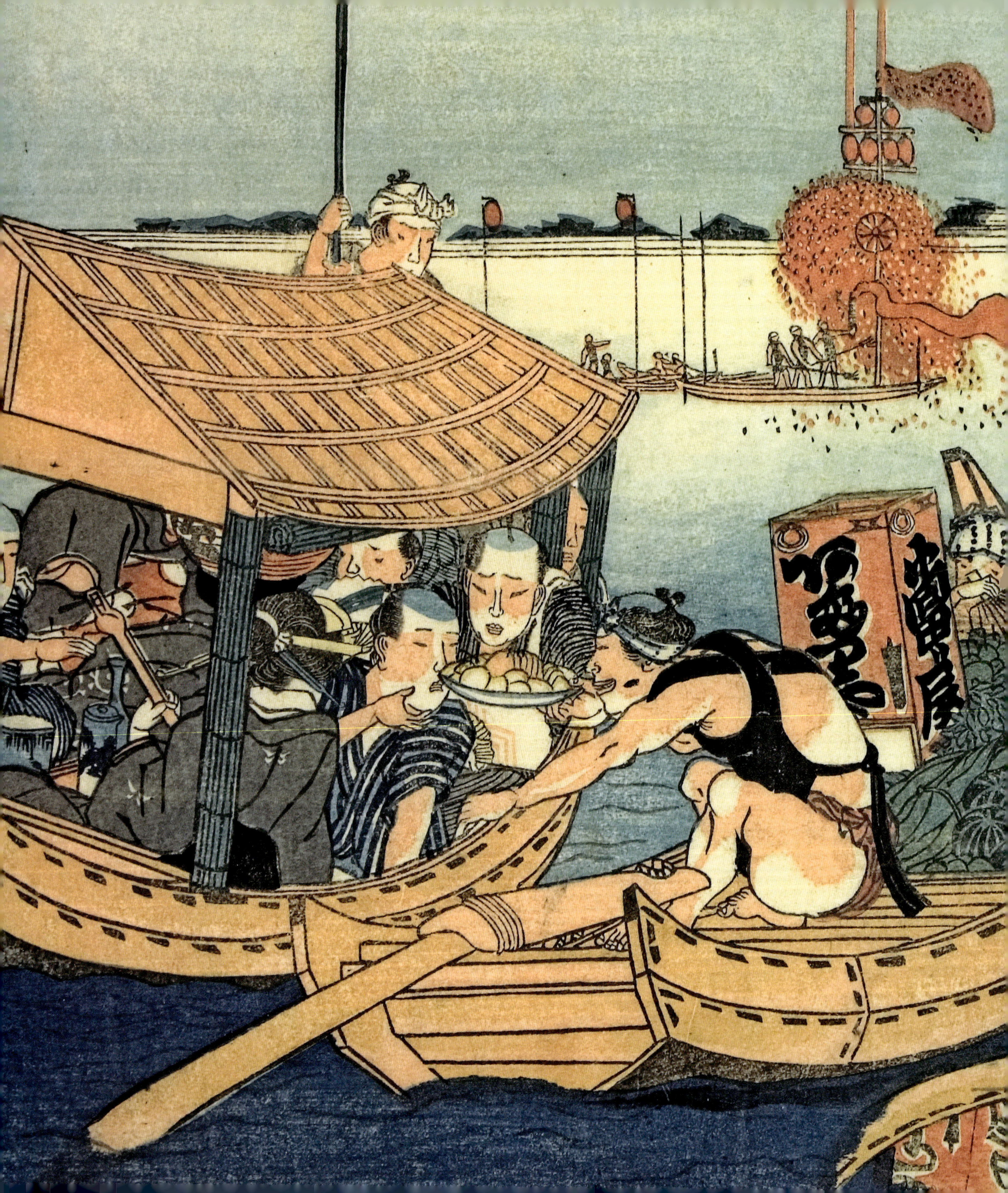

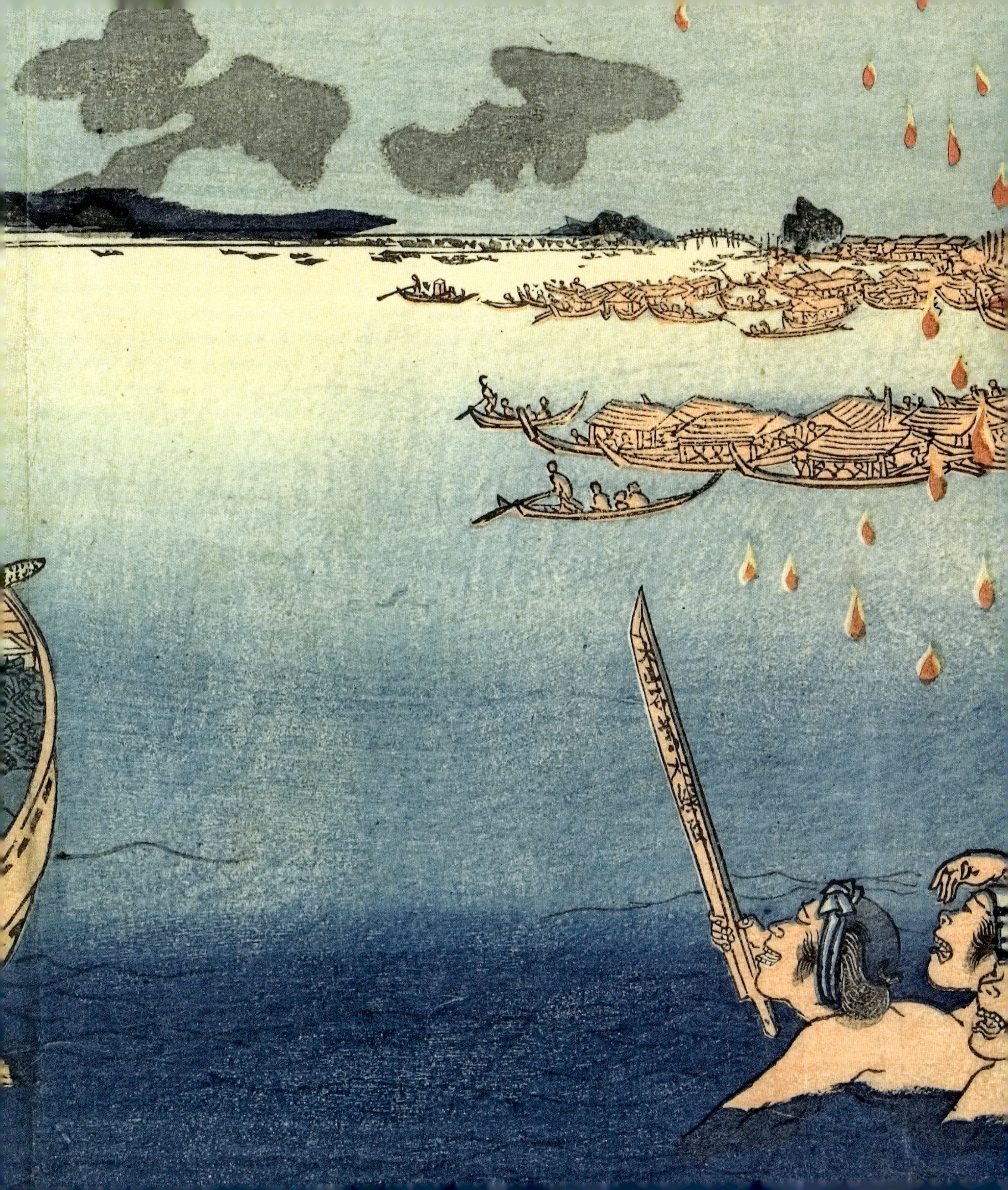

85

Rocks and crabs at the Sumida river, Edo

early 1830s

Colour woodblock, *ōban*, published by Yamaguchiya Tōbei, 24.2 × 36.5 cm

PRINT TITLE
'Picture of Successful-deal Pine Tree, Edo' (*Tōto shubi no matsu no zu*)

ARTIST'S SIGNATURE
Ichiyūsai Kuniyoshi ga (in rectangular cartouche)

ARTIST'S SEAL
toshidama

CENSORSHIP SEAL
kiwame

COLLECTOR'S SEAL
(*verso*) Werner Schindler

Takashima Masao Collection, Japan

REFERENCES
Springfield 1968, no. 22; Tsuji 1970, no. 44; *Ukiyo-e taikei* 1974, no. 30; Riccar 1978, no. 3; Keyes 1984, pl. 38; MSU 1991, no. 11; Suzuki 1992, no. 3; Itabashi 1994, Kuniyoshi no. 8; Mainichi Shinbunsha 1995, no. 73; Nagoya 1996, nos 181–2; Isao 2008, p. 26

The viewpoint is an eccentric one, as is often the case in Kuniyoshi's landscapes. The artist transports the viewer to the foot of a stone embankment on the Sumida river in Edo, where crabs scuttle in crevices and a sea louse clings to a rock. Yellow flowers dangle on spindly stems. This is anything but a picturesque view of 'Successful-deal Pine Tree' (*Shubi no matsu*), the famous landmark on the river that is here relegated to the distance (see cat. 66). A fisherman sitting in his boat is the only sign of human life, and even he is almost obscured by the foreground rock.

Shaded modelling of the rock and embankment, fitful ragged clouds printed in shades of Prussian blue, deep spatial recession towards the low horizon and closely observed drawing of the aquatic creatures – all these are features of Kuniyoshi's style at its most European. He may have been encouraged to adopt them by Aōdō Denzen's and other Japanese artists' experiments in this direction, but the way in which he combines these elements would seem to reflect his own, idiosyncratic artistic personality. This was one of the key works analysed by Tsuji Nobuo to support his characterisation of the artist as belonging to the 'lineage of original thinkers – the avant-garde of Edo' (*kisō no keifu, Edo no avangarudo*; Tsuji 1970).

An earlier impression, in the Ainsworth Collection, has printed blue ripples at the water's edge, along with pale pink and green on the rock and stone embankment, instead of the brown seen here (Keyes 1984, pl. 38). That impression also lacks a large part of the blue cloud formation at the top left.

Five designs from this series are known (they are reproduced in MSU 1991, nos 11–15). They all bear titles that include the name of a neighbourhood in the same way: *Tōto [name of neighbourhood] no zu* (*Picture of [...], Edo*). Most of the locations are unusual and the views are all eccentric to some degree, generally featuring a low vantage point. The prints share a focus on European stylistic elements and on mundane activities, such as people walking in the rain, caulking a boat, fishing for eels or pointing at a roadside statue. Roger Keyes has argued that three more landscapes with similar cartouches and signatures belong to the series: 'The Night Attack, Act Eleven of *Treasury of Loyal Retainers*' (cat. 79), 'Okane, Strongwoman of Ōmi province' (Suzuki 1992, no. 61) and 'Mt Asama seen from Usui Pass' (Riccar 1978, no. 35) (Keyes 1984, p. 187).

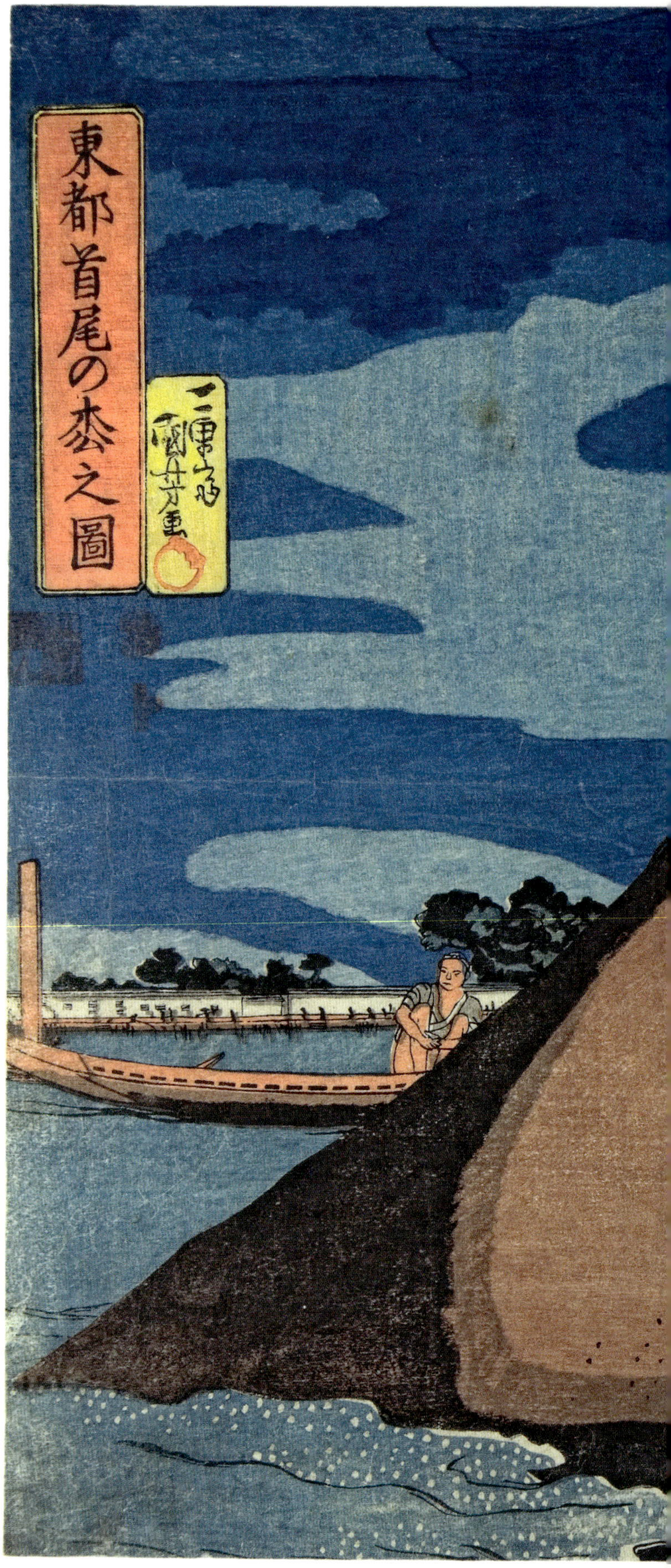

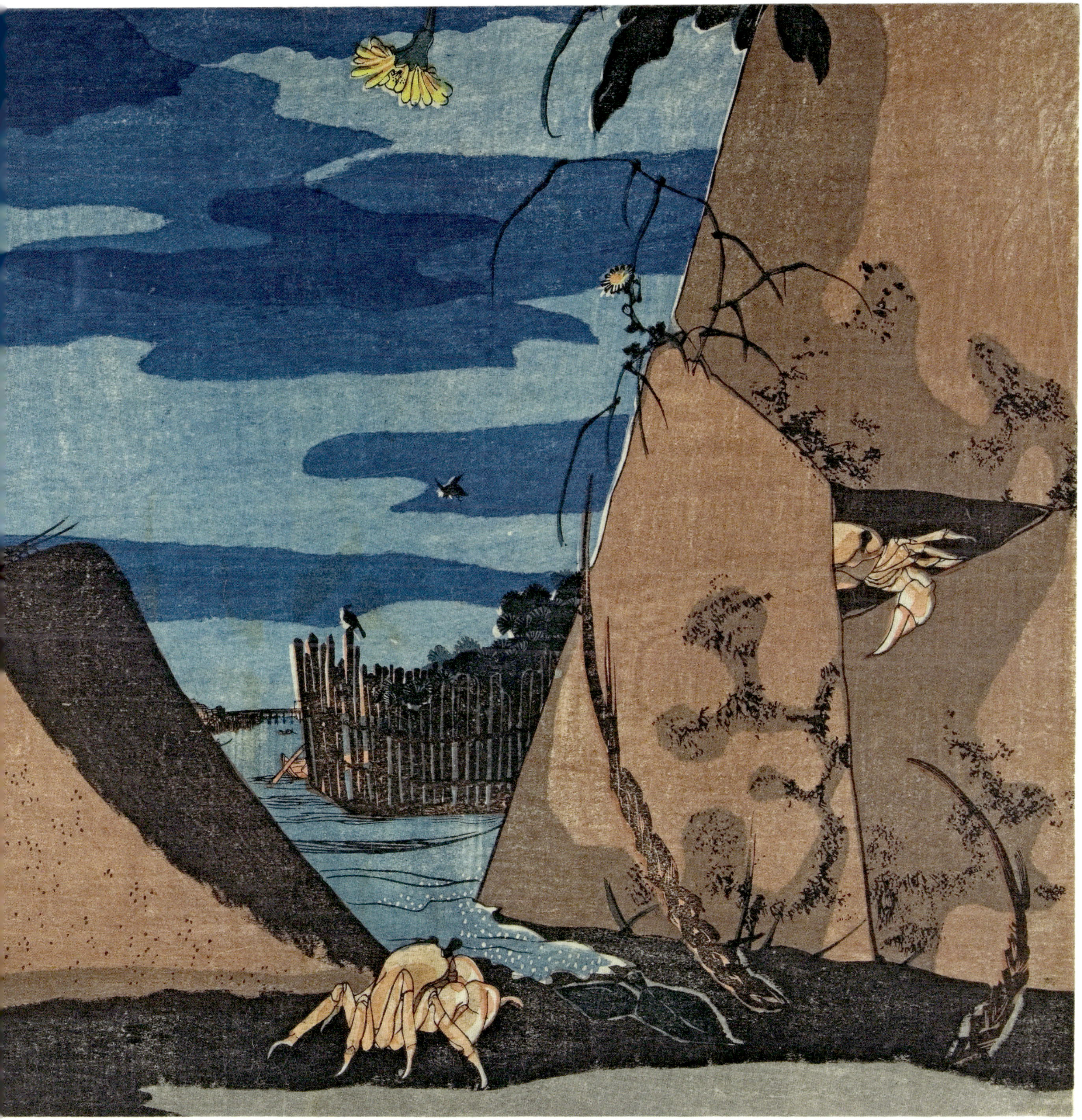

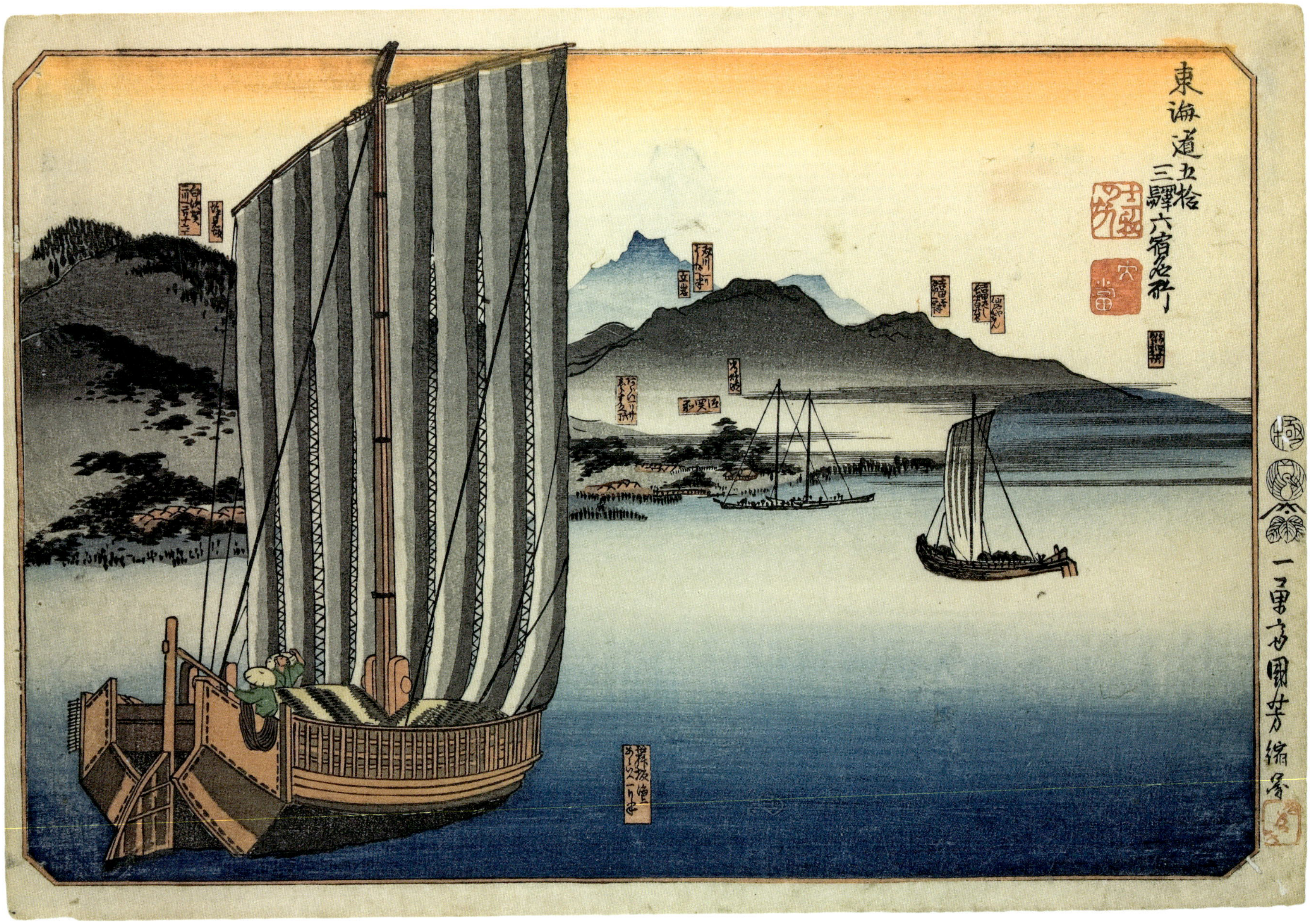

東海道五拾三驛六宿名所
一勇斎國芳緒筆

86

Ships between Maisaka and Arai

mid-1830s

Colour woodblock, *ōban*, published by Tsuruya Kiemon and Tsutaya Kichizō, 24.8 × 36.7 cm

SERIES TITLE
'Fifty-three Stations of the Tōkaidō Road, Six Famous Places [Together]' (*Tōkaidō gojūsan-eki rokushuku meisho*)

ARTIST'S SIGNATURE
Ichiyūsai Kuniyoshi *shukuzu* (reduced picture by Ichiyūsai Kuniyoshi)

ARTIST'S SEAL
Yanaki

American Friends of the British Museum (The Arthur R. Miller Collection) 03302

REFERENCES
Springfield 1968, no. 37; Riccar 1978, no. 26; Springfield 1980, no. 53; HUT, vol. 5, 1989, BW no. 48; Suzuki 1992, no. 40; Mainichi Shinbunsha 1995, no. 85; Amsterdam 1998, no. 213

A ship at full sail leads the viewer's gaze across the sea towards a distant shoreline. In a bold compositional gesture, the tip of the mast and one corner of the sail extend beyond the frame of the image. A small note near the bottom of the print, next to the ship, states 'One and a half *ri* [about 6 km] by sea from Maisaka to Arai'. Another adds that at Arai, where Lake Hamana (in modern Shizuoka prefecture) flows into the Pacific ocean, there is an official checkpoint. Further notes guide the viewer up the slope on the left towards Shirasuka, and through distant hills towards, successively, the post-stations of Futakawa, Yoshida and Goyu. The journey along the eastern coastal road, the Tōkaidō, had begun in Edo (modern Tokyo) and will end at the imperial city of Kyoto.

Around 1833–34 the publishers Takenouchi Magohachi and Tsuruya Kiemon achieved a sensational success with Hiroshige's series of prints 'Fifty-three Stations of the Tōkaidō Road' (*Tōkaidō gojūsan-tsugi no uchi*). The present series is thought to have been created in 1834–35, in response to this 'Tōkaidō boom'. It, too, was issued by two firms, Tsuruya Kiemon and Tsutaya Kichizō, but, rather than picturing each post-station on a single sheet, it telescopes the long road into a sequence of images featuring three to six places each. Most show a vignette of human activity in one foreground corner, set off against a panoramic landscape in the distance. All twelve designs have survived (they are illustrated in Suzuki 1992, nos 33–44).

This is a fine early impression, with much subtle gradation of the colours. The two red seals at top right, alongside the series title, read 'from twelve sheets' (*jūni-mai no uchi*) and 'great hit' (*ō-atari*). The red seal that appears in the lower right corner, beneath the artist's signature, reads 'Yanaki', which may derive from 'Yanagiya', the name of the indigo-dyeing business run by Kuniyoshi's father (personal communication from Iwakiri Yuriko). Later printings lack this seal.

CONCISE ILLUSTRATED BIOGRAPHY OF MONK NICHIREN

(Cats 87, 88)

Monk Nichiren (1222–1282) is a major figure in Japan's religious history. In 1253 he founded the Nichiren sect in Kamakura to propagate the belief that the true essence of Buddhist law is found in the teachings of the *Lotus Sutra*. Frequently at odds with better-established sects, Nichiren was banished twice, first to Tatsunokuchi in Fujisawa and then to Sado island, before being pardoned and permitted to return to Kamakura.

Kuniyoshi's series features ten famous episodes from Nichiren's life, principally demonstrations of his miraculous spiritual powers. It is unusual for a whole series of full-colour ukiyo-e prints to be devoted to a popular religious subject in this way. The year 1831 marked the 550th anniversary of the monk's death, but the form of Kuniyoshi's signature suggests a publication date of *c.* 1835–36. Suzuki Jūzō reproduces all ten designs (Suzuki 1992, nos 178–87).

87

Monk Nichiren in the snow at Tsukahara

c. 1835

Colour woodblock, *ōban*, published by Iseya Rihei, 24.8 × 37 cm

SERIES TITLE
'Concise Illustrated Biography of Monk Nichiren' (*Kōso go-ichidai ryakuzu*)

PRINT TITLE
'In the Snow at Tsukahara, Sado Island' (*Sashū Tsukahara setchū*)

ARTIST'S SIGNATURE
Ichiyūsai Kuniyoshi hitsu

ARTIST'S SEAL
toshidama

CENSORSHIP SEAL
kiwame

American Friends of the British Museum (The Arthur R. Miller Collection) 12110

REFERENCES
Springfield 1968, no. 17; *Ukiyo-e taikei* 1974, no. 31; Hillier 1976, no. 836; Riccar 1978, nos 184–6; Springfield 1980, nos 31–3; Robinson 1982, no. S6.10.; Amsterdam 1984, no. 215; Keyes 1984, pl. 131; HUT, vol. 12, 1988, BW no. 133; MSU 1991, no. 62; TNM 1991, no. 181; Suzuki 1992, no. 183; Baur 1994, no. G365; Nihon Ukiyo-e Kyōkai 1995, no. 161; Mainichi Shinbunsha 1995, no. 179; Nagoya 1996, no. 90; Amsterdam 1998, no. 208; Isao 2008, p. 51

Nichiren is shown trudging through deep snow on the hillside at Tsukahara during his exile on Sado island. Corpses were abandoned on this forlorn moor and the monk intoned prayers for their salvation. Travel hat tilted against the elements, he cuts a lonely figure. In addition to the white dots carved into the blocks, shell-white pigment has been flicked with a brush onto the surface of the print to suggest snow falling more densely.

Several scholars have pointed out that Kuniyoshi borrowed a large section of the composition – the village nestling along the shoreline at the foot of the mountain – from an illustration in the book *Bunpō sansui ikō* (*Posthumous Manuscript of Landscapes by Bunpō*, 1824) that had been drawn originally by the Kyoto artist Kawamura Bunpō (1779–1821) and prepared for publication after his death by Kawamura Kihō. Such borrowings were not unusual, and ukiyo-e artists 'mined' Bunpō's book on more than one occasion (Tinios 2004).

Many different printings of Kuniyoshi's design exist. One main variation concerns the printed horizon line, which some impressions lack. Most scholars have agreed with Suzuki Jūzō that impressions including the horizon line are the earliest (Suzuki 1992, p. 206), but Matthi Forrer disagrees (Baur 1994, no. G365). Many variations are found in the colouring and pattern of wiping used for the village houses, and Nichiren's stole is sometimes green, not orange. A dramatically different printing shows the entire hillside and village printed darkly, in black and shades of grey (Mainichi Shinbunsha 1995, no. 179).

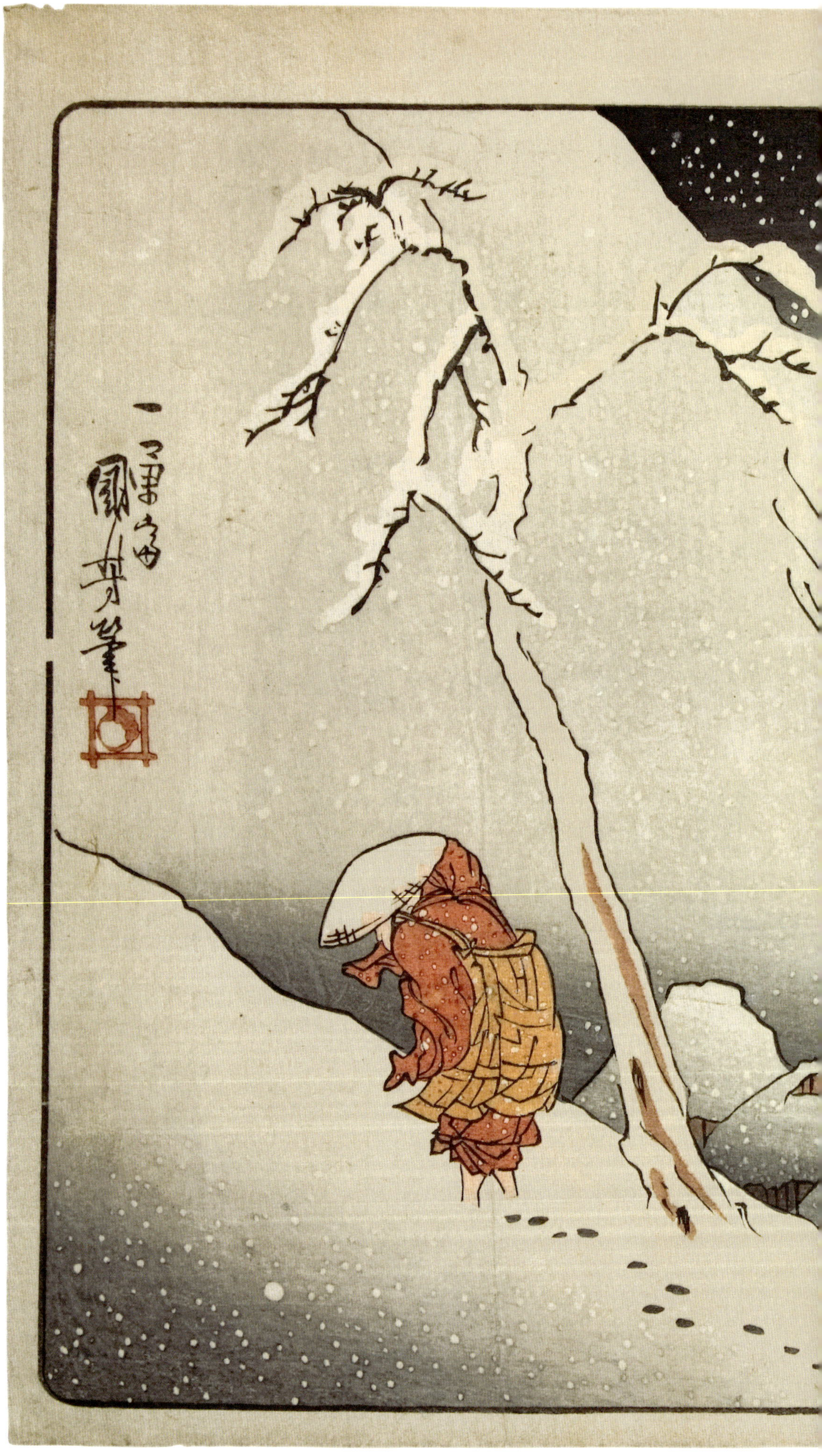

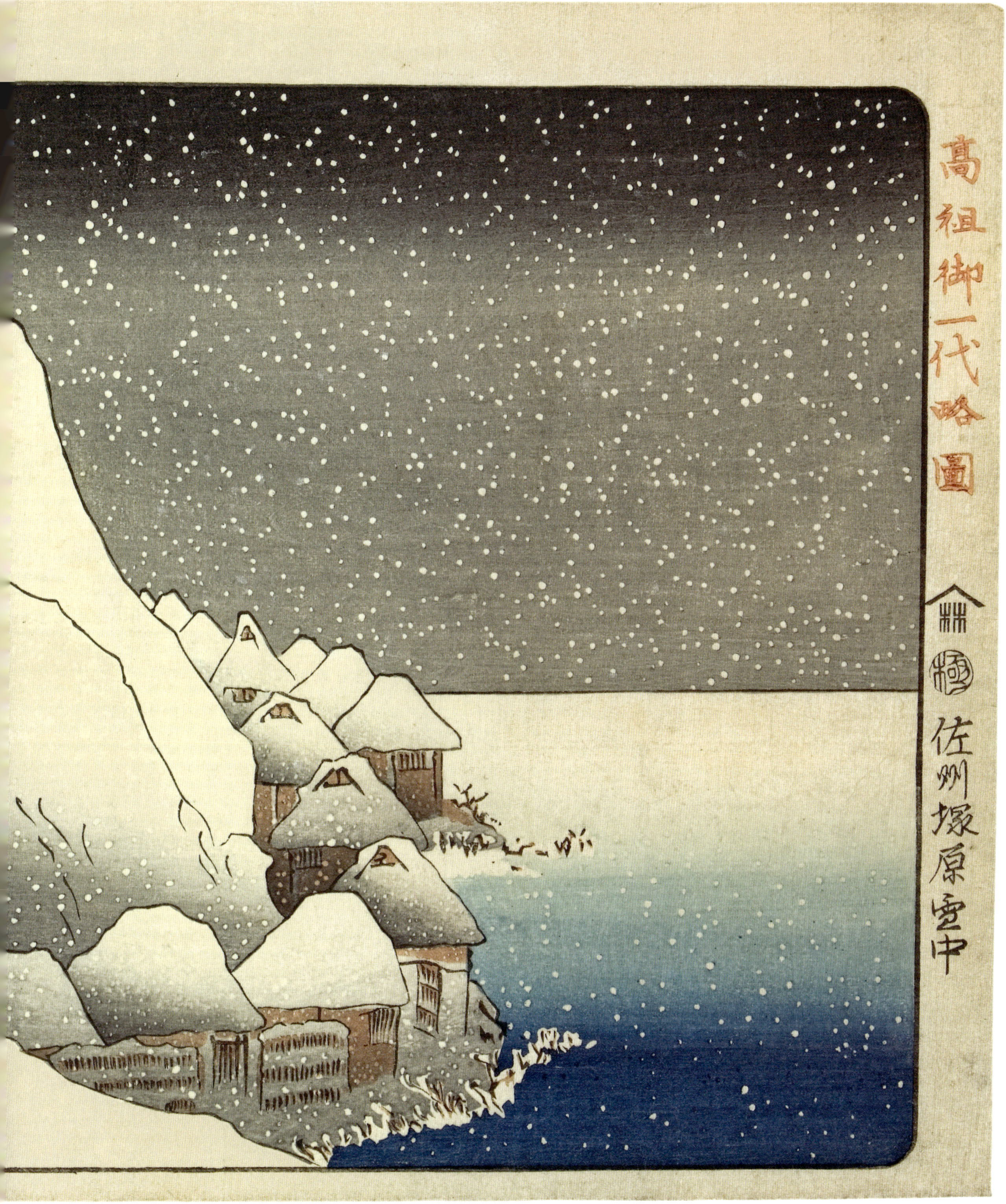
高祖御一代略圖
佐州塚原雪中

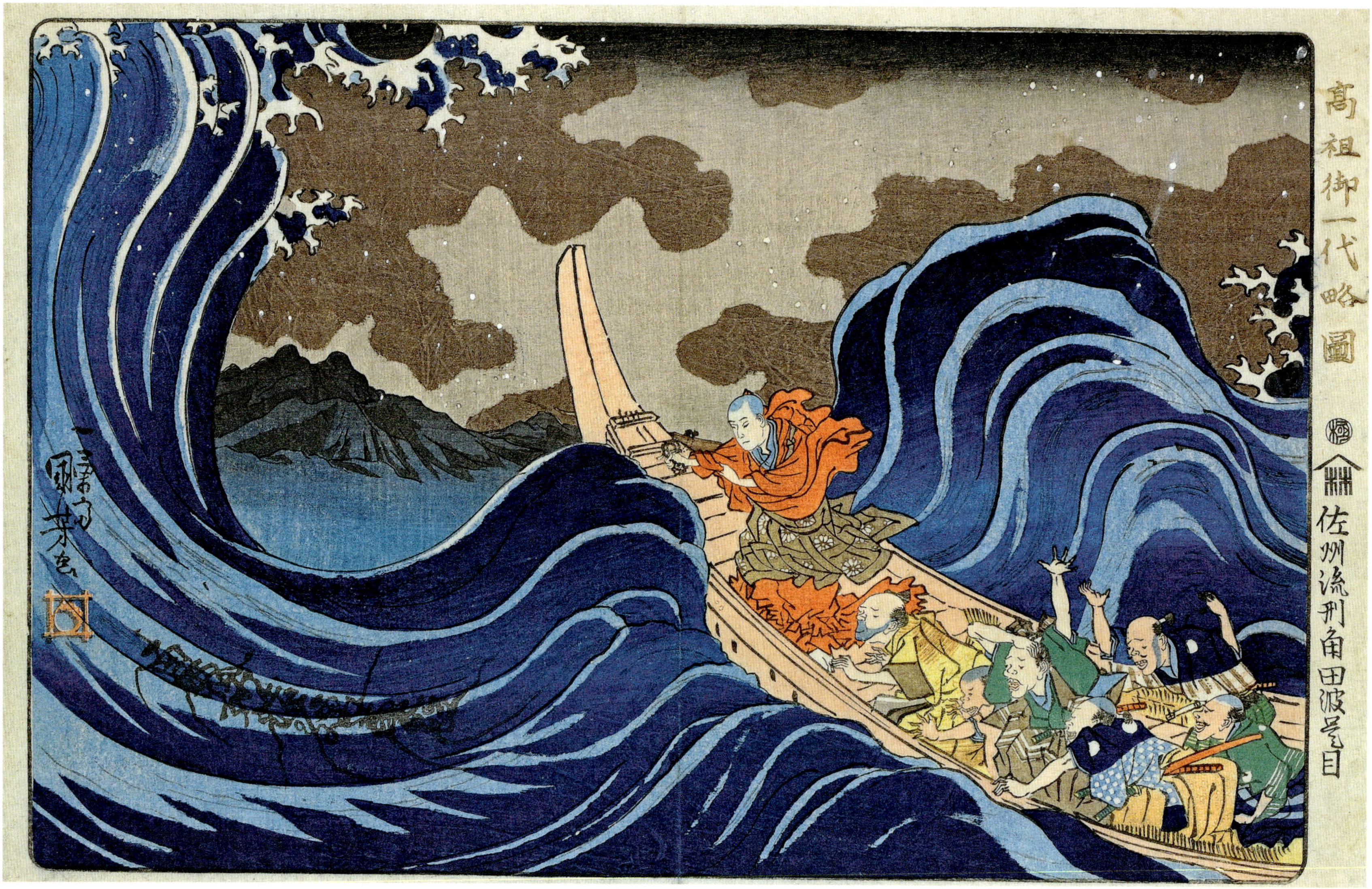

88

Monk Nichiren calms the waves at Kakuta

c. 1835

Colour woodblock, *ōban*, published by Iseya Rihei, 24 × 37.3 cm

SERIES TITLE
'Concise Illustrated Biography of Monk Nichiren' (*Kōso go-ichidai ryakuzu*)

PRINT TITLE
'Banishment to Sado Island: Sutra Title on the Waves at Kakuta' (*Sashū rukei kakuta nami daimoku*)

ARTIST'S SIGNATURE
Ichiyūsai Kuniyoshi ga

ARTIST'S SEAL
toshidama

CENSORSHIP SEAL
kiwame

The British Museum, JA 1913.4-15.010

REFERENCES
Robinson 1961, no. 23; Springfield 1968, no. 18; Hillier 1976, no. 835; Riccar 1978, no. 183; Robinson 1982, no. S6.9; Amsterdam 1984, no. 213; Keyes 1984, pl. 126; HUT, vol. 3, 1988, BW no. 40; HUT, vol. 5, 1989, BW no. 42; Nihon Ukiyo-e Kyōkai 1990, no. 1–73; TNM 1991, no. 180; Suzuki 1992, no. 182; Baur 1994, no. G370; Mainichi Shinbunsha 1995, no. 178; Nagoya 1996, no. 93; Amsterdam 1998, no. 207; Ōta 1999, no. 68

The ship taking Nichiren into exile on Sado island met with a terrible storm at Kakuta. Taking a pole, the monk calmly wrote the mantra (*daimoku*) 'Hail to the Miraculous Law of the Lotus Sutra' (*Namu myōhō renge kyō*) on the waves, whereupon the storm abated. The characters of the mantra remained afloat on the sea. This design is the most dynamic in the series, the treatment of the wave somewhat reminiscent of Hokusai's famous print 'The Great Wave' of just a few years earlier.

The earliest impressions show small, black, triangular shapes scattered across the top of the design (later removed, as in the present print) in a technique known as 'wasted carving' (*muda-bori*). The shapes were cut into the key-block to indicate the position of the shell-white pigment that would be flicked onto the finished print with a brush to suggest sea spray. Earlier printings also have a larger number of colours, additional gradated printing in the sky and distant mountains, and a band of lighter blue gradated horizontally across the sea so as to illuminate the mantra on the waves (Suzuki 1992, no. 182).

89

Tamura ferry on the Ōyama road

c. 1842

Colour woodblock, *ōban*, published by Wakasaya Yoichi, 25.2 × 35.8 cm

PRINT TITLE
'View of Tamura Ferry on the Ōyama Road, Sagami Province' (*Sōshū Ōyama-michi Tamura no watashi no kei*)

ARTIST'S SIGNATURE
Ichiyūsai Kuniyoshi ga (in gourd-shaped *Yoshi* cartouche)

American Friends of the British Museum (The Arthur R. Miller Collection) 17601

REFERENCES
Robinson 1961, no. 47; Hillier 1976, no. 834; Riccar 1978, no. 36; Springfield 1980, no. 59; Suzuki 1992, no. 48; Nagoya 1996, no. 194; Madison 2007, no. 105

This is a summer view of Tamura ferry, on the pilgrimage road from Edo to Ōyama ('Great Mountain') in Sagami province – the mountain seen here in the distance. Pilgrimage to the Ōyama Afuri shrine, where prayers were thought to encourage rainfall, was permitted only for twenty days in late summer, from the twenty-seventh day of the sixth month to the seventeenth of the seventh month. At Tamura, in the foreground in the print, pilgrims had to take a boat across the Sagami river to Ichinomiya on the far bank. Kuniyoshi shows those waiting at the ferry eating watermelon; many have removed some of their clothes in the summer heat. The vista is broad and inviting, the trees lush with foliage. Extensive use of shading and modelling gives body to the foliage, mountains and figures. The clouds, too, are essentially European in conception.

The publisher of this print, Wakasaya Yoichi, issued two related landscapes that depict pilgrims making ritual ablutions beneath the Ōtaki and Rōben no taki waterfalls at the sacred mountain in Ōyama (Suzuki 1992, nos 49–50). The three designs may have been intended for a more extensive series that never came about. Oka Yasumasa has suggested that the basic composition of Kuniyoshi's print and the figure on horseback being led by a groom derive from a small copperplate print by the Kyoto artist Gengendō I (Matsumoto Yasuoki, 1786–1867) entitled 'View of the Fuji River on the Tōkaidō Road' (*Tōkaidō Fujikawa chōbō no zusha*). In turn, Gengendō I may have based his design on an imported French print. Though the precise date of his print has not been established, it must have been created before *c.* 1847 (Oka 1992, pp. 158–67, figs 35, 36).

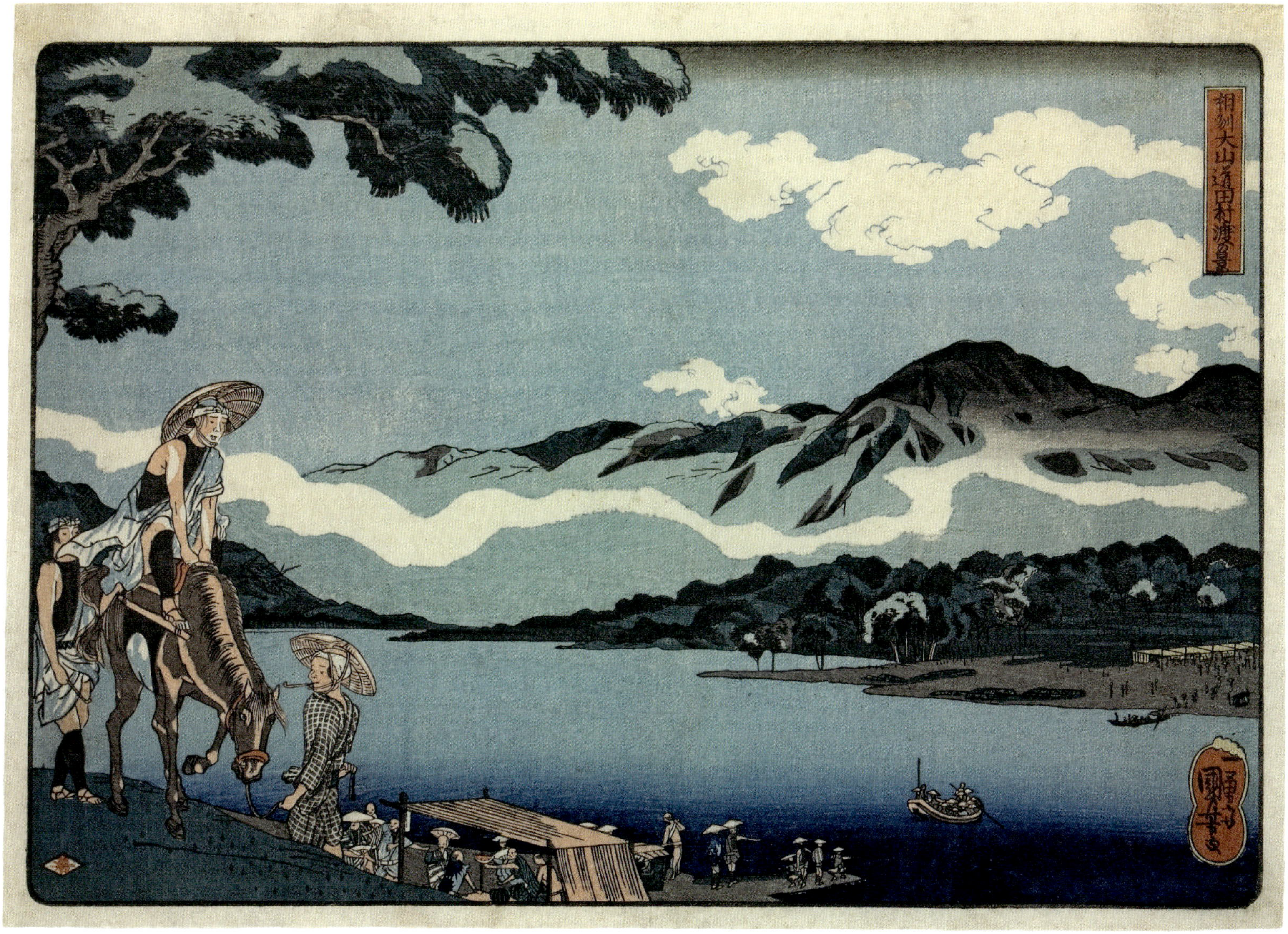

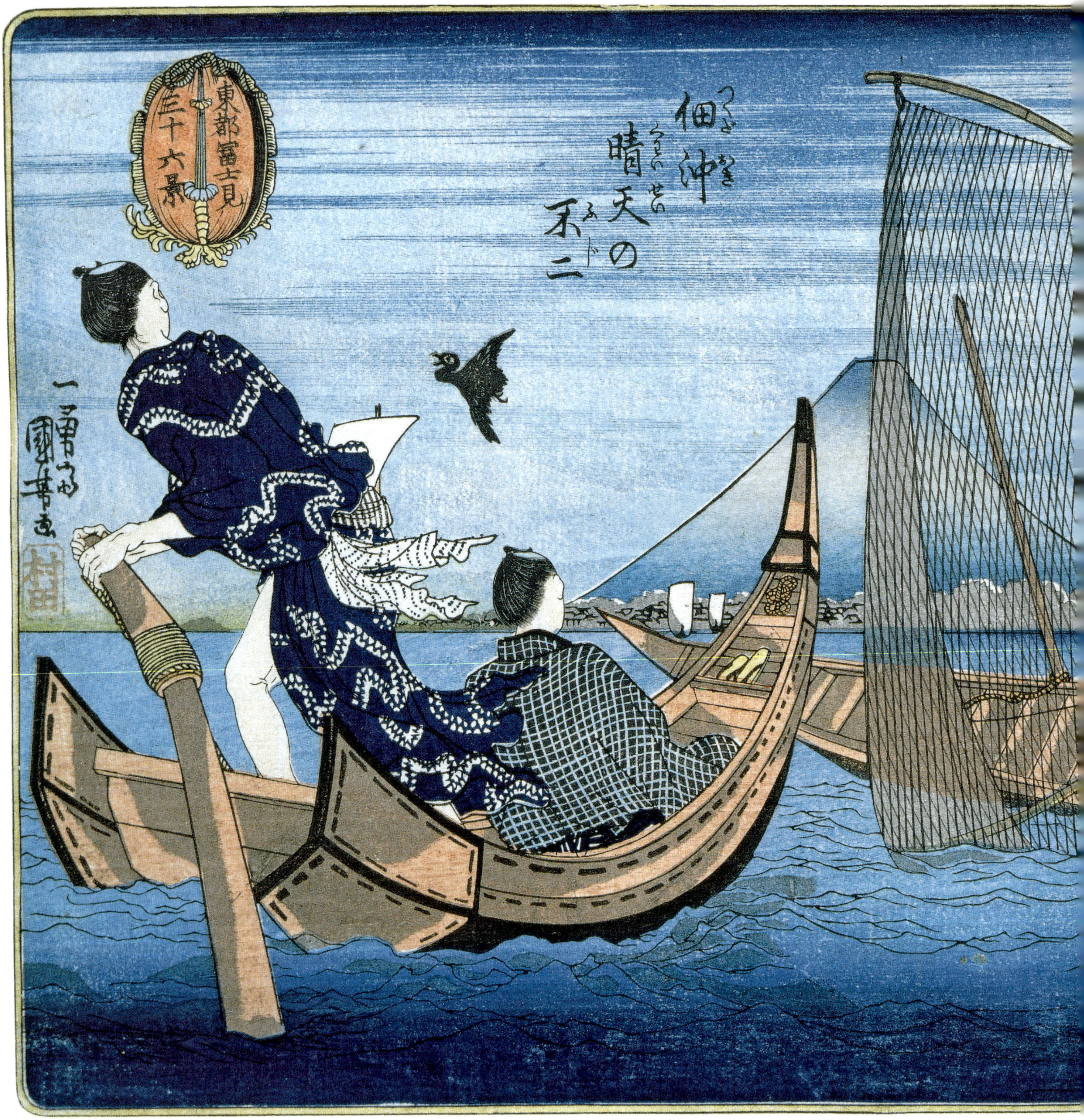
東都富士見
三十六景
佃沖
晴天の
不二
一勇斎国芳画

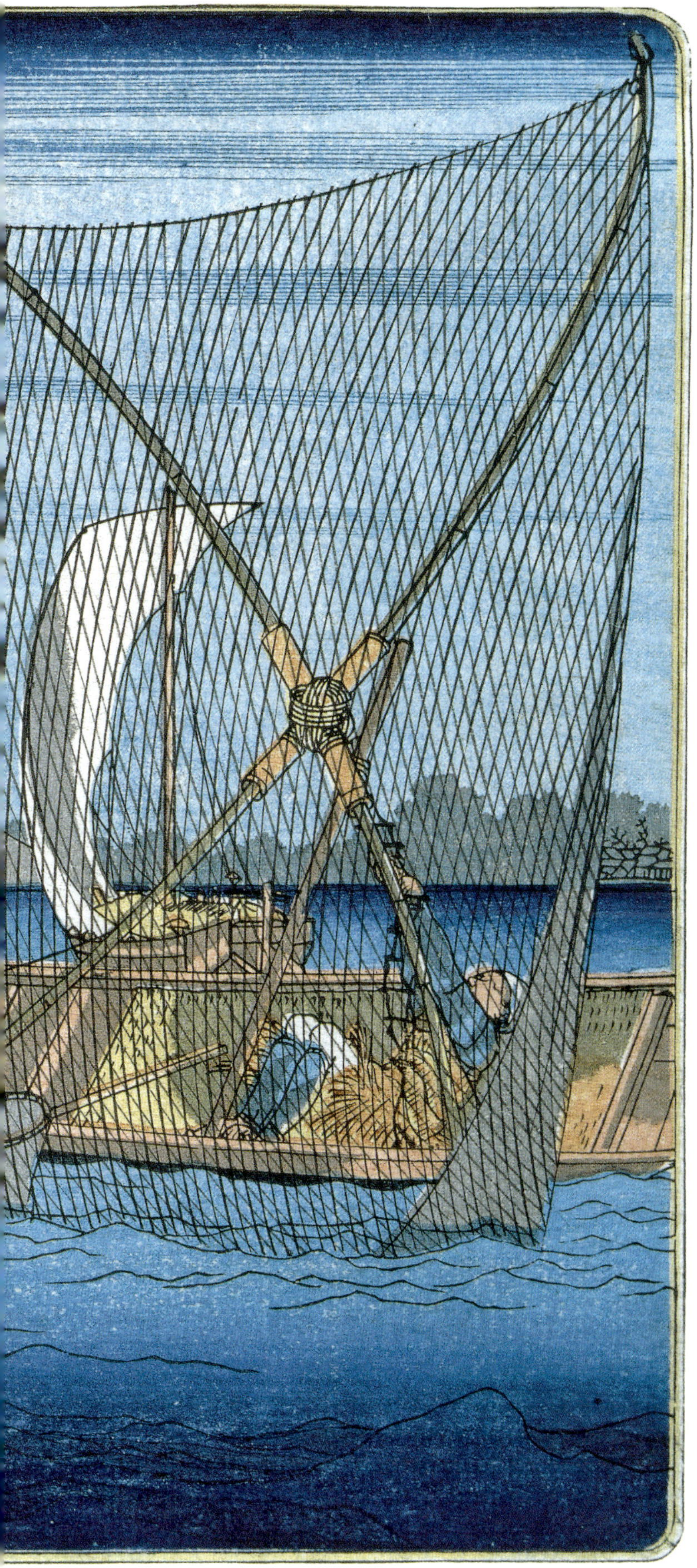

90

Mt Fuji seen from boats in Edo bay

1843–44

Colour woodblock, *ōban*, published by Murataya Jirōbei, 23.1 × 34.5 cm

SERIES TITLE
'Thirty-six Views of Fuji from Edo' *(Tōto Fujimi sanjū-rokkei)*

PRINT TITLE
'Fuji in Clear Weather, from off Tsukuda Island' *(Tsukuda oki kaisei no Fuji)*

ARTIST'S SIGNATURE
Ichiyūsai Kuniyoshi ga

CENSOR'S SEAL
Mura (trimmed)

Victoria and Albert Museum, London, E.2269-1909

REFERENCES
Robinson 1961, no.41; Springfield 1968, no.81; Riccar 1978, no.19; Springfield 1980, no.74; HUT, vol.5, 1989, no.57 (this impression); HUT, vol.7, 1990, BW no.135; V&A 1991, no.96 (this impression); Suzuki 1992, no.29; Itabashi 1994, Kuniyoshi no.15; Nagoya 1996, no.197; Amsterdam 1998, no.222

At water level in Edo bay, the viewer seems to be moving along behind the fast 'boar's tusk boat' (*choki-bune*) with its single passenger. Both ferryman and passenger gaze towards the distant towering presence of Mt Fuji, spectacularly visible in the fine weather. A fisherman's skiff cuts across the composition. Its occupant braces his feet against the gunwale as he strains to haul in a large 'four-armed net' (*yotsude-ami*), the skiff tilting dramatically in the process. The boats' curves echo the slopes of Mt Fuji and accentuate their elegance. Behind the skiff more boats are heading towards the horizon at full sail. A breeze causes the ferryman's cotton sash and robe to flutter; a cormorant flies over the water. The low viewpoint and the European-style shading seen here distinguish many of Kuniyoshi's Edo cityscapes (see also cats 81–5).

The compositional ploy of depicting Mt Fuji as seen through a net was used by Hokusai in volume three of his illustrated book *Fugaku hyakkei* (*One Hundred Views of Mt Fuji*). That volume may not have been published until *c.* 1849, several years later than the present print. On the other hand, the title of Kuniyoshi's series (from which five designs are currently known) certainly alludes to that of Hokusai's well-known *Fugaku sanjū-rokkei* (*Thirty-six Views of Mt Fuji*) of *c.* 1830–33. A *kyōka* or haiku poem is printed in the sky in the earliest impressions of the series, but was subsequently omitted, as here. The present design originally bore a haiku by one Shinnichian Kinga describing how the shadow of Fuji cooled the boat's path. (For illustrations of early printings of all five designs, see Nagoya 1996, nos 195–9.) The margin of this impression has been trimmed, removing the single 'Mura' censorship seal.

ONE HUNDRED POEMS BY ONE HUNDRED POETS

(Cats 91–7)

The original *Hyakunin isshu* (*One Hundred Poems by One Hundred Poets*) was a collection of poems in the standard *tanka* form of thirty-one syllables, each written by a different author. The hundred verses, selected in the 1230s by the renowned poet and scholar Fujiwara no Teika (1162–1241), range in date from the seventh century to Teika's own day and were intended as a historical survey representing the very best in Japanese poetry. *One Hundred Poems* has remained the most authoritative collection of its kind; traditionally, many people have attempted to memorise its entire contents. An edition annotated by Ozaki Masayoshi and entitled *Hyakunin isshu hitoyo-gatari* was published in Osaka in 1833, and this seems to have a triggered a *Hundred Poems* craze. Kuniyoshi's series, which aims to provide pictorial evocations, some historical, some contemporary, of the 'heart' (*kokoro*; that is, the essence) of each poem, formed part of this 'boom'. Indeed, as Iwakiri Yuriko has pointed out, the Sōjō Henjō design copies the composition of the illustration and the interpretation of the poem in Ozaki's book (Nagoya 1996, p. 242). Joshua Mostow has retranslated the *Hundred Poems* collection and described in fascinating detail its cultural afterlife in texts and images (Mostow 1996). The translations given in the entries below are his.

Each print bears a rectangular text cartouche. This contains the classical poem, followed by the name of the section in the classical anthology in which it can be found ('love poems', 'autumn poems' and so forth) and the title of that anthology. The rest of the text explains the imagery and meaning of the poem for a popular audience, sometimes beginning with the formula 'The essence of the poem is' (*Uta no kokoro wa*). The designs are numbered. Since only fifty-eight have been identified (all listed and described in Robinson 1982, series S.19), the series doubtless never reached completion. The Miller Collection includes forty-five of them (10601–45). Just one print bears the personal censorship seal 'Taka', so the incomplete series is thought to have been issued *c.* 1842, as the Tenpō publishing regulations were being introduced (see pp. 21–2). A series with such an exalted literary character accorded well with the moralising aims of the Tenpō reforms.

91

Emperor Kōkō and his attendants in snow

c. 1842

Colour woodblock, *ōban*, published by Ebisu, 36.9 × 24.5 cm

SERIES TITLE
'One Hundred Poems by One Hundred Poets' (*Hyakunin isshu no uchi*)

PRINT TITLE
'Kōkō Tennō' (no. 15)

ARTIST'S SIGNATURE
Ichiyūsai Kuniyoshi ga

ARTIST'S SEAL
toshidama

POEM
Kimi ga tame / haru no no ni idete / wakana tsumu / waga koromode ni / yuki wa furitsutsu

American Friends of the British Museum (The Arthur R. Miller Collection) 10614

REFERENCES
Springfield 1968, no. 55; Hillier 1976, no. 839; Riccar 1978, no. 192; Robinson 1982, no. S19.15; Mostow 1996, pp. 187–9

'For my lord's sake / I went out into the fields of spring / to pick young greens / while on my robe / the snow kept falling and falling.'

KŌKŌ TENNŌ

The emperor is shown looking back over one shoulder as he walks up a hillside in deep snow. He wears high wooden clogs, but his attendants and page boy appear to be bare-footed. One attendant protects him with a parasol and another carries a woven basket of young greens; like the hats, both objects are partly coated with snow.

The poem comes from the spring section of *Kokinshū* (commissioned *c.* 905). It was written by Emperor Kōkō (830–887) when still a prince to accompany a gift of young greens, which were customarily gathered and eaten at New Year. The text comments that they provided protection from all kinds of malady.

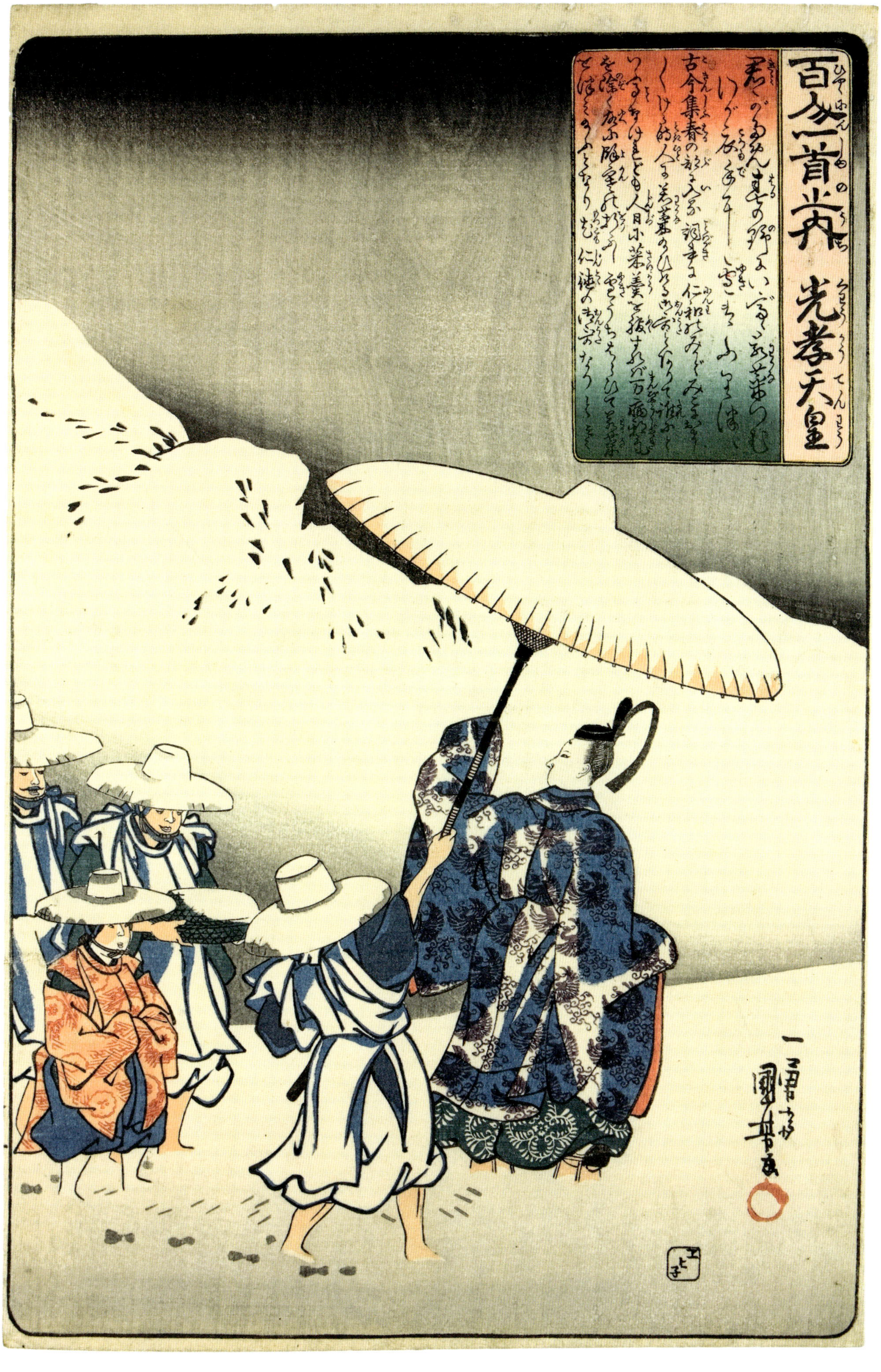
百人一首之内
光孝天皇
一勇斎國芳画

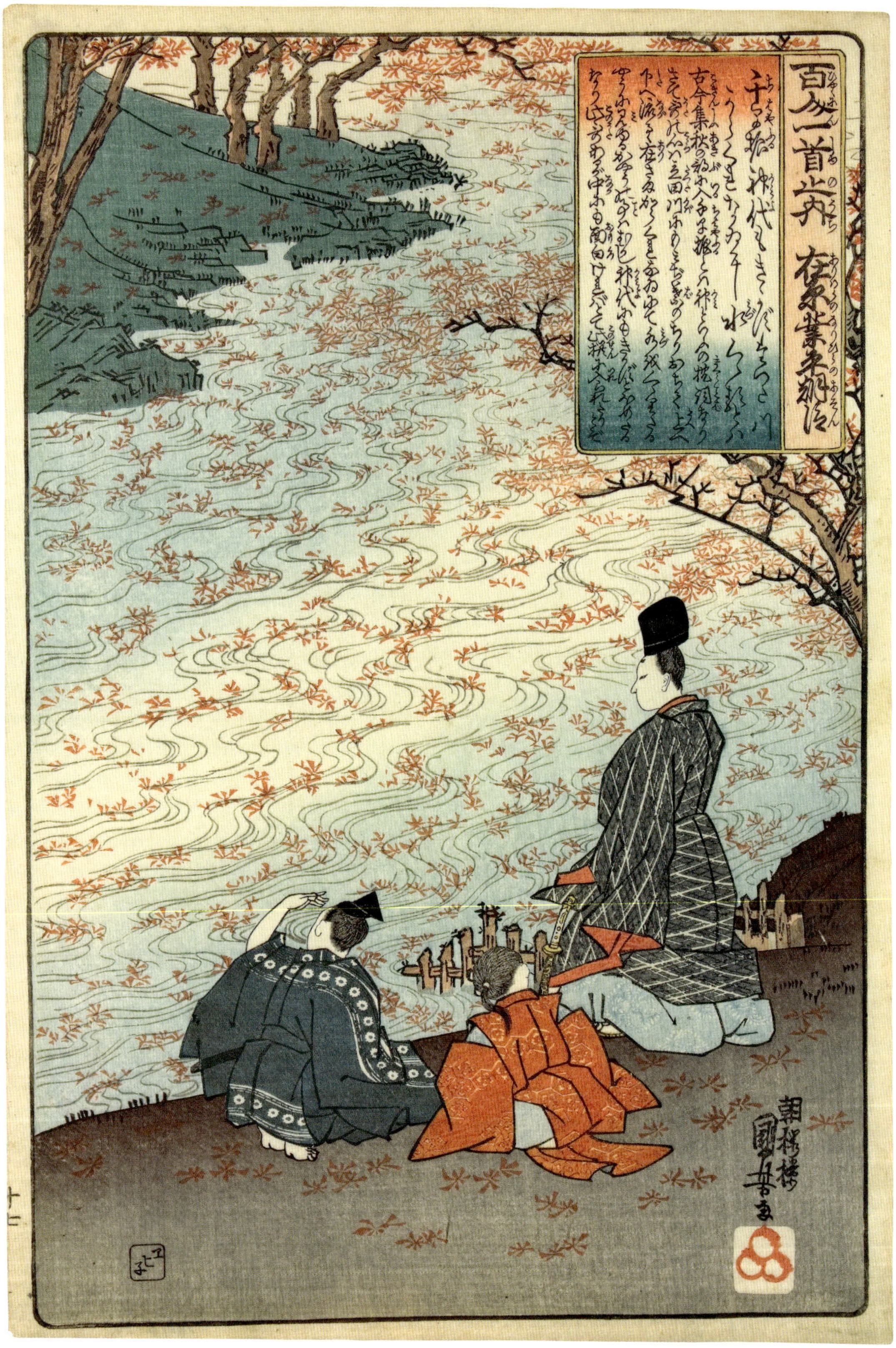

92

Courtier Ariwara no Narihira and his attendants admire autumn leaves on the Tatsuta river

c. 1842

Colour woodblock, *ōban*,
published by Ebisu,
36.8 × 25.3 cm

SERIES TITLE
'One Hundred Poems by One Hundred Poets' (*Hyakunin isshu no uchi*)

PRINT TITLE
'Ariwara no Narihira no Ason' (no. 17)

ARTIST'S SIGNATURE
Chōōrō Kuniyoshi ga

ARTIST'S SEAL
triple *toshidama*

POEM
Chihayaburu / kamiyo mo kikazu / Tatsutagawa / kara-kurenai ni / mizu kuguru to wa

American Friends of the British Museum (The Arthur R. Miller Collection) 10615

REFERENCES
Robinson 1961, frontispiece; Springfield 1980, no. 79; Robinson 1982, no. S19.17; HUT, vol. 3, 1988, no. 50; Yamaguchi 1991, Kuniyoshi no. 48; Suzuki 1992, no. 190; Mostow 1996, pp. 192–4

'Unheard of / even in the legendary age / of the awesome gods: / Tatsuta River in scarlet / and the water flowing under it.'

ARIWARA NO NARIHIRA NO ASON

Kuniyoshi pictures the scene in accordance with the headnote in *Ise monogatari* (*Tales of Ise*, mid-tenth century), which reads: 'A certain man [Narihira], off on an excursion with some imperial princes, once composed this poem on a bank of the Tatsuta river' (McCullough 1968, p. 141). The lyrical image shows Narihira standing at the water's edge, gazing pensively as two companions sit respectfully beside him. Delicate gradation in the area of the river has created a lighter band down the centre, which seems almost to sparkle, combining with the scattered leaves and elegantly eddying river to entrance the eyes – an effect unparalleled even in the age of the gods, the poet remarks.

The verse first appeared in the autumn section of *Kokinshū*. Its author, Ariwara no Narihira (825–880), was thought to be the protagonist of the later *Tales of Ise*, which also contains the poem. The *Tales* established the traditional view of him not only as a skilful poet, but also as a handsome and sensitive lover. He was included among the Six Immortals of Poetry and the Thirty-six Immortals. The headnote in *Kokinshū* states that Narihira was inspired to compose the verse not by a natural scene, but by a screen painting belonging to the Second Ward Empress that depicted autumn leaves floating down the Tatsuta river. The earliest versions of the poem featured an image of blue cloth that had been tie-dyed with scarlet, but later commentators reinterpreted this to mean blue water flowing under a carpet of scarlet leaves (Mostow 1996, p. 192).

93

Palanquin bearers on a road at night

c. 1842

Colour woodblock, *ōban*, published by Ebisu, 36.4 × 25 cm

PRINT TITLE
'Ōe no Chisato' (no. 23)

SERIES TITLE
'One Hundred Poems by One Hundred Poets' (*Hyakunin isshu no uchi*)

ARTIST'S SIGNATURE
Ichiyūsai Kuniyoshi ga

ARTIST'S SEAL
Kuniyoshi

POEM
Tsuki mireba / chiji ni mono koso / kanashikere / waga mi hitotsu no / aki ni wa aranedo

American Friends of the British Museum (The Arthur R. Miller Collection) 10619

REFERENCES
Springfield 1968, no. 57; Riccar 1978, no. 191; Robinson 1982, no. S19.23; HUT, vol. 3, 1988, BW no. 39; Yamaguchi 1991, Kuniyoshi no. 47; Suzuki 1992, no. 188; Nagoya 1996, no. 96; Mostow 1996, pp. 210–12

'When I look at the moon / I am overcome by the sadness / of a thousand, thousand things – / even though it is not autumn / for me alone.'
ŌE NO CHISATO

Two porters are carrying their empty palanquin along a country road at night. A village and woodlands can be seen in the distance and beside the road stands a small statue of the deity Jizō, protector of travellers. If the mountain in the background is Mt Tsukuba, as its shape suggests, the scene could be taking place on the Japan embankment (Nihon-tsuzumi), which led to Yoshiwara pleasure quarter in Edo. The men might then be on their way to collect a patron after a night of revelry. One porter turns his head from the viewer to gaze at the full moon, beautifully printed with a double halo and seemingly emitting a bright, clear light. Kuniyoshi thus illustrates in a striking way the text's claim that everyone in this world is affected by the melancholy of autumn, making a workman representative of humanity as a whole. Two puppies doze: animals are oblivious to such emotions. All this differs markedly from conventional images of the scene, which showed the courtier–poet himself looking at the moon.

The poet Ōe no Chisato (active *c.* 889–923) was a nephew of Ariwara no Narihira (see cat. 92). This verse was included in the autumn section of *Kokinshū*.

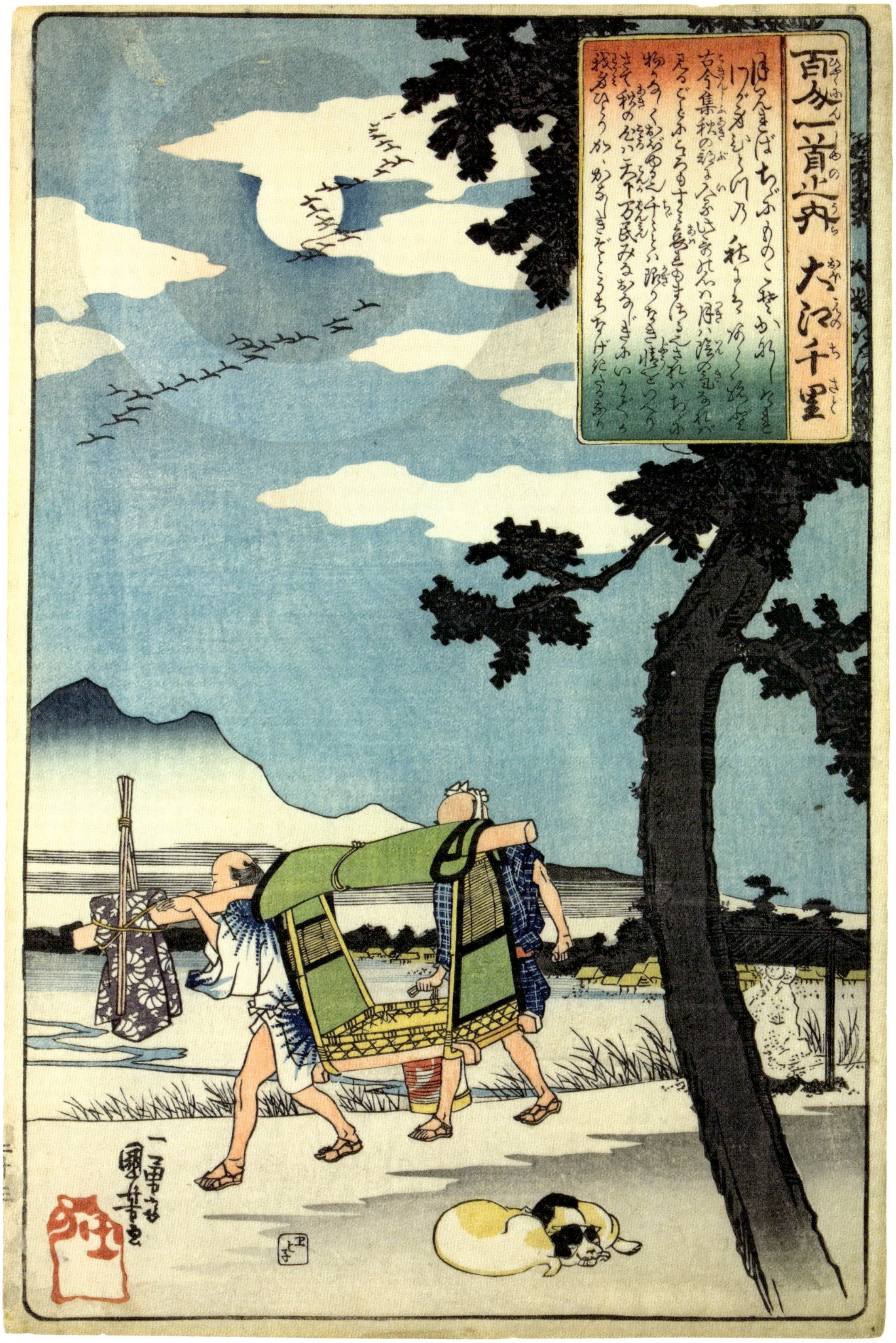

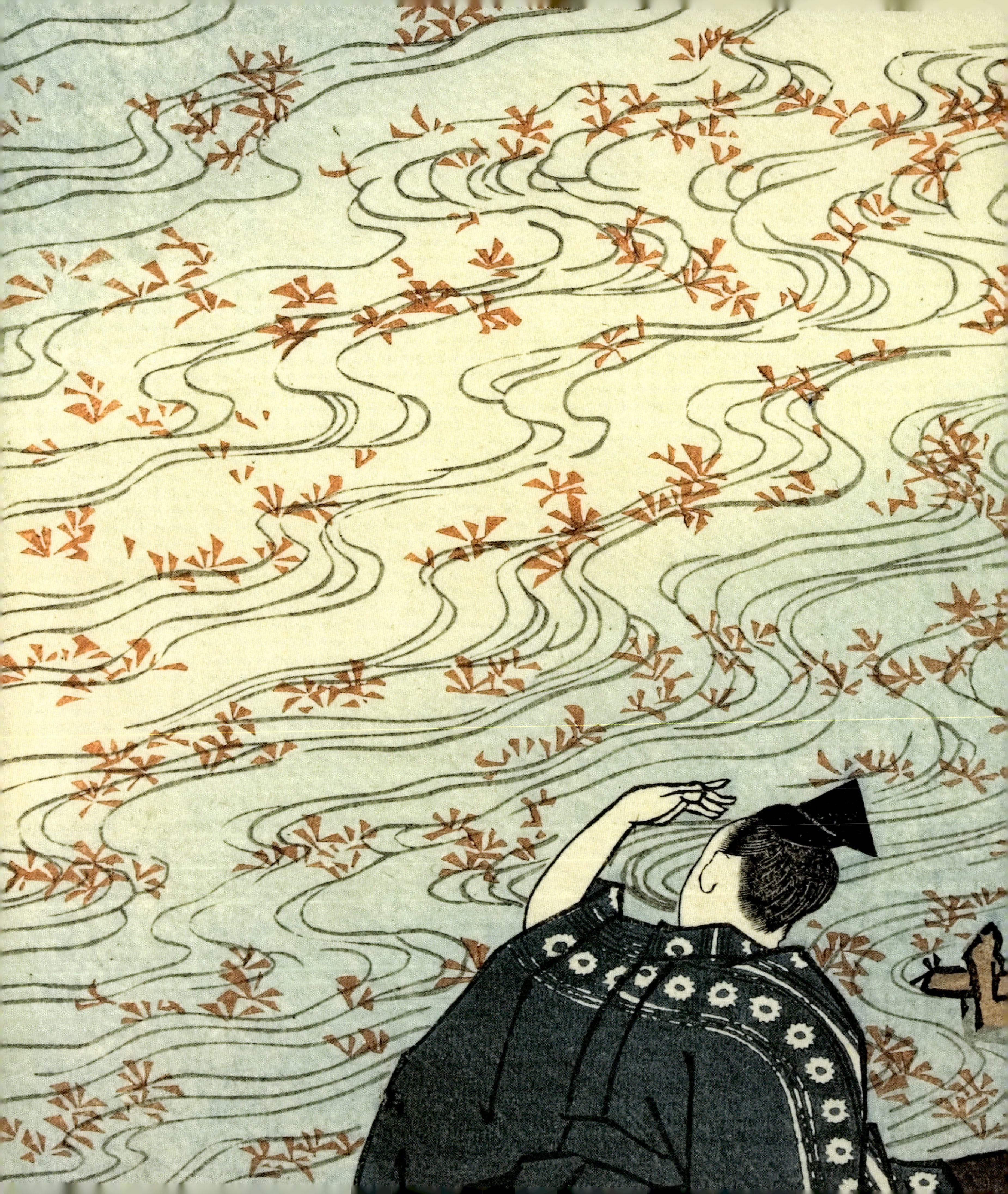

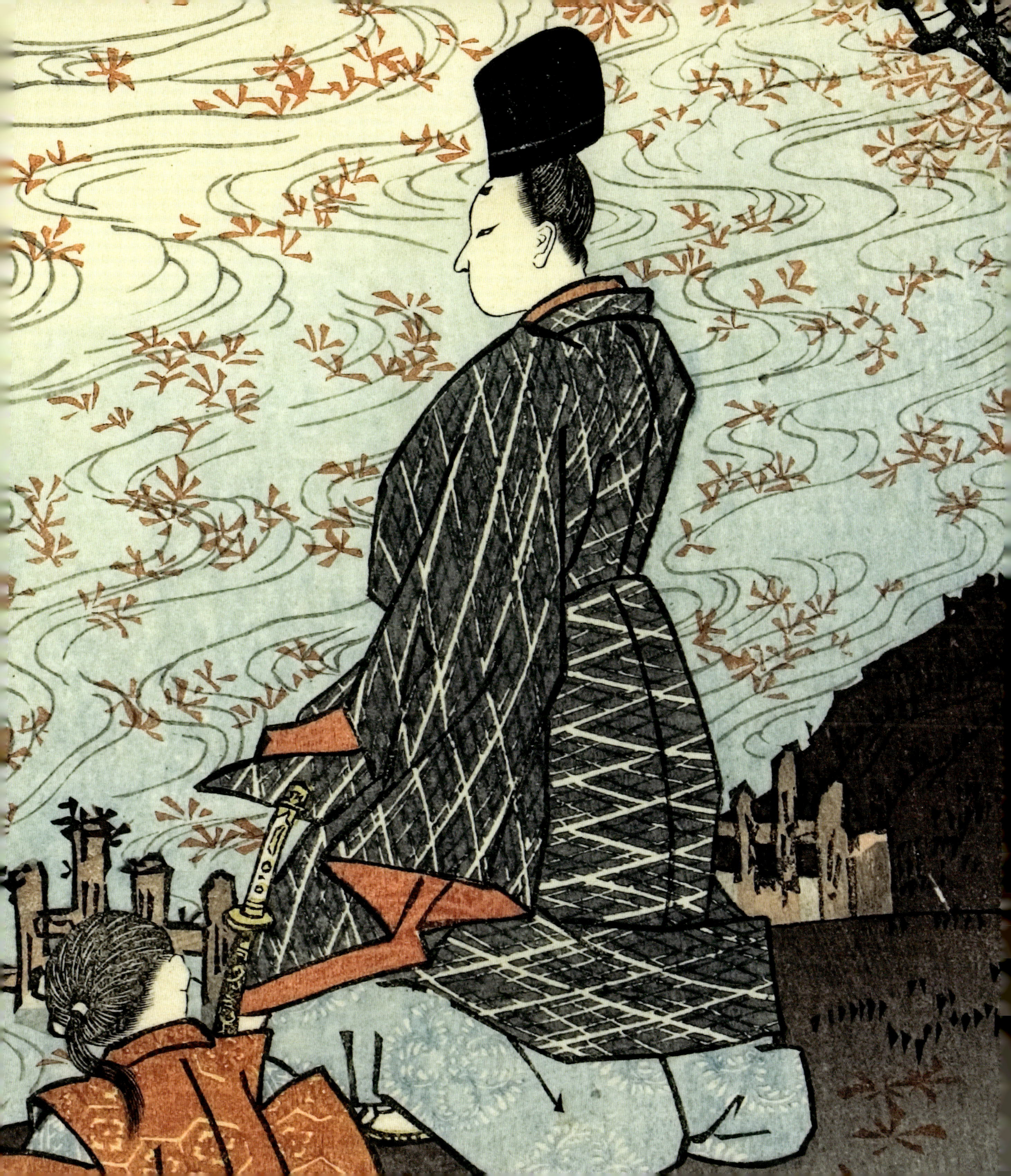

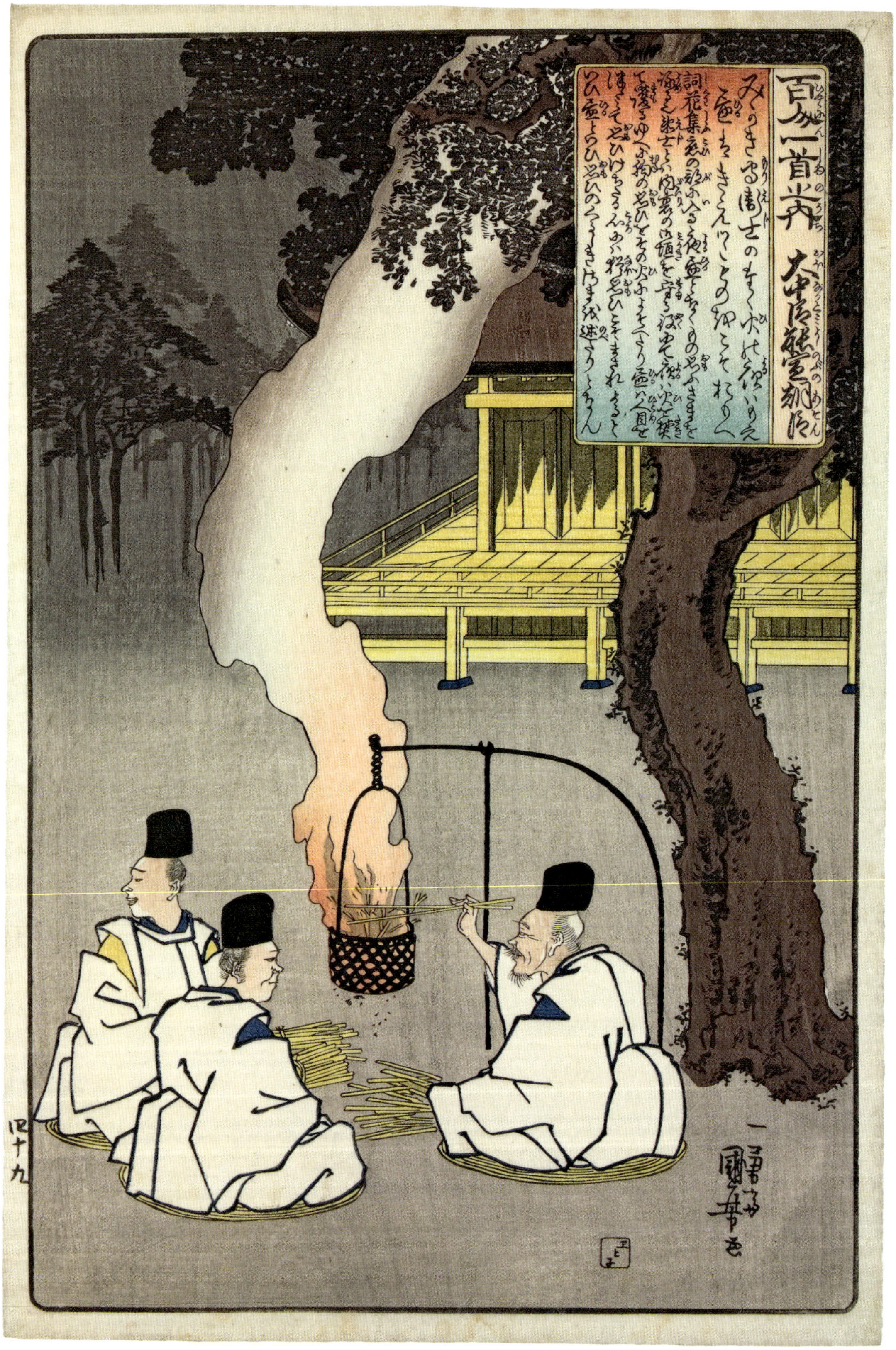

94

Three palace guards around a fire at night

c. 1842

Colour woodblock, *ōban*, published by Ebisu, 37.2 × 25.5 cm

SERIES TITLE
'One Hundred Poems by One Hundred Poets' (*Hyakunin isshu no uchi*)

PRINT TITLE
'Ōnakatomi no Yoshinobu no Ason' (no.49)

ARTIST'S SIGNATURE
Ichiyūsai Kuniyoshi ga

POEM
Mi-kakimori / eji no taku hi no / yoru wa moe / hiru wa kietsutsu / mono o koso omoe

American Friends of the British Museum (The Arthur R. Miller Collection) 10629

REFERENCES
Illing 1980, no. 11; Robinson 1982, no. S19.49; Mostow 1996, pp. 287–9

'Like the fire the guardsman kindles / guarding the imperial gates: / at night burning, / in the day exhausted, / over and over, so I long for her.'

ŌNAKATOMI NO YOSHINOBU NO ASON

Three palace guards are seated around their watch fire at night, one tending with tongs to the fire in a hanging brazier. The rising smoke has delicate bands of wiped colour and the fire illuminates a section of the branches above their heads. Nocturnal gloom engulfs the trees in the distance. As in cat. 93, Kuniyoshi focuses on ordinary people, the low-ranking guards who are chatting convivially, and does not include the courtier-poet shown in more conventional illustrations of the scene.

The text states that the poem by Ōnakatomi no Yoshinobu (921–991) comes from the love section of the anthology *Shikashū* (commissioned in 1144) and interprets the verse to mean that the fire of palace guards at night is like the burning desire of love. In the daytime people should try to hide their feelings from the eyes of others; yet the pangs of love continue to grow and cause pain.

Later printings left out the wiped pale colours in the smoke, changed the colour of the ground to pink and omitted the mid-grey block used to print some of the distant trees (Illing 1980, no. 11).

95

The spirit of Retired Emperor Sutoku and a stormy sea

c. 1842

Colour woodblock, *ōban*, published by Ebisu, 37.1 × 25.5 cm

PRINT TITLE
'Shutoku-in' (no. 77)

SERIES TITLE
'One Hundred Poems by One Hundred Poets' (*Hyakunin isshu no uchi*)

ARTIST'S SIGNATURE
Ichiyūsai Kuniyoshi ga

ARTIST'S SEAL
Yo, with *toshidama*

POEM
Se o hayami / iwa ni sekaruru / takigawa no / warete mo sue ni / awan to zo omou

American Friends of the British Museum (The Arthur R. Miller Collection) 10639

REFERENCES
Robinson 1961, no. 31; Riccar 1978, no. 196; Springfield 1980, no. 82; Robinson 1982, no. S19.77; HUT, vol. 3, 1988, no. 52; Nagoya 1996, no. 97; Mostow 1996, pp. 369–71; Amsterdam 1998, no. 29; Smithsonian 2002, no. 123

'Because the current is swift, / even though the rapids, / blocked by a boulder, / are divided, like them, in the end, / we will surely meet, I know.'

SHUTOKU-IN

After the defeat of his faction in the Hōgen civil war of 1156, Retired Emperor Sutoku (1119–1164; 'Shutoku' on the print) was exiled to Shikoku island in Sanuki province, where he later died. Kuniyoshi chooses not to illustrate the poem, but to depict a dramatic episode from Sutoku's life. From exile the emperor sent sets of sutras to Kyoto as offerings in memory of his deceased father, Retired Emperor Toba. When they were refused and returned to him, Sutoku cast them into the sea in a rage. He then ravaged the realm in the form of a *tengu*, a winged creature, half man, half bird. Versions of this tale appeared in the novels *Ugetsu monogatari* (*Tales of Moonlight and Rain*), by Ueda Akinari, and *Chinsetsu yumihari-zuki* (*Strange Tales of the Bow Moon*), by Takizawa Bakin (Nagoya 1996, p. 242). Kuniyoshi's image shows Sutoku as a ghostly apparition with wild, flowing hair, the sleeves of his pale court robes flapping like the wings of a *tengu* as he bellows across a stormy sea while lightning plays around the rocky promontory.

The poem, by contrast, evokes unwavering affection in the face of rejection and comes from the love section of the *Shikashū* anthology, commissioned by Sutoku-in himself in 1144. According to the commentary, the verse's meaning is truly profound in its use of the metaphor of a fast-flowing river whose waters are temporarily divided by a rock, but inevitably flow together again further downstream.

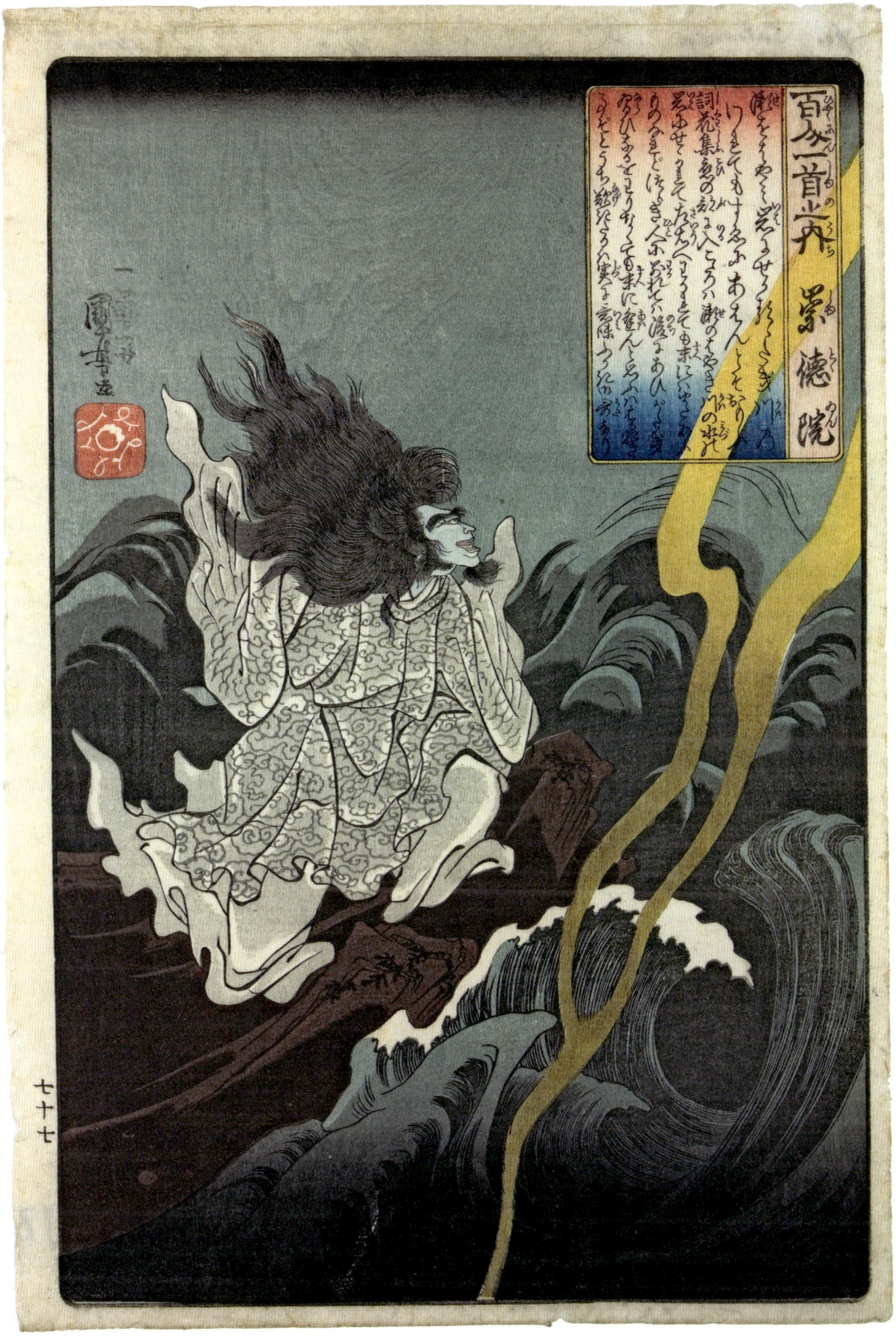

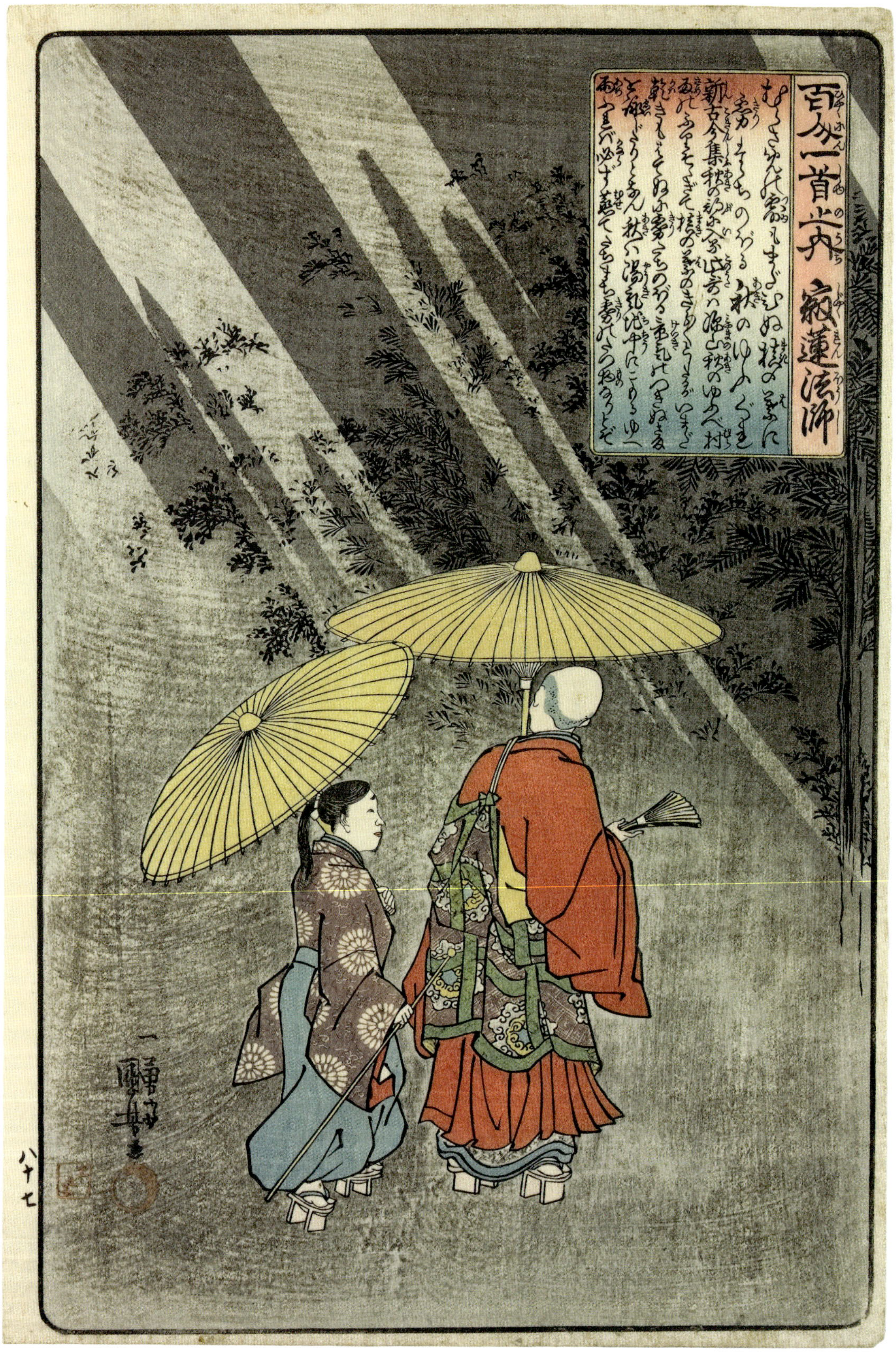

96

Monk Jakuren and his attendant in evening rain

c. 1842

Colour woodblock, *ōban*, published by Ebisu, 36.9 × 25.3 cm

PRINT TITLE
'Jakuren-hōshi' (no. 87)

SERIES TITLE
'One Hundred Poems by One Hundred Poets' (*Hyakunin isshu no uchi*)

ARTIST'S SIGNATURE
Ichiyūsai Kuniyoshi ga

ARTIST'S SEAL
toshidama

POEM
Murasame no / tsuyu mo mada hinu / maki no ha ni / kiri tachinoboru / aki no yūgure

American Friends of the British Museum (The Arthur R. Miller Collection) 10644

REFERENCES
Robinson 1982, no. S19.87; Mostow 1996, pp. 398–9; Amsterdam 1998, no. 30

'While the raindrops of / the passing shower have not yet dried from / near the leaves of the evergreens / the mist is already rising, on / this autumn evening.'

JAKUREN-HŌSHI

Dressed in richly coloured ecclesiastical garb, Monk Jakuren turns from the viewer to gaze into the gloom of an autumn shower falling on a grove of Chinese black pines (*maki*). The angle of his head and the way he holds the fan suggest rapt appreciation of the gentle natural beauty of the scene. A pageboy walks behind, carrying a stick. The grey pigments used in the background were mixed with lead white, which has tarnished to produce a pleasing mottled patina.

Jakuren-hōshi was the priestly name of the courtier born Fujiwara no Sadanaga (d. 1202), a nephew of the great poet Shunzei. The verse comes from the autumn section of the *Shin-Kokinshū* anthology, commissioned in 1201 by Emperor Go-Toba, with Jakuren as one of its editors. The text comments that, since the earth retains residual heat from the sun in autumn, any rain will quickly turn to vapour and rise as mist.

97

Women carrying buckets of brine for salt

c. 1842

Colour woodblock, *ōban*,
published by Ebisu,
36.3 × 24.7 cm

PRINT TITLE
'Inpumon'in no Ōsuke' (no. 90)

SERIES TITLE
'One Hundred Poems
by One Hundred Poets'
(*Hyakunin isshu no uchi*)

ARTIST'S SIGNATURE
Chōōrō Kuniyoshi ga

POEM
Misebaya na / ojima no ama no / sode dani mo / nure ni zo nureshi / iro wa kawarazu

American Friends of the British Museum (The Arthur R. Miller Collection) 10645

REFERENCES
Riccar 1978, no. 193; Robinson 1982, no. S19.90; Mostow 1996, pp. 406–8

'How I'd like to show him! / The sleeves of the fishermen / of Male Island, / when it comes to wet, are wet indeed, / but their colour doesn't change!'
INPUMON'IN NO ŌSUKE

Two women are shown at the seashore collecting brine in yoked buckets to make salt. The robe of the woman closest to the viewer bears a bold pattern of seashells. Mt Fuji appears in the distance.

The verse is by the twelfth-century female poet Inpumon'in no Ōsuke, who served Princess Ryōshi, daughter of Emperor Go-Shirakawa. It was included in the love section of the *Senzaishū* anthology, commissioned in 1183. The poem responded to a verse of some two hundred years earlier by the male poet Shigeyuki, who had likened his sleeves moistened by tears of love to the sleeves of fishermen soaked by the sea on the beach at Matsushima. The text on the print explains that Inpumon'in no Ōsuke's angry riposte proposes that men's tears do not stain because, unlike hers, they are not heartfelt, crimson tears – that is, tears of blood.

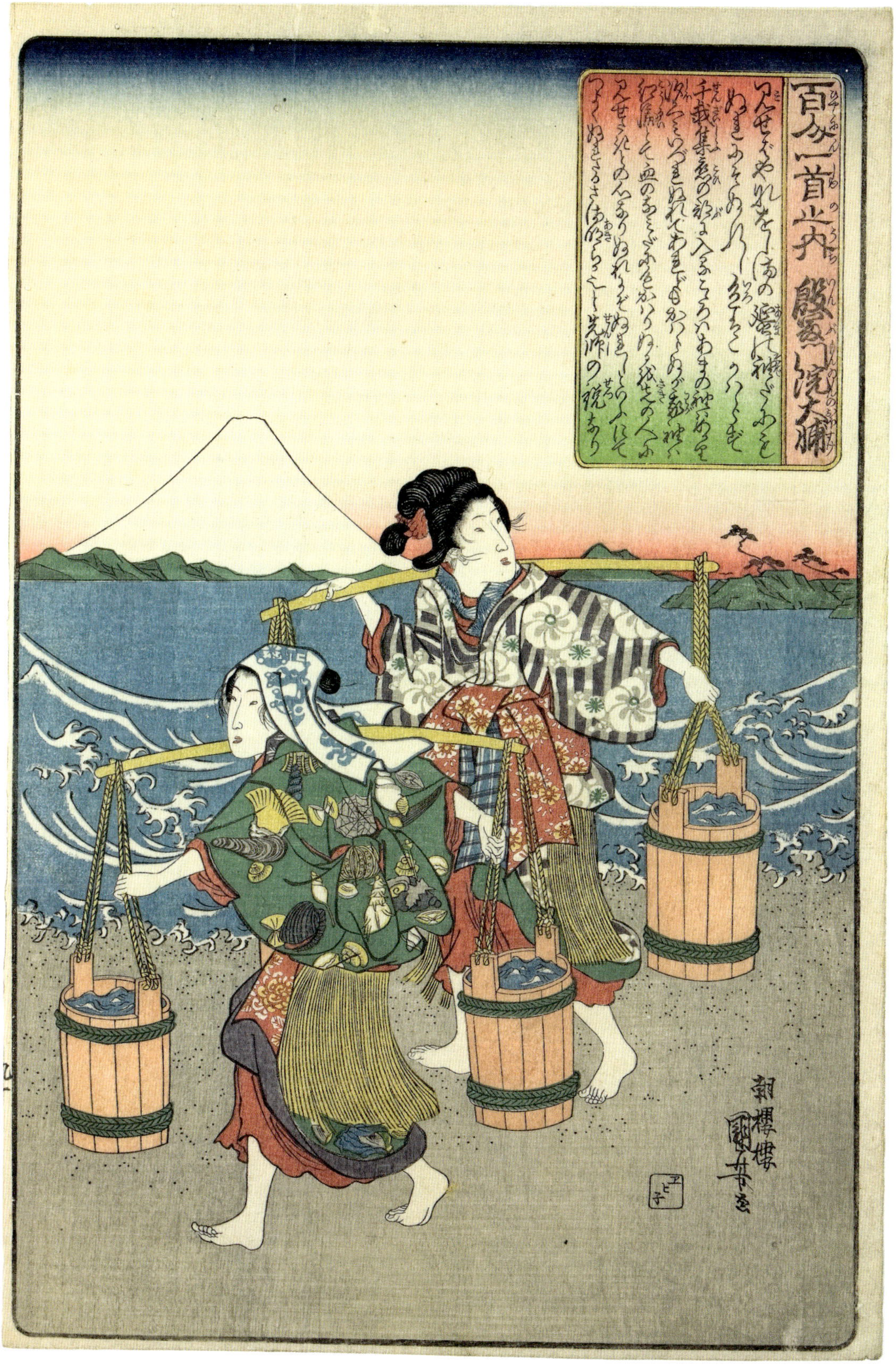

TWENTY-FOUR PARAGONS OF FILIAL PIETY FOR CHILDREN

(Cats 98–101; fig. 3)

The 'Twenty-four paragons of filial piety' (*Nijūshi-kō*) consisted of Chinese stories about children who behaved towards their parents in an exemplary, self-sacrificing manner. Considered the supreme Confucian virtue in China, filial piety (*kō*) ranked second in the samurai-dominated society of Edo-period Japan after feudal loyalty (*chū*). The Chinese tales were attributed to the Yuan-period author Guo Jujing (Yizi, 1260–1368). In Japan they first became a common subject in paintings and illustrated manuscripts of the Muromachi period (1336–1573), before featuring in printed illustrated books and woodblock prints in the Edo period. Several ukiyo-e artists had produced versions before Kuniyoshi, but the stories took on a new resonance in the moralising ethos promoted by the authorities during the Tenpō reforms of the 1840s.

Despite the Chinese origin of the tales, Kuniyoshi's style in this series is at its most European. (In his prints of the *Water Margin* tale [cats 3–10] he had already used European stylistic features when depicting a Chinese subject.) Recent research by Japanese scholars has revealed some of the artist's sources. He clearly copied some figures and other motifs directly from illustrations in European books, notably *Gedenkwaerdige Zee- en Lant-Reize door de voornaemste Landschappen van West en Oost Indien* of 1682, by Jan (Johannes) Nieuhof (1618–1672) (Katsumori 2000; Katsuhara 2006; see also pp. 23–4, figs 6–8). In other cases he borrowed motifs from prints by Japanese artists working in a European-influenced style, such as Aōdō Denzen (1748–1822). In yet other instances he took his cue from illustrations in Japanese books that were themselves adaptations of European sources, for example reusing figures from *Kōmō zatsuwa* (*Dutch Miscellany*, 1787), edited by Morishima Chūryō (1756–1810), that had been modelled on ones in *Het Groot Schilderboek* (*Great Book of Painting*, 1707) by the Dutch artist Gerard de Lairesse (1640/41–1711) (Oka 1992, pp. 155–61; Suzuki 1992, p. 208). Further research promises to disclose more borrowings of this kind.

Each of the fifteen published designs known from the series includes a rectangular cartouche containing a synopsis of the child's exemplary behaviour. Robinson lists and describes fourteen of the prints (Robinson 1982, series S13). Small black and white illustrations of all fifteen designs have been reproduced elsewhere (MSU 1991, pp. 151–2). A publisher's advertisement for the series appears in an illustrated novel issued in 1844, so the fourteen designs that do not bear censorship seals are thought to have been published *c.* 1843 (Nagoya 1996, p. 244). The moralising theme was of precisely the kind being encouraged by the authorities in the Tenpō reforms.

The fifteenth design, the story of Yan Zi (Jap. En Shi), has a censorship/date seal of 1853. In addition, two block-ready drawings for unpublished designs in the set have survived, both showing a censorship/date seal of 1857 (Suzuki 1992, p. 208, figs 25, 26). It would seem, then, that the series was set aside after fourteen designs, taken up again after a gap of some ten years and then abandoned for good.

A preparatory drawing and a block-ready drawing for a Lady Tang (Jap. Tō Fujin) print are known, the latter bearing Kuniyoshi's signature in the style of the later 1850s (both formerly Scheiwe Collection; Essen 1972, nos 538, 540). The style and position of the cartouches in the two drawings suggest that the design formed part of the present set. On the other hand, the group of prints published *c.* 1843 had included Lady Tang and it seems odd that Kuniyoshi should have designed another.

98

Wang Bao visits the tomb of his mother during a thunderstorm

c. 1843

Colour woodblock, *ōban*, published by Wakasaya Yoichi, 23.9 × 37 cm

PRINT TITLE
'Ō Hō [Wang Bao]'

SERIES TITLE
'Twenty-four Paragons of Filial Piety for Children' (*Nijūshi-kō dōji kagami*)

ARTIST'S SIGNATURE
Ichiyūsai Kuniyoshi ga

American Friends of the British Museum (The Arthur R. Miller Collection) 16912

REFERENCES
Robinson 1982, no. S13.14

The text tells how Wang Bao's mother was frightened of thunder. After her death, Wang Bao would hurry to her grave whenever there was thunder and lightning, walking around it and telling her not to be afraid. In particularly severe storms he would put his arms round the grave-marker and shed tears. 'There are few examples of such deep filial piety in this world.'

Three figures in Chinese attire scatter in alarm at the thunder and lightning playing around a roofed red structure next to a large tree. The tree marks the grave. In the pitch-black clouds behind it can be seen the ring of drums beaten by the god of thunder to produce peals of thunder.

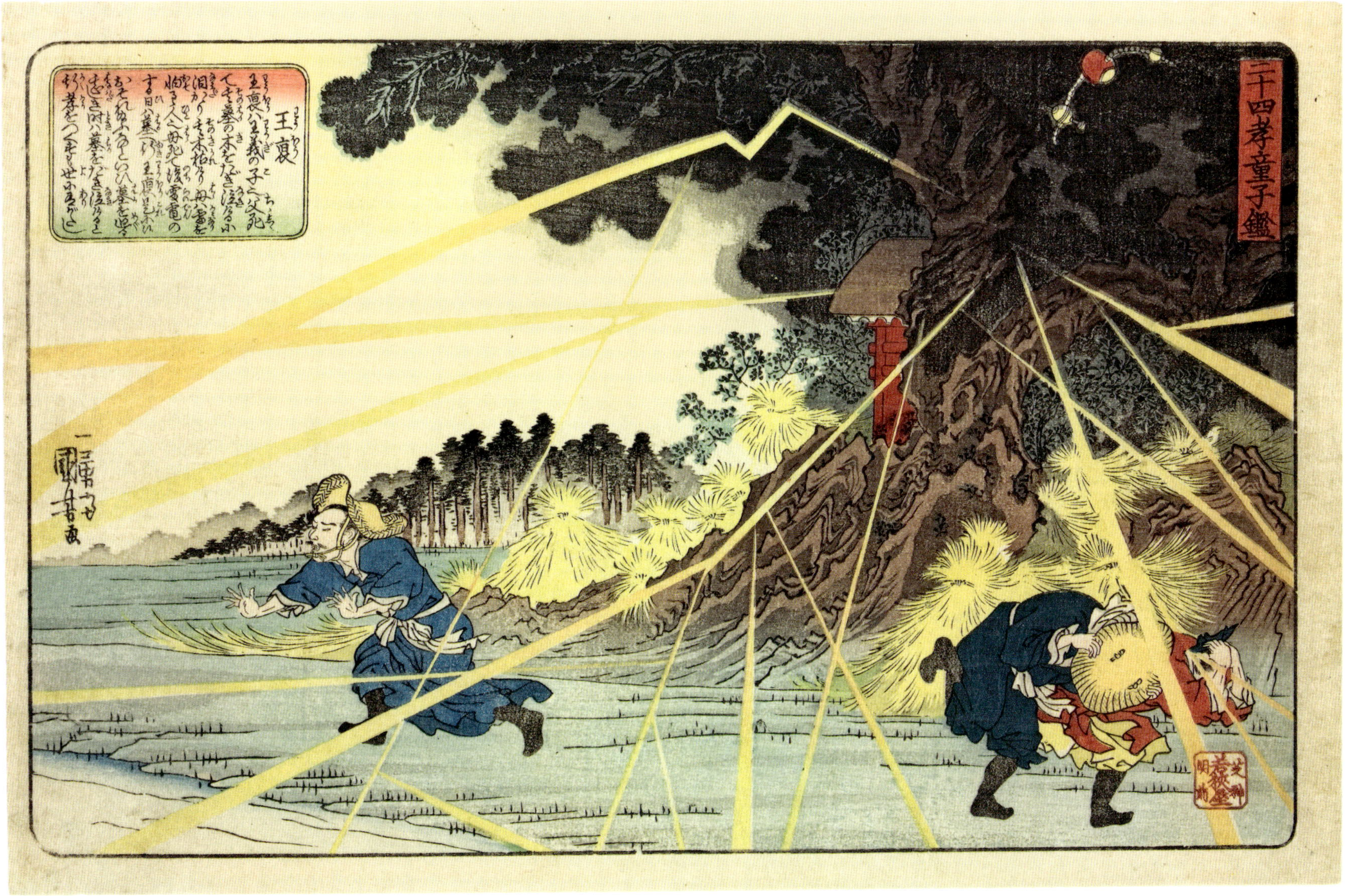

99

Dong Yong bids farewell to the heavenly weaver

c. 1843

Colour woodblock, *ōban*, published by Wakasaya Yoichi, 24.1 × 36.3 cm

SERIES TITLE
'Twenty-four Paragons of Filial Piety for Children' (*Nijūshi-kō dōji kagami*)

PRINT TITLE
'Tō Ei [Dong Yong]'

ARTIST'S SIGNATURE
Ichiyūsai Kuniyoshi ga

American Friends of the British Museum (The Arthur R. Miller Collection) 16908

REFERENCES
Springfield 1980, no. 138; Robinson 1982, no. S13.10; HUT, vol. 3, 1988, BW no. 38; MSU 1991, no. 67; Suzuki 1992, no. 197; Nagoya 1996, no. 109; Isao 2008, p. 31

The text on the print tells how Dong Yong was so poor that he had to sell himself into service in order to pay for his father's funeral. On the road back to his master's house after the funeral, Dong encountered a beautiful woman. She accompanied him home and stayed for one month, weaving two hundred bolts of silk cloth, with which Dong repaid his debt. Then she revealed herself to be an angel (*tennyo*) and flew back into the sky. The text comments: 'This is how the angel assisted Dong Yong's filial feelings.'

The gateway in Kuniyoshi's print looks Chinese, as do the hairstyles and robes of some of the figures. By contrast, the angel and the ship at sail are distinctly European in appearance. Indeed, the composition as a whole reflects European influence. The figure facing the viewer in a blue robe was actually adapted from a depiction of an unclothed native Brazilian woman in Nieuhof's *Gedenkwaerdige Zee- en Lant-Reize* (p. 24, fig. 8). Oka Yasumasa has argued that Kuniyoshi based the angel on the frontispiece in De Lairesse's *Groot Schilderboek* and that the objects she is holding are palm leaves (Oka 1992, pp. 155–7). The poses of the two figures, however, differ considerably. It seems likely that European sources also existed for the other figures.

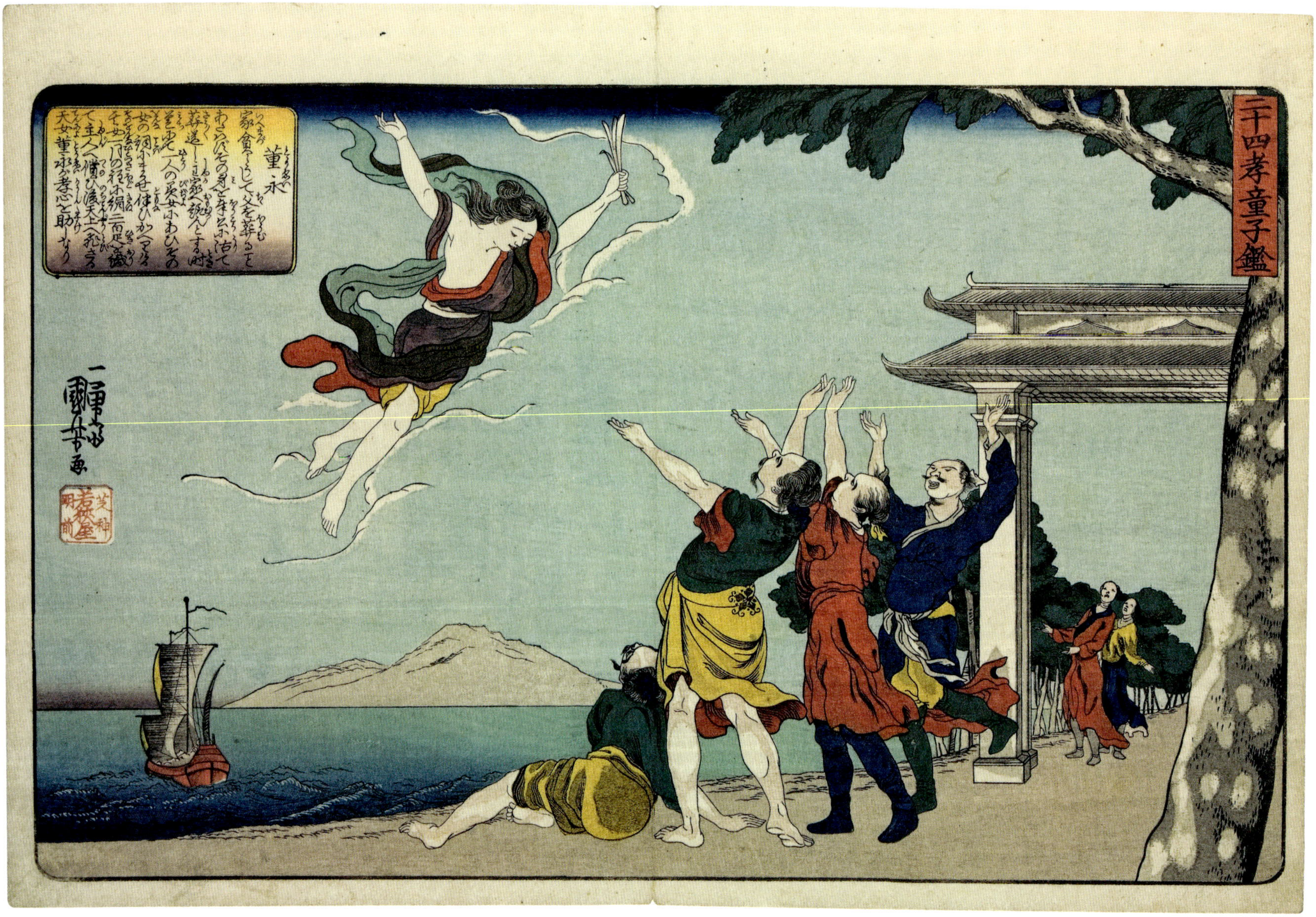

100

Preparatory drawing for the print 'Dong Yong'

c. 1843

Ink on paper,
23.7 × 31.6 cm

COLLECTOR'S SEAL
Theodor Scheiwe

The British Museum, JA 1992.4-8.01

REFERENCES
Essen 1972, no. 537

This first-stage preparatory drawing for the design of Dong Yong shows Kuniyoshi working out his ideas. At this early point in the creative process he clearly planned the angel in the sky quite differently, only later developing the much more active pose seen in the finished design. The two versions may reflect separate European sources. The sketch has just one foreground figure, presumably Dong Yong, instead of the four in the print. The drawing shows Kuniyoshi altering the angle of Dong's left leg, raising it to make it more dynamic and thereby changing the pose of Nieuhof's Brazilian woman on which he had based the figure (p. 24, fig. 8). To make this correction he drew on a piece of thin paper pasted over the area around the leg. For the block-ready drawing, a neat tracing would have been made from this sketch and possibly from others as well. In the working drawing no mountains appear on the low, distant horizon.

The verso of the thin sheet of paper bears an unrelated sketch of a figure on horseback. This shows through clearly on the recto, where the motif appears upside down in the sky.

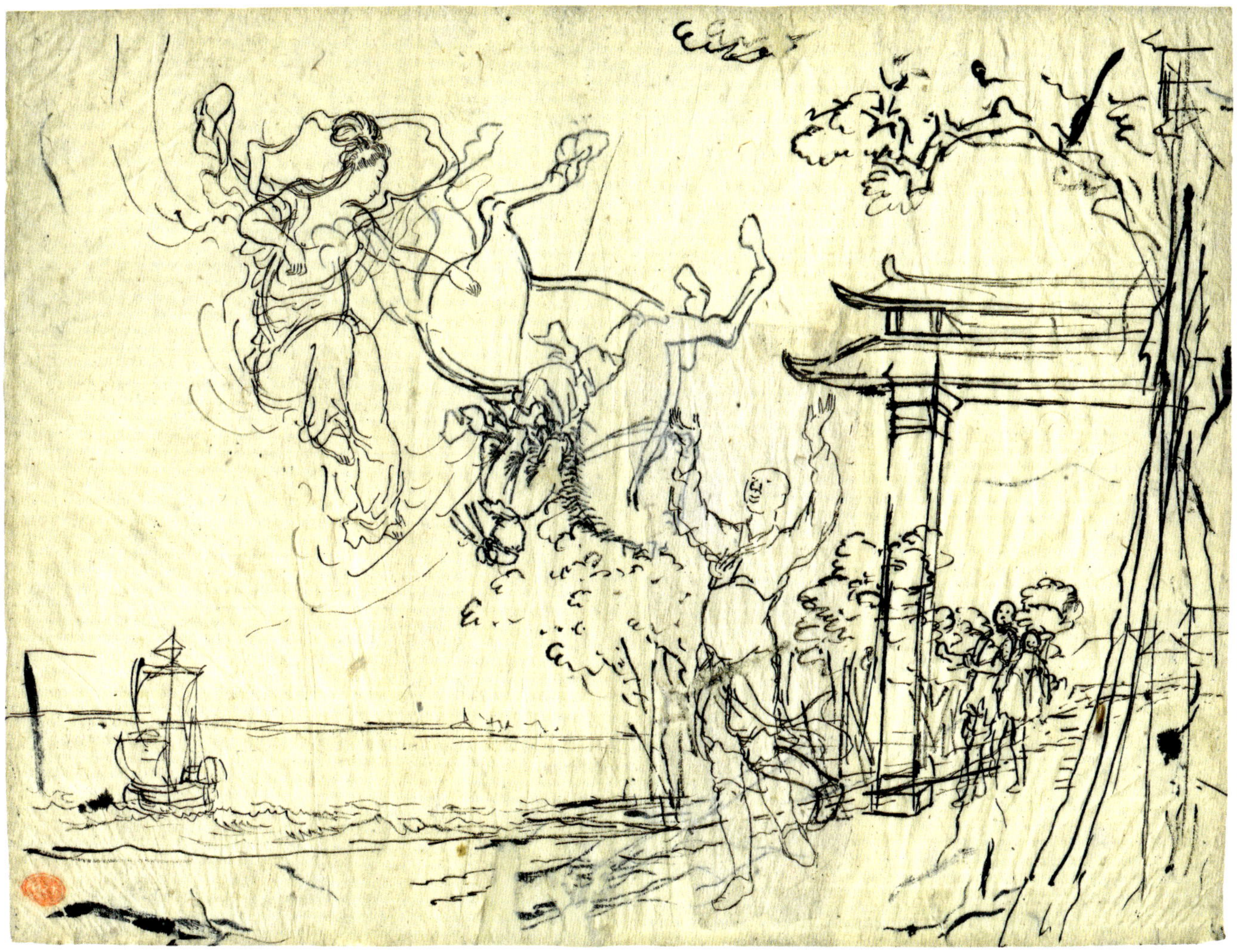

101

Yang Xiang rescues his father from a tiger

c. 1843

Colour woodblock, *ōban*, published by Wakasaya Yoichi, 26 × 37.4 cm

SERIES TITLE
'Twenty-four Paragons of Filial Piety for Children' (*Nijūshi-kō dōji kagami*)

PRINT TITLE
'Yō Kō [Yang Xiang]'

ARTIST'S SIGNATURE
Ichiyūsai Kuniyoshi ga (in oval cartouche)

American Friends of the British Museum (The Arthur R. Miller Collection) 16907

REFERENCES
Riccar 1978, no. 204; Springfield 1980, no. 140; Robinson 1982, no. S13.9; HUT, vol. 12, 1988, BW no. 134; Amsterdam 1998, no. 218

The commentary relates how Yang Xiang and his father were in the mountains when a tiger appeared and threatened to eat the older of the two. Unperturbed, Yang faced the beast and yelled at it, offering himself as prey in place of his father. The tiger dropped its tail and fled. Father and son had been saved 'thanks to [exemplary] filial behaviour'.

Kuniyoshi adds drama to the scene by including a rushing mountain torrent and gusts of driving rain. The red autumn foliage of the creeper winding around the pine provides a contrasting touch of lyricism.

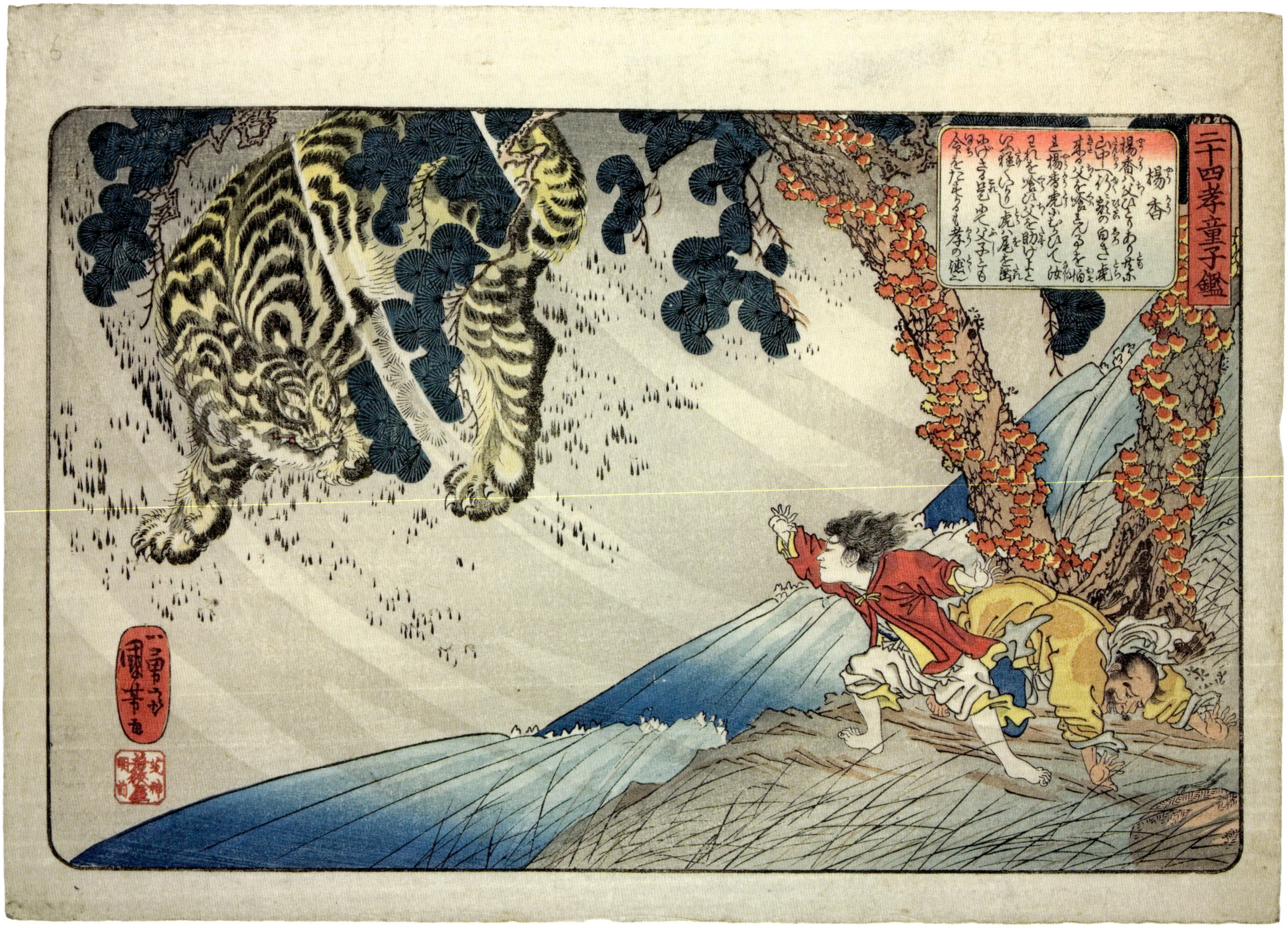

102

Lady Kayō shoots an arrow into the eye of Princess Sai

1849–50

Colour woodblock, *ōban*, no publisher's mark (originally published by Iseya Chūsuke), 37.2 × 25.3 cm

PRINT TITLE
'India: Lady Kayō shoots an arrow into the eye of Princess Sai to console King Hanzoku' (*Tenjiku, Kayō fujin Sai-ki ga manako o ite Hanzoku-ō o nagusamu*)

SERIES TITLE
'Pictures of the Spirit Fox in Three Lands' (*Sangoku yōko zue*)

ARTIST'S SIGNATURE
Ichiyūsai Kuniyoshi ga (in gourd-shaped *Yoshi* cartouche)

ARTIST'S SEAL
Yoshikiri

CENSORS' SEALS
Fuku and Muramatsu

American Friends of the British Museum (The Arthur R. Miller Collection) 07003

REFERENCES
Robinson 1982, no. S66.3; Suzuki 1992, no. 159; Mainichi Shinbunsha 1995, no. 184; Nagoya 1996, no. 77; Amsterdam 1998, no. 84

The cruel scene takes place in the garden of the palace of King Hanzoku in India. Princess Sai had criticised the king for neglecting affairs of state as a result of his infatuation with Lady Kayō. In revenge Lady Kayō brought about the princess's downfall by making false accusations against her. Tied to a tree in the presence of the king, Princess Sai is tortured to death by Lady Kayō, who shoots arrows into her eyes, ears and mouth. The costumes in Kuniyoshi's print appear more European than Indian, and it would seem that the European style was the artist's default choice when depicting 'foreign' scenes, be they European, Chinese or Indian.

The print is one of six known from the series 'Pictures of the Spirit Fox in Three Lands' (*Sangoku yōko zue*), which revolves around an evil, nine-tailed white fox that adopts the guise of beautiful women in three lands: Lady Kayō in India (three designs), Princess Da Ji in China (one) and Lady Tamamo-no-mae in Japan (two). In part the prints were adapted from the illustrated novel *Ehon Tamamo monogatari* (*Picture Book: Tales of Lady Tamamo*) of 1805, written and illustrated by the Osaka artist Okada Gyokuzan (1737–1812). The composition of the present print, for example, derives substantially from the corresponding image in the novel, but places greater emphasis on exotic, foreign stylistic elements (Nagoya 1996, p. 239).

Two publishers, Iseya Chūsuke and Echizenya Hachiemon, collaborated on issuing the series. Although the colours in this impression are bright and have not faded, the absence of the mark of the original publisher, Iseya, probably indicates that it comes from a slightly later printing.

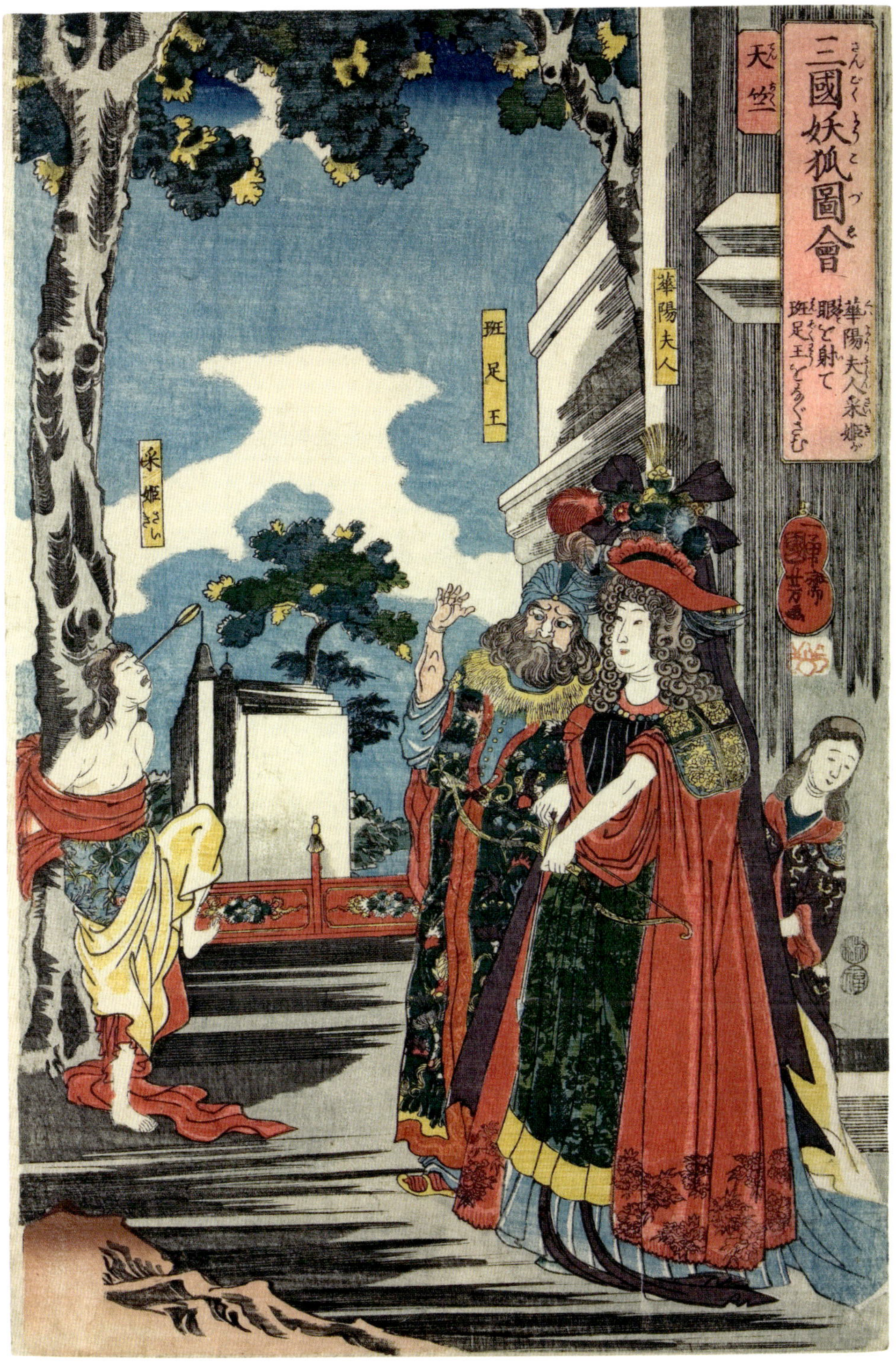

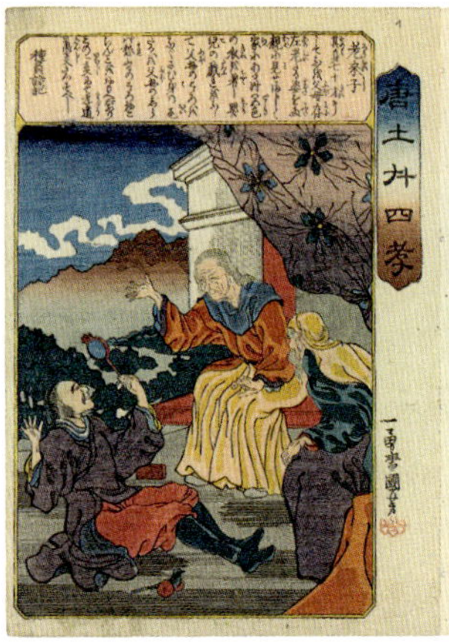

103.7

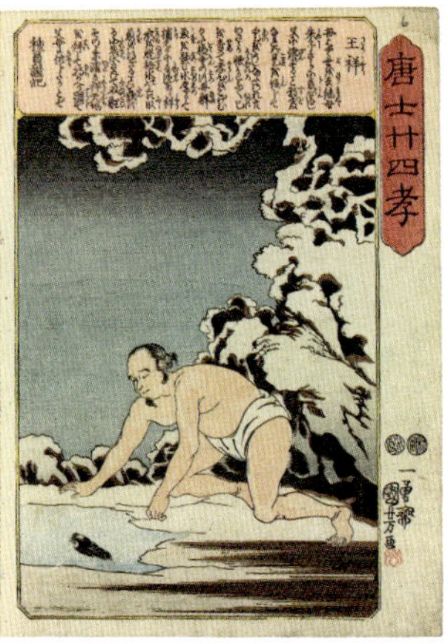

103.6

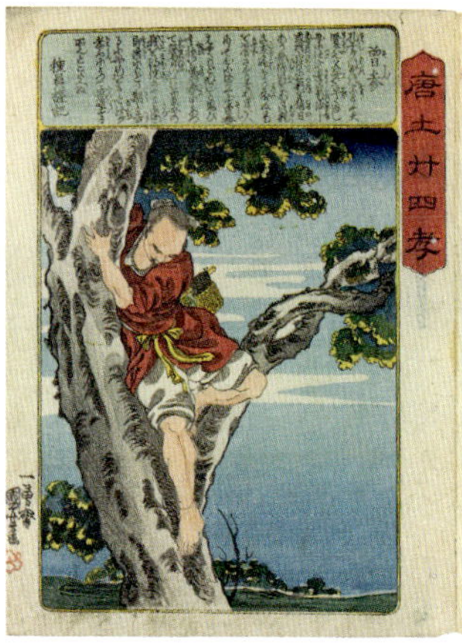

103.5

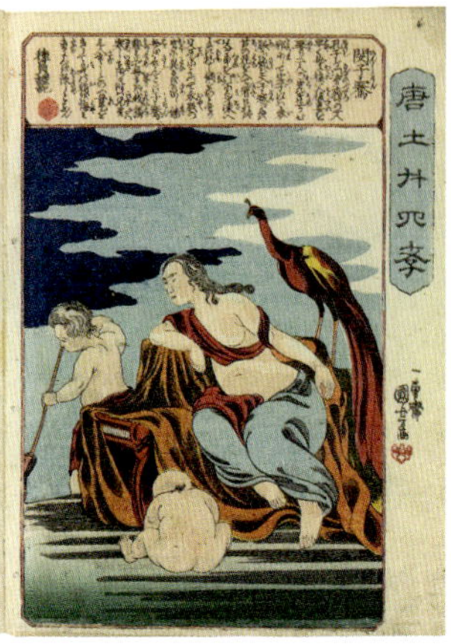

103.4

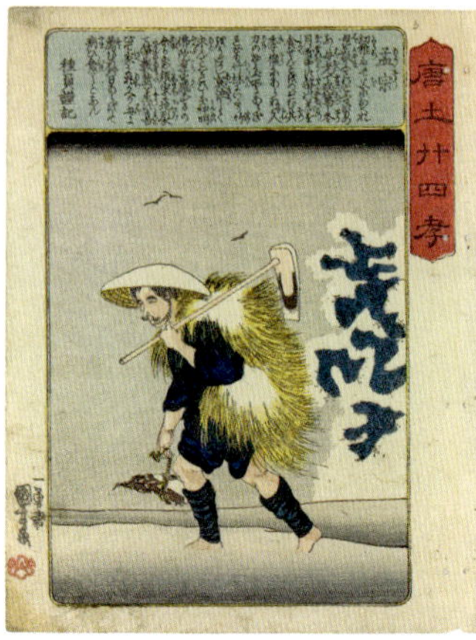

103.3

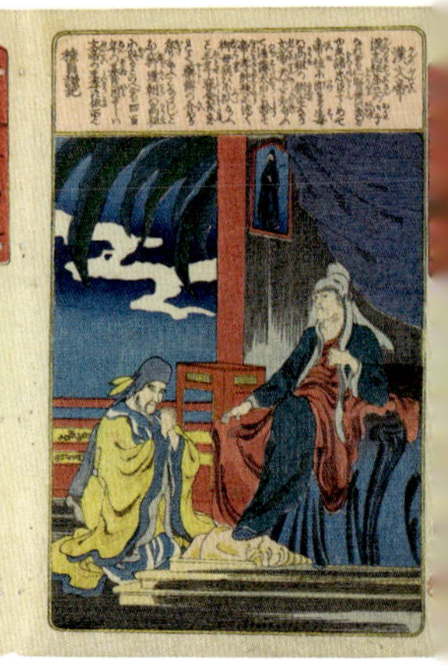

1

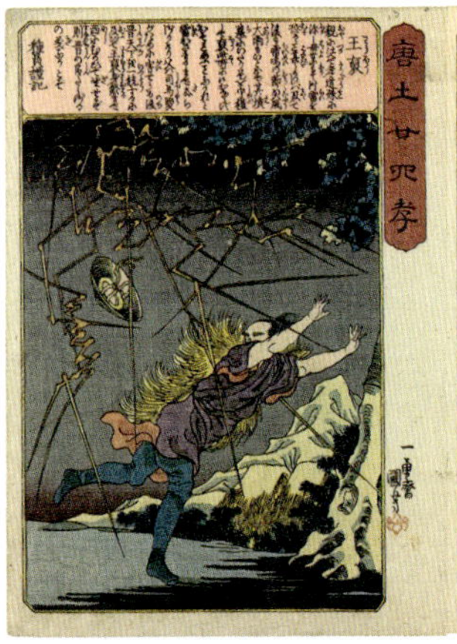

103.13

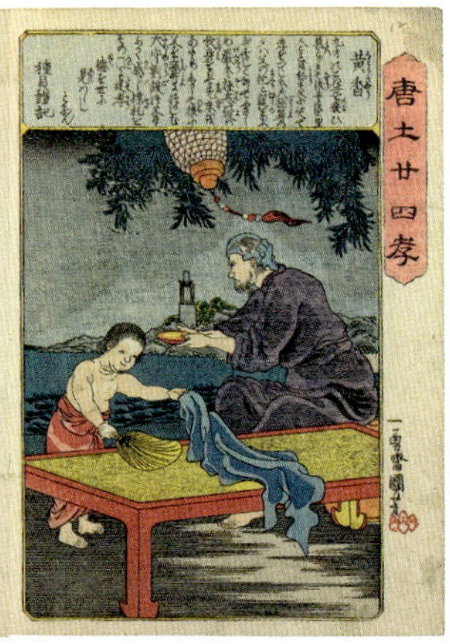

103.12

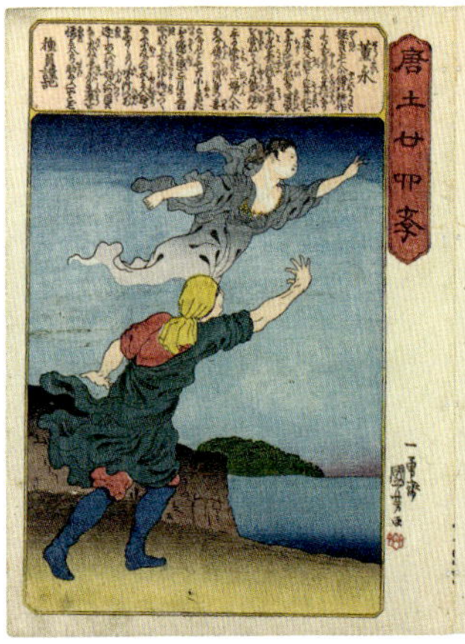

103.11

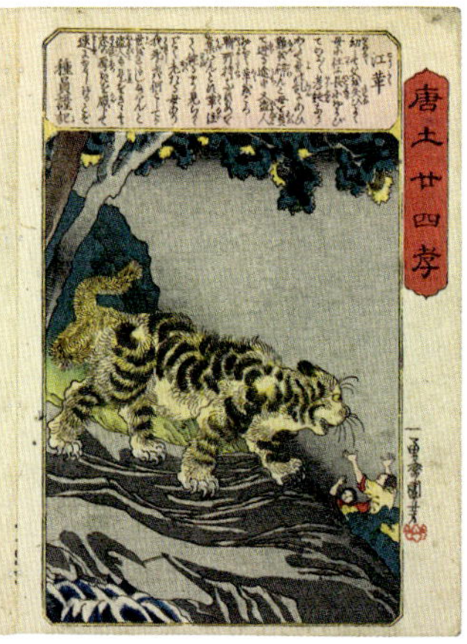

103.10

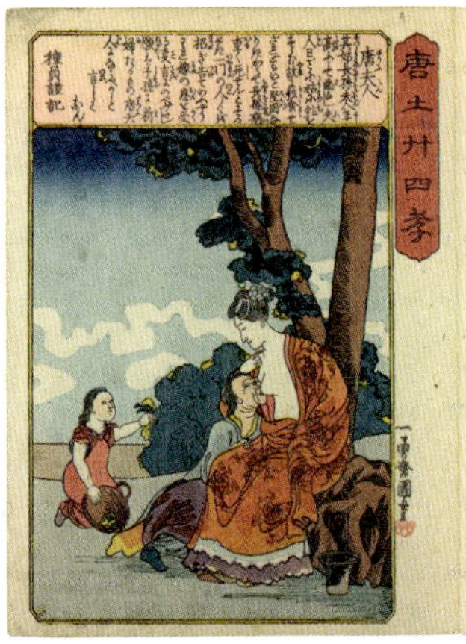

103.9

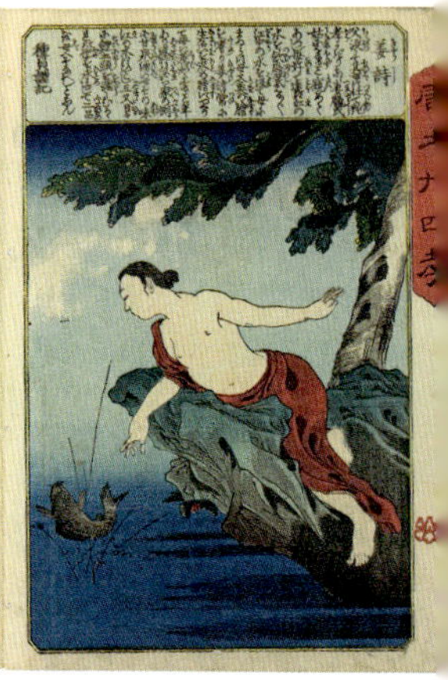

1

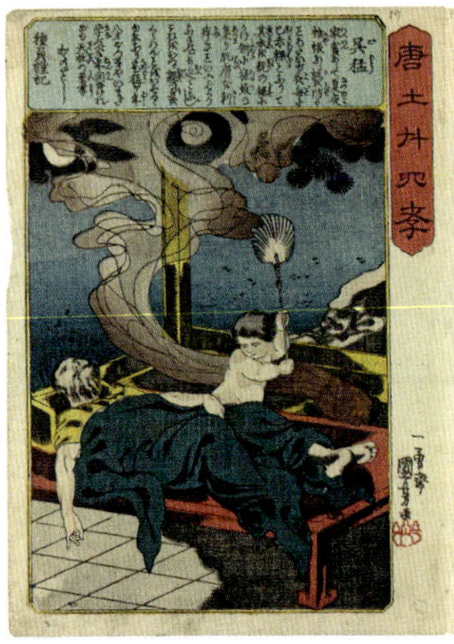

103.19

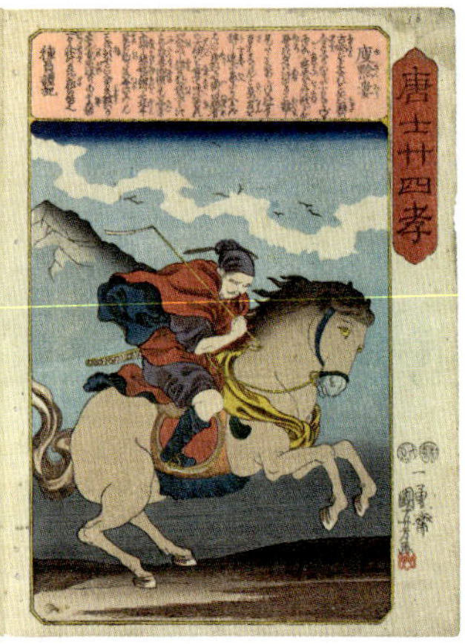

103.18

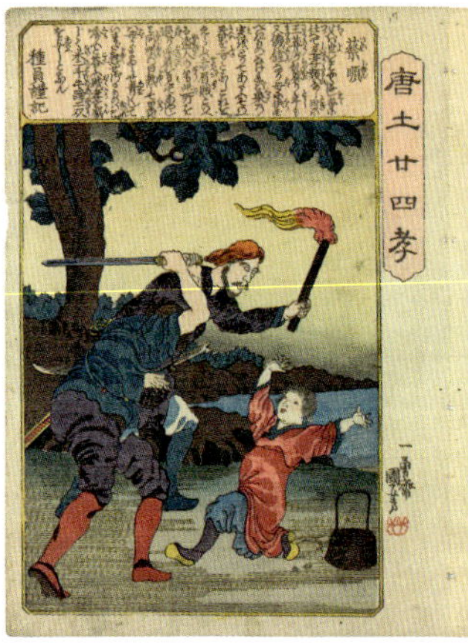

103.17

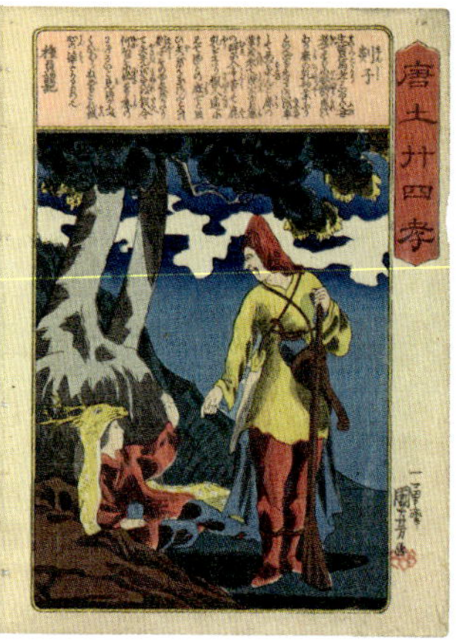

103.16

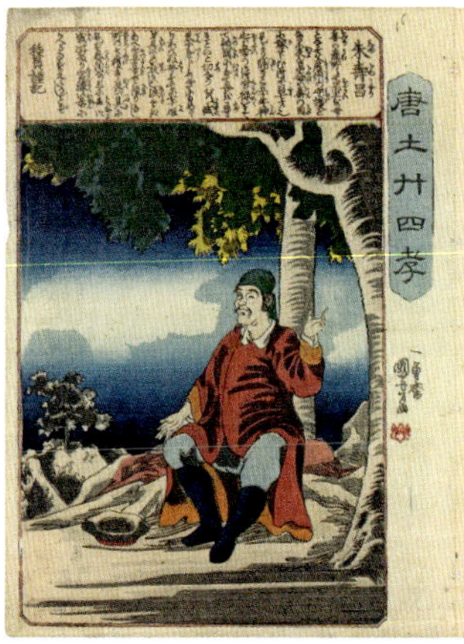

103.15

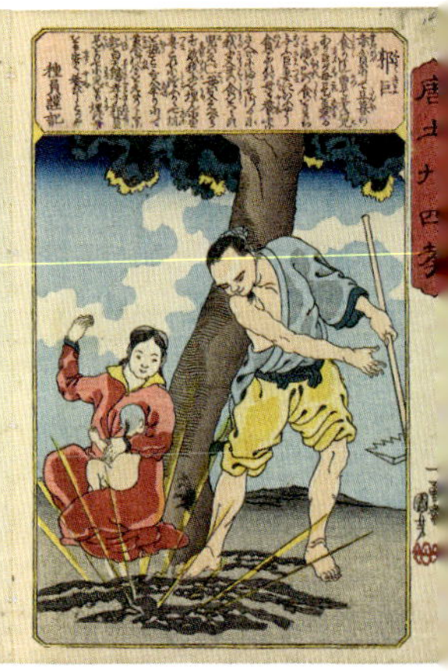

10

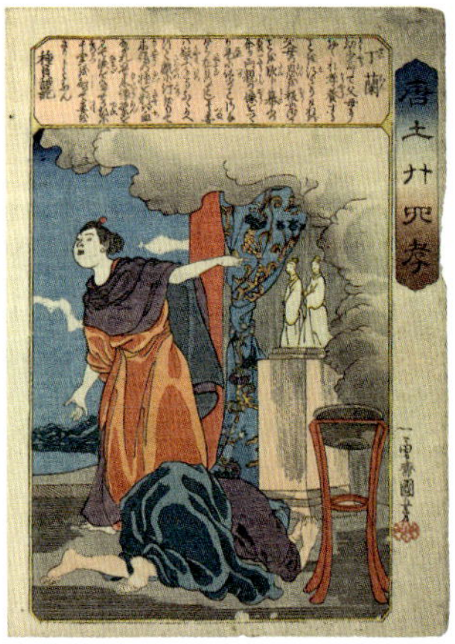

103.24

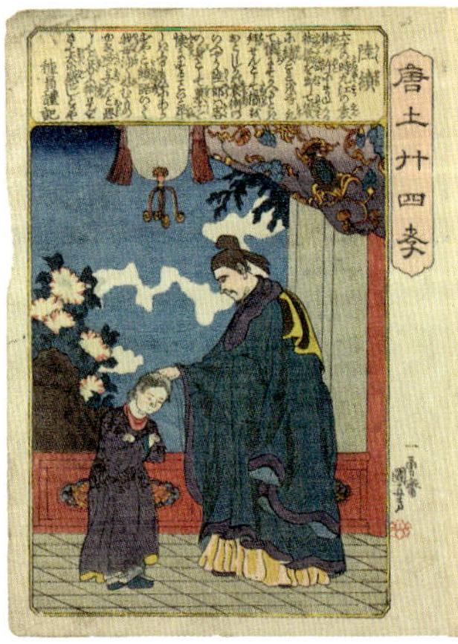

103.23

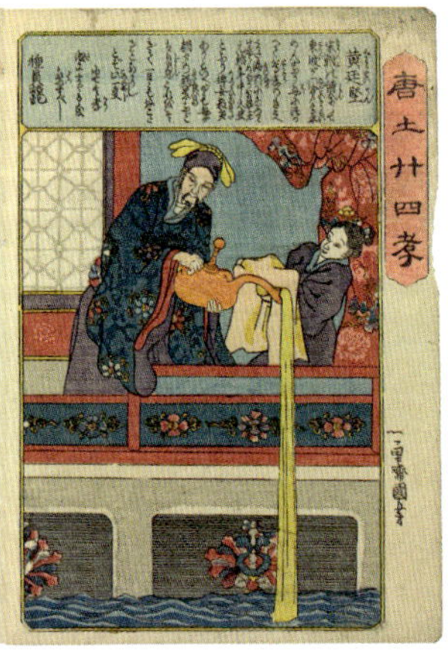

103.22

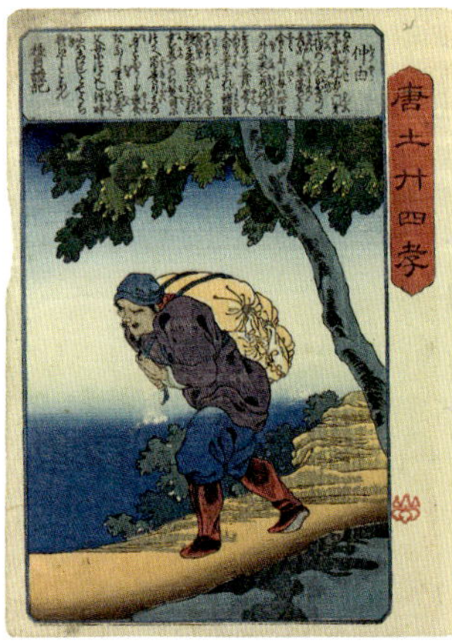

103.21

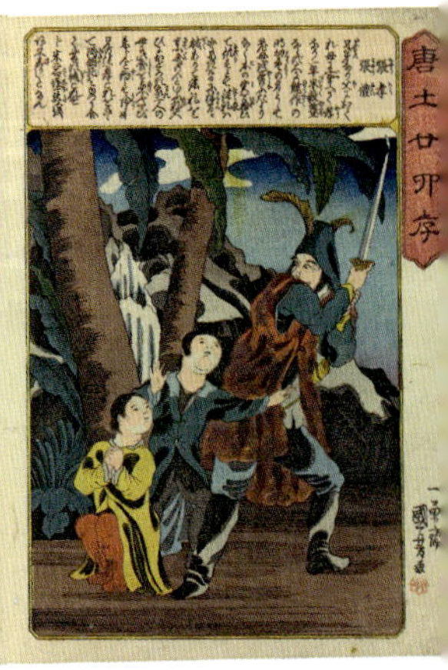

10

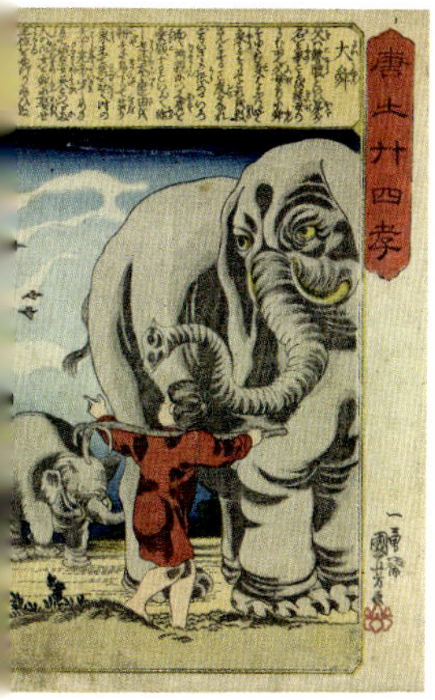

103.1

TWENTY-FOUR PARAGONS OF FILIAL PIETY IN CHINA

(Cat. 103)

This series on the twenty-four Chinese paragons of filial piety is slightly later than the other included here (cats 98–101 and fig. 3, where more information on the subject will be found). The prints, in the smaller, *chūban* format, were originally bound together and issued as a folding album. Two prefaces – missing from the Miller Collection, which otherwise has the complete set in the form of a sewn book (17001, 01-024) – are printed in white characters against a black background, in imitation of Chinese stone rubbings. They include a description of the exotic, European-influenced style as 'Dutch painting full of flesh colour'. One is signed 'Musa Dōjin of Kyoto', while the publisher's seal on the other reads 'Dainandō'. Nothing is known about the preface author or the publisher, so the circumstances surrounding the production of the series remain obscure. The texts above each picture, written by Ryūkatei Tanekazu, recount the story of each child. Iwakiri Yuriko has detected in these commentaries and in some of Kuniyoshi's illustrations the influence of the book *Nijūshi-kō eshō* (*Selected Pictures of the Twenty-four Paragons of Filial Piety*), published in Osaka in 1842 (Nagoya 1996, p. 244). Sources for several figures and animals in the prints have recently been discovered among the illustrations in Nieuhof's *Gedenkwaerdige Zee-en Lant-Reize* and in an edition of *Aesop's Fables* (Katsumori 2000; Katsuhara 2006).

The series is thought to date from 1848–50: two of the designs bear the twin censorship seals of Murata and Mera. Some impressions of the prints have surface burnishing (*shōmen-zuri*), apparently in imitation of the varnish applied to European oil paintings.

103.4

Min Ziqian [R], one of the twenty-four Chinese paragons of filial piety

1848–50

Colour woodblock, *chūban* album, no publisher's seal, 24.9 × 19.1 cm (covers)

SERIES TITLE
'Twenty-four Paragons of Filial Piety in China' (*Tōdo nijūshi-kō*)

PRINT TITLE
'Bin Shiken [Min Ziqian]

ARTIST'S SIGNATURE
Ichiyūsai Kuniyoshi ga

ARTIST'S SEAL
Yoshikiri

American Friends of the British Museum (The Arthur R. Miller Collection) 17001-04

The text describes how Min Ziqian's father remarried when the boy's mother died and had two more sons with the stepmother. The stepmother dressed her offspring in clothes padded with cotton wadding, but stuffed Min's garments with nothing more than flowers from reeds. The father did not realise this until Min became so cold that he dropped the rope with which he was pulling his father's cart. Min dissuaded the angry father from divorcing his second wife, saying that he (Min) was now the only son suffering from cold, whereas if the stepmother left them all three would be affected. Hearing this, the stepmother was moved to improve her behaviour towards Min. Kuniyoshi's image shows her relaxing on a 'European' couch while Min sweeps the floor.

103.5

Zeng Can [L], one of the twenty-four Chinese paragons of filial piety

1848–50

Colour woodblock, *chūban* album, no publisher's seal, 24.9 × 19.1 cm (covers)

PRINT TITLE
'So Shin [Zeng Shen]'

SERIES TITLE
'Twenty-four Paragons of Filial Piety in China' (*Tōdo nijūshi-kō*)

ARTIST'S SIGNATURE
Ichiyūsai Kuniyoshi ga

ARTIST'S SEAL
Yoshikiri

American Friends of the British Museum (The Arthur R. Miller Collection) 17001-05

REFERENCES
Robinson 1961, no. 39; Riccar 1978, no. 199; Robinson 1982, no. S60; Suzuki 1992, no. 200; Nagoya 1996, nos 111–2; Ōta 1999, no. 81; Isao 2008, p. 30

The text describes how Zeng Can behaved extremely dutifully towards his mother after his father died. When he was collecting firewood in a mountain forest one day, his mother received a visit from a close friend of her son who had travelled a great distance. Worried that she would not be able to accord the visitor proper hospitality on her own, she bit her finger in vexation. Zeng immediately felt a pang in his chest and realised that his mother must be apologising to the visitor for his absence. He rushed home to tell his mother what had happened and she was deeply moved by his filial piety (see also p. 22, fig. 3).

Most images of the tale depict Zeng hurrying home, but Kuniyoshi shows him climbing down from a tree, where he has been gathering branches for firewood, an axe tucked into his belt at the back. This print ranks among Kuniyoshi's most European.

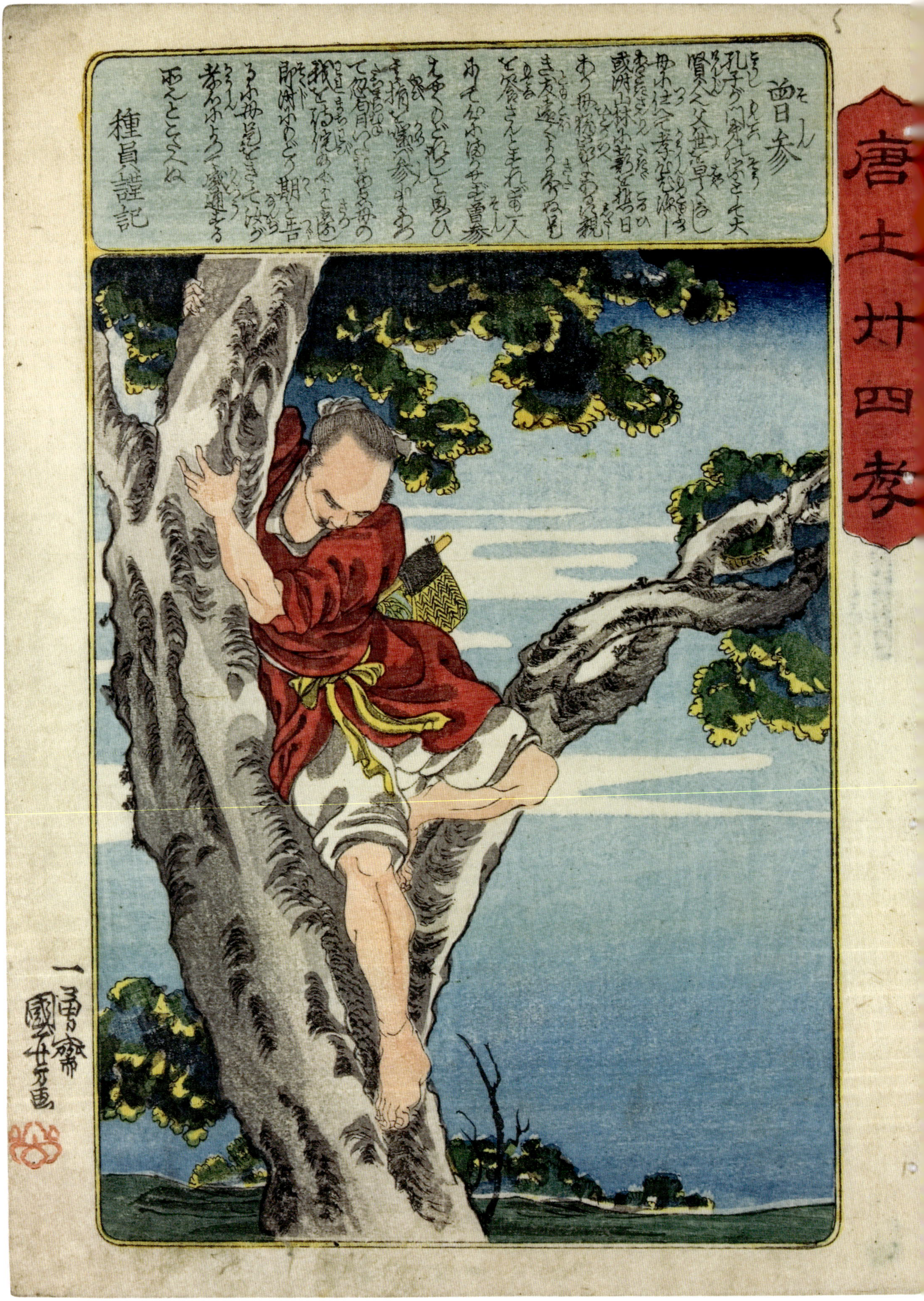

唐土廿四孝
曾参
種員謹記
一勇斎國芳画

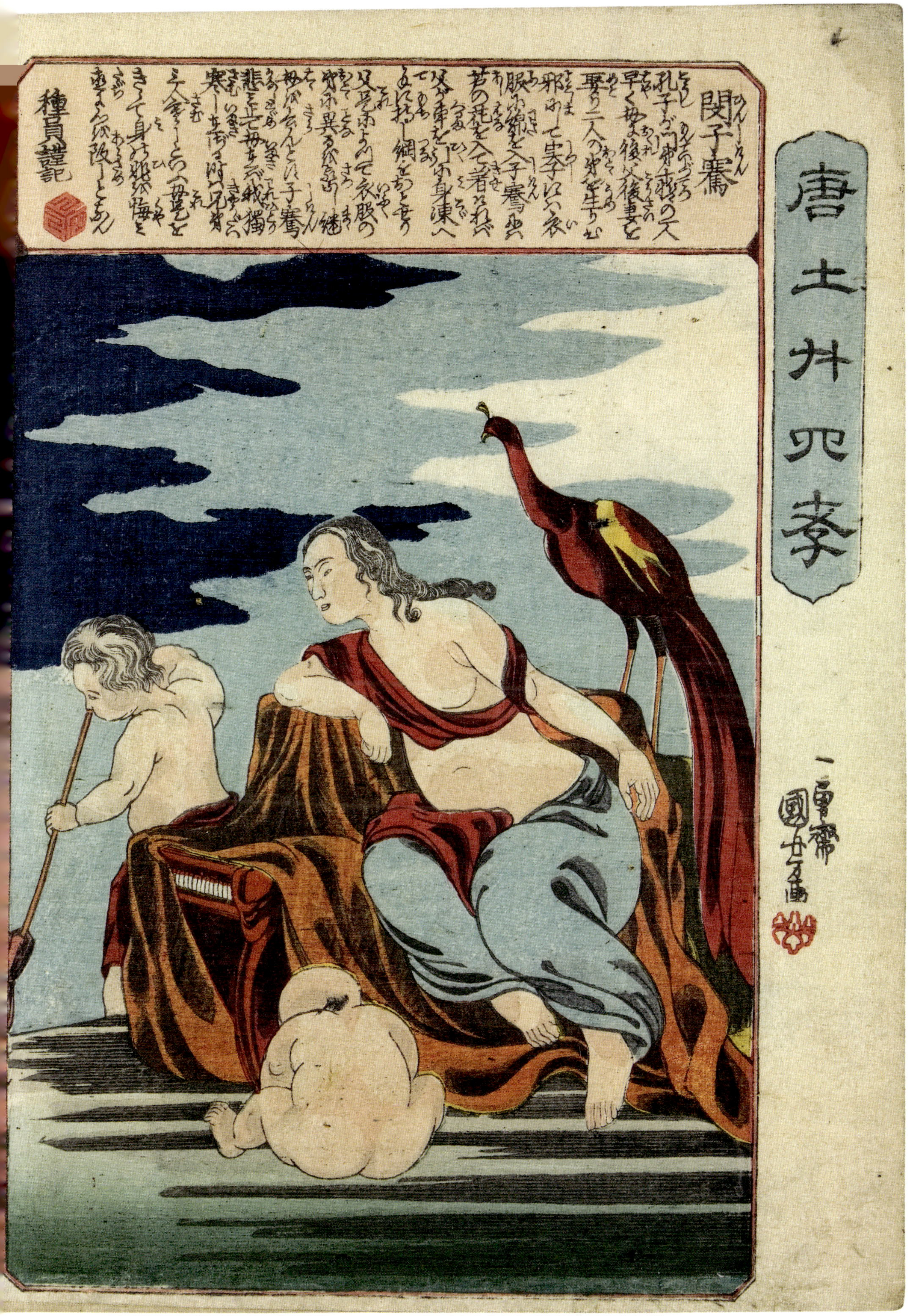
唐土廿四孝
閔子騫
種員謹記
一勇齋國芳画

4

THEATRE

Popular Kabuki theatre was the most important arena for expressing and exploring the collective values of the townspeople of Edo. Performances were staged all year round in three theatres licensed by the authorities, with breaks every few months to prepare new programmes. Favourite plays – some historical, featuring fictionalised samurai heroes (*jidai-mono*), and some 'domestic', revolving around the lives of townspeople (*sewa-mono*) – were constantly rewritten and developed as vehicles for star actors. Female roles were taken by specialist male actors called *onnagata*. Performances would typically alternate nuanced, realistic passages with spectacular scenes full of action and stage tricks. Music, sound effects, onstage chanting and elegant dances performed by the actors were important additional elements in the day-long programme.

Kuniyoshi's early period of artistic activity overlapped with the final years of the great playwright Tsuruya Nanboku IV (1755–1829), whose works either were sombre and psychologically acute or featured magical and supernatural themes. Plays of the latter kind showcased the talents of Onoe Kikugorō III (1784–1849) in a role such as the Spirit of the Cat Stone (Neko-ishi no Kai), complemented by the sensational mechanical tricks of Hasegawa Kanbei's sets (cat. 106).

The leading actor of the time was Ichikawa Danjūrō VII (1791–1859), an extremely versatile artist who was particularly acclaimed for bombastic heroic roles in the 'rough stuff' (*aragoto*) style in which his family had specialised for generations (cats 104, 105). Kabuki was a major target of the Tenpō reforms of 1841–43: Danjūrō VII was banished from Edo in 1842 for infringing sumptuary laws (he was not permitted to return until 1849); the three theatres were required to move away from the centre of the city; and prints of actors and stage scenes were banned under publishing regulations introduced in the sixth month, 1842. Restrictions were relaxed gradually from 1846, but for many years afterwards neither actors' names nor their crests could be shown on prints.

Danjūrō VII's handsome son Ichikawa Danjūrō VIII (1823–1854) was the heartthrob actor of the day. He was even written as a character into the best-selling illustrated novel *Jiraiya gōketsu monogatari* (*Tale of the Hero Jiraiya*), which featured the exploits of a glamorous robber (cat. 117). In 1854, at the age of thirty-two (thirty-one by Western reckoning), Danjūrō VIII suddenly committed suicide. In 1849, when he travelled to meet his father in Osaka, Kuniyoshi had designed a magnificent, de-luxe *surimono* print as a tribute from two clubs of Edo fish merchant poets (cat. 110); now, in 1854, the artist created a haunting memorial portrait in a grand triptych format (cat. 118).

Another popular amusement in Edo were *misemono* – entertainments in temporary street-side booths to which the public paid admission. One such spectacle was based on a votive painting commissioned from Kuniyoshi by a brothel owner in 1855 for the temple Sensō-ji, in which the artist depicted the climax of the murderous tale *Hag of Hitotsuya*. The *misemono*, mounted in 1856 by the craftsman Matsumoto Kisaburō, took the form of life-size 'living dolls' (*iki-ningyō*) that re-enacted the scene from the tale. This, in turn, inspired several prints by Kuniyoshi (cat. 119). During the artist's later years, such interplay between Kabuki theatre, *misemono* entertainments and ukiyo-e prints and illustrations was particularly widespread.

104

Kabuki actor Ichikawa Danjūrō VII as Arajishi Otokonosuke

1828

Colour woodblock with metallic pigment and embossing, *shikishi-ōban surimono*, 20.4 × 17.8 cm

ARTIST'S SIGNATURE
Ichiyūsai Kuniyoshi ga

PRINTER
Shinzō

POEMS
Wakaba sasu / komatsu no hoka ni / futamata no / ōne mo hikan / kyō no ne-no-hi no.
TAKARA NO FUNAUTA [R]

Yama to iu / yama no naka ni mo / nuki-idete / ōkina mono yo / Fuji no hatsuyume.
HŌSHITEI [L]

American Friends of the British Museum (The Arthur R. Miller Collection) 21604

REFERENCES
Amsterdam 1984, no. 199; Nagoya 1996, p. 280, no. 35; Amsterdam 1998, pp. 252–3

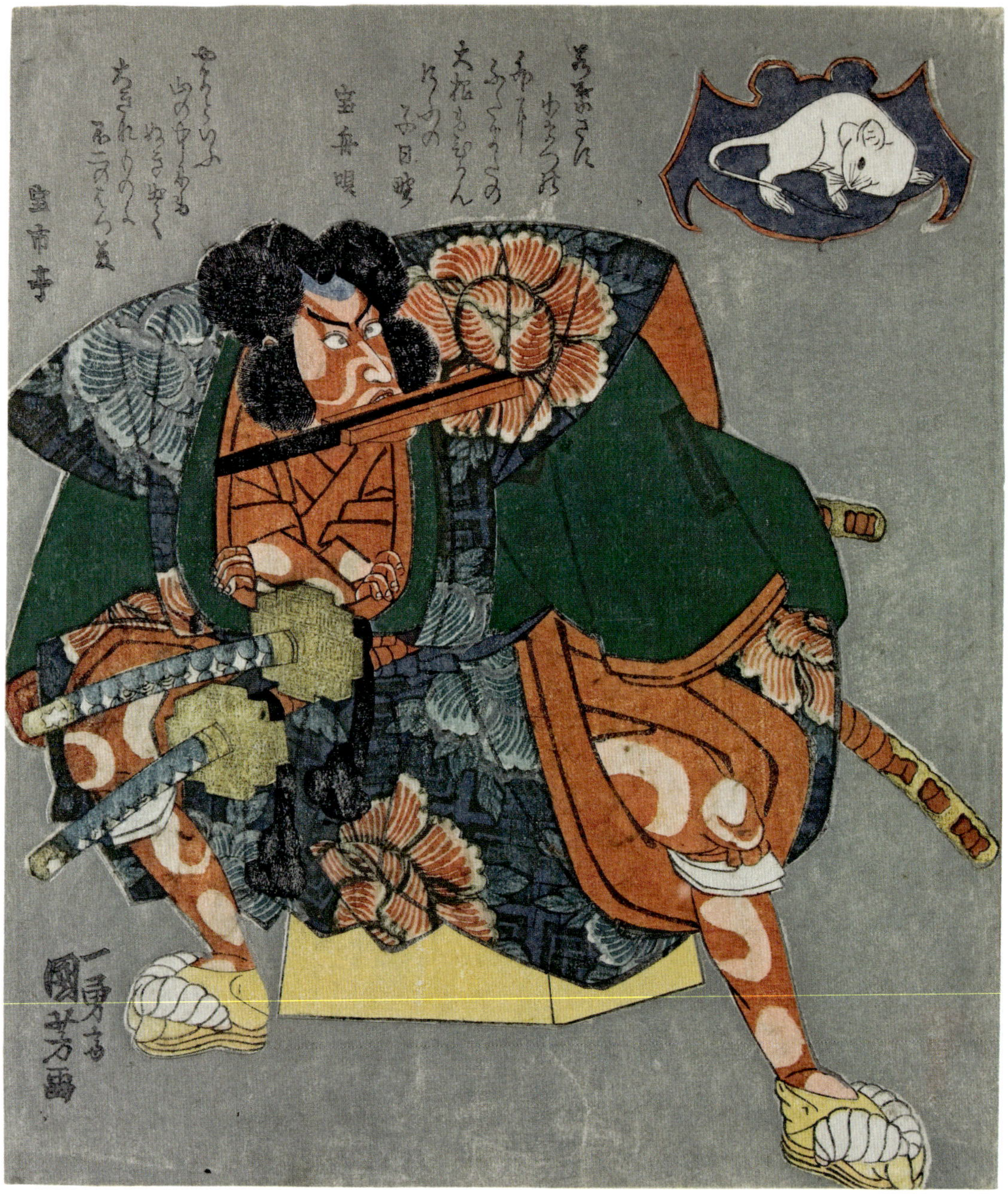

Ichikawa Danjūrō VII is portrayed in the muscular heroic role of Arajishi Otokonosuke, literally 'Wild Lion Macho Man'. Otokonosuke's adversary is a large evil rat with magic powers, represented here by the small white rat in the auspicious bat-shaped cartouche in the top right corner at which he is glaring. The scene is known as 'Under the floorboards' (*Yukashita*). At night, Otokonosuke is keeping watch over his lord from beneath the floorboards when he is surprised by a giant rat with a hand scroll in its mouth. The scroll, which contains a secret list of conspirators needed by the lord's loyal supporters, has been stolen by the rat. The rat is a magic guise adopted by the evil retainer Nikki Danjō, leader of the conspiracy. Treading its head under his foot, Otokonosuke strikes the rat on the head with the iron fan that the print shows clenched between his teeth. The actors generally presented this as a 'stage pose' tableau (*mie*) on a mechanical platform (*seri*) that rose from under the main stage.

During the 1660s a major succession dispute and factional struggle took place within the Date clan of Sendai. The scene described above was included in some Kabuki plays that alluded to this historical event. The bombastic role of Otokonosuke was typical of the 'rough stuff' (*aragoto*) style cultivated by the Ichikawa Danjūrō line of actors. Ichikawa Danjūrō VII (1791–1859) played the role several times in the course of his long career. His formal shoulder wings and leggings (*kamishimo*) here feature a large peony motif and a stylised 'triple rice-measure' (*mimasu*) crest printed with powdered brass – both emblems of the Danjūrō line. The same *mimasu* crest appears on the guards of his unnaturally large swords. Seated on a stool while he keeps watch, the actor pulls apart the collar of his robe from inside and strikes a defiantly combative pose.

The print is likely to have been produced for the New Year of 1828, which was a rat year in the zodiac cycle. Hence Kuniyoshi's design probably relates to the role, notable for its association with rats, rather than to a particular performance of the play. This suggestion is borne out by the two poems printed at the top, which contain imagery typical of the New Year, not of Kabuki.

105

Kabuki actor Ichikawa Danjūrō VII subdues a constable

early 1830s

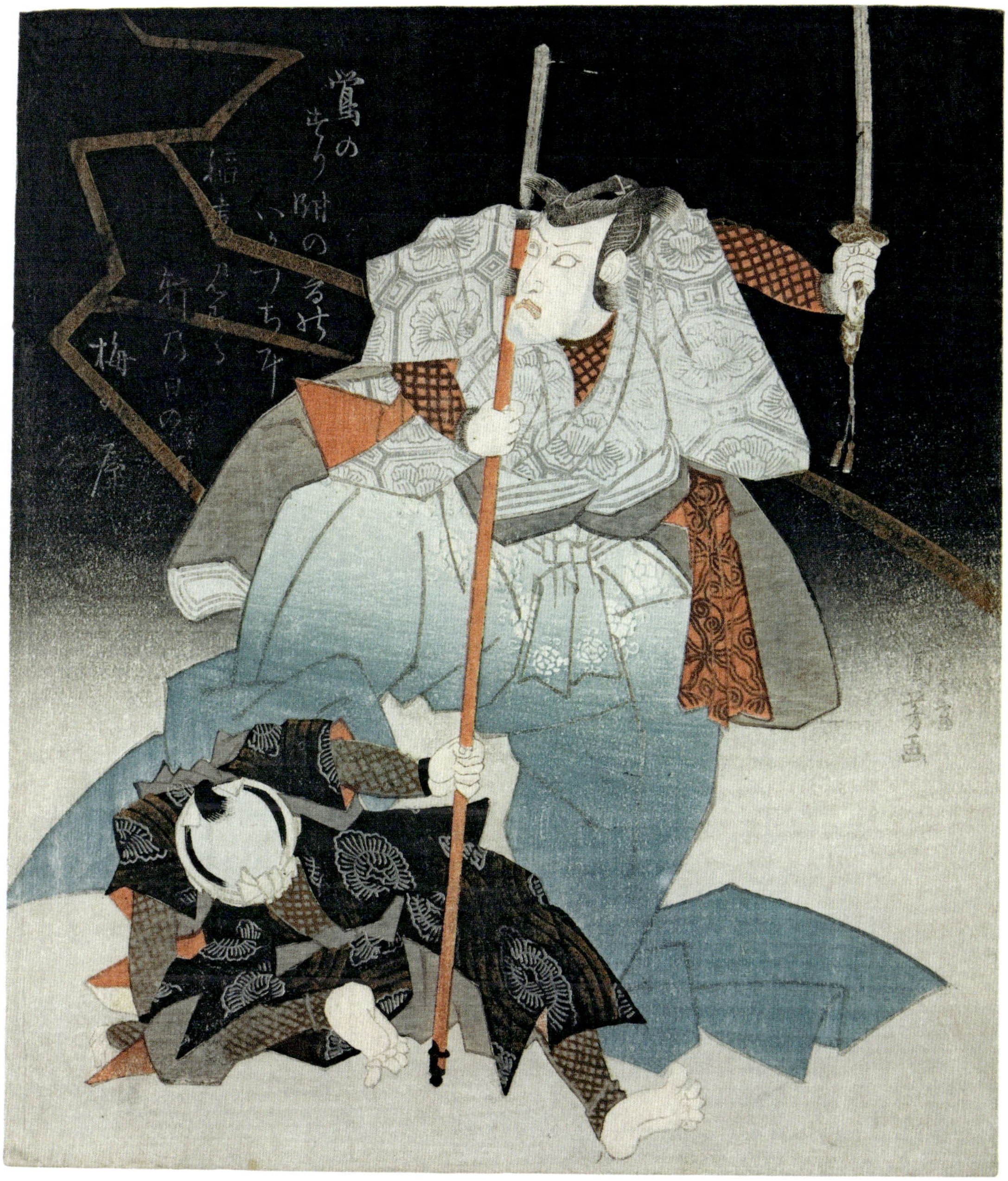

Colour woodblock with metallic pigments and embossing, *shikishi-ban surimono*, 20.9 × 18.3 cm

ARTIST'S SIGNATURE
Ichiyūsai Kuniyoshi ga

POEM
Uguisu no / surie no oto no / ikazuchi ni / inazuma misuru / noki no hi no kage.
UMENOYA

American Friends of the British Museum (The Arthur R. Miller Collection) 21601

REFERENCES
Berlin 1990, no. 65 (with alternative poem by Ichijuen Kageyoshi); Nagoya 1996, p. 280, no. 36 (with alternative poem by Ichijuen Kageyoshi); Chiba 1997, no. 140; Amsterdam 1998, p. 253

Danjūrō VII appears in a resolute stage pose, with one foot inside long trailing leggings (*naga-bakama*) placed firmly on the back of a hapless, cowering constable (*torite*), who has obviously failed to arrest him. The role is not known but, as the actor's muscular stance makes clear, he is performing in the 'rough stuff' (*aragoto*) style that was the forte of the Danjūrō line. Bracing himself against the constable's pike, he defiantly brandishes an unsheathed sword, as lightening forks dramatically around the pair.

Typically, *surimono* would be privately distributed at the New Year by the poet (or poets) whose name they bear, in this case Umenoya Kakuju (1801–1856), patron and lifelong friend of Kuniyoshi (see also pp. 29–30). A passionate Kabuki fan, Umenoya spared no expense in this image of the 'superstar' of the Edo stage. Metallic pigments have been used extensively: brass on the arm guards, leggings and hilt of the sword (to give the effect of gold); tin in the stylised peony motif on Danjūrō's robe (to suggest silver); and copper for the lightning.

New Year poems were required to include elements appropriate to the season, here the warbler (which first sings when the plum blossom opens) and spring sunshine. Umenoya contrives to reconcile these peaceful images with references to the fight scene on a stormy night: 'The sound of the warbler's / bird food being ground / echoes like thunder / as sunlight pierces the eaves / like streaks of lightening' (trans. John T. Carpenter).

Asano Shūgō records another printing (with a verse by Ichijuen Kageyoshi), which, he surmises, is slightly later (Chiba 1997, p. 174).

106

Kabuki actor Onoe Kikugorō III [C] as the Spirit of the Cat Stone

1835

Colour woodblock, *ōban* triptych, published by Izumiya Ichibei, 36.7 × 25.5 [R], 36.9 × 25.2 [C], 36.8 × 25.5 cm [L]

PRINT TITLE
'From the Fifty-three Stations of the Tōkaidō Road [Scene at Okazaki]' (*Gojūsan-tsugi no uchi [Okazaki no ba]*)

ARTIST'S SIGNATURE
Ichiyūsai Kuniyoshi ga

CENSORSHIP SEAL
kiwame

American Friends of the British Museum (The Arthur R. Miller Collection) 19408

REFERENCES
Robinson 1961, no. 72; Isao and Iwakiri 1999, nos 67–9; Ōta 1999, no. 134; Hiraki 2006, p. 52; Isao 2008, pp. 40–1

The great Kabuki actor Onoe Kikugorō III was much loved for his interpretation of supernatural roles. Here he is shown playing Neko-ishi no Kai, the Spirit of the Cat Stone. He is dressed as an old woman in the 'twelve-layered' brocade robes of a court lady, but sprouts a cat's ears and paws. Neko-ishi has conjured up the terrifying monster cat that glares at the viewer beneath the tattered reed blind of a lonely inn at Okazaki on the Tōkaidō road. Two heroes try to subdue the cat spirit: Shirasuga Jūemon, played by Mimasu Gennosuke I, on the right, who is dressed as an itinerant monk with tall basket hat, and Inabanosuke, played by Ichimura Uzaemon XII, on the left, who has drawn his sword. An illustrated novel in *gōkan* format based on this performance provides more detail about the scene. It describes how the heroes see the shadow of a giant cat on the reed blind. When they pull this down the shadow disappears and is replaced by an old woman in court robes who is blackening her teeth, depicted here on the centre sheet (Isao and Iwakiri 1999, nos 67–9). A shadow cast inside the standing lantern in the left and central sheets shows a cat licking the bowl of lamp-oil, a famous moment in the theatrical presentation. Smaller cats wearing headscarves dance crazily around the fire. The scene comes from the play *Ume no haru gojūsan-tsugi* (*Plum Spring: The Fifty-three Stations*), performed at the Ichimura theatre, Edo, from the second month of 1835.

The play was based on a successful work by the great playwright Tsuruya Nanboku IV (1755–1829) that had first been performed in the sixth month, 1827: *Hitori-tabi gojūsan-tsugi* (*Solitary Travels along the Fifty-three Stations*). This wove together several supernatural tales associated with places along the Tōkaidō road and showcased the acting talents of Kikugorō III and the sensational mechanical tricks of Hasegawa Kanbei's sets. Some of these elements were retained in the play of 1835. The idea for the present scene is said to have come to Nanboku IV when his pet cat brought him a colour woodblock print of a court lady holding a fan and when his maid cast an eerie shadow while pouring oil into the lantern in his study (Iizuka 1926, pp. 557–62). The story seems to have been adapted from another legend, associated with Okabe, further along the Tōkaidō road, in which a mountain cat took on the guise of an old woman to prey on travellers at a lonely inn. Warriors were sent to subdue her and she was finally turned into a giant rock shaped like a reclining cat.

Another printing is known (reproduced in Isao 2008, for example). This shows the title presented in white reserve on the grey background so as to read, on the right sheet, 'From the Fifty-three Stations of the Tōkaidō Road' (re-cut, since the characters are shaped differently from those in the present impression) and, on the left sheet, 'Scene at Okazaki' (not included here).

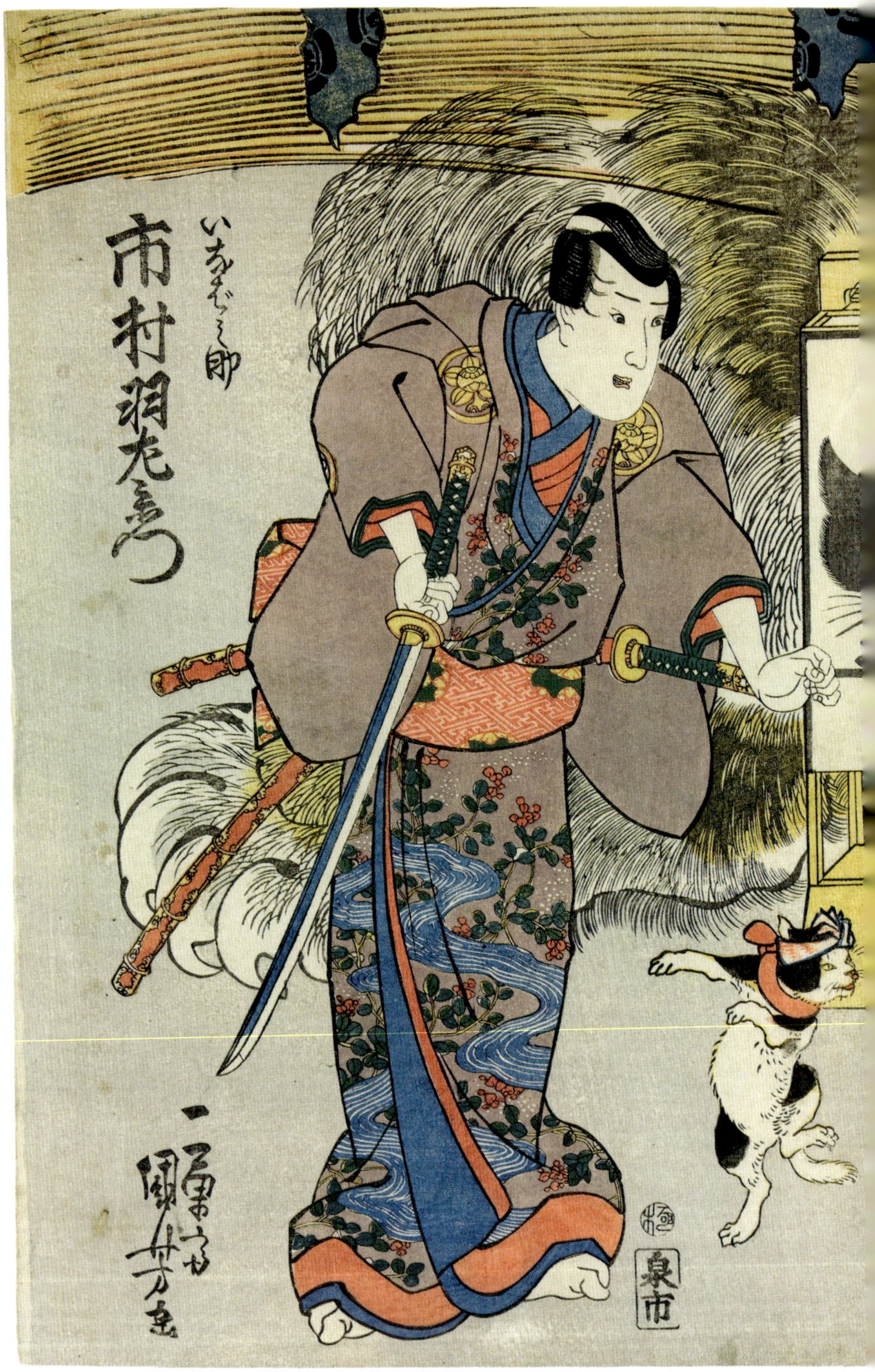

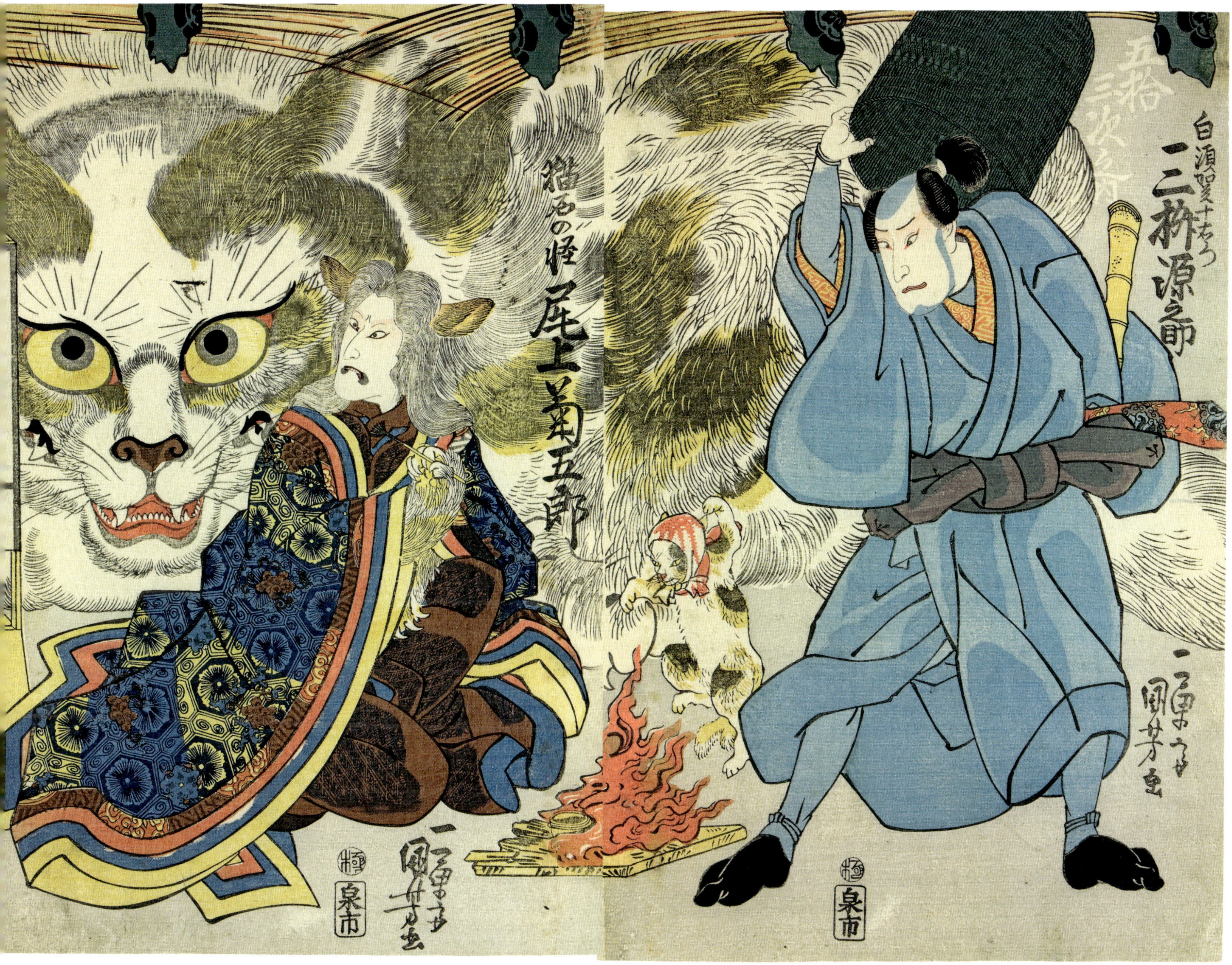
猫石の怪 尾上菊五郎
極
泉市
三枡源之助
極
泉市

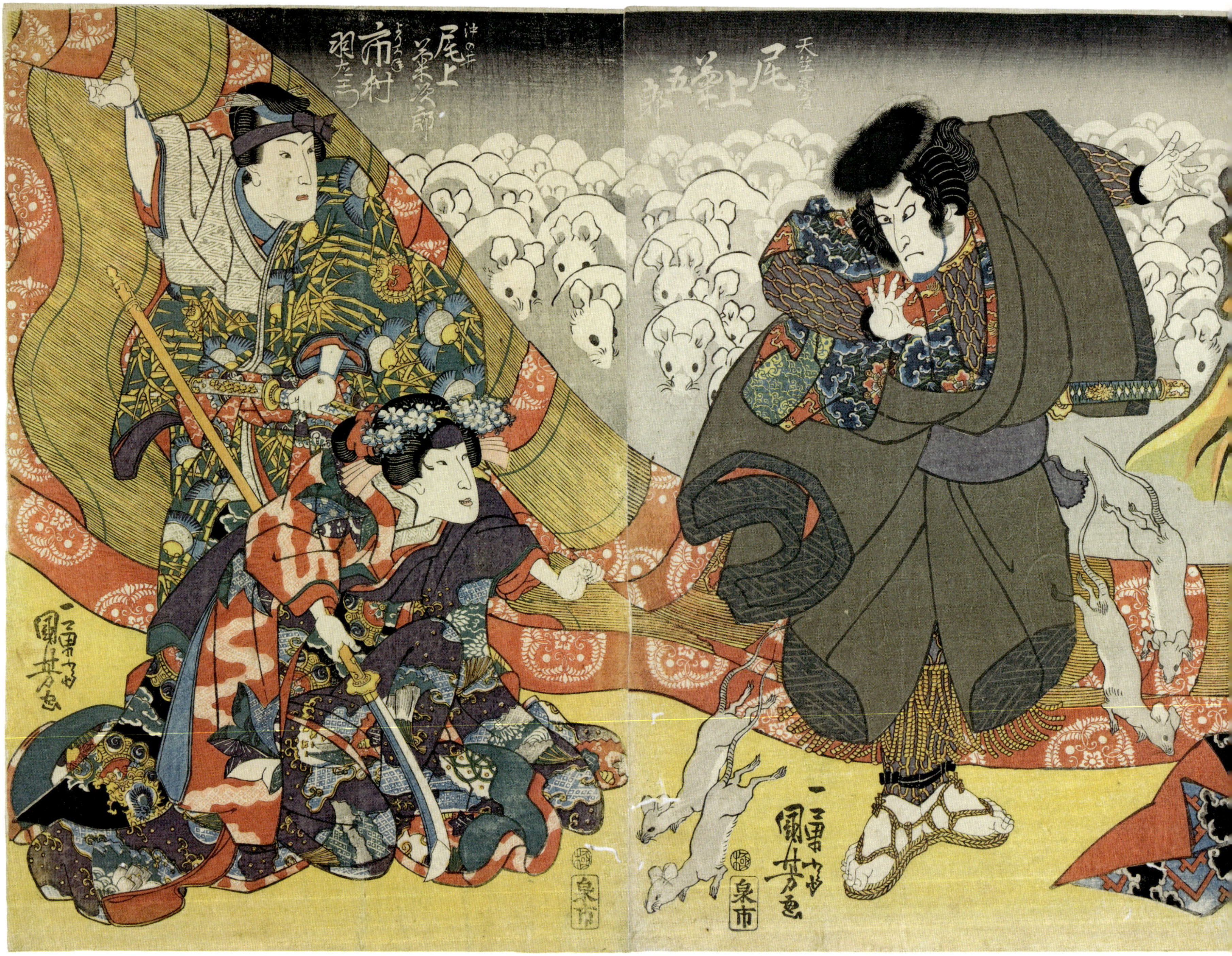

泉市
泉市

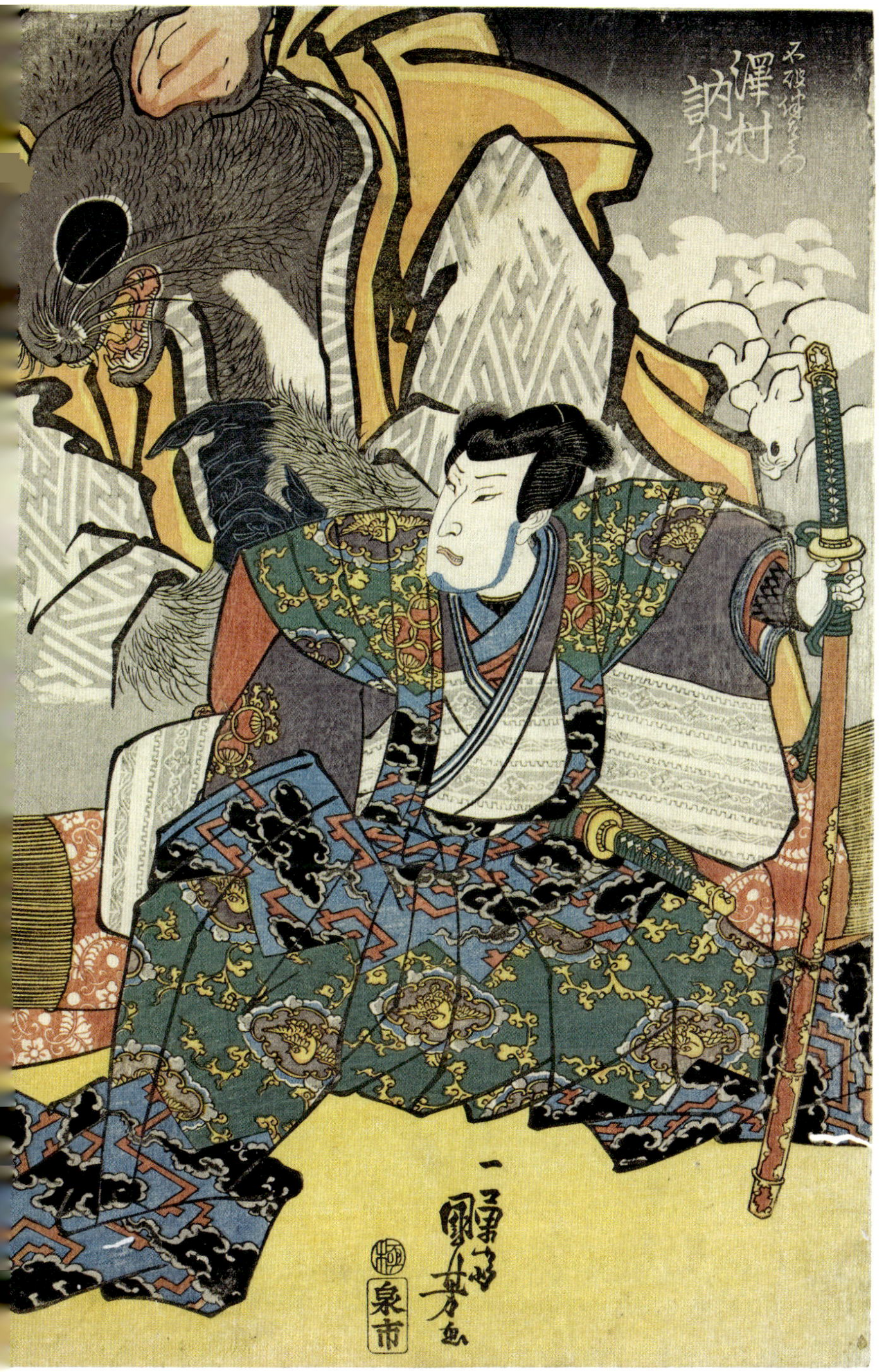

107

Kabuki actor Onoe Kikugorō III [R] as Tenjiku Kaja conjuring up rats

1836

Colour woodblock, *ōban* triptych, published by Izumiya Ichibei, 37.4 × 25.7 [R], 37. 4 × 26 [C], 37.4 × 25.5 cm [L]

ARTIST'S SIGNATURE
Ichiyūsai Kuniyoshi ga

CENSORSHIP SEAL *kiwame*

American Friends of the British Museum (The Arthur R. Miller Collection) 19609

REFERENCES
Springfield 1968, no.44 (right sheet only)

Kabuki actor Onoe Kikugorō III, known for his supernatural roles, plays Tenjiku Kaja ('Young Tenjiku') and is shown on the centre sheet conjuring up a horde of rats, led by a giant rat dressed in priestly attire. The animals swarm out from behind a rolled reed blind that has collapsed onto the stage. The other three characters prepare to defend themselves: Fuwa Banzaemon, on the right sheet, played by Sawamura Tosshō I; the woman Okinoi, played by Kikugorō's pupil Onoe Kikujirō II, and (Ashikaga) Yorikane, played by Ichimura Uzaemon XII, on the left. The play, called *Kuruwa kuruwa Date no ōyose* (*Coming! Coming to the Pleasure Quarter: Great Gathering of the Date Clan*), was performed at the Ichimura theatre, Edo, from the second month, 1836.

Detailed records of the plot have apparently not survived. As so often with Kabuki in the later Edo period, it seems to have combined several well-known stories – in this case, at least three. The 'Date' of the title evokes the world of plays based on feuding within the Date clan of Sendai in the 1660s. Lord Ashikaga Yorikane figures in some versions of that story, which invariably featured a much-loved scene in which the evil Nikki Danjō summons a horde of rats and himself takes the form of a large rat (see also cat. 104). In one of the earliest Kabuki plots to have survived from the seventeenth century Fuwa Banzaemon, shown on the right with the customary lightning pattern on his long, trailing leggings (*naga-bakama*), rivals Nagoya Sanza for the affections of the courtesan Katsuragi. Tenjiku Kaja, the central figure in the triptych, with his wig of wild hair, is a variant of Tenjiku Tokubei ('Indian Tokubei'), who uses magic learned on trips to South India to conjure up giant toads (see also cat. 117) and other creatures to attack his enemies.

Letters written by the author Takizawa Bakin (1767–1848) record that 'superstar' rivals Ichikawa Danjūrō VII and Kikugorō III were originally billed to appear together in this production and that Bakin's *Satomi hakkenden* (*Eight Dogs of the Satomi*) would form part of the story (see also cat. 20). However, after a disagreement about the allocation of roles Danjūrō left to perform at the rival Morita theatre (*Kabuki nenpyō* 1961, pp. 325–6). The performances were praised nonetheless and the play became a hit.

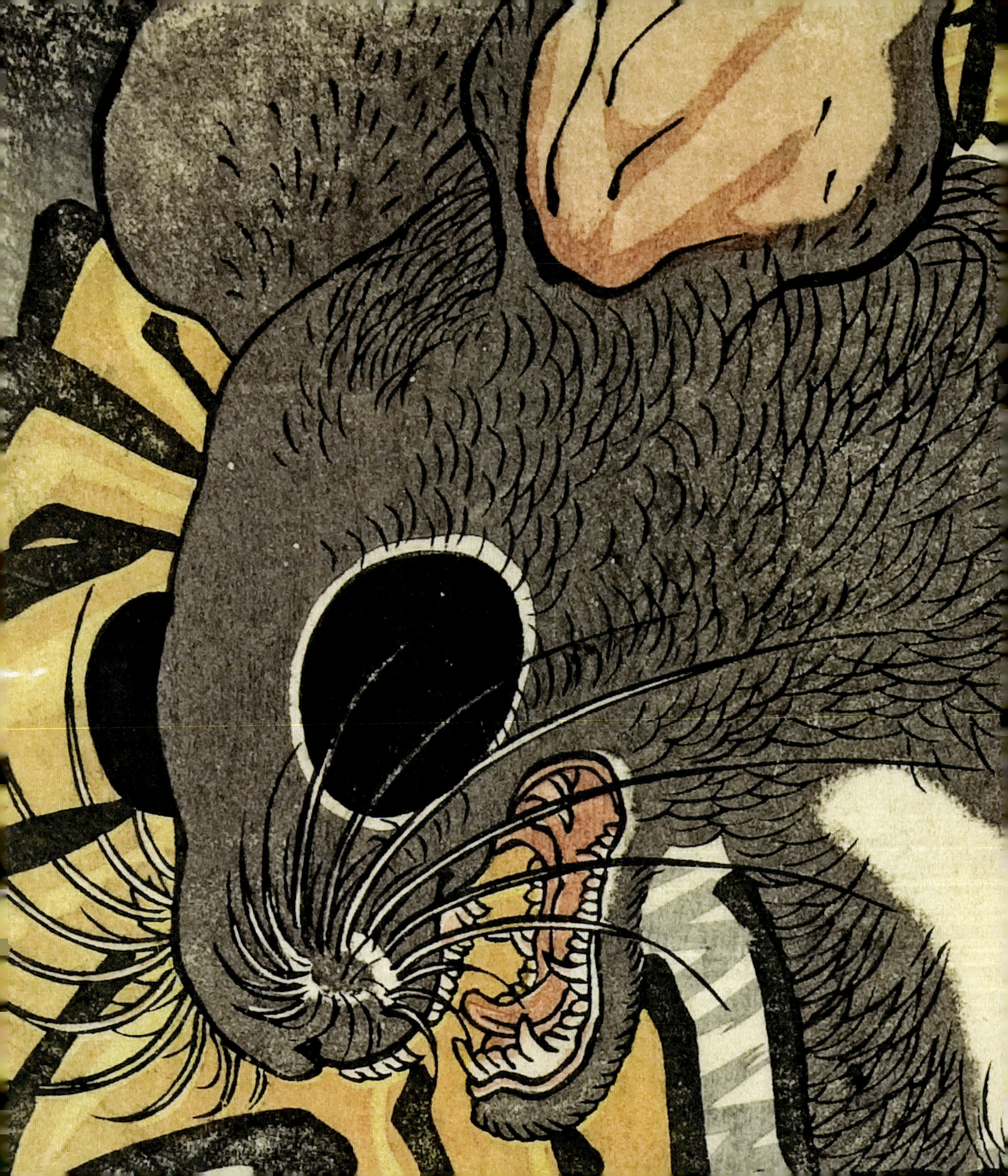

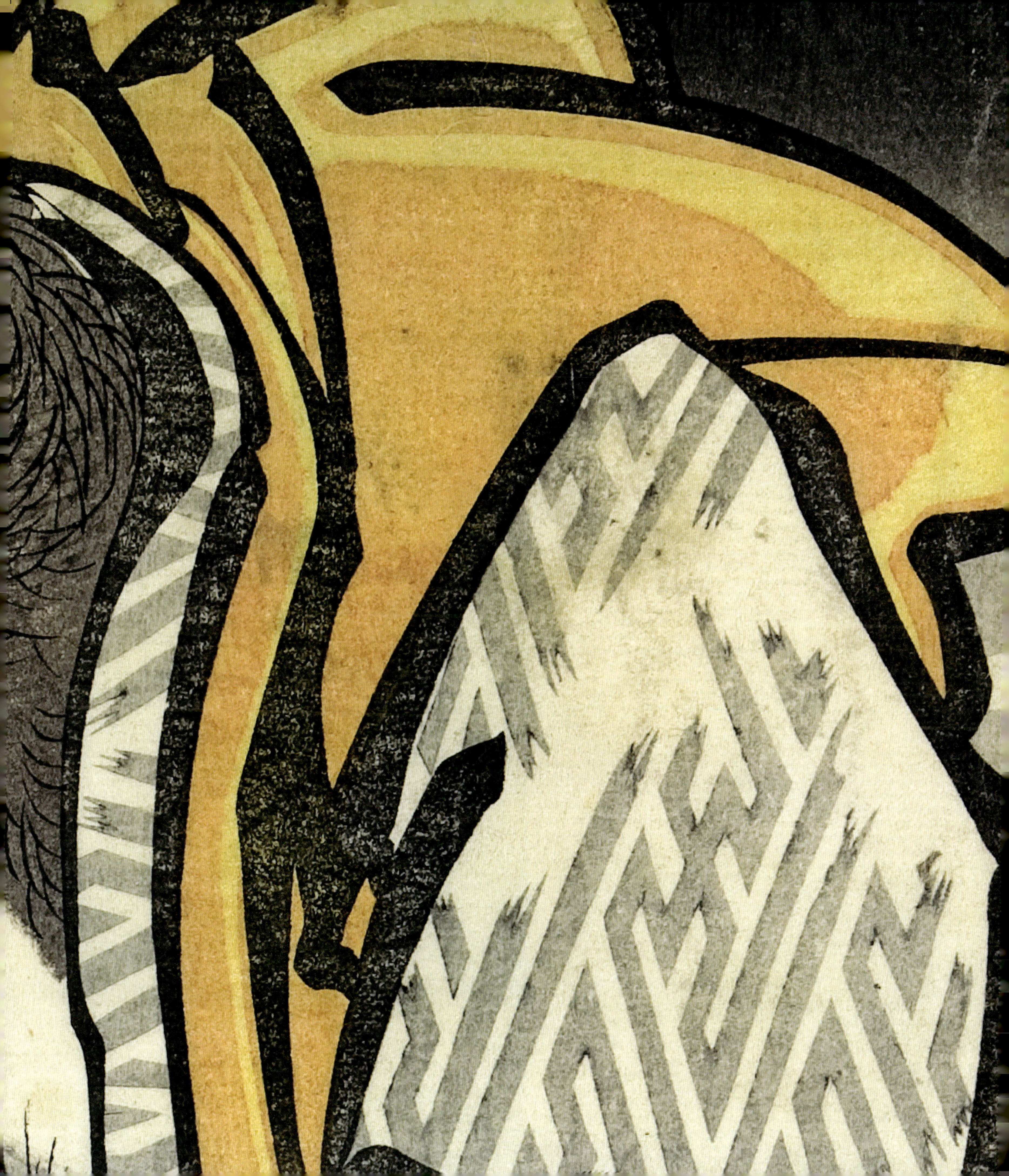

108

Kabuki actor Ichikawa Ebizō V as the pirate Kezori Kuemon

1840

Colour woodblock, *ōban*, published by Fujiokaya Hikotarō, 37.7 × 25.4 cm

PRINT TITLE
'Ichikawa Ebizō as Kezori Kuemon' (*Ichikawa Ebizō, Kezori Kuemon*)

ARTIST'S SIGNATURE
Ichiyūsai Kuniyoshi ga (in gourd-shaped *toshidama* cartouche)

CENSORSHIP SEAL
kiwame

POEM
Kuemon ga / serifu mawashi no / yoseba-guchi / waza ni koku su no / koshirae mo yoshi.
RIKUDAEN

Jeffrey Pollard and Ooi-Thye Chong Collection, USA

REFERENCES
Robinson 1961, no. 75; Suzuki 1992, no. 304; Mainichi Shinbunsha 1995, no. 134; Nagoya 1996, no. 124 (all the above with alternative poem by Umenoya); Amsterdam 1998, no. 161 (this impression)

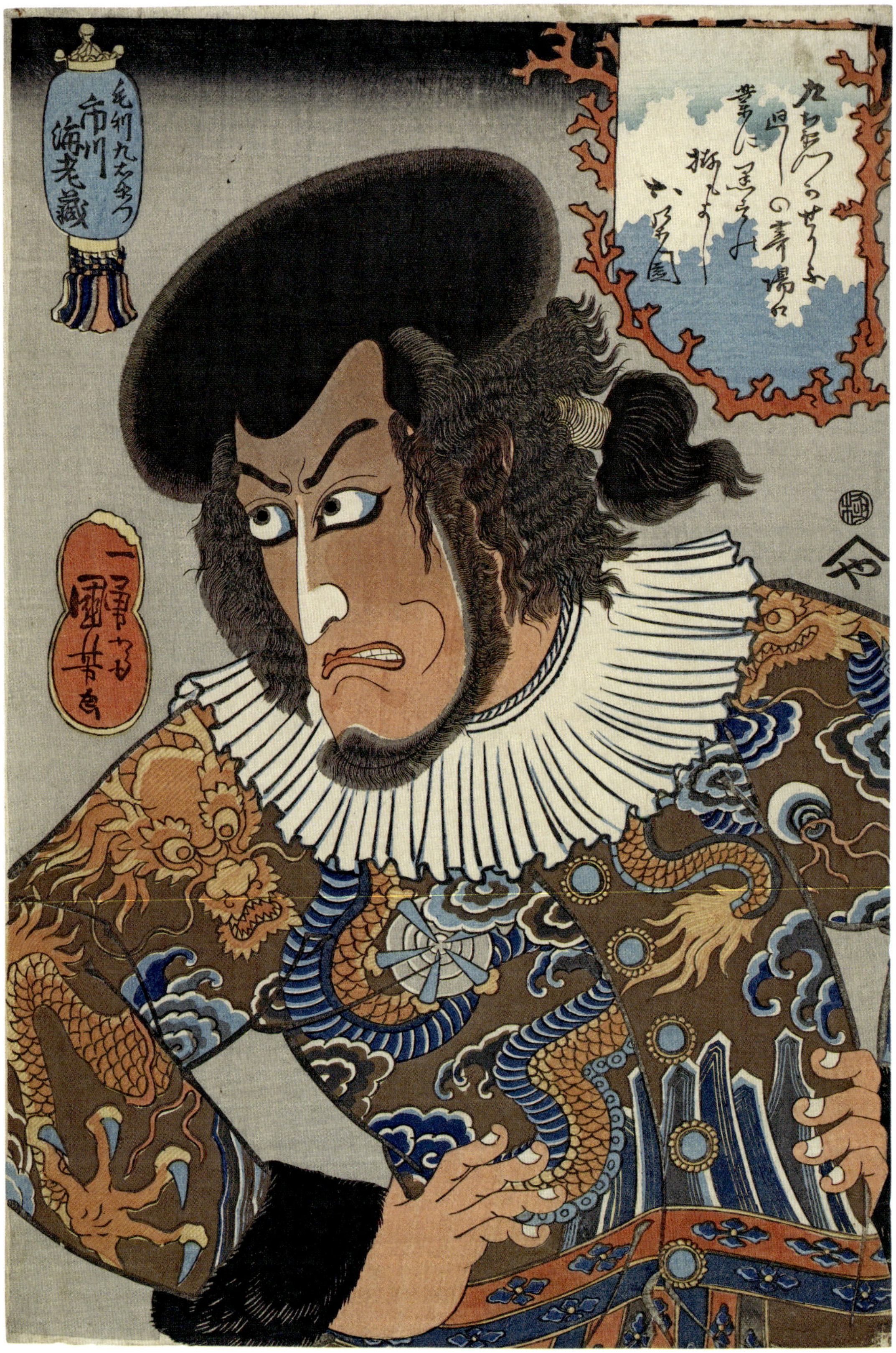

Ichikawa Ebizō V (the former Danjūrō VII) appears as Kezori Kuemon, a pirate captain and smuggler. He wears an exotic, Chinese-style brocade costume, decorated with dragons and featuring a pleated collar. Hands planted firmly on hips, Kuemon leans forward with a threatening glare in a stage pose known as 'watching the tide' (*shiomi no mie*). His ship is bound for Hakata in Kyushu. One of his passengers, Komatsuya Sōshichi, a young merchant from Kyoto, is travelling to meet his lover, the courtesan Kojorō, who works in the Okuda brothel at Hakata. When Kuemon realises that Sōshichi has been spying on his smuggling activities, he orders him to be thrown into the sea (the full plot is given in Herwig 2004, pp. 114–19). It is a sign of Kuemon's rough, outlandish character that he is bearded and sports a bristling, ringleted stage wig – a variant of the curly-style (*kusetsuki*) stage wig typically worn by seafarers who have returned from foreign travels.

The play was *Koi minato Hakata no hitofushi* (*Haven of Love: A Hakata Piece*), performed at the Nakamura theatre, Edo, from the eighth month, 1840. The original version was a puppet play by Chikamatsu Monzaemon, first performed in 1718 and taking its cue from several incidents in recent years in which smugglers had been executed by the authorities.

From late 1834 to early 1835 Ebizō had toured to places as distant as Nagasaki, the sole port open to foreign trade in the west of Japan. In his 1837 and 1840 performances as Kuemon he entertained the audience by peppering his speech with Nagasaki argot and showing off some of the exotic foreign goods he had acquired there. Spectators were particularly stunned by the splendid embroidery of five-clawed dragons on his costume, like the robe of a Chinese official (Iizuka 1926, pp. 760–3).

This is one of nine half-length actor portraits for performances in the seventh and eight months, 1840. The prints were probably sponsored by Umenoya Kakuju and other poets. Another of them depicts Sawamura Tosshō I as Komatsuya Sōshichi, from the same play (Iwakiri 1992a, p. 7, fig. 5; personal communication). A different edition of the present design carries a poem by Umenoya, in place of the verse by Rikudaen, inside the cartouche with the border of red coral at top right (Suzuki 1992, no. 304). It is not clear which printing is the earlier.

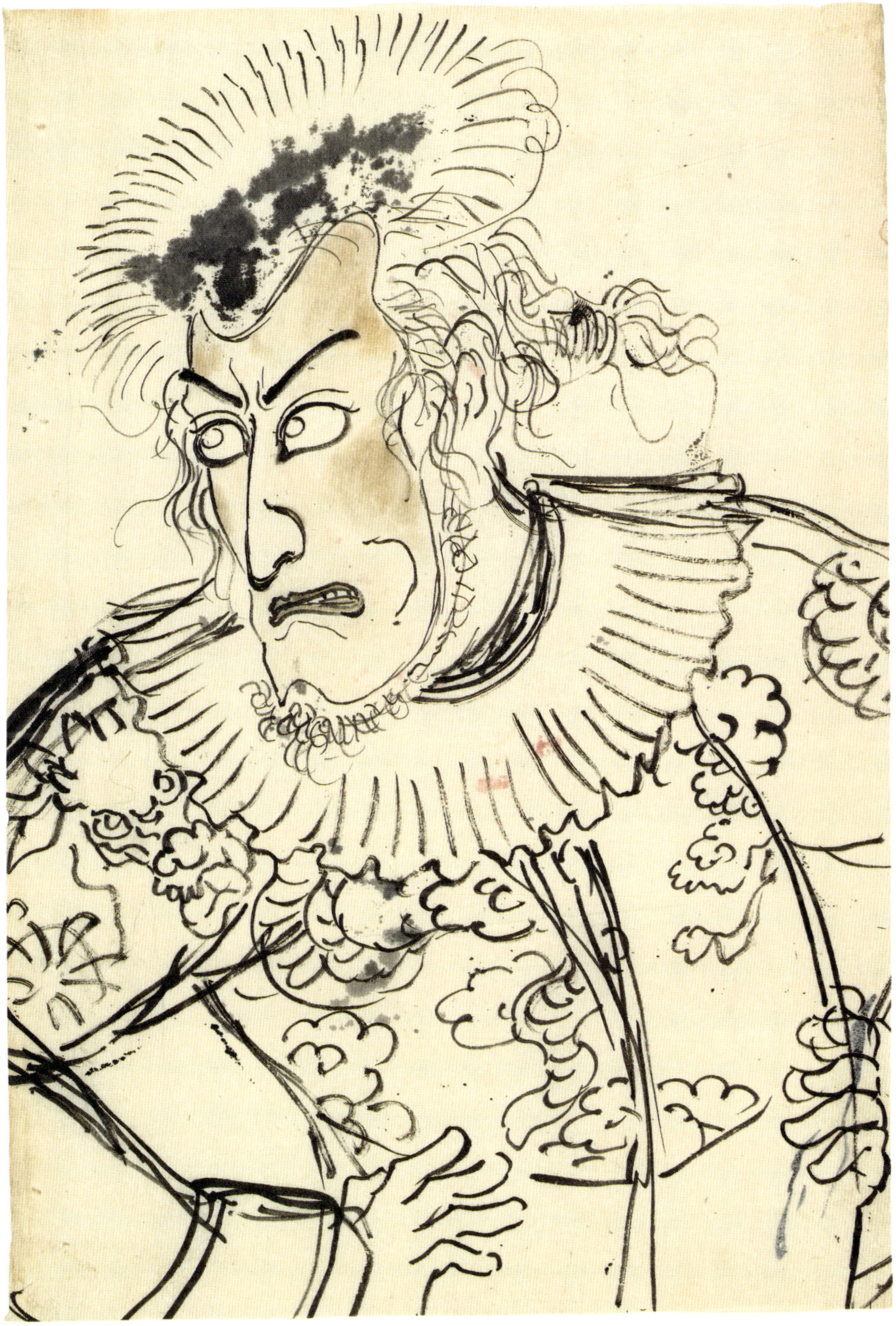

109

Preparatory drawing for the print
'Ichikawa Ebizō V as Kezori Kuemon'
1840

Ink and slight colour on paper,
31.5 × 22.1 cm

Jeffrey Pollard and Ooi-Thye Chong Collection, USA

REFERENCES
Sotheby's 1993, lot 268; Amsterdam 1998, no. 160

Kuniyoshi's vigorously brushed lines look set to jump off the page in this preparatory drawing for the portrait of Ebizō V as Kuemon (cat. 108). The sheet has almost certainly been trimmed on all sides, giving the figure even greater prominence than in the print. Ebizō V (Danjūrō VII) had especially large eyes, and stage glares (*nirami*) belonged among the specialities of the Danjūrō line of actors. The drawing shows Kuniyoshi boldly reworking the outlines of the arms and collar several times in search of a suitably strong pose, whereas the facial features seem to have come to him more easily, doubtless because he was following the conventional 'likeness' (*nigao*) established by artists for depicting individual actors. The lines of the beard and wig, although rudimentary, are highly expressive. A cloud-like smudge of black ink suffices to indicate the wig's mop of bristling hair. The pale red highlights on the face were reproduced in the finished print, using an extra block for this subtle colour effect.

The drawing was originally the forty-eighth in a collection of fifty pasted into a scrap-album that bore the title 'Kuniyoshi rough sketches, no. 37' (*Kuniyoshi sōkō, sanjū-shichi*) in large written characters on its cover. This 'no. 37' came from a group of five such albums sold at auction in 1993 and then broken up (Sotheby's 1993), one of which was inscribed 'no. 60'. Two similar albums, 'no. 39' and 'no. 48' (see pp. 28 and 29, fig. 15), have survived intact in the Victoria and Albert Museum, London, which purchased them in 1889 from the Paris dealer Siegfried Bing. A large group of loose-leaf drawings by Kuniyoshi, formerly in the collection of Ferdinand Lieftinck (1879–1959), was acquired by the National Museum of Ethnology, Leiden, in 1958 (Robinson 1953; Forrer 1988, pp. 18–19). Many of them may have been removed from similar albums. It has been suggested that the albums either functioned as a studio reference during Kuniyoshi's lifetime or were assembled by pupils as a record after his death. Evidently, at least sixty existed, each probably containing some thirty to fifty working drawings.

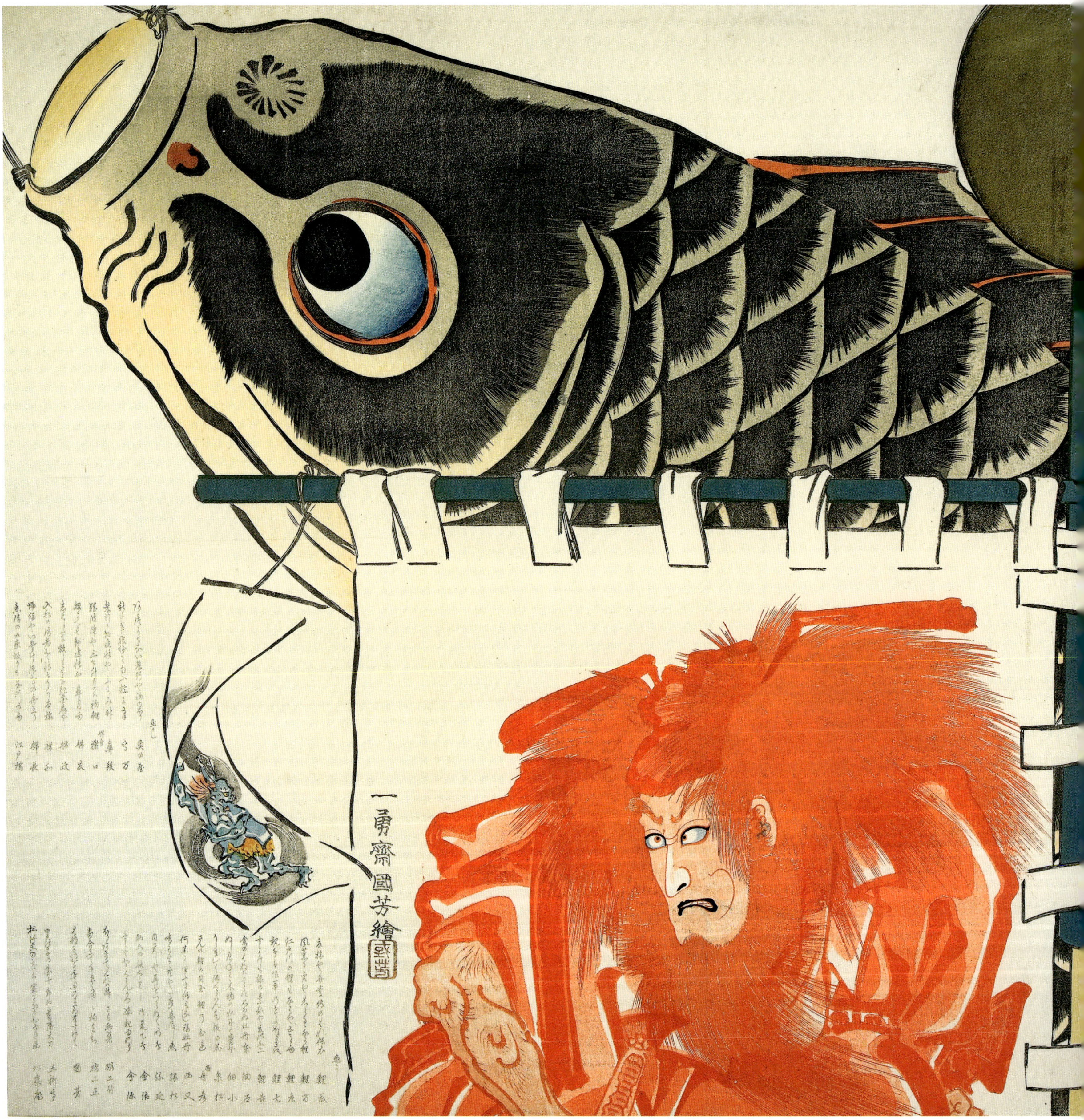
一勇齋國芳繪

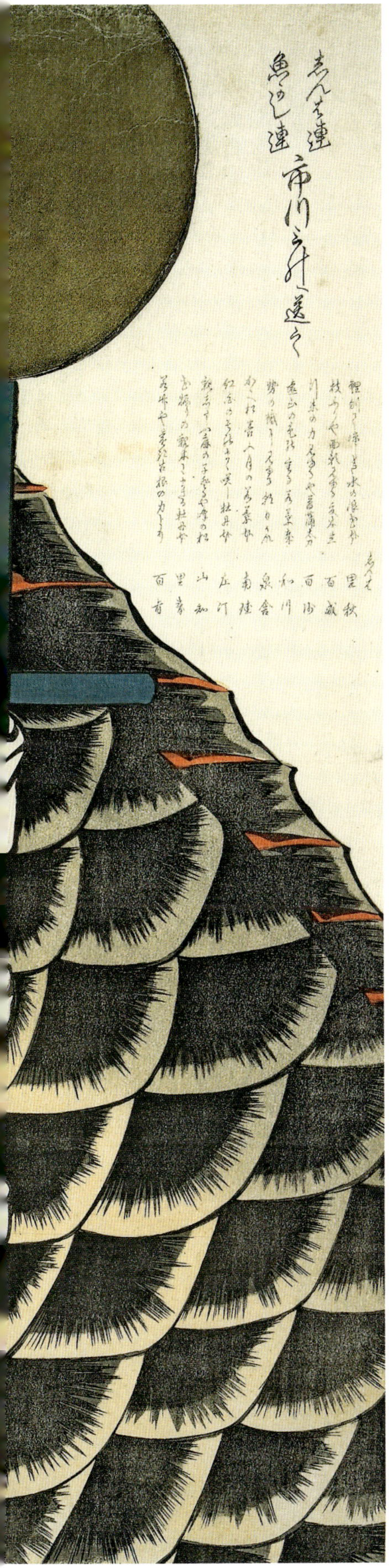

110

Shōki banner and carp streamer for the Boys' Festival

1849

Colour woodblock with metallic pigment and embossing, *zenshi-ban surimono*, 43.2 × 56.6 cm

PRINT TITLE
'Gift from the Shinba and Uogashi Clubs to Ichikawa Sanshō [Danjūrō VIII]' (*Shinba-ren Uogashi-ren Ichikawa Sanshō e kore o okuru*)

ARTIST'S SIGNATURE
Ichiyūsai Kuniyoshi e (picture by Ichiyūsai Kuniyoshi, on banner)

ARTIST'S SEAL
Kuniyoshi (on banner)

The British Museum, JA 1906.12-20.01342 (Arthur Morrison Collection)

REFERENCES
Springfield 1968, no. 131; Riccar 1978, no. 293; Springfield 1980, no. 195; HUT, vol. 3, 1988, no. 55; Suzuki 1992, no. 461; Itabashi 1994; Kuniyoshi no. 117; Mainichi Shinbunsha 1995, no. 192; Nagoya 1996, no. 224; Amsterdam 1998, no. 199; Ōta 1999, no. 182; Isao 2008, p. 83

A giant carp streamer appears to leap over the bristling figure of Shōki the Demon-queller (Zhong Kui in his native China), who is painted in red on a cloth banner attached to a pole capped by a metal ball. Families placed such streamers and banners outside their houses for the Boys' Festival, celebrated each year on the fifth day of the fifth lunar month.

Several hundred copies of this grand, privately commissioned *surimono* would have been printed, to honour the young Kabuki star Ichikawa Danjūrō VIII (Sanshō). The commission came from two groups of haiku poets, the Shinba and Uogashi, whose members were mostly prosperous Edo fish merchants. Following successful farewell performances in Edo in the third month, 1849, Danjūrō VIII was about to visit his father in Osaka. Danjūrō VII had been living there in exile for most of the period since 1842, when he had fallen foul of sumptuary laws issued as part of the Tenpō reforms.

The *surimono* contains many witty elements and is most lavishly produced: brass powder has been printed on the metal ball and the 'stitching' on the banner's loops has been heavily embossed into the paper. Boys' Festival imagery was appropriate, since Danjūrō VIII was travelling to Osaka in the fifth month. A carp trying to leap up a waterfall symbolised manly perseverance, but was also one of the family emblems of the Danjūrō line of actors. The painting of Shōki includes facial features that would instantly have been recognised as those of Danjūrō VII by his legions of fans and it shows him performing a 'stage glare' (*nirami*) to frighten the small demon painted on the dangling paper tag. Images of Shōki printed or painted in red were thought to ward off smallpox.

The Shinba group's poems appear in the top right corner, those by the Uogashi group at bottom left. The verses mainly praise Danjūrō VIII, but the hope is also expressed that his father will soon be pardoned and permitted to return to Edo. One poem each by Kuniyoshi, the block-cutter Yokokawa Hori-Take (Takejirō) and the printer Surikō Masa appears towards the end of the Uogashi group. It is be assumed that these three collaborated on the print. Asano Shūgō notes the existence of a different printing, in which many of the Uogashi group's poems have been changed (Nagoya 1996, no. 224).

The British Museum preserves another large *surimono* produced on the same occasion. It shows an album open at portraits of Danjūrō VII and Danjūrō VIII by Kuniyoshi, surrounded by a still life of a gourd vine and a writing case by Shibata Zeshin (JA 1906.12-20.01344; reproduced in HUT, vol. 3, 1988, no. 57).

111

Teruuji at an abandoned temple

1849–51

Colour woodblock, *ōban* triptych, published by Sawaya Kōkichi, 37.6 × 25.3 [R], 37.2 × 25.3 [C], 37.6 × 25.4 cm [L]

PRINT TITLE
'Up-to-date Teruuji in an Old Picture at an Old Temple' (*Imayō Teruuji furudera no kozu*)

ARTIST'S SIGNATURE
Ichiyūsai Kuniyoshi ga (in gourd-shaped *Yoshi* cartouche)

ARTIST'S SEAL
Yoshikiri

CENSORS' SEALS
Kinugasa and Watanabe

American Friends of the British Museum (The Arthur R. Miller Collection) 18913

REFERENCES
Kondo 1982, fig. 12; Yamaguchi 1991, Kuniyoshi no. 38

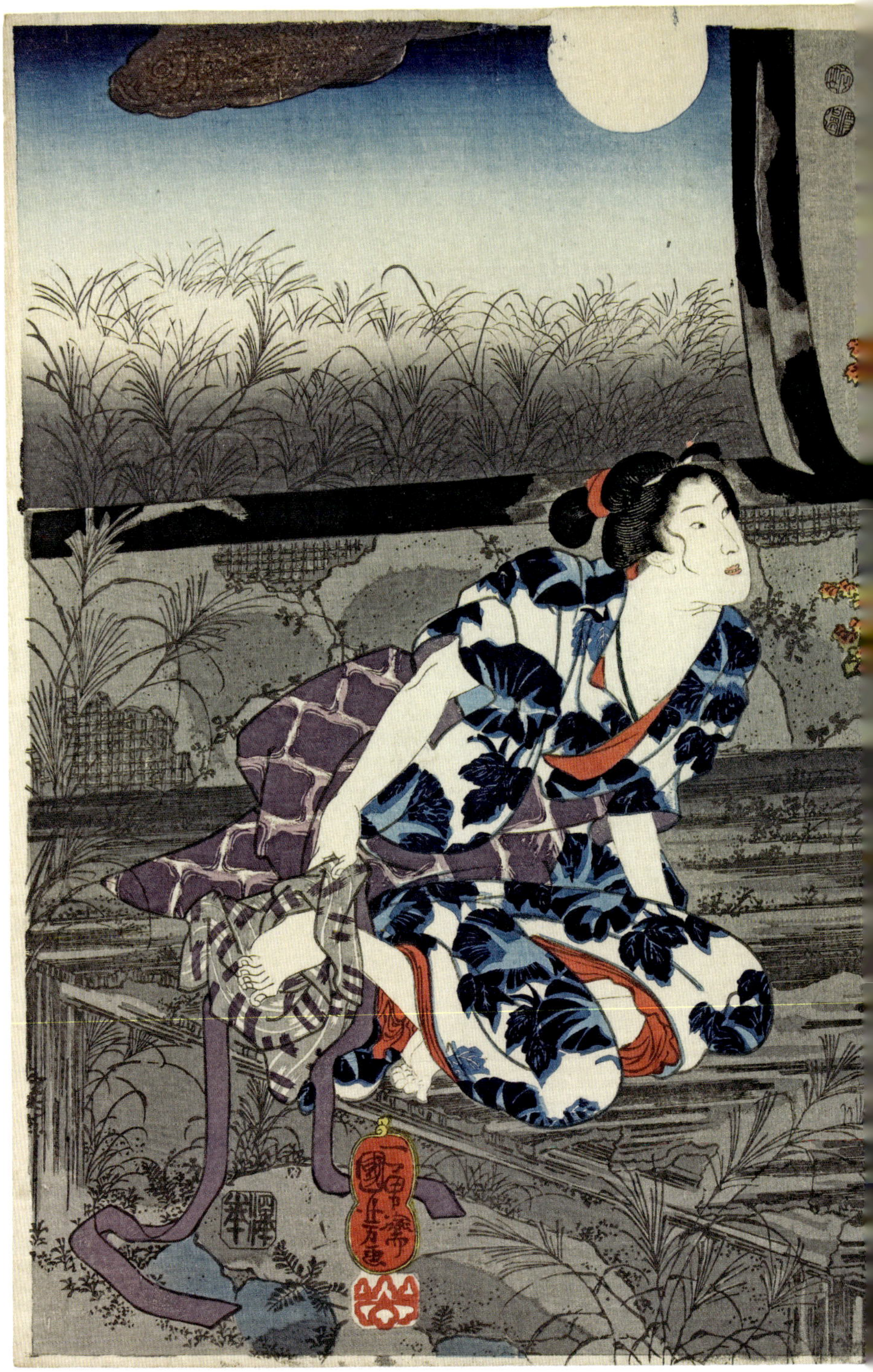

The setting is an abandoned temple on a lonely moonlit moor. Teruuji, standing in the centre, offers a hand towel to his lover Tasogare, who kneels on the ruined veranda wiping her feet with a cloth. From the next room they are spied on by a mysterious female figure dressed in the elaborate costume of a Nō drama, wielding a red and white stage 'wand' in one hand and gripping the cords of a she-devil (Hannya) mask in her teeth. She is Shinonome, Tasogare's mother, who has stolen an heirloom sword that Teruuji is searching for. In the next scene, wearing the she-devil mask, she will attack the lovers and threaten Tasogare with the sword. The design is a tour de force of cutting and printing, particularly in the way it captures the effect of the painting peeling from the sliding panels that separate the two rooms.

The phenomenally successful illustrated novel *Nise Murasaki inaka Genji* (*A Fake Murasaki and a Rustic Genji*), with text by Ryūtei Tanehiko and illustrations by Utagawa Kunisada, appeared serially in the *gōkan* format from 1829 to 1842. It was an elaborate rewriting – in some senses a parody – of the classic novel *Genji monogatari* (*Tale of Genji*) of c. 1000. The Tenpō reforms curtailed publication in 1842 and Tanehiko committed suicide the following year, possibly as a result of official harassment in response to his involvement in *Nise Murasaki inaka Genji* and its spin-off erotic works. In 1847 the publisher Tsuruya Kiemon and others began issuing a sequel entitled *Sono yukari hina no omokage* (*Linking to it, Vestiges of the Countryside*). This and other publications related to the novel of 1829–42 prompted two rival Kabuki plays on the theme, performed at the Nakamura and Ichimura theatres in the eighth and ninth months of 1851, respectively. Both productions featured a scene with Shinonome, Mitsuuji (the equivalent of Kuniyoshi's Teruuji; see below) and Tasogare accompanied by onstage musicians.

Kuniyoshi's print would not seem to depict a specific stage performance. In fact, it includes many elements borrowed from Kunisada's illustrations for the novel of 1829–42, notably the peeling painting of the court carriage (from part V, vol. 2, published in 1831). Eiko Kondo pointed out that Kuniyoshi's hero is called Teruuji, not Mitsuuji (his name in the novel), and detected in the conflation of 'Teru' and 'uji' the influence of the sequel novel of 1847, in which the hero's name was changed from Mitsuuji to Terumoto (Kondo 1982, p.87).

Kunisada was by far the most prolific artist in generating book illustrations and prints relating to the 1829–42 novel. Kuniyoshi was here responding to the craze.

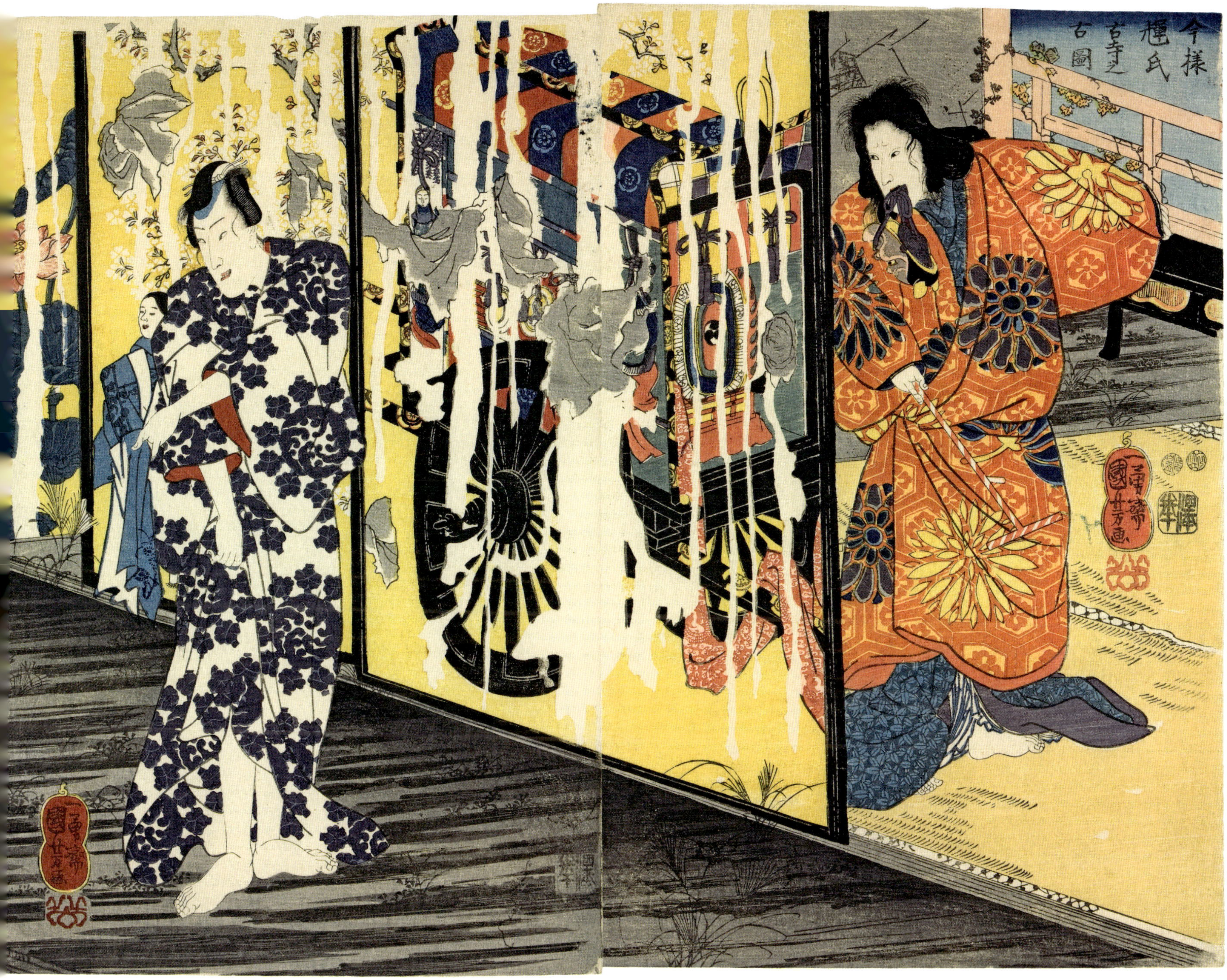
今様
櫃氏
古寺之
古圖

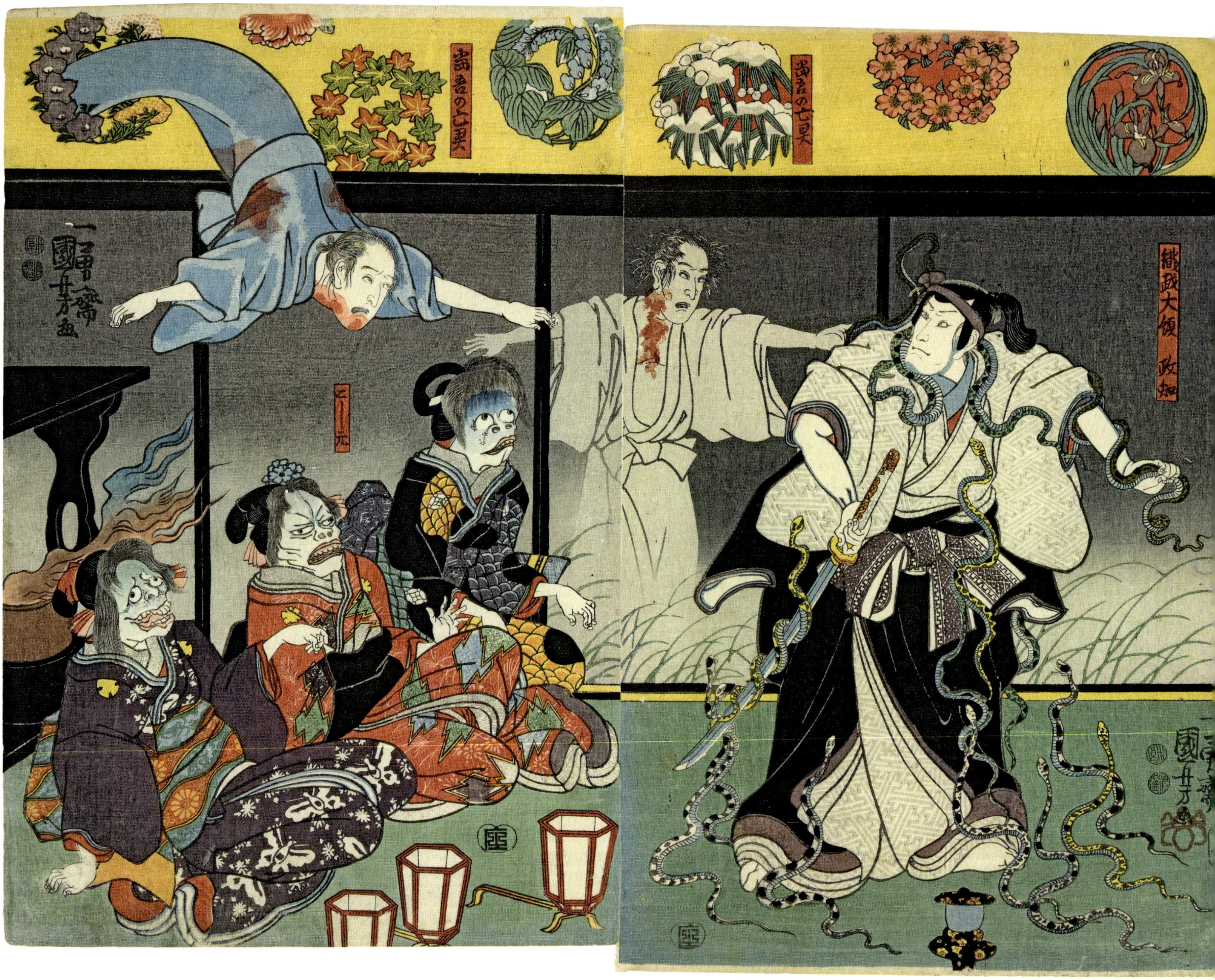

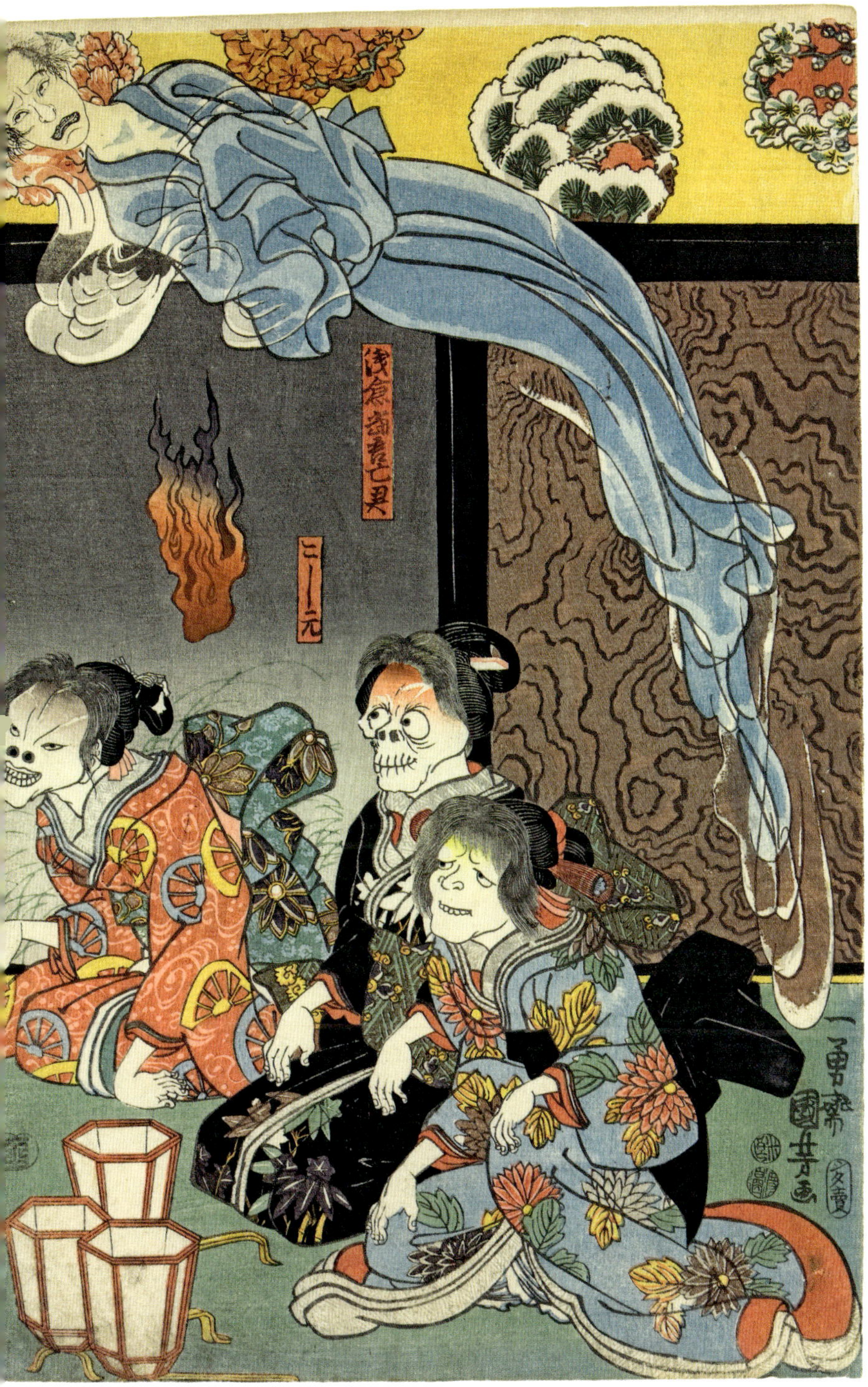

112

The ghost of Asakura Tōgo attacks Orikoshi Masatomo

1851

Colour woodblock, *ōban* triptych, published by Hayashiya Shōgoro, 37 × 25.2 [R], 36.6 × 24.9 [C], 36.6 × 25.2 cm [L]

ARTIST'S SIGNATURE
Ichiyūsai Kuniyoshi ga

ARTIST'S SEAL
Yoshikiri (paulownia crest, centre sheet)

CENSORS' SEALS
Mera and Watanabe

RETAIL SEAL
shita-uri (discreet sale)

American Friends of the British Museum (The Arthur R. Miller Collection) 19612

REFERENCES
Yamaguchi 1991, Kuniyoshi no. 33

Lord Orikoshi Masatomo (centre), played by Bandō Hikosaburō IV, wears pale clothes and a purple headband, both indicating his invalid state. He is sinking into madness, assailed from every side in his mansion by the ghost of Asakura Tōgo, played by Ichikawa Kodanji IV, who appears on all three sheets. The 'ghost' tumbles out of a trap door in the decorated panels above the sliding doors. Snakes writhe towards and over Orikoshi, one winding its way up his sword. The faces of his ladies-in-waiting (*koshimoto*), seated on either side, have turned into skulls. Tōgo had led an unsuccessful protest on behalf of the suffering farmers of Sakura, even petitioning the shogun directly, and for this he and his family were tortured and crucified. His ghost is now exacting revenge.

The play *Higashiyama Sakura sōshi* (*The Higashiyama Story Book*), performed from the eight month of 1851 at the Nakamura theatre in Edo, was enormously popular, running for more than a hundred days. Written by Segawa Jokō III, it interwove a well-known account of an actual farmers' revolt in the 1640s with *Nise Murasaki inaka Genji* (*A Fake Murasaki and a Rustic Genji*), a version of the classic Genji novel then in vogue (see cat. 111). It belonged among the few Kabuki plays of the Edo period that dealt directly with the problems of the rural poor, and the element of protest it contained has been seen as evidence of the authorities' weakening power in the years following the Tenpō reforms. The seal 'discreet sale' (*shita-uri*) on the centre and right sheets of Kuniyoshi's triptych was probably applied together with the censors' seals. It was used sporadically from the third month of 1850 to the twelfth of 1853, apparently to reinforce an instruction to print shops not to display actor prints prominently. It may have been timed to coincide with the return of Ichikawa Ebizō V from exile (Iwakiri 2002, pp. 27–9).

Kuniyoshi designed a number of prints related to the play: the Miller Collection alone contains three more triptychs, showing farmers protesting in front of Orikoshi's mansion (19813), the torture of Tōgo and his family (19812) and another scene with the haunting of the ailing Orikoshi (19505). Perhaps the artist sympathised strongly with the farmers. Three acts of the play have appeared in English translation (Brandon and Leiter 2002, pp. 220–7).

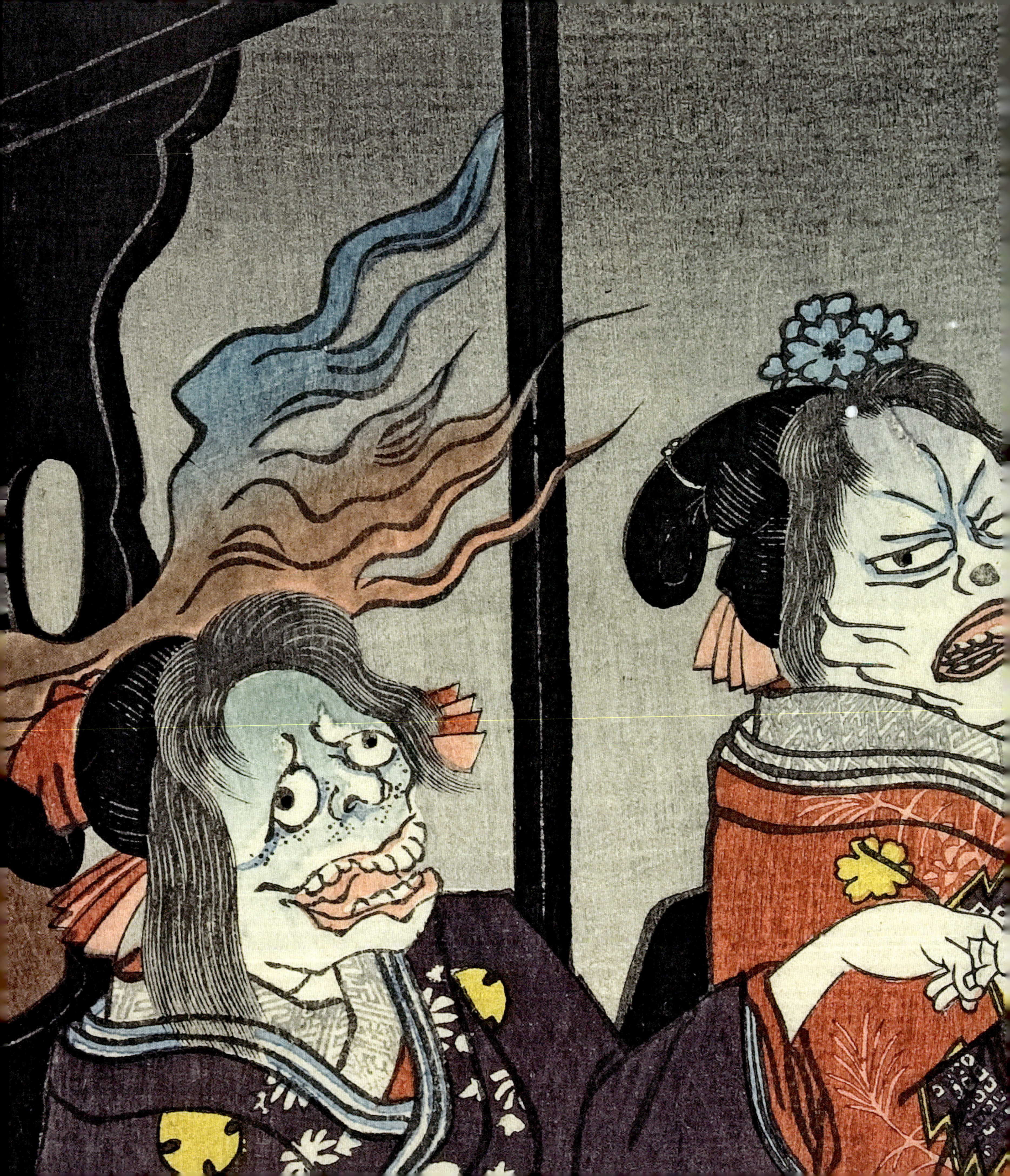

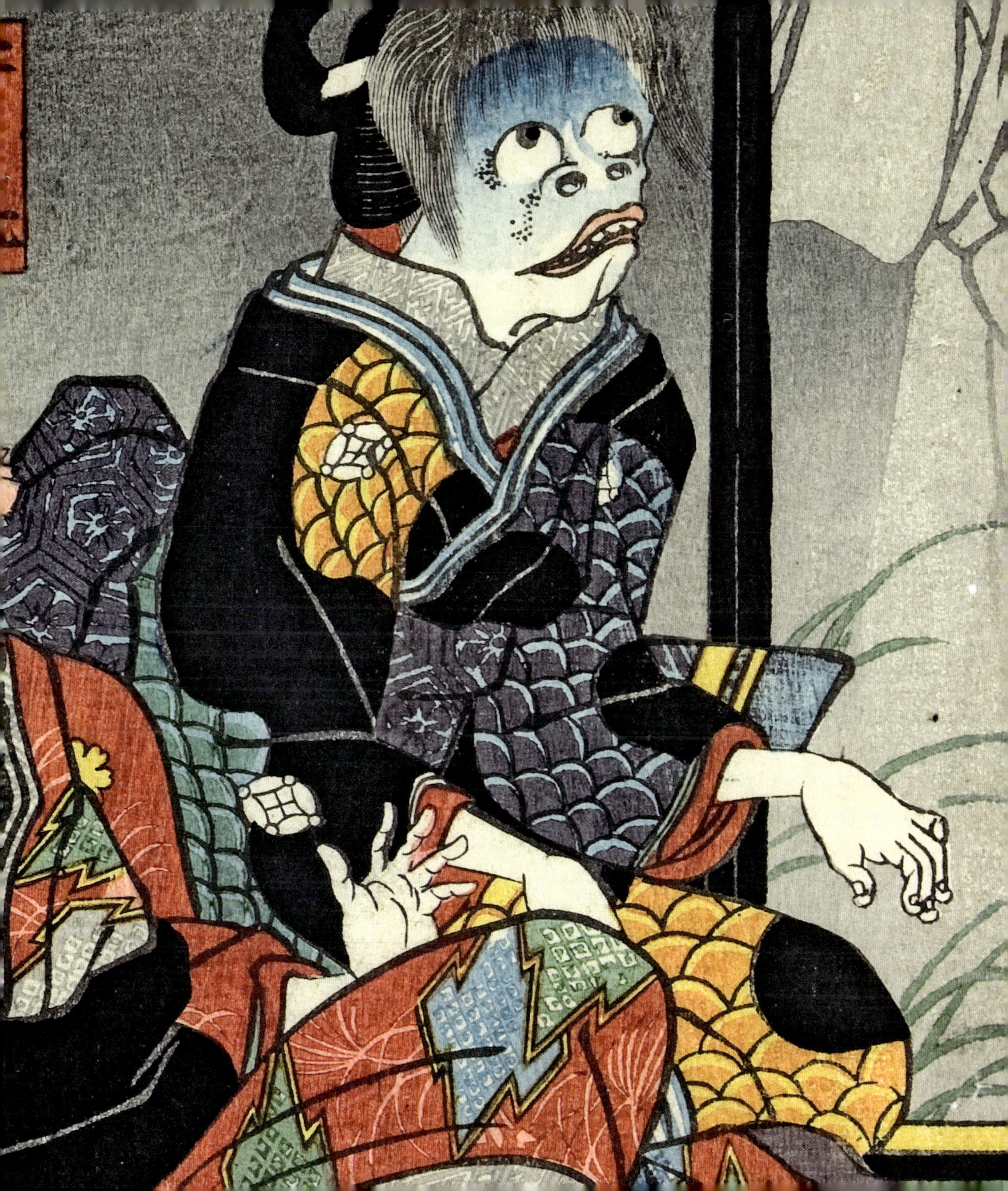

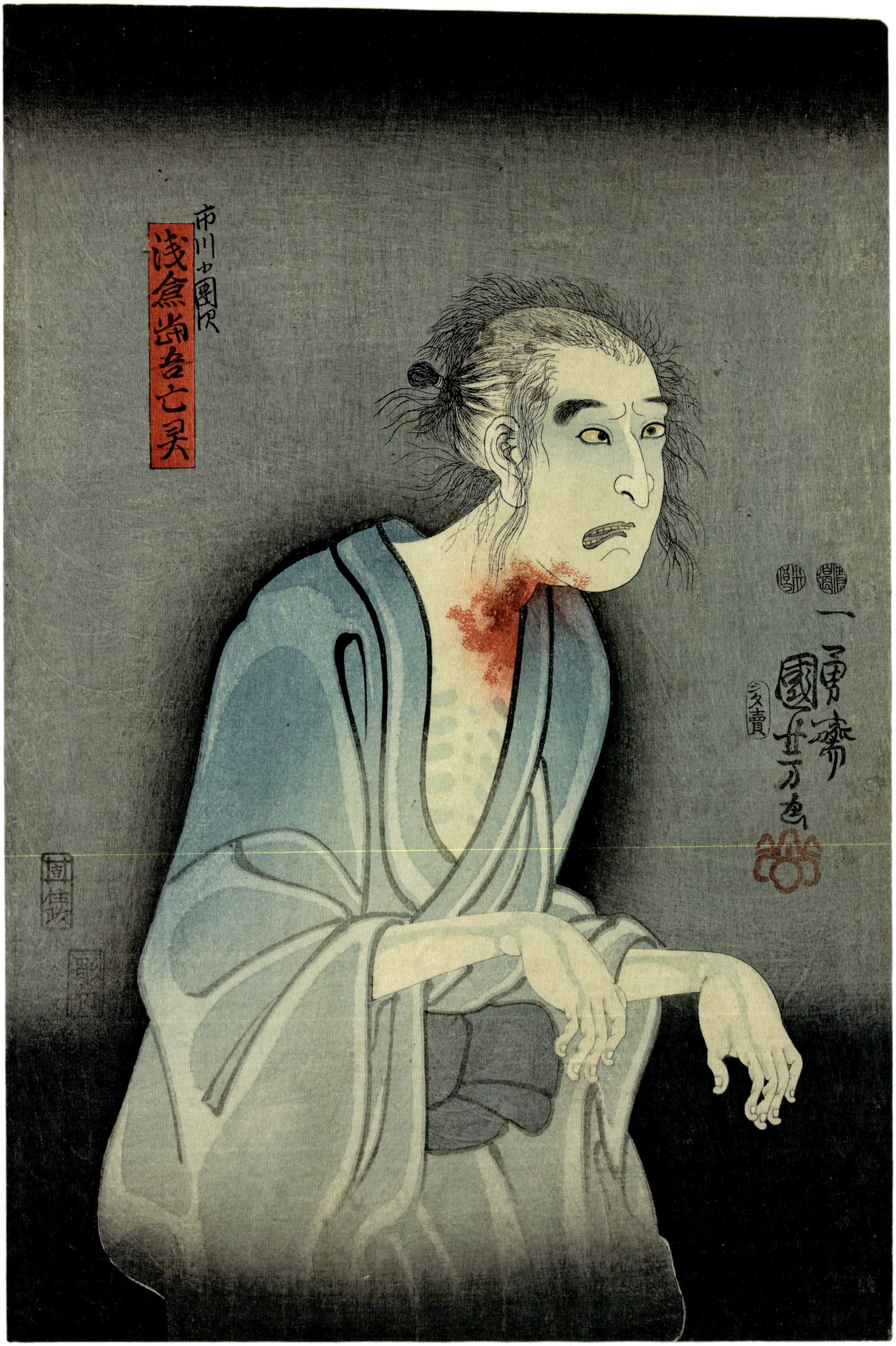
市川小團次
浅倉当吾亡霊
一勇齋國芳画

113

Kabuki actor Ichikawa Kodanji IV as the ghost of Asakura Tōgo

1851

Colour woodblock, *ōban*, published by Sumiyoshiya Masagorō, 36.5 × 24.8 cm

ARTIST'S SIGNATURE
Ichiyūsai Kuniyoshi ga

ARTIST'S SEAL
Yoshikiri

BLOCK-CUTTER'S SEAL
Hori-Take (Yokokawa Takejirō)

CENSORS' SEALS
Mera and Watanabe

RETAIL SEAL
shita-uri (discreet sale)

American Friends of the British Museum (The Arthur R. Miller Collection) 21325

REFERENCES
(left sheet only) Robinson 1961, no. 76; Springfield 1968, no. 135; Itabashi 1994, Kuniyoshi no. 54; Amsterdam 1998, no. 177; (both sheets) Riccar 1978, no. 292; Yamaguchi 1991, Kuniyoshi nos 31–2; Suzuki 1992, nos 313–14; Mainichi Shinbunsha 1995, no. 136; Nagoya 1996, no. 129; Madison 2007, no. 120

This wonderfully gruesome image shows the ghost of Asakura Tōgo played by Ichikawa Kodanji IV. Looming out of the shadows, he has come to assail Lord Orikoshi Masatomo, who had ordered Tōgo's torture and crucifixion for leading a farmers' protest (see also cat. 112). A companion sheet (below) shows Bandō Hikosaburō IV as Orikoshi, who is losing his reason and has drawn his sword to repel the ghost's attack.

The print testifies to the outstanding skill of 'Carver Take' (Hori-Take), the trade name of the master block-cutter Yokokawa Takejirō, whose seal nestles modestly in the shade behind the ghost's back. His cutting of the ghost's thin, wispy hair is particularly effective. The unknown printer made an important contribution to the success of the image, the smooth transition from figure to shadow at the bottom, the black 'halo' around the shoulders and the congealed blood at the neck all adding to its ghoulishness. A touch of glue was printed on each sickly eye. A previous owner has written the actor's name in brush characters at top left, next to the red cartouche containing the printed role name.

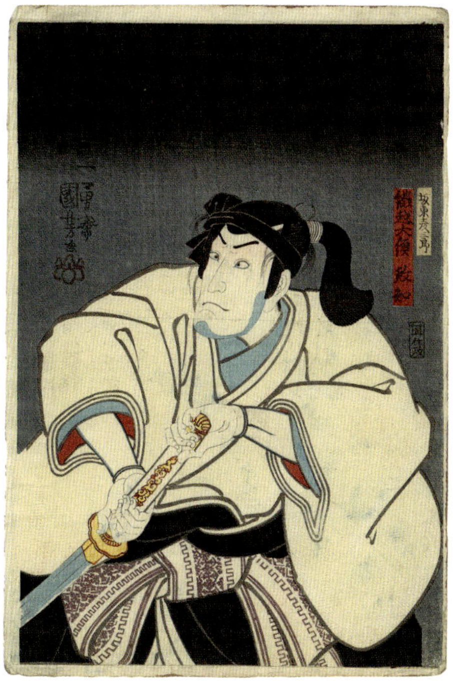

Bandō Hikosaburō IV as Orikoshi Dairyō Masatomo, 1851. Colour woodblock print, published by Sumiyoshiya Masagoro, 37.1 × 25.7 cm.
Museum of Fine Arts, Boston (William Sturgis Bigelow Collection), 11.38270

THIRTY-SIX FASHIONABLE RESTAURANTS IN EDO

(Cats 114, 115)

Each print features a half-length portrait of a Kabuki actor in a role. The role is given in every case, but lingering censorship restrictions forbade the actors to be named. However, famous performers would be recognised by their fans, since print artists consistently rendered their 'likeness' (*nigao*) in the same way. Across the top of each design is an inset landscape showing a famous restaurant in the city of Edo. These were drawn by Kuniyoshi's daughters, Tori and Yoshi, or by other pupils of his. The district is mentioned, but not always the restaurant, apparently as an invitation to the viewer to deduce its name from that of the role or from the accessories carried by the actor. The series, its title containing a punning reference to the classical Thirty-six Immortals of Poetry (*Sanjū-rokkasen*; see cats 56–8), was a collaborative venture between the publishers Yamamoto Heikichi, Yamaguchiya Tōbei and Mitaya Kihachi. Sixteen of the projected thirty-six designs have been identified (personal communication from Iwakiri Yuriko). They bear date seals ranging from the eleventh month of 1852 to the second month of 1853.

In the intercalary second month of 1852 Kunisada began designing a series of half-length actor portraits set against reworked versions of Hiroshige's well-known landscape views of the Tōkaidō road, originally published some twenty years previously. The overwhelmingly positive public response encouraged Kunisada to produce similar portraits with landscapes in the course of the summer, grouping them into series on ever more inventive themes. That year he created more than three hundred such designs, each series issued by several publishers in collaboration (Izzard 1993, p. 173). Kuniyoshi was moved to produce series of the same kind to meet the apparently insatiable demand. In a series such as 'Auspicious Pictures of Land and Sea' (*Sankai medetai zue*; cats 71–3), published in the seventh and eight months of 1852, he applied the successful formula to prints of beautiful women.

114

Kabuki actor Onoe Kikugorō III as Old Man Kasahara

1852

Colour woodblock, *ōban*, published by Yamamoto Heikichi, 37.4 × 25.7 cm

PRINT TITLE
'Nihonbashi, Kasahara-ō'

SERIES TITLE
'Thirty-six Fashionable Restaurants in Edo' (*Tōto ryūkō sanjūroku kaiseki*)

ARTIST'S SIGNATURE
Ichiyūsai Kuniyoshi ga (in gourd-shaped *Yoshi* cartouche)

ARTIST'S SEAL
Yoshikiri

CENSORS' SEALS
Mera and Watanabe

DATE SEAL
11th month, 1852

American Friends of the British Museum (The Arthur R. Miller Collection) 00201

REFERENCES
Keyes 1989, no. 227

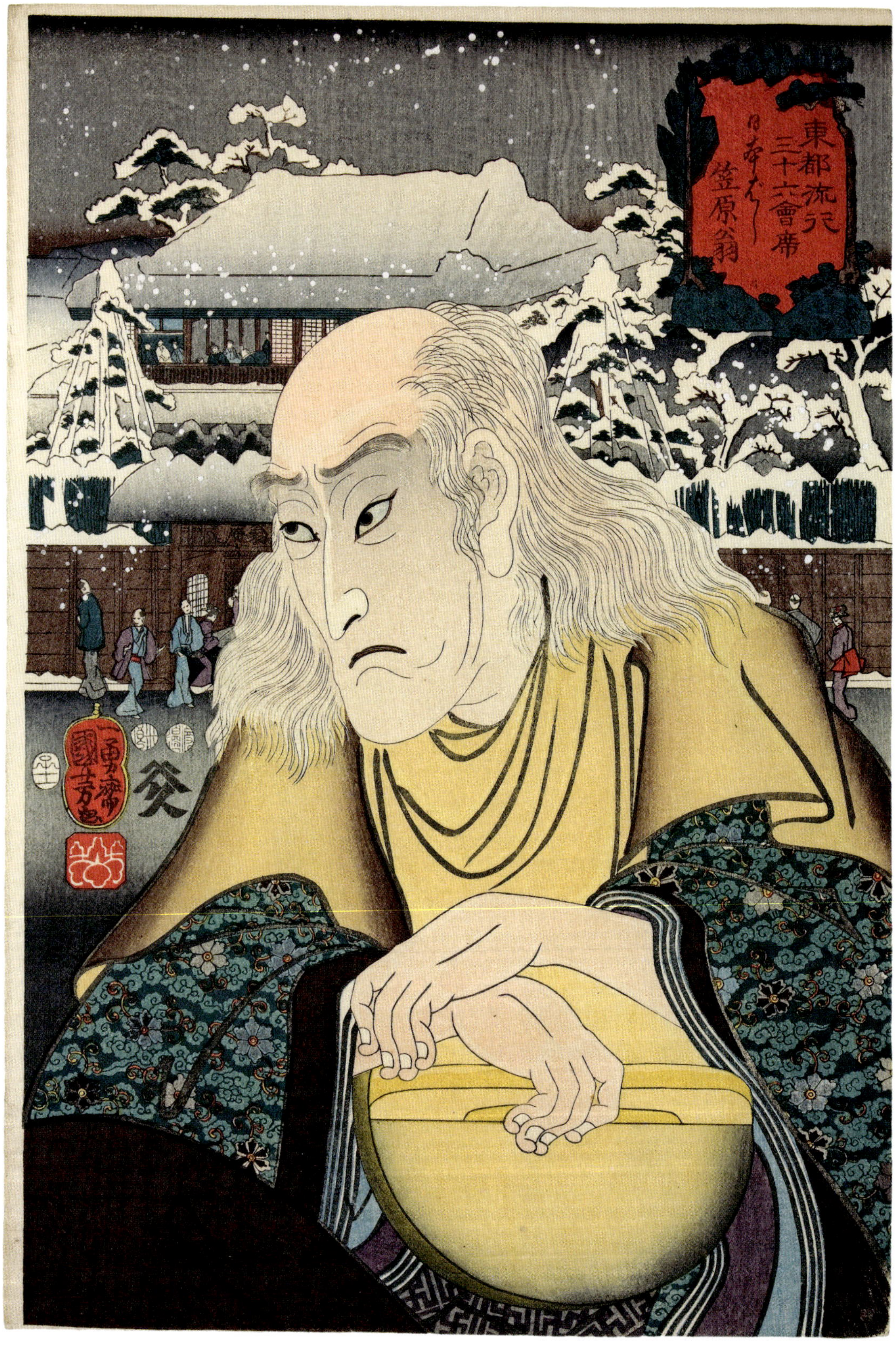

This is a posthumous portrait of Onoe Kikugorō III (1784–1849), who had been much admired for the delicacy and realism of his acting, especially in the supernatural roles in which he excelled (cats 106, 107). Here he plays Kasahara-ō (Kasahara Zuiōken; Old Man Kasahara), a sword master who in Kabuki teaches the warrior Miyamoto Musashi to fight with a weapon in each hand. Kasahara gets Musashi to practice against a wooden pot lid, which he is holding in the print. Thus prepared, Musashi takes revenge on his father's killer, Sasaki Ganryū. In reality, Miyamoto Musashi (1584?–1645) was a renowned warrior, who founded the 'Two Sword School' (Nitōryū) of swordsmanship.

The name of the restaurant appears on the signboard hanging in the gateway, barely visible to the left of the actor's eyes: 'Okina-an' ('Cottage of the Old Man'), evidently a punning reference to the name of the Kabuki character. The old man's portrait is drawn with considerable gravitas, even pathos, and his long white hair has been sensitively rendered by the block cutter. In this early printing thick white pigment has been flicked over the background landscape to suggest falling snow.

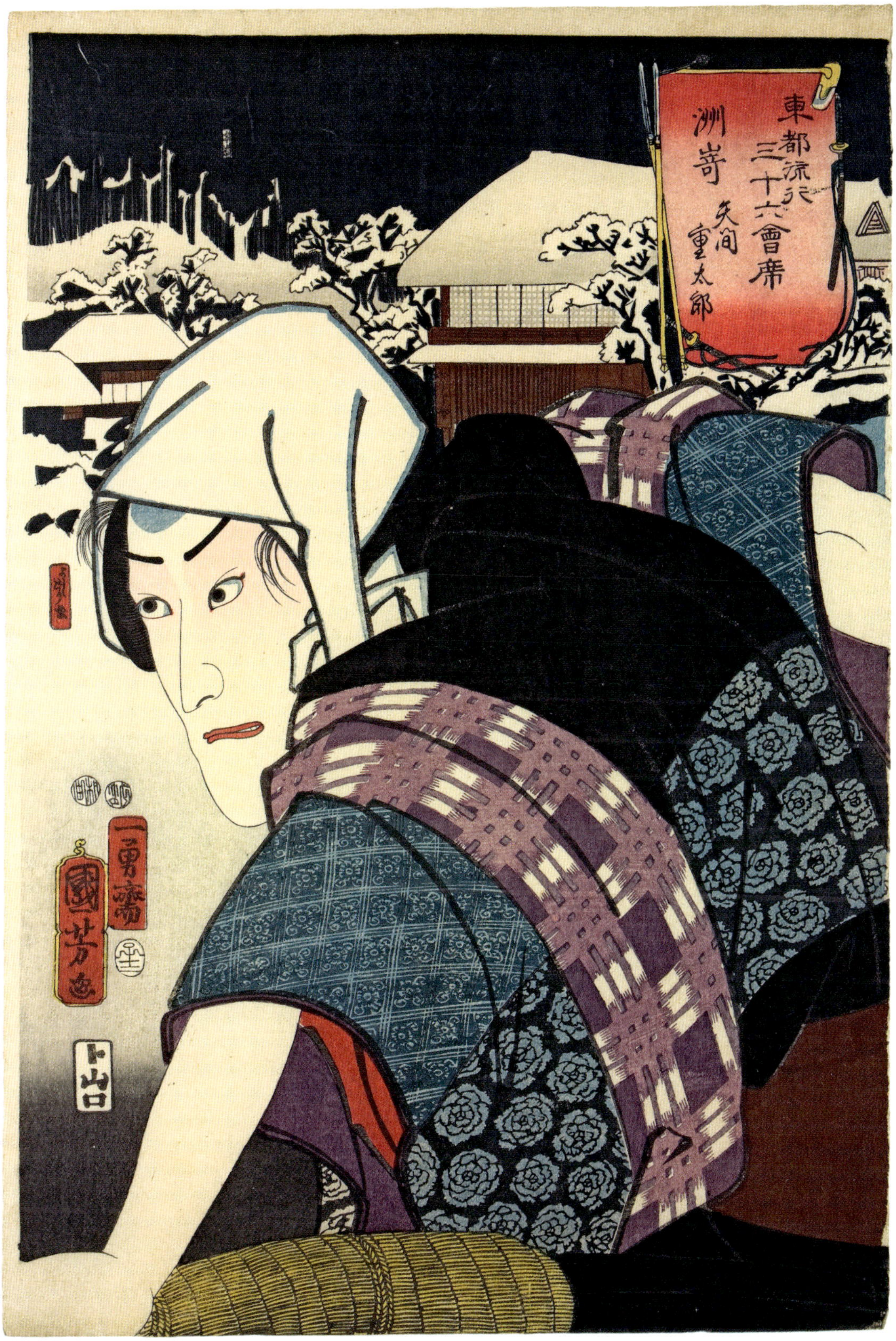

115

Kabuki actor Ichikawa Danjūrō VIII
as Yazama Jūtarō
1852

Colour woodblock, *ōban*,
published by Yamaguchiya Tōbei,
37.6 × 25.8 cm

SERIES TITLE
'Thirty-six Fashionable Restaurants in Edo'
(*Tōto ryūkō sanjūroku kaiseki*)

PRINT TITLE
'Suzaki, Yazama Jūtarō'

ARTIST'S SIGNATURE
Ichiyūsai Kuniyoshi ga
(in double rectangular *Yoshi* cartouche)

ARTIST'S SIGNATURE (INSET LANDSCAPE)
Yoshitori ga

CENSORS' SEALS
Kinugasa and Murata

DATE SEAL
12th month, 1852

American Friends of the British Museum
(The Arthur R. Miller Collection) 00208

Yazama Jūtarō is one of the forty-seven loyal retainers who avenged the death of their lord, Enya Hangan, in the Akō vendetta of 1701–03 (see cats 41–9). Disguised as an outcast (*hinin*), he is shown secretly delivering a bundle of swords concealed in a straw bale. Unbeknown to Jūtarō, his wife, O-Rie, has become a streetwalker in order to support Jūtarō's aged parents while he is in hiding. The two meet by accident on a snowy night and O-Rie tries in vain to persuade her husband to come home. The moral of the scene is clear: neither should be ashamed of their lowly status as outcast or streetwalker, since it furthers their cause of avenging Jūtarō's lord (Herwig and Mostow 2007, pp.218–19).

Ichikawa Danjūrō VIII performed the role in *Chūkō kanagaki kōshaku* (*A Lecture on Loyalty in Simple Language*) at the Kawarasaki theatre, Edo, from the eleventh month, 1852. This play was a variant of the famous *Kanadehon chūshingura*, a drama on the subject of the Akō vendetta written in 1748. In the print Danjūrō VIII's handsome features stare out resolutely from beneath the raffish headscarf: this may be the moment when he meets his wife and realises she has become a prostitute. Roles of robbers and ne'er-do-wells were this actor's forte.

Susaki was an entertainment neighbourhood along the waterfront of Fukagawa, overlooking Edo bay. The Kiba lumber yards can be seen behind the snow-covered buildings in the background landscape by Yoshitori.

116

Kabuki actor Ichikawa Danjūrō VIII as Misuji no Tsunagorō (left)

1851

Colour woodblock, *ōban* diptych, published by Sanoya Kihei, 37.8 × 25.7 [R], 37.8 × 25.2 cm [L]

ARTIST'S SIGNATURE
Ichiyūsai Kuniyoshi ga

ARTIST'S SEAL
Yoshikiri

CENSORS' SEALS
Mera and Watanabe

RETAIL SEAL
shita-uri (discreet sale)

American Friends of the British Museum (The Arthur R. Miller Collection) 18207

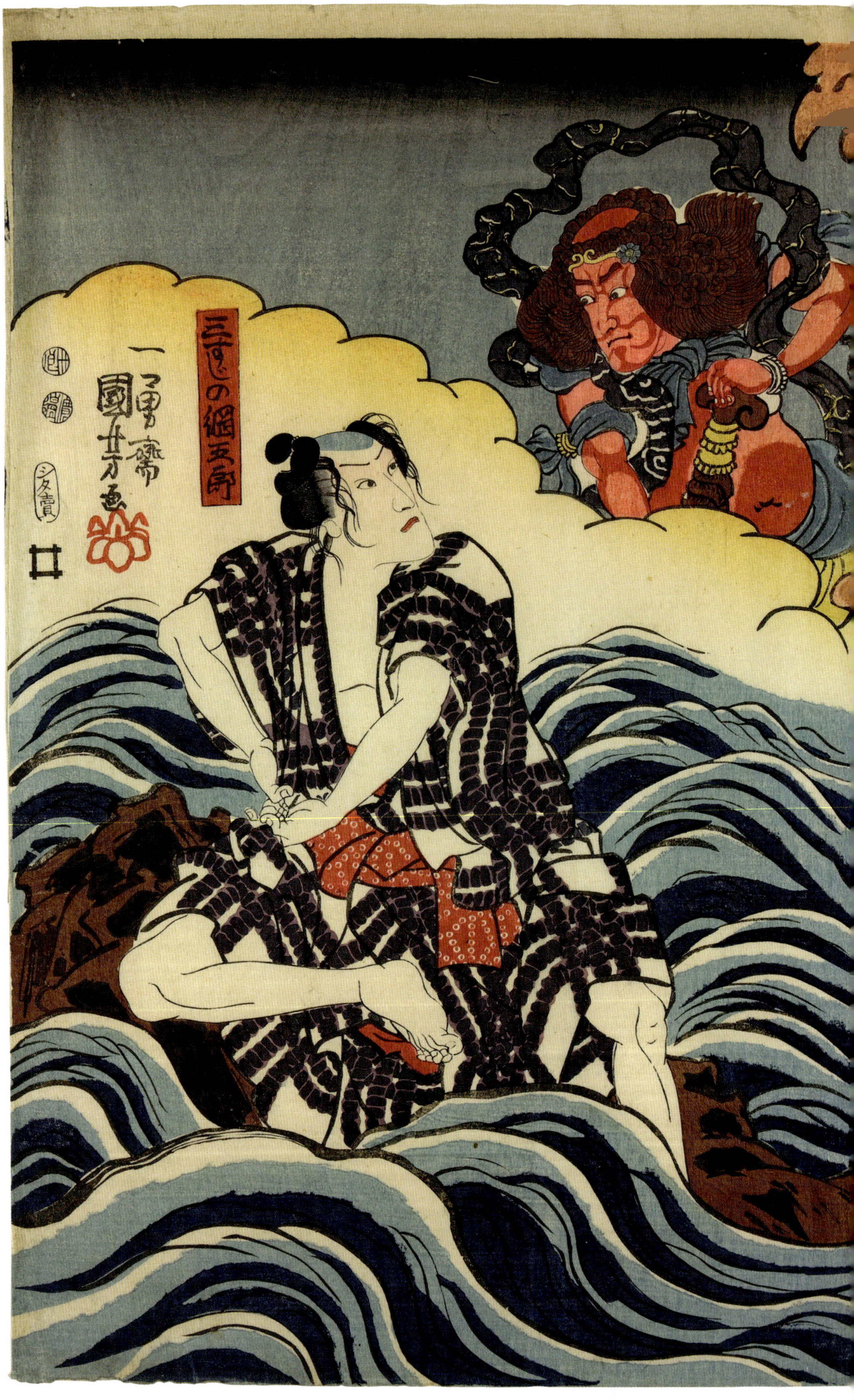

Ichikawa Danjūrō VIII was the heartthrob young Kabuki actor of his era. Fans must have been thrilled to see him depicted in this way, with wet dishevelled hair and quite scantily clad in a cotton robe, wringing out the end of one sleeve as he perches on a rock in the middle of a fast-flowing river. He looks up to the emanation in the sky of Buddhist deity Fudō Myōō, the 'Immovable King of Light', surrounded by flames and carrying a sword to cut through ignorance and a rope to snare enemies of the faith. Accompanying Fudō to the right and left are his child acolytes Kongara, played by Bandō Shūka, and Seitaka, played by Ichikawa Kuzō II.

The print names the character seated on the rock as Misuji no Tsunagorō. This suggests that Kuniyoshi based his design on a draft version of the play, because by the time of the performances this character had developed into 'Hiranoya Tokubei, later Honchōmaru Tsunagorō'. The play was *Shinpan koshi no shiranami* (*Newly Published: Bandit of the River Crossing*), presented at the Ichimura theatre, Edo, from the ninth month of 1851, a story that featured a female bandit and formed the second part of *Genji moyō furisode* (*hinagata*) (*Model for a Robe in Genji Pattern*), one of two rival productions mounted at the Nakamura and Ichimura theatres in the autumn of that year (see cat. 111). Theatrical records indicate that the print shows a scene in which Tokubei was rescued from drowning by Fudō's rope. They reveal further that Danjūrō VIII played both roles, Tokubei and Fudō, by performing a lightning costume change, or *haya-gawari* (*Kabuki nenpyō* 1961, pp. 553–4; *Zoku kabuki nendaiki* 1925, pp. 604–5). The part of Fudō was a speciality of the Ichikawa Danjūrō lineage and the play featured as one of the 'Eighteen Famous Kabuki Plays' (*Kabuki jūhachiban*) codified in 1832 by Danjūrō VII, when he passed on the Danjūrō acting name to his son. Close connections existed between the Danjūrō line of actors and the cult of the deity Fudō Myōō at the Narita Fudō temple. Some even regarded the actors as 'living emanations' (*bunshin*) of Fudō. In 1851 Danjūrō VIII was playing Fudō for the second time and, since he was mentioned as returning to form after illness, the performance may have been put on partly in gratitude to the deity.

Kuniyoshi designed a half-length portrait of Danjūrō VIII in the same scene, published in the seventh month of the following year, 1852, in the series 'Parody of the Twelve Zodiac Signs' (*Mitate jūnishi no uchi*). That print gives the character's name as Tsunagorō (Amsterdam 1998, no. 178).

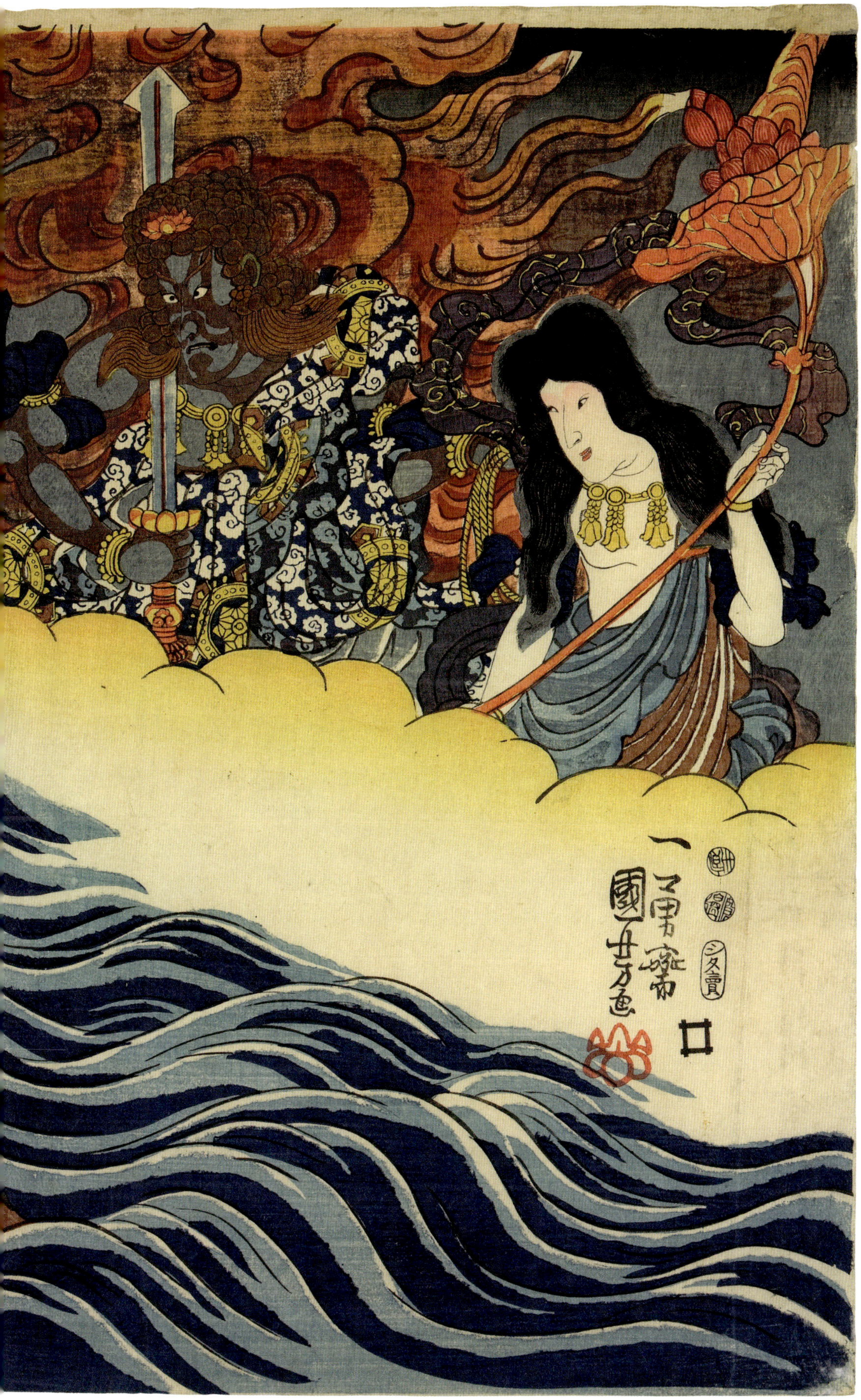
一勇斎國芳画

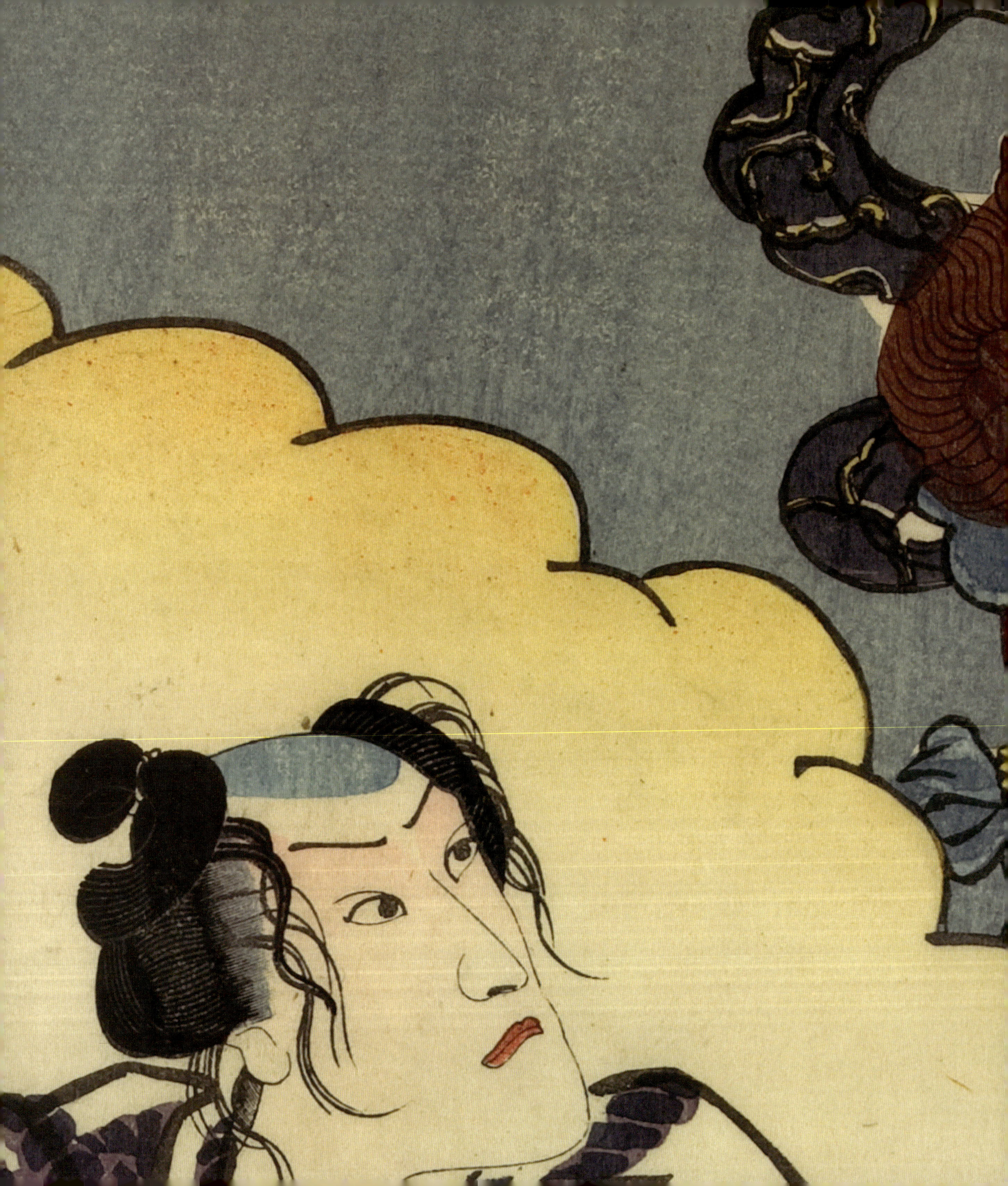

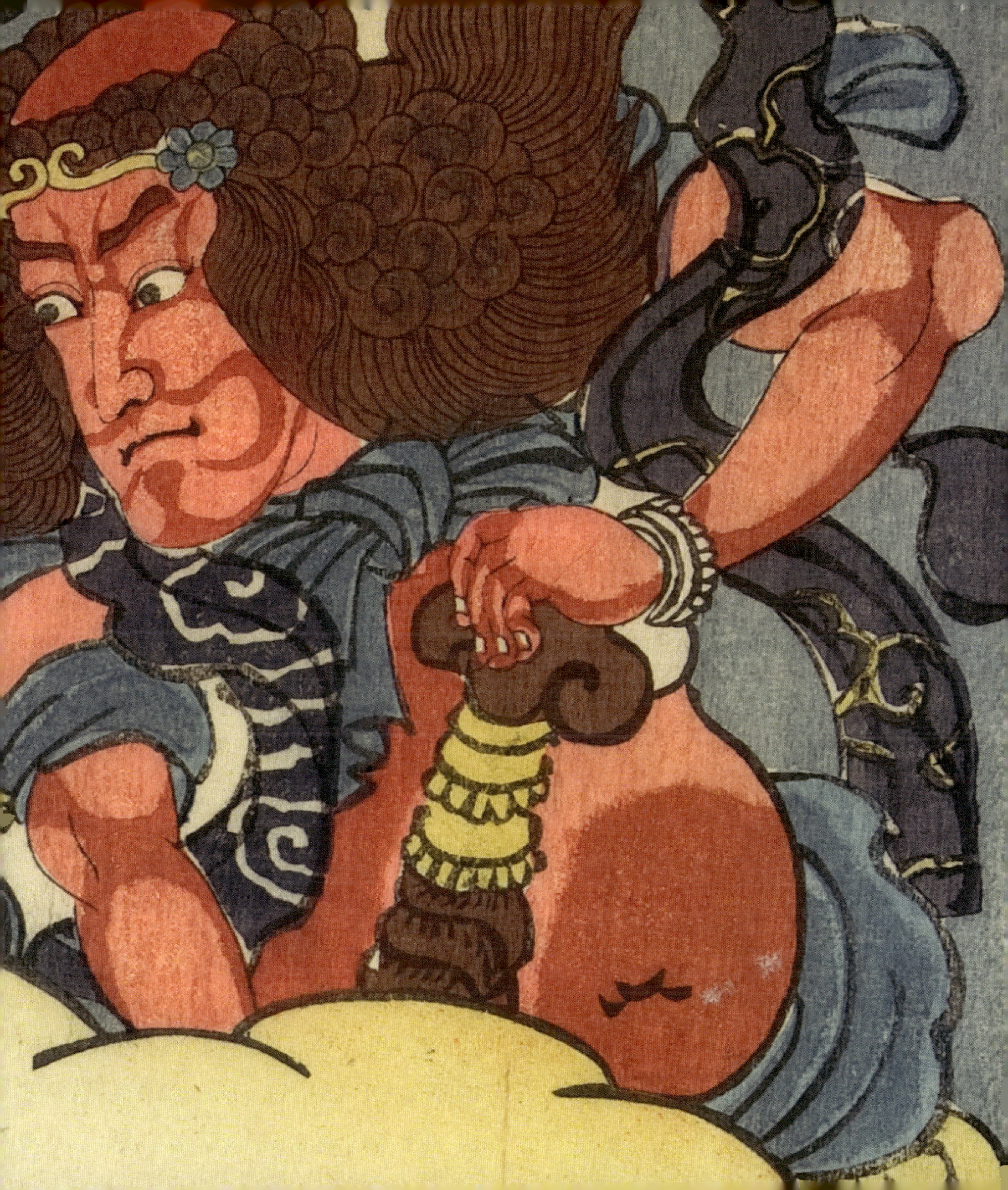

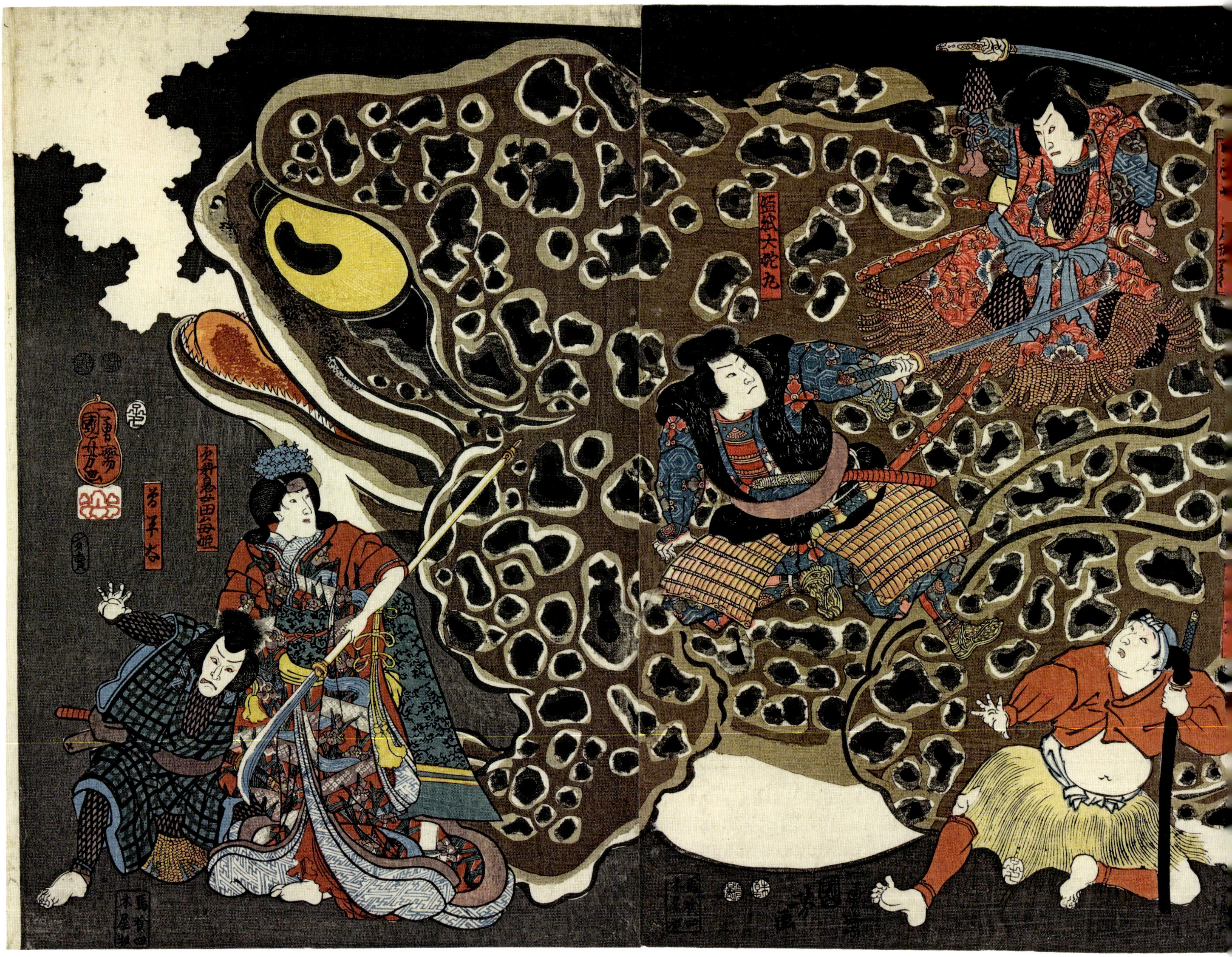

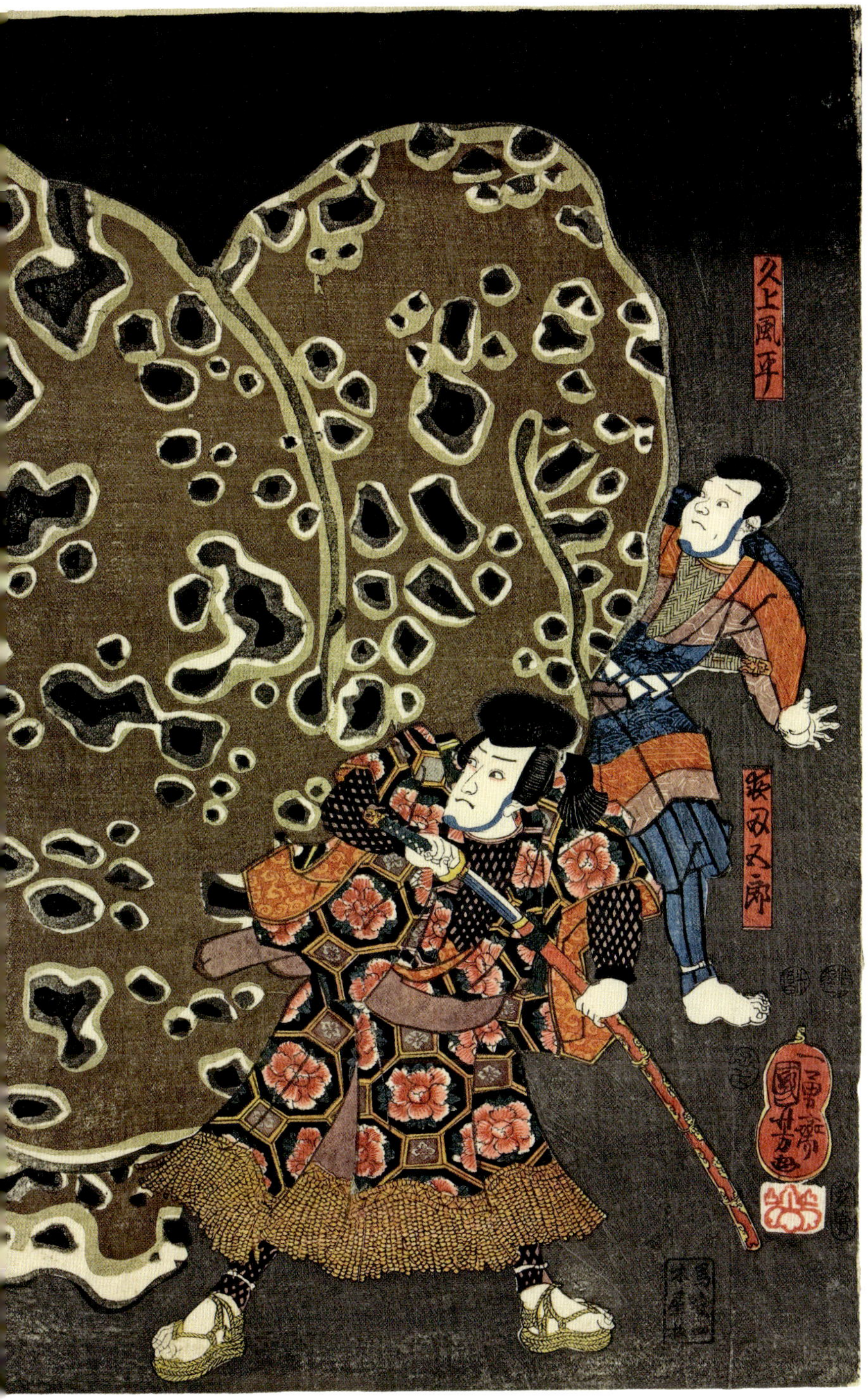

117

Kabuki actor Ichikawa Danjūrō VIII as Jiraiya (centre), with a monster toad

1852

Colour woodblock, *ōban* triptych, published by Kiya Sōjirō, 37.1 × 25.5 [R], 36.9 × 24.8 [C], 37 × 25.9 cm [L]

ARTIST'S SIGNATURE
Ichiyūsai Kuniyoshi ga (in gourd-shaped *Yoshi* cartouche)

ARTIST'S SEAL
Yoshikiri

CENSORS' SEALS
Mera and Watanabe

DATE SEAL
7th month, 1852

RETAIL SEAL
shita-uri (discreet sale)

American Friends of the British Museum (The Arthur R. Miller Collection) 19504

Swinging a sword above his head, the robber Jiraiya, played by Ichikawa Danjūrō VIII, sits on top of the giant toad in the centre sheet. In a secret hideout on Mt Myōkō he has learned the magic art of conjuring toads from his teacher, Senso Dōjin, and intends to use it to destroy his master's enemy Orochimaru, who conjures giant snakes. On the right sheet, drawing his sword, is Yashagorō, played by Ichikawa Kuzō II. Back on the centre sheet, Orochimaru, played by Arashi Rikan III, is shown climbing up the side of the toad as he lunges at Jiraiya with his sword. On the left sheet, the female role specialist Iwai Kumesaburō III plays Princess Tagoto, a halberd-wielding young samurai woman. The print does not, in fact, depict an actual stage scene and may have been issued in advance of the play *Jiraiya gōketsu monogatari* (*Tale of the Hero Jiraiya*), performed at the Kawarasaki theatre, Edo, from the seventh month of 1852.

Jiraiya was a Chinese bandit of the Ming period (1368–1644). Early nineteenth-century stories in Japan transformed him into a Japanese robber, and these tales were adapted for illustrated fiction and Kabuki theatre. A *gōkan*-format novel with the title *Jiraiya gōketsu monogatari* (*Tale of the Hero Jiraiya*), which began serial publication in 1839, enjoyed particular success. Its authors, who included Mizukaki Shōgan and Ryūkatei Tanekazu, regularly incorporated references to the actor Danjūrō VIII into the narrative. Kuniyoshi was one of several artists who illustrated the novel at different times during its publication. The immensely popular eponymous play of 1852, written by a leading playwright, Kawatake Shinshichi II (later Mokuami), and starring Danjūrō VIII, formed the culmination of endeavours to bring together the actor and the character.

Kuniyoshi based his depiction of the giant toad on an illustration of 1850 by Kunisada published in the *gōkan* novel. He expanded the double-page black and white illustration into a full-colour three-sheet print, converting the faces of the main figures into likenesses of Kabuki actors. In the event, however, no such scene was performed in the Kawarasaki production.

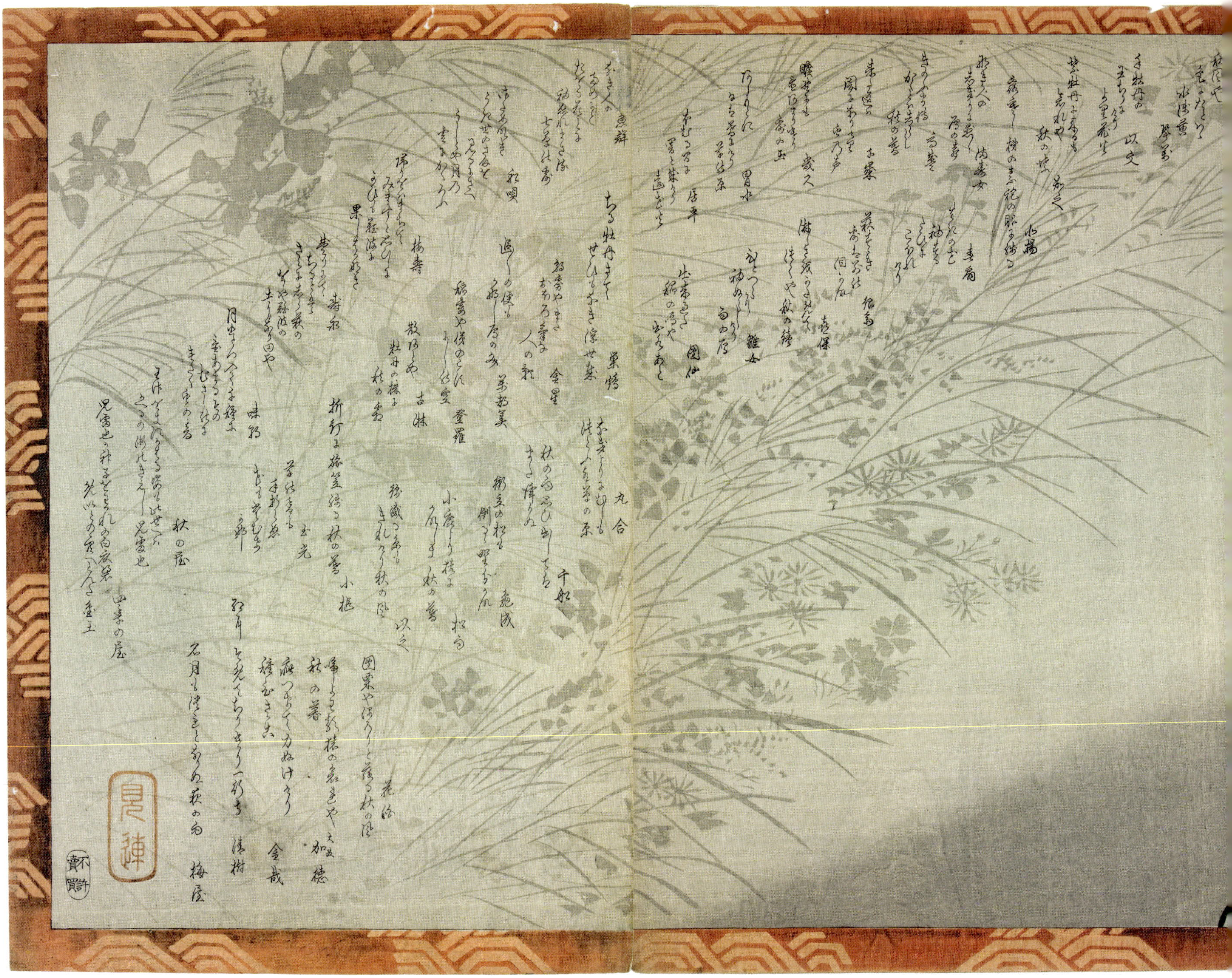

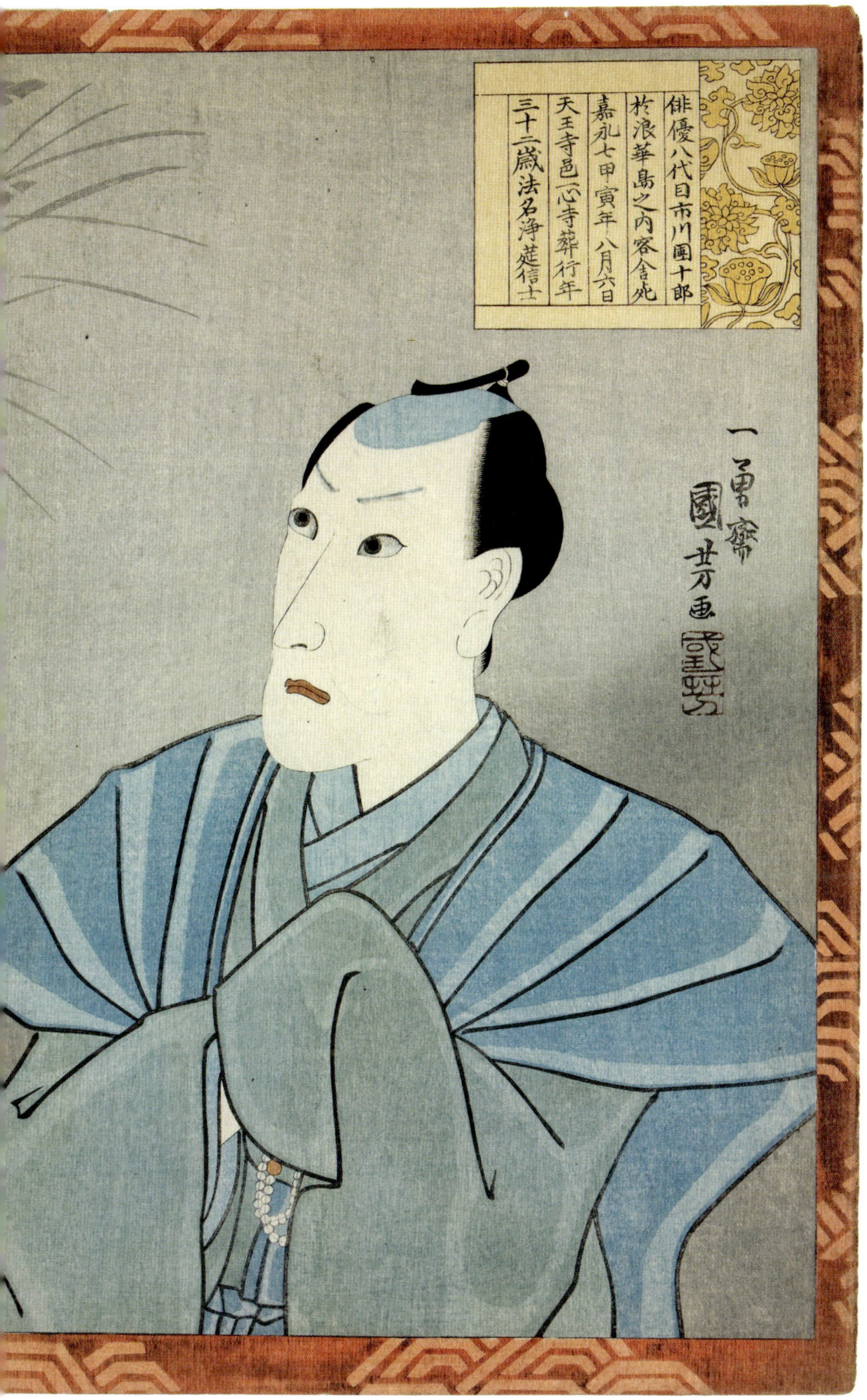

118

Memorial portrait of the Kabuki actor Ichikawa Danjūrō VIII

1854

Colour woodblock, *ōban* triptych, publisher unknown, 36.7 × 25.1 [R], 36.8 × 24.5 [C], 36.7 × 24.7 cm [L]

ARTIST'S SIGNATURE
Ichiyūsai Kuniyoshi ga

ARTIST'S SEAL
Kuniyoshi

RETAIL SEAL
fukyo baibai
(sale and purchase not permitted)

American Friends of the British Museum (The Arthur R. Miller Collection) 21003

REFERENCES
Suzuki 1992, no. 320; Nagoya 1996, nos 131–2; Chiba 1997, no. 41

Ichikawa Danjūrō VIII unexpectedly committed suicide while on tour in Osaka, during the night of the fifth to the sixth day of the eighth month, 1854. He was only thirty-two years old (thirty-one by Western reckoning) and his death came as a tremendous shock to his fans and fellow actors alike. The tragic news soon reached Edo and as many as three hundred 'death pictures' (*shini-e*) were rapidly produced by publishers to meet the enormous public demand, particularly among female fans (Danjūrō VIII was unmarried). The many reasons advanced for his suicide have included the challenges faced by an Edo star acting in Osaka, persecution by his father's mistress, O-Tame, and massive debts (Nishiyama 1979, p. 209).

Necessarily produced quickly, memorial prints of actors were often designed anonymously and sometimes crudely. They generally showed the deceased in pale blue monk's robes and carrying prayer beads; inscriptions gave his age at the time of death, his posthumous Buddhist name and his burial place, and usually included a deathbed poem. Some of Danjūrō VIII's death pictures show him lying in state like the deceased Buddha and surrounded not by all the earth's creatures, as was customary, but by hordes of lamenting women. The present triptych, lavishly and sensitively produced, emphasises the ethereal, otherworldly beauty for which the actor was celebrated. A Buddhist rosary is just visible beneath the sleeve of his pale blue death robes. The two remaining sheets are given over to several dozen memorial haiku by a group styling itself 'Ken-ren' in the red oblong seal at bottom left. The final poem is by Umenoya Kakuju, a patron and friend of Kuniyoshi who was an ardent theatregoer and may well have sponsored the print and organised its production (Iwakiri 1992a, p. 11). Another, smaller seal in the bottom left corner reads 'sale and purchase not permitted' (*fukyo baibai*): the memorial, then, was made for private distribution, not commercial sale. Behind the poems appears a haunting design of delicately gradated autumn grasses, appropriate both to the season of Danjūrō's passing and to the sadness it provoked.

119

Life-size dolls of *The Hag of Hitotsuya*

1856

Colour woodblock, *chūban* triptych, published by Daikokuya Kinnosuke, 25.2 × 18.2 [R], 25.2 × 18.2 [C], 25.2 × 18.2 cm [L]

PRINT TITLE
'Fashionable Living Dolls' (*Fūryū ningyō*)

ARTIST'S SIGNATURE
Ichiyūsai Kuniyoshi ga (in double rectangular cartouche)

ARTIST'S SEAL
Yoshikiri

CENSORSHIP SEAL
aratame

DATE SEAL
2nd month, 1856

American Friends of the British Museum (The Arthur R. Miller Collection) 22216

REFERENCES
Suzuki 1992, no. 351

A withered hag grasps her daughter by the hair and menaces her with a kitchen knife. The daughter looks at her tormentor with a terror-stricken, pleading expression. On the left sheet a youth dozes, head on arm, apparently oblivious to the attack. The setting is Hitotsuya, a lonely house on the moor of Asajigahara near Asakusa, where the old woman preys on travellers who seek lodging, crushing them with a great stone as they sleep and then stealing their belongings. On this occasion her daughter is smitten with the charms of the innocent lodger and tricks the mother into attempting to kill her in place of the stranger. Filled with remorse, the hag throws herself into a nearby pond, which is thereafter known as Old Woman Pond (Uba-ga-ike). Unbeknown to either of them, the youth was a manifestation of Kannon, the Buddhist deity of mercy, who had come to the house in disguise to put an end to the woman's ghastly crimes. Kannon is worshipped at Sensō-ji, the temple that to this day forms the heart of the Asakusa district.

Kuniyoshi produced many versions of the subject, the earliest perhaps a triptych print of *c.* 1840 in which the hag's attack is depicted most dramatically (Suzuki 1992, no. 218). In the second month of 1855 he completed a large votive painting of the scene for Sensō-ji, to a commission by the owner of the prestigious Okamoto brothel in Yoshiwara. The painting has survived earthquake, fire and war and until recently could still be admired hanging in the eaves inside the temple's main hall of worship (Naitō 1998, no. 31).

The late Edo period saw the heyday of a kind of popular attraction known as *misemono* – street-side entertainments offered in temporary booths to which the public paid admission. In the first month of 1856 the craftsman Matsumoto Kisaburō of Kumamoto exhibited 'living dolls' (*iki-ningyō*) in the Okuyama district, just to the north-west of Sensō-ji. These were realistic, life-size models of characters from sensational stories or legends. One of the tableaux Matsumoto presented to great acclaim was based on Kuniyoshi's votive painting of the Hitotsuya legend. In turn, Kuniyoshi modelled the composition of the present triptych, published in the second month of that year, on Kisaburō's dolls. In the third month another maker of *iki-ningyō*, Ōe Chūbei of Osaka, put on a rival display at the temple Eitai-ji in Fukagawa. This, too, included a Hitotsuya scene, and Kuniyoshi again made prints of it, as he did of many other living-doll displays. Popular culture in the late Edo period evinced a widespread taste for mimicking one thing by another in a vivid and sensational way. The interplay between Kabuki theatre, *misemono* entertainments and ukiyo-e prints and illustrations was particularly intense (Kinoshita 1993, chapters 2, 3).

Drawing no. 13 in 'Kuniyoshi rough sketches, no. 19' (*Kuniyoshi sōkō, jūkyū*), one of five albums of Kuniyoshi drawings auctioned in 1993 (see cat. 109), included preparatory sketches for the heads of all three figures.

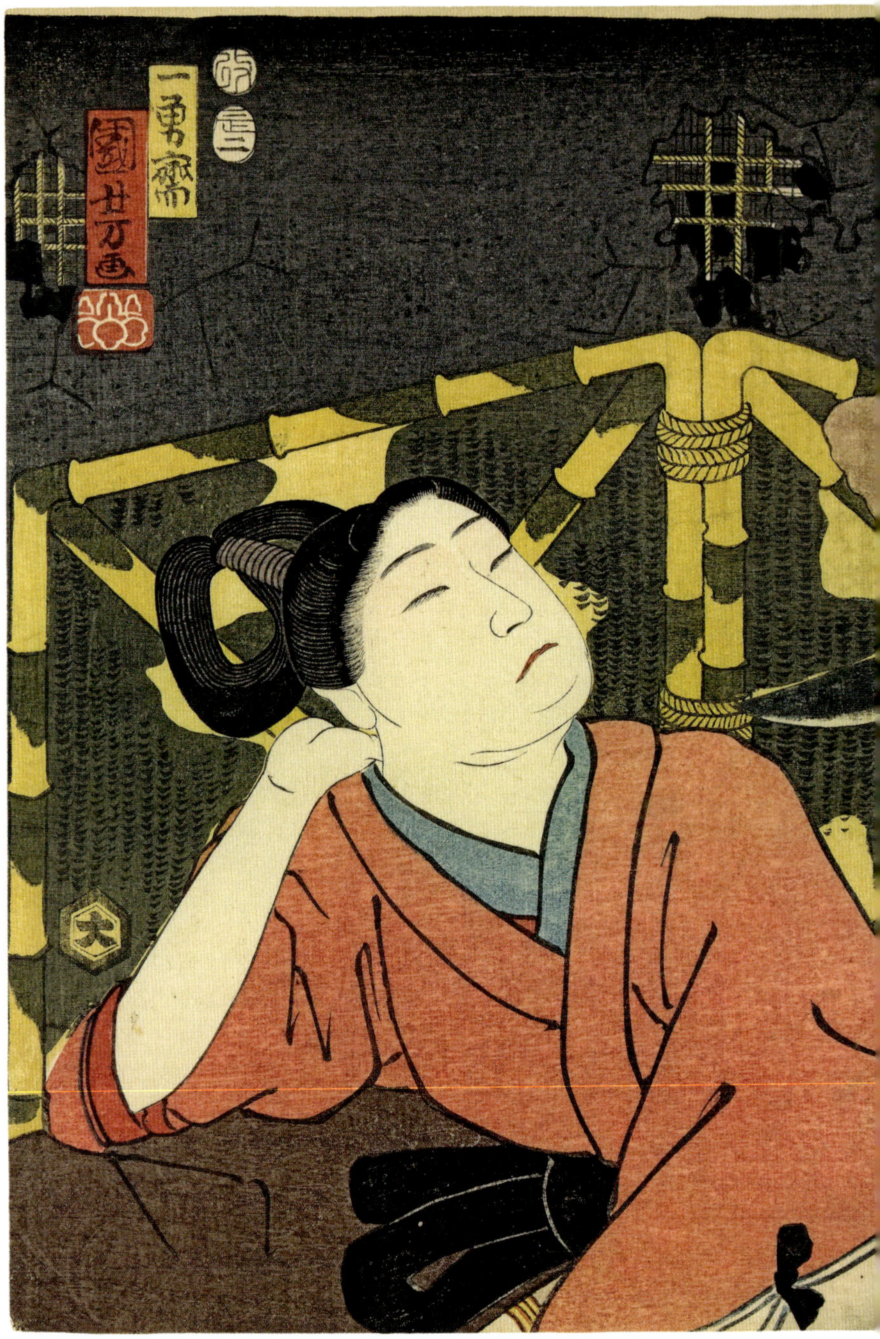

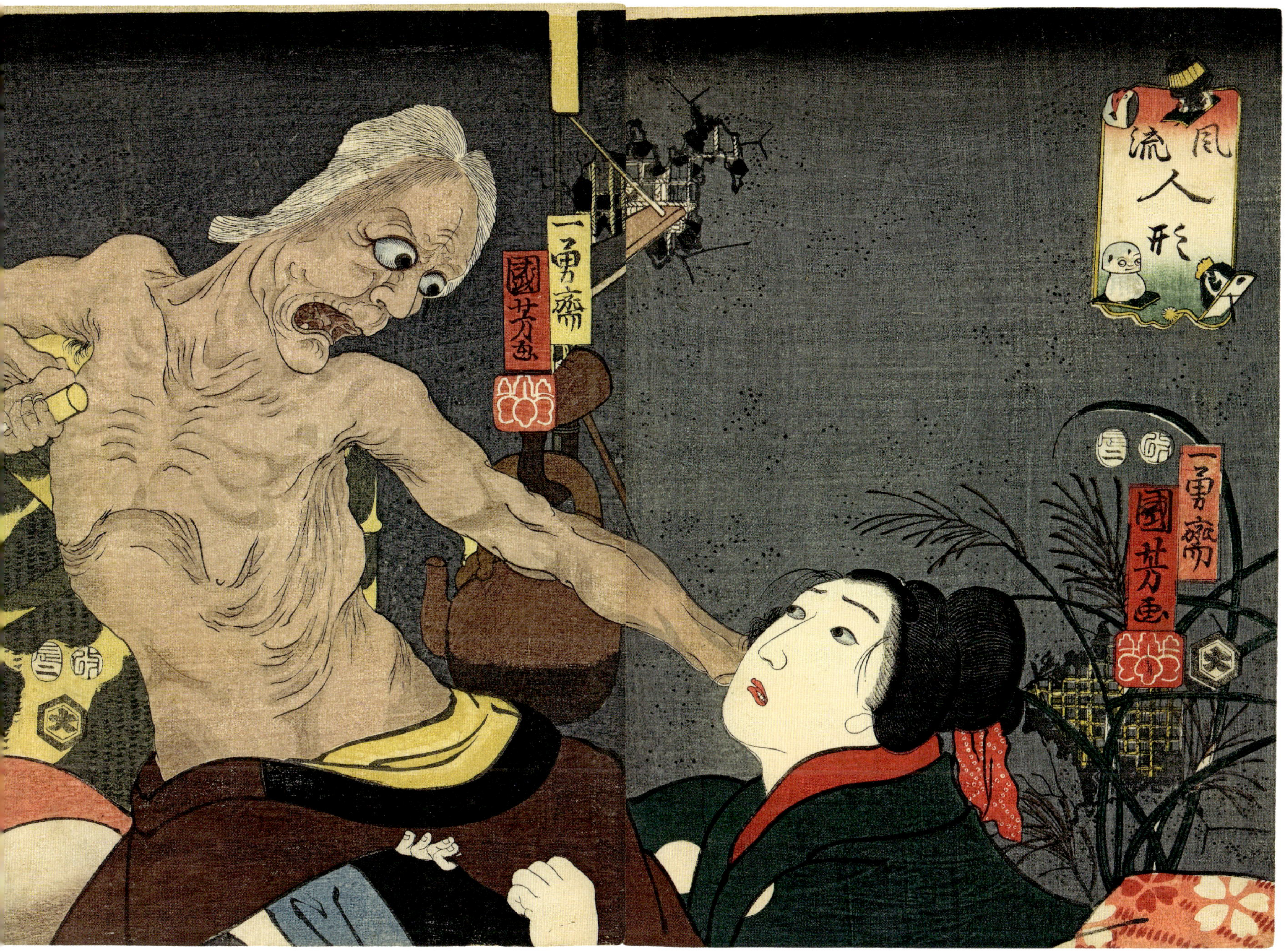
風流人形
一勇斎
國芳画
一勇斎
國芳画

5

HUMOUR

Kuniyoshi created some of the most comical images in Japanese art. They are often highly sophisticated works in which visual humour operates in collusion with conceptual cleverness (p.22, fig.4). Particularly appealing are the many prints populated by animals. Sometimes animals engage in human activities; elsewhere they are allowed to give free rein to their innate characteristics. Always they are brimming with energy. Kuniyoshi loved cats, and several designs show the artist at work in their company. There was a long tradition in Japanese art of using animal imagery to comment in a gently satirical way on human affairs. The various bans and restrictions imposed as part of the Tenpō reforms of 1841–43 presented Kuniyoshi with a unique opportunity to mobilise the animal kingdom in protest. When Yoshiwara pleasure quarter burned down at the end of 1845 and the public hungered for information about the 'temporary quarters' (*karitaku*) established elsewhere in Edo, Kuniyoshi, who was now not permitted to produce pictures of courtesans, responded by populating an entire temporary quarter with sparrows impersonating courtesans, clients and workers (cat. 126).

Kuniyoshi is today admired first and foremost for his prints of warriors, yet evidence exists to suggest that at the start of his career it was his comic works that found favour with the public. An official record of important events noted that during the Tenpō era (1830–44) Kuniyoshi's 'crazy pictures' (*kyōga*) and Hiroshige's landscapes were particularly popular (see also p.22). The cultures of East Asia accorded great respect to states of 'inspired madness' (*kyō*), sometimes fuelled by drink. 'Crazy verse' (*kyōka*) became the most popular kind of amateur poetry in Edo in the late eighteenth century, with thousands becoming members of verse clubs. Kuniyoshi played a crucial part in the development of the 'crazy pictures' genre, which, initially at least, aimed out to present comic visual equivalents of well-known phrases and sayings (p.23, fig.5; cat. 121). His pupil Kawanabe Kyōsai (1831–1889) took up this work where Kuniyoshi left off.

Humorous prints assumed a new importance as a result of the ban imposed in the sixth month, 1842, on prints of actors, courtesans and geisha. In terms of subject-matter, they were largely unaffected by the ban, and they were also well equipped to comment on social affairs. Kuniyoshi quickly placed his humorous visual vocabulary at the service of complex satires. In these 'weird and unusual pictures' (*kikai no zu*), as officials described them, or 'riddle pictures' (*hanjimono* or *hanji-e*) Kuniyoshi circumvented censorship of prints commenting on current affairs. He used comic and imaginative displacement to create new and unsettling imagery that the public endowed with meanings critical of the times. Such were the famous Earth Spider triptych (cats 124, 125) of 1843 and the Floating-world Matabei diptych of 1853 (p.30, fig. 16).

There are signs that the ban on Kabuki prints began to be relaxed officially in 1846, although actors' names and crests could still not be included. Perhaps, then, Kuniyoshi's playful images of actors in the form of cats (cat. 127), turtles (cat. 130), characters from Ōtsu paintings (cat. 129) and even graffiti (cat. 128) should be viewed as a riotous celebration of the authorities' grudging permission for actor 'likenesses' (*nigao-e*) to be published again.

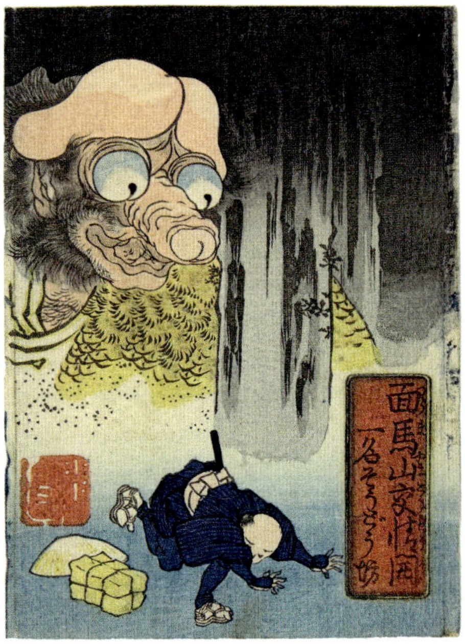
120.5

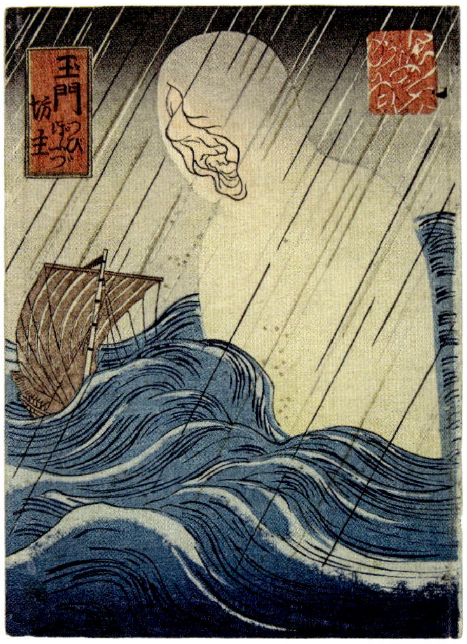
120.4

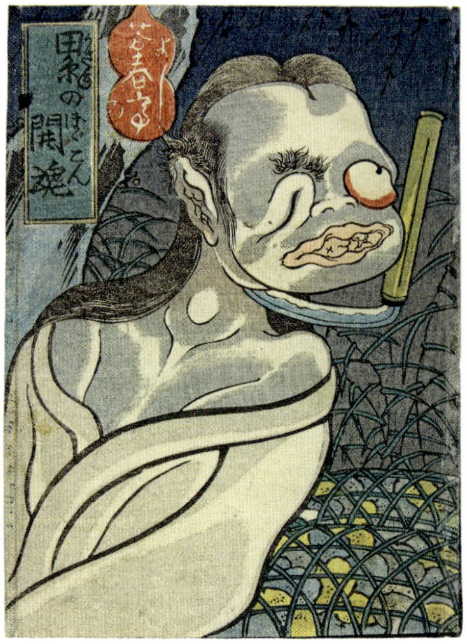
120.3

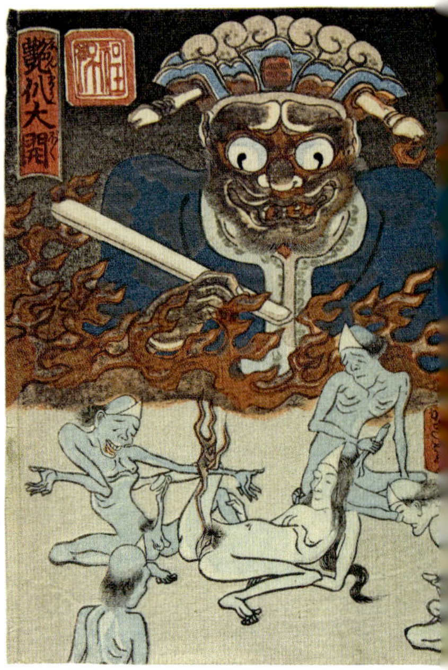

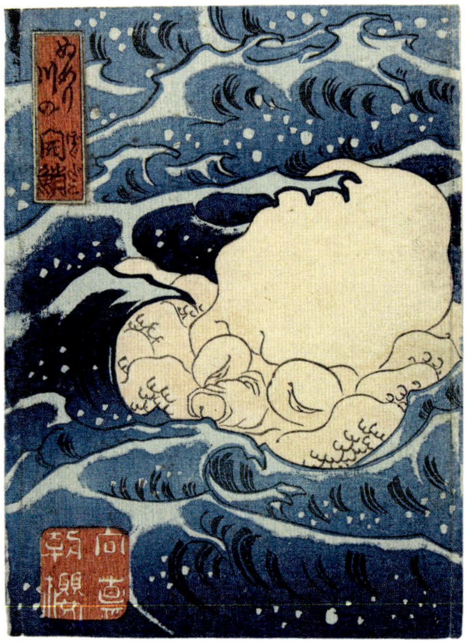
120.9

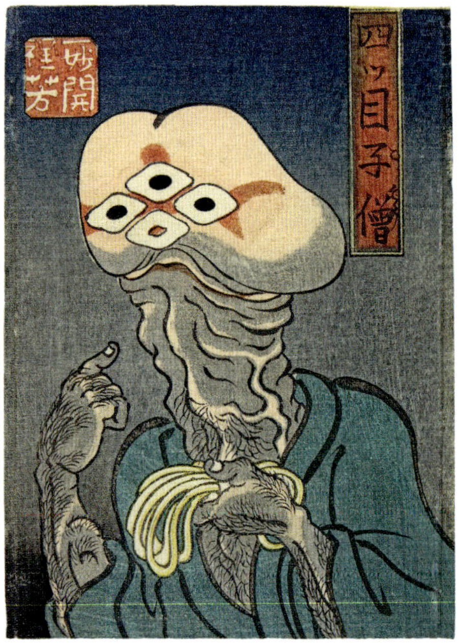
120.8

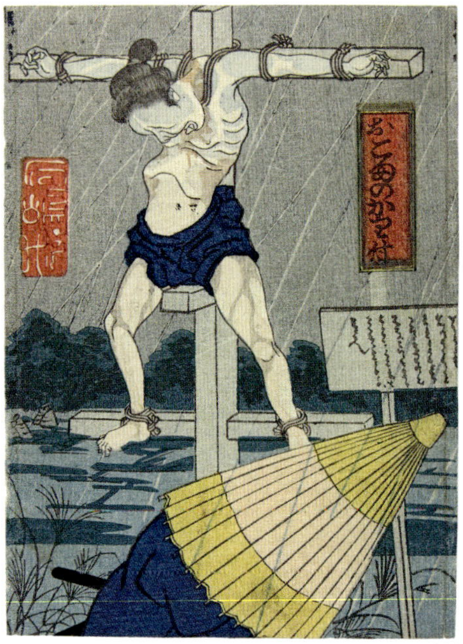
120.7

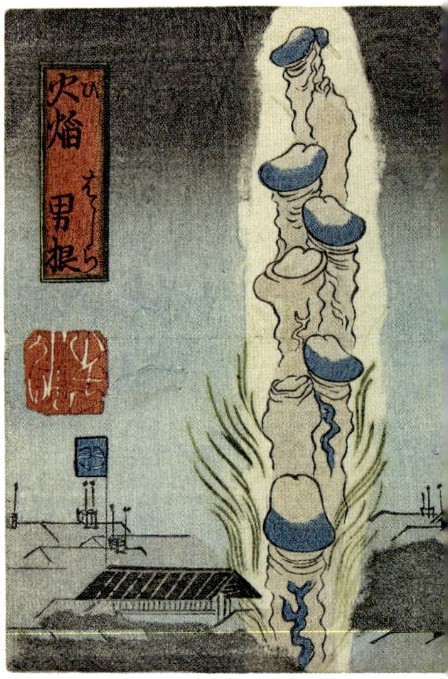

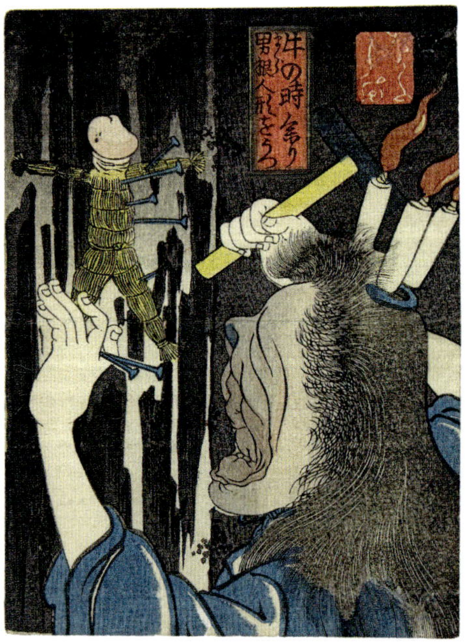
120.13

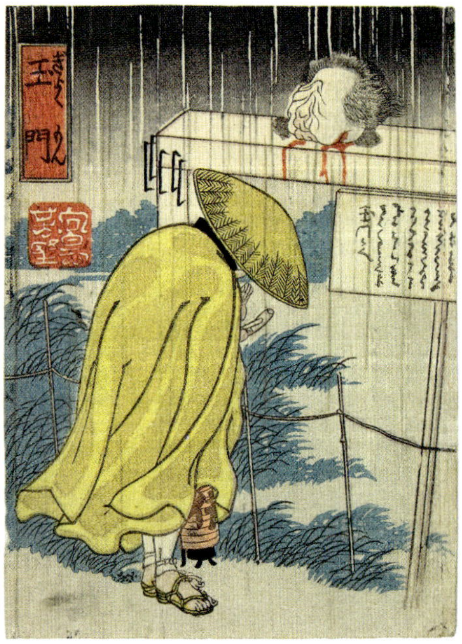
120.12

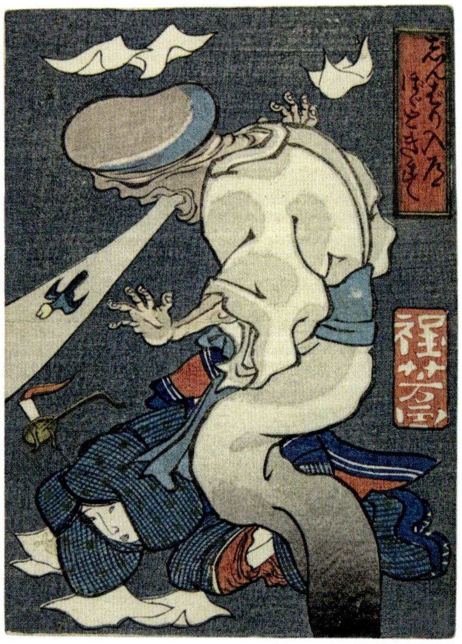
120.11

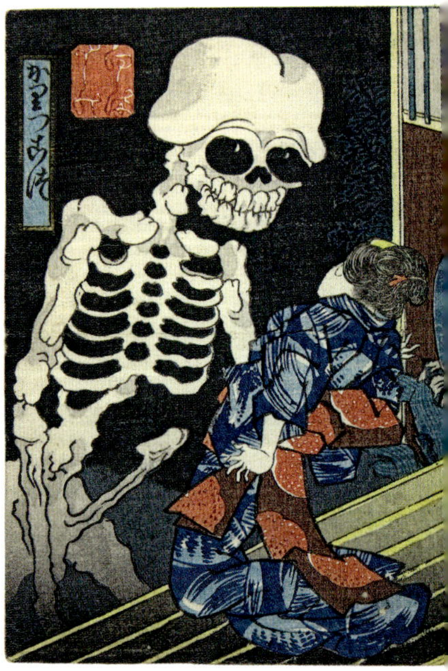

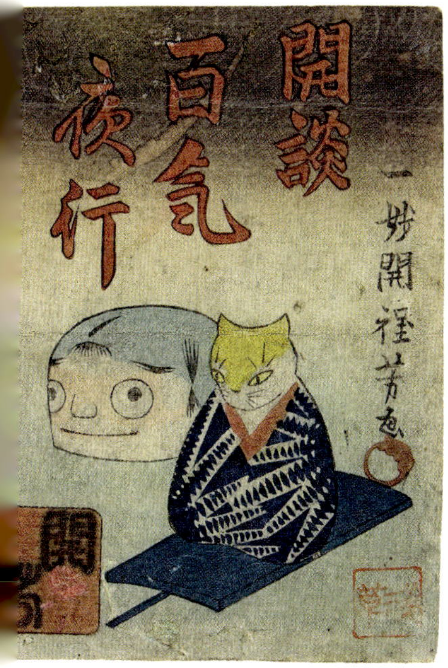

120.1

120

Comic erotic prints of demons

c. 1836

Colour woodblock with metallic pigments, series of twelve erotic *koban* prints with printed wrapper, publisher unknown (sizes given below)

SERIES TITLE
'Ghost Story: Night Procession of the Hundred Demons' (*Kaidan hyakki yagyō*)

ARTIST'S SIGNATURE
Ichimyōkai Hodoyoshi ga (on wrapper)

ARTIST'S SEAL
toshidama, Asakusa, Boboyoshi (on wrapper)

Takashima Masao Collection, Japan

REFERENCES
Hayashi 1964, p. 164; Yoshida 1971, pp. 231–3; Inagaki 1991, nos 179–86; Shirakura 2007, p. 126

THE SERIES CONSISTS OF THE FOLLOWING DESIGNS:

120.1 Cover: 'Jumping doll' (*tobiningyō*).
A toy in the shape of a cat-person.
12.8 × 9.2 cm

120.2 'Sexy Prick, Big Pussy' (*Enmara daibobo*).
Enma, king of hell, presides over lovemaking between the hungry dead (*gakidō*).
12.9 × 9.6 cm
SEAL
Boboyoshi.

120.3 'Pussy Spirit of Kasane' (*Kasane no bobokon*).
Disfigured Kasane had been murdered by her husband Yoemon with a sickle beside the Kinu river.
13 × 9.5 cm
SEAL
Hōshuntei Yoshino.

120.4 'Cunt Monk' (*Tsubi bōzu*).
Umi-bōzu (sea monk) was a large demon that emerged from the sea to haunt ships.
12.9 × 9.7 cm
SEAL
Ichimyōkai in.

120.5 'Consoling Pussy of Horse Face Mountain, Sometimes Called Monk Riot' (*Tsuramayama dōjō-bobo, ichimei Sōdō-bō*).
Monk Sōjō taught military arts to Ushiwaka-maru, the young Yoshitsune, at Kuramayama.
13 × 9.6 cm
SEAL
Hodoyoshi.

120.6 'Pillar of Flames' (*Hi-hashira*).
A flaming pillar of penises rises above the roofs of Yoshiwara pleasure quarter, which was frequently destroyed by fire.
13 × 9.4 cm
SEAL
Ichimyōkai.

120.7 'Crucifixion of Okoma' (*Okoma no karitsuke*).
Okoma, sentenced to be executed at Suzu-ga-mori for murdering her husband, was pardoned after petitioning by her lover Saiza.
12.9 × 9.6 cm
SEAL
Mukōjima Yoshino.

120.8 'Four-eyed Acolyte' (*Yotsume kozō*).
Hitotsume kozō (one-eyed acolyte) was a much-feared demon. This four-eyed version holds *Higo-zuiki*, dried stems of sweet potato that were used as a sex toy.
12.9 × 9.5 cm
SEAL
Ichimyōkai Hodoyoshi.

120.9 'Octo-pussy of the Numeri River' (*Numerikawa no bobo-dako*).
Large octopuses were hunted at the mouth of the Nameri river in Etchū province (modern Toyama prefecture; see also cat. 71).
12.9 × 9.6 cm
SEAL
Mukōjima Chōō.

120.10 'Penis Skeleton' (*Karikkotsu*).
A penis skeleton menaces a woman who has come onto the veranda at night.
12.8 × 9.3 cm
SEAL
Mukōjima Yoshino.

120.11 'Licentious Priest with Angry Pussy' (*Jinbari nyūdō bobo dokisu*).
12.8 × 9.3 cm
SEAL
Hodoyoshi ga.

120.12 'Jewel Gate', i.e. vulva **(*Gyokumon*).**
An executed criminal's head was sometimes publicly displayed at the entrance to a prison (*gokumon*).
13 × 9.6 cm
SEAL
Mukōjima Yoshino.

120.13 'Nailing a Dick Doll at the Hour of the Ox' (*Ushi no toki mairi mara ningyō o utsu*).
A woman wanting to kill a man who had spurned her was supposed to don a crown of candles, go to a shrine at the hour of the ox (about 2 am) and nail a straw figurine of the man to a sacred tree. Seven days later he would die.
12.9 × 9.3 cm
SEAL
Mukōjima.

Male and female sex organs are drawn in the guise of various demons. The prints bear explicit titles, which often include puns on the names of the demons. The tone is generally comic and parodic, although certain images are sadistically violent. The imagery known as 'Night Procession of the Hundred Demons' (*Hyakki yagyō*) originated in the medieval period and embodied the belief that inanimate objects develop souls after one hundred years and move about in procession at night, threatening anyone whom they encounter. The demons parodied in the present series, however, are closer to those in illustrated books of ghosts by the artist Toriyama Sekien (1712–1788), published between 1776 and 1784. Katsukawa Shunshō (d. 1792) had already produced a comic erotic parody of demon imagery with his *Hyaku bobo-gatari* (*One Hundred Tales of Pussy*), which appeared in 1771, and in 1825 Kunisada created a three-volume erotic work on the theme, *Hyakki yagyō* (*Night Procession of the Hundred Demons*).

Kuniyoshi created some thirty-three explicitly erotic printed works in the course of his career (Shirakura 2007, pp. 251–2). Most were produced between 1828 and 1839, before erotica were suppressed in the early to mid-1840s as a result of the Tenpō reforms. He returned to the genre when enforcement of the reforms had slackened, designing seven further works between 1846 and 1859. His erotica generally take the then standard form of lavishly colour-printed books in three volumes and feature explicit scenes of lovemaking, coupled with pornographic stories. The content of 'Ghost Story: Night Procession of the Hundred Demons' is therefore unusual among his erotic works and allowed him to give full rein to his taste for the macabre and grotesque. The erotic art-names he assumes for the series include Hodoyoshi ('Just Right') and Boboyoshi ('Good Pussy'). The title could also be translated in erotic terms as 'Pussy Stories: One Hundred Night Ejaculations'.

Hayashi Yoshikazu dated the series c. 1829 (Hayashi 1964, p. 164), but this has recently been disputed. The earliest known occurrence of the art-name 'Chōōrō' in Kuniyoshi's oeuvre is on a fan print of 1836. The use of 'Chōō' in the present series, the appearance of the name 'Mukōjima' (the neighbourhood on the east bank of the Sumida river to which Kuniyoshi probably moved in the mid-1830s) and the style of the characters with which the erotic art-name 'Hodoyoshi' is written on the wrapper suggest a date of c. 1836 (personal communication from Iwakiri Yuriko).

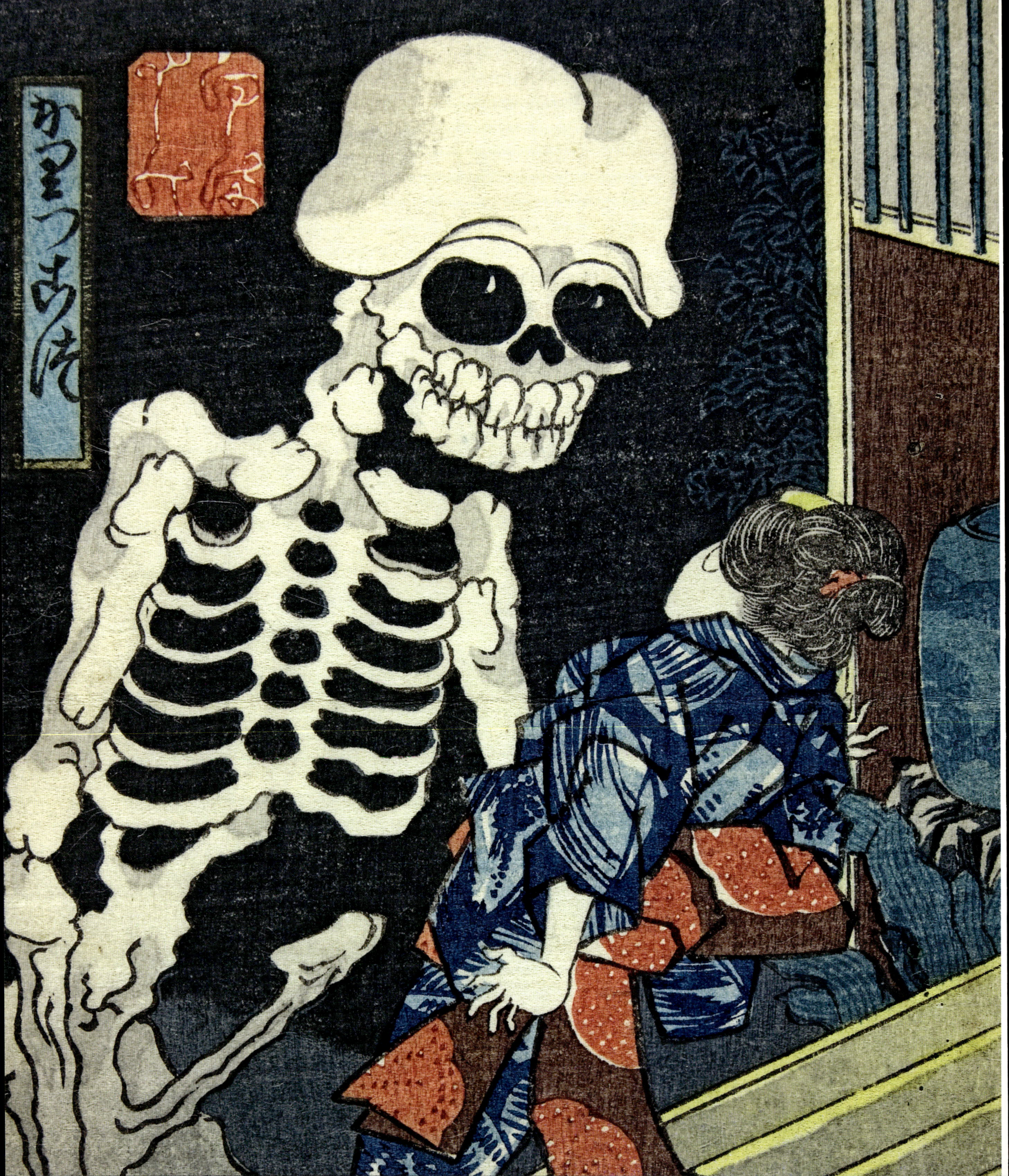

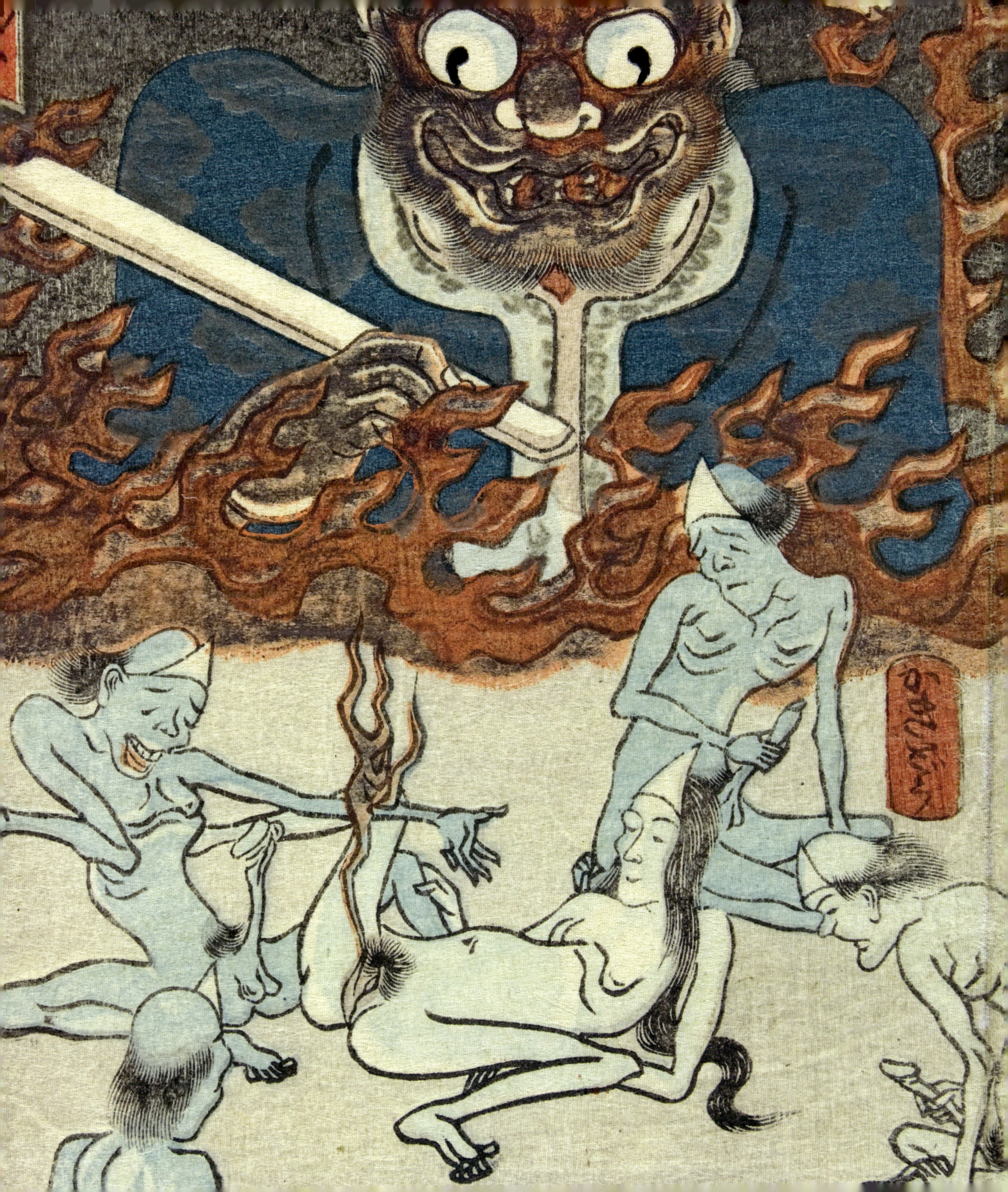

121

Phoenix and lobster,

1839–41

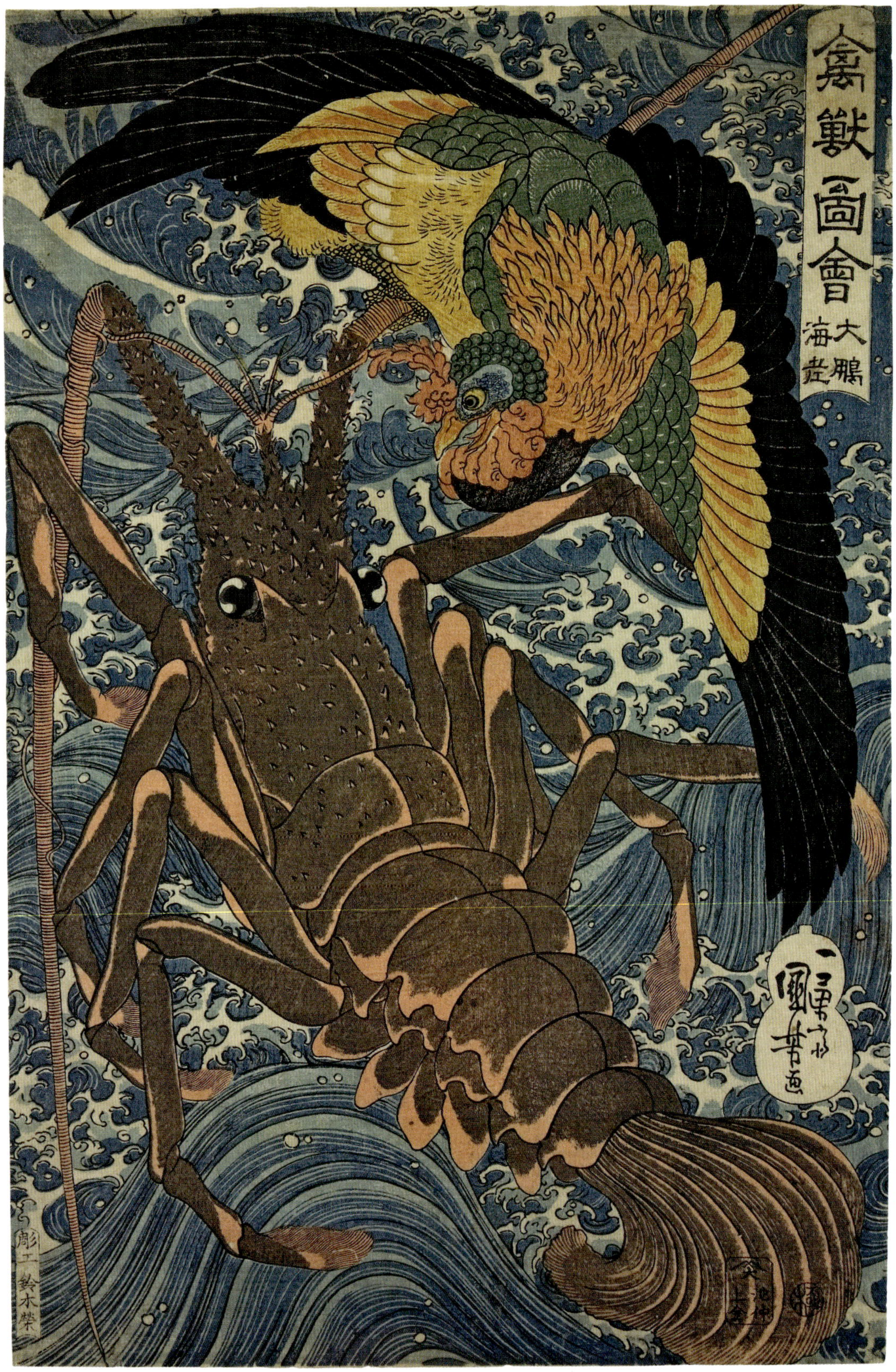

Colour woodblock, *ōban*, published by Jōshūya Kinzō, 37.7 × 25.4 cm

SERIES TITLE
'Birds and Beasts' (*Kinjū zue*)

PRINT TITLE
'Phoenix, Lobster' (*Taihō, ebi*)

ARTIST'S SIGNATURE
Ichiyūsai Kuniyoshi ga (in gourd-shaped cartouche)

BLOCK-CUTTER
Suzuki Ei

CENSORSHIP SEAL
kiwame

American Friends of the British Museum (The Arthur R. Miller Collection) 02401

REFERENCES
Riccar 1978, no.210; Springfield 1980, no.56; Yamaguchi 1991, Kuniyoshi no.46; Suzuki 1992, no.449; Nagoya 1996, no.213; Amsterdam 1998, no.242

A giant phoenix perches on the long whisker of a large lobster, while behind them waves swirl. This densely packed image plays with customary notions of scale. Suzuki Jūzō has shown that it illustrates a religious parable told by the great Zen prelate Ikkyū (1394–1481) and suggests that Kuniyoshi may have known this from *Ikkyū-banashi* (*Ikkyū's Tales*), a popular book of the monk's sayings first published in 1668. In the tale, which Ikkyū used to hint at metaphysical dimensions not easily grasped by human understanding, the phoenix is a creature of the northern oceans and decides to journey south. After flying a great distance, it becomes tired and perches on what it takes to be the branch of a tree. The 'branch' is, in fact, the whisker of a giant lobster that lives in the southern oceans. The lobster undertakes to continue the phoenix's journey, but eventually wearies and decides to rest in a cave. This turns out to be the ear of a giant turtle, which continues the journey and never returns (Suzuki 1992, no.449).

Five designs from the series are known, most of them showing fantastic or mythical creatures (four are illustrated in Suzuki 1992, nos 449–52). In the earliest printings of the present design the title and signature cartouches have a yellow background. In this impression the deep blue of the waves is not as dark as in other published impressions; also the body of the lobster is printed in pale ink, rather than in a second shade of orange, as is more commonly encountered.

122

Octopus games

1840–42

Colour woodblock, *ōban*, published by Fujiokaya Hikotarō, 36.7 × 24.4 cm

PRINT TITLE
'Fashionable Octopus Games' (*Ryūkō tako no asobi*)

ARTIST'S SIGNATURE
Ichiyūsai Kuniyoshi giga (Playfully drawn by Ichiyūsai Kuniyoshi)

CENSORSHIP SEAL
kiwame

American Friends of the British Museum (The Arthur R. Miller Collection) 21402

REFERENCES
Inagaki 1991, no. 50

Octopuses re-enact human amusements using leaves from sweet potato plants as hats, weapons and other objects. Their snub-nosed faces with bulging eyes are fixed in a comic, frowning expression. Kuniyoshi has no other ambition than to make viewers laugh, even as they admire the energy and economy of his drawing. Five scenarios are being acted out: an acrobat with musician and announcer (*Karuwaza, hayashi, kōjō*, top right), the duel between Benkei and Ushiwaka (*Benkei, Ushiwaka*, top left; see cat. 21), a street merchant selling candy, with children (*Oman-ga-ame, kodomo*, centre right), a 'sparrow' dance (*Suzume-odori*, centre left) and a sumo judge with wrestlers (*Sumō gyōji, torikumi*, bottom right).

Kuniyoshi did much to develop comic prints as a separate genre, in particular with images in which animals mimic the activities of humans.

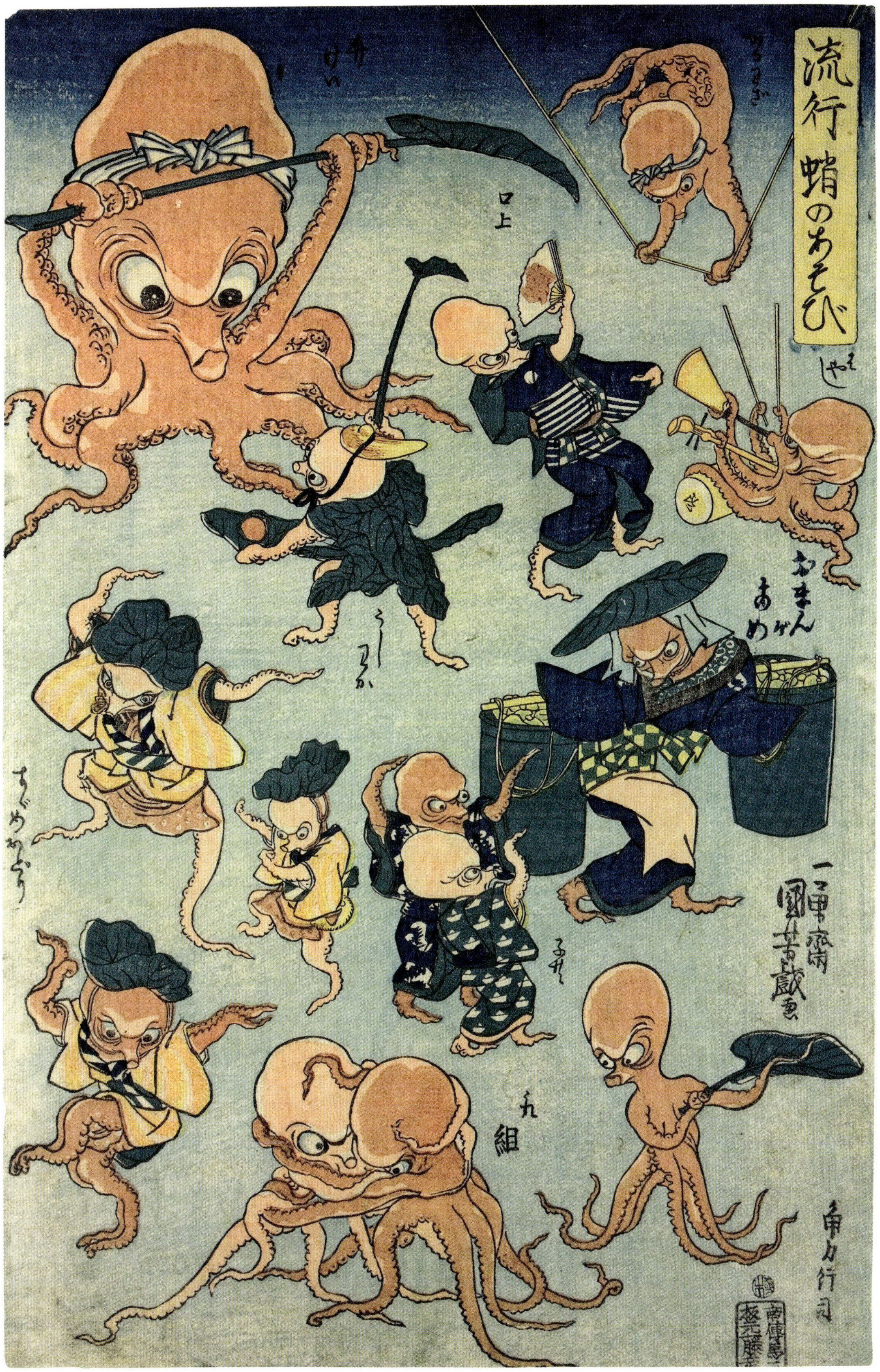

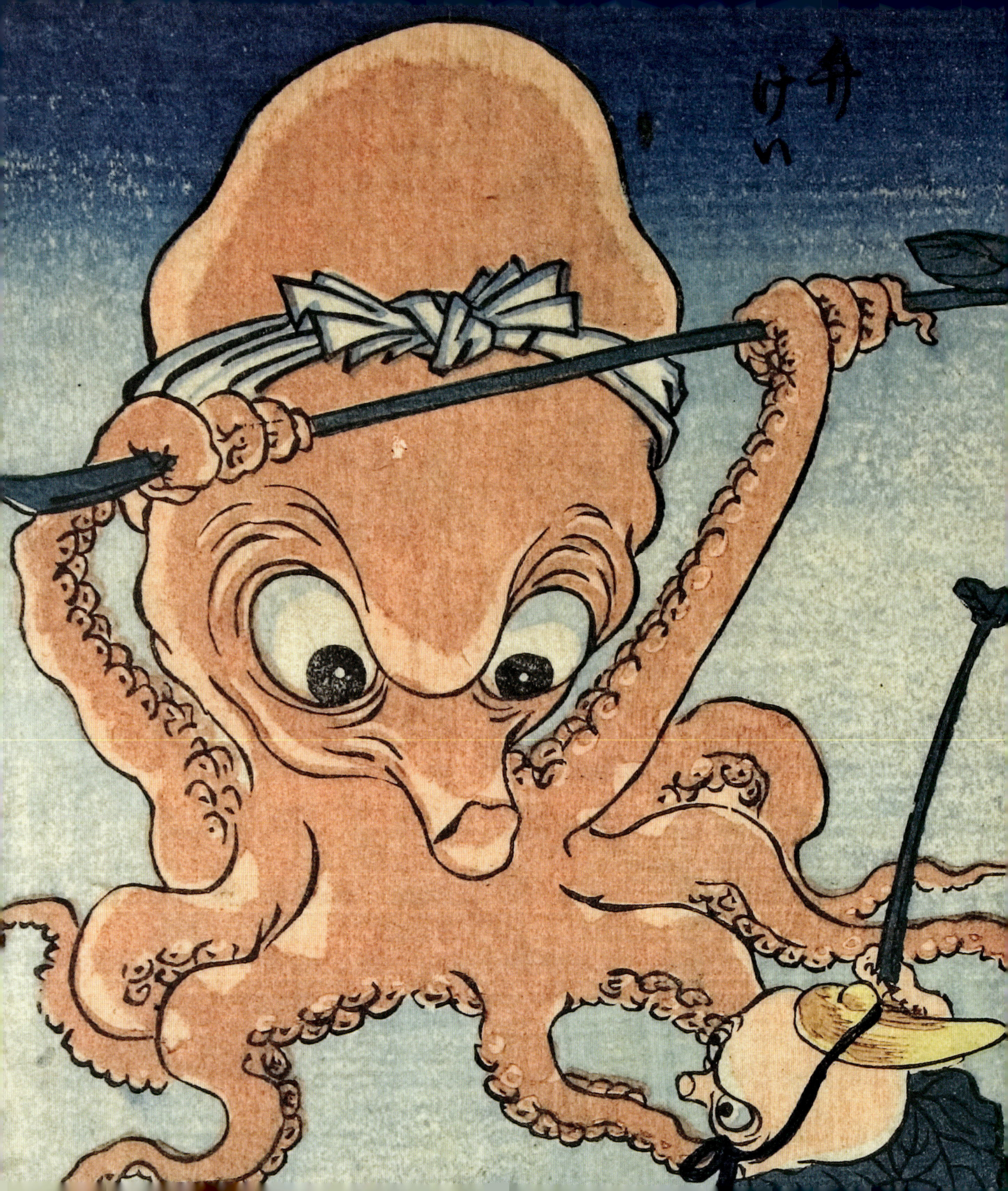
弁けい

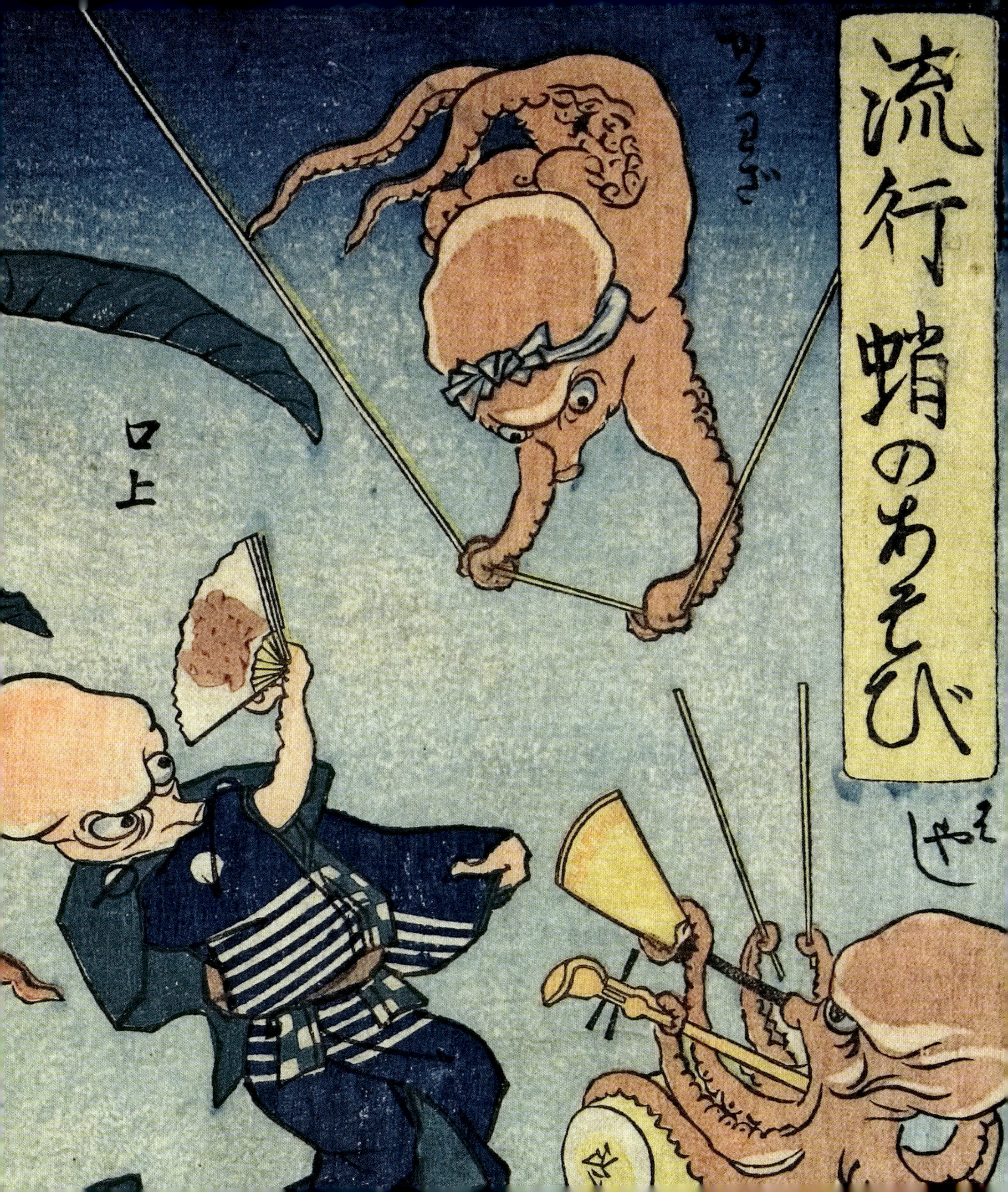
流行 蛸のあそび
口上

123

Textile pattern of people

1840–42

Colour woodblock, *ōban*, published by Yamamoto Heikichi, 24.7 × 36.6 cm

PRINT TITLE
'Textile Pattern of People to Stop You Yawning' (*Akubi-dome jinbutsu sarasa*)

ARTIST'S SIGNATURE
Ichiyūsai Kuniyoshi giga (Playfully drawn by Ichiyūsai Kuniyoshi, in rectangular cartouche)

CENSORSHIP SEAL
kiwame

American Friends of the British Museum (The Arthur R. Miller Collection) 21417

REFERENCES
Brussels 1989, no. 894; Suzuki 1992, no. 381; Mainichi Shinbunsha 1995, no. 142; Nagoya 1996, no. 230

The semi-naked male bodies, mostly clad in nothing but loincloths, grab each others' torsos, arms, legs and heads in a never-ending tangle. Men of all ages and classes, from courtiers to workmen, are represented. It is impossible to determine where one body ends and another begins, a puzzle that is intended 'to stop you yawning', as the title has it. The inscription in the yellow box beneath the title reads: 'Using fourteen bodies it looks like thirty-five people' (*Jūyon-nin no karada nite sanjūgo-nin ni miyuru*). *Sarasa* is a kind of cotton cloth printed with a complex pattern, which at this time was generally imported into Japan from southern India.

Another printing of the design is known. It shows a green box for the inscription beneath the title, rather than the yellow one seen here.

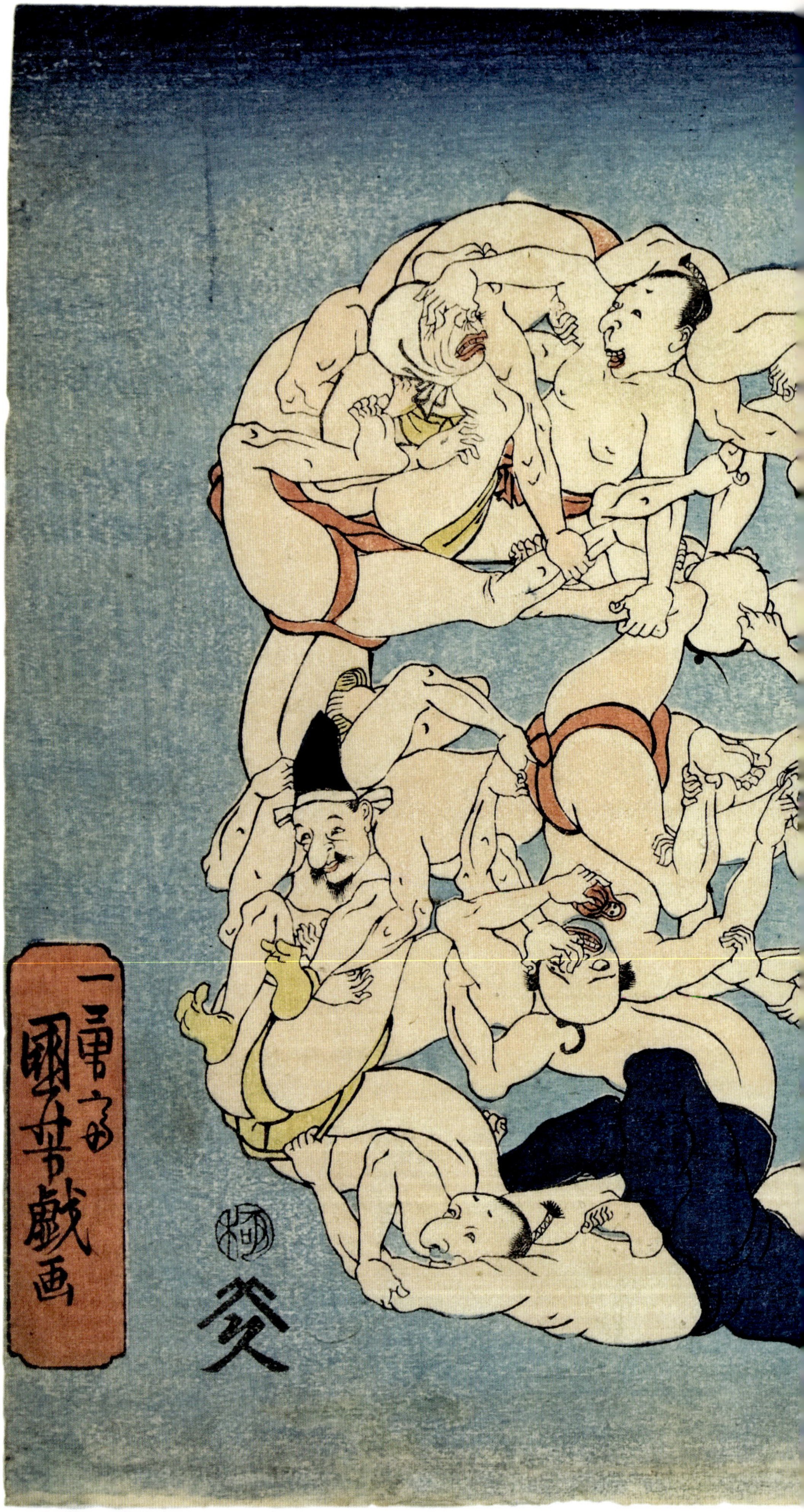

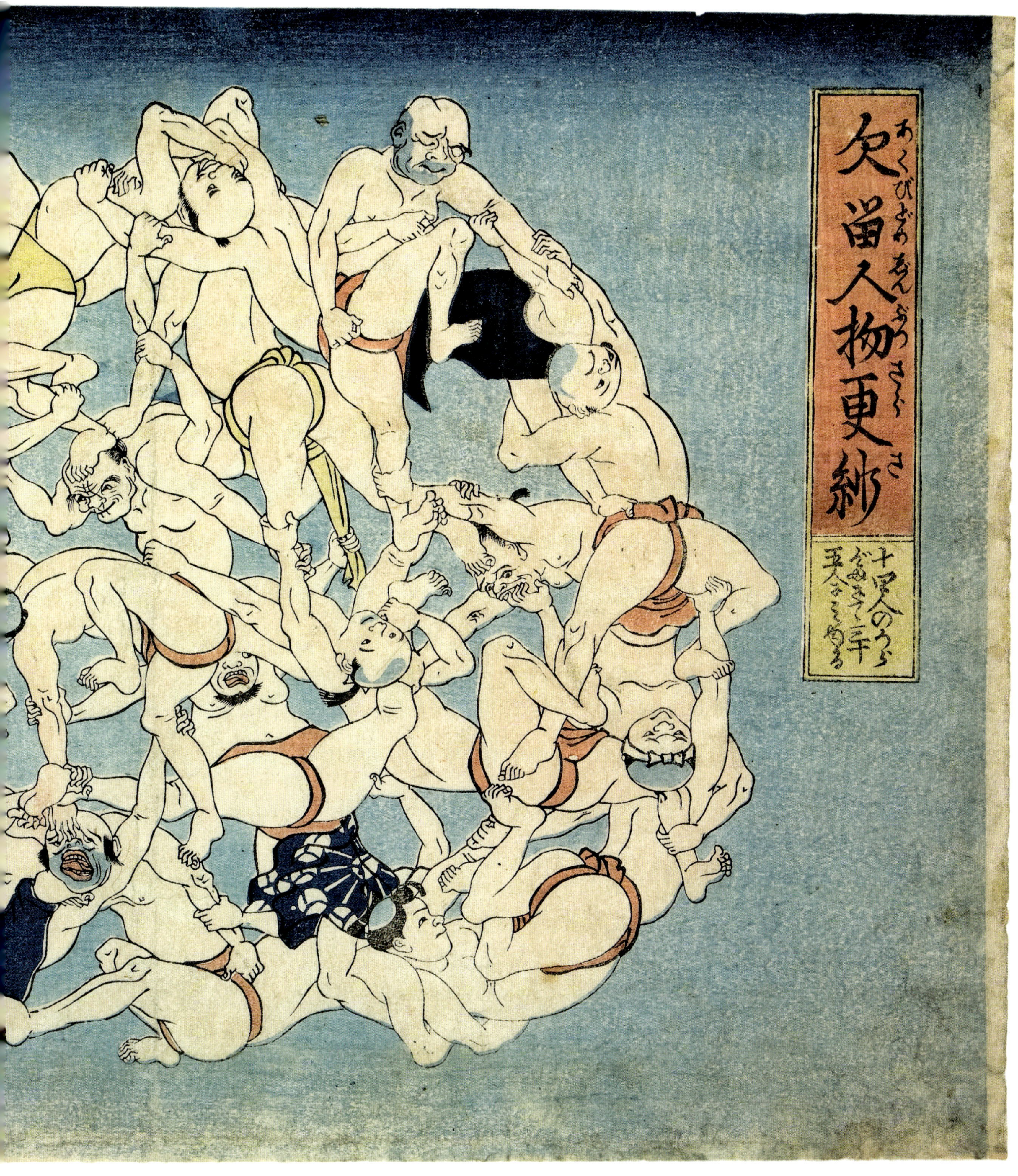
欠留人物更紗

124

The Earth Spider conjures up demons at the mansion of Minamoto no Raikō (original edition)

1843

Colour woodblock, *ōban* triptych, published by Ibaya Senzaburō (publisher's mark on all three sheets), 35.8 × 24.9 [R], 35.8 × 24.7 [C], 35.8 × 24.3 [L]

PRINT TITLE

'The Earth Spider Conjures Up Demons at the Mansion of Minamoto no Raikō' (*Minamoto no Yorimitsu-kō no yakata ni tsuchigumo yōkai o nasu zu*)

ARTIST'S SIGNATURE

Ichiyūsai Kuniyoshi ga (all three sheets)

Victoria and Albert Museum, London, E.10535-1886

REFERENCES

Robinson 1961, no. 42; Springfield 1968, no. 137; Hillier 1976, no. 842; Riccar 1978, no. 278; Springfield 1980, no. 114; Robinson 1982, no. T128; HUT, vol. 5, 1989, no. 49; V&A 1991, no. 93; Inagaki 1991, no. 176; Thompson 1991, fig. 35; Suzuki 1992, no. 441; Mainichi Shinbunsha 1995, no. 141; Nagoya 1996, nos 260–1; Ōta 1999, nos 162–3; Isao 2008, pp. 60–1

125

The Earth Spider conjures up demons at the mansion of Minamoto no Raikō (pirated edition)

1843 (?)

Colour woodblock, *ōban* triptych, published by Ibaya Senzaburō (publisher's mark on left sheet only), 35.5 × 25.8 [R], 35.2 × 25.7 [C], 35.7 × 25.9 cm [L]

PRINT TITLE

'The Earth Spider Conjures Up Demons at the Mansion of Minamoto no Raikō' (*Minamoto no Yorimitsu-kō no yakata ni tsuchigumo yōkai o nasu zu*)

ARTIST'S SIGNATURE

Ichiyūsai Kuniyoshi ga (left sheet only)

American Friends of the British Museum (The Arthur R. Miller Collection) 20906

The warrior hero Minamoto no Yorimitsu (or Raikō, d. 1021), on the right, dozes on his sickbed. His bodyguards were nicknamed the 'Four Heavenly Kings' (Shitennō): on the centre sheet Watanabe no Tsuna and Sakata no Kintoki play *go*; but Urabe no Suetake, on the right sheet, close to Yorimitsu, and Usui no Sadamitsu, on the left sheet, look about apprehensively. Although they cannot see it, the evil Earth Spider, Tsuchigumo, conjures up a battle between rival armies of demons to torment Yorimitsu's feverish dreams. Kuniyoshi has greatly increased the number and types of demons in comparison with a version he produced some twenty years earlier (cat. 2): there are now over fifty.

Kuniyoshi may have taken inspiration for his striking exhibition of devilry from *Hyakki yagyō* (*Night Procession of the Hundred Demons*; see cat. 120). Melinda Takeuchi has suggested many other sources, Chinese, Japanese, medieval, modern, theatrical, literary, Buddhist and supernatural (Takeuchi 1987). But how did contemporary viewers 'read' the image? The triptych became a *cause célèbre* and reactions to it are recorded in several documents, among them *Fujiokaya nikki* (*Fujiokaya Diary*), a detailed journal kept by the bookseller Sudō (Fujiokaya) Yoshizō, and *Tenpō zakki* (*Miscellaneous Records of the Tenpō era*). In 1973 the historian Minami Kazuo analysed possible sources and demonstrated that, whatever Kuniyoshi's intention, the image was widely interpreted as a 'riddle picture' (*hanji-mono*) satirising the Tenpō reforms, which were still being implemented when the print was issued in the eighth month of 1843 (Minami 1973).

The ailing Yorimitsu was generally identified with the ineffectual Shogun Tokugawa Ieyoshi (ruled 1837–53). Urabe no Suetake soon became associated with the senior councillor Mizuno Tadakuni (1794–1851), the hated chief architect of the Tenpō reforms, since the two men coincidentally shared a family crest consisting of a water plantain (*omodaka*). *Tenpō zakki* correlated the various demons with the many professions that the reforms suppressed or restricted, such as prostitution, ballad singing by women and hairdressing by women. In addition, two impressions are known to have existed with small labels to indicate which demon represented which profession. The demon/profession correspondences in these three sources sometimes differ considerably. The nine-skulled standard in the top right of the centre sheet, for example, is said to represent either the leading 'ten guilds of wholesalers' (*tokumi-doiya*) or brothels. Nevertheless, about seventy per cent of the correspondences relate to the same four categories: restrictions on luxury items, social customs, performing arts and religious practices. It is clear that many people made the image a focus for venting frustration at the reforms' severity. 'Riddle pictures' were to become a major new genre of political satire in the late Edo period, and this triptych is a significant early instance in Japan of what might be called a 'political cartoon'.

Fujiokaya nikki describes how the print's publisher took fright when it achieved acclaim as a satire, deciding to avoid punishment for himself and the artist by recalling all stocks and planing the blocks. That winter, however, a version was designed by Utagawa Sadahide in a reduced format and issued by a different publisher, the otherwise unknown Hisatarō. Some impressions were printed without demons and sold openly for thirty-six *mon* per triptych; others with demons were sold discreetly for one hundred *mon* to those who requested them. Hisatarō was arrested and, after twenty days in handcuffs, fined three *kan mon* (about 3,000 *mon*), as was Sadahide. A set of twelve small calendar pictures on the theme by Utagawa Yoshitora was subsequently issued in a wrapper for three *monme* (about 200 *mon*). Large fines were again imposed on publisher and artist, and on several print sellers, and some of those punished also spent periods in handcuffs. Yoshitora, like Sadahide, was fined three *kan mon* (*Fujiokaya nikki*, vol. 2, 1988, pp. 413–14). *Ukiyo no arisama* (*The Way of the Floating World*, 1806–46), an anonymous chronicle thought to have been written by a physician in Osaka, records that 2,000 impressions of one version of the design (it is not clear which) were sent to print shops in Kyoto and 2,000 more to Osaka, selling very well in both places after initial public hesitation (Minami 1973, p. 124).

The survival of three printings of Kuniyoshi's design, the first authorised, the others pirated, confirms its popularity, the blocks having been completely re-cut in each case. (No impressions of the Sadahide and Yoshitora versions have come to light.) The earliest surviving printing, assumed to comprise impressions sold before stocks were withdrawn and the original blocks planed, bears Ibaya Senzaburō's trademark and Kuniyoshi's signature on each sheet. Two blocks, mid-grey and dark-grey, were used for the Earth Spider, and there is flesh-coloured modelling on Yoritomo's face and hand. The mouth of the pox-covered female demon holding a large brush on the centre sheet is slightly open and her teeth are visible (see cat. 124; Springfield 1968, no. 137; Suzuki 1992, no. 441; Isao 2008, pp. 60–1). The second printing, a re-cut, pirated edition, shows the publisher's mark and artist's signature on the left sheet only. The Earth Spider is printed with a single block, and there is no colouring on Yorimitsu's face or hand. The mouth of the female demon on the centre sheet is closed. In general the printing is less rich (see cat. 125 and the impression in the National Museum of Scotland, Edinburgh, A.1887.745.68.1). In the third printing, a pirated edition even more crudely re-cut and printed, the block-cutter abbreviated and misinterpreted many details. Again, the publisher's mark and artist's signature appear on the left sheet only. There is no use of gradated printing (*bokashi*) along either edge of the divide between the realm of the demons and the green floor of Yorimitsu's mansion (see the impression in the William Sturgis Bigelow Collection, Museum of Fine Arts, Boston, 11.30462-4).

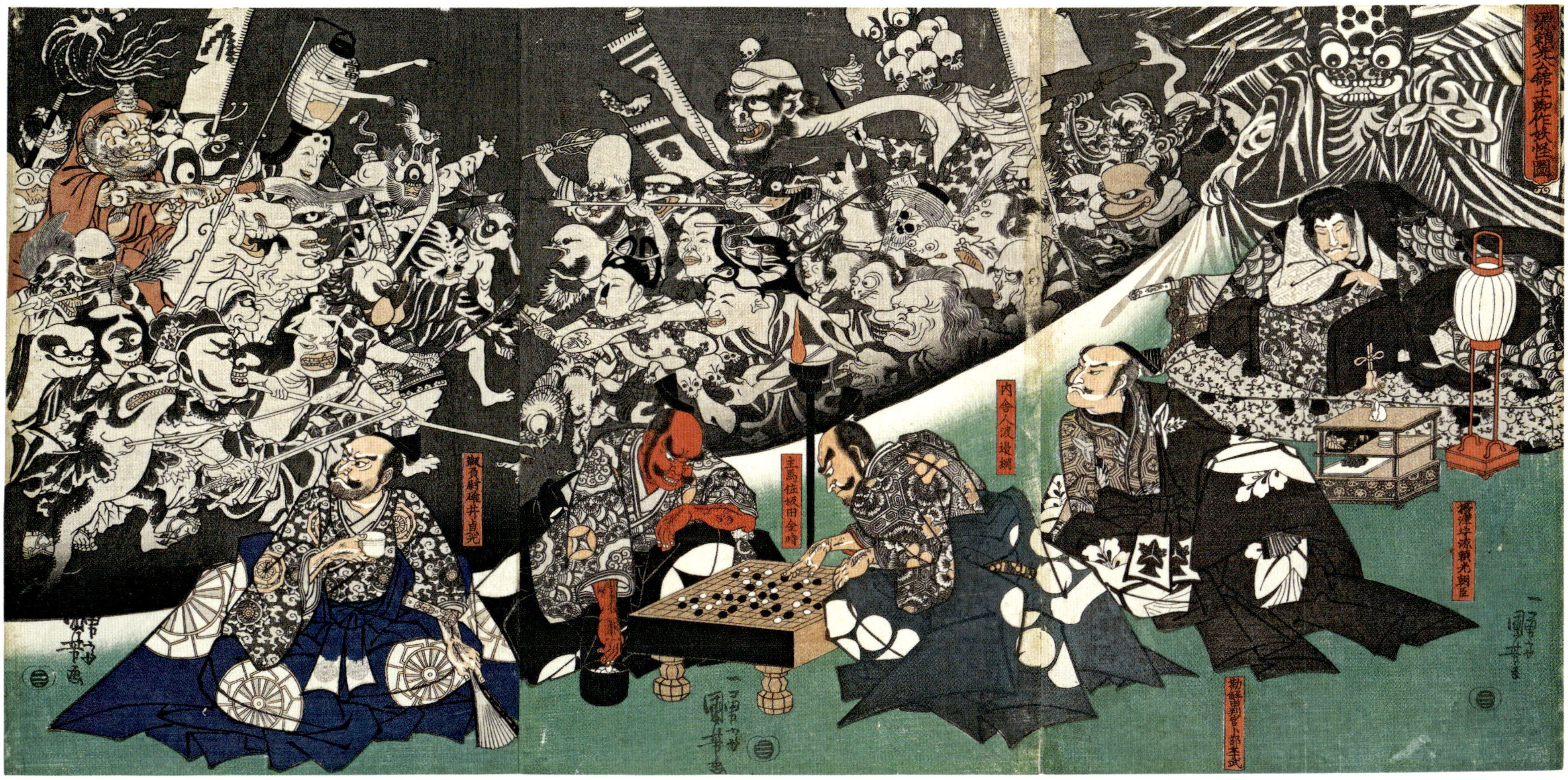

124

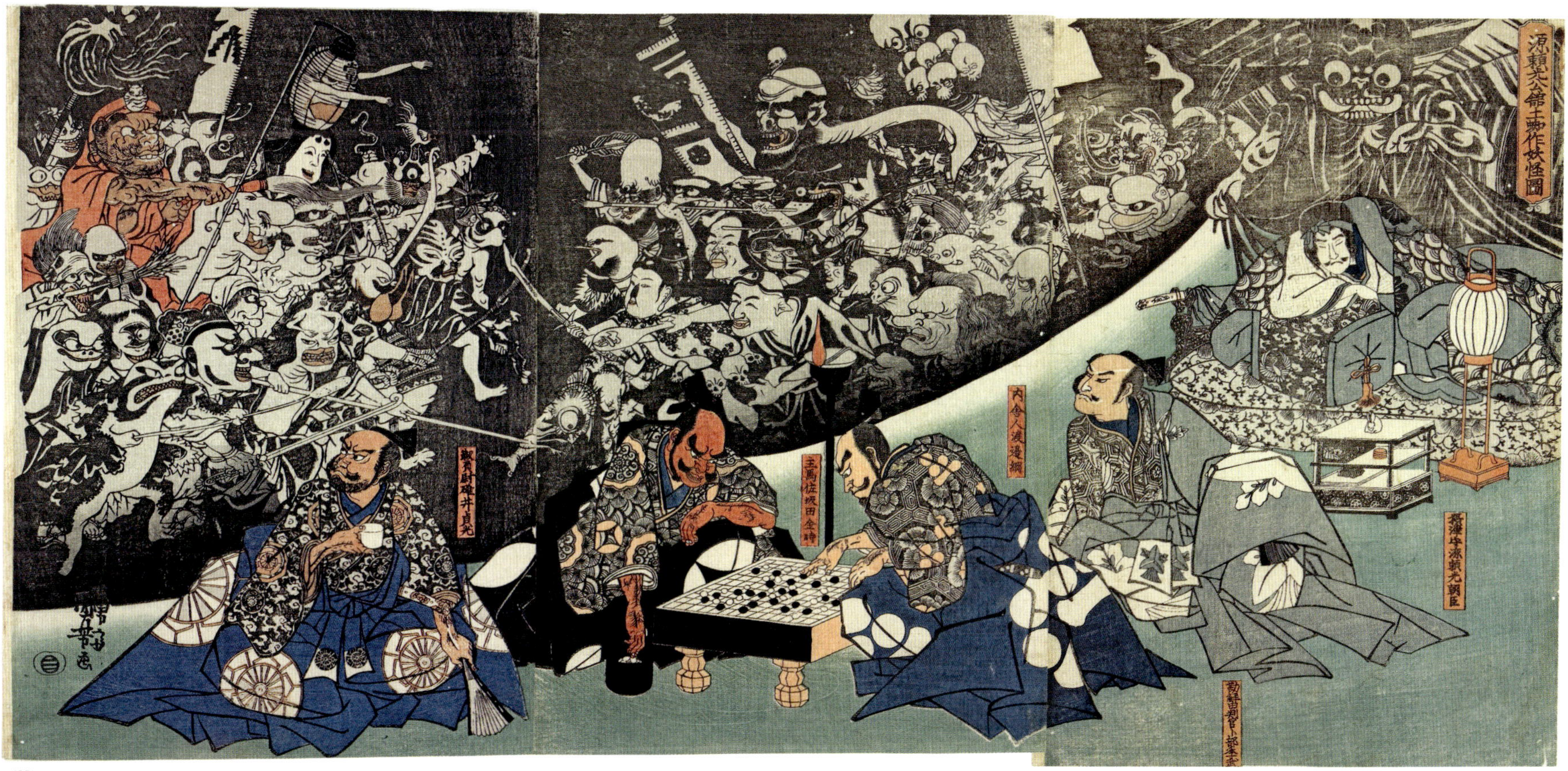

125

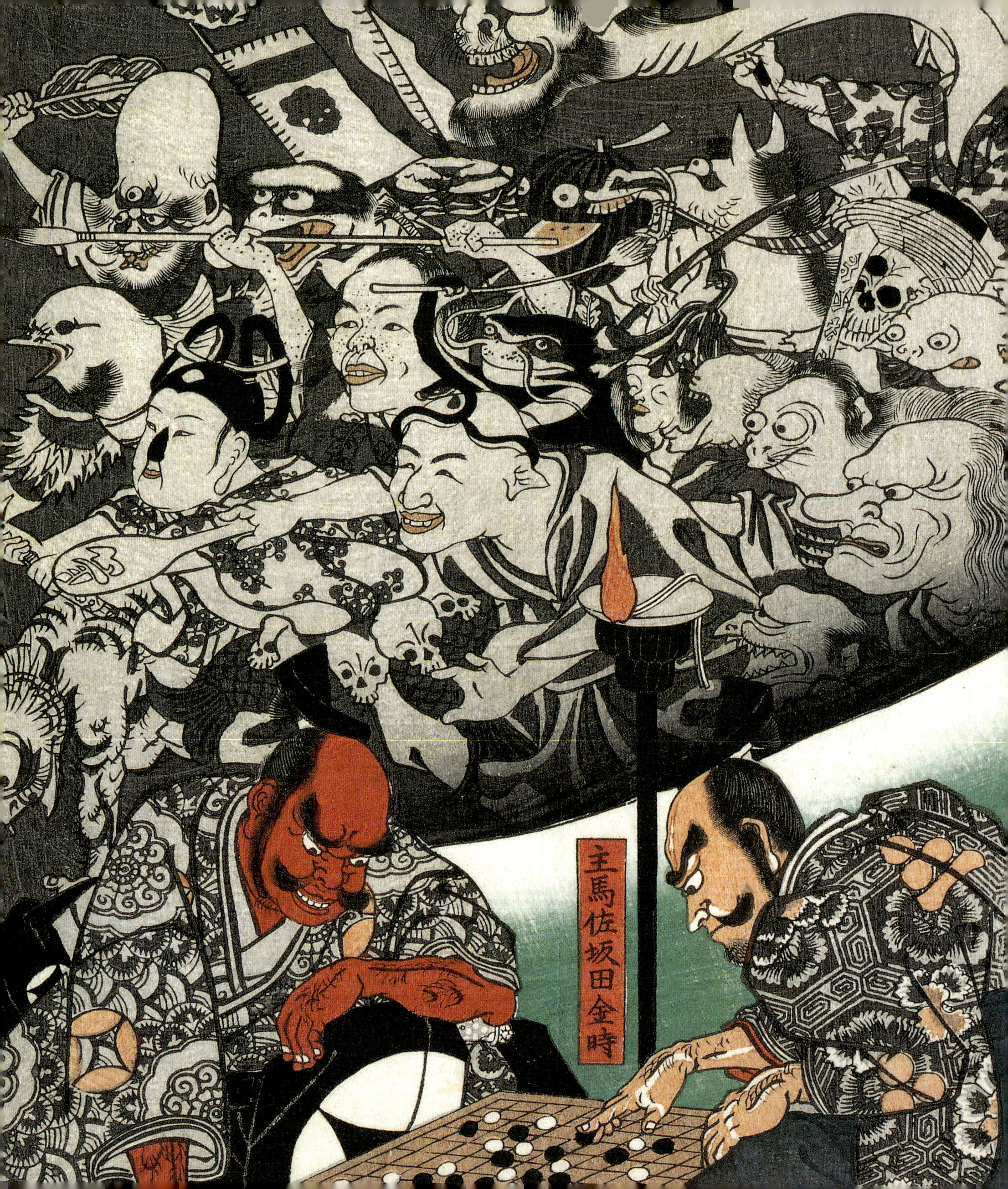
主馬佐坂田金時

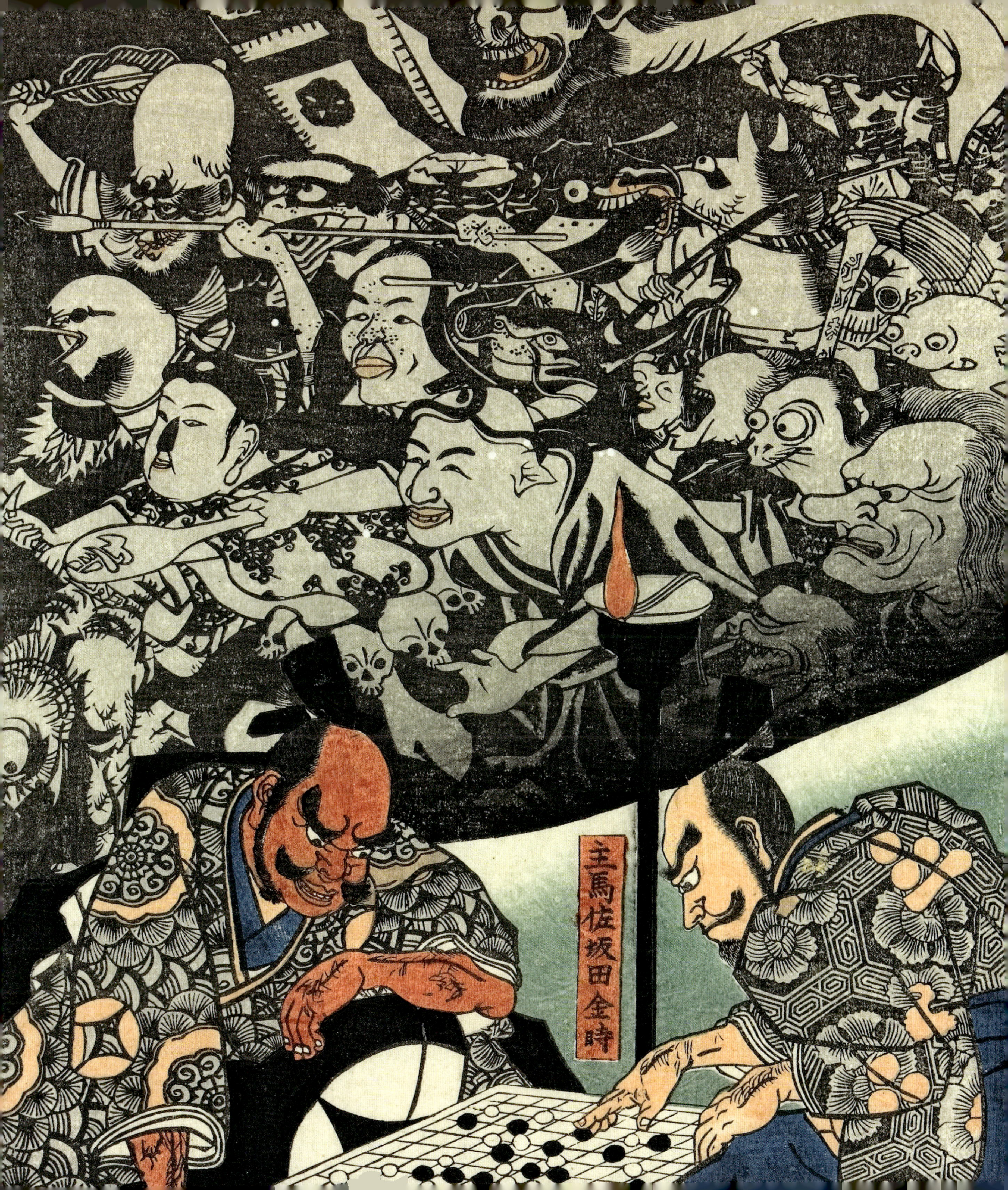
主馬佐坂田金時

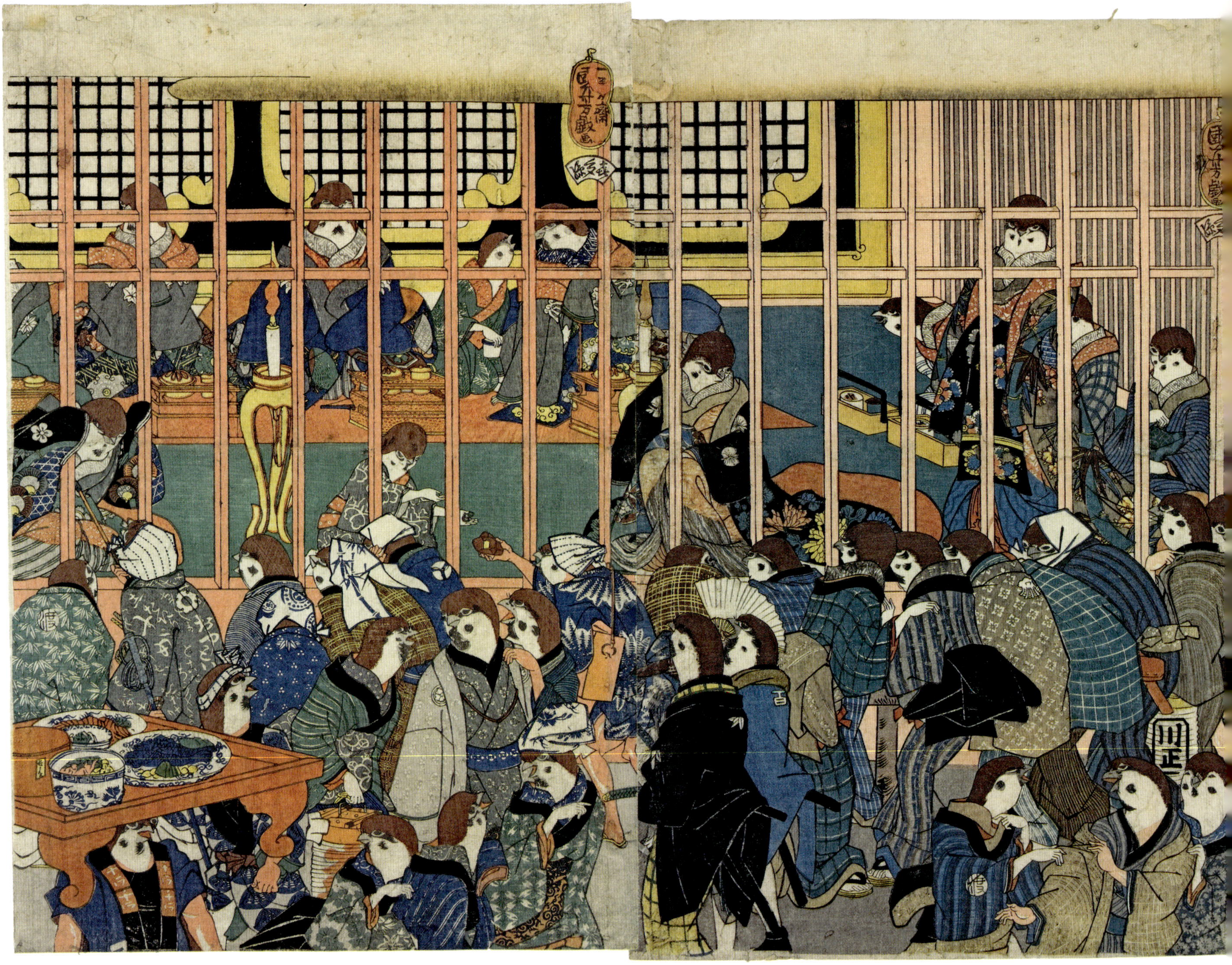
一勇斎国芳戯画
川正

126

Sparrows impersonating a brothel scene

1846

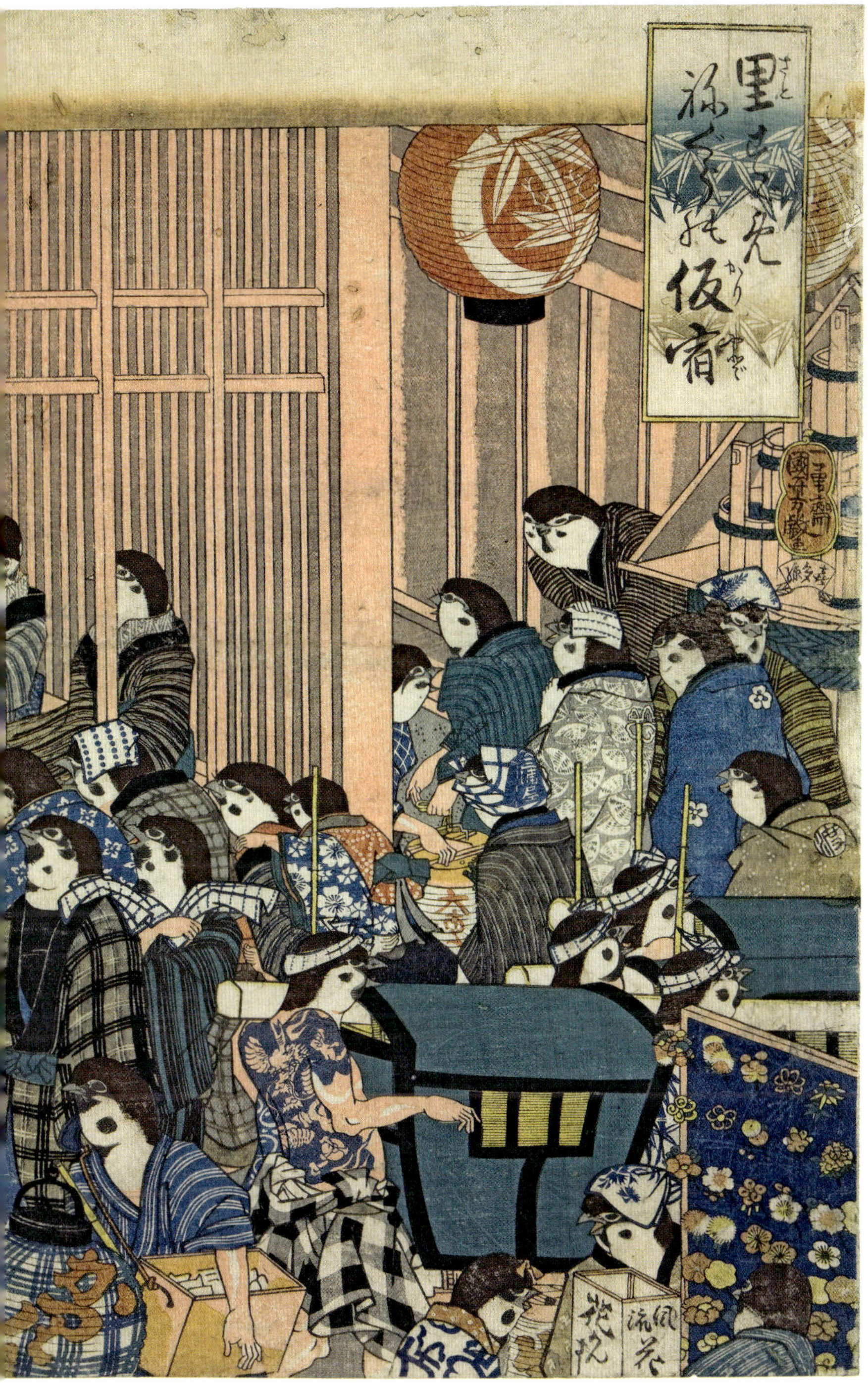

Colour woodblock, *ōban* triptych, published by Kitaya Magobei, 36.8 × 25.7 [R], 37 × 25.7 [C], 37.3 × 25.5 cm [L]

PRINT TITLE
'Village Sparrows: Temporary Shelter in the Nest' (*Sato suzume negura no kariyado*)

ARTIST'S SIGNATURE
Ichiyūsai Kuniyoshi giga (Playfully drawn by Ichiyūsai Kuniyoshi, in gourd-shaped *Yoshi* cartouche)

CENSOR'S SEAL
Watari (on three sparrows' robes)

American Friends of the British Museum (The Arthur R. Miller Collection) 19207

REFERENCES
Springfield 1968, no.88; Riccar 1978, no.273; Springfield 1980, no. 141; Inagaki 1991, no.44; Suzuki 1992, no.411; Itabashi 1994, Kuniyoshi no.90; Mainichi Shinbunsha 1995, no. 160; Nagoya 1996, nos 262–3; Ōta 1999, no. 178; Isao 2008, pp.60–1

Sparrows imitate, in minute detail, a scene in a pleasure quarter. Male pleasure-seekers, mainly workmen wearing rakish head-cloths, stare through the open lattice at courtesans seated in the 'display room' (*harimise*) of a brothel. The women are dressed in their finery and have smoking sets in front of them. On the right sheet tattooed porters carry a wealthy customer in a palanquin, while a street trader sells decorative floral hairpins. On the left sheet a large tray-table of food for a party is borne aloft, above the heads of the crowd.

In the twelfth month of 1845 Yoshiwara pleasure quarter was completely destroyed by fire. As was the custom, the authorities permitted the brothels to reopen in 'temporary lodgings' (*karitaku*) in the unlicensed quarters dotted all over the city, until Yoshiwara could be rebuilt. The Tenpō reforms included a regulation forbidding the depiction in prints of courtesans and geisha. Kuniyoshi has responded to this with remarkable inventiveness and wit, providing the public with desired information about the 'temporary lodging'. 'The village' (*sato*) was a common way of referring to Yoshiwara, and 'sparrow' (*suzume*) also described a man who knew his way around town.

Based on an analysis of passages from *Shichū torishimari ruishū, Shomotsu nishiki-e no bu* (*Collection of City Prosecutions: Book and Colour Print Section*), a document in the National Diet Library, Tokyo, Suzuki Jūzō recounts the story surrounding the censorship of this image. The city official (*nanushi*) who was duty censor for the month in question, Watanabe Shōemon, suffered a stroke and therefore entrusted his personal censorship seal to his son, who was to mark the finished preparatory drawings with it. Warming to his task, the son playfully impressed the seal onto the costumes of three sparrow figures (on the far right of the right sheet, in the centre foreground of the centre sheet and on the far left of the left sheet), as if it were a personal crest decorating their robes. This lapse in the seriousness expected of a city official came to the attention of the chief investigator (*onmitsu-gakari*), who reported the matter to the North City Magistrate, Tōyama Kagemoto. Tōyama required Watanabe to resign from his post as censor in the fifth intercalary month of 1846 (Suzuki 1992, p.235).

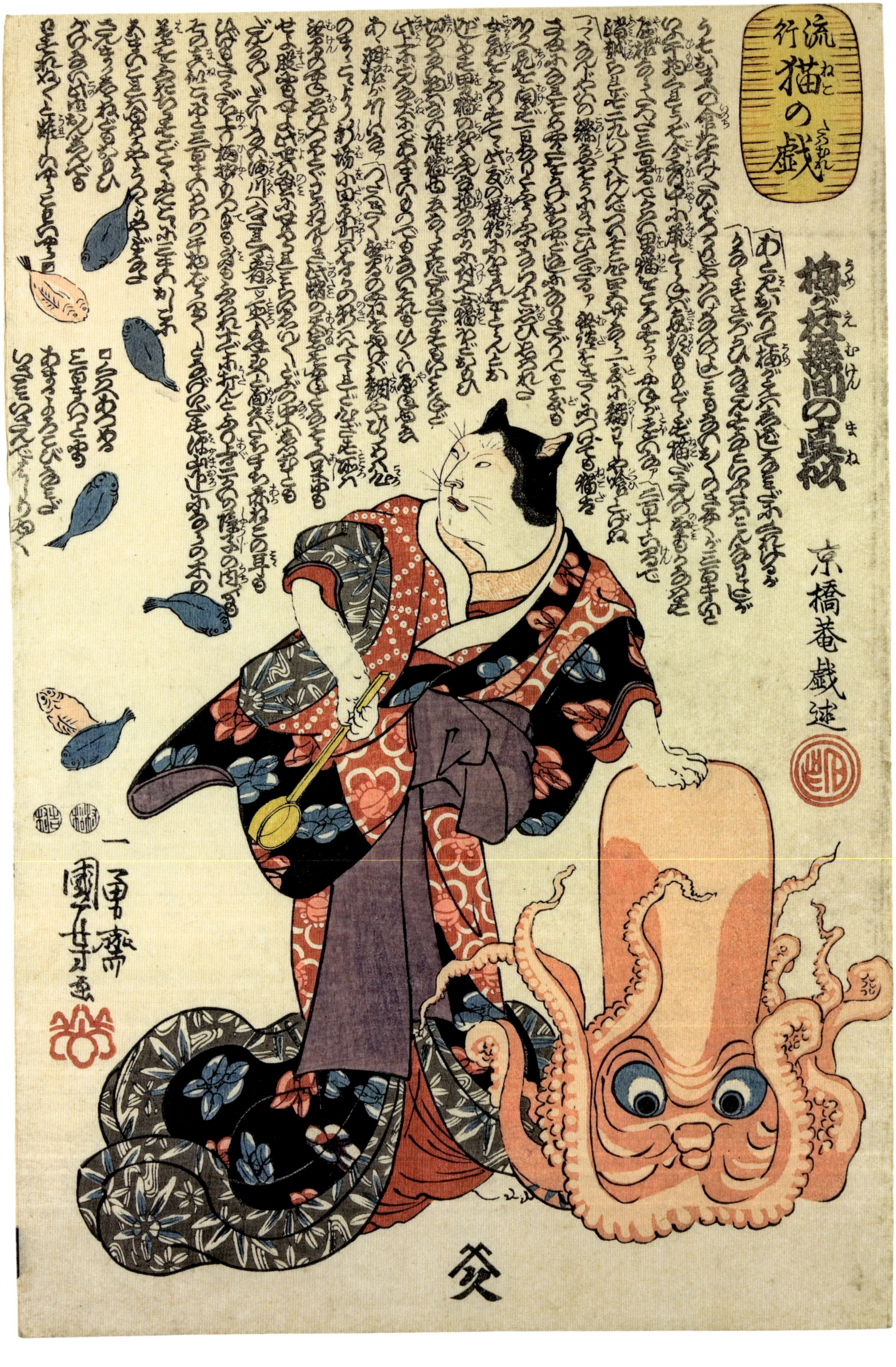
流行猫の戯
梅が枝無間の真似
京橋菴戯述
一勇斎国芳画

127

Cat impersonating a scene from Kabuki

c. 1847

Colour woodblock, *ōban*, published by Yamamoto Heikichi, 35.5 × 24.4 cm

SERIES TITLE
'Fashionable Cat Games' (*Ryūkō neko no tawamure*)

PRINT TITLE
'Parody of Umegae Striking the Bell of Limitless [Hell]' (*Umegae muken no mane*)

ARTIST'S SIGNATURE
Ichiyūsai Kuniyoshi ga

ARTIST'S SEAL
Yoshikiri

CENSORS' SEALS
Muramatsu and Yoshimura

American Friends of the British Museum (The Arthur R. Miller Collection) 03901

REFERENCES
Inagaki 1991, no. 12; Amsterdam 1998, no. 233; Hiraki 2006, p. 45

A cat impersonating a female Kabuki character has struck an octopus on the head with a wooden scoop and now watches with evident satisfaction as dried mackerel tumble down on the left.

The origins of this image are complex. At the temple Kansen-ji at Sayo no Nakayama in Tōtōmi province (the western part of modern Shizuoka prefecture) there was a famous bell called *Muken no kane* ('Limitless Bell'). Striking it supposedly brought boundless riches in this world and 'limitless hell' (*muken-jigoku*) in the next. In a Kabuki play of the Kyōhō era (1716–36) the actor Segawa Kikunojō I parodied this legend on stage for the first time, by tapping a stone water basin with a wooden scoop. The scene became an integral part of the puppet/Kabuki play *Hiragana seisuiki* (*Beginner's Version of the Rise and Fall of the Heike and Genji Clans*), first performed in 1739. Chidori has sold herself into prostitution as the courtesan Umegae so as to raise money to help her beloved Genta restore his honour. He now needs an additional three hundred gold *ryō* coins to redeem his pawned armour and join the battle of Ichinotani (which took place in 1184). With the legend of the Bell of Limitless Hell in mind, Umegae (Chidori) strikes the water basin in the garden with a scoop and swears to sell her soul. Three hundred coins rain down from the balcony above. The money is not the result of a miracle, however, but has been cast down by Genta's mother, Enju, who had secretly witnessed her pledge and taken pity on the couple (Herwig 2004, pp. 130–7).

Kuniyoshi and the author Santō Kyōzan (1769–1858), cat-lovers both, collaborated on a highly inventive novel in *gōkan* format, in which famous Kabuki actors and stage scenes were impersonated by cats. The novel, entitled *Oborozuki neko no sōshi* (*Hazy Moon Cat Tales*) and issued in seven parts from 1841 to 1849, with a hiatus in 1843–44 caused by the Tenpō reforms, was a runaway best-seller. The present design comes from a spin-off series of colour prints by Kuniyoshi with texts by Kyōzan (signed 'Kyōkyoan'). The texts, which are full of references to cats, parody the libretti of the Kabuki plays. For several years after the 1842 publishing regulations it was forbidden to draw recognisable likenesses of Kabuki actors, so this kind of comically 'displaced' actor print must have been popular with theatre fans. The title cartouche has the shape of a *koban* gold coin and alludes to the popular phrase 'gold coin for a cat' (*neko ni koban*), the equivalent of the English 'pearls before swine'. Five designs in the series are known (four are listed in Tsuda 2006, p. 28).

There are many playful feline references in the design. A cat's preference for an octopus over a stone water basin requires no explanation; neither does the substitution of dried mackerel for gold coins. The robe of the 'courtesan' ought to be decorated with plum motifs, in allusion to her name Umegae (*ume* means 'plum'), but close examination of what look like pink and white plum blossoms on the red background shows them to be stylised cat collars and bells. Similarly, the repeating 'floral' pattern on the black surcoat turns out to consist of clusters of clam shells.

Inagaki Shin'ichi publishes a transcription of the full text on the design (Inagaki 1991, pp. 18–19).

128

Graffiti caricatures of Kabuki actors

c. 1848

Colour woodblock, *ōban*, published by Ibaya Senzaburō, 36 × 25.2 cm

SERIES TITLE
'Storehouse of Treasured Goods: Scribblings on the Wall' (*Nitakara-gura kabe no mudagaki*)

ARTIST'S SIGNATURE
Ichiyūsai Kuniyoshi ga (as graffito)

ARTIST'S SEAL
Yoshi (paulownia crest, as graffito)

CENSORS' SEALS
Hama and Kinugasa

American Friends of the British Museum (The Arthur R. Miller Collection) 12401

REFERENCES
Riccar 1978, no. 268; Springfield 1980, no. 158; Amsterdam 1984, no. 224; Brussels 1989, no. 903; HUT, vol. 5, 1989, BW no. 54; Nihon Ukiyo-e Kyōkai 1990, no. 1–75; V&A 1991, no. 103; Yamaguchi 1991, Kuniyoshi no. 85; MSU 1991, no. 27; Suzuki 1992, no. 405; Mainichi Shinbunsha 1995, no. 161; Nagoya 1996, no. 271; Madison 2007, no. 119

An ardent theatre fan with a more than modest talent for drawing has taken a nail and scratched caricature portraits of his favourite Kabuki actors into the white plaster of a storehouse wall. The authorities might have banned the production and sale of lavish actor prints in the Tenpō reforms of the 1840s, but the groundswell of support from the populace for their stage heroes could not be so easily halted and it has found expression in this outlaw form. The graffiti artist has even had the temerity to sign his work in forceful, scratched characters rendered in white reserve along the grey section of wall at the bottom: 'Ichi-yū-sai Kuni-yo-shi ga' (drawn by Ichiyūsai Kuniyoshi). The signature is followed by the 'scratched' trademark of the publisher Ibaya Senzaburō, who has recorded this masterpiece of street art for posterity in a colour woodblock print.

That, at least, is the conceit of the print. Kuniyoshi has transformed his habitually suave style so as produce 'clumsy', but energetic and endearing likenesses – a way of deflecting any objections from the censor. In elevating the caricature style of drawing to the realm of sophisticated art, the print constitutes an important precursor of modern manga. Tinkering with the standard 'likeness' (*nigao-e*) painstakingly developed by leading print artists to depict an actor was a delicate matter, and in some cases the graffitist has added little 'picture riddles' (*hanji-mono*) alluding to the actor's name to make it clear who is represented – for, even after the ban on actor portraits was relaxed at the end of 1846, it was still forbidden to name them or show their acting crests. Thus, bottom left, 'pagoda' (*tō*) + 'elephant' (*zō*) = Tōzō, referring to Azuma Tōzō V. In the top left corner the street artist/theatre fan breaks into an exclamation of praise for a performance, as if calling out from the audience 'Well done! Well done!' (*Shimeta, shimeta*).

The actors have been identified by Suzuki Jūzō as follows, with supplementary research by Iwata Hideyuki (as published in Nagoya 1996, p. 270):

Bandō Hikosaburō IV, top right, with his *kuji-bishi* ('nine-line rhombus') crest

Bandō Mitsugorō IV as Priest Shunkan, bottom right, the arrow (*ya*) in a target (*mato*) alluding to his house name, Yamatoya

Onoe Matsusuke III, top centre, with the needle of a pine (*matsu*) referring to his name

Fujikawa Kayū III, a female role specialist, centre, with the actor's crest in the shape of a fan

Ōtani Tomoemon IV, top left

Nakamura Gennosuke II, centre left, the plum (*bai*) and *shamisen* (musical instrument) alluding to his pen-name, Baisha

Azuma Tōzō V, bottom left, the pagoda (*tō*) and elephant (*zō*) alluding to his name.

Five designs are known from the series 'Storehouse of Treasured Goods: Scribblings on the Wall' (*Nitakara-gura kabe no mudagaki*). When turned into a question as *Nita ka?*, the beginning of the title becomes a pun: 'Do they look like them [the actors]?' Three of the five prints have a yellow section at the bottom of the wall and have been dated *c.* 1847 on the basis of the actors and roles portrayed. The remaining two designs, including the present sheet, show a grey section at the bottom and have been dated *c.* 1848, since the print not included here contains a portrait of Ichikawa Danjūrō VIII as Fuwa Banzaemon, a role he performed at the Ichimura theatre from the third month of 1848. All five designs are illustrated as nos 270–1 in Nagoya 1996, which also provides detailed information on the identifications.

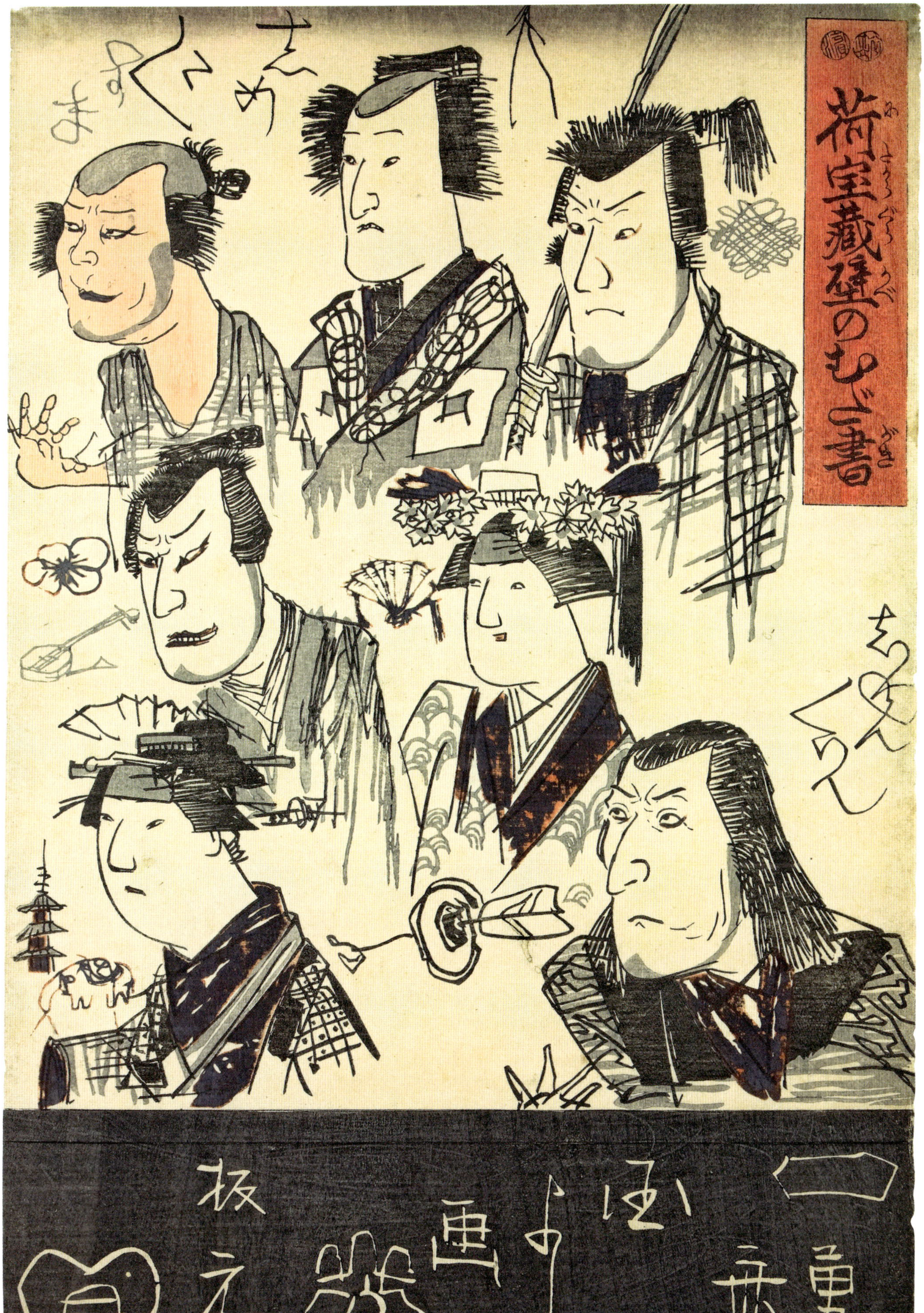
荷宝蔵壁のむだ書
一勇斎
板元

129

Self-portrait painting Ōtsu pictures

1848

Colour woodblock, *ōban* triptych, published by Minatoya Kohei, each sheet approx. 36.4 × 25.2 cm

PRINT TITLE
'Ōtsu Pictures for the Times: A Rare Thing You've been Waiting For'
(*Toki ni ōtsu-e kitai no maremono*)

ARTIST'S SIGNATURE
Ichiyūsai Kuniyoshi ga

ARTIST'S SEAL
Yoshikiri

BLOCK-CUTTER
Hori-Takichi

CENSORS' SEALS
Hama and Kinugasa [R];
Mera and Murata [C,L]

Fitzwilliam Museum, Cambridge, given by T. H. Riches 1913 (P.3656-R)

REFERENCES
Springfield 1968, no. 35; Riccar 1978, no. 279; HUT, vol. 5, 1989, BW no. 33; Keyes 1989, no. 165; Inagaki 1991, no. 81; Thompson 1991, fig. 39; Suzuki 1992, no. 442; Minneapolis 1994, no. 25; Cambridge 1997, no. 53 (this impression); Amsterdam 1998, fig. 15; Ōta 1999, no. 157; Isao 2008, p. 84

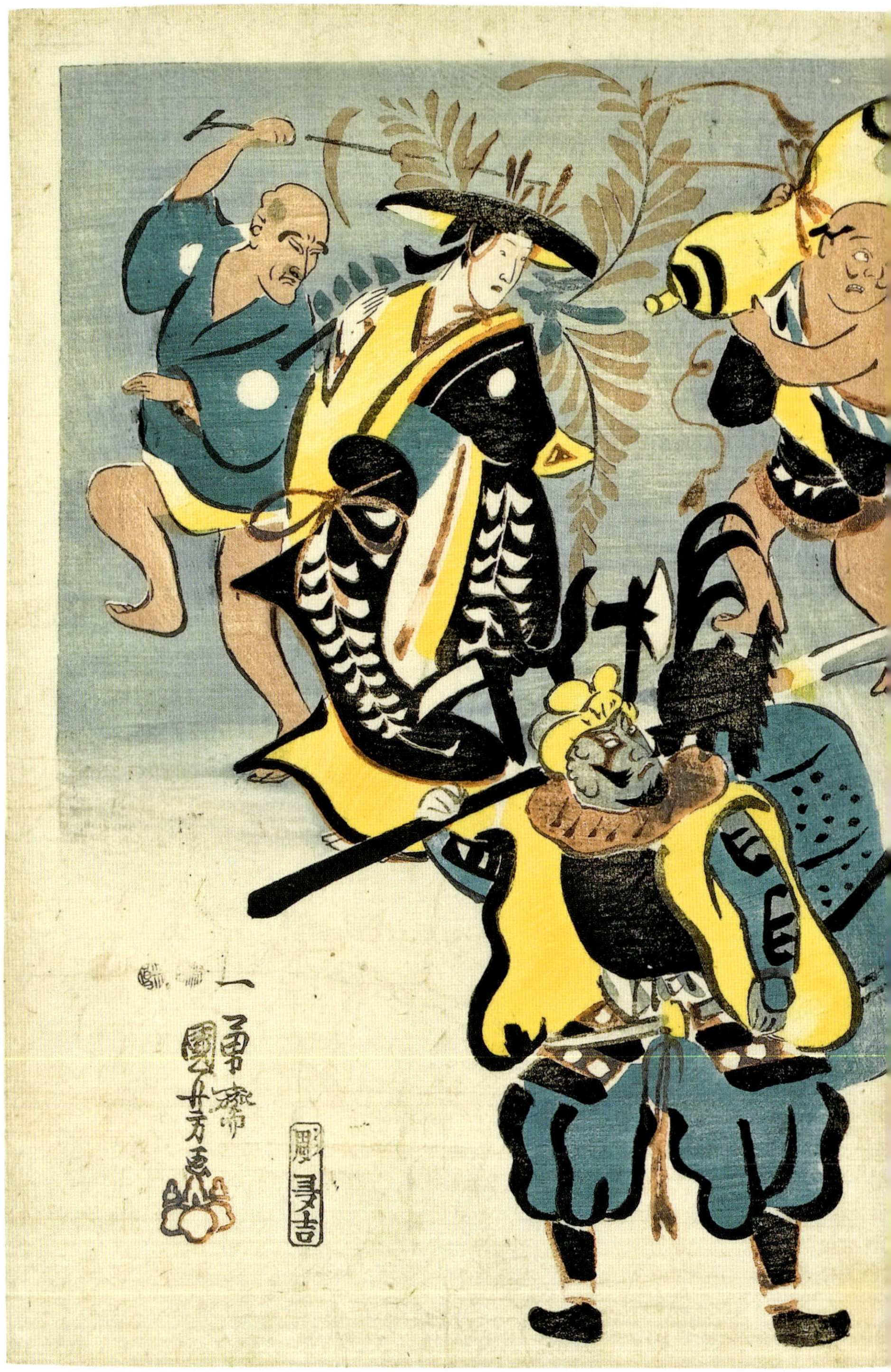

Colourful characters from Ōtsu folk paintings have come to life and stand in a circle looking at their creator, the painter, who is seated in the centre. 'Ōtsu pictures' (*Ōtsu-e*) were a lively kind of folk painting made in and around the village of Ōtsu in Ōmi province (modern Shiga prefecture) as souvenirs for travellers along the Tōkaidō road. The silhouetted figures on the fluttering sheets of paper in Kuniyoshi's print indicate that the characters have emerged from his paintings. Lest there be any doubt that the artist is Kuniyoshi, the fan at his side bears a large version of his *Yoshikiri* seal and a pet cat looks up to gain its master's attention (Kuniyoshi was a cat-lover). Tantalisingly, one of the Ōtsu paintings dances in the air right in front of the painter's face. Kuniyoshi included some half-dozen self-portraits in his prints and book illustrations, but without exception he either hides his face or averts it from the viewer. Such playful, self-effacing modesty was expected of a true 'Edokko', an artisan or merchant son of Edo.

Perhaps, then, the 'Rare Thing You've Been Waiting For' mentioned in the title is not Kuniyoshi's never-to-be-seen face, but the 'likenesses' (*nigao*) of leading Kabuki actors 'hidden' in the Ōtsu characters. By 1848 the Tenpō reforms' publication regulations had been relaxed sufficiently for artists to be permitted once more to design recognisable images of actors, provided they were not named. The present print should therefore be regarded simply as one of Kuniyoshi's playfully inventive 'crazy pictures' (*kyōga*). The actors and their roles depicted have been identified by Suzuki Jūzō. Anti-clockwise from the right, they are: Ichikawa Kodanji IV as Thunder God (*Kaminari*), an unknown actor as Catfish with a Gourd (*Hyōtan namazu*), Onoe Kikujirō (?) as Young Falconer (*Takajō wakashu*), Ichikawa Kuzō II as Samurai Footman (*Yakko*), Ōtani Hiroemon as Daikoku (*Gehō*), Iwai Kumesaburō III as Ushiwaka-maru, Nakamura Utaemon IV as Demon Reciting Buddhist Prayers (*Oni nenbutsu*), Nakayama Bungorō as Drunkard Samurai Footman (*Sakanomi yakko*), Onoe Baikō IV as Wisteria Maiden (*Fuji musume*), Seki Sanjūrō III as Blind Musician (*Zatō*) and Ichikawa Danjūrō VIII as Benkei Carrying the Bell (*Tsurigane Benkei*; see also cats 23, 24).

Suzuki Jūzō reproduces an impression from the earliest printing of the design, which has the entire background printed blue and a wiped horizontal band of black across the top (Suzuki 1992, no. 442, and Miller Collection 21002). There, as here, the orange lead (*tan*) pigment has tarnished black in many places.

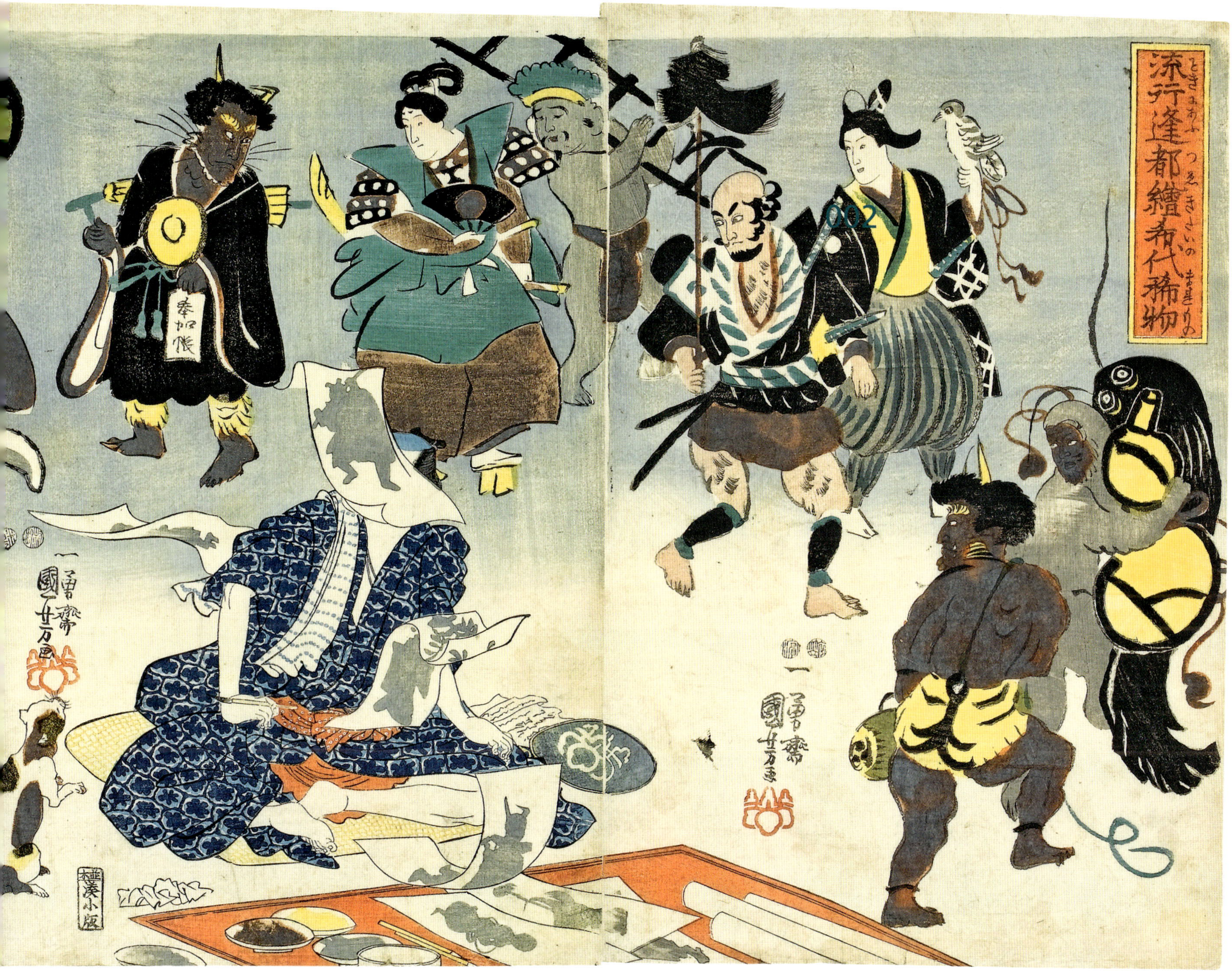
流行逢都繪希代稀物
一勇斎國芳画
一勇斎國芳画
002

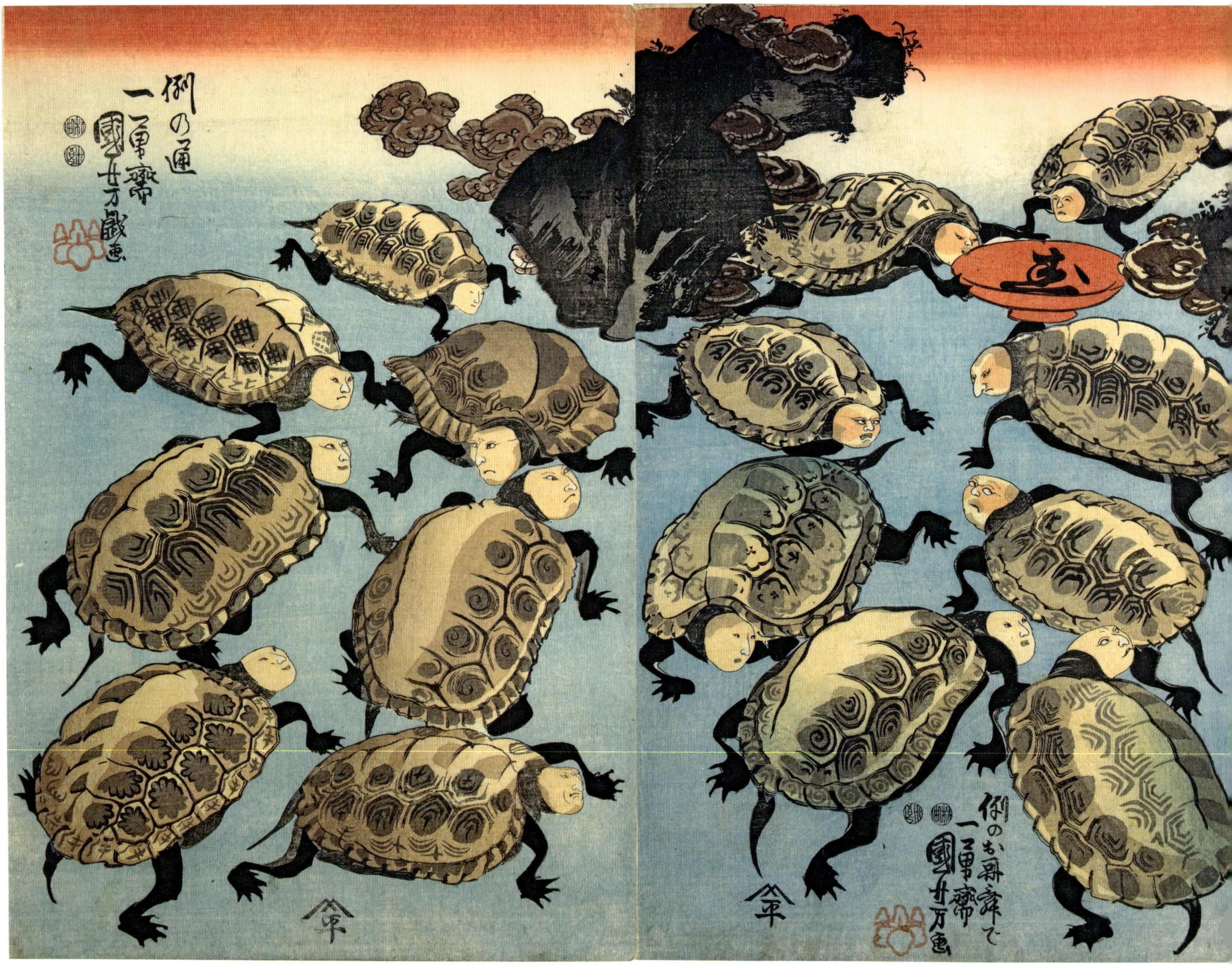
例の通
一勇斎
國芳戯画

130

Kabuki actors as turtles

1848

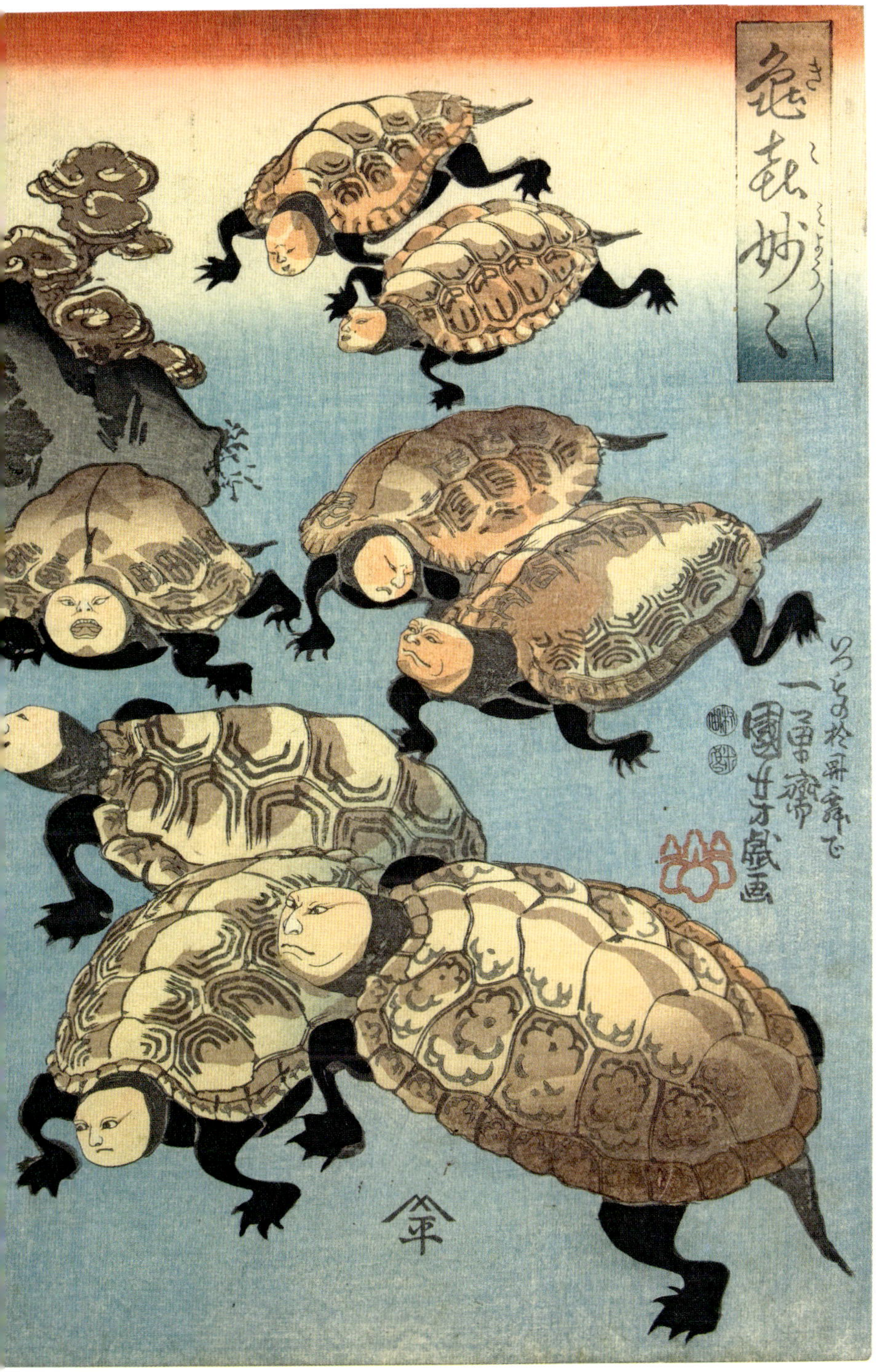

Colour woodblock, *ōban* triptych, published by Nomuraya Tokubei, 36.2 × 25 [R], 36.3 × 24.7 [C], 36.2 × 25 cm [L]

PRINT TITLE
'Turtle Fun: Wonderful, Wonderful' (*Kiki myōmyō*)

ARTIST'S SIGNATURES
Itsumo no o-kabu de Ichiyūsai Kuniyoshi giga ('Playfully drawn by Ichiyūsai Kuniyoshi, with the usual treatment' [R]);

Rei no o-kabu de Ichiyūsai Kuniyoshi ga ('Drawn by Ichiyūsai Kuniyoshi, with the normal treatment' [C]);

Rei no tōri Ichiyūsai Kuniyoshi giga ('Playfully drawn by Ichiyūsai Kuniyoshi, as normal' [L])

ARTIST'S SEAL
Yoshikiri

CENSORS' SEALS
Mera and Murata

The British Museum JA 1907.5-31.0638

REFERENCES
Springfield 1968, no. 107; Riccar 1978, no. 275; HUT, vol. 3, 1988, BW no. 34 (this impression); Keyes 1989, no. 192; Inagaki 1991, no. 145; Thompson 1991, fig. 33; Suzuki 1992, no. 398; Nagoya 1996, no. 269

The picture teems with turtles, most of them heading towards the red lacquer saké cup, from which one is already drinking. Growing on the rocks are clumps of fungus. All this imagery is auspicious. Turtles were thought to live for ten thousand years and to be inordinately fond of wine: the saké cup here is inscribed with the character for 'long life' (*kotobuki*). As in China, certain types of sacred fungus were believed to confer immortality when eaten.

In each of his inscriptions Kuniyoshi points out that the subject is treated in his 'usual' or 'normal' way (i.e. playfully). On close scrutiny it turns out that the heads of all twenty-three turtles have been drawn with likenesses (*nigao*) of Kabuki actors. Despite gradual relaxation of the ban on actor prints after 1846, it was still forbidden to name actors or show their crests; so the likenesses here are abetted by distinctive 'markings' on each turtle shell, which allude to the relevant actor's name either in the form of a stylised version of his stage crest or in some other way. Thus, the 'senior' turtle in the bottom right corner is Nakamura Utaemon IV and the stylised plum blossom pattern on his shell refers to his family's acting crest. Similarly, the turtle at centre left on the left sheet depicts Ichikawa Danjūrō VIII and the pattern on the shell – three squares, one inside the next – represents a stylised version of his 'triple rice-measure' (*mimasu*) crest. Katsuhara Ryōta and Suzuki Jūzō have identified nearly all the actors and deciphered most of their shell markings (Suzuki 1992, pp. 233–4).

Kiki myōmyō is a stock emphatic expression meaning 'Strange, strange, wonderful, wonderful'. In the context of the punning print title, although the first two characters are still pronounced *kiki*, their meaning changes to 'turtle fun'.

An entry in *Fujiokaya nikki* (*Fujiokaya Diary*) for the fourth month of 1848 records that the publisher, expecting the triptych to sell well, had one thousand sets printed, pricing them at sixty *mon* each. In the event, it proved a flop and only one hundred and fifty were sold (*Fujiokaya nikki*, vol. 3, 1988, p. 246). Suzuki observes, however, that later printings have survived, which suggests that the design eventually became popular enough to merit reprinting, albeit with less sophisticated effects (the gradated printing on the shell of Utaemon IV, bottom right, and at other places in the design is omitted) (Suzuki 1992, pp. 233–4).

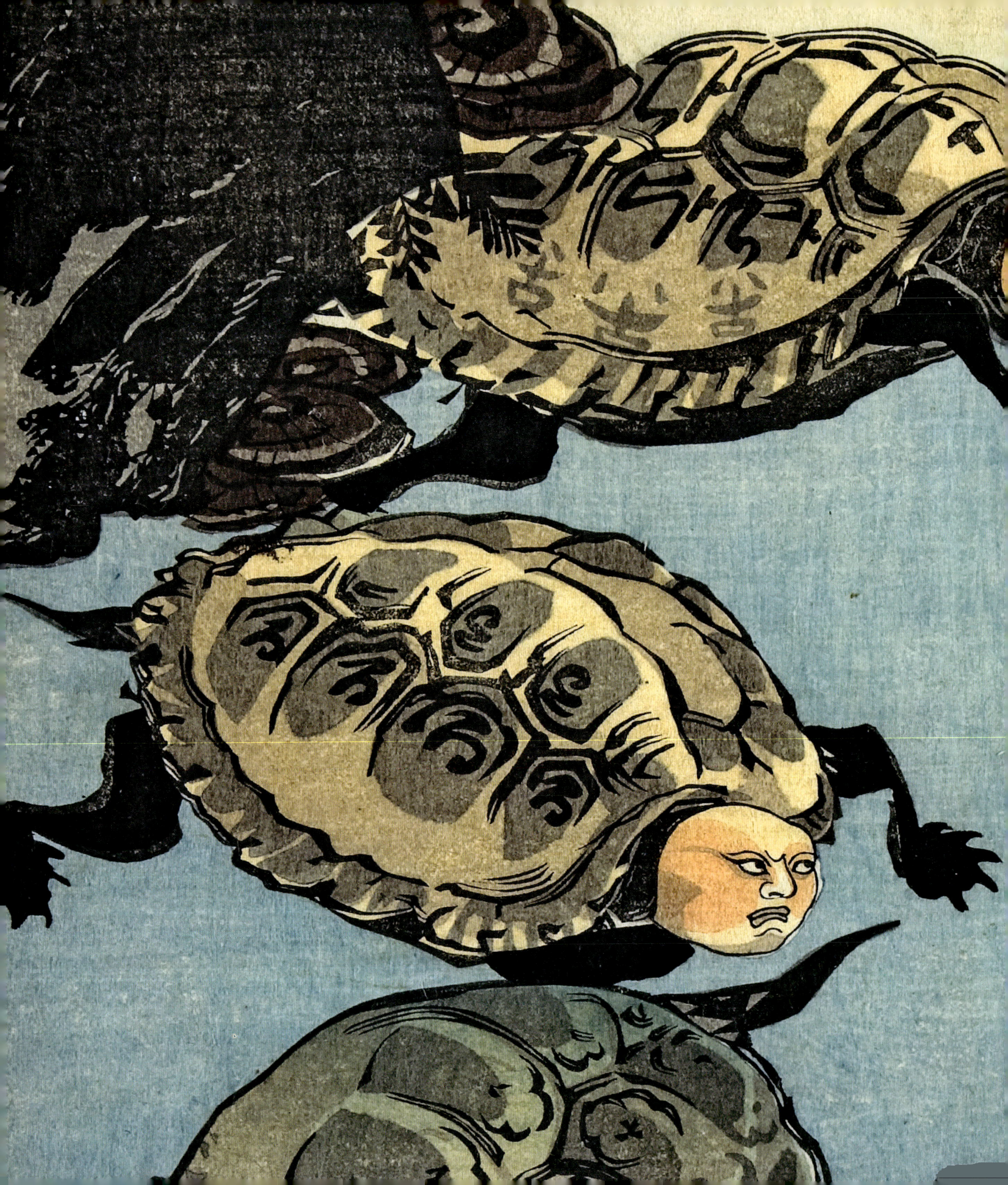

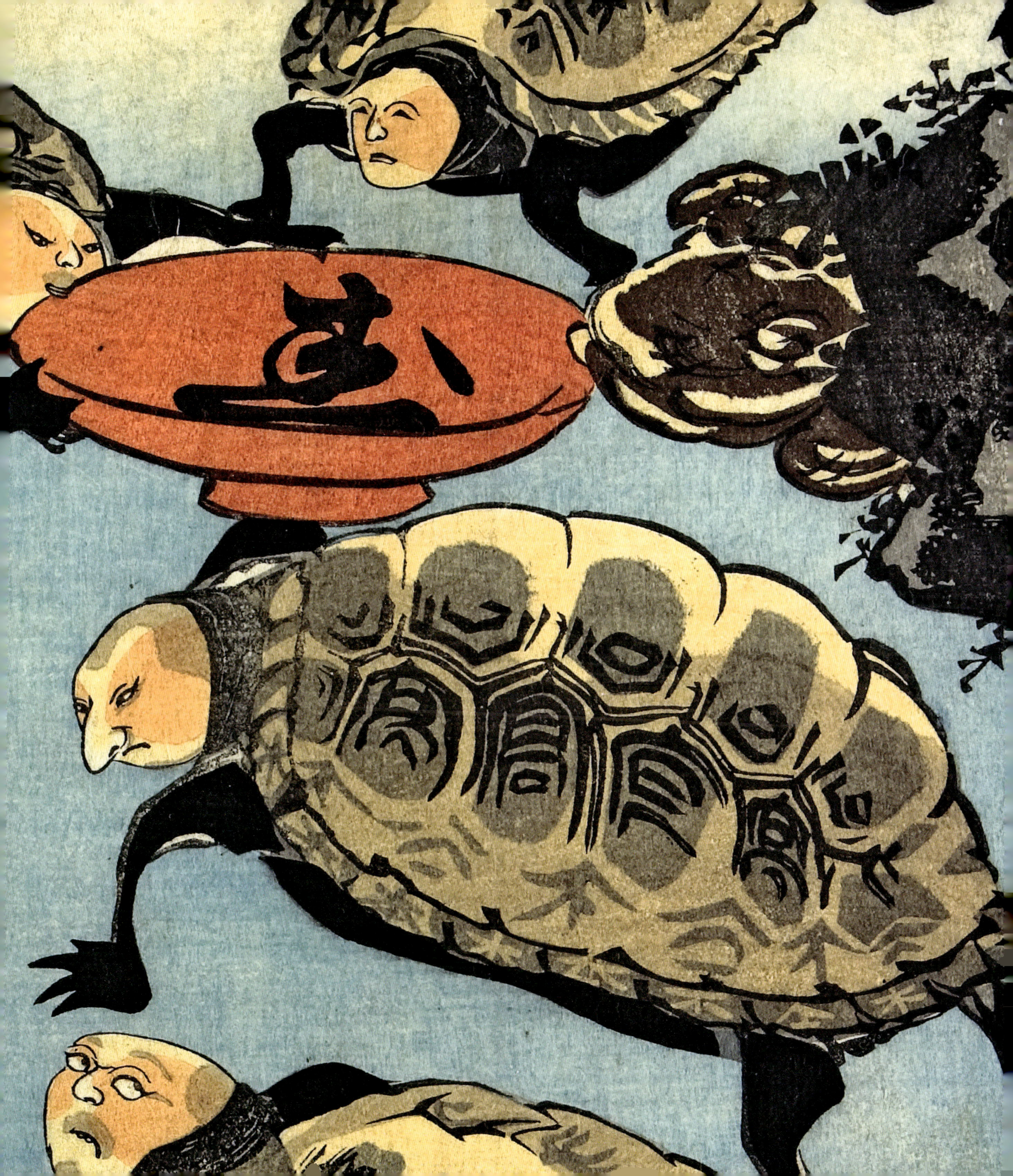

131

Original cherrywood printing block for 'He looks fierce but he's a really great guy'

c. 1847

Cherrywood printing block, 39.6 × 27 × 1.7 cm

ARTIST'S SIGNATURE
Ichiyūsai Kuniyoshi giga (playfully drawn by Ichiyūsai Kuniyoshi)

ARTIST'S SEAL
Yoshikiri

CENSORS' SEALS
Hama and Kinugasa

PUBLISHER'S MARK
Izutsuya Bunsuke, Nagoya (inserted later)

Andō Osamu Collection, Japan (courtesy of Katsuhara Ryōta)

REFERENCES
Nagoya 1996, no. 310

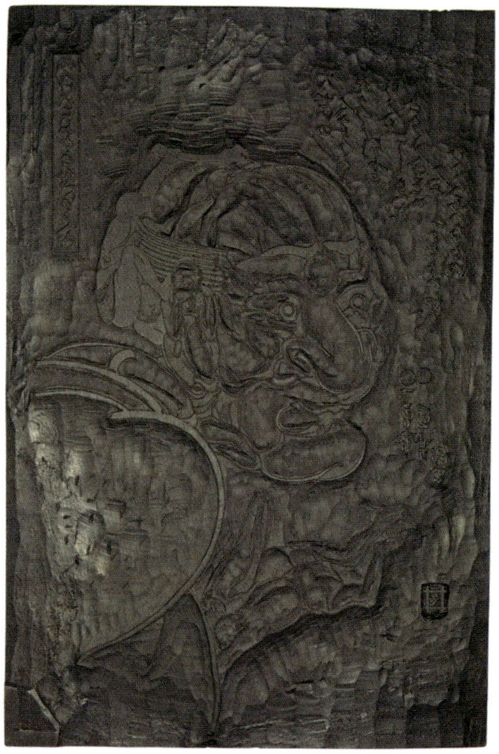

132

Modern proof impression of 'He looks fierce but he's a really great guy'

PUBLISHER'S MARK
Izutsuya Bunsuke [Nagoya] (plugged), 39.3 × 27 cm

ARTIST'S SIGNATURE
Ichiyūsai Kuniyoshi giga (playfully drawn by Ichiyūsai Kuniyoshi)

ARTIST'S SEAL
Yoshikiri

CENSORS' SEALS
Hama and Kinugasa

Andō Osamu Collection, Japan (courtesy of Katsuhara Ryōta)

REFERENCES
Nagoya 1996, no. 311

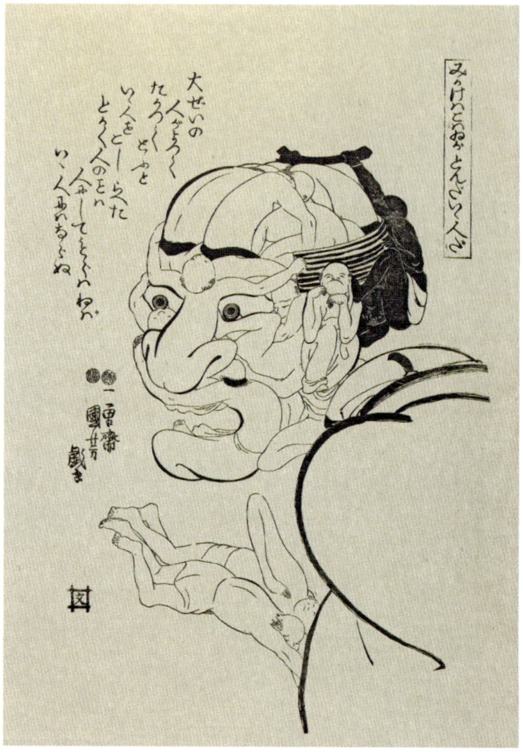

133

He looks fierce but he's a really great guy

c. 1847

Colour woodblock, *ōban*, published by Fujiokaya Hikotarō, 36.8 × 25.1 cm

PRINT TITLE
'He looks fierce but he's a really great guy' (*Mikake wa kowai ga tonda ii hito da*)

ARTIST'S SIGNATURE
Ichiyūsai Kuniyoshi giga (playfully drawn by Ichiyūsai Kuniyoshi)

ARTIST'S SEAL
Yoshikiri

CENSORS' SEALS
Hama and Kinugasa

INSCRIPTION
Ōzei no hito ga yotte takatte tōto ii hito o koshiraeta / tokaku hito no koto wa hito ni shite morawaneba ii hito ni wa naranu

Takashima Masao Collection, Japan

REFERENCES
Springfield 1968, no. 101; Hillier 1976, no. 846; Riccar 1978, no. 266; Springfield 1980, no. 155; HUT, vol. 11, 1988, no. 137; MSU 1991, no. 71; Suzuki 1992, no. 382; Itabashi 1994, Kuniyoshi no. 91; Tokyo Shinbun 1994, no. I-51; Nagoya 1996, no. 281; Amsterdam 1998, no. 231

Semi-naked figures huddle together to form a half-length portrait of a man: 'He looks fierce but he's a really great guy'. The pattern on his robe, a circle crossed by three horizontal lines, reveals his identity: he is Asaina Saburō, a historical figure who became a hero in popular late Edo-period fiction, including an illustrated novel in *yomihon* format by Takizawa Bakin entitled *Asaina shima-meguri no ki* (*Record of Asaina's Travels to Various Islands*, 1815–26). Asaina's fictional journeys in foreign lands, where he met inhabitants who looked very different from the Japanese, became an important popular arena for exploring the politically charged subject of Japan's foreign relations (Kurushima, in Asano and Yoshida 1997). In Kuniyoshi's print, for example, two black men form the hair, one holding aloft a piece of black coral to suggest a topknot. Two pink figures in black loincloths make the eyebrows.

How did Kuniyoshi come up with the striking idea of combining figures into a face? No direct models exist in Japanese art and it is tempting to suggest that a European image in the tradition of Giuseppe Arcimboldo (1527–1593) fired his imagination. The composite heads in the currently accepted corpus of autograph works by Arcimboldo consist exclusively of vegetables, fruits, flowers and animals (Vienna 2007). However, several works formerly attributed to the artist feature naked children's bodies arranged to form the head of their murderer, King Herod (see, for example, Geiger 1954, pls 81–3). Unless a more definite correlation can be established, any connection must remain conjectural.

Four published designs by Kuniyoshi are known in which figures form a head (Suzuki 1992, nos 382–5; see also cats 134, 135). There is also one unpublished drawing in Leiden, entitled 'An Honest Man' (*Shōjiki na hito*; Amsterdam 1998, no. 268). In a further print the twelve animals of the zodiac come together to create a human head (Suzuki 1992, no. 386).

The moralising text at the upper left perhaps testifies to the lingering spirit of the Tenpō reforms. It may be roughly translated as follows: 'A large crowd of people got together, hugged one another and finally managed to create a good person. At any rate, in human affairs, if people do not imagine themselves in the situation of other people, then they will never make a good person.'

The original cherrywood printing block for the design has survived. On the reverse it bears four small designs by Kuniyoshi for an illustrated novel in *gōkan* format, *Kogane-giku hana no miyakoji*, part three, which was published by Mikawaya Tetsugorō in 1848 (Nagoya 1996, no. 312). The single-sheet print would have been considered more important; that side of the block would therefore have been cut earlier and the design published before the book illustrations were carved on the reverse. Since the print bears the twin censorship seals that were introduced in 1847, it is thought to have been issued in the course of that year. The block was later sold to Izutsuya Bunsuke, a Nagoya publisher, who inserted his trademark on a newly carved plug of wood and printed another edition of the design. A modern proof impression taken from the block shows the Izutsuya trademark to the left of the man's hand.

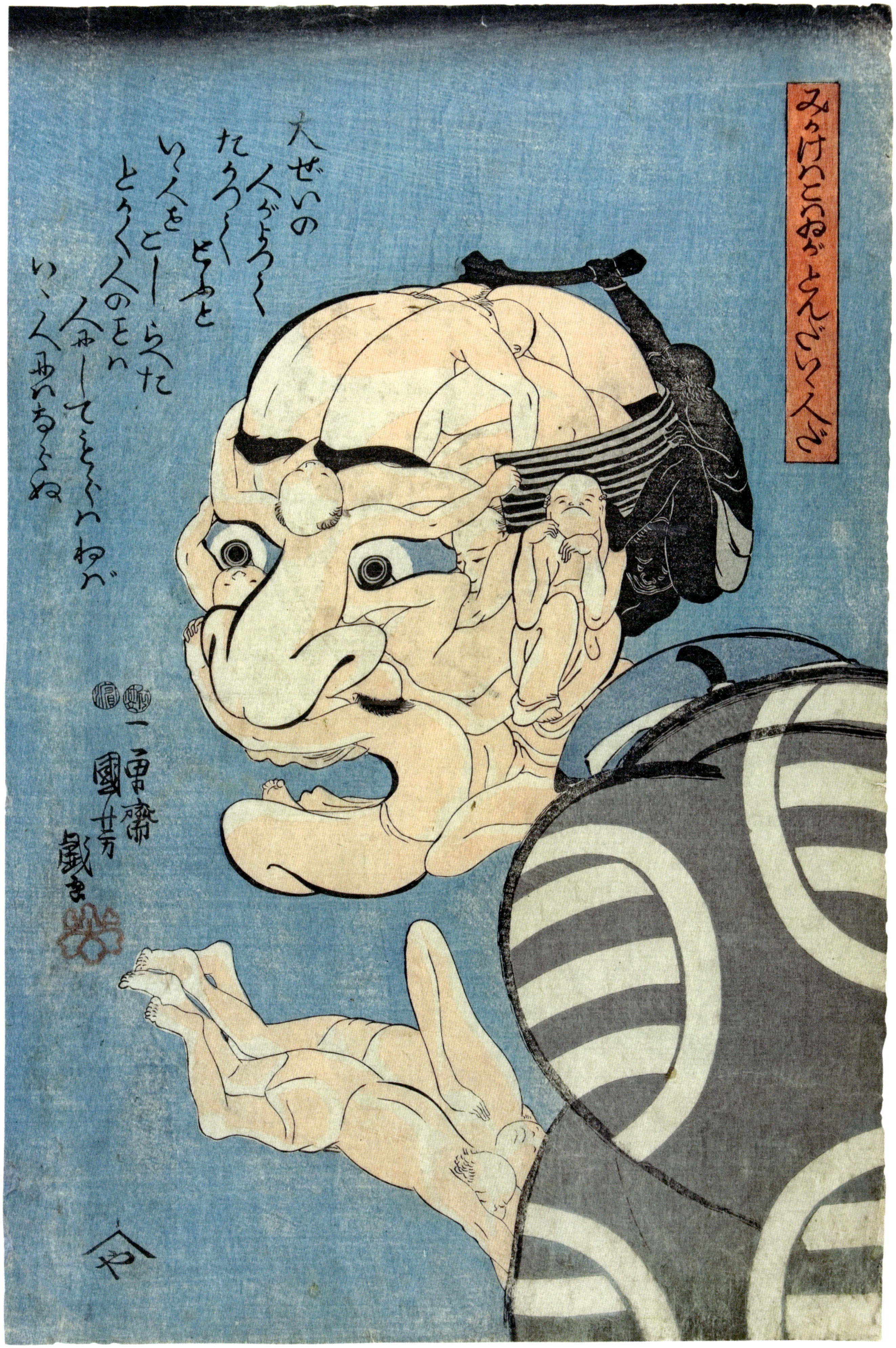
みかけハこハゐがとんだいゝ人だ
一勇齋国芳戯画

134

Men come together and make a man

c. 1847

Colour woodblock, *ōban*, published by Yamatoya Kyūbei, 36 × 24.1 cm

PRINT TITLE
'Men come together and make a man' (*Hito katamatte hito ni naru*)

ARTIST'S SIGNATURE
Ichiyūsai Kuniyoshi giga (Playfully drawn by Ichiyūsai Kuniyoshi)

ARTIST'S SEAL
Yoshikiri

CENSORS' SEALS
Muramatsu and Yoshimura

INSCRIPTION
Hito-ōki / hito no naka ni mo / hito zo naki / hito ni nare hito / hito ni nase hito

American Friends of the British Museum (The Arthur R. Miller Collection) 21404

REFERENCES
Springfield 1968, no. 100; Riccar 1978, no. 264; Springfield 1980, no. 153; Venice 1987, p. 236; HUT, vol. 11, 1988, no. 139; Brussels 1989, no. 908; Suzuki 1992, no. 383; Tokyo Shinbun 1994, no. I-55; Mainichi Shinbunsha 1995, no. 146; Nagoya 1996, no. 283; Amsterdam 1998, no. 232; Ōta 1999, no. 168

A group of men with shaved heads have come together to make a head. The eye and hair are formed by their black loincloths, the eyebrow by a black belt. The black topknot consists of a portable writing set (*yatate*), held in the hand of one man's outstretched arm. The shoulder and back are formed by a group of figures wearing identical green robes who lie next to one another in a huddle. The moralising poem (*dōka*) inscribed at the top repeats the character for 'man' (*hito*) no less than seven times and can be tentatively translated as: 'In any great man among men / there is no man at all. / Some people become people, / other people make people.'

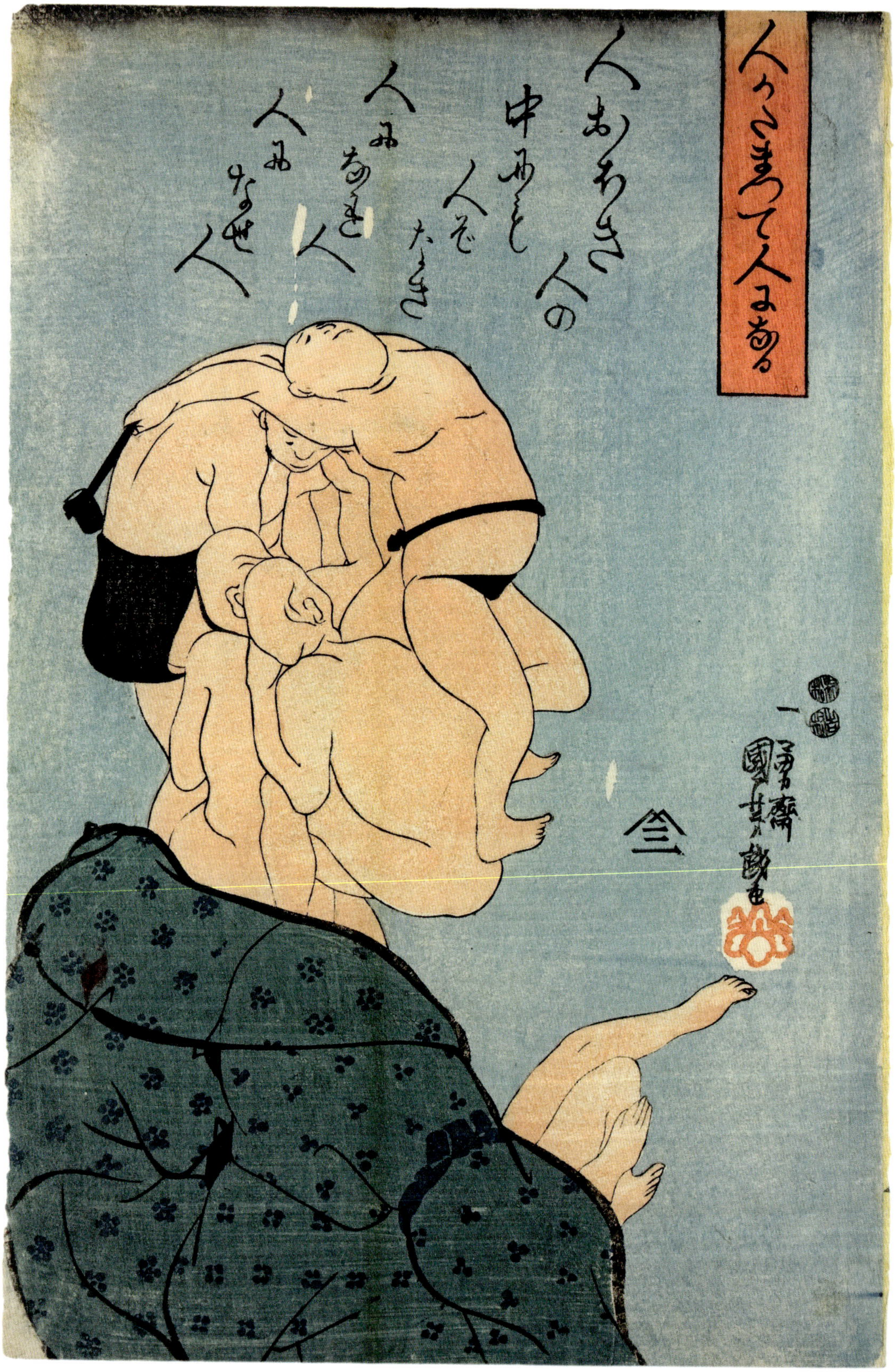

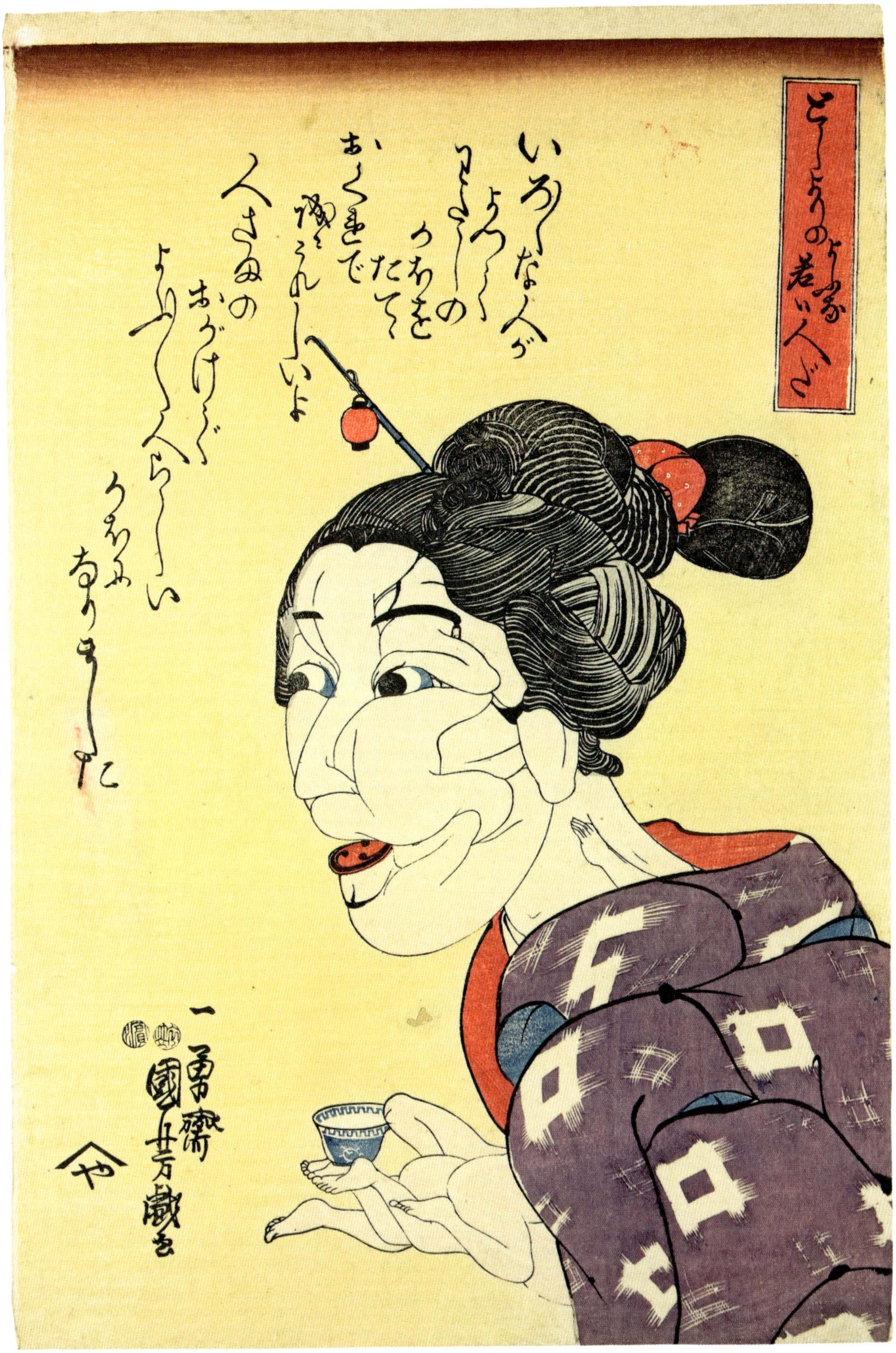

135

Young woman who looks like an old lady

c. 1847

Colour woodblock, *ōban*, published by Fujiokaya Hikotarō, 38.2 × 25.9 cm

PRINT TITLE
'It's a young woman who looks like an old lady' (*Toshiyori no yō na wakai hito da*)

ARTIST'S SIGNATURE
Ichiyūsai Kuniyoshi giga (Playfully drawn by Ichiyūsai Kuniyoshi)

CENSORS' SEALS
Hama and Kinugasa

INSCRIPTION
Iroiro na hito ga yotte watashi no kao o tatete okure de makoto ni ureshii yo / hito-sama no o-gake [o-kage] de you you hito-rashii kao ni narimashita

American Friends of the British Museum (The Arthur R. Miller Collection) 21408

REFERENCES
Riccar 1978, no. 265; Springfield 1980, no. 154; Venice 1987, p. 235; HUT, vol. 11, 1988, no. 136; Brussels 1989, no. 907; Suzuki 1992, no. 385; Tokyo Shinbun 1994, no. I-53; Mainichi Shinbunsha 1995, no. 144; Nagoya 1996, no. 280; Amsterdam 1998, no. 230; Ōta 1999, no. 167

The young woman is holding a small saké cup and leans forward with her mouth open, ready for a chat. Her hair is formed by three women wearing striped robes who huddle so that their heads meet. One holds a lantern on a bamboo pole, which becomes a decorative hairpin. The bun and its red ribbon are made by two crouching women. The eyes are circles of black hair left on the shaved heads of two naked boys who hold aloft sickles to form the eyebrows. The mouth may consist of a child's miniature hand-drum. The woman's clothing is composed of male figures wearing matching purple robes with white ikat-dyed flashes. The blue of their shaved heads, with the faces averted from the viewer, becomes the lining of the woman's summer robe, visible through its open seams.

The title may claim that the young woman looks like an old lady, but she herself is delighted with her appearance: 'I'm terribly happy that so many different people came together to make my face for me. Thanks to these kind people, it really has turned into quite a "personable" face.'

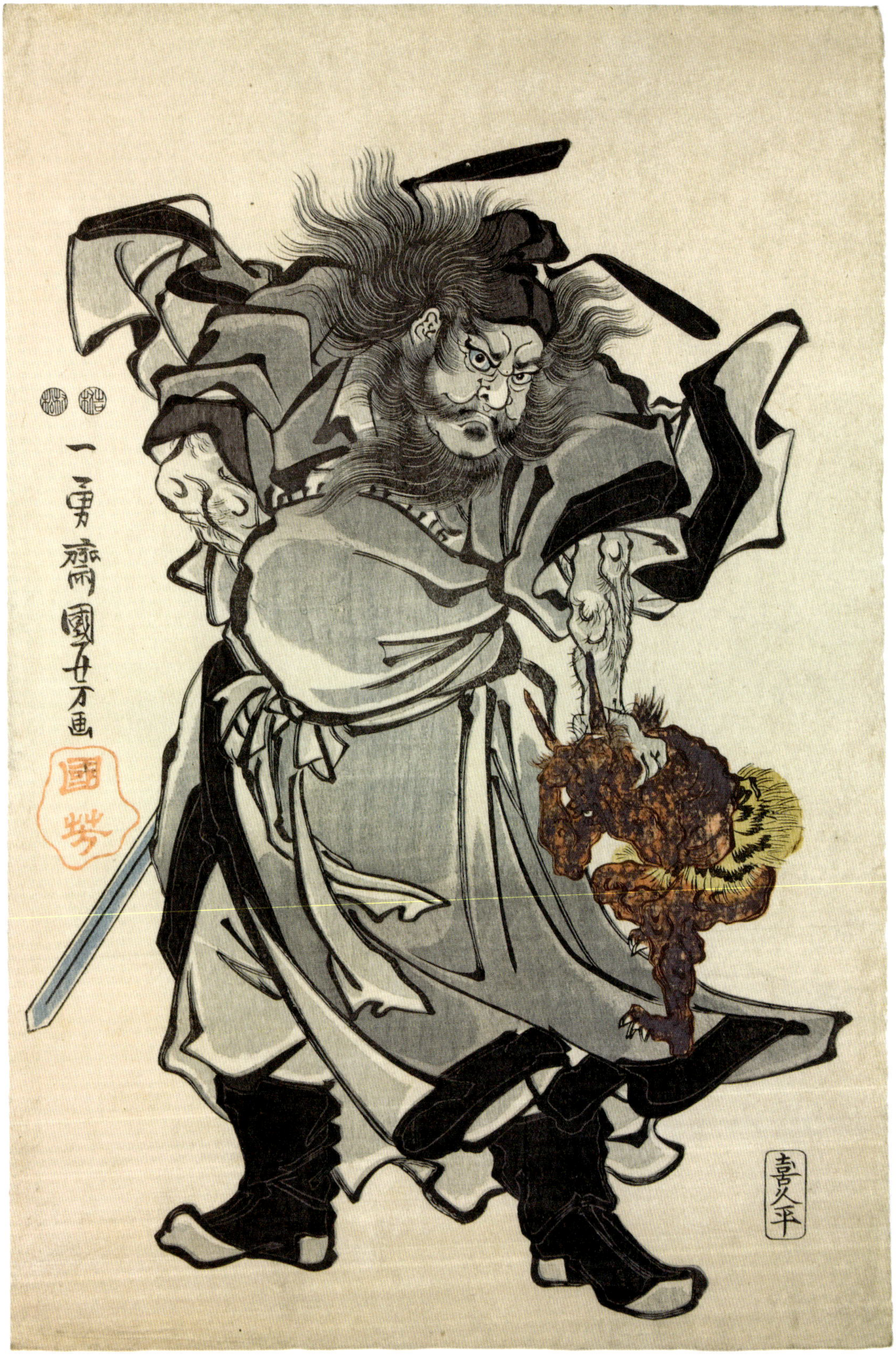

136

Shōki the demon-queller

c. 1847

Colour woodblock, *ōban*, published by Kikuhei, 37.5 × 25.3 cm

ARTIST'S SIGNATURE
Ichiyūsai Kuniyoshi ga

ARTIST'S SEAL
Kuniyoshi

CENSORS' SEALS
Muramatsu and Yoshimura

American Friends of the British Museum (The Arthur R. Miller Collection) 21410

REFERENCES
Robinson 1963, no. 23; Brussels 1989, no. 900

Shōki (Zhong Kui in his native China) was a legendary hero who drove away demons. He was said to have subdued a demon that troubled the sleep of Emperor Xuanzong (ruled 713–56) of the Tang period. Ashamed at failing the imperial examinations, Zhong had allegedly committed suicide in earlier times and was now rendering posthumous service to the emperor in gratitude for the honourable burial he had been accorded. He is generally depicted, as here, with a ferocious stare, bristling hair and beard, a Chinese scholar's robes and cap, and tall boots. He invariably chases off small demons with a long, straight sword.

In Japan, Shōki's auspicious image was displayed annually for the Boys' Festival, the fifth day of the fifth lunar month. A red image of Shōki was considered effective against smallpox (see also cat. 110). Kuniyoshi's treatment of the figure is painterly, the lines tapering and swelling in the manner of a scroll painting executed in brush and ink. Indeed, the signature and seal resemble those generally seen on his autograph hanging scroll paintings, not on his woodblock prints. The body of the cowering demon is printed in orange lead pigment (*tan*), which has tarnished black. Yonemura and Suzuki reproduce other Shōki prints by Kuniyoshi from around this time (Smithsonian 2002, nos 102–3; Suzuki 1992, no. 226, dated third month, 1854).

137

Arhat Handaka conjures up a dragon

late 1840s or early 1850s

Hanging scroll; ink and light colour on paper, 125 × 51.2 cm

ARTIST'S SIGNATURE
Ichiyūsai Kuniyoshi

ARTIST'S SEAL
Kuniyoshi

The British Museum JA 1913.5-1.0360, given by Sir W Gwynne-Evans, Bt. Ex-coll. Arthur Morrison

REFERENCES
Robinson 1961, no. 98; Clark 1992, no. 158; Amsterdam 1998, no. 278

Handaka (Panthaka in Sanskrit) is one of the sixteen arhats, disciples of the Buddha Sakyamuni who use their supernatural powers to protect the faith during the period between Sakyamuni's death and the coming of Maitreya, the Buddha of the future. Handaka's attribute is a begging bowl from which a dragon emanates in a rain cloud. In Kuniyoshi's humorous treatment, the holy man pokes at the diminutive dragon with one finger and the creature bristles back at him angrily. The work was clearly painted at speed: the texture of the trails of cloud flying upwards from the dragon suggests that it may even have been done spontaneously at a party, with the paper laid on tatami matting. The energetic brushwork has produced richly contrasting ink tonalities. The monk's stole worn by Handaka has slipped off one emaciated shoulder, the shape of which echoes comically the bony protrusion on the top of his head. The hem of his dark monastic robe curls into fantastic flourishes.

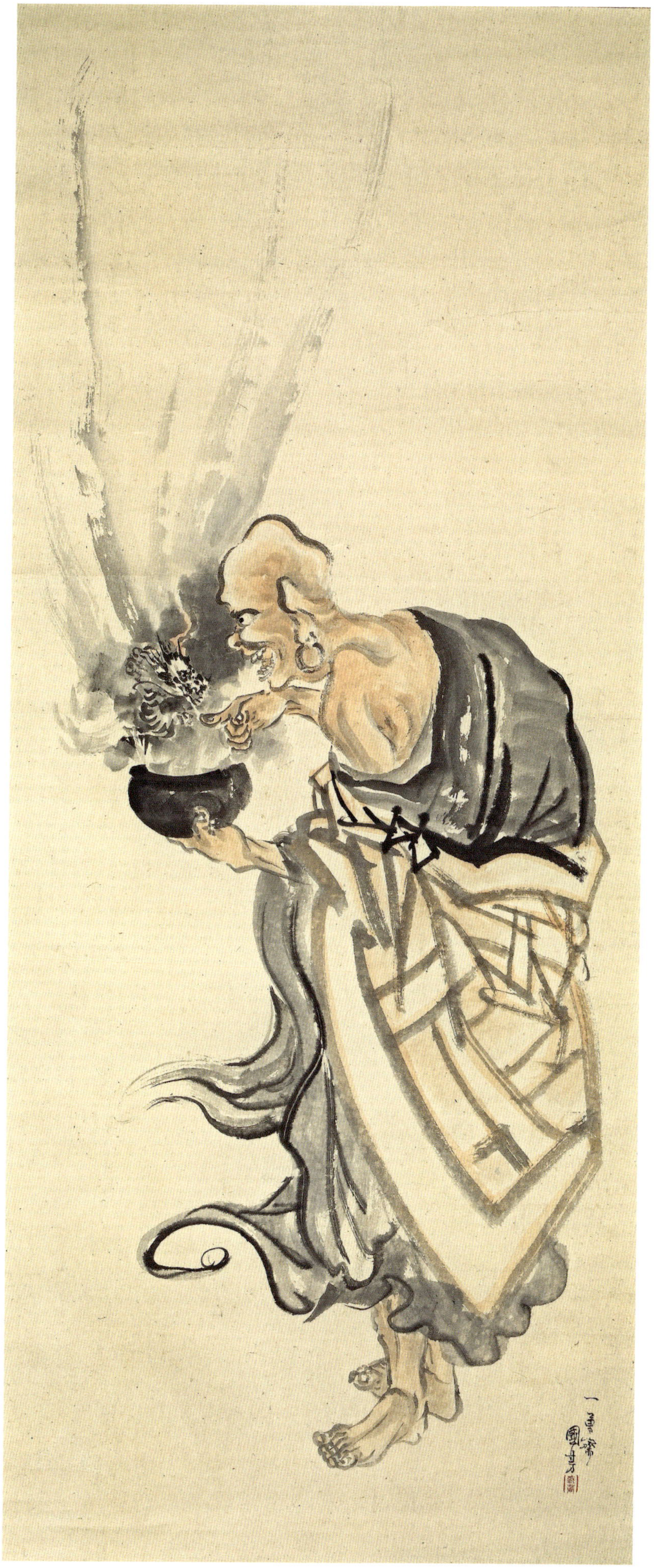

GLOSSARY

aragoto
'rough stuff': the bombastic, muscular style of Kabuki acting, typically as performed by the Ichikawa Danjūrō lineage.

chū-tanzaku
'medium poem slip': a print format measuring approximately 39 × 12 cm, obtained by cutting a full-size sheet into four vertical strips.

chūban
'medium sheet': a print format measuring approximately 26 × 19.5 cm, obtained by cutting a full-size sheet in four.

e
'picture': used as a prefix or suffix to denote a painting, print or brush drawing.

ehon
'picture book': a printed book containing mainly pictures.

ehon banzuke
'illustrated booklet': typically, an illustrated synopsis of a Kabuki play.

ema
a votive painting presented to a temple or shrine and hung on public display.

ga
'picture' or 'painting': when used after a print artist's signature the term means 'designed by'.

gōkan
'combined volume': a genre of illustrated fiction popular in the mid-nineteenth century, with pictures by artists of the ukiyo-e school, and colour-printed wrappers, covers and frontispiece illustrations; generally published serially over a number of years.

haikai
see 'haiku'.

haiku
(also *haikai*): a succinct verse form of seventeen syllables, often on natural subjects relating to the seasons.

hanshita-e
'block-ready drawing': a neat, detailed brush drawing on thin paper, prepared by the ukiyo-e artist to be pasted directly onto the cherrywood printing block as a guide to the block-cutter. (See also p. 28.)

Kabuki
Popular type of drama that evolved in the seventeenth century and features a wide range of fantastical, historical and urban themes. Performances generally last all day and are dominated by hereditary acting families, with female roles played by specialist male actors. Spectacular stage tricks are often an important element, along with music and dance interludes.

key-block
(also line-block): the printing block cut from the *hanshita-e* and used to print the lines of a design, before areas are printed from separate colour blocks.

kiwame
'examined': a small round seal containing the character for *kiwame*, employed by censors to mark an approved *hanshita-e* and then cut into the printing block; in use from 1791 to 1842.

koban
'small sheet': a print format measuring approximately 23 × 16.5 cm, obtained by cutting a smaller full-size sheet in four.

kōdan
oral tales, especially military chronicles, recited to a paying public.

kyōgen
comic plays that originated in the medieval period, typically performed between more serious Nō plays in the course of a day-long programme.

kyōgō-zuri
'proof print': a set of proofs taken from the 'key-block' and given to the artist for him to indicate the arrangement of colours and write notes on patterns and special printing effects; used by the block-cutter to prepare the colour blocks.

kyōka
'crazy verse': a popular verse form of thirty-one syllables, typically a parody of a classical poem or a light-hearted poem filled with wordplay.

line-block
see 'key-block'

meimeiden
'individual stories': tales of warriors and their associates who participated in group vendettas, notably 'Chūshingura', the story of revenge taken by loyal retainers of the Akō fief.

misemono
a street-side entertainment offered in a temporary booth to which the public paid admission.

mitate-e
a type of image that establishes playful, and often tenuous, connections between two apparently unrelated subjects.

naga-ōban
'tall large sheet': a rare vertical print format measuring approximately 52 × 18.5 cm.

nigao-e
'likeness picture': a recognisable portrait of a Kabuki actor, drawn in accordance with stylised conventions perfected by each leading print artist.

Nō
A form of drama, developed in the medieval period, on highly poetic ghost and Buddhist subjects. Costumes are of brilliant brocade and the main performers generally wear masks of character types. Narration and music is provided by onstage musicians.

ōban
'large sheet': a print format measuring approximately 39 × 26 cm, obtained by cutting a full-size sheet in half.

ōgi
a folding fan, sometimes with a painted or printed image attached to its bamboo spines.

Ōtsu-e
'Ōtsu picture': a genre of folk painting, with a stock range of comic characters, that originated in and around the village of Ōtsu in Ōmi province (modern Shiga prefecture).

shikishi-ban
'square sheet': a print format measuring approximately 20 × 18 cm, obtained by cutting a full-size sheet in six and generally used for *surimono*.

shini-e
'death picture': a memorial print issued to mark the death of a celebrity, generally a Kabuki actor.

shita-e
'preparatory drawing': a print artist's rough brush drawings, which were worked up into a *hanshita-e*.

surimono
'printed thing': a de luxe print, typically commissioned by poets to complement their verses with inventive designs, published privately and often distributed at the New Year holiday.

tengu
mythical creatures, half bird and half man.

uchiwa
rigid, round summer fan mounted on a handle and decorated with a painting or print.

ukiyo-e
'picture of the floating world': painting or print, typically showing a Kabuki actor, a courtesan, landscape, warrior or comic subject, produced in the period *c.* 1670 to *c.* 1910; also, the school of popular artists who designed these images.

yomihon
'book to read': a long, serial novel, typically a richly imaginative adventure story taking place in China or Japan, interspersed with full-spread illustrations by an ukiyo-e artist.

yotsugiri-ban
'sheet cut in four': a print format measuring approximately 19.5 × 13 cm, obtained by cutting an *ōban* in four, i.e. by cutting a full-size sheet in eight.

zenshi-ban
'full-size sheet': a print format measuring approximately 39 × 53 cm and consisting of a full-size, uncut sheet.

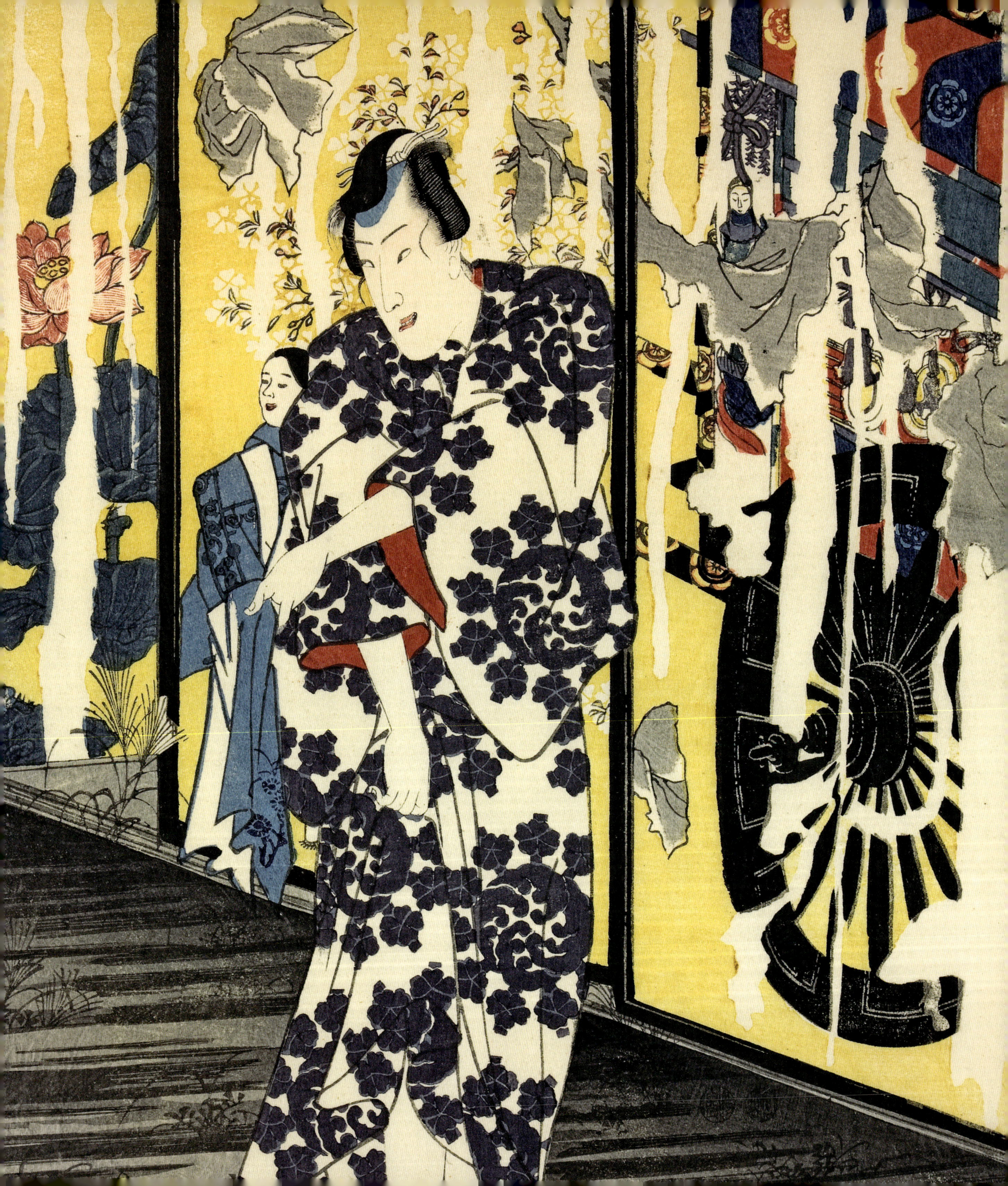

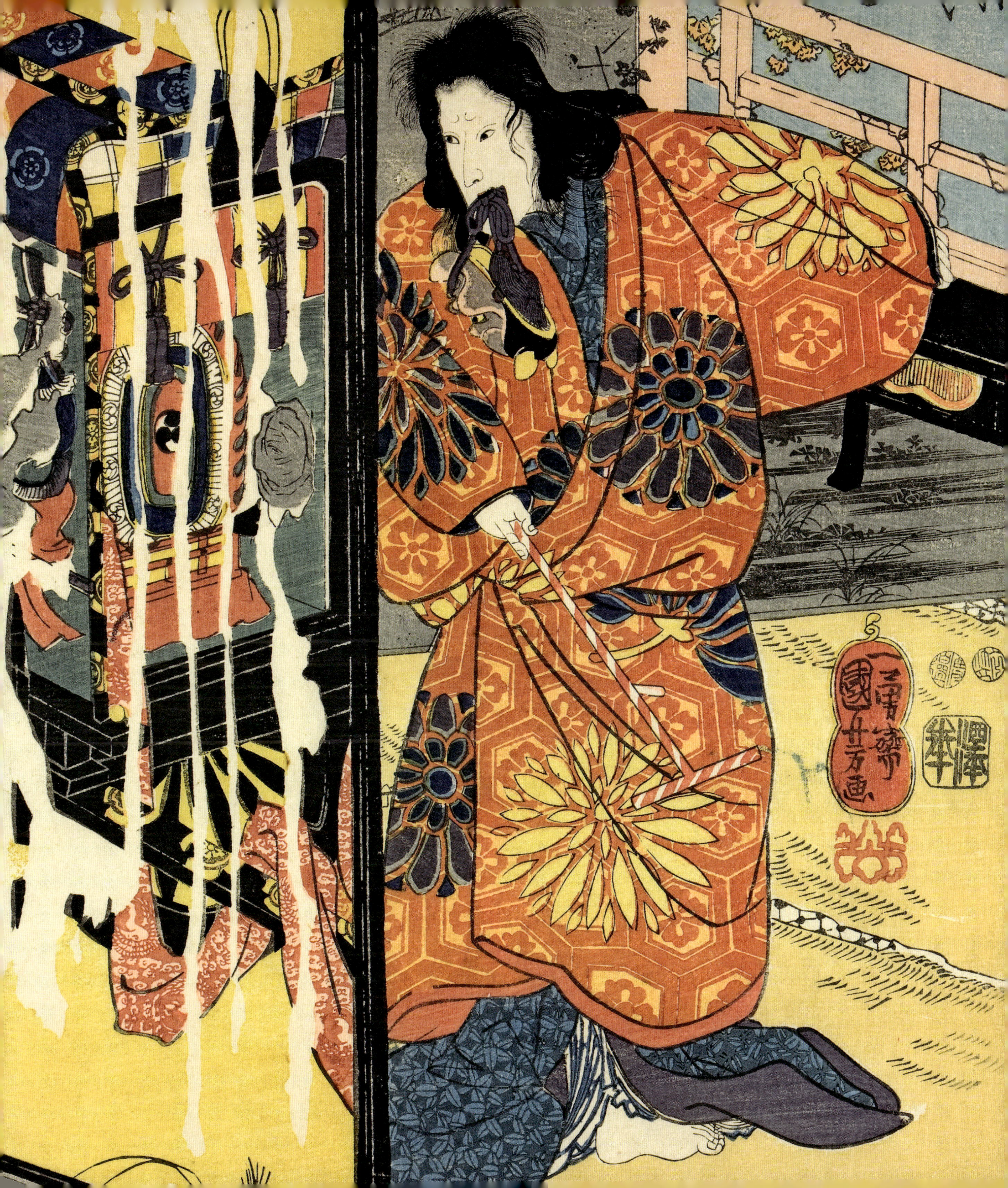
一勇斎國芳画

BIBLIOGRAPHY

AMSTERDAM 1984
Amsterdam, Rijksmuseum, Rijksprentenkabinet, *Japanese Prints IV: Hiroshige and the Utagawa School*, by Charlotte van Rappard-Boon, Amsterdam 1984.

AMSTERDAM 1998
Amsterdam, Rijksmuseum Vincent van Gogh, *Heroes and Ghosts: Japanese Prints by Kuniyoshi (1797–1861)*, ed. Robert Schaap, exh. cat., Leiden 1998.

ASANO AND CLARK 1995
Asano Shūgō and Timothy Clark, *The Passionate Art of Kitagawa Utamaro*, 2 vols, exh. cat., British Museum, London, et al., London 1995.

ASANO AND YOSHIDA 1997
Asano Shūgō and Yoshida Nobuyuki, eds, *Ukiyo-e o yomu*, vol. 6, *Kuniyoshi*, Tokyo 1997.

BADEN-BADEN 1984
Baden-Baden, Staatliche Kunsthalle, *Aus der fliessend-vergänglichen Welt: Japanische Pinselzeichnungen und Holzschnittbücher von 1600 bis 1900*, by Katharina Schmidt et al., exh. cat., Baden-Baden 1984.

BAREN NO KAI 1990
Baren no Kai, ed., *Ukiyo-e: Kōki Utagawa-ha*, exh. cat., Denki Bunka Kaikan Gararii, Nagoya 1990.

BAUR 1994
Geneva, Collections Baur, *The Baur Collection: Japanese Prints*, vol. 2, by Matthi Forrer, Geneva 1994.

BERLIN 1990
Berlin, Museum für Ostasiatische Kunst, *Surimono*, by Steffi Schmidt and Setsuko Kuwabara, exh. cat., Berlin 1990.

BINYON 1916
Laurence Binyon, *A Catalogue of Japanese and Chinese Woodcuts… in the British Museum*, London 1916.

BOLITHO 1989
Harold Bolitho, 'The Tempō crisis', in Marius B. Jansen, ed., *The Cambridge History of Japan*, vol. 5, *The Nineteenth Century*, Cambridge 1989, pp. 116–67.

BRANDON AND LEITER 2002
James R. Brandon and Samuel L. Leiter, eds, *Kabuki Plays on Stage*, vol. 3, *Darkness and Desire, 1804–1864*, Honolulu 2002.

BRUSSELS 1989
Brussels, Musées Royaux d'Art et d'Histoire, *Estampes Japonaises*, by Chantal Kozyreff, exh. cat., Brussels 1989.

CAMBRIDGE 1997
Cambridge, Fitzwilliam Museum, *Prints of the Floating World: Japanese Woodcuts from the Fitzwilliam Museum, Cambridge*, by Craig Hartley, London 1997.

CHIBA 1997
Chiba-shi Bijutsukan, *Suijin-tachi no okurimono: Edo no surimono ten*, by Asano Shūgō, exh. cat., Chiba 1997.

CHRISTIE'S 1989
New York, Christie's, *Japanese Prints and Drawings from the Collection of the late Theodor Scheiwe, Part I*, auction cat., 21 March 1989.

CHRISTIE'S 1989A
New York, Christie's, *Japanese Prints and Drawings from the Collection of the late Theodor Scheiwe, Part II*, auction cat., 16 October 1989.

CHRISTIE'S 2007
London, Christie's, *The Dynamic World of Utagawa Kuniyoshi: The B. W. Robinson Collection*, auction cat., 7 November 2007.

CLARK 1992
Timothy Clark, *Ukiyo-e Paintings in the British Museum*, exh. cat., British Museum, London 1992.

CLARK 1993
Timothy Clark, *Demon of Painting: The Art of Kawanabe Kyōsai*, exh. cat., British Museum, London 1993.

CLARK ET AL. 2001
Timothy Clark et al., *The Dawn of the Floating World (1650–1765): Early Ukiyo-e Treasures from the Museum of Fine Arts, Boston*, exh. cat., Royal Academy of Arts, London 2001.

DE BRUIJN 1983
R. De Bruijn, 'Kuniyoshi and his Prophet', *Andon: Bulletin of the Society for Japanese Arts and Crafts (Verenigung voor Japanse Kunst)* 11, 1983, pp. 13–22.

EDO-GAKU JITEN 1984
Nishiyama Matsunosuke et al., eds, *Edo-gaku jiten*, Tokyo 1984.

EDO-TOKYO 1999
Edo-Tokyo Hakubutsukan, ed., *Genroku ryōran*, exh. cat., Tokyo 1999.

ESSEN 1972
Essen, Villa Hügel, *Ukiyo-e: Die Kunst der heiteren vergänglichen Welt, Japan 17.–19. Jahrhundert: Sammlung Scheiwe*, by Rose Hempel, exh. cat., Essen 1972.

FAGIOLI 1985
Marco Fagioli, *Utagawa Kuniyoshi: 90 Disegni*, Florence 1985.

FAULKNER 2001
Rupert Faulkner, *Hiroshige Fan Prints*, London 2001.

FISCHER 2000
Felice Fischer, *The Arts of Hon'ami Kōetsu*, exh. cat., Philadelphia Museum of Art, Philadelphia 2000.

FORRER 1988
Matthi Forrer, *Drawings by Utagawa Kuniyoshi from the Collection of the National Museum of Ethnology, Leiden*, Leiden 1988.

FOXWELL 2004
Chelsea Foxwell, 'The Double Identity of Chūshingura: Theatre and History in Nineteenth-century Prints', *Impressions: The Journal of the Ukiyo-e Society of America* 26, 2004, pp. 23–43.

FRENCH 1977
Calvin French, *Through Closed Doors: Western Influence on Japanese Art, 1639–1853*, exh. cat., University of Michigan Museum of Art, Ann Arbor, et al., Rochester, MI, 1977.

FUJIOKAYA NIKKI
Kinsei shomin seikatsu shiryō, Fujiokaya nikki, ed. Suzuki Tōzō and Koike Shōtarō, 15 vols, Tokyo 1987–95.

GENEVA 1978
Geneva, Musée d'Art et d'Histoire, *Kuniyoshi 1798–1861: Une collection particulière*, exh. cat., Geneva 1978.

GEIGER 1954
Benno Geiger, *I Dipinti Ghiribizzosi di Giuseppe Arcimboldi*, Florence 1954.

GUDHJ
Genshoku ukiyo-e dai hyakka jiten, ed. Nihon Ukiyo-e Kyōkai, vol. 2, *Ukiyo-eshi*, Tokyo 1982; vol. 3, *Yōshiki, chōshō, hanmoto*, Tokyo 1982; vol. 9, *Sakuhin 4, Hiroshige – Kiyochika*, Tokyo 1981.

HALFORD 1956
Aubrey S. and Giovanna M. Halford, *The Kabuki Handbook*, Rutland, VT, and Tokyo 1956.

HAMADA 1973
Hamada Giichirō, ed., *Edo bungaku chimei jiten*, Tokyo 1973.

HAYASHI 1964
Hayashi Yoshikazu, *Enpon kenkyū: Kuniyoshi*, Tokyo 1964.

HAWLEY 1975
W. M. Hawley, *Pictorial Biography of Toyotomi Hideyoshi, the Unifier of Japan; Ehon Toyotomi Kunkoki by Ichiyusai Kuniyoshi, from the Woodblock Edition of 1855–1884*, Los Angeles 1975.

HAYWARD GALLERY 2004
London, Hayward Gallery, *Eyes, Lies and Illusions: The Art of Deception*, ed. Laurent Mannoni et al., exh. cat., London 2004.

HERWIG 2004
Henk J. Herwig and Arendie Herwig, *Heroes of the Kabuki Stage*, Leiden 2004.

HERWIG AND MOSTOW 2007
Henk J. Herwig and Joshua S. Mostow, *The Hundred Poets Compared: A Print Series by Kuniyoshi, Hiroshige and Kunisada*, Leiden and Boston 2007.

HILLIER 1976
Jack Hillier, *Japanese Prints and Drawings from the Vever Collection*, 3 vols, London 1976.

HIRAKI 2006
Tokyo, Hiraki Ukiyo-e Zaidan, ed., *Nyantomo neko-darake / Cats of Many Varieties*, exh. cat., Tokyo 2006.

HOKKAIDŌ 2000
Hokkaidō-ritsu Asahikawa Bijutsukan, eds, *Utagawa Kuniyoshi ichimon no zenbō ten*, exh. cat., Asahikawa 2000.

HOUSTON 2003
Houston, Museum of Fine Arts, *The History of Japanese Photography*, by Anne Wilkes Tucker et al., exh. cat., Houston 2003.

HUT
Hizō ukiyo-e taikan, ed. Narazaki Muneshige, vol. 3, *Daiei Hakubutsukan III*, Tokyo 1988; vol. 5, *Bikutoria Arubaato Bijutsukan II*, Tokyo 1989; vol. 7, *Gime Bijutsukan II*, Tokyo 1990; vol. 11, *Jenoba Tōyō Bijutsukan II*, Tokyo 1988; vol. 12, *Berurin Tōyō Bijutsukan*, Tokyo 1988; suppl. vol., *Chesutaa Biiti, Kerun…*, Tokyo 1990.

IIJIMA 1894/1941
Iijima Kyoshin, *Ukiyo-eshi Utagawa retsuden*, Tokyo 1894; rev. Tamabayashi Seirō, Tokyo 1941.

IIZUKA 1926
Iizuka Tomoichirō, *Kabuki saiken*, Tokyo 1926.

ILLING 1978
Richard Illing, *Later Japanese Prints*, Oxford 1978.

ILLING 1980
Richard Illing, *The Art of Japanese Prints*, London 1980.

INAGAKI 1991
Inagaki Shin'ichi and Isao Toshihiko, *Kuniyoshi no kyōga*, Tokyo 1991.

INAGAKI 2003
Inagaki Shin'ichi, 'Kuniyoshi no hyaku-mensō', *Ukiyo-e geijutsu* 145, January 2003, pp. 69–74.

ISAO 2008
Isao Toshihiko, *Motto shiritai Utagawa Kuniyoshi: Shōgai to sakuhin*, Tokyo 2008.

ISAO AND IWAKIRI 1999
Isao Toshihiko and Iwakiri Yuriko, *Kuniyoshi yōkai hyakkei*, Tokyo 1999.

ISHII 1929/2005
Ishii Kendō, *Nishiki-e no hori to suri*, Tokyo 1929; rev. Yamashita Tsuneo, Tokyo and Kyoto 2005.

ITABASHI 1994
Tokyo, Itabashi Kuritsu Bijutsukan et al., ed., *Supuringufiirudo Bijutsukan hizō ukiyo-e meihin ten/Ukiyo-e from the Museum of Fine Arts, Springfield*, exh. cat., Tokyo 1994.

IWAKIRI 1992A,B
Iwakiri Yuriko, 'Umenoya to Kuniyoshi', *Ukiyo-e geijutsu* 105, July 1992, pp. 3–13 (part one) [a]; 106, November 1992, pp. 3–10 (part two) [b].

IWAKIRI 2001
Iwakiri Yuriko, 'Utagawa Kuniyoshi *Honchō Suikoden gōketsu (gōyū) happyakunin no hitori* ni tsuite', *Ukiyo-e geijutsu* 138, January 2001, pp. 3–27.

IWAKIRI 2002
Iwakiri Yuriko, 'Tenpō kaikaku to ukiyo-e', *Ukiyo-e geijutsu* 143, March 2002, pp. 3–33; 145, January 2003, p. 88 (corrigenda).

IWAKIRI 2007
Iwakiri Yuriko, 'Tenpō jūsan-nen no kakari-nanushi no aratame ni tsuite', *Ukiyo-e geijutsu* 154, July 2007, pp. 88–91.

IZZARD 1993
Sebastian Izzard, *Kunisada's World*, exh. cat., Japan Society, New York 1993.

JOLY 1908
Henri L. Joly, *Legend in Japanese Art*, London 1908.

KABUKI JITEN 1983
Kabuki jiten, ed. Hattori Yukio et al., Tokyo 1983.

KABUKI NENPYŌ 1961
Kabuki nenpyō, by Ihara Toshirō, vol. 6 [1816–53], Tokyo 1961.

KATSUHARA 2006
Katsuhara Ryōta, 'Nyūhofu chō *Tōzai kairiku kikō* to Kuniyoshi no yōfū hanga', *Ukiyo-e shunjū*, 2nd ser., no. 1, January 2006, pp. 6–29.

KATSUMORI 2000
Katsumori Noriko, 'Tairō kara Kuniyoshi e: Bijutsu ni miru ransho juyō no katachi', *Kōbe Shiritsu Hakubutsukan kenkyū kiyō* 16, March 2000, pp. 17–44.

KAWAZOE 2008
Kawazoe Yū, *Edo no taishū geinō: Kabuki, misemono, rakugo*, Kyoto 2008.

KEYES 1981
Roger Keyes, 'Kuniyoshi's Low Tide at Susaki, A Five Panel Surimono', *Andon* 3, 1981, pp. 77–9.

KEYES 1984
Roger Keyes, *Japanese Woodblock Prints: A Catalogue of the Mary A. Ainsworth Collection*, Allen Memorial Art Museum, Oberlin, OH, 1984.

KEYES 1985
Roger Keyes, *The Art of Surimono… in the Chester Beatty Library, Dublin*, 2 vols, London 1985.

KEYES 1989
Roger Keyes, *The Male Journey in Japanese Prints*, Berkeley, Los Angeles and London 1989.

KING AND IWAKIRI 2007
James King and Iwakiri Yuriko, *Japanese Warrior Prints (1646–1905)*, Leiden and Boston 2007.

KINOSHITA 1993
Kinoshita Naoyuki, *Bijutsu to iu misemono*, Tokyo 1993.

KLOMPMAKERS 1988
Inge Klompmakers, *Of Brigands and Bravery: Kuniyoshi's Heroes of the Suikoden*, Leiden 1988.

KONDO 1982
Eiko Kondo, 'Inaka Genji Series', in Matthi Forrer, ed., *Essays on Japanese Art Presented to Jack Hillier*, London 1982, pp. 78–93.

KORNICKI 1998
Peter Kornicki, *The Book in Japan: A Cultural History from the Beginnings to the Nineteenth Century*, Leiden 1998, repr. Honolulu 2001.

KRUML 1973
London, Richard Kruml, *Ichiyusai Kuniyoshi (Catalogue 9)*, dealer's cat., London 1973.

KRUML 1989
London, Richard Kruml, *Surimono (Catalogue 23)*, dealer's cat., London 1989.

LOEWENSTEIN 1922
Fritz E. Loewenstein, *Die Handzeichnungen der japanischen Holzschnittmeister*, Plauen 1922.

McCULLOUGH 1968
Helen Craig McCullough, *Tales of Ise*, Stanford, CA, 1968

McCULLOUGH 1985
Helen Craig McCullough, *Brocade by Night: 'Kokin wakashū' and the Court Style in Japanese Classical Poetry*, Stanford, CA, 1985.

MACHIDA 1995
Machida Shiritsu Hakubutsukan, ed., *Bakumatsu no fūshiga: Boshin sensō o chūshin ni*, exh. cat., Tokyo 1995.

MACHIDA 2003
Machida Shiritsu Kokusai Hanga Bijutsukan, ed., *Ukiyo-e dai musha-e ten*, exh. cat., Tokyo 2003.

MADISON 2007
Madison, WI, Chazen Museum of Art, *Competition and Collaboration: Japanese Prints of the Utagawa School*, by Laura Mueller, exh. cat., Leiden and Boston 2007.

MAINICHI SHINBUNSHA 1995
Mainichi Shinbunsha, ed., *Edo no geki-gaka: Kuniyoshi no sekai ten*, exh. cat., Tokyo 1995.

MINAMI 1973
Minami Kazuo, 'Ka'ei-ki no ukiyo-e to Edo no hyōban', *Ukiyo-e geijutsu* 36, March 1973, pp. 5–14.

MINAMI 1973A
Minami Kazuo, 'Kuniyoshi ga *Minamoto no Yorimitsu-kō no yakata ni tsuchigumo yōkai o nasu zu* to minshū', *Nihon rekishi* 302, July 1973, pp. 119–26.

MINAMI 1974
Minami Kazuo, 'Tenpō kaikaku to ukiyo-e', *Kokugakuin zasshi* 75, no. 10, October 1974, pp. 18–34.

MINAMI 1981
Minami Kazuo, 'Utamaro to Toyokuni no hikka ni tsuite', *Ukiyo-e shūka furoku* 11, February 1981, pp. 1–8.

MINNEAPOLIS 1994
Minneapolis Institute of Arts, *Ōtsu-e: Japanese Folk Paintings from the Harriet and Edson Spencer Collection*, by Matthew Welch, Minneapolis 1994.

MOSTOW 1996
Joshua S. Mostow, *Pictures of the Heart: The Hyakunin Isshu in Word and Image*, Honolulu 1996.

MSU 1991
Meihin soroimono ukiyo-e, ed. Suzuki Jūzō, vol. 7, *Kuniyoshi, Eisen*, Tokyo 1991.

NAGOYA 1991
Nagoya-shi Hakubutsukan et al., eds, *Hokusai: Fukutsu no gajin-damashii*, exh. cat., Nagoya 1991.

NAGOYA 1996
Nagoya-shi Hakubutsukan et al., eds, *Tanjō 200-nen kinen: Utagawa Kuniyoshi ten*, exh. cat., Nagoya 1996.

NAITŌ 1998
Naitō Masato, *Utagawa Kuniyoshi*, Shinchō bijutsu bunko 22, Tokyo 1998.

NAKAU 1998
Nakau Ei, *Ukiyo-e Chūshingura no sekai*, Tokyo 1998.

NEWLAND 2005
Amy Riegle Newland, ed., *The Hotei Encyclopedia of Japanese Woodblock Prints*, 2 vols, Amsterdam 2005.

NIHON KEIZAI SHINBUN 1985
Nihon Keizai Shimbun, ed., *Shindoraa korekushon ukiyo-e meihin ten/Masterpieces of Ukiyo-e Prints from the Schindler Collection*, exh. cat., Tokyo Matsuzakaya Ginza, Tokyo 1985.

NIHON UKIYO-E KYŌKAI 1974
Nihon Ukiyo-e Kyōkai, ed., *Berurin Kokuritsu Hakubutsukan shozō mesaku ukiyo-e ten*, exh. cat., Uehonmachi Kintetsu Hyakkaten, Osaka, Tokyo 1974.

NIHON UKIYO-E KYŌKAI 1995
Nihon Ukiyo-e Kyōkai, ed., *Gurabuhōn korekushon – Ukiyo-e meihin ten*, exh. cat., Matsuzakaya (Ueno), Tokyo, 1995.

NIHON UKIYO-E KYŌKAI 1990
Nihon Ukiyo-e Kyōkai, ed., *Doitsu Puruberaa korekushon ukiyo-e hanga meihin ten*, exh. cat., Matsuzakaya, Osaka, et al., Tokyo 1990.

NISHIYAMA 1979
Nishiyama Matsunosuke, 'Ichikawa Danjūrō no daidai', in Gunji Masakatsu, ed., *Nihon no koten*, vol. 20, *Kabuki jūhachiban*, Tokyo 1979, pp. 196–210.

NUT 1995
Nikuhitsu ukiyo-e taikan, ed. Kobayashi Tadashi, vol. 6, *Azabu Bijutsu Kōgeikan*, Tokyo 1995.

OKA 1992
Oka Yasumasa, *Megane-e shinkō*, Tokyo 1992.

OSADA 2002
Osada Kōtoku, *Kuniyoshi sakuhin mokuroku (nishiki-e hen)*, Tokyo 2002.

ŌTA 1986
Tokyo, Ōta Kinen Bijutsukan, ed., *Utagawa-ha ten*, exh. cat., Tokyo 1986.

ŌTA 1987
Tokyo, Ōta Kinen Bijutsukan, ed., *Utagawa Kuniyoshi giga ten*, exh. cat., Tokyo 1987.

ŌTA 1999
Tokyo, Ōta Kinen Bijutsukan, ed., *Kuniyoshi geijutsu no zenbō*, exh. cat., Tokyo 1999.

PITTSBURGH 1976
Pittsburgh Museum of Art, Carnegie Institute, *Eight Hundred Years of Japanese Printmaking: From the Collection of Dr. and Mrs. James B. Austin*, by Roger Keyes and James B. Austin, Pittsburgh 1976.

PLAKS 1987
Andrew H. Plaks, *The Four Masterworks of the Ming Novel*, Princeton, NJ, 1987.

RICCAR 1978
Tokyo, Riccar Bijutsukan, ed., *Utagawa Kuniyoshi ten / Exhibition of Ukiyo-e by Kuniyoshi*, exh. cat., Tokyo 1978.

RICCAR 1979
Tokyo, Riccar Bijutsukan, ed., *Utagawa Kuniyoshi Suikoden / Exhibition of Suikoden by Kuniyoshi*, exh. cat., Tokyo 1979.

ROBINSON 1953
Basil W. Robinson, *Summary Catalogue of Drawings by Utagawa Kuniyoshi in the Collection of Ferd. Lieftinck*, Groningen 1953.

ROBINSON 1961
Basil W. Robinson, *Kuniyoshi*, London 1961.

ROBINSON 1963
Basil W. Robinson, *Kuniyoshi: Ein Meister des japanischen Farbholzschnitts*, Essen 1963.

ROBINSON 1982
Basil W. Robinson, *Kuniyoshi: The Warrior Prints*, Oxford 1982.

ROBINSON AND MILLER 1996
Basil W. Robinson and Arthur R. Miller, 'Supplement to *Kuniyoshi: The Warrior Prints*', typescript, 1996.

SCHACK 1975
Gerhard Schack, *Japanische Handzeichnungen von Itchō, Hokusai, Kuniyoshi, Kyōsai, Chinnen, Eisen, Hiroshige, Kunisada, Hokkei, Hokuba, Isai*, Hamburg 1975.

SHIBUI 1983
Shibui Kiyoshi, ed., *Nikuhitsu ukiyo-e bijinga shūsei*, 2 vols, Tokyo 1983.

SHICHŪ TORISHIMARI RUISHŪ
Dai Nihon kinsei shiryō, Shichū torishimari ruishū, ed. Tokyo Daigaku Shiryō Hensanjo, vols 18–21, *Shomotsu nishiki-e no bu* 1–4, Tokyo 1988–94.

SHIRAKURA 2007
Shirakura Yoshihiko, *E-iri shunga ehon mokuroku*, Tokyo 2007.

SHŌTŌ 2003
Tokyo, Shibuya Kuritsu Shōtō Bijutsukan, ed., *Musha-e: Edo no hiiroo dai zukan*, exh. cat., Tokyo 2003.

SMITH 2003
Henry D. Smith II, 'The Capacity of Chūshingura', *Monumenta Nipponica* 58, no. 1, Spring 2003, pp. 1–42.

SMITH 2005
Henry D. Smith II, 'Hokusai and the Blue Revolution in Edo Prints', in John T. Carpenter, ed., *Hokusai and his Age*, Amsterdam 2005, pp. 235–69.

SMITHSONIAN 2002
Washington, D.C., Smithsonian Institution, *Masterful Illusions: Japanese Prints in the Anne van Biema Collection*, by Ann Yonemura, Washington, D.C., 2002.

SOTHEBY'S 1997
London, Sotheby's, *Highly Important Japanese Prints from the Henri Vever Collection: Final Part*, auction cat., 30 October 1997.

SPRINGFIELD 1968
Springfield Museum of Fine Arts, ed., *The Raymond A. Bidwell Collection of Prints by Utagawa Kuniyoshi (1798–1861)*, Springfield, MA, 1968.

SPRINGFIELD 1980
Springfield Museum of Fine Arts, *Utagawa Kuniyoshi: An Exhibition of the Work of Utagawa Kuniyoshi based on the Raymond A. Bidwell Collection of Japanese Prints at the Springfield Museum of Fine Arts*, by Merlin C. Dailey, exh. cat., Springfield, MA, 1980.

STRANGE 1924
Edward F. Strange, *Tools and Materials Illustrating the Japanese Method of Colour-Printing*, Victoria and Albert Museum, London 1924.

SUZUKI 1985
Suzuki Jūzō, *Ukiyo-e hakka*, vol. 7, *Kuniyoshi*, Tokyo 1985.

SUZUKI 1992
Suzuki Jūzō, *Kuniyoshi*, Tokyo 1992.

SUZUKI AND OKA 1969
Suzuki Jūzō and Oka Isaburō, *Masterworks of Ukiyo-e: The Decadents*, Tokyo, New York and San Francisco 1969.

TAKEUCHI 1987
Melinda Takeuchi, 'Kuniyoshi's Minamoto Raikō and the Earth Spider: Demons and Protest in Late Tokugawa Japan', *Ars Orientalis* 17, 1987, pp. 5–38.

THOMPSON 1991
Sarah E. Thompson with H. D. Harootunian, *Undercurrents in the Floating World: Censorship and Japanese Prints*, exh. cat., Asia Society, New York 1991.

TINIOS 1996
Ellis Tinios, *Mirror of the Stage: The Actor Prints of Kunisada*, exh. cat., Leeds University Art Gallery, Leeds 1996.

TINIOS 2004
Ellis Tinios, 'Borrowed Landscapes: The Exploitation of Maruyama-Shijō Book Illustrations by Ukiyo-e Artists', in Amy Reigle Newland, ed., *The Commercial and Cultural Climate of Japanese Printmaking*, Amsterdam 2004, pp. 165–70.

TINIOS 2007
Ellis Tinios, 'Warrior Prints and the Double-edged Sword of Loyalty', in Madison 2007, pp. 37–43.

TNM 1991
Tokyo National Museum / Tokyo Kokuritsu Hakubutsukan, ed., *Matsukata korekushon ukiyo-e meihin ten / Ukiyoe from [the] Matsukata Collection*, exh. cat., Tokyo 1991.

TNM 2005
Tokyo National Museum / Tokyo Kokuritsu Hakubutsukan, ed., *Hokusai ten*, exh. cat., Tokyo 2005.

TOKUNO 1892 / 1982
T. Tokuno, ed. S. R. E. Koehler, *Japanese Wood-cutting and Woodcut Printing*, Washington, D.C., 1892; rev. Peter Morse, 'Tokuno's Description of Japanese Printmaking', in Matthi Forrer, ed., *Essays on Japanese Art Presented to Jack Hillier*, London 1982, pp. 125–34.

TOKYO SHINBUN 1973
Tokyo Shinbun, ed., *Ikiteru ukiyo-e: Horimono ten*, exh. cat., Shinjuku Odakyū Hyakkaten, Tokyo 1973.

TOKYO SHINBUN 1994
Tokyo Shinbun, ed., *Disguised Vision*, exh. cat., Isetan Museum of Art, Tokyo 1994.

TOKYO STATION GALLERY 2004
Tokyo Station Gallery, ed., *Kuniyoshi, Kyōsai*, exh. cat., Tokyo 2004.

TSUDA 2006
Tsuda Mayumi, 'Utagawa Kuniyoshi ga *Oboro-zuki neko no sōshi* to neko zu', *Ukiyo-e geijutsu* 152, July 2006, pp. 27–42.

TSUJI 1970
Tsuji Nobuo, *Kisō no keifu: Matabei-Kuniyoshi*, Tokyo 1970.

UKIYO-E TAIKA SHŪSEI 1931
Ukiyo-e taika shūsei, ed. Sasakawa Rinpū et al., vol. 17, *Kunisada, Kuniyoshi*, Tokyo 1931.

UKIYO-E TAIKEI 1974
Ukiyo-e taikei, by Suzuki Jūzō, vol. 10, *Kunisada, Kuniyoshi, Eisen*, Tokyo 1974.

UKIYO-E TAISEI 1931
Ukiyo-e taisei, ed. Yoshida Teruji, vol. 11, *Haitai jidai II*, Tokyo 1931.

V&A 1991
London, Victoria and Albert Museum, *Masterpieces of Japanese Print [sic.] (The European Collection): Ukiyo-e from the Victoria and Albert Museum*, by Rupert Faulkner, Tokyo, New York and London 1991.

VARSHAVSKAYA 2005
Elena Varshavskaya, *Heroes of the Grand Pacification: Kuniyoshi's 'Taiheiki eiyūden'*, Amsterdam 2005.

VENICE 1987
Venice, Palazzo Grassi, *The Arcimboldo Effect*, exh. cat., Venice 1987.

VIENNA 2007
Vienna, Kunsthistorisches Museum, *Archimboldo (1526–1593)*, exh. cat., Vienna 2007.

WARD 1976
Sidney C. Ward, *One Hundred Surimono in the Collection of Sidney C. Ward*, n.p. (privately published) 1976.

WASEDA 1992–93
Tokyo, Waseda Daigaku Engeki Hakubutsukan, ed., *Chūshingura (jō, ge)*, 2 vols, Tokyo 1992–93.

WEINBERG 2000
David R. Weinberg, *Kuniyoshi: The Faithful Samurai*, Leiden 2000.

YAMAGUCHI 1991
Yamaguchi Kenritsu Bijutsukan, ed., *Ukiyo-e Utagawa-ha 3 kyōshō ten: Kunisada, Kuniyoshi, Hiroshige no sekai*, exh. cat., Yamaguchi 1991.

YOSHIDA 1971
Yoshida Teruji, *Ukiyo-e higa no kenkyū*, Tokyo 1971.

YURA 1979
Yura Tetsuji, ed., *Sōkō Nihon ukiyo-e ruikō*, Tokyo 1979.

ZOKU KABUKI NENDAIKI 1925
Zoku kabuki nendaiki, ed. Hirotani Yūtarō, Tokyo 1925.

Relevant websites
www.britishmuseum.org/research
www.kuniyoshiproject.com
www.mfa.org/collections

INDEX

All references are to page numbers; those in **bold** type indicate catalogue plates, and those in *italic* type indicate essay illustrations

L

M

N

O

Benefactors of the Royal Academy of Arts

ROYAL ACADEMY TRUST

Major Benefactors

The Trustees of the Royal Academy Trust are grateful to all its donors for their continued loyalty and generosity. They would like to extend their thanks to all those who have made a significant commitment, past and present, to the galleries, the exhibitions, the conservation of the Permanent Collection, the Library collections, the Royal Academy Schools, the education programme and other specific appeals.

HM The Queen
The 29th May 1961 Charitable Trust
Barclays Bank
B.A.T. Industries Plc
Big Lottery Fund (formerly New Opportunities Fund)
John Frye Bourne
British Telecom
Mr and Mrs John Burns
Mr Raymond M Burton CBE
Sir Trevor Chinn CVO and Lady Chinn
The Trustees of the Clore Foundation
The John S Cohen Foundation
Sir Harry and Lady Djanogly
The Dulverton Trust
Alfred Dunhill Limited
The John Ellerman Foundation
The Eranda Foundation
Ernst and Young
Esso UK Plc
The Foundation for Sport and the Arts
Friends of the Royal Academy
Jacqueline and Michael Gee
Mr Mark Getty
Glaxo Holdings plc
Diane and Guilford Glazer
Mr and Mrs Jack Goldhill
Maurice and Laurence Goldman
Mr and Mrs Jocelin Harris
The Philip and Pauline Harris Charitable Trust
The Charles Hayward Foundation
Heritage Lottery Fund
Mr Damien Hirst
IBM United Kingdom Limited
The Idlewild Trust
Lord and Lady Jacobs
The J P Jacobs Charitable Trust
The Japan Foundation
Gabrielle Jungels-Winkler Foundation
Mr and Mrs Donald P Kahn
The Lillian Jean Kaplan Foundation
The Kirby Laing Foundation
The Kresge Foundation
The Kress Foundation
The Lankelly Foundation
The Leverhulme Trust
Lex Service Plc
The Linbury Trust
Sir Sydney Lipworth QC and Lady Lipworth
John Lyons Charity
Ronald and Rita McAulay
McKinsey and Company Inc
John Madejski OBE DL
Her Majesty's Government
The Manifold Trust
Marks and Spencer
The Mercers' Company
Mr and Mrs Minoru Mori
The Monument Trust
The Henry Moore Foundation
The Moorgate Trust Fund
Robin Heller Moss
Museums and Galleries Improvement Fund
National Westminster Bank
Stavros S Niarchos
The Peacock Trust
The Pennycress Trust
P F Charitable Trust
The Pilgrim Trust
The Edith and Ferdinand Porjes Trust
John Porter Charitable Trust
The Porter Foundation
Rio Tinto Plc
Mr John A Roberts FRIBA
Simon and Virginia Robertson
The Ronson Foundation
The Rose Foundation
Rothmans International Plc
Mrs Jean Sainsbury
The Saison Foundation
The Basil Samuel Charitable Trust
Mrs Coral Samuel CBE
Sea Containers Ltd
Shell UK Limited
Miss Dasha Shenkman
William and Maureen Shenkman
The Archie Sherman Charitable Trust
Sir Hugh Sykes DL
Sir Anthony and Lady Tennant
Ware and Edythe Travelstead
The Trusthouse Charitable Foundation
The Douglas Turner Trust
Unilever plc
The Weldon UK Charitable Trust
The Welton Foundation
The Weston family
The Malcolm Hewitt Wiener Foundation
The Maurice Wohl Charitable Foundation
The Wolfson Foundation
and others who wish to remain anonymous

PATRONS

The Royal Academy is delighted to thank all its Patrons for generously supporting the following areas over the past year: exhibitions, education, the Royal Academy Schools, the Permanent Collection and Library, and Anglo-American initiatives; and for assisting in the general upkeep of the Academy.

Platinum

Mrs Allen
Mr and Mrs John Coombe
Mr and Mrs Patrick Doherty
Mrs Helena Frost
Lady Getty
Janicke and Leif Höegh
Mr Frederik Paulsen
Mr and Mrs David Shalit

Gold

Sir Ronald Cohen
Lady Gosling
Michael and Morven Heller
Anya Hindmarch
Mr and Mrs Ronald Lubner
Prof and Mrs Anthony Mellows
Lady Jane Rayne
Mrs Inna Vainschtock
Mr and Dr Winkler

Silver

Mrs Gary Brass
Mrs Elie Brihi
Mrs Debbie Burks
Sir Charles and Lady Chadwyck-Healey
Mr and Mrs Chapman Stoller
Sir Trevor Chinn CVO and Lady Chinn
John C L Cox CBE
Mary Moore Danowski
Miss Ellison
Mr and Mrs Eric Franck
Jaqueline and Jonathan Gestetner
Patricia and John Glasswell
Lady Gosling
Mr and Mrs Alan Hobart
Mr and Mrs Jon Hunt
S Isern-Feliu
Mrs Raymonde Jay
Mr Nand Khemka and Princess Jeet Nabha Khemka
Mrs Aboudi Kosta
Lady Lever of Manchester
Mark and Liza Loveday
Mr and Mrs Richard Martin
The Mulberry Trust
Mr and Mrs D J Peacock
The Lady Henrietta St George
Mr and Mrs Schneer
Mr and Mrs Kevin Senior
The Countess of Shaftesbury
Mrs Stella Shawzin
Richard and Veronica Simmons
Jane Spack
Sir James and Lady Spooner
Mrs Elyane Stilling
Sir Hugh Sykes DL
Group Captain James Tait
Mr Mikhail Trushin

Bronze

Agnew's
Mr Peter Allinson
Mrs Marina Atwater
Jane Barker
Stephen Barry Charitable Settlement
James M Bartos
The Duke of Beaufort
The Bellinger Donnay Charitable Trust
Mrs J K M Bentley/Summers Art Gallery
Konrad O Bernheimer
Mrs Charles Brocklebank
Lord Browne of Madingley
Mrs Alan Campbell-Johnson
Mr F A A Carnwath CBE
Jean and Eric Cass
Mr and Mrs George Coelho
Denise Cohen Charitable Trust
Carole Conrad
Mrs Cathy Corbett
Mr and Mrs Sidney Corob
Julian Darley and Helga Sands
The Countess of Dartmouth
Mr Davis and Ms Roboz
Peter and Kate De Haan
Ms Davina Dickson
Mrs Dobell-Wood
Dr Anne Dornhorst
Lord Douro
Sir Philip Dowson CBE PPRA and Lady Dowson
Mr and Mrs Maurice Dwek
Mr Eddis
Lord and Lady Egremont
Mary Fedden RA
Mr and Mrs David Fenton
Bryan Ferry
Mrs Donatella Flick
Mrs George Fokschaner
Lord and Lady Foley
Mrs Jocelyn Fox
Mr Monty Freedman
Arnold Fulton
Mark Glatman
Mrs Godwin
Mrs Val Gooding
Nicholas and Judith Goodison
Piers and Rosie Gough
David and Lesley Haynes
Mr Andreas Heeschen
Mr and Mrs Christoph Henkel
Ms Joanna Hewitt
Mrs Jasmine Horowitz
Mrs Pauline Hyde
Sir Martin and Lady Jacomb
Harold and Valerie Joels
Dr Elisabeth Kehoe
Mr and Mrs James Kirkman
Norman A Kurland and Deborah A David
The de Laszlo Foundation
Joan H Lavender
Mr George Lengvari and Mrs Inez Lengvari
Miss R Lomax-Simpson
The Marquess of Lothian
Mr and Mrs Henry Lumley
Miss Jane McAusland
Gillian McIntosh
Mr and Mrs Magan
Mr and Mrs Eskandar Maleki
Mr Michael Manser RA and Mrs Jose Manser
Mr Marcus Margulies
Mr and Mrs Stephen Mather
Zvi and Ofra Meitar Family Fund
Mrs Michael Moore
Mrs Alan Morgan
Dr Ann Naylor
Ann Norman-Butler
North Street Trust
Mr Georg von Opel
Mr Michael Palin
John H Pattisson
Mr Philip Perry
Mr and Mrs Anthony Pitt-Rivers
John and Anne Raisman
Mr and Mrs Ian Rosenberg
Lord Rothschild
Lady (Robert) Sainsbury
Mrs Sirkka Sanderson
H M Sassoon Charitable Trust
Carol Sellars
Dr Lewis Sevitt
Major General and Mrs Shaw
Mrs Lesley Silver
Alan and Marianna Simpson
Mr and Mrs Mark Franklin Slaughter
Mr Smith
Brian D Smith
Mr and Mrs David T Smith
Lord Sterling of Plaistow
Mrs D Susman
Lord and Lady Taylor
Miss M L Ulfane
Mrs Norah de Vigier
Ms Walkey
John and Carol Wates
Mrs Weinstock
Edna and Willard Weiss
Anthony and Rachel Williams
and others who wish to remain anonymous

BENEFACTOR PATRONS

The Peter Boizot Foundation
Mr and Mrs William Brake
Mrs Mary Graves
Mrs Sue Hammerson
The Lord Marks of Broughton
Sir Anthony and Lady Tennant

BENJAMIN WEST GROUP PATRONS

Chairman

Lady Judge

Platinum

Dean Menegas

Gold

Lady J Lloyd Adamson

Silver

Mr and Mrs Paul Collins
Kim Dunn
Charles and Kaaren Hale
Lady Judge
Scott and Christine Morrissey
Mr and Mrs John R Olsen
Wendy Becker Payton
Frank and Anne Sixt

Bronze

Ms Ruth Anderson
Mrs Alan Artus
Tom and Diane Berger
Mrs Brooks and Mr Medland
Debra Cajrati Crivelli
Mr and Mrs Gunnar L Engstrom
Mrs Clare Flanagan
Cyril and Christine Freedman
Mr Andrew Hawkins
Suzanne and Michael Johnson
Charles G Lubar
Mr and Mrs Patrick Mahon
Neil Osborn and Holly Smith
Ms Theresa A Parker
Lady Purves
Mr and Mrs K M Rubie
Sylvia Scheuer
Mr and Mrs Thomas Schoch
Carole Turner Record
Frederick and Kathryn Uhde
Mr and Mrs Ullmo
Mr John D Winter
Mary Wolridge
and others who wish to remain anonymous

SCHOOLS PATRONS GROUP

Chairman

Mr John Entwistle OBE

Platinum

Mr Campbell Rigg
Matthew and Sian Westerman

Gold

Mr and Mrs Paul Myners

Silver

Lord and Lady Aldington
Mr John Entwistle OBE
Mr Philip Marsden

Bronze

Ian and Tessa Ferguson
Julia Fuller and David Harding
Prof Ken Howard RA and Mrs Howard
Mr Trevor Pickett
Mr Peter Rice
Anthony and Sally Salz
Mrs Inge Borg Scott
Mr Ray Treen
and others who wish to remain anonymous

CONTEMPORARY PATRONS GROUP

Chairman

Susie Allen

Patrons

Mr Tarek Aguizy
Mrs Alan Artus
Viscountess Bridgeman
Dr Elaine C Buck
Miss Camilla Bullus
Jenny Christensson
Mr Gus Danowski
Mary Moore Danowski
Helen and Colin David
Chris and Angie Drake
Dr Yvonne von Egidy-Winkler
Ms Lissa Engle
Belinda de Gaudemar
Ms Soma Ghosh
Mrs Selima Gürtler
Caroline Hansberry
Mrs Susan Hayden
Dr David Landau CBE
Mazen and Mireille Masri
Mrs Penelope Jane Mather
Angela Nikolakopoulou-Koulakoglou
Barbara Pansadoro
Mr Andres Recoder and Mrs Isabelle Schiavi
Sir John Rose
John Tackaberry
Mrs Inna Vainschtock
Lawton Wehle Fitt
Cathy Wills
Mary Wolridge
and others who wish to remain anonymous

TRUSTS AND FOUNDATIONS

The Peter Boizot Foundation
The Bomonty Charitable Trust
The Charlotte Bonham-Carter Charitable Trust
William Brake Charitable Trust
C H K Charities Limited
The Carlton House Charitable Trust
The Coutts Charitable Trust
Alan Cristea Gallery
The Dovehouse Trust
D'Oyly Carte Charitable Trust
The Gilbert & Eileen Edgar Foundation
The Fenton Arts Trust
The Flow Foundation
The Gatsby Charitable Foundation
Goethe Institut London
Heritage Lottery Fund
Institut für Aulandsbeziehungen e.V.
Stanley Thomas Johnson Foundation
The Emmanuel Kaye Foundation
The Kindersley Foundation
Lapada Association of Art and Antiques Dealers
The de Laszlo Foundation
The David Lean Foundation
The Leche Trust
The Leverhulme Trust
The Maccabaeans
The McCorquodale Charitable Trust
Marsh Christian Trust
The Paul Mellon Estate
The Mercers' Company
The Millichope Foundation
The Mulberry Trust
The National Manuscripts Conservation Trust
Newby Trust Limited
North Street Trust
The Old Broad Street Charity Trust
P F Charitable Trust
The Peacock Charitable Trust
The Stanley Picker Trust
The Pidem Fund
Edith and Ferdinand Porjes Charitable Trust
Pro Helvetia
Mr and Mrs J A Pye's Charitable Settlement
The Radcliffe Trust
The Rose Foundation
The Schroder Charity Trust
The Archie Sherman Charitable Trust
The South Square Trust
Oliver Stanley Charitable Trust
The Peter Storrs Trust
Joseph Strong Frazer Trust
The Swan Trust
Swiss Cultural Fund in Britain
Sir Jules Thorn Charitable Trust
The Patricia Turner Foundation
Albert Van den Bergh Charitable Trust
The Celia Walker Art Foundation
The Spencer Wills Trust
The Harold Hyam Wingate Foundation
Hazel M Wood Charitable Trust
The Worshipful Company of Painter-Stainers

AMERICAN ASSOCIATES OF THE ROYAL ACADEMY TRUST

Burlington House Trust
Mr and Mrs James C Slaughter

Benjamin West Society
Mrs Walter H Annenberg
Mr Francis Finlay
Mrs Deborah Loeb Brice

Benefactors
Mrs Nancy B Negley
Mrs Edmond J Safra
Mr and Mrs Albert H Small
The Hon John C Whitehead
Mr and Mrs Frederick B Whittemore

Sponsors
Mrs Russell B Aitken
Ms Britt Allcroft
Mr and Mrs Stephen Bechtel
Mrs Sylvia K Hassenfeld
Mrs Drue Heinz HON DBE
David Hockney RA
Mr Arthur L Loeb
Mr and Mrs Hamish Maxwell
Mrs Lucy F McGrath
Ms Diane A Nixon
Mr Arthur O Sulzberger and Ms Allison S Cowles
Mr Vernon Taylor Jr
Mr and Mrs Dave Williams

Patrons
Ms Helen Harting Abell
Mr and Mrs Steven Ausnit
Mr Donald A Best
Mrs Mildred C Brinn
Mrs Benjamin Coates
Mrs Mary Sharp Cronson
Anne S Davidson
Ms Zita Davisson
Mr and Mrs Stanley De Forest Scott
Mrs June Dyson
Mrs Barbara Fox-Bordiga
Mr and Mrs Lawrence S Friedland
Mr and Mrs Leslie Garfield
Mr C Hugh Hildesley
Dr Bruce C Horten
The Hon W Eugene Johnston and Mrs Johnston
Mr William W Karatz
The Hon Philip Lader and Mrs Lader
Mr and Mrs Daniel Leab
Ms Brenda Neubauer Straus
Mr and Mrs Wilson Nolen
Mr and Mrs Jeffrey Pettit
Cynthia Hazen Polsky and Leon B Polsky
Lady Annie Renwick
The Hon Frederick W Richmond
Mr and Mrs Peter M Sacerdote
Ms Louisa Stude Sarofim
Mrs Frances G Scaife and Mr William G Dagit
Mrs Frederick M Stafford
Mr and Mrs Stephen Stamas
Ms Joan Stern
Ms Elizabeth F Stribling and Mr Guy Robinson
Mr Martin J Sullivan OBE
Dr and Mrs Robert D Wickham
Mr Robert W Wilson

Donors
Mr James C Armstrong
Mr Constantin R Boden
Mrs Edgar H Brenner
Mr and Mrs Philip Carroll
Mr and Mrs Reginald B Collier
Mr and Mrs Howard S Davis
Ms Jody Donohue
Mr and Mrs William J Doody
Mrs Beverley C Duer
Mr Robert H Enslow
Mr Ralph A Fields
Mrs Katherine D Findlay
Mr and Mrs Christopher Forbes
Mr and Mrs Gordon P Getty
Mrs Betty N Gordon
Mr O D Harrison Jr
Mr and Mrs Gustave M Hauser
Mrs Judith Heath
Ms Elaine Kend
Mr and Mrs Nicholas L S Kirkbride
Mr and Mrs Gary Kraut
The Hon Samuel K Lessey Jr
Mr Henry S Lynn Jr
Ms Clare E McKeon
Ms Christine Mainwaring-Samwell
Ms Barbara T Missett
The Hon William Nitze and Mrs Nitze
Mrs Charles W Olson III
Mrs Patsy Preston
Mrs Nanette Ross
Laura Christman and William Rothacker
Mr Mark Schneider
Mrs Martin Slifka
Mrs Sharon Tedesco
Mrs Judith Villard
Mr and Mrs William B Warren

Corporate And Foundation Support
American International Group, Inc.
Annenberg Foundation
Bechtel Foundation
The Blackstone Charitable Foundation
The Brown Foundation
Fortnum & Mason
Gibson, Dunn & Crutcher
The Horace W Goldsmith Foundation
Hauser Foundation
Leon Levy Foundation
Loeb Foundation
Henry Luce Foundation
Lynberg & Watkins
Sony Corporation of America
Starr Foundation
Thaw Charitable Trust

CORPORATE MEMBERS OF THE ROYAL ACADEMY

Launched in 1988, the Royal Academy's Corporate Membership Scheme has proved highly successful. Corporate membership offers benefits for staff, clients and community partners and access to the Academy's facilities and resources. The outstanding support we receive from companies via the scheme is vital to the continuing success of the Academy and we thank all members for their valuable support and continued enthusiasm.

Premier Level Members
A T Kearney Limited
Accenture
The Arts Club
The Bank of New York Mellon
Barclays plc
Booz & Company
CB Richard Ellis
Deutsche Bank AG
Ernst & Young LLP
GlaxoSmithKline plc
Goldman Sachs International
Hay Group
HSBC plc
Intercontinental London Park Lane
Kleinwort Benson
LECG Ltd
Lombard Odier Darier Hentsch
Northern Trust
Schroders plc
Smith and Williamson
Standard Chartered

Corporate Members
All Nippon Airways
Apax Partners
Arcadia Group plc
BGC Brokers L.P.
BNP Paribas
The Boston Consulting Group
Bovis Lend Lease Limited
British American Business Inc.
British American Tobacco
Calyon
Capital International Limited
Christie's
Citi
Clifford Chance LLP
Concateno plc
Control Risk Group
Curzon Partnership LLP
Denton Wilde Sapte
Diageo plc
Doll
Eurohypo AG
F & C Asset Management plc
GAM
Heidrick & Struggles
Insight Investment
ITV plc
John Lewis Partnership
JP Morgan
KPMG
Lazard
London College of Fashion
Louis Vuitton
Man Group plc
Mizuho International plc
Momart Limited
Morgan Stanley
Navigant Consulting
Nedrailways
Novo Nordisk
Osborne Samuel LLP
Pentland Group plc
Rio Tinto
Roger Vivier
The Royal Society of Chemistry
Skadden, Arps, Slate, Meagher & Flom LLP
Slaughter and May
Société Générale
Theo Fennell
Timothy Sammons Fine Art Agents
Trowers & Hamlins
Veredus Executive Resourcing
Weil, Gotschal & Manges
Windsor Partners Limited

SPONSORS OF PAST EXHIBITIONS

The President and Council of the Royal Academy would like to thank the following sponsors and benefactors for their generous support of major exhibitions in the last ten years:

2009
Premiums and RA Schools Show
Mizuho International plc
RA Outreach Programme
Deutsche Bank AG

2008
GSK Contemporary
GlaxoSmithKline
Byzantium 330–1453
J. F. Costopoulos Foundation
A. G. Leventis Foundation
Stavros Niarchos Foundation
Travel Partner: Cox & Kings
Miró, Calder, Giacometti, Braque: Aimé Maeght and His Artists
BNP Paribas
Vilhelm Hammershøi: The Poetry of Silence
OAK Foundation Denmark
Novo Nordisk
240th Summer Exhibition
Insight Investment
Premiums and RA Schools Show
Mizuho International plc
RA Outreach Programme
Deutsche Bank AG
From Russia: French and Russian Master Paintings 1870–1925 from Moscow and St Petersburg
E.ON
2008 Season supported by Sotheby's

2007
Paul Mellon's Legacy: A Passion for British Art
The Bank of New York Mellon
Georg Baselitz
Eurohypo AG
239th Summer Exhibition
Insight Investment
Impressionists by the Sea
Farrow & Ball
Premiums and RA Schools Show
Mizuho International plc
RA Outreach Programme
Deutsche Bank AG
The Unknown Monet
Bank of America

2006
238th Summer Exhibition
Insight Investment
Chola: Sacred Bronzes of Southern India
Travel Partner: Cox & Kings
Premiums and RA Schools Show
Mizuho International plc
RA Outreach Programme
Deutsche Bank AG
Rodin
Ernst & Young

2005
China: The Three Emperors, 1662–1795
Goldman Sachs International
Impressionism Abroad: Boston and French Painting
Fidelity Foundation
Matisse, His Art and His Textiles: The Fabric of Dreams
Farrow & Ball
Premiums and RA Schools Show
The Guardian
Mizuho International plc
Turks: A Journey of a Thousand Years, 600–1600
Akkök Group of Companies
Aygaz
Corus
Garanti Bank
Lassa Tyres

2004
236th Summer Exhibition
A. T. Kearney
Ancient Art to Post-Impressionism: Masterpieces from the Ny Carlsberg Glyptotek, Copenhagen
Carlsberg UK Ltd
Danske Bank
Novo Nordisk
The Art of Philip Guston (1913–1980)
American Associates of the Royal Academy Trust
The Art of William Nicholson
RA Exhibition Patrons Group
Vuillard: From Post-Impressionist to Modern Master
RA Exhibition Patrons Group

2003
235th Summer Exhibition
A. T. Kearney
Ernst Ludwig Kirchner: The Dresden and Berlin Years
RA Exhibition Patrons Group
Giorgio Armani: A Retrospective
American Express
Mercedes-Benz
Illuminating the Renaissance: The Triumph of Flemish Manuscript Painting in Europe
American Associates of the Royal Academy Trust
Virginia and Simon Robertson
Masterpieces from Dresden
ABN AMRO
Classic FM
Premiums and RA Schools Show
Walker Morris
Pre-Raphaelite and Other Masters: The Andrew Lloyd Webber Collection
Christie's
Classic FM
UBS Wealth Management

2002
234th Summer Exhibition
A. T. Kearney
Aztecs
British American Tobacco
Mexico Tourism Board
Pemex
Virginia and Simon Robertson
Masters of Colour: Derain to Kandinsky. Masterpieces from The Merzbacher Collection
Classic FM
Premiums and RA Schools Show
Debenhams Retail plc
*RA Outreach Programme**
Yakult UK Ltd
Return of the Buddha: The Qingzhou Discoveries
RA Exhibition Patrons Group

2001
233rd Summer Exhibition
A. T. Kearney
Botticelli's Dante: The Drawings for Dante's Divine Comedy
RA Exhibition Patrons Group
The Dawn of the Floating World (1650–1765). Early Ukiyo-e Treasures from the Museum of Fine Arts, Boston
Fidelity Foundation
Forty Years in Print: The Curwen Studio and Royal Academicians
Game International Limited
Frank Auerbach, Paintings and Drawings 1954–2001
International Asset Management
Ingres to Matisse: Masterpieces of French Painting
Barclays
Paris: Capital of the Arts 1900–1968
BBC Radio 3
Merrill Lynch
Premiums and RA Schools Show
Debenhams Retail plc
*RA Outreach Programme**
Yakult UK Ltd
Rembrandt's Women
Reed Elsevier plc

2000
1900: Art at the Crossroads
Cantor Fitzgerald
The Daily Telegraph
232nd Summer Exhibition
A. T. Kearney
Apocalypse: Beauty and Horror in Contemporary Art
Eyestorm
The Independent
Time Out
Chardin 1699–1779
RA Exhibition Patrons Group
The Genius of Rome 1592–1623
Credit Suisse First Boston
Premiums and RA Schools Show
Debenhams Retail plc
*RA Outreach Programme**
Yakult UK Ltd
The Scottish Colourists 1900–1930
Chase Fleming Asset Management

*Recipients of a Pairing Scheme Award, managed by Arts + Business. Arts + Business is funded by the Arts Council of England and the Department for Culture, Media and Sport

OTHER SPONSORS

Sponsors of events, publications and other items in the past five years:

Carlisle Group plc
Castello di Reschio
Country Life
Guy Dawson
Derwent Valley Holdings plc
John Doyle Construction
Dresdner Kleinwort Wasserstein
Lucy Flemming McGrath
Foster and Partners
Goldman Sachs International
Gome International
Gucci Group
Rob van Helden
Michael Hopkins & Partners
IBJ International plc
Martin Krajewski
Harvey and Allison McGrath
Marks & Spencer
Morgan Stanley Dean Witter
Prada
Radisson Edwardian Hotels
Richard and Ruth Rogers
Strutt & Parker